Personality and Intelligence at Work

Personality and Intelligence at Work examines the increasingly controversial role of individual differences in predicting and determining behaviour at work. It combines approaches from organisational psychology and personality theory to critically examine the physical, psychological and psychoanalytic aspects of individual differences, and how they impact on the world of work.

Topics covered include the role of IQ at work as the best predictor of success, but also the importance of increasingly recognised social intelligences such as emotional intelligence (EI). The significance of personality traits and the impact of temperaments on work performance are also examined, and the methods used to assess work behaviour and potential are reviewed. Psychological tests, which measure personality traits, are questioned as accurate predictors of behaviour at work, alongside other factors such as job satisfaction, productivity, absenteeism and turnover.

This new, thoroughly revised and updated edition of *Personality at Work* provides a comprehensive review of the relevant literature from psychology, sociology and management science. It will be of interest to students of organisational psychology and business and management studies, as well as HR professionals.

Adrian Furnham is Professor of Psychology at University College London and a Fellow of the British Psychological Society. He is on the editorial board of a number of international journals, as well as the past elected president of the International Society for the Study of Individual Differences. He believes work is more fun than fun and considers himself to be a well-adjusted workaholic.

Personality and Intelligence at Work

Exploring and explaining individual differences at work

Adrian Furnham

Routledge
Taylor & Francis Group

LONDON AND NEW YORK

First published 2008
by Routledge
27 Church Road, Hove, East Sussex BN3 2FA

Simultaneously published in the USA and Canada
by Routledge
270 Madison Avenue, New York, NY 10016

Routledge is an imprint of the Taylor and Francis Group, an Informa business

Copyright © 2008 Psychology Press

Typeset in Times New Roman by
RefineCatch Limited, Bungay, Suffolk
Printed and bound in Great Britain by
TJ International Ltd, Padstow, Cornwall

British Library Cataloguing in Publication Data
A catalogue record for this book is available from the British Library

Library of Congress Cataloging-in-Publication Data
Furnham, Adrian.
    Personality and intelligence at work: exploring and explaining individual
differences at work / Adrian Furnham
    p. cm.
ISBN 978–1–84169–585–3 (hardcover)—ISBN 978–1–84169–586–0 (pbk)
1. Personality and occupation.   2. Prediction of occupational success.   3.
Employees—Psychological testing.   4. Work—Psychological aspects.   5.
Personality and intelligence.   6. Individual differences.   I. Title.
   BF698.9.O3F867   2007
   155.2′2—dc22

                                           2007020404

ISBN 978–1–84169–585–3 (hbk)
ISBN 978–1–84169–586–0 (pbk)

For:

**The Memsahib and the Dauphin:
Godspeed and Hamba Kahle**

Contents

x   *Contents*

Figures

Foreword

The day after the terrorist attacks of September 11 2001, *Le Monde*'s former editor, Jean-Marie Colombani, wrote, "Today, we are all Americans." Since then, French attitudes toward Americans have had their share of ups and downs, an oscillation that seems to occur in the political relationships among all countries. Relations among nation-states are complex, and political sentiments – ally one month, foe the next – seemingly change with the seasons.

Academic sentiments do not wax and wane so quickly or clearly as political ones, which make them slower to form, but also longer lasting. The case of individual differences is a good example. Whilst differential psychology (the study of individual differences) was considered by many to be a discredited area roughly a generation ago, today few would disagree that sentiments have changed rather dramatically. Moreover, although I'm unaware of any polling data on the subject, I venture that few expect the academic currency of dispositional explanations to deflate anytime soon.

Though differential psychology probably reached its nadir well before Mischel's famous 1968 book, its resurgence is relatively easier to trace. Most prominent in changing opinion were the twin studies – studies that showed that identical twins, even when reared apart – bore striking similarities in terms of their intelligence, personality, and just about any other measurable individual difference. Equally striking, though less acknowledged, was the relative lack of importance of shared environment (parental practices, educational background, socioeconomic status) on these variables.

Another major factor was the promulgation and acceptance of taxonomies for classifying the myriad attributes that characterise people. In the area of intelligence, there is the *g* factor, to denote general mental ability. In personality, there are five factors – the so called "Big Five". Of course, there are multiple aspects of intelligence, and five factors hardly describe everything about an individual's personality. But scientific progress often depends on classifications, and differential psychology has been no exception.

A third factor explaining the ascendance of dispositional factors has been slower to develop but no less significant in its importance. Study-by-study, often one trait and one criterion variable at a time, research has slowly but inexorably accumulated showing that personality and intelligence matter to virtually every important criterion in organisations: job performance, job attitudes, withdrawal, leadership, creativity, adaptation to change, and so on. The debate over individual differences is no longer over whether they matter, but how much they matter, or by what reasons they matter.

It is in this last area – this so-called third factor – where the author, Adrian Furnham, has contributed most significantly. As perhaps the most productive psychologist alive in

Europe who has studied personality before it was fashionable, or even broadly acceptable to do so, Furnham is in a unique position to provide both a historical and
contemporary perspective on this field. And provide a perspective he does. I know of
no other book which so thoroughly considers the effect of personality and cognitive
ability on a host of criteria that matter to organisations and to those of us who study
organisational behaviour. Never one to run away from controversy, Furnham also
responds to some of the remaining criticisms of personality and individual differences.
In this writer's opinion, the book is equally valuable in taking stock of all that has been
accomplished, and in pointing to areas where we can build on the past successes.

As Thomas Kuhn so accurately observed, revolutions in science are rare. Just as a
political revolution will only last if institutions are put in place to solidify the change,
scientific revolutions only have lasting impact when they are followed by the more
quotidian empirical studies that substantiate and refine the paradigm shifts (what Kuhn
called "normal science"). Both personality and intelligence research have advanced
because the revolutions – the paradigm shifts – have been closely followed by normal
science. As a normal scientist (apologies for the double entendre), Furnham's work
has played no small role in substantiating the paradigm shift, and this book does an
excellent job of reviewing his and others' contributions. As he notes in concluding this
book, "It is a good time to be alive for a differential psychologist interested in the world
of work."

As a result of the contributions of Furnham and other personality and organisational psychologists, it is not a great exaggeration to paraphrase Colombani: Today,
we are all dispositionalists.

Timothy A. Judge
Gainesville, Florida, USA
October 31, 2007

Preface

This book is a "sort of" second edition of *Personality at Work*, if such a thing is possible. In fact, less than a quarter of this book retains anything of the structure and content of the earlier book, which I am happy to say remains in print after 15 years.

There are various reasons why *that* book is so different from *this*. The *first* reason is the sheer amount of research that has gone on over the past decade or so. Whilst personality psychologists were for a long time "married" to clinicians, and then to social psychologists, there has been over the past 10–15 years a happy and fruitful relationship with work (I/O) psychology. Work psychologists have embraced individual difference and been particularly interested in understanding the mechanisms and processes that account for the variation everyone notices with respect to work motivation and productivity. It has been observed that the most productive worker produces 2.5 more "output" than the least productive worker. The question is what part stable individual differences play in all this *and* how the process works.

The *second* reason is the development of research in personality psychology itself. From 1970 to 1990 the shadows of the person–situation debate lingered such that the quality and quantity of research in differential psychology suffered. This is certainly not true today. Indeed the field is expanding. And with work, as in behaviour genetics, and neuropsychology we are really beginning to understand the origin and consequences of individual differences. It is an exciting time to be a differential psychologist.

Third, the increase in sophistication in research methods, particularly meta-analysis and structural equation modelling, means important discoveries are being made. Good meta-analyses provide an excellent method to "summarise" what has been found in a particular area and spot patterns. Researchers are able to examine, classify and critique all studies done in a particular area, often over an extensive time period, to find what has been learnt.

Further, structural equation modelling, particularly when it is on longitudinal data, offers an important way to see causal patterns through multiple variables. Inevitably issues dealt with in this book are multi-causal. Simple questions like "What motivates people to work harder?" or "How can we reduce accidents?" always involve a large number of intra- and inter-individual interactions, as well as situational factors. Structural equation modelling and similar techniques offer an excellent path through the complexities.

Fourth, whereas this area was seen to be mainly a research area at the interface of personality and work psychology, it has become apparent that other disciplines are taking an active interest in how individual differences influence work outcomes. This includes psychiatrists with their interest in personality disorders, social psychologists interested in how attitudes, beliefs and values at work influence outcome and human-resource experts interested in concepts like competence. Equally, economists, ergonomists, environmental psychologists and organisations-behaviour researchers (sociology of work) have become crucially interested in some of the central questions addressed in this book. New chapters in this book reflect those developments.

I have also been involved in the assessment and coaching of senior managers and it is quite impossible to imagine how one might explain obvious, dramatic and stable individual differences in productivity and satisfaction by anything else than personality and intelligence variables. I also believe that business (organisational) psychologists really cannot avoid getting involved in real-world problems and issues. As applied psychologists they need to validate their theories and methods by applying them in the real world. Equally, I believe it behoves consultants to make the time to consult the latest works from academia.

Various chapters from this book have appeared elsewhere in other papers, chapters and books that I have written, though all have been updated.

I have been particularly lucky over the past five or six years to have been helped, stimulated and challenged by bright PhD students (Dino, Joanna, Mark, Tomas); thoughtful and generous academic colleagues (Chris, Robert, Joyce); practical managerial consultants (Andrew, David, Mike, John) as well as editors of learned journals and quality newspapers.

To be a little more specific: As to students and ex-students I am grateful to Mark Batey for sharing his extensive knowledge of all aspects of the topic of creativity and helping so much with the chapter in that area. Next Dr K. V. Petrides is not only my major source of wisdom for emotional intelligence and trait theory but an excellent companion to help evaluate all modern trends in psychometrics. Joanna Moutafi has certainly helped me analyse interesting data sets provided by business psychologists. Tomas Chamorro-Premuzic has been a wonderfully efficient and extremely thoughtful colleague helping me particularly to understand the relationship between personality and intelligence. I am both enormously proud of them and very grateful to them. They will see many of their ideas in the book and I happily acknowledge their contribution to my thinking and writing.

As regards academic colleagues, I benefit regularly from the intellectual as well as material generosity of Bob and Joyce Hogan. They are wonderfully feisty, courageous and iconoclastic. Both are rigorous and imaginative and joyful slaughterers of shibboleths, myths, political correctness and the like. They have also supported me financially for which I am always grateful. Chris McManus is an amazingly talented colleague and I always benefit from our mid-corridor exchanges. Similarly Chris Jackson is a long-standing friend with a brilliant eye for patterns in data that I miss.

Of course I am ever grateful to friends and colleagues who are consultants. In particular I would like to thank Andrew Lambert and Mike Haffenden for commissioning research from me but also allowing me to report some of it in this book. I have been both challenged and rewarded at Kaisen Consulting and David Pendleton at The Edgecumbe Group has helped me by providing rich data. John Taylor, friend, fellow trainer and co-author has also helped me more than he knows by encouraging me to be clearer and answer specific problems.

But my greatest help, albeit sternest critic is, of course, my lovely, elegant and very clever wife with whom I discuss everything. At one stage in the writing of this book I had two weekly columns in national newspapers both on the topic of this book and found in the Appointment pages. Having discussed my ideas and written these pieces they were evaluated by Alison. I got away with nothing: some articles were rejected out of hand; others had as much red pen as blue; but some got through. She clarifies my thinking, vastly improves my sentence structure and sharpens up the structure. It is totally appropriate the book is dedicated to her and my fine son Benedict who may one day read this book.

Adrian Furnham
London 2007

1 Individual differences at work

Introduction

This book is an attempt to provide a critical, comprehensive, and contemporary review of the management science, psychiatric, psychological and sociological literature at the interface of differential and occupational psychology. The focus of the book concerns the role of individual differences, specifically personality and intelligence, in predicting, explaining and maintaining all behaviour at work from accidents and absenteeism to job satisfaction and workplace sabotage.

This area of research has shown a strong resurgence of interest with many albeit rather different books with similar titles. Thus we have *Personality at Work* (Fontana, 2000); *The Owner's Manual for Personality at Work* (Howard & Howard, 2001); the edited *Personality and Work* (Barrick & Ryan, 2003), as well as *Personality and the Fate of Organizations* (Hogan, 2006). Each asserts the importance of individual differences in understanding behaviour at work.

One might plot the interest organisational psychologists have had over the last 100 years in individual differences. There could be many criteria: the *first* is academic books and papers published on the topic; a *second* is evidence of consultancy where management trainers and advisors have used tests for selection and development to help companies improve their efficiency and effectiveness. *Third*, one could look at companies and see when, which, and why they used personality tests.

It seems, over the twentieth century, that there were *four* periods of change. The *first* was during wars (notably the Great War and the Second World War). With high numbers of conscripted soldiers it is important to determine both their aptitudes and temperament for specialist jobs. Hence, testing is used widely by armies and institutions doing person/job fit. *Second*, there is always growth of tests when there is great economic decline or change often because the number of job applicants increases. Organisations often find tests a cheap and efficient way of improving their selection decisions. *Third*, when test publishers come into being and management consultants find tests useful in training and development there is often substantial growth in test usage in business, as both sell tests aggressively. But, *fourth*, there are also periods when test usage declines. This may occur through a change in the law that, for instance, necessitates tests to show substantial evidence that they are not biased against certain groups. It may also occur if there are high-profile litigation cases where testees successfully sue organisations because of the misuse of tests.

Differential psychology is split very dramatically into two areas that are central to the theme of this book: *tests of power* (intelligence testing) and *tests of preference* (personality testing). No one doubts that both personality *and* intelligence predict education, health and work outcomes. However, these two areas of psychology have until recently not been very clearly integrated (Chamorro-Premuzic & Furnham, 2005). It is important to understand these two solid foundations of differential psychology as well as how they are related.

The two disciplines of differential psychology

Two presidents of the American Psychological Association pointed out in their state-of-the-art address that there seemed, in psychology, a great division between *experimental psychology*, which sought to discover universal laws of human behaviour, and *correlational* psychology, which sought to describe and explain individual differences (Cronbach, 1957).

Cronbach (1957) noted that experimental psychologists are embarrassed and annoyed by individual differences, which they often treat as error variances. Yet, this variability is the very essence of correlational or differential psychology. Thus, we have experimental and personality psychologists with different perspectives and agendas.

Eysenck (1981) pointed out that a science of psychology can not properly function without *both* branches, which are indispensable to a proper understanding of people. More than that, one cannot properly exist without the other. Individual differences interact in almost every case with experimental and situational factors to produce results profoundly different for individuals of different personalities, different capacities and different motivations. Consequently, he argued, studies in experimental, social, educational, clinical or industrial psychology that do not take into account personality factors (using that term in its widest sense as referring to individual differences in temperament, intelligence, character, attitudes, aptitudes, etc.) inevitably throw away a great deal of potential information, and enlarge the error term in their analysis to an unacceptable degree for scientific progress. Main experimental effects are frequently swamped by interaction effects, and these are lost when we do not include personality in the research design. Conversely, the concepts and laws of experimental psychology are vital to any scientific understanding or interpretation of the results of work in personality. Eysenck believed that if we are to explain the major factors of personality in scientific terms, we must make appeal to the concepts used in experimental *and* physiological psychology. Only in this way, by the integration of the two disciplines of scientific psychology, he suggested, can we hope to build up a unitary science, as opposed to that "collection of chapter headings" of which William James spoke so disparagingly. Despite the obvious commonsensical nature of this observation the two worlds of correlational and experimental psychology remain steadfastly separated. Whilst there are divisions within each camp, nevertheless there is still mutual distrust and suspicion between these two groups who largely ignore one another.

Differential psychology is itself split into two definable groups: those who study *personality* traits and those who study *intelligence* (Table 1.1). Various researchers (Ackerman, 1994; Anastasi, 2004; Eysenck, 1967) have made various conceptual distinctions between the two areas.

The delineation is relatively clear. Intelligence researchers are interested in ability, primary intellectual or cognitive ability, always measured by power tests with right or wrong answers. Intelligence tests are often called cognitive or cognitive ability tests. Nearly all ability tests are timed. Intelligence tests tap into maximal performance to

Table 1.1 The two pillars of differential psychology

Personality	Intelligence
Typical performance	Maximal performance
Preference tests	Power tests
Non-ability	Ability
Non-cognitive	Cognitive

Table 1.2 Distinguishing between intelligence and personality

Dimension	Intelligence	Personality
Trait	Unidirectional ("little of" to "much of")	Bidirectional (polar extremes)
Trait to item relationship	Strictly monotonic	Not necessarily monotonic
Goals and optimal assessment situation	Test situation requiring maximal performance	Real-life situation
Motivation in taking the instrument	High motivation	Tends to vary
Instructions	To do one's best	To provide a candid response
Criteria for evaluating responses	Veridical criterion	Direction/intensity (no correct response)
Stability of the instrument	Relatively stable	Tends to fluctuate
Reliability of the instrument	Generally high	Varies from high to low
Interpreting results	Relatively straightforward	More open and controversial
Practical utility	Moderate	Low to moderate

Source: Most and Zeidner (1995). Reproduced with permission of Plenum Publishers.

see what a person is capable of. Intelligence researchers are essentially interested in describing the processes and mechanics underlying problem-solving ability.

Personality researchers on the other hand look at how people naturally or typically behave. They look at preferences and habitual ways of behaving. They are as much interested in perceptions and emotions as cognitions. Personality tests are rarely timed and often point out that they do not have right or wrong answers.

Most and Zeidner (1995) listed 10 dimensions upon which these two constructs differed (Table 1.2).

The "neat" distinction between the two areas has, of course, attracted the attention of those who are interested in the measuring and explaining of things from the other perspective. Thus, for a long time now, we have had power or objective tests of personality and self-assessed tests of intelligence (see Chapter 7).

There is a long history to objective personality tests. Cattell (1957) defined an objective personality test as any test showing reasonable variability that could be objectively scored and the purpose of which was indecipherable to the subject. Cattell and Warburton (1967) compiled an impressive compendium of over 800 objective personality and motivation tests for use in experimental research. Over the years, various tests have been devised to measure particular traits. Thus, Wallace and

Newman (1990) related motor speed (trace on a circle template as slowly as possible) to impulsivity because people high in impulsiveness should be less able to measure their approach behaviour.

There remains an interest in objective personality tests (Karp, 1999) but this research is found more in the applied, clinical literature than the academic, personality area (Cimbolic et al., 1999; Schmidt & Schwenkmezger, 1994; Schwenkmezger et al., 1994).

One reason why objective tests are attractive to researchers is that they supposedly reduce the possibility of faking. Indeed Elliott et al. (1996) demonstrated that an objective test (time taken to trace a circle) is more resistant to failing than self-report personality questionnaires.

The rise in interest in genetic and biological markers of personality may mean a great rise in interest in this sort of measure of personality. Indeed for nearly forty years there has been an interest in the relationship of personality and salivation (Corcoran, 1964; Deary et al., 1988). It may well be that mouth swabs will replace personality questionnaires in the next decade!

Equally recently there has been renewed interest in self-assessed or self-estimated intelligence. There are also questionnaires that measure things such as Typical Intellectual Engagement (TIE; Ackerman & Goff, 1994), which are closely related to measures of intelligence. Indeed it has been suggested that certain personality traits, like Openness-to-Experience, which is associated with curiosity and a life of the mind (i.e. interested in aesthetics, etc.), are *proxy* measures of intelligence. Some even call the dimension *intelletance*.

But for the organisational psychologist interested in the topic of assessment and selection, there is an interesting paradox and conundrum. It is essentially whether selection tests are really measures of maximal personality and typical intelligence: assessing people using measures of intelligence and personality to predict job success. Do they respond, as asked typically, on the personality measure? Or do they respond maximally in the sense that they give the most desirable answers. Further, do they, once they have acquired the job, behave maximally according to their ability (Hofstede, 2001; Klehe & Anderson, 2005) or typically according to their usual pace?

It is well known that people dissimulate in any form of self-report measure, be it interview or questionnaire. They try to form a good impression or, worse, perhaps they are completely lacking in self-awareness and self-insight so cannot rather than will not report on their actual beliefs and behaviour. They answer untypically in the sense that they often under-report their neuroticism and over-report their conscientiousness. In fact this is not a serious psychometric problem (Dilchert et al., 2006; Furnham, 1986) from a predictive validity point of view but it does mean that the profile is not typical. By processes of impression management, selective memory, and presentational skills the interviewee turns a test supposedly of typical performance into one of maximal performance.

Equally most people will try hard to "do well" on any cognitive ability test they are confronted with. However, once they have obtained the job it is not always certain that they will exercise the same effort. At work, then, typical performance occurs when: people are unaware that they are being observed or evaluated; people are not consciously trying to do their best; people work over a longer period of time. On the other hand, maximal performance is more likely to occur when: people know they are being evaluated; people understand and accept instructions to maximise effort; people are observed for a short enough time period to keep them focused on the task at hand.

Thus, people can invest full, intermediate or virtually no effort in a task. In this sense we can have typical or maximal personality and intelligence. Nevertheless it is traditional to think of intelligence tests as those requiring maximal performance and personality tests those requiring typical performance.

The relationship between personality and intelligence

As noted above, relatively few researchers have taken an interest in both personality *and* intelligence. They seem to be attracted to either one or the other area. There are, of course, exceptions like the two great University College London trained psychometricians Hans Eysenck and Raymond B. Cattell.

But over the years there have been numerous essays, chapters and edited books that have attempted to address precisely that issue (Collis & Messick, 2001; Saklofske & Zeidner, 1995).

Zeidner (1995) has argued that there appear to be seven major ways of thinking about the relationship:

1 "Intelligence is the independent variable, whereas personality is the dependent variable.
2 Intelligence is the dependent variable, whereas personality is the independent variable.
3 Intelligence and personality show a bidirectional relationship, with reciprocal determinism existing between the two constructs.
4 The observed personality–intelligence relationship is artefactual, with a third extraneous variable responsible for the observed relationship between the constructs.
5 Personality is an intervening or 'nuisance' variable intervening between the intelligence construct (as input) and manifest level of intelligence (as output, evidenced in intelligence test scores).
6 Personality is a moderator variable, moderating the relationship between intelligence and a criterion variable of interest.
7 Intelligence is a moderator variable, moderating the relationship between personality and a criterion outcome variable" (p. 316).

It is agreed that it is too simplistic to think of personality and intelligence acting independently on some measurable work-related variable like output. Whilst it could be expected that bright, stable, conscientious people would produce more in relatively complicated jobs it is equally possible that either personality or intelligence acts as a moderator or mediator variable in that relationship.

More recently, researchers have proposed models that specifically examine the relationship between personality and intelligence. They proposed a model that subjectively assessed intelligence at its centre. More recently they asked what personality and intelligence have in common (Chamoro-Premuzic & Furnham, 2006). They proposed seven things: (1) they are both latent psychological constructs; (2) their effects are manifested and observed in behavioural differences between individuals; (3) such differences can be quantified with standardised psychometric instruments; (4) both variables occupy a central position in the history of differential psychology; (5) they are largely genetically determined; (6) individual scores show relatively little variability over the life span; and (7) they are predictors of individual differences in a wide range of outcomes including performance in educational and occupational settings. They proposed a new concept called intellectual competence or the intelligence personality, which is the individual's capacity to acquire and consolidate knowledge throughout the life-span, which is dependent on ability, personality and self-insight. These factors help to explain the development of ability, how confidence affects this development and how people perform on day-to-day tasks.

The idea of a moderator and mediator variable can best be described diagrammatically (Figure 1.1).

In this relationship, the direct relationship between intelligence and some outcome variables is mediated by personality. Thus, brighter people might be less productive if very neurotic, but much more productive if very conscientious. In this sense intelligence is moderated by personality. Equally it may be that conscientiousness is moderated by intelligence in that it is only moderately or above average intelligent people who are more productive if they are conscientious.

Equally, personality or intelligence could be a mediator variable (Figure 1.2). The important point to note is that any direct relationship between either personality or intelligence at work may be moderated or mediated by the other. In this sense it seems always important to measure both variables in research exercises.

The relationship between personality and intelligence has been explored over the years in single studies as well as meta-analyses. They are not always comparable because they use different measures or systems of personality. Consider the following, the celebrated meta-analysis of Ackerman and Heggestad (1997). It examines the relationship between the Big Five personality variables and five measures of cognitive ability (Table 1.3).

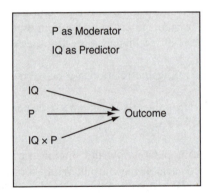
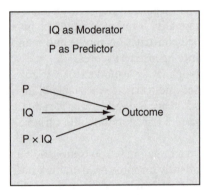

Figure 1.1 Moderator: Third variable that effects zero-order correlations between other two variables.

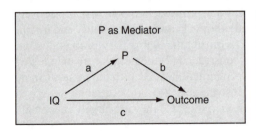
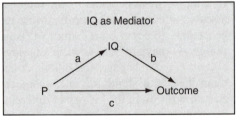

Figure 1.2 Mediator: When a and b are controlled, previously significant path c is not.

Table 1.3 Personality correlates of psychometric intelligence: The Big Five and ability test scores

	N	E	O	A	C
General intelligence (psychometric *g*)	−.15*	.08*	.33*	.01	.02
Crystallised intelligence (*gc*)	−.09*	.11*	.30*	.04	−.05
Cognitive speed	−.04	.06*	−.05	.04	.04
Visual perception	−.04*	.06*	.24*	.02	−.10
Mathematical/numerical ability	−.17*	.09*	.01	−.05	−.15*

Notes: * *p* < .05. N = Neuroticism; E = Extraversion; O = Openness; A = Agreeableness; C = Conscientiousness.
Source: Table and results derived from Ackerman and Heggestad's (1997) meta-analysis of 135 samples.

Table 1.4 Big Five predictors of fluid intelligence (*gf*)

	gf	
	β	*t*
Neuroticism	−.07	−3.32*
Extraversion	−.09	−3.68*
Openness	.12	5.51*
Agreeableness	.00	0.14
Conscientiousness	−.13	−5.81*
Regression model	$F(5, 2625) = 15.40*$	
Adjusted R^2	.03	

Note: *p* < .05.
Source: From Moutafi et al. (2005). Copyright © Elsevier 2005, with permission from Elsevier.

It shows five things. *First*, whatever the measure of cognitive ability used Neuroticism is negatively correlated with *all* measures: the more neurotic a person, the less well they perform on intelligence tests. *Second*, extraverts seem to do better than introverts on intelligence tests, but the correlations are very modest. *Third*, Openness is most strongly related to cognitive ability measures but not all of them. *Fourth*, the trait of Agreeableness seems quite unrelated to cognitive ability test scores. *Fifth*, Conscientiousness is modestly negatively associated with cognitive ability.

A recent study showed similar findings (Moutafi et al., 2005). This is a regression in which traits are related to intelligence and the amount of variance accounted for (Table 1.4).

Three observations are worth making about this table. *First*, the pattern of results is similar except in this study Extraversion is negatively correlated with intelligence. However, the amount of variance accounted for by intelligences remains modest. *Second*, the results seem to indicate that four of the five personality traits are related to intelligence. *Third*, the strongest predictor of intelligence test scores in this study body is low Conscientiousness. Correlations are consistent but modest. The question remains how to explain the relationship (Chamorro-Premuzic & Furnham, 2005).

Explaining the relationship

Personality traits do significantly and systematically relate to intelligence test scores. But how does one explain the nature of that relationship?

Neuroticism

There are a number of different "models" to explain the relationship between Neuroticism and cognitive ability. Nearly all researchers, whether they have focused on trait or state anxiety (which are themselves highly correlated) and children, students or the adult population have found anxiety fairly strongly related to reduced academic performance.

There has, however, been more disagreement as to the mechanism or process that explains that finding. Anxiety causes worry (the cognitive aspect of anxiety) and tension/ nervousness, which affects working memory. A number of models have been proposed. Mueller (1992), for instance, has produced a self-efficacy model (shown diagrammatically in Figure 1.3). It shows that low self-efficacy leads to worry and thence anxiety and thereafter poor test performance. Believing themselves to be poor at tests subjects feel less interested in preparing or trying hard and therefore actual low competency results, which leads on to trait anxiety and a vicious circle.

Dobson (2000) suggested a not dissimilar model (Figure 1.4).

This model suggests that trait anxiety (i.e. neurotic) individuals experience particular stress and threat in testing situations, which increases their state anxiety. Thus, high trait plus higher state anxiety influences thinking, which reduces scores on tests.

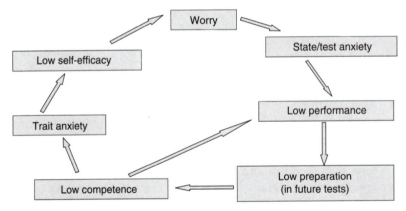

Figure 1.3 A hypothetical model for the processes underlying the relation between anxiety and test performance (based on Mueller, 1992).

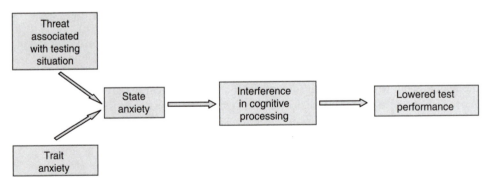

Figure 1.4 Model of the relationship between Neuroticism and academic success (Dobson, 2000). Copyright © 2000 Blackwell Publishing. Used with permission of Wiley-Blackwell Publishing Ltd.

These two models are not contradictory. They both attempt to explain how the trait anxiety in Neuroticism leads to state anxiety and, thus, poor performance.

There are at least three important complicating factors in all this. The *first* concerns the relationship between trait and state anxiety. Moutafi et al. (2006) tested two models, which are shown in Figure 1.5.

They were able to show in an experimental study that involved inducing state anxiety that there was evidence for Model 2, namely that whilst trait anxiety (i.e. Neuroticism) is correlated with test performance the causal path is from trait to state anxiety and thence to reduced performance. This shows clearly that it is the anxiety component of Neuroticism that causes reduced test performance.

A *second* issue is whether any relationship between anxiety and test performance is linear or curvilinear. Thus, it has been suggested that a certain amount of anxiety may be good for test performance. To be concerned to do well leads to more and better preparation. But too much anxiety could cause both a kind of preparation phobia and also poor performance at the task.

A *third* issue concerns sex differences in that there is an interaction between gender and Neuroticism and cognitive ability (Figure 1.6). Females have slightly higher Neuroticism scores than males but it may well be their culturally socialised attitude to testing that interacts with state anxiety.

Hence, the possibility of the model above, which may help to explain sex differences in top university final exams, where males tend to outperform females in most subjects at the top universities. This model has yet to be tested but suggests the following. According to all test norms females tend to have higher Neuroticism scores than males. Further, compared to males, females experience greater evaluation apprehension and self-doubt about their abilities (Chamorro-Premuzic & Furnham, 2005). This causes an increase in state anxiety, cognitive processing problems and lowered performance. Males, on the other hand, with lower Neuroticism and higher self-belief see tests more as a challenge than a threat. This in turn leads to greater positive arousal and higher scores.

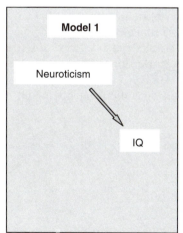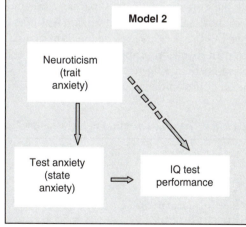

Figure 1.5 Two models representing Neuroticism being directly related to intelligence and the relationship between Neuroticism and intelligence being mediated by test anxiety affecting IQ test performance. (From Moutafi et al., 2006.) Copyright © 2006, with permission from Elsevier.

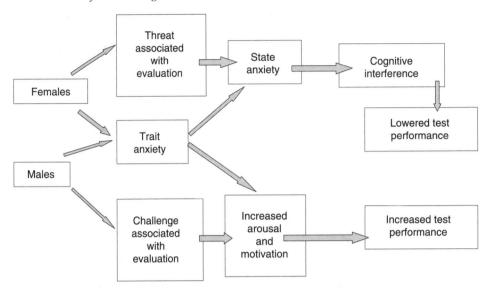

Figure 1.6 Sex differences in the interactive effect of Neuroticism and evaluative pressure on academic performance.

The argument, however, is clear. It is not that Neurotics are less intelligent but that their neurosis affects their test performance. This, of course, has implications for how best to measure the "true" cognitive ability of anxious individuals. Equally, it may explain the consistent literature which shows that Neuroticism is consistently and significantly related to poor performance and lower satisfaction at work (Furnham, 2005b).

Extraversion

Of all the personality factors perhaps the most confusion and equivocal findings concern the dimension of Extraversion–Introversion. From a cognitive psychology perspective Matthews (1999) has detailed the cognitive processes associated with Extraversion and Introversion (Table 1.5). It suggests that Extraversion is positively related to some aspects of intelligence and not others.

The literature on the relationship between Extraversion and intelligence is equivocal,

Table 1.5 Test related features to high and low Extraversion

Extraversion level	*High*	*Low*
Divided attention	+	−
Long-term memory	−	+
Reflective problem solving	−	+
Resistance to distraction	+	−
Retrieval from memory	+	−
Short-term memory	+	−
Vigilance	−	+

Source: Adapted from Matthews (1999).

but there is a consistency in that all correlations are small. It has been noted that the relationship between Extraversion and educational success does change with age, ranging from positive ($r = .10$ to $r = .20$) in primary school to negative at university ($r = -.10$). It is also related to the type of test (i.e. how long it is) and the particular ability being measured.

It has been suggested that Extraversion has educational (and test-taking benefits) in primary school, but that at university the correlation is negative. Perhaps it is the sociability of Extraverts and their boredom susceptibility that means they choose social interaction over exam preparation.

Wolf and Ackerman (2005) recently published a long-awaited meta-analytic investigation of the relationship between Extraversion and intelligence. This updated previous meta-analyses. The results showed that the overall correlation was $-.04$, which meant it had gone from slightly positive to slightly negative but that the effect sizes were very small. They did, however, recommend splitting Extraversion into two distinct but related factors of *social potency* (broad interpersonal effectiveness and a desire to make an impact on others) and *social closeness* (warmth and need for intimacy). Overall the relationship was lower for social closeness than social potency. This supports the Eysenckian perspective (Chamorro-Premuzic & Furnham, 2005). It seems that, overall, there is little correlation between Extraversion and intelligence test scores.

Openness

Some synonyms for Openness are intelletance or intellectual competence and it is no surprise that, of all the trait variables, it tends to show highest correlations with intelligence in the region of $r = .30$ (Ackerman & Heggestad, 1997; Chamorro-Premuzic & Furnham, 2005; McCrae, 1987). The high correlations between Openness and Ackerman and Goff's (1994) typical engagement concept gives some insight into the process or mechanism that explains the relationship. This is also related to Cattell's (1987) *investment theory*. This essentially suggests that open, curious individuals read more, explore their environment and seek out answers to many questions. In doing so they acquire a large knowledge base, which is related to crystallised intelligence. Thus, open people do well on intelligence tests. Furthermore, this grows as they get older. Openness is associated with intellectual curiosity, a life of the mind, imagination and artistic sensitivity. It is also related to need for cognition.

Openness is also correlated with creativity. Open individuals tend to have a wide range of interests, they often tend to have unusual thought processes and they get to be known for making unconventional judgements. They value intellectual matters and are questioning. Therefore, it is no surprise that the correlations between intelligence tests (both fluid and crystallised) and creativity and measures of Openness are significant and positive and usually in the range $r = .2$ to $r = .5$. Of all the personality traits it is Openness that can best serve as a proxy for intelligence, because it is so (relatively) highly correlated with it.

Agreeableness

Agreeableness is consistently shown to be essentially unrelated to intelligence. Agreeable people tend to be altruistic, compassionate and modest. They tend to be straightforward and not particularly competitive. This can mean that they might not "try hard" at certain tests lest they "show up" others less talented than themselves. Their modesty is not necessarily an index of low self-confidence or self-esteem but it could influence certain lecture situations in these ways. Nearly all individual studies and meta-analyses have shown near zero correlations between trait Agreeableness and intelligence test scores.

Conscientiousness

Over the past decade a number of studies using different cognitive ability measures have come to very much the same conclusion. There is a small ($10 < r < .20$), *negative* relationship between Conscientiousness and intelligences. Furnham (2005b) listed the results reproduced in Table 1.6, which show very consistent patterns, despite very different population groups and measures of intelligence.

How to explain these results? This is particularly problematic given the well-replicated finding that Conscientiousness positively predicts work outcomes. The puzzle is this: Conscientiousness predicts success at work; Intelligence predicts success at work; Conscientiousness is negatively related to intelligence.

Thus, paradoxically, persistent, self-disciplined and achievement-striving individuals appear to do *less well* on intelligence tests. It is possible that at least in competitive environments like elite universities less-intelligent individuals have to work harder to succeed. Those who know they are very bright can afford to prepare less and "wing it". However, in the world of work preparation pays off and this accounts for hard work leading to success. One clue to this puzzle may, however, lie in a more fine-grain analysis at the facet (primary factor) rather than at the domain (superfactor) level. That is, some measures of Conscientiousness contain facets associated with dutifulness and diligence (which are correlated with Obsessiveness) but also facets associated with achievement orientation and efficiency. It is quite possible that the former are negatively associated with intelligence test taking while the latter are positively associated.

Whilst it is still fashionable always to separate the measurement and conceptualisation

Table 1.6 Correlations between Conscientiousness and intelligence measures

Measure of IQ	r	p	N
1 Graduate Managerial assessment (Abstract)	− .11	< .01	900
Watson–Glaser Critical Thinking Appraisal *g*	− .13	< .001	900
g	− .14	< .001	900
2 Graduate Managerial Assessment (Abstract)	− .11	< .001	2658
3 General Reasoning test Battery 1 – Numerical reasoning	− .12	< .05	201
GRTB 2 – Verbal Reasoning	− .23	< .001	201
GRTB 2 – Abstract Reasoning	− .26	< .001	201
4 Raven's Standard Progressive Matrices	− .02	< .05	182
5 Baddeley Reasoning test	− .21	< .05	100
6 General Reasoning test Battery 2 – Numerical reasoning	− .20	< .001	4625
GRTB 2 – Verbal Reasoning	− .26	< .001	4625
GRTB 2 – Abstract Reasoning	− .16	< .001	4625
g	− .25	< .001	4625

Source: Derived from Furnham (2005b).

of personality and intelligence it is clear that they are related to each other in systematic ways. Most applied researchers have tended to look at one or other, rather than both of these variables, when trying to predict and understand individual differences in work-related behaviour.

Personality psychology

For over a century, personality psychologists have pursued the task of attempting to arrive at a clear, replicable, universal and accepted taxonomy of traits. The idea is that taxonomisation precedes explanation and that once the *periodic table* of personality is known the harder, perhaps more important, task of understanding the aetiology and processing of traits can begin. It has not, however, been until the last 15 to 20 years that this has even begun to happen.

There are almost 20,000 trait words in English. Some are used by psychologists in a "technical" sense, and others are almost ignored by trait researchers. Lay people describe and explain behaviour that they see (in others) by the use of trait words, e.g. "He is an extravert", "She is impulsive", "They are neurotic". However, because these words are used to describe and explain, this does not mean that they are always scientifically useful. Even some psychologists never escape the tautological loop of, for example, saying that an extravert is impulsive and sociable, and that sociable and impulsive people are extraverts, but then never offering an *explanation* for the origins of traits and the mechanisms and processes whereby they influence behaviour.

Digman (1990b) traced the history of classificatory work (often factor analysis) of personality dimensions over a 40-year period. Despite the use of rather different methods, samples and terms, it appears to be possible to align radically different theories in order to show their overlap.

Cattell and Eysenck, whose work on personality demanded research for over 30 years (1945–1975), have a lot in common, but also showed some important differences. Both sought, through factor analysis, to "let reality reveal itself". Cattell began with lexical criteria, by using 171 trait names for this factor analysis. Using different types of data (self-report, observational and objective), he made many discoveries and conducted many exploratory factor analyses on many data sets. He settled on 16 factors, which can be described in either technical or everyday language.

Eysenck argued that it was better to develop and test theories (a practice now called confirmatory factor analysis), rather than to discover factors. He set about measuring and testing the two Galen-inspired "superfactors". Over 40 years of research he developed the gigantic three model with his super-traits of Extraversion, Neuroticism and Psychoticism.

However it was the work of Costa and McCrae (1992) among others that led to the near-universal acceptance of the famous five-factor model. Costa and McCrae (1995b) believed that earlier criticisms that personality traits were either simple descriptions or cognitive fictions could now be refuted in part because of evidence of the heritability of most personality traits. However, it should not be assumed that the five-factor model is without critics (Block, 1995).

Nevertheless, the fact that so many personality researchers are working within the five-factor model framework must be good for an erstwhile fragmented field. There is an impressive research library on the social behaviour correlates of the Big Five described in this book.

Most scientists and lay people believe in the *causal primacy* of traits. Although it is agreed that this works at many levels, and can be indirect, it is assumed that internal, stable traits shape and structure (and hence predict) behaviour. Furthermore, most agree that traits are fundamental (biologically based, and stable over time), not simply a superficial mask that is negotiable in different social encounters.

Trait psychologists aim to develop a comprehensive but parsimonious and powerful theory of personality. For nearly 100 years the psychometric approach has been characterised by the construction and refinement of questionnaires through multivariate statistics. The fundamental aim is to develop reliable and valid measures that accurately measure the fundamental traits. Some theories attempt to combine measures of ability, motivation, personality and mood, but most stick to traits alone.

The issue of stability over time is more difficult to demonstrate because of the necessity for longitudinal research, but it is interestingly counter-intuitive. However, in recent research Deary (2004) has shown the remarkable evidence of the stability of performance on IQ tests with an $r = .69$ over a 60-year period. Studies conducted over 10 to 30 years report correlations of .65 to .80. Furthermore, using different tests and different methods over long periods of time, it is possible to demonstrate an impressive level of stability (Conley, 1985). The results of these studies are surprisingly unequivocal. There is overwhelming evidence for the *stability* of personality traits (particularly Extraversion, Neuroticism and Conscientiousness) and intelligence over time (Costa & McCrae, 1992). For many individuals, this is self-evidently true of others, if not of themselves. Many people like to believe that they have changed, almost always for the better (being wiser, more mature and more insightful), but that others have not – but in this they are mistaken!

In fact, there is also impressive evidence that the structure and correlates of traits are consistent across cultures (Eysenck & Eysenck, 1985). Thus, traits seem to be remarkably resilient. Only major trauma seems to change personality, which implies that the situations and interactionists may be overstressing the role of social and contextual variables in changing or shaping behaviour.

McCrae and Costa (1995) argued that:

1   "Personality traits are not descriptive summaries of behaviour, but rather dispositions that are inferred from and can predict and account for patterns of thoughts, feelings and actions.

2   Scientific evidence for the existence of traits is provided (in part) by studies that show patterns of covariation across time, twin pairs, and cultures – covariation that cannot be readily explained by such alternatives as transient influences, learned responses and cultural norms.

3   Patterns of covariation provide non-circular explanations, because observation of some behaviours allows the prediction of other, non-observed behaviours.

4   Psychological constructs give conceptual coherence to the covarying patterns of thoughts, feelings and actions; good constructs have surplus meaning that points beyond the known correlates of a trait.

5   Trait explanations are not themselves mechanistic; the mechanisms through which they operate may or may not be specified in a psychological theory.

6   When trait standing in an individual is assessed using a validated method, knowledge of the trait's manifestations can legitimately, albeit fallibly, be invoked to explain that individual's behaviour.

7   Personality traits are hypothetical psychological constructs, but they are presumed to have a biological basis.
8   Over time, traits interact with the environment to produce culturally conditioned and meaning-laden characteristic adaptations (such as attitudes, motives, and relationships).
9   Specific behaviours occur when these characteristic adaptations interact with the immediate situation; traits are thus best construed as indirect or distal causes of behaviour" (p. 248).

Others assert that traits are necessary but not sufficient to explain social behaviour. Diener (1996), like others, believes that we need more than traits to explain individual differences in behaviour. He dismisses the idea that traits are mere labels without true explanatory power. He notes:

[T]rait correlations do not explain underlying processes, other variables are inevitably important at least in some instances, and traits do not explain intra-individual variation. . . . We need to understand how traits influence behaviour and how they interact with the environment. We need to understand how traits arise and how they are stored in the nervous system.

(p. 437)

Deary and Matthews (1993) argued that the trait approach is not only "alive and well", but flourishing. They highlight various "bright spots" in current trait theory:

1   Growing agreement concerning the number, character and stability of personality dimensions.
2   A greater understanding of the heritability of personality traits, and hence a greater appreciation of the role of the environment.
3   A growing sophistication of research, which aims to elucidate the biological and social bases of trait differences.
4   An appreciation of the extent to which personality differences predict outcomes, or act as moderators, in cognitive and health settings.

They assert, as many others have done before them, two fundamental points:

1   *The Primary Causality of Traits* – the idea that causality flows from traits to behaviour and that, although there is a feedback loop, it is less important.
2   *The Inner Locus of Traits* – the idea that traits describe the fundamental core qualities of a person that are latent rather than manifest.

The causes of personality traits have always been acknowledged to be both biological and social. The evidence for the former is primarily based on behaviour genetics. The fact that there were so many competing theories, typologies and measures of traits did not serve the trait position well. The pre-paradigmatic state of affairs meant that it was difficult to take the trait arguments seriously. However, there is growing consensus over the emergence of the "Big Five" as fundamental higher-order orthogonal factors. The 1980s and 1990s have been dominated by the five-factor model (FFM) of traits; What this means is that many personality psychologists have accepted that there are five fundamental (higher-order) orthogonal (independent of one another) personality traits (these will be described later). The origin of the model lies in very different methods and areas. It is open to question how much agreement there really is for this position, when Eysenck (1992) claims 3 factors, Cattell (1957) 16 factors and Brand (1994) 6 factors, and furthermore, the labelling of the factors within the Big Five tradition is not consistent.

Essentially, differences between the various theorists can in part be resolved by understanding a few salient issues. *First*, researchers have used rather different methods, such as studies of natural language in questionnaire construction, and this has naturally had an effect on the labelling of the factors. *Second*, different factor-analytical methods yielded two different results. The dispute between Cattell and Eysenck is really about whether to use an orthogonal or oblique rotation – the former trying to render factors independent of one another and the latter attempting to maximise variance. *Third*, a number of researchers have concentrated on "unpacking" some of the fundamental traits, rather than looking at the relationship between them – i.e. they investigate them at rather different levels. Hence there appears to be more disagreement than there really is.

What is true, however, is that personality psychology after two decades of decline and disrepair (1965–1985) is now flourishing. There are half a dozen international scientific journals dedicated to personality research and flourishing societies. Once again clinical, education and organisational psychologists have become aware that to understand the issues that concern them they need to be cognisant of, and take into account, personality traits. This book is concerned with how traits influence behaviour in the workplace.

Seven approaches to personality at work

An examination of the highly diverse, dispersed and divergent literature concerning personality at work has highlighted seven rather different approaches to the topic (Furnham, 1991a).

Classic personality theory

This approach starts with a theory of personality and relates empirically assessed measures (as the independent variable) to various work-related behaviours. The personality variable chosen may vary on a number of dimensions:

- Single or multiple traits are measured. A single trait might be considered, e.g. self-monitoring (Snyder, 1975), or locus of control (Rotter, 1966) or alternatively a trait system, bound up in an elaborate theory like that of Eysenck (1967), or Cattell (1957). It is frequently the case that multiple traits are used, as single trait theories are usually not as rich a source of hypotheses.
- Cognitive or biological-based traits are measured. For instance, some "traits" or personality dimensions are quite clearly conceived of in cognitive terms, e.g. belief systems such as conservatism (Wilson, 1973) or attributional styles. These cognitive traits refer to the way people perceive the world, or attribute the cause of their own or others' behaviour. On the other hand, some traits, e.g. extraversion (Eysenck, 1967) or sensation-seeking (Zuckerman, 1979), are conceived of in biological terms such that the person's behaviour is a function of biological differences. Both approaches seem equally popular.

- "Normal" and "Abnormal" traits can be measured. For instance, some traits are clearly conceived of in terms of abnormal behaviour like depression, psychopathy or hypochondriasis, which measures some aspect of "abnormal" behaviour that, though valid and indeed at times quite relevant to work-related behaviours, seem less useful than "normal" traits, because many working people do not exhibit these traits to any degree. This is, however, not true of neuroticism, which is very common.
- Dynamic vs. Stylistic traits. This is the distinction made between Freudian/neo-Freudian ideas (such as the oral or anal personality, which supposedly measure deep-seated, possibly unconscious, needs and fears) and stylistic traits, which do not presume the same aetiology (in childhood) or processes. To date, however, very few Freudian personality tests have been applied to the workplace save perhaps Kline's (1978) work on the oral and anal personality.

The basic tenet of this "classic personality theory" approach is to measure personality as the independent variable and see how it correlates with some (often rather arbitrarily chosen) work-related behaviour. In criticism of this approach, it should be pointed out that:

- So far, the approach has been piecemeal and there is very little evidence of a concerted, systematic and programmatic research effort, which is perhaps not that unusual.
- Sometimes this research has been laboratory based and hence it frequently has poor ecological validity.
- The selection of work-related variables is somewhat random and based on convenience because researchers are either unable to get better measures or, indeed, are not sure what to look for.
- Essentially, studies such as these are nearly always seen by personality researchers simply as supporting evidence for their ideas.

Compared to the extensive research on the relationship between personality and, say, learning, mental health or social behaviour, the extant research from classic personality theory on occupational and organisational variables has been disappointing.

Classic occupational psychology/organisational behaviour

This approach starts with some work-related variable, be it conceived at the individual, group or organisational level, and examines its personality correlates. Again, the independent variables may be conceived of, or measured, quite differently:

- Self-report vs. behavioural. Some variables are measured by questionnaire ratings or interviews, while others are measured by actual behaviour such as absenteeism, produce made or sold, or number of promotions. Both self-report and behavioural measures are subject to different forms of systematic error.
- Single vs. aggregate measures. The work-related behaviour may be a single, one-off assessment, or an aggregate measure made up either from different parts (i.e. combining superior, subordinate, self and colleague assessments) or measurements conducted over time. Clearly, in terms of reliability and representativeness, aggregate measures are preferable.

- Within vs. between organisations. Sometimes variables are examined only within an organisation while others are compared between organisations. The clear advantage of the latter approach is that one can control for organisational variables, which are quite likely to have major effects.

Researchers in this tradition are usually interested in examining personality correlates of specific work behaviours that might help personnel and human resource professionals select, appraise, promote or train individuals. But this research has a number of limitations:

- The choice of personality variables has been arbitrary and uninformed. Some personality tests have been favoured mainly because they have been commercially exploited rather than because they are reliable and valid. Some outdated tests, largely forgotten and condemned by psychometricians, remain a popular choice and hence seriously threaten the nature of the results.
- Similarly, statistical analyses have been simple and naive. As a rule simple correlations have been computed rather than partial correlations or even more preferably multivariate statistics to prevent type II errors (finding more significant differences than actually occur). Given that both independent and dependent variables are multi-factorial, it is essential that sufficiently robust and sensitive multivariate statistics are used to analyse results.
- Studies in this area are frequently exploratory and are atheoretical rather than based on a sound theory or programmatic research endeavour. As a result, interesting results are rarely followed up and the theoretical implications rarely exploited.
- Often, researchers ignore possible organisational and societal factors that either directly or indirectly affect the dependent variable. That is, work-related behaviours are rarely solely under the control of the individual and may be moderated by powerful organisational factors, which need to be taken into account.

The occupational psychology and organisational behaviour literature is diverse, often poor but sometimes very good. Alas, the good research and theorising is difficult to find and limited in both quantity and scope.

The development of a work-specific individual difference measure

A third approach is to develop a personality measure aimed at predicting exclusively a specific work-related behaviour (like absenteeism) and to use this measure to predict that behaviour. This is not necessarily tautological though at first it may seem so. A fairly large number of these measures already exist. But they are highly varied and may be:

- Narrow vs. wide in conceptualisation. For instance, the personality measures might attempt to predict a specific (narrow) form of occupational behaviour, such as absenteeism, or a much wider range of occupational behaviours such as satisfaction or productivity. It is probably true that the former is a much more common approach than the latter.
- Single vs. multiple traits. That is, the measure (usually a questionnaire) could be multi-dimensional supposedly measuring many different behaviours/beliefs at work or a single trait measure, that only measures one dimension.

- Self-report vs. behaviour. There is no reason why the individual-difference measure need necessarily be self-report based. It could well be biographical, behavioural or physiological and, indeed, all have been used at one time or another to try to predict work-related behaviour.
- Attitudinal vs. attributional. Most of these measures are of the self-report kind but some are attitudinal, systematically examining work-related attitudes and beliefs, while others are quite specifically concerned with attributional styles.

The approach of the development of a work-specific individual difference measure has been adopted by those from both personality and occupational psychology traditions. However, there are a number of self-evident draw-backs. These include:

- Rarely, if ever, do researchers pay much attention to the aetiology of the trait or dimension being measured. This could be an important feature in understanding developmental features associated with the trait.
- Almost by definition the measures have limited applicability, as they are designed specifically for the workplace and are therefore presumably restricted to it in terms of predictability.
- Frequently, but not always, the background theoretical work on the processes, mechanisms and phenomena associated with the trait (which explains how and why the trait determines behaviour) is not done sufficiently or sufficiently well, no doubt because the task is seen primarily as an applied one.
- As mentioned above, there is frequently a confounding or overlap between the independent and dependent variable such that it is very circular and tautological. Thus, some measures ask a person with whom they communicate at work and then proceed to determine through sociometric analysis their communication patterns. Tautological research can be a waste of time.

There is clearly still much scope for this approach to personality at work. The current literature shows sporadic rather than sustained effort and some evidence of faddishness regarding the choice of both independent and dependent variable. Nevertheless, there is some considerable evidence that this approach may prove very fruitful, e.g. the work on occupationally salient attributional style (Furnham et al., 1994).

The concept of "fit" and "misfit" at work

Probably because of its intuitive appeal this approach has a fairly long history (Pervin, 1967). The idea is quite simple: based on personality, predispositions, some jobs are more suitable for the individual than others. Based on a comparable analysis of both the person and the job it may be possible accurately to measure the degree of fit (which is desirable) or misfit (undesirable). The work of Holland (1985) is most relevant here. Variations on this theme include:

- Whether the analysis is based more on jobs or individuals. Clearly, to obtain a measure of fit, *both* people and jobs need to be analysed and measured, however the measurement of the one is nearly always based on the concepts/language developed by the other. In most cases, and for obvious reasons, the conceptual language of fit is based on personality or individual differences rather than jobs.

- Impressionistic vs. "geometric". A second crucial feature is whether the concept of "fit" is simply subjectively impressionistic or rather that it is objective, measurable and "geometric". Few would argue that the former approach is the more desirable but there are certain difficulties associated with the latter approach, notably the complexity of the multi-dimensional geometric model.
- Similarity vs. complementarity. There is extensive, if somewhat equivocal, literature on similarity and attraction between individuals, which offers three hypotheses: similar people are attracted; the attraction of opposites; and the concept of complementarity. Though there is no evidence for the attraction of opposites concept (which in the context of Pervin's work becomes the misfit hypothesis), it remains uncertain whether the similarity or complementarity hypothesis is to be supported.

This approach, like the others, is not without its problems:

- Pattern vs. formulae? One approach to this area is to devise a limited number of types (of people and/or job) and show their relationships in some mosaic or pattern. This allows for some nice geometric (Euclidean) calculations. On the other hand it may be possible to write a formula that expresses fit in the form of simultaneous equations.
- "Fit" studies are by definition correlational and not causal, hence it is not possible to infer directionality such as the idea that misfit *leads to* absenteeism. Indeed, it is quite possible and feasible to derive hypotheses and explanations with fit as the dependent, not the independent, variable.
- Everything in this approach is based on the veridical nature, sensitivity, comprehensiveness and clarity of conceptualisation of the variables that make up the fit. Where, for instance, these are conceived too vaguely or widely, the resultant fit measures are practically worthless.

This remains one of the most promising areas of research, notwithstanding these problems, because of its predictive power. Predictably, the concept of fit has been particularly popular in such research areas as vocational choice and "problems" at work, for example stress and health. However, the real promise of the fit–misfit literature lies in predicting motivation and satisfaction at work, an area still currently neglected.

Longitudinal studies of people in work

It is almost universally recognised that longitudinal research is invaluable in examining how a multitude of variables (personality, psychographic, demographic) change over time, relate to one another at different periods, and *predict* behaviour. That is to say, the concept of cause is best examined longitudinally. However, it is also widely recognised that longitudinal research is fiendishly difficult, expensive and problematic. Nevertheless, some studies have examined personality at work over time.

Again studies come in many different forms:

- Short, medium vs. long time spans. It is not always clear what comprises a "longitudinal" time span – a year, five years, ten years? Studies of less than a couple of years, though longitudinal, can not reveal substantial differences that operate over longer periods such as decades. On the other hand, studies carried out over very long periods (twenty years or more) have difficulties in accounting for drop-outs, etc.

- Within or between organisations. Some organisations have sponsored or allowed research to be conducted within their, albeit very large, organisation. Within-organisation studies, by definition, seriously restrict the range and type of variable that can be examined. On the other hand, between-organisational studies (following individuals over time) frequently do not allow for sufficient comparisons.
- Retrospective vs. prospective. Some longitudinal studies are done by archival research, where past records are compared to current data. Given that these records exist, such studies are robust, useful and sensitive. Alternatively, one can begin a study now and plan it into the future. The latter approach is clearly preferable because one has more control over what is measured, how and when.

Longitudinal research only has problems if it is done badly or, of course, if it is discontinued for one reason or another. Scarcity of resources means that frequently good research is not done. Most common problems are:

- Too few subjects, or not knowing whether "drop-outs" occur for systematic reasons. Tracing people's behaviour at work over lengthy periods is difficult but restricting numbers because of costs only limits the generalisability of the research.
- Poor measurements of the variables. Either because one is limited to the organisation's own records (such as application and assessment forms), or because measurement techniques have substantially improved over the years, early measures may be psychometrically unsound, thus threatening the quality of the results.
- Restricted range of variables. Studies done on particular individuals (a class of students), or of employees from a particular organisation, by definition are restricted and thus may not be reliable. In addition between-organisation variables cannot be considered. Clearly, this is only important if these unmeasured variables are significant, but one can only know this if they are examined.

A few good longitudinal studies of this sort exist, but they too have their limitations, and it is highly desirable, if we are to understand personality differences at work, that more research of this sort be done.

Biographical or case-history research

This approach, akin to the "great-man" theory of history, examines in detail the life of one individual to see what clues it provides as to which biographical factors predict job success. There are not many examples of this approach but those that exist do differ on various criteria:

- Individuals vs. groups. Some approaches consider only the lives of particular individuals, while others consider a whole family (a dynasty), or people who have attended a particular institution and done well later in life.
- Monetary vs. "other" success criteria. It is rather difficult to decide which criteria of success (or failure) are appropriate to use in order to select the "successful" people to examine.
- Impressionistic vs. scholarly. Some studies on successful entrepreneurs are in the

"best seller" tradition where the "readability" of the story is more important than obtaining or understanding the facts. On the other hand, scholarly biographies are rarely sweepingly interpretative as to how, when and why biographical factors predict occupational success.

The biographical approach is intuitively appealing, and often most interesting to the general public, but it is very uncertain to what extent it can and does inform the issue of personality determinants of work success. Major problems include:

- Only highly successful people are considered. Thus, there is a very serious sampling problem because there appears to be no theoretical reason why particular people are chosen for analysis. This means that the data available are highly unrepresentative.
- There is almost never a control group. That is, there is no comparison person or group to compare to those studied in detail. It is therefore impossible to understand precisely which factors do or do not relate to occupational success.
- Atheoretical research means no systematic testing of hypotheses. Rarely, if ever, are biographers led to attempt to seek out particular facts to test hypotheses.

Meta-analyses of studies

Any reviewer trying to understand which, how, when and why personality variables predict job success has an almost impossible task in attempting to find and evaluate and understand 100 years of research on the topic. However, over the past 20 years or so researchers have been doing meta-analyses (Hunter & Schmidt, 1990). They have argued that this form of analysis corrects for error and bias in research findings. Some of the most impressive and comprehensive examples of this work have been done by Ones and her colleagues (Ones et al., 2006).

Meta-analysis essentially involves collecting together all studies that fulfil a particular set of criteria and then doing an analysis of some systematic results. Thus, meta-analyses have been done on the relationships between intelligence test scores and training outcome as well as productivity at work (see Chapter 6). Before being put into these analyses studies have to fulfil certain criteria usually associated with the instruments used, experimental findings and the data reported. Some researchers are stricter than others but all strive to be as inclusive and comprehensive as possible.

Thus, while individual studies may show conflicting results a meta-analysis of many (if not nearly all) studies in an area shows a clear trend. Further, the meta-analyses reveal a number of important indices that reveal the relationship between variables. This often painstaking task has been very important in the area of personality and intelligence at work. Meta-analyses have shown systematic explicable relationships between personality and intelligence test scores as well as the relationship between personality and work outcomes and intelligence and work outcomes. As a consequence it has been possible to show that intelligent, stable, open, conscientious people tend to be most successful at work.

Personality and organisational behaviour

Interestingly, although lay people view individual differences and personality as the most central, crucial, salient and interesting of psychologists' many missions, academic psychologists, particularly industrial/organisational (I/O) psychologists, still tend to take the opposite view. Despite the fact that some I/O psychologists usually proclaim that personality testing is neither useful in selection, nor in the prediction of productivity, many human resources personnel as well as negotiators and economic columnists stress the importance of understanding individual differences. Of course, the word "personality" is used differently: lay people usually mean public reputation and psychologists usually mean structure, and dynamic inner processes, which are private. "Personality" refers to stylistic consistencies in social behaviour, which are a reflection of an inner structure and process.

Most lay people are type- rather than trait-theorists (see Chapter 4). Types are categories, syndromes, trait summaries. They are the oldest and simplest way to classify people, hence their abiding popularity, but still find a role in modern psychology. Traits refer to single dimensions made up of related components. Thus, the trait of neuroticism, isolated by many researchers as a fundamental and unique trait, includes behaviours and cognitions associated with guilt, low self-esteem, depression, phobia, anxiety, and psychosomatic illnesses. Both trait and type theories provide useful heuristics with which to describe people. However, lay people shy away from using "negative" traits like neuroticism preferring more "positive" traits such as insightfulness. While lay people prefer to look for positive correlates of occupational success, many psychologists are interested in (equally predictive) negative correlates of success (see Chapter 5). It seems as if laymen infer failure from success while psychologists infer success variables, processes, structures and criteria from failure.

The ease of construction and the apparent fame (and money) that may be associated with the development of an eponymous personality test means that thousands have been published. Many are very poor, with little or no theoretical (or even clear) conceptualisation, psychometric properties, or worse, external validity. A review by Guion and Gottier (1965) was highly influential in this rejection of standard personality measures for personnel selection, no doubt because of the quality of so many of the tests used. However, a major criticism of this review was that they did not group studies according either to the tests used, the constructs upon which they were based, or the organisational criteria needed. Recent meta-analysis has been much more positive but the 1970s and 1980s showed evidence of a crisis in personality theory, which may account, in part, for the paucity of good research over the period. The issues that seemed most important were:

- Situationism – the idea that in many (work) situations, inter-individual variability in behaviour is low and personality differences are likely to have little predictive power. This theory, which has been largely disproved, suggested that personality traits were both unreliable and invalid because the major determinants of behaviour were not inside individuals but rather external, situational factors. Spurious and dubious arguments have now been settled and personality theory thrives. Yet they are seen as a resurgence among work psychologists to deny or downplay the crucial role of personality at work.
- Paradigm uncertainty – rather than see some consensus about the nature, structure and processes involved in personality, the field appears to have been further subdivided, with an earlier onslaught being from constructionists who argued that personality is a construct of the observer. However, there is more and more evidence that mainstream personality theorists are accepting the evidence of both

the fundamental (five) dimensions of personality and the biological structures determining them.

- Personality (and criterion) measurement – few measures *aggregate* multiple-act criteria or observations to provide more robust measures that reduce error variance. Once this error has been reduced, the relationship between personality measures and occupational behaviour becomes much more apparent. Previously weak findings may be simply due to measurement error rather than actual weak relationships.
- Performance consistency – not all behaviours are as consistent as others and performance distributions should be considered before predictions are made. That is, neither individual difference nor occupational behaviour can be assured to be consistent in occurrence, because both are shaped (reinforced and inhibited) by other external and structural factors. Presumably it is possible to document when, where and why behavioural consistency does and does not exist.
- Time – different types of criteria are more or less valid as predictors of occupational behaviour depending upon *when* the criterion is measured. Thus, for a person new in a job, ability will be more predictive than personality, but their role is likely to be reversed later in the same job.

A number of reviewers have pointed out the poor regard with which personality theory used to be held in I/O psychology, for example Bernadin and Beatty (1984): "The research on individual-difference variables has not borne much fruit. Rating accuracy appears to be more related to situation-specific variables than to individual characteristics" (p. 246).

Staw et al. (1986) noted that: "The field is no longer interested in what the individual brings to the work-setting in terms of behavioural tendencies, traits, and personality" (p. 57). The situation remains the same today. Thus Murphy and Dzieweczynski (2005) concluded: "The validity of measures of broad personality traits is still low, personality tests used in organisations are still poorly chosen, and links between personality and jobs are poorly understood. Personality measures are unlikely to achieve the degree of acceptance given to cognitive tests because of differences in the domains, differences in the tests and differences in the environments in which cognitive tests versus personality inventories and developed" (p. 343).

Hogan (2005b) in also critical in arguing that personality researchers do not agree on a research agenda and have little regard for practical applications. Further, test publishers seem quite unconcerned with measurement validity.

As has been pointed out previously, many organisational, occupational and industrial psychologists have historically not had much time for personality theories, constructs and measures. Certainly the only really powerful approach to receive any attention in this area is the trait approach, within a nomothetic framework, as opposed to cognitive or "self" approaches, conceived in an idiographic framework. Idiographic, or case-study, methods have usually been seen by psychologists in this area to be too unscientific to yield data of sufficient generalisability.

According to Weiss and Adler (1984), personality variables have taken two major roles in organisational behaviour research. To some extent, individual difference variables have had a central role in theory. Such variables as self-esteem, self-actualisation, expectancy-valence, need for achievement, and fear of failure are individual difference personality factors that "drive" various theories of job motivation and performance.

Other individual difference variables are seen more as moderator variables, explaining the link between job (dis)satisfaction and absenteeism. A second role has been in the design of studies, where individual differences are seen as either independent, dependent, moderator or all three variables. Naturally, cognitive and motivational factors have been concentrated on most.

Weiss and Adler (1984) described four representative areas in occupational psychology where personality constricts had been used:

1 Job scope – where motivational variables have been used extensively, e.g. locus of control and higher-order needs.
2 Leadership – researchers have long sought after personality traits linked to leadership, a concept that has been shown to have statistically significant (but not strong) direct and interactive effects on work behaviour.
3 Employee withdrawal – the scattered and diverse literature has looked at personality correlates of turnover, absenteeism, and lateness.
4 Goal setting – the idea that personality relates to level of aspiration is only comparatively recent.

However, over the past 20 years many of these areas, particularly leadership have been addressed (Judge et al., 2002b, 2004). In a later review, Adler and Weiss (1988) seemed more optimistic as a result of I/O researchers' "consideration of contextual variables and specification of criterion constructs that might relate to the personality variables of interest" (p. 311).

They reviewed a dozen or so studies on topics such as goal setting, charismatic leadership and job attitudes. They make three telling points about job attitudes: (1) The fact that job attitudes are consistent over time and across situations is in accordance with a dispositional explanation; (2) Unstable attitudes do not necessarily imply a situational explanation or rule out a dispositional one; and (3) The fact that dispositional traits might not account for more of the variance than situational factors does not mean that they are not worthy of investigation.

However, since the early 1990s there has been a massive resurgence in the interest in personality traits and their behavioural predictive power. Hogan nearly 15 years ago (1991) concluded his review of individual differences and personality in the I/O literature thus:

- The criticism of personality, popular in the 1970s and 1980s, is no longer valid.
- Much of early personality theory had a clinical bias and hence many measures are not really appropriate for predicting occupational behaviour.
- Factor-analytic research suggests five major independent traits relevant to social behaviour: neuroticism (adjustment); extraversion (sociability); conscientiousness (responsibility); agreeableness (warmth) and culture (imaginativeness).
- The relevance of accuracy of social perception for interviewing, selection and performance appraisal links personality and occupational psychology.
- Meta-analysis of 25 years of literature suggests that personality inventories can make valid contributions to personnel selection and assessment.
- One cannot forget the importance of measures, people, criteria and situations as moderator variables.

Recent reviewers and critics are much more optimistic and positive about the possibility of finding powerful relationships between personality (individual) difference variances and occupational behaviour. Yet much work remains to be done, both theoretical and empirical.

Longitudinal studies at work

Most researchers agree that longitudinal studies (well designed, planned and executed) are by far the best types of research, as they are the best naturalistic studies able to sort out cause and correlation. However, they are difficult, expensive and by definition time consuming.

Yet there are various studies that have examined the relationships between personality and work over time. Harrell and Harrell (1984) looked at personality differences between people who reached general management early, in contrast to those who held more specialised jobs. MBA students were tested five years after graduation. Over 90% ($N = 434$) responded, who by that time were in a variety of jobs. Four scales of the MMPI showed significant differences. General managers were higher than consultants on *Pd* (Psychopathic deviate). This presumably reflected a need for autonomy or independence. General managers were higher than marketeers, consultants, and engineers on *Pa* (Paranoia), all at .05 level. This presumably reflected intensity and sincerity. General managers were higher at the .5 level than Accounts on *Ma* (Hypomania), which probably meant energy level. General managers were lower on *Si* (Social introversion) than accountants (.01 level) and production men (.05 level), meaning that general managers were more socially extraverted.

Also, Harrell et al. (1977) tested 266 graduates, 5 and 10 years after graduating. A regression analysis was performed aiming to regress a battery of personality data (with 31 different scales); a "high earner's scale", which measured leadership, energy, sociability, and dominance; age of entrance to university, and graduation grade-point average. Age, grade-point average and the "higher earner's scale" correlated significantly with five-year earnings. Whereas the Strong Vocational Interest Blank Managerial Orientation correlated positively with five-year earnings, the SVIB engineer correlated negatively. The results were repeated on the 10-year group and the results were much the same. Overall, the personality data from the MMPI did not prove significant.

Anderson (1977) tracked 90 entrepreneurs over a 2.5-year period, following the debilitating effects of a natural disaster. He looked at their locus of control (as measured by the Rotter scale); their perceived stress, their various coping behaviours and their performance in the organisation. Those with the more healthy and adaptive internal locus of control tended to experience low stress and employed more task-centred and less emotion-centred coping behaviours than externals. Interestingly, successful internals became more internal and unsuccessful externals more external over this period. The cross-lagged correlation coefficients suggested that locus of control influences performance, which in turn operates as a feedback mechanism and influences locus of control.

Hinrich's (1978) study followed 47 people who had been assessed on various dimensions over an 8-year period. Ratings of aggressiveness, persuasiveness, oral communication, self-confidence and test ratings on ascendancy and self-assurance were most strongly related to performance 8 years later. The two simple ratings – overall rating and general-management evaluation – correlated .58 with the ratings 8 years later. The

Gordon Personal Profile and various value ratings used in this study seemed excellent predictors 8 years on.

Brousseau (1978) followed 116 engineers, scientists, and managers employed by a large petroleum company over 5.9 years. They were given the Guilford–Zimmerman Temperament Survey, which was used to derive four characteristics: (1) Active Orientation – outgoing, optimistic, lively and risky; (2) Philosophical Orientation – serious minded and liking self-analysis; (3) Freedom from Depression – energetic, seldom tired, vigorous, non-neurotic; and (4) Self-confidence – seldom hurt or disappointed.

These scores were related to five characteristics of the person's job: skill variety, task identity, task significance, autonomy and feedback. The results showed that active orientation (extraversion) and freedom from depression (non-neuroticism) were related to task identity, task significance and job summary. The results provide some support for the overall theory, which proposes that an individual's life-orientation and level of emotional well-being is influenced by the stimulus complexity of their job experience.

Schneidman (1984) interviewed 11 lawyers in the 1980s who had been interviewed by Terman in the 1920s. Occupational success seemed related to contentment, self-confidence, openness, spontaneity, and freedom from feelings of hostility, irritability and dissatisfaction. But, of course, in studies such as this it is not easy to separate cause and effect.

Kohn and Schooler (1982) examined data collected in 1964 from 3101 men (a representative male sample) and a follow-up of a quarter of that number (who were still under 65 years of age) 10 years later. They were particularly interested in the reciprocal effects of job conditions and personality.

They consistently found evidence of the reciprocal effects of job conditions on personality and vice versa. They noted:

> Jobs that facilitate occupational self-direction increase men's ideational flexibility, and promote a self-directed orientation to self and to society; jobs that limit occupational self-direction decrease men's ideational flexibility and promote a conformist orientation to self and to society. The analysis further demonstrates that opportunities for exercising occupational self-direction, especially for doing substantively complex work, are to a substantial extent determined by the job's location in the organisational structure with ownership, bureaucratisation, and a high position in the supervisory hierarchy all facilitating the exercise of occupational self-direction. Those findings provide strong empirical support for the interpretation that class-associated conditions of work actually do affect personality. The longitudinal analysis also provides evidence of other job-to-personality effects, the most important being that oppressive working conditions produce a sense of distress. . . . In short, occupations self-direction, ideational flexibility, and a self-directed orientation are intertwined in a dynamic process through which the individual's place in the stratification system both affects and is affected by his personality.

(pp. 1281–1283)

Inwald (1988) did a five-year, follow-up study of 219 correction officers who were hired in a one-year period. He was particularly interested in whether test results, as well as psychological interpretations and interviews, could predict 28 officers who were "terminated". Test results proved to be the best predictors but although they could identify up to 75% of those sacked, it scored "false hits" in as many as a third of the cases. The Inwald Personality Inventory proved particularly useful at predicting subsequent sackings, and was, of course, much cheaper and efficient than interviews. Inwald recognised that termination did not represent the only or the best assessment criterion, but was impressed that personality inventory scores could predict so well into the future.

In an extensive longitudinal study Mortimer et al. (1986) followed 512 young men to see how social, family, and personality factors affected their occupational attainments. The study had a number of quite specific questions it aimed to address. These included: Are individual psychological attributes mainly formed by the end of adolescence, or do they continue to change over time in response to major life experiences encountered in adulthood? What is the effect of social structure, particularly occupational location on occupational attainment? How does family life affect work and vice versa, and what is the effect of both on personality?

Through path analysis they sought answers to both psychological and sociological questions, such as whether socioeconomic origins or psychological/personality factors together, or individually, determine occupational success. The results showed a pervasive impact of the father–son relationship on such things as achievement-related attitudes, but early assistance and support was highly rated. The two measures of family influence – socioeconomic status and paternal support – appeared to have both short- and long-term effects.

Because this study examined attitudes, values and experiences *before* people joined the labour market, it was possible to examine self-selection and self-fulfilling characteristics. Results showed that self-confidence indirectly influenced work autonomy a decade later through its influence on intrinsic skills.

Mortimer et al.'s data seem to suggest that the "psychological" variables that they measured, namely self-competence, work involvement, people-oriented values, intrinsic values, and extrinsic values were fairly stable over time. The authors therefore concluded that an individual's sense of identity and values is largely formed by the end of adolescence. However, the results also indicated that experiences of autonomy in the work environment do, and can, influence self-competence.

Still by far the most interesting and unique study, however, was that of Howard and Bray (1988), who followed managers for 20 years; having attended assessment centres at joining, 8 years later, and 20 years after that. The sample consisted of over 422 men who joined Bell in the 1950s. In the 1950s they were assessed according to their: Family and educational background; Lifestyles (9 categories were devised such as parental-familial; religious humanism); Work interests; Work history; Expectations and work preferences; Work attitudes (10 areas were considered such as supervision, satisfaction, and salary); Personality and motivation (various standard questionnaires that yielded seven measures: self-esteem, leadership, motivation, positiveness, impulsivity, affability, and ambition); Abilities (administrative, interpersonal, and cognitive); Overall assessment evaluations (seven dimensions being administrative skills, interpersonal skills, intellectual ability, advancement motivation, work involvement, stability of performance, and independence).

The authors were interested in the "harbingers of career advancement", the seeds of personal adjustment and how changing times and lifestyles affected the work force. Most pertinent for this book is how personality changed over time. The most dramatic change was in ambition, which dropped steeply in the first 8 years and then again by year 20. Graduates, more ambitious to begin with, actually dropped more steeply.

Self-esteem remained much the same, as did impulsivity, but affability did not drop much over time. Yet, achievement orientation (having a challenging job or a difficult assignment) increases over time. Aggression and autonomy went up over the years, while deference abasement and endurance tended to drop.

Ability measures, on the other hand, tended to change less dramatically though there were numerous and noticeable differences between college and non-college graduates. Thus, administrative skills and work involvement tended to increase with graduates over the 20-year period, while they decreased for non-graduates. This may or may not be explained by intelligence.

This extremely rich and detailed account considers, among other things, the effects of career advancement. For instance, they examined how attitudes had changed from time 1 (MPS 0) to time 20 (MPS 20). What it showed was that over time, attitudes change, such that low scorers get lower and high scorers get higher. In 6 of the 10 cases where differences were noticeable, this "lens" effect occurred. Similarly personality and motivational changes were noted. Self-esteem did not change much but other changes are certainly worth noting:

- Ambition continued to differentiate workers most sharply, with the disparity growing slightly larger over time (i.e. lack of ambition led to less advancement, which self-fulfilled the lack of ambition).
- Leadership motivation clearly distinguished the job-level groups over time, but the higher-level men increased in this desire while the lower-level men decreased.
- Affability declined for all groups, particularly those at the top, but, interestingly, increased for the very bottom group.

Howard and Bray (1988) "cut" the data yet another way by looking at how the various measures related to personal adjustment twenty years on. They found five of the six personality and motivational factors were related to adjustment ratings. Findings showed:

- The poorly adjusted gave up readily on career aspirations, while the very opposite was true of the well adjusted.
- Positiveness and self-esteem become even more pronounced, over time, in their relatedness to adjustment.
- The relationship between affability and adjustment, while virtually very strong, reduces over time.

This remarkable study allowed for the examination of the correlates of managerial potential. At the very beginning of their time with the company, employees were rated on a 5-point potential scale – that is, potential that the person would reach a fairly high position in the company. This rating was fairly consistently related to personality factors. The higher-rated potential managers were characterised by strong desires to achieve as leaders and professionals. They had a greater ambition to advance, while the lower-rated potential managers indicated in their interviews that job security was most valued. The relationship of the adjusted conformity and positive factors to potential, was consistent with the relationship of potential to the Positiveness factor. The Positiveness factor indicated that the higher-potential managers had higher general adjustment, optimism, and self-confidence as rated from the projective exercise.

Similarly, personality and motivational factors were logically, and frequently strongly, correlated with ratings of adjustment. Ambition and Positivity were equally related to Management potential and Adjustment, while Positiveness and Adjusted Conformity were predominantly related to Adjustment. Equally, the Self-Esteem factor correlated significantly with Adjustment, but not with Management potential.

There are also recent studies on the stability of intelligence over time (Whalley & Deary, 2001) and the surprising extent to which intelligence test scores predict so many life-relevant variables over the life span (Gottfredson & Deary, 2004; see Chapter 6). Certainly, despite what many people like to believe the evidence is that all individuals are surprising stable over time and across social situations. There have been many important and interesting longitudinal studies that followed participants for over 20 years (Caspi, 2000; Caspi & Roberts, 2001). They have tended to show modest but predictable correlation between childhood temperament, adult personality traits as well as outcome variables. Most provide impressive evidence of stability over time but relatively few of the more recent studies have considered work outcomes over time. Consistency rather than change is the norm. Thus, work-related behaviour of individuals is likely to endure if closely related to individual difference.

The importance of these longitudinal studies cannot be underestimated, because unlike most cross-sectional studies they are able to disentangle cause and effect as well as test for moderator and mediator variables. What most of these careful studies have demonstrated is that, first, most individual differences do not change much over time and, second, that they relate directly and systematically to occupational behavioural variables like position, promotion history, and salary.

Conclusion

This book is about individual differences and their impact on all working behaviours. Various chapters look at the data and theories on personality traits, types and temperaments, as well as cognitive and social intelligences and when, how and why they relate to work behaviours. However, it goes further to look at dysfunctional behaviours at work, creativity and work and the concept of competence.

This chapter considered how personality and intelligence are related: that is why there are replicable, explicable and therefore predictable relationships between test scores on these two measures. However, what is important to bear in mind is that *both* are important in predicting work-related outcomes. Further, there are many other concepts like creativity, psychopathology or competence, which are hybrids between the two concepts. Each will be addressed in this book.

The research on individual differences at work spans a century. There have been times of great research endeavour and times of cynical lethargy inspired by the belief that individual differences are not very important. Whilst the 20-year period from 1960 to 1980 was dominated by scepticism, the period since then has been a great renaissance on the part of many researchers. Most importantly, personality psychologists have taken much more interest in work variables and work psychologists in individual differences. Despite the cost and difficulty of longitudinal studies and meta-analyses it is perhaps these two research traditions that have been most important in demonstrating the relevance of individual difference at work.

Furthermore, there is now a healthy debate and dialogue between researchers from different areas and that can only be good for the field.

2 Methods to assess work behaviour and potential

Introduction

Inevitably, nearly everyone in an organisation is, at some point, in the business of assessment of others. Many senior staff and all HR professionals are in the business of *selection*. Most managers, even supervisors, are required to assess their staff regularly using *appraisal* systems. Nearly all managers, particularly at more senior levels, are mandated with *development* and *training* responsibilities, which involve assessment. And even the "lowliest of staff" are now frequently required to assess (rate) their boss in 360° feedback exercises.

However, evaluation and assessment is different from appraisal. Performance appraisal and assessment are, in many ways, about the same thing. However, the average, rather poorly done, performance evaluation process is not really as well planned as an assessment (Jeanneret & Silzer, 2000, p. 6).

Evaluation or assessment is typically focused on summarising current behaviour and dispositions, whilst assessment is typically focused on predicting future behaviour and performance potential. Often evaluation depends almost exclusively on the evaluator's observational skills, while assessment often depends on both reliable psychological tools and the assessor's observational skills. Usually evaluation uses techniques that are rarely researched or validated, while assessment uses tools and techniques that have been researched and validated. Sometimes evaluation involves an evaluator who is poorly trained, often subjective and influenced by "organisation hearsay", while, ideally, assessment involves an assessor who is highly trained, objective, and removed from organisational influence. Often evaluation assesses only a small subset of skills and behaviours or "fashionable" performance areas, while good assessment assesses a standard and comprehensive set of skills, abilities, and characteristics. It is not unusual for evaluation to become contaminated by other organisational systems like compensation. However, hopefully, assessment maintains independence from organisational systems. Evaluation can summarise conclusions inconsistently or poorly, but good assessment documents conclusions in a consistent and professional manner.

Most people know that assessment of personality, ability and potential really matters, particularly at work. It has been estimated that the difference between a *good* and an *average* worker will be between 40% and 70% of their salary. In other words on an average salary of £30,000, there may be around £15,000 difference to the value of the organisation between the good employee compared to the strictly average employee.

For a very long time, and still today, selection follows a traditional path: advertisement, application form, references and interview. Arnold et al. (2005) list seven commonly used methods, interviews, psychometric tests, references, biodata, work-sample tests, handwriting analysis and assessment centres. Each of these will be reviewed in this chapter. Essentially all methods can be grouped under four headings: (1) *Self-report* (what people say about themselves in interviews or on personality/preference tests, or completing biographical reports); (2) *Observational data* (what other people say about them in references or at assessment centres); (3) *Test data* (showing how they perform on very specific tests such as cognitive ability tests); and (4) *Bio-logical/physiological data* (which involves a comprehensive analysis of brain and body functioning).

There have been a number of important developments particularly through psycho-metric assessment methods. These are a regular source of popular and academic debate (Barrett, 2003). In all assessment there is an *ideal* process and an *actual* process. Doyle (2003, p. 260) notes that the ideal process and actual process are frequently very different from each other. He argues that seven questions should be, but are often not, asked: (1) What does the job entail? (2) What sort of people could do it? (3) Where can I find such people? (4) How would I recognise someone who could do the job/be the best at it? (5) How can I avoid bias? (6) How will I know that I've go the best person/got the selection process right? and (7) What's it worth to get it right? These seven questions suggested by Doyle all have action implications. They are all important questions and they underline the complexity of the activity if it is to be done properly.

Assessment is about finding people who *can* and *will* work in a particular job. It is also about understanding their preferences, particularities and peccadilloes *and* making sure that they are well managed and developed to get the best out of them.

A great deal of assessment employs psychological tests (of power and preference) of one sort or another. Psychological tests refer, essentially, to a standardised series of questions or problems that attempts to assess a particular human characteristic (ability, attitudes, knowledge, interests, personality, skills). A psychometric test is usually one that has been thoroughly investigated to examine its *reliability* (gives similar answers on various different occasions) and *validity* (measures what it says it measures). The terms reliability and validity may well have different meanings depending upon whether one is a psychometrician (academic/scientist) or a practitioner. Whilst the technical meaning will be followed here practitioners may think of reliability as agreement by the candidate and validity as positive reactions by the candidate themselves.

Tests differ enormously. For instance there are group vs. individually administered tests. Some require a one-to-one administrator, others can be easily and effectively be run in largish groups. There are "objective" vs. open-ended tests. The former requires the choice of several responses; the latter means one has to generate the response. Equally one could distinguish between pen-and-paper vs. performance tests, the latter involve the manipulation of apparatus, equipment or even tools, and power vs. speed tests. A number of these will be considered in this chapter.

The use of tests in selection and assessment

There are references to crude selection tests in the Bible. Gideon used a "drinking test" to select soldiers (Judges 7: 4–7). The ancient Chinese used a range of tests to select their mandarins. In the nineteenth century people used graphology, astrology, etc. Work-sample tests were used before the first war in America. They were later used extensively in the First and Second World Wars.

The first intelligence tests were constructed in 1904 and used extensively in the Great War. Similarly, it was in the First World War that personality tests were first used to *select out* men who could not stand the stress of continuous battle. The first group exercises and assessment centres (War Office Selection Board; Civil Service Selection Board) were used by the British army in the early 1940s.

It is important to know the history of assessment methods in order to know what is simply being repackaged and updated as well as what is actually new. Equally it is important to know what techniques have fallen out of favour (e.g. graphology) and why (because it proved invalid). In fact most of the techniques used today are well established. Thus while there has been development, progress and revision in nearly every assessment method most have a long history associated with them.

There has, in fact, been an important resurgence of interest and research in psychometrics and psychometric testing. Partly because of increasing agreement about the dimensions of both personality and intelligence and partly as a function of the increased sophistication of researchers, there is a new spirit of enthusiasm and optimism.

Enthusiasm for testing waxes and wanes in organisations and society at large. Economic conditions, test publisher activity, celebrated court cases, and changes in the law are all important. Yet the most central question underlying the whole testing enterprise is test validity. Overall psychometric tests used in the workplace have come out of rigorous scientific assessments rather well.

Note what Goldberg (2005, personal communication) concludes in a provocative but fully documented paper:

> Once upon a time, many folks thought it cool to disparage the predictive utility of personality measures, especially those based on self-reports. Over the past two decades, such a jaundiced view has been shown to be false. Specifically, we now know that well-constructed measures of personality traits predict *the most important life* events (e.g. health-related behaviours and outcomes, including morbidity and mortality; job performance, including leadership styles; educational achievement, even after controlling for cognitive test scores; relationship outcomes, including marital failure; and of course virtually all serious mental disorders, including drug and alcohol abuse). Moreover, personality measures predict these criteria *far more validly* than do most medical/biological measures predict diseases, including obesity and diabetes, cholesterol and heart disease, and smoking and lung cancer.
>
> How could this overwhelming body of evidence have been overlooked? First of all, one must acknowledge the general disdain on the part of some sceptics for psychological as opposed to biological measures of individual differences. Probably of more importance, however, are the metrics used to establish effect size in psychology as compared to medicine. In general, psychologists use effect size measures (such as the correlation coefficient) that include the entire distribution of research participants, not simply its tails. In contrast, odds ratios and the like can be constructed from extreme groups, thus excluding the vast majority of folk in the middle of the distribution. Clearly, effect size measures based on extreme groups can appear to be much larger than those based on the entire sample.
>
> One lesson that we should all have learned by now is that even small effects can be of enormous importance when the outcome is momentous enough: Clinical trials have been stopped on the basis of correlations in the .02 to .05 range, when based on large samples (ensuring that the results are reliable), and when the outcome

is mortality. Because the effect sizes for personality measures are far larger than that, even against the criterion of mortality, at least some personality measures should routinely be included in most if not all epidemiological surveys.

In many sectors and in many countries, there appears to be a renewed interest and faith in the ability of tests to validly identify those likely to be superior performers at work. They are seen to be both cost-efficient and highly effective.

Costing assessment and assessment trends

What is the ratio of the *best to worst* performers in any job? That is, assuming we could get a sensitive and accurate measure of various people's performance, how much more productive (measured by quality or quantity) is the best worker (in the top 10%) from the worst/least-effective worker (bottom 10%).

The answer depends on the job, but the simple rule appears to be that the best produce about *twice* as much as the worst and that this increases for more difficult and complex jobs. It is, therefore, possible to calculate the difference between good and bad workers in any job. Another rule of thumb for researchers appears to be 40–70%. That is, the difference between good and bad workers is between 40% and 70% of their salary whereas the difference between the best and worst may be much higher. So the rule of thumb (Cook, 2004) is: "The value of a good employee minus the value of a poor employee is roughly equal to the salary paid for the job."

Thus, at £60,000 you may assume that you are getting around £81,000 worth from the good, and £39,000 from the bad, but £102,000 from the best and £18,000 from the worst. Whilst these exact calculations are in dispute everyone hopefully recognises the importance of selecting the right people.

There are also ways of calculating the *return* on selection, investment of time and money. The calculation is based on five factors that are put into a formula, they are: (1) the validity of the test; (2) the calibre of the recruits; (3) the distinction in value between good and bad employees; (4) the cost of selection; and (5) the proportion of applicants selected.

So, using this formula, it is quite possible to show that on a set salary of say £30,000 the saving for the organisation (per annum) by selecting good, over poor, candidates maybe £5000 per annum. This number is multiplied by the number of candidates.

One can also use these formulae to determine when it is a good idea to invest more in selection procedures. The answer is clear. Spending more money on selection assessment is a good idea when, first, the calibre of the recruitment is high, rather than uniformly average, and, second, when employees differ quite widely in their worth to the organisation, i.e. procedure has high validity.

Cook (2004, p. 281) looking at the value of good employees concludes:

- "Utility theory deals with the cost-effectiveness of selection.
- People vary in the amount of work they do, and in the value of their work to the organisation.
- It is possible to estimate how people vary by various techniques, including rational estimates.
- Estimates of how much people vary can be used to determine when selection is cost-effective (and when it is not).

- Estimates of how people vary can also be used to estimate on selection programmes.
- Utility estimates do not seem to impress managers all that much.
- Some preliminary evidence suggests that good selection may improve an organisation's profitability."

There have been various surveys of employers asking *what* selection methods they used. Whilst their results give a quick and useful snapshot, they have many limitations. This includes the (un)representative nature of the sample; the fact that important distinctions are rarely made between senior/junior jobs or between which tests they use and why. However, what the results show is surprisingly similar between countries, sectors and job levels.

A British study (Hodgkinson et al., 1995) of 176 UK employees showed the following rank order from most- (always) to least- (never) used methods: interview; references; application form; ability test; personality test; assessment centre; structured interview; and biodata. However, a similar American Study (Rynes et al., 1997) of 251 employers showed a rather different pattern: references; structured interview; drug test; school/university grades; interview; work trial; work sample; ability test; personality test; assessment centre; and biodata.

Overall, however, an unstructured interview, references and some application-form data seem to be collected for nearly *every* selection task. Paradoxically these have been shown to be some of the *least* valid ways to assess people. However, there is much less agreement about job analysis. Whilst text books all argue that job analysis should precede person specification and then person assessment, this is almost never done. Indeed many organisations appear to be neither very interested in, nor skilled at, job analysis.

What is changing in assessment? Are there any clear definable trends? In 2000 three Belgian researchers (Lievens et al., 2002) asked 16 HR specialists to list and describe three current or future trends they considered to be important in personnel selection (Table 2.1).

Table 2.1 Current trends in personnel selection

Trend/challenge in personnel selection	*Frequency*
1 E-recruitment, e-assessment, online recruiting and testing, Internet selection, the Internet, Web-based testing, technological challenges, integration of selection into human resource information systems, video-based tests.	21 (28)
2 Competency-based selection, competency-based interviewing, competencies, competency management, competency-based assessment (and development).	15 (20)
3 Selection in tight labour markets, job marketing, human resource marketing, shrinking labour force, employer brand marketing, war for talent.	9 (12)
4 Emotional Intelligence	8 (11)
5 International selection, expatriate selection, selection in the EU, globalisation.	6 (8)
6 Specialisation of consultancy firms, increasing competition.	2 (3)
7 Impact of legislation.	2 (3)
8 Outsourcing of selection	2 (3)
9 Team selection	2 (3)
10 Miscellaneous (only once mentioned)	9 (12)

Note: Each participant was asked to list three trends. However, not all participants listed three trends; $n = 26$; percentages are shown in parentheses.

Source: Lievens et al. (2002).

They believed they could detect *four* themes of importance:

1   *Labour market shortages*: Shortages across Europe have led many companies to rethink their strategy and process to ensure it is fair to all concerned and that they can attract and correctly identify talented individuals.
2   *Technological developments*: Two issues are relevant; the administration of tests via computers as well as recruitment and testing on-line via the Internet.
3   *Applicant perceptions*: This refers to the perceptions of applicants as to the fairness and validity of the assessment process. This is, in part, not only an impression-management task for all organisations, but also refers to the effect of assessment methods on job acceptance and subsequent performance.
4   *Construct-driven approaches*: This refers to being clear about what one is trying to assess and why. That is having a theory and evidence for the factors/constructs that one is trying to assess and showing their predictive validity.

Lievens et al. conclude:

> Although the four trends were discussed separately, it is clear that they are related. For example, the use of technology in personnel selection and the constructs measured affect applicants' perceptions of the selection procedure. Another example is the relationship between labour market shortages and applicant perceptions. On the one hand, it is clear that applicants' perceptions of the treatment in selection procedures will impact on the image of companies as employers and their attractiveness for prospective applicants on the labour market. On the other hand, labour market shortages may also impinge upon applicant perceptions in the selection process. After all, in labour markets which favours the applicant, people's perceptions of apparently poor treatment by a recruiting organisation will likely be more negative than under more neutral labour market conditions. Moreover, higher-performing applicants may well be knowledgeable of their market value and have possible opportunities for employment with other competitor employers.
>
> (p. 595)

More recently Anderson et al. (2004) also identified four major themes for future research and practice in selection.

1   *Bi-modal prediction*. This means that because jobs are changing so much and so rapidly, recruiters and selectors have first to predict the likely components of a changeable work role and then, second, address the issue of person–work role fit. There are four questions associated with this: How can organisations select for highly changeable job roles, newly created jobs and flexible forms of working? How can job analysis techniques be made flexible enough to measure future task elements? To what extent is the traditional method able to deal with unstable criteria measurement problems? What is the validity of measures of cognitive ability for changeable work roles?
2   *Multilevel fit*. There can be person–job, person–team and person–organisation fit, misfit and neutral fit. Questions for this issue are: How can one select for these three different types of fit concurrently? How can ideas of person–job fit be expanded to take into consideration other types of fit? How can one balance these types of fit?

3   *Applicant reactions and decision making.* This refers to what candidates see or think about the way they are assessed and any effects on their decision making. Questions of relevance include: How do applicants process the information they receive in the assessment process? How do applicant perceptions relate to other criteria like validity and adverse impact?

4   *Tension between research and practice.* Here they distinguish good *pragmatic* science, and *popularist* science (low on rigour), *pedantic* science (low on practical relevance) and *puerile* science (low on both).

Bartram (2004) also lists some emerging trends that he observes concerning assessment in organisations. These include:

- Trying to find tests that work and are useful in a multinational global business environment.
- A desire for computer-based expert systems that provide job analysis/competency profiling and tests/rank orders candidates with respect to those criteria.
- An increase in computerised testing.
- Concern with employee honesty and dependability.
- Concern with test security and protecting all assessment from compromise through coaching.
- A search for valid predictors that minimise adverse impact (i.e. illegal or non-sensible discrimination).
- Tests that can pick up knowledge, abilities and traits that are useful for thriving in a flexible work situation.

Kwiatkowski (2003) points out that changes occur in who organisations want in their organisation; who they choose to do the assessing; how the assessments should be done; whether diversity issues need to be confronted and whether to seriously consider what employees want. He points out various trends: assessment for working in teams (tele-workers) is central; the idea of selecting for cultural organisational fit (not job–person fit) remains important; small-to-medium sized enterprises are growing and appearing more and more to need (and value) assessment; many organisations now outsource HR functions like assessment and will continue to do so; line managers are encouraged to do assessment for more junior staff; new techniques being considered are neurological functioning and genetic testing; individuals will be encouraged to have and be able to produce authenticated, portable assessment profiles, which they can take from job to job and save them repeating assessments; psychometric tests are here to stay and are growing, especially integrity tests; Internet assessment is growing and will continue to do so; diversity of workforces is increasing; as workers are harder to recruit and retain very different groups (in terms of demography and attitudes), will have to be sought and assessed; organisations are becoming very sensitive to what employees want, which affects how, when and where they apply.

The above observations have various contradictions, i.e. assessment is outsourced but more line managers are encouraged to do it. However, these inconsistencies could be resolved by pointing out that different sectors (i.e. public vs. private) and different-sized companies (large, medium, small) in different countries respond rather differently to assessment issues.

Most of the work on trends is speculative rather than empirically based, but that is the very nature of futurology. However, there appears to be enough agreement between different writers to suggest it is possible to make good predictions as to what is coming down the assessment track at least in the forthcoming three to five years. All seem to suggest an increase rather than a decrease in the use of psychometric tests of personality and ability.

Cognitive and mental-ability tests

This refers to achievement, aptitude or mental-ability tests. Many terms cover the same areas: ability achievement, cognitive ability, mental ability and intelligence tests. These are distinct from social intelligence tests, creativity or divergent-thinking tests (see Chapter 6).

Academic research has shown that, quite consistently, cognitive ability accurately predicts job performance across *all* jobs but particularly in *complex* jobs. Many believe that intelligence is the *single best* predictor of (senior, managerial) work performance. All recent research points to the predictive power of cognitive ability and, hence, the importance of using these tests in selection (see Chapter 6).

The recent research evidence is very clear. The single best predictor of success in complex, changing, managerial jobs is intelligence. Brighter people learn faster; they have a greater store of knowledge; and they tend to be intellectually more self-confident. They analyse problems more efficiently and are less threatened by change. One can, of course, be too bright for the job if it is unskilled or unchallenging.

Many of these issues will be discussed in Chapter 6. What is true, however, is that for the vast majority of organisations who use tests they show a much greater use of personality-type preference tests than ability-type power tests. This is ironic since the validity of the latter is considerably higher than the former. Scepticism and cynicism about the use of ability tests have many historic roots. However, it does seem the case that there is now sufficient evidence to suggest that appropriately chosen and administered cognitive ability tests are highly valid assessment tools.

Personality tests

The "bottom line" in this complex and very hotly debated area is this. The validity of personality tests in predicting future work performance depends on (a) the test, (b) the criteria that one is trying to predict, and (c) the population sample. The tests are at their most useful/accurate when a good, well-validated test is used and the criteria are clear, well measured and theoretically related to the trait measured.

Over about 100 years of research and disagreement researchers have (for the most part) agreed on what is the underlying structure (i.e. personality, periodic table) of traits. There are five, and this is now called the Big Five (see Chapter 4).

Recent studies have shown that two of these are relevant to all jobs, namely Neuroticism and Conscientiousness. Successful managers have a clear profile: they tend to be low on Neuroticism (i.e. very stable), low on Agreeableness, average on Openness, highish on Extraversion and very high on Conscientiousness. Different jobs require different profiles but there are none where high Neuroticism and low Conscientiousness are an advantage.

The concept is relatively straightforward. There are five, higher-order, orthogonal (unrelated to each other) traits that are stable over time and consistent across situations. They are the best way of parsimoniously describing an individual's personality. Further, these personality factors predict how, why and when individuals behave as they do in and out of work. Arnold et al. (2005) concluded: "the literature suggests that when used appropriately, personality measures can add significant incremental validity in a selection process, over and above cognitive ability testing" (pp. 186–187).

Cook (2004, pp. 171–172) provides a useful bullet-point summary of the current research on this topic.

- "Personality is a vaguer and more diffuse concept than ability, and there are many models of personality.
- Personality is most conveniently assessed by inventory or questionnaire. It can also be assessed by interview, assessment centre, references or peer ratings.
- Personality inventories are written by a variety of methods which generally overlap to some extent, including internal analysis by statistics, and external analysis comparing groups of people with known characteristics.
- The big five factor model is widely accepted, but may not give the best prediction of work behaviour. Other models exist.
- Personality inventories have limited value in predicting how well a person can do a job.
- Personality inventories may be more successful in predicting effort driven citizenship, leadership, motivation or career success.
- Personality inventories may also be more successful in predicting avoidance of deviant or problematic behaviour at work.
- Preliminary results suggest that the relationship between team personality and team performance may be complex, and that low scorers may be able to hold back the entire group.
- Personality inventories are self-reports and not tests, and can be faked. Faking appears to affect the outcome of selection.
- Personality tests are also widely used to screen out people with problem characteristics, such as violent tendencies, deviant sexual impulses or dishonesty.
- Screening tests for employee honesty are surprisingly successful.
- Gender differences are often found with personality tests, but ethnicity differences do not seem to be a problem.
- Personality inventories have been criticised on the grounds that some of their questions are unduly intrusive."

As we shall see in Chapter 4, early reviews and meta-analyses about the validity of personality tests at work led to general scepticism on the part of academics for over 20 years. However, since the 1980s there has been good accumulating evidence of the validity of particular tests and measures of particular traits to predict a whole range of work outcomes (Robertson & Smith, 2001; Schmidt & Hunter, 1998). Experts in the area are now convinced of the validity and, thus, of the utility of personality tests in assessment of individuals at work.

Assessment is a central issue in organisational psychology. There are numerous issues that never go away and get continually debated.

Three crucial assessment issues

Many issues are important in the use of psychometric tests in selection and development but just three of those frequently debated will be considered here.

The old chestnuts of validity and reliability

Do tests give the same answers on all occasions or are they influenced by all sorts of temporary factors? This is the issue of reliability. A test cannot be valid if it is not reliable. Validity is the single, simply most important issue and it asks the question: Does the test really measure what it says it measures? This effectively means: Do test scores predict some work criterion? The problem starts with defining and measuring some actual criterion. This is a major problem.

Cook (2004, p. 239) notes: "Whatever criterion or measure of work performance is used will be imperfect. The most frequently used criterion is the supervisor rating, which is convenient and inclusive, but frequently also biased. Objective criteria such as output, absence or sales are complex, being shaped by many forces. They are also often unreliable. Increasing attention is being paid to other aspects of workplace behaviour, such as organisational citizenship. Work performance changes over time, but remains constant enough to make selection a viable enterprise. The criterion is important because it focuses the employer's mind on what they actually mean by good work performance."

There are all sorts of reasons why tests produce unreliable results. Cohen et al. (1988, p. 19) list various factors that reduce test reliability:

- "the amount of test anxiety they are experiencing and the degree to which that test anxiety might significantly affect the test results
- capacity and willingness to cooperate with the examiner or to comprehend written test instructions
- the amount of physical pain or emotional distress being experienced
- the amount of physical discomfort brought on by not having enough to eat, having had too much to eat, or other physical conditions
- the extent to which they are alert and wide awake as opposed to 'nodding out'
- the extent to which they are predisposed to agreeing or disagreeing when presented with stimulus statements
- the extent to which they have received prior coaching
- the importance they attribute to portraying themselves in a good – or bad – light, and
- the extent to which they are, for lack of a better term, 'lucky,' and can 'beat the odds' on a multiple-choice achievement test (despite the fact that they may not have learned the subject matter)."

Despite this long list of reasons why tests may not be reliable, there is good evidence of their test–retest reliability over long periods of time. Indeed they appear to be considerably more reliable than many medical tests (e.g. blood pressure) that we assume are very reliable. Tests *have* to be valid and reliable. But there are many different types of validity. Anderson and Cunningham-Snell (2000, p. 81) describe in straight-forward language the most important types:

1   "*Predictive validity*, the extent to which selection scores predict future job perform-ance. Successful applicants are tracked through the selection process and after a period of employment with the organisation a subsequent measure of performance is obtained. The selection and criterion ratings are correlated.

2   *Concurrent validity*, the extent to which selection scores predict current perform-ance. Selection techniques are administered to existing job incumbents and correl-ated with ratings of job performance taken over the same time period.

3   *Construct validity*, the extent to which selection accurately measures the constructs or dimensions it was designed to assess. The selection method is correlated with another method which is known to accurately reflect the construct.

4   *Content validity*, the extent to which the selection process adequately samples all the important dimensions of the job. This requires a thorough examination of the job description and job specification.

5   *Face validity*, the extent to which the applicant perceives the selection method to be relevant to the job.

6   *Parallel reliability*, the measurement consistency. Each candidate completes two equivalent selection methods and the two scores are correlated.

7   *Test–retest reliability*, the measurement consistency. Candidates complete the same selection method at two time points. The two scores are then correlated.

8   *Split-half reliability*, the measurement consistency. Items from a measure are divided into two halves (e.g. odd-numbered versus even-numbered items) and the scores from each half are correlated."

Each and all of these types of reliability and validity are important. These could provide an excellent checklist for anyone thinking of using any test. The question is, simply, is there evidence for each of these measures of validity and reliability in the test manual?

After considering this theory area, Cook (2004, p. 218) concludes:

- There are various ways to validate selection methods.
- Criterion validation is the traditional method which correlates predictor scores with work performance scores. This is the most convincing approach, since it relies on empirical evidence. However, statistical problems can arise, such as leverage, non-linearity or suppressor variables. Criterion validation requires fairly large numbers.
- Content validation focuses on the content of what people need to know in order to do the job, and does not require large numbers. However, it is only suitable for assessing fairly specific skills and knowledge.
- A pool of experts can estimate a test's likely validity for a particular job fairly accurately.
- Construct validation relies on attributes that people need to do a particular job (e.g. ambition or mechanical comprehension). It is probably more useful to the psych-ologist who is trying to develop a theoretical model than to the everyday selector.
- Synthetic validation relies on assembling batteries of tests that are geared to a list of competences generated by job analysis. Synthetic validation is suitable for large workforces with a wide variety of jobs, some of which have only a few people doing them.
- Predictive and concurrent validation ought to differ a great deal, but do not seems to differ that much in practice.

- Validation is necessary to ensure that the test is selecting good applicants and rejecting poor ones.
- Validation may also be needed if the test that is being used creates adverse impact.

Test validity is critically important and clearly misunderstood. Hogan et al. (1999) claim that:

> Personality assessment has a job to do, and the job is to predict behaviour. Specifically the job is to predict individual differences in people's potential for getting along and getting ahead, and most importantly in their occupations. Well-constructed personality tests do not measure dimensions that exist inside people. When people respond to items on personality tests, they are essentially responding to questions from an anonymous interviewer. Personality tests elicit self-presentations that are characteristic features of a person's interpersonal style. If we find that persons with high scores on certain test scales are described by their peers as weak, anxious and indecisive, this does not mean that we have measured a trait for submissiveness. It means, rather, that we have developed a statistical procedure for predicting how that person is likely to be described by others. Personality measurement concerns probabilities, and can be compared to measurement in petroleum geology. We know that certain critical signs co-vary with the presence or absence of certain desired characteristics – oil or a behavioural tendency. The presence of the critical signs means that there is some probably – but no certainty – that the desired characteristics will be present. In both kinds of measurement, the possibility of misdiagnosis is always present. The fact that a person receives a high score on a measure of, for example, submissiveness means that this person will probably be described by others as timid and unassertive. It does not tell us why the person behaves so as to make others describe him/her in that way.
>
> (p. 8)

It is often surprising to academic researchers that test reliability and validity are not the primary reasons for practitioner choosing and using tests. Many take this for granted – often on very poor evidence – and are more concerned with how well tests will be received in the organisation. Organisational politics often seem more important than psychometric validity.

Most well-established tests have been subjected to continuous disinterested validation research. There is now impressive evidence for the validity of many personality tests, which should guide researchers and assessors on the ones to use.

Acceptability of selection and assessment methods to candidate

Organisations are becoming more concerned with the candidates' reactions, particularly in times of labour shortages. Some have been known to whistle-blow to the press and even advocate a boycott on purchasing the products of organisations whose assessment methods are thought of as biased, unfair or inappropriate.

The following conclusions can be drawn from various more-recent studies in the area (Cook, 2004): "Candidates like interviews, work samples and assessment centres. Candidates dislike biodata, peer assessment, and personality tests. The more job-related the method (simulations, interviews, concrete ability tests) the more they are as seen to be fair. Candidates do not like being assessed on aspects of themselves (i.e. personality) which they believe they cannot (easily) change."

This is an important issue and has involved researchers trying to devise tests with high face validity. Thus, Furnham et al. (2006) have devised a proof-reading test that correlates highly with measures of intelligence. Giving a candidate an intelligence test may be popular but most individuals accept a proof-reading test in a selection exercise because proof-reading is so relevant to many jobs. In this sense, assessors have to try to hide what the test is actually measuring because of the importance of candidate reactions.

What is acceptable or desirable by a candidate may not, however, be the same for an assessor. The cost, time-taken, fakeability and validity of tests has also to be taken into consideration. There is, therefore, nearly always a trade-off between the needs and desires of the selectors and those selected.

Test coaching, practice and dissimulation

Can people be taught how to "do better" on both personality and ability tests. The issue for personality is about dissimulation: Impression management and faking good. For the test constructor, it is about getting accurate and honest scores. For the practising HR manager, it is about getting accurate test scores.

Many people reject all preference (self-report) tests because respondents are potentially dissimulating: They respond in the way they believe helps them achieve their ends but not honestly. There are various ways to try to "catch" liars and dissimulators. These include having lie tests as well as attempting to construct the profiles of these typical responses.

There has been a lot of debate around the use of ipsative measures, which are forced choice. These are known to improve (that is reduce) dissimulation but have other consequences that threaten the validity of the tests.

Detractors argue that dissimulation is not a serious problem. If it were there would be a much lower range of scores, because all would go for a, or the, desirable profile. Second, no tests would have any validity evidence because faked scores would not predict anything. This is self-evidently not true. Some argue that this is not a problem of people deliberately lying, but rather that they are unable to tell the truth because they do not have sufficient insight to do so (Furnham, 1986).

The issue is more controversial with ability tests. The question is simple and fundamentally important. Can individuals, by practice and coaching, improve their test scores? The answer is *yes*. But the more interesting and difficult question is, *by how much?*

Practice involves learning from one's own experience while coaching involves active teaching. Both are effective but the effects of coaching are achieved quite quickly and, thereafter, there is little benefit. It is also known that some tests – like the famous Raven's Progressive Matrices – are much less resistant to training. The more abstract the task, the less it seems vulnerable to coaching.

It has been argued that coaching and practice actually give a better, truer picture of a person's ability. Practice improves self-confidence and reduces test anxiety. It does not make tests less accurate but often provides a fairer picture on the maximal performance.

Te Nijenhuis et al. (2001) concluded: "Although practice and coaching do have clear, substantial effects, they do not seem to undermine the value of testing strongly. It is beyond dispute that test takers have every right to prepare themselves as thoroughly as possible for test taking. In the case of students trying to get a good education and job applicants trying to get the job, individuals are clearly not wasting their time in their attempt to increase their scores by test preparation. Familiarity with tests is important, and most students do not take the test 'cold'. However, it should not be forgotten that the effects of coaching reach their maximum within a few hours of training. A test-wise strategy for test takers would be to focus practice and coaching on tests with low to medium levels of cognitive complexity: they offer the largest gains. A good counter-strategy for testing agencies would be to use primarily tests with high *g* loadings, to devise several parallel versions of tests, or even to construct new tests (or unearth and polish old ones from archives) that are built on principles not covered in test preparation booklets" (p. 305).

Eight questions and answers about contemporary assessment

Furnham and Lambert (2005) set out to answer various questions of interest to those working in this area.

1. What are the assessment methods most frequently used by major employers and what are they each used for?

Most organisations make two very important distinctions – Selection vs. Development (Training) and Senior vs. Middle/Junior Management. This provides a neat 2 × 2 grid.

Assessment methods are used specifically for selection purposes and/or development purposes. Selection may be for graduate trainees, for junior management and senior management. This is nearly always selection from the "outside" although it may in rare instances involve promotion from within. Most organisations seem to believe, however, that they know about individuals already working in the organisation so there is less need for any sort of formal assessment.

There are other factors as well that impact on the choice of assessment method:

1   *Select in or select out*: Is the organisation growing or shrinking? Is it actively recruiting or evaluating whether people should keep their jobs?
2   *Mass vs. individual*: What is the size of the group that is being assessed? Some organisations who either have high turnover or massive growth, expect to have to assess many hundreds of individuals per annum. This inevitably affects how they go about cost-effective, and valid, testing.
3   *General vs. specialist*: Whether they are attempting to select highly specialistic individuals with specific experience and educational qualifications or those selected for more general supervisory or managerial roles.
4   *In-house vs. outsourced*: Some organisations buy-in specialist consultants to do their assessment. Others prefer to do the whole thing in-house.
5   *Psychometric vs. "evaluative" (judgemental)*: Is the process one of applying a range of standard tests of different sorts or is it based on the expert evaluation of individuals dealing – "softer", non-numeric, self-report data.

A central question for assessors is what to assess, before worrying about how most effectively to do it. This process is at least a guide to what needs to be assessed in terms of the individual. Not everyone would necessarily agree with the list but it shows the way in which non-academic, highly practical researchers think. Organisations do, however, frequently use different methods depending on who they are selecting. There are usually three groups involved:

Graduate selection This only occurs if the organisation is big, growing, and has an active programme aimed at encouraging high-quality graduates. Numbers range from 20 to over 100. It seems that there are three approaches here. *First*, the assessment centre: Despite the cost (time and money) some organisations trust an assessment centre approach that may be in-house, or bought in. Traditionally it will involve testing, interviews, group work and in-tray exercises. These may be as short as half a day or as long as two days. *Second*, the traditional trio of application form, interview and references conducted by HR specialists. This would involve some selection via application-form data; a variety of different interviews (structured/unstructured; team/single, etc.) and the collection of references by letter or telephone. *Third*, the line manager selection usually by (only) interview or job try-out work sample. The idea here is to give line managers training in selection so that they can do the assessment for which they take responsibility. This nearly always involves some interviews. In some organisations that is all that is done.

Middle to senior managers This nearly always involves the standard trio:

1   *Interviews*: Usually the more senior the job, the more people want to have a "look at" the candidate. This may mean board-style interviews where a largish group (up to 10) interview a candidate or they have sequential interviews.
2   *References*: Some organisations remain "old-fashioned" by simply asking candidates to nominate various people who know them and who are then contacted and asked to write unstructured references. Others send out questionnaires to candidate-nominated people.
3   *Application form*: Sometimes these are used for early sorting – i.e. deciding that a person does not have the qualifications necessary for the job. It seems, however, that relatively few organisations "score" applications or invest much time and effort in their design.

The main issues here are whether the managers are assessed by HR specialists alone, with line managers or by line managers themselves. The history and size of the organisation dictate this.

Very senior (CEO level) individuals   It may seem either ironic or paradoxical that the *more* senior the person the *less* he/she appears to be assessed by: any objective tests (certainly of ability); more junior people in the organisation (i.e. upward evaluation); more internal than external people.

Frequently the task of both finding and assessing a top manager is given to headhunters/search consultants and specialist consultants. They frequently use only two methods in their assessment:

Interview This is often *long* (up to 4 hours), *structured* (by the need to evaluate competencies), and driven by *critical incidences*. It may be done by more than one consultant at a time (to improve *reliability*). It is nearly always portrayed, rather than as a selection interview, as an in-depth, walk-through life of an individual. Furthermore, the interviewers nearly all contract to give the individual *full feedback* on their observations. This has two important functions: first it ensures the greater buy-in of those asked to take part and second it means that the assessment exercise also has a developmental function both for those selected and those not selected. Clients and interviewees set a lot of store by this.

References   Usually the more senior the job the more the views of others are consulted. This is rather different from the traditional method, often used with middle- to junior-ranking staff, when the candidate nominates one or two people who are contacted by post and asked to comment on any aspect of the candidate. These references have the following characteristics: They are numerous, often being around 6 people in total. It is established beforehand by discussions with the candidate and his/her boss that they are appropriate in the sense that they *know* the individual *well*, have full experience and understanding of their abilities, aptitude and style from various perspectives. This looks very much like the multi-source perception one finds in the 360° literature. These referees are interviewed either face-to-face or by telephone for around 20–40 minutes. These interviews are semi-structured and designed to get a rich, even complex picture of all aspects of the candidate. Referees are assured anonymity and hence encouraged to be completely frank about the candidate. Previously it was found that free-response written references tended to be very bland and tended to be over-positive with possibly important negative features ignored because of concerns with litigation.

Head hunters and search consultants tend to take the information that they have acquired and process it to form a report. Most have a preferred format though they all, of necessity, agree a list of criteria with the client beforehand. These reports are for both clients and candidate, though the former may receive more information than the latter, either given verbally or in a separate document. Most refrain from strong accept/ reject recommendations, believing that the clients should ultimately make this decision themselves.

Choosing a psychological test

The considerations listed by Groth-Marnet (1984, p. 7) are displayed in Box 2.1. This is a very useful, if demanding, check-list. But which tests do businesses currently use?

Brown (1999) did a telephone interview of 190 British organisations that used personality questions. Ten tests were frequently used and in order of popularity they were:

1   Occupational Personality Questionnaire (OPQ; 33%),
2   Fifteen Factor Questionnaire (15FQ; 26%),
3   16 Personality Factor Questionnaire Form A/B (16PF; 20%),
4   16 Personality Factor Questionnaire Version 5 (16PF-5; 20%),
5   Thomas International Personality Profile Analysis (PPA; 8%),
6   Myers-Briggs Type Indicator (MBTI; 8%),
7   Occupational Personality Profile (OPP; 5%),
8   PA Preference Inventory (PAPI; 2.5%),
9   Firo B (2.5%),
10   Rapid Personality Questionnaire (RPQ; 1%).

Box 2.1 Issues to address when evaluating a psychological test

---

Theoretical orientation

1   Do you adequately understand the theoretical construct the test is supposed to be measuring?
2   Do the test items correspond to the theoretical description of the construct?

Practical considerations

1   If reading is required by the examinee, does his ability match the level required by the test?
2   How appropriate is the length of the test?
3   Does the examiner require additional training? If so, how can this be acquired?

Standardisation

1   Is the population to be tested similar to the population the test was standardised on?
2   Was the size of the standardisation sample adequate?
3   Have subgroup norms been developed?

Reliability

1   Are reliability estimates sufficiently high (generally .90 for clinical decision making and .70 for research purposes)?
2   What implications do the relative stability of the trait, the method of estimation reliability, and the test format have on reliability?

Validity

1   What were the criteria and procedures used to validate the test?
2   Has the test been constructed so as to produce accurate measurements?
3   Will the test produce accurate measurements within the context and purpose for which you would like to use it?

The majority that used tests for both recruitment and development indicated a 50–50 ratio. However, personality tests were used more for recruitment than development overall. In all, 39% of those surveyed used tests more for recruitment as opposed to 20% who used them more for development, i.e. number of tests used: 10 or less (8%); 11–50 (38%), 51–100 (24%), 101–150 (6%), 151–200 (4%), 201–250 (1%), 251–300 (4%), 301–400 (3%), 401–500 (3%) 1000+ (2%) and no response (4%). Most organisations gave verbal feedback only (50%) but 43% gave both verbal and written feedback.

In response to the question, "Where feedback is given is it linked to job demands?" 53% of those who gave feedback indicated that they linked their feedback, to some extent, to the job demands. Those surveyed were also asked if they gave feedback to the decision maker prior to giving feedback to the respondent and 73% of those who gave feedback said they did.

In her discussion of this literature, Brown (1999) mentioned the following points: As many as 17% of the sample use tests without any training qualifications or registration.

It is encouraging that most people give feedback on their results. Organisations use their data more for norming references than criteria comparisons. That is, they compare staff more to population norms than use tests for actuarial predictions

In 2001 the American Management Association had a review on workplace testing. They got 1627 usable responses. The data refer to those tested for selection (i.e. applicants) and those tested who were in the organisation for developmental or promotional prospects.

Psychological measurement   Of the respondent firms, 29% employed one or more of the forms of psychological measurement listed in the AMA questionnaire. The share has dropped precipitously over recent years, from 48% in 1998 to 33% in 1999 and 2000, and to 29% in 2001. Skill shortages may explain this; when mission-critical positions go unfilled in a tight labour market, companies may well take shortcuts in the application and evaluation process.

It should come as little surprise that an assessor's training, expertise and area determine their use of tests. One study in America illustrates this (Ryan & Sackett, 2000, p. 57). This showed that cognitive ability tests were used about 20% of the time in applicant testing but that interest inventories were only used about 8% of the time. The results illustrated overall that tests (ability and personality) are indeed used frequently (Table 2.2).

This illustrates three interesting things: All use interviews. Well over three quarters use both ability and personality tests. There are many dramatic differences in which personality and ability tests various groups use.

Table 2.2 Percentage of assessors using assessment methods and specific tests

Assessment methods	
Personal history form	81.9
Ability tests	74.3
Personality inventories	78.9
Projective tests	41.7
Simulation exercises	28.8
Interview	95.5
Specific tests	
WAIS-R	18.0
Wonderlic	6.3
Watson Glaser-CTA	19.6
EAS	9.8
Wesman PCT	9.2
GZTS	18.4
MMPI	24.4
MBTI	14.9
16PF	26.9
EPPS	8.2
CPI	19.3
TAT	20.9
Rorschach	14.2
Sentence completion	8.9

2. What are the strengths and weaknesses of each assessment method (in relation to their use as perceived by different groups)?

There are three sorts of data to answer this question. The first is the evaluation of *academic experts*. They are interested primarily in validity, but other factors as well. Naturally, there is not full agreement but clear trends in that direction can be seen. What these reviews lead one to conclude from the two criteria set are the following: *First*: assessment centres and peer ratings are perhaps the best selection methods to use. The former is very expensive and the latter very cheap. *Second*: many well-known methods are of very limited validity (i.e. interviews, references). *Third*: surprisingly little is known about the potential bias of these tests.

Schmitt (1989) argued for both the validity of, but also fairness in, employment selection. Subgroup means refers to the fact that these tests show results for different groups of people (i.e. male vs. female, black vs. white, old vs. young). This is obviously an important area of bias. Hence Table 2.3. The bigger the subgroup means, the more the potential bias in these tests, which differentiate between various groups based on gender, age, race, etc.

Anderson and Cunningham-Snell (2000) make an interesting and important distinction between validity (i.e. predictive accuracy) and popularity (Table 2.4).

Cook (2004, pp. 283–287) notes that there are six useful criteria for judging selection tests:

1   "*Validity* is the most important criterion. Unless a test can predict productivity, there is little point in using it.
2   *Cost* tends to be accorded far too much weight by selectors. Cost is not an important consideration, so long as the test has validity. A valid test, even the most elaborate and expensive, is almost always worth using.
3   *Practicality* is a negative criterion – reason for not using a test.
4   *Generality* simply means how many types of employees the test can be used for.
5   *Acceptability* to candidates is important, especially in times of full employment.

Table 2.3 Level of validity and subgroup mean difference for various predictors

Predictor	Validity	Subgroup mean difference
Cognitive ability and special aptitude	Moderate	Moderate
Personality	Low	Small
Interest	Low	?[a]
Physical ability	Moderate–high	Large[b]
Biographical information	Moderate	?
Interviews	Low	Small (?)
Work samples	High	Small
Seniority	Low	Large (?)
Peer evaluations	High	?
Reference checks	Low	?
Academic performance	Low	?
Self-assessments	Moderate	Small
Assessment centres	High	Small

Notes: [a]"?" Indicates either a lack of data or inconsistent data. [b]Mean differences largely between male and female subgroups. From Schmitt (1989). Copyright © 1989 John Wiley & Sons Limited. Reproduced with permission.

Table 2.4 The distinction between predictive accuracy and popularity

Predictive accuracy	Validity coefficients
Perfect prediction	1.00
Assessment centres promotion	0.68
Work samples	0.54
Ability tests	0.54
Structured interviews	0.44
Integrity tests	0.41
Assessment centres performance	0.41
Biodata	0.37
Personality tests	0.38
Unstructured interviews	0.33
Self-assessment	0.15
References	0.13
Astrology	0.00
Graphology	0.00

Popularity	%
Interviews	97
References	96
Application forms	93
Ability tests	91
Personality tests	80
Assessment centres	59
Biodata	19
Graphology	3
Astrology	0

Adapted from Anderson and Snell (2000).

6   *Legality* is another negative criterion – a reason for not using something. It is often hard to evaluate, as the legal position on many tests is obscure or confused."

He provides an assessment of different types on these criteria (Table 2.5).

Cook (2004) provides six criteria of choice, all important and all different. This implies that many organisations have to make a trade-off, i.e. cost for validity, practicality for generality. Second, whilst some methods do well at some criteria and poorly at others, very few succeed at all criteria: Assessment centres probably do best.

Cook's (2004, pp. 386–387) commentary is as follows:

Cost Interview costs are given as medium/low, because interviews vary so much and because they are so much taken for granted that few estimates of their cost have been made. Structured interview costs are high, because the system has to be tailor-made and requires a full job analysis. Biodata costs are given as high or low; the cost is high if the inventory has to be specially written for the employer, but it be might be low if a "ready-made" consortium biodata could be used. The cost of using educational qualifications is given as nil because the information is routinely collected through application forms.

Table 2.5 Summary of 12 selection tests by six criteria

Selection test	Validity	Cost	Practicality	Generality	Acceptability	Legality
Interview	Low	Medium/low	High	High	High	Uncertain
Structured interview	High	High	?Limited	High	Untested	No problems
References	Moderate	Very low	High	High	Medium	Some doubts
Peer rating	High	Very low	Very limited	Very limited	Low	Untested
Biodata	High	High/low	High	High	Low	Some doubts
Ability	High	Low	High	High	Low	Major problems
Psychomotor test	High	Low	Moderate	Limited	Untested	Untested
Job Knowledge	High	Low	High	Limited	Untested	Some doubts
Personality	Variable	Low	High	High	Low	Some doubts
Assessment	High	Very high	Fair	Fair	High	No problems
Work sample	High	High	Limited	Limited	High	No problems
Education	Moderate	Nil	High	High	Untested	Major doubts

Source: From Cook, M. (2004). *Personnel selection: Adding value through people*. Copyright © 2004 John Wiley & Sons Ltd. Reproduced with permission.

Practicality This means that the test is not difficult to introduce, because it fits into the selection process easily. Ability and personality tests are very practical because they can be given when candidates come for interview, and they generally permit group testing. References are very practical because everyone is used to giving them. Assessment centres are only fairly practical, because they need a lot of organising, and do not fit into the conventional time of selection procedures. Peer assessments are highly impractical because they require applicants to spend a long time with each other. Structured interviews may have limited practicality, because managers may resist the loss of autonomy involved. Work-sample and psychomotor tests have limited practicality, because candidates have to be tested individually, not in groups.

Generality Most selection tests can be used for any category of worker, but true work samples and job knowledge tests can only be used where there is a specific body of knowledge or skill to test, which in practice means skilled manual jobs. Psychomotor tests are only useful for jobs that require dexterity or good motor control. Peer ratings can probably only be used in uniformed disciplined services. Assessment centres tend to be restricted to managers, probably on grounds of cost, although they have been used for humbler posts.

Legality Assessment centres, work samples and structured interviews probably do not cause legal problems, but educational qualifications and mental ability tests most certainly do. The position on other measures, such as biodata, remains uncertain. Taking validity as the over-riding consideration, there are seven classes of test with high validity, namely peer ratings, biodata, structured interviews, ability tests, assessment centres, work-sample tests and job-knowledge tests. Three of tests have very unlimited generality, which leaves biodata, structured interviews, ability tests and assessment centres.

- Biodata do not achieve quite such good validity as ability tests, and are not as transportable, which makes them more expensive.
- Structured interviews have excellent validity but limited transportability, and are expensive to set up.
- Ability tests have excellent validity, can be used for all types of jobs, are readily transportable, and are cheap and easy to use, but fall foul of the law in the USA.
- Assessment centres have excellent validity, can be used for most grades of staff and are legally fairly safe, but are difficult to install, and expensive.
- Work samples have excellent validity, are easy to use and are generally quite safe legally, but are expensive, because they are necessarily specific to the job.
- Job-knowledge tests have good validity, are easy to use, and are cheap because they are commercially available, but they are more likely to cause legal problems because they are usually paper-and-pencil tests.
- Personality inventories achieve poor validity for predicting job proficiency, but can prove more useful for predicting how well the individual will conform to the job's norms and rules.
- References have only moderate validity, but are cheap to use. However, legal cautions are tending to limit their value.

Another recent summary by Arnold et al (2005) is presented in Table 2.6.

Table 2.6 A summary of studies on the validity of selection procedures

Selection method	Evidence for criterion-related validity	Applicant reactions	Extent of use
Structured interviews	High	Moderate to positive	High
Cognitive ability	High	Negative to moderate	Moderate
Personality tests	Moderate	Negative to moderate	Moderate
Biodata	Can be high	Moderate	Moderate
Work-sample tests	High	Positive	Low
Assessment centres	Can be high	Positive	Moderate
Handwriting	Low	Negative to moderate	Low
References	Low	Positive	High

Source: From Arnold et al. (2005). Reprinted with permission from Pearson Education.

What is perhaps most noticeable about these tables is their *similarity*, despite the fact that they maybe based on a different database. Occasionally an individual technique, such as a structured interview, is judged fair to average (in terms of validity) by one and as good to excellent by another but overall the results are robust. Assessment centres, work-sample tests and cognitive ability tests are usually judged most valid in all reviews. This is not surprising as many are basing their assessments on the same data. What we can say, therefore, is that among academic reviewers there remains good consensus as to the efficacy of different assessment methods.

3. What is new in the area? (What has been introduced or changed and what is the reaction?)

There are a number of new definable products, trends and developments in the area. These are driven by various factors:

- *Changes in the law*: Legal changes, litigation, etc., have driven some issues (i.e. integrity testing, diversity training).
- *Changes in business*: As many organisations attempt to restructure and become more flexible, they become concerned with specific issues (i.e. spotting potential high flyers).
- *Ideas of gurus*: Popular books highlight various concepts, issues or measures, which are enthusiastically embraced by business people.
- *Recommendations of consultants/academics*: They often have their own agenda, which might or might not be related to the above.

Thus, it is possible to see the emergence of various concepts, products and measures used to assess people for jobs and help develop them. Further, just as some of these products begin to emerge, others tend to wane. Thus, 360° evaluation/feedback is probably at its zenith but it is now much less popular than it has been. Equally, outward-bound/outdoor training to strengthen team work seems on the wane.

Many of the new issues are covered later in this book like emotional/social intelligence, the dark side of behaviour at work, behaviour in teams, etc. However, two issues are worth mentioning briefly here.

Diversity

This is a very important, but rather unclear, area. One issue of considerable concern is how tests might differentiate, but also discriminate against, certain groups typically based on things like age, ethnicity and gender (Ones & Anderson, 2002; Wareing & Fletcher, 2004). The issue, of course, is bias and how to deal with it through the development of new tests, the dropping of some/all tests, or statistical techniques, like different group cut-off scores, different norms, etc. (Van de Vijver & Phalet, 2004). This is the issue of adverse impact, which is frequently the topic of court cases.

In this area some issues are "hotter" than others. Without doubt the two hottest are race and gender. However, the issue of age differences has emerged as important, particularly with age discrimination legislation. Some deny that there are any race or gender differences in intelligence, despite the test evidence in this area. This prevents people using ability tests and sometimes personality tests. There are small consistent sex differences in ability tests. From all the recent hotly disputed data, it is possible to conclude that:

1   Gender differences in general intellectual ability are small but predictable (Jackson & Rushton, 2006).
2   Secular changes have diminished gender differences in special ability scores.
3   Mean differences in verbal ability and mathematical ability in the general populace have virtually disappeared.
4   Males appeared to be more variable in a number of ability measures and this difference in variability, particularly at the high end of the distribution of ability, may contribute to an excess number of males above relatively high cutting scores.
5   There are small but consistent gender differences on tests of spatial ability. The magnitude of the difference appears to vary with the type of test and may be as high as 0.75 standard deviation units in favour of males over females for tests of mental rotation.

Organisations believe that hiring people from more diverse backgrounds is both a necessity and is very desirable. They believe it enhances their image with minority groups but sometime realise that it may cause conflicts. They have begun to recognise that people from different groups may, and indeed do, have different work styles, motivations, developmental needs and career aspirations.

The assessment issue (as opposed to the management issue) is how to find, recruit, and select and then develop people with diverse interests, abilities and needs. There are also concerns about how culture filters the way people behave during assessments, which affects their outcomes. Thus, in most assessment situations selectors are trying to measure things like a candidate's skill, knowledge, attitudes, motives, values and competencies. However, the difference in the cultural background of assessor and the assessed may easily lead to misinterpretation.

Fairness is one issue, but a second is whether there are real, and important, differences between individuals. Although issues of race and gender are apparently too hot to handle it is possible to look at age difference. Employing older people or retaining older people in the workforce is now a big issue: so selectors and researchers have tried to ask questions about how they may be different.

Four things influence an older worker's ability and productivity. First their *physical and mental health*, which influences all aspects of their social functioning. Next their *education and ability*. The third factor is their *motivation and attitude to work*. Finally, there is *the nature of the work* itself, with its peculiar and particular set of mental and physical demands.

Older workers can bring wise judgement and social competence. Many have greater acceptance and credibility with customers than young people. They have often built up useful and supportive networks, both inside and outside the organisation. Many enjoy and have got used to lifelong learning and continuing education: "learning a little each day, makes it far easier to stay". Further, many are marked by old-fashioned values of commitment and loyalty.

Teaching older workers means applying what we know about adults' education more carefully. Their education works best when: people are taught with meaningful and familiar materials; people can self-pace their own learning; people have training on a weekly basis rather than in blocks, that is, *distributed* vs. *massed* learning; people practise with new materials; and people can call on special tutors and peers for help.

Older people tend to have lower educational qualifications having left school earlier. Many of them never had the option of further or higher education and may, therefore, have less confidence in their ability – unlike the me-generation who believe they are extremely talented and deserving. They can be less motivated to take part in work training that they might believe "shows them up". After all, most have fairly limited experience of training. But if the training is adapted to their needs they can make excellent and very grateful students.

Recruiting, selecting and developing people from non-diverse backgrounds is a real, important and continuing challenge. As the workplace swells with migrant labour with different educational, work-experience and socioeconomic backgrounds, it remains an important challenge to assess people accurately and fairly.

The issues of increasing demographic diversity in the workplace and the possibility of assessment methods discriminating unfairly, inappropriately and illegally is likely to remain an important, if not a growing issue, for those involved in assessment, selection and training at work.

Self-awareness

The goal of a great deal of developmental work is to increase an individual's self-awareness. There are many ways of thinking about self-awareness. One is about congruency between self and others: that is, it is defined as "the extent to which an individual sees themselves as others see him or her". Within the definition, the preferred tool is multi-source, multi-rater systems or 360° feedback to increase self-awareness.

Fletcher and Bailey (2003) have listed six benefits of using 360° feedback to increase self-awareness:

- "It is inherently fairer and has greater accuracy in representing performance because it offers a more rounded assessment of the individual, not just the top-down perspective of conventional appraisal.
- It is an empowering mechanism, in that it allows subordinates to exert some influence over the way they are managed; the same is true for peers, who can reflect back and perhaps alter the way a colleague performs as a member of the team.

- It enhances awareness of the organisation's competency framework, because staff completing the questionnaires may (depending on how the questionnaire is presented) become familiar with the competencies and the behaviours associated with each one.
- It has powerful development and learning potential – if used sensitively and with the right kind of support mechanisms. The impact of this kind of feedback is, as anyone who has used it knows, quite strong and can motivate changes in behaviour.
- It brings about a culture change in organisations, whereby individuals become more ready to seek, give and accept feedback in a constructive manner, and so enhance communication and openness.
- It increases self-awareness, that is the extent to which an individual's self-assessment of performance is congruent with how colleagues perceive that performance" (pp. 395–396).

Self-awareness in senior and middle managers is seen to be very important. It is believed to be related to the capacity for self-criticism, to awareness of others' emotions and, of course, to emotional intelligence.

Most of the concern with self-awareness is awareness of social behaviours – that is how people "come across" in social settings. However, there is also an interest in, and concern with, an accurate appreciation of one's actual abilities and potential. This means having a sensible and realistic appreciation of what one can do (ability) and what, even with effort and training, one is less good at.

Those who overestimate their abilities suffer *hubris*, those that underestimate them suffer *humility*. Furnham (2001a) has conducted various studies that have shown consistent sex differences in self-estimated intelligence. Males give higher scores than females. Further, outliers who believe that they have high IQs (which tests reveal they do not have) appear more likely to be male, while those who underestimate their scores are females. The central question is what are the consequences of these accurate or inaccurate self-beliefs about ability? The self-confidence that results from believing (accurately or not) that one is intelligent may be as functional in work settings as the actual ability itself. Further, humility on the part of females may mean that they are easily overlooked in selection and promotion decisions, particularly when they are based on interviews.

A great deal of therapy and training is dedicated to improving a person's self-insights and awareness, which is increasingly thought of as an excellent but simple measure of mental health.

4. What guiding principles and processes do large employers use in choosing, using, evaluating different assessment methods?

There appear to be *five* factors that determine when, why and how an organisation uses any particular assessment method. The first is the *sector* they operate in. This determines the type of assessment that is done. Does the organisation have generalised vs. specialised staff; do they mainly assess graduates or senior managers; what sort of biographical and skills profile are they looking for? Thus, a bank may have very different procedures for call-centre staff, branch mangers and senior managers. Equally, public sector administrative type organisations assess very differently from say entrepreneurial selling companies.

Second, is the *history* of the organisation. Most organisations have historical precedents, particularly big public companies. They may have successfully used a system or method like assessment centres and be happy with them. Often in small companies it is the opinion of strong-minded bosses that affects choice of, and rejection of, particular methods. It is not unusual to find bigger more bureaucratic organisations sticking with particular assessment methods even though they have not fully assessed them.

Third is the issue of the use of *consultants*. Consultants have preferred assessment methods. Clinically oriented and head-hunter consultants rely very heavily on long structured interviews and observer reports. Test publisher consultants often "push" particular tests that they know about and are comfortable with. Organisations have a love–hate relationship with consultants who they periodically change. These changes lead to different, possibly contradictory advice with the effect that assessment methods may equally suddenly be introduced or dropped.

A fourth important factor is *staff and applicant reactions*. Organisations are more than ever PR and litigation conscious. They are increasingly sensitive to assessor satisfaction with the process. If people think it is unfair or inaccurate they increasingly complain. This can cause organisations to drop certain techniques quite dramatically. There is often a difficult tension and trade-off between assessment methods, validity and acceptability. That is, the assessor may find that whilst the evidence points to both cost-effectiveness and validity for a particular method (e.g. intelligence testing) assessors seem very unhappy about its use. Equally, they may favour methods such as the unstructured interview that provides remarkably little validity. Organisations differ in their sensitivity to feedback and its assessment however.

Finally, the *training and background* of senior HR managers are important, and inevitably the background of the senior person in selection, recruitment and appraisal. Just as the use of consultants can make a big difference in what assessment methods are chosen, so the background and training of those who take the manager decisions are important. A senior HR manager may come from a PR or IR background; they may have particular qualifications or not; they may be psychology graduates or postgraduates. Further, they may have had many HR jobs in different companies and been fully exposed to a range of assessment techniques. Their education and experience are often driving forces in further decision making.

5. *What practical lessons can be learnt that indicate good practice in the area?*

Furnham and Lambert (2005) from their case studies of half a dozen organisations concluded thus:

A. Assessment is important   Selection and development can have massive immediate and dramatic economic consequences. Mistakes in selection and promotion can be extremely costly to the individual and the organisation. Whilst all people are developable, there are limits to their development. People need to be assessed for their general and specific development capability.

B. Assessment is expensive   Good assessment methods cost in time and money. Disinterested but competent consultants come at a high price. Assessment centres are very expensive. It is a question of balance for many to try to decide on the optimal or ideal cost–benefit analysis for the whole section enterprise. Thus, references are cheap but 360° packages are expensive. A great deal of thought needs to be given to this. It is difficult to cost assessment methods. How to cost a selection interview? This could include recruitment cost as well as interviewers' time (as a function of their salary). Psychological tests are easier to cost and may range from relatively simple pen-and-paper tests from £5 to £30 to on-line tests with extensive and impressive feedback reports costing up to £500 each. Assessment centres typically cost out at £1000 per day, making a typical 3-day assessment cost £3000 whether they are successful or not. Reference collecting is perhaps the cheapest of all methods. Cost is covered by the work of Cook (2004) described earlier.

C. Validate one's own processes Most organisations are *amnesic* in the sense that they forget to analyse the past. Because of time and expertise constraints they do not always look back at their records to validate their processes. Have they selected poor performers: if so when, how and why? Sometimes they examine spectacular successes and failures but that rarely validates their own procedure.

D. Senior managers are ambivalent about development Younger managers seek out opportunities to learn and develop but this can be very threatening to older senior managers who believe it good for their staff but not them. They claim that serious time constraints limit their development needs. Thus, organisations have to be careful not to waste time, money and good will by trying outside coaching, many MBAs and the like to develop managers who can't or won't change or are the in the job only for a few years.

E. The spend on assessment may be wrong Some organisations spend a lot on selecting junior people but little on their development and vice versa for very senior people – unless they hire head hunters to do the job for them. This is not just a matter of due diligence. Senior people are less often assessed for their ability because their experience and track record act as proxy resources. But do they? Equally little attention may be paid to the dark-side, select-out variables, that may be important in senior managers.

F. Assessment needs to look at dynamics Most people are assessed and selected for a particular job or role. Hence, one begins with a job analysis. However, it is increasingly being realised that all job roles are more flexible and jobs more changeable that ever before. Further, many people are selected to be high flyers in the sense that one is trying to assess people for a variety of roles. Thus, one feature that assessors need to consider is dynamics – that is those characteristics like intelligence, openness, tolerance of ambiguity that predict how people will survive, dive or thrive in changeable circumstances.

6. How effective are the methods perceived to be in terms of identifying the right people (i.e. validity) and cost effectiveness?

Questions about validity and cost are crucially important. If you present a group of people with a list of assessment methods and ask them, from their personal and professional experience, to rate or rank them first for validity and second for cost, the following would probably emerge. The methods at the top (most valid) and the bottom (least valid) would probably be *much the same*. That is, most agree that work samples, assessment centre and cognitive ability tests are valid, while graphology and unstructured interviews are much less valid and reliable. Whereas there is disagreement among individuals from different groups around such things as personality tests, this is usually due to: not making the distinction between different types of tests; basing opinions on different data sets; having a strong personal vested interest in one test or other; having had very different educational and occupational experiences.

The same issues may be applicable to cost effectiveness. There are, however, huge differences in costs of each preferred method be it psychometric test or 360°. Doing the assessment "in house" is obviously a very different business from outsourcing it. By definition certain methods like assessment centres are going to be very expensive while others like work-sample tests or references may be very cheap. Obviously the cost (in time and money) vs. effectiveness (validity) trade-off is one of the most important decisions in this whole area.

7. What changes have been made (or require to be made) why and how?

As noted earlier, there are all sorts of issues that drive a particular organisation to change their assessment strategies. Some, like the civil service or military, seem only to tinker with aspects of the well-established procedure. Others are more fashion conscious in the sense they hear about, and include new concepts, measures, etc., like trying to assess *emotional intelligence* or using *360° feedback* extensively. Still others find they are in difficulty and therefore instead of recruiting and selecting, they have to assess redundancy and deselection.

There are, however, a number of issues that seem to be fairly widely considered by organisations.

The web

Chapman and Webster (2003) have pointed out that the new assessment technologies (predominantly the web) have specific goals. Namely to: improve efficiency; enable new screening tools; reduce costs; standardise the HR system; expand the applicant pool; promote the organisational image; and increase applicant convenience.

However, there are also unintended effects. Thus, the use of the Internet does expand the applicant pool but also increases the number of under-qualified and out-of-country applicants. It is easy to be *flooded with inappropriate applicants*. There is also a *loss of the personal touch* that both assessor and assessee value and respect. There are also concerns about *cheating* if tests are used. Finally, there are still concerns about *adverse impact*, which means that certain groups simply do not have access to the technology.

HR technology remains a challenge. The hopes of individuals have been very high but not all the experiences have been positive. Nonetheless, it seems to be the future. Internet advertising and recruitment seems very cost effective. Young people expect it.

But can one do good assessment via the Internet? Does this exclude certain groups? Are the results different from pen-and-paper tests? The growth of Internet recruitment is with us (Potosky & Bobko, 2004). Not only is there web-based testing and application form processing but also web-based coaching. Young et al. (2004) describe how a database of interlinked coaching templates can be used to do very efficient loadings on the web. The Internet has changed the world and will continue to do so. How it affects assessment is a critical issue. This is perhaps the fastest and most pervasive change around.

Applicants' reaction to testing

Organisations are naturally concerned that their assessment methods are seen to be just, fair, modern and scientific. This has a major effect on the reputation of the organisation. Big organisations see their assessment technique as a PR opportunity. They see it as helping them in the "war for talent". They are also very nervous if senior managers reject a particular method.

Various studies have looked at test-taker attitudes and reactions. Lievens et al. (2003) asked applicants to rate eight measures on three criteria (see Table 2.7).

Interviewers' beliefs about the validity of tests and of their fairness had little impact. But the more people thought tests were valid, the more they thought personality and cognitive ability tests were fair.

In a useful review study, Truxillo et al. (2004) looked at both "soft" and "hard" outcomes of applicants' perceptions of fairness of assessment procedures. The following were their findings. For *soft outcomes* when people feel the process is fair they: express more satisfaction with it; feel more attracted to the assessing organisation; intend to recommend the organisation to others; get a strong sense of self-efficacy; feel motivation to take the tests; do not intend to proceed with legal action. On the other hand, for *hard outcomes* reactions include: withdrawing the application if assessment was felt unfair; reapplication after rejection; great belief in testing validity; greater commitment to organisation. They point out that many factors influence perceptions of fairness. These include: applicants' expectations of assessment; applicants' familiarity with the selection process; applicants' personality; applicants' socioeconomic status and national culture.

Assessment also has issues around privacy. Organisations do themselves a favour in explaining assessment procedures in training and considering the possibility of selection unfairness.

Hausknecht et al. (2004) found that four sets of factors predicted applicants' perceptions. They were the *personal characteristics* of the applicant (their work and test experience, age, sex and personality), the *nature of the job* they were applying for (e.g. how attractive it was); the *organisation* (history, resources), but most importantly the *process outcome* (intrusions into privacy). All these factors determined the candidates' test anxiety and motivation and, most importantly, their belief in the justice of the whole experience. The techniques they thought most valid and fair were interviews and work samples followed by cognitive ability tests and then followed by personality tests, honesty tests, biodata and graphology.

Table 2.7 Evaluating different selection techniques

Technique	Overall fairness	Scientific value	Job relatedness
1 Work samples	Very high		Very high
2 Biography			Very high
3 Structured interviews	Very high		Very high
4 Unstructured interviews			
5 Personality tests			
6 Cognitive ability tests		High	
7 Personal references	Low	Very low	Low
8 Graphology	Very low	Very low	Very low

Source: Based on Lievens et al. (2003)

Organisations are now beginning to adapt their whole assessment strategy on the basis of the feedback they get specifically around appropriateness, ability, fairness, and validity.

Assessing for redundancy and adverse impact

Assessment methods can be used for both select *in* and select *out* decisions. But there are two senses on select in. First, most assessment is involved in selecting an individual for a position. There is, however, also selecting an individual to be removed from a position.

When organisations restructure or downsize, they have to make decisions about who to keep and who to let go. Sometimes organisations are over-staffed, sometimes roles change. A central question is what assessment methods can best be used to help make these important decisions. In an interesting and current case study Bywater and Thompson (2005) looked at the use of personality questionnaires in making people redundant at the Royal Mail.

They argued that redundancy settings differ from recruitment and developmental settings in three important ways: "In redundancy situations the candidates will be completing the questionnaire in a situation of high stakes and competition with other candidates, for a limited number of roles. In redundancy situations the candidates are internal to the organisation and may thus have a clearer idea of what the organisation is looking for at the end of the process. Finally, in a redundancy situation the candidates are likely to be feeling a degree of breach in their 'psychological contract' with the organisation. This is likely to reduce the honesty for their answers, and thus the usefulness of the information that they convey, still further" (p. 8).

They asked a number of centrally important questions and attempted some practical advice on how to deal with them:

1   Can candidates fake personality tests? Yes. . . .
2   Can candidates guess the desired profile? Not really. . . .
3   Does the context have any effect on the psychometrics of the questionnaire? Yes . . . reliability drops.

Adverse impact concerns are growing; particularly in litigious America: Assessors have to seriously think about the real possibility that the methods they use discriminate and differentiate in ways they neither expect nor plan.

In an up-to-date and useful summary of the area, Cook (2004, pp. 268–269) concludes:

• "Fair employment law covers gender, ethnicity, disability, religion and age (in the USA).
• Most fair employment selection cases involve adverse impact, not direct discrimination. Adverse impact means that fewer minority applicants are successful. If the success rate for minority applicants is less than four-fifths that of the majority, adverse impact is established.
• Getting the numbers right (i.e. ensuring that there are the right proportions of women and minorities in the workforce) can be difficult, as there are legal restrictions on how employers can achieve this.
• A selection method that creates adverse impact must be proved – in court – to be

valid, the employer must also show that there is no possible alternative that is equally valid but which will not create adverse impact.

- American researchers are trying combinations of tests to try to find one that will prove valid but create no adverse impact.
- Differential validity means that a test has different validity for minority and majority people. North American research has not found evidence of differential validity. Virtually no research had been reported on this issue outside North America.
- Disability discrimination legislation affects selection in different ways. Adverse impact claims cannot be made. The employer must not use any health-related enquiries as part of the selection process, and must try to adapt selection tests to disabled applicants.
- In the UK far fewer unfair selection cases have been brought, and the position is still much more open.
- Other countries in Europe and elsewhere, have adopted the same basic adverse impact model."

When companies shrink and have to lay off staff, they often use simple formulae (first in, first out or last in, first out) to make decisions who to keep and who to lose. Whilst other methods may be thought of as fairest by certain groups, it certainly is not based on either performance data (such that there is available) or psychometric assessment, which may be considered the wiser decision. Equally having a wise, legal and transparent policy for ensuring no adverse impact for certain groups is also a wise business decision.

8. What do suppliers and consultancies think about current trends?

Until the early 1980s the use of psychological tests of ability and personality in British industry was comparatively unknown. The British were always sceptical about psychology and believed one could "sum up" a person pretty well with a glance at a CV, the grip of the handshake, the steadiness of the eye and a few perspicacious questions at the traditional interview.

But *three* things happened in the early 1980s to make testing not only "sexy", but almost a requirement for HR professionals who talked about best practice and psychometric insight. Sudden rises in unemployment led to unprecedentedly large numbers of job applicants, which the old system could not cope with. Next there were some stories, perhaps even fables, from people like the, then, new head of British Leyland (Sir Michael Edwardes) who claimed that through judicious use of tests (more to fire than hire people) he turned around the whole company.

However, it was the third factor that proved most important and long lasting. This was the establishment, and aggressive marketing, of test publishers, one of whom still dominates the market. Consultants soon jumped on the band wagon and by the 1980s psychometric testing was all the rage. Graduates on the milk round sometimes reported that they had taken the same test six times while middle-aged executives could be seen on trains reading paperbacks with titles like "Know Your Own Personality" and "Know Your IQ" in anticipation of a terrifying testing session to determine whether they were "let go" in the new round of restructuring.

Demand was met by supply. There was a sudden growth in test publishers and, for the first time, Americans found the British interested in using the tests. Paradoxically, as both personality theory and classic psychometrics were in decline in the groves of academia there was a massive popular interest in the topic.

Testing was not a flash in the pan. Certainly some people remained sceptical – a number even became cynical – but too many people had too much at stake. Consultants made a lot of money, either testing people and writing reports, or else training HR people to "certify" them to use the tests themselves. Test inventors and publishers had a field day. And HR professionals enjoyed the credibility that testing gave them. It should be acknowledged, of course, that testing also did make a difference. It certainly helped in decision making and gave users a new vocabulary to describe and analyse people. The enthusiasm for the concept of competency in fact revived interest in testing rather than quenching it.

There have been blips in the field. Some damming evaluations have been published in top journals. Employers have been sued, and others have been publicly ridiculed by their choice of test, and also, more frequently, by the use of items in the test. The point about litigation is important. Tests seem to becoming caught up in our litigious society much as other recruitment and promotion processes are.

What is the state-of-the-art twenty years on? Is there a decline in test usage because of disappointment in what testing could do? Did having expectations raised lead to cynicism, scepticism and a major decline in interest? The answer appears to be no. Every so often a new idea comes along that helps the testing business. Perhaps the latest one is emotional, social or perhaps spiritual intelligence. Despite, or perhaps because of, the concept being all things to all men, it soon developed a following and it did not take long for entrepreneurs to realise its potential. Tests of all sorts with no known validity soon appeared and now they can be down loaded from the web, almost free of charge.

It seems the case that employment "contracts" differ hugely between three kinds of business: bureaucracies, "family" businesses and fast-moving/ultramodern concerns (Furnham & Lambert, 2005). These are not mutually exclusive categories but this categorisation seems appropriate to examine the way industry uses tests.

Bureaucracies are centralist, procedural and uniform. The Civil Service is like this but then so are many of the utilities, large multinationals, airlines and the like. They tend to use testing because it makes the playing field more level and manageable. They emphasise propriety and fairness. They take a long time deciding *on* a test, once they had taken a long time deciding *to* test. But once the decision has been made they tend to be loyal to the test even if the results are not fully exploited.

"Family" businesses are the second category and these tend to be dominated by one leader. These may have an enthusiastic advocate of testing as their leader, in which case testing happens. More usually, the task for any key employee is that he/she gets on with the leader, irrespective of what the tests say. They emphasise the boss's judgement and the inevitability of having to make that relationship work. By definition some are almost test addicts, the others test phobics. Often these attitudes are based not on thoughtful contemplation but often some random experience they had when first encountering a test and their reaction to it.

The third category is the *new electronic industries*. Fast-moving, ultramodern companies are having to move at breakneck speed. They eschew procedures that slow them down and are happy to make and re-make decisions. If people work out, fine. If they do not, fine (they can go). If tests help make better selection and training decisions use them. Whatever the test, if it does the job, fine. There is little test loyalty just opportunistic pragmatism.

Psychometric testing is alive and well. Its market is segmented by company type, each of which uses tests for quite different reasons. But 20 years of testing has had an effect on both tester and testee. The British use psychobabble and psychometric speak with a new confidence. "I am an extraverted non-completer-finisher"; "I don't like my boss because he is an INTJ"; "I am not surprised she can't get a job with that Wanted Control score" are all not unfamiliar lines at chattering-class parties. Testing, it seems, will be with us for some time yet.

Recommendations: Lessons from experience

After their desk-based (review) and interview-based (case study) research on the current use (and abuse) of various assessment and selection methods used in large multi-national companies, Furnham and Lambert (2005), concluded with 10 lessons that may be of use and interest to those involved in these areas.

1. Amateurism will not do

The whole business of selection and development requires technical knowledge. One needs to know what methods are available and how to be able to wisely access then assess each – assessment methods themselves need assessment. This requires a reasonable amount of technical knowledge about psychometrics test publishing, etc. Even if many of the assessments are to be outsourced, managers need to know how to differentiate between various consulting groups offering the same service. In a sense, this is meta-assessment: the judicious assessment of assessment measures.

Uninformed purchasers of methodologies and consultancies can be at the mercy of over-priced, invalidated and legally "dubious" methodologies. Organisations, then, would do well to ascertain the knowledge base they have *in house*. This audit would then allow them to consider recruiting, training and updating those whose job it is to run or monitor the assessment process.

Assessment is a complex, costly and important business at all levels but particularly important at more senior levels. It cannot and should not be left to people whose knowledge and skills in this area are insufficient or outdated. Perhaps an organisation should consider spending a percentage of its assessment budget (say 10% per annum) making sure that all assessors are sufficiently professional and up to speed in the area.

2. Learning from the past

Store data and validate the process. Organisations should carefully store all their assessment data. Once a system is set up this is not a particularly difficult or time-consuming business. There are, however, legal implications related to storing this information electronically.

Validating one's approach is an important and much-neglected task, which provides three very important features. First, it helps build up *company norms*. That is, it shows how people who have been accepted *and* rejected score on any exercise. This is particularly important where tests are imported from other countries (i.e. America) and/or have poor or few normative data sets.

More importantly, this information gives very valuable data on the validity of the methods in the organisation. By linking assessment scores with an individual's progress one may determine if, whether and when they will be able to predict all sorts of job outcomes like absenteeism, accidents, probation, promotion and derailment.

Third, they can also provide interesting *developmental data* if any of the tests are run again. This means that it is possible to compare scores on, say, recruitment, end of probation, promotion, etc., to see if and whether people have changed. This is particularly important for measures of skills and knowledge.

The amnesic organisation wastes money by not validating its *own* procedures. The best way to do this is to keep every one's assessment data on file and to periodically see whether it has predictive value.

3. Spend assessment money in proportion to job value

From an assessment point of view, many HR people believe that (very) senior managers have to be treated with "kid-gloves". Many would never dare even considering giving them an intelligence test or indeed testing their technical knowledge. Many are not even given personality tests. The best one can hope for is a structured interview but even that does not often happen.

So, the paradox is that the most senior and arguably, therefore, the most important people in the organisation undergo the least valid assessment method. Least time and money (excluding head-hunter fees) is spent on the highest paid. The central question is whether that money is well spent, there is a recruitment issue and a selection issue. Senior people who often have very significant financial responsibilities need to be carefully selected particularly in terms of their abilities, their stress-coping styles and their potential to derail.

A mini-assessment centre may be devised for senior appointments. This can (and should) be constituted so as to maintain the self-esteem of candidates but also comprehensively test their knowledge, skills and flexibility. Just as they may be required to have a good health check, so they may also be required to have a good psychological strength. Discounting recruitment fees, the time, money and energy spent on assessment should be (directly) proportioned to the value of the job to the organisation.

4. Assess for a failure as well as success

Most assessment is the hunt for any measurement of characteristics that assessor wants. Traditionally assessors specify the desirable competencies of the individual and then try to gauge them.

Very rarely do assessors specify what they *do not want* apart from the choice of the competencies that they do not want. Just as doctors look for both signs of health *and* illness so assessors need to be able to specify factors that they believe would lead candidates to fail or derail.

It is known that any form of negative information obtained via application form, interview or reference seems to count more highly than positive information. Thus, knowing a person has very poor education history, or indeed had a criminal record or a history of mysterious illnesses, may count against them quite unfairly.

Assessors need to know what factors lead to management failure. These include a whole range of mental illnesses both neurotic and psychotic. Recent work on the personality disorders has been particularly illuminating with regard to management failure. Narcissism and evidence of psychopathic tendencies have been shown to be highly predictive of serious derailment.

A search through the file of failed managers often throws up most useful evidence of patterns of biological markers of failure. These should help assessors develop a list of things that they really should look for signs of in the process.

5. *Study the job market*

The demographics of the job market change quite radically. Hence, one had a "war for talent", recruiting the older workers, assessing diversity, etc. In the business of strategic planning organisations often do a projected analysis. That is, they try to specify the number and type of jobs they are going to require, given job growth or retrenchment or relocation, or whatever, of their organisation. Presuming that this is or even can be reasonably well done the question therefore arises as to where to get these future employees.

Political, social or economic change can very rapidly change the job market. The demographic profile of a nation can change dramatically with immigration. Equally, highly skilled jobs may be able to command higher and higher remuneration if too many employers chose too few individuals.

Market forces have a high impact on salaries. All organisations need to benchmark their compensation and benefit packages regularly. But, more importantly, they need to know where to recruit. The issue for assessment is having sufficient flexibility in the methodology to adapt it to a very different work force. Thus, if one is to assess large numbers of people whose mother tongue is not English, it is important not to have assessment tools that discriminate against them. Equally, older people do not always perform as well on some tasks as younger people. The job market influences recruitment, which impacts on assessment.

6. *Assessment is an HR, IR and PR business*

How people are assessed has many consequences. First, assessment can lead to good or bad PR. There are often newspaper reports of highly aggressive candidates who thought their assessment unfair, biased or discriminating. Whether it be the ubiquitous "milk round", or high-level board appointments, organisations must be aware that their assessment methods may be under close security. Assessment needs to be seen to be open and fair to candidates. Hence organisations may have to consider the occasional trade-off between an assessment method that has proven validity but which is not seen to be acceptable to many candidates.

Assessment is also about an IR issue as labour unions often have strong, clear policies about how, when and why individuals are assessed for promotion, redundancy, etc. Assessment, in short, can lead to disputes and even strikes. It is important to get all parties "on board" in the design, delivery and execution of assessment at all levels. It is nearly always better to sort out this at the planning stage than when things go wrong.

Assessment should always be a primary HR function. Whilst it is very important to encourage non-HR people to develop expertise in this area and take full responsibility for their decisions, it should be HR that holds the central planning role for all assessment. Hence, the importance of being up to date in the whole assessment area.

7. *Differentiate between selection and development*

It is possible to use selection data for development purposes. Thus, when a person has gone through a rigorous data-gathering selection process they may be very eager to get feedback on that process for developmental purposes. In this sense the two activities may look much the same.

However, it is important to distinguish between the two. Thus, it may well be that a particular process or instrument that is useful in development may not be so useful in selection and vice versa.

Among other things, the purpose of development is to increase self-awareness, boost self-confidence, explore and exploit talents. To do this, people need to reflect, to experiment and to take risks in a safe environment. It may be that certain psychometric tests of highly dubious psychometric validity are very useful in helping people talk and think about themselves. Equally, some exercises from an assessment centre may be highly diagnostic of a particular state but have relatively little value for development purposes.

Both assessment and development should be ongoing processes. Many organisations pay lip service to development often because they don't know what they should be doing in the area. Further, they also believe that assessment is more-or-less a one-off business done when an individual joins an organisation or a particular department. Just as health is or should be regularly monitored so should an individual's progress in the job.

8. *Updating job analysis and competency profiles*

Jobs change more than people. The attitude and climate of organisations change as they grow or decline. The skill sets, attitudes, expectations and opportunities for individuals change. Some jobs change dramatically in the skills they require while some (rather few) remain much the same over time. Some assessment is for specific jobs. Other types of assessment are for careers where an individual might be expected to take on various jobs. In the former instance it is important to keep up to date as to job and role requirements. Technological and legal changes can have a powerful impact on how jobs are done. Within a very short period one technology replaces another and job incumbents have to learn to use it and job applicants need to be conversant in it.

This inevitably means that competency profiles have to change related to job demands. The more dynamic and fast-changing the market in which the organisation is working, the more important it is to update both job analysis and the competency profiles that match it.

Assessing people for longer-term senior management careers is less dependent on specific job analysis. There will always be a need for planning and people skills. However, if there are rather different career tracks to the top in different organisations it may be a good idea to attempt to describe the particular capabilities associated with that track and be aware of changes along the way.

9. *Evaluate cost: The value of efficient assessment*

Assessment can be very expensive. Using head hunters to do recruitment and designing in a running assessment centre can be prohibiting exposure. Often HR people are required to justify the amount of money spent on assessment.

It is, therefore, very useful to learn how to do a return-on-investment calculation to show the benefits of selection. It should be remembered that the data from this work suggest the following. Money spent on selection is best spent when first the overall calibre of the recruits is high and varied (as opposed to uniformly mediocre); where the employees differ a lot in their worth to the organisation and where the selection process is known and valued.

By using this method it is possible to cost the saving per employee. When assessors are confronted with objectives or queries regarding their methods or costs it is desirable and impressive to have a clear argument as to know why the money is spent.

Essentially the point to be made is simple. The cost of invalid or inappropriate assessment is far higher in the long term than those involved in selecting the right people for the job. As has been remarked before, if you think education is expensive try ignorance.

10. Keep up to date on both research and legal issues

It is very easy for assessors to get out of touch both about the law as well as research. HR directors now find they are occasionally challenged by candidates over their assessment methods. Getting expert advice can be expensive. Prevention is better than cure. It is important that assessors keep up with local and European employment legislation. Indeed, they really need to make a virtue of their squeaky-clean, totally open and fair assessment methods.

Keeping up with the law may mean attending seminars and reading reports. The same is true for keeping up with the social science research on assessment methods. Academics and researchers are frequently surprised by how ignorant and out of date some organisations are in their assessment methods. Many have been superseded or were of very little validity in the first place. There is good disinterested research assessing assessment methods. As one of their primary personal development tasks, all assessors need to make sure that they are up to date and able to provide probing and insightful questions to potential suppliers be they test publishers or consultants.

The advantages and disadvantages of testing

From a practical point of view, it may be useful to consider arguments for and against using tests in the work-place.

Advantages

- Tests provide numeric information that means individuals can more easily be compared on the same criteria. In interviews, different questions are asked of different candidates, and the answers often forgotten. Tests provide comparable profiles.
- With data-based records one can trace a person's development over time. In fact, by going back to test results kept in a person's file one can actually see if, and by how much, the tests were predictive of occupational success (see Chapter 1).
- Tests give explicit and specific results on temperament and ability rather than vague, ambiguous, coded platitudes that are so often found in references. A percentage or a sten score (provided of course that it is valid) makes for much clearer thinking about personal characteristics than terms like satisfactory, sufficient or high-flyer. Good norms demonstrate a candidate's relative scores.

- Tests are fair because they eliminate corruption, favouritism, old-boy, Mason – or Oxbridge – networks from self-perpetuating. That is, if a person does not have the ability or has a "dangerous" profile they will not be chosen irrespective of their other "assets".
- Tests are comprehensive in that they cover all the basic dimensions of personality and ability from which other occupational behaviour patterns derive. A good test battery can give a complete picture of individual functioning.
- Tests are scientific in that they are soundly empirically based on proven theoretical foundations – that is, they are reliable, valid and able to discriminate the good from the mediocre and the average from the bad.
- Tests increase the behavioural conceptual language of those who use them. This gives those who are not trained in personality theory a very useful set of concepts they can use to identify and distinguish human characteristics in the workplace.
- Empirical data resulting from the tests can be used to settle empirical arguments. That is, objective numbers provide the sort of clear evidence to justify decisions.
- Tests give testers and testees alike, interesting and powerful insights into their own beliefs and behaviours. They might also be used to explain to candidates why they have been rejected.

Disadvantages

- Many of these tests are fakeable – that is, people like to describe themselves in a positive light and receive a "desirable" score so that they may be accepted. Yet this faking in a way reflects their "real" personality. Also, some tests have lie scores to attempt to overcome this. The effects of this distortion, however, are not major.
- Some people do not have sufficient self-insight to actually report on their own feelings and behaviour – that is, it is not that people lie but that they cannot, rather than *will not*, give accurate answers about themselves (some tests only look for simple behavioural data to overcome this).
- Tests are unreliable in that all sorts of temporary factors – test anxiety, boredom, weariness, a headache, period pains – can lead people to give different answers on different occasions. Although this is partly true, this factor only makes a small difference.
- Most importantly some tests maybe invalid – they do not measure what they say they are measuring and these scores do not predict behaviour over time. For many tests this is indeed the Achilles heel and they are lamentably short of robust proof of their validity. It is supremely important that tests have predictive and construct validity.
- They might be able to measure all sorts of dimensions of behaviour but not the crucial ones to the organisation like trustworthiness, and likelihood of absenteeism. Buying personality tests is like having a set menu and what many managers want is an à la carte menu where they can select only what they want.
- People have to be sufficiently literate or articulate to do these tests, not to mention sufficiently familiar with North American jargon. Many organisations therefore believe their work force could not do them properly, they would take up too much time, or would cause needless embarrassment.
- There are no good norms at least for the populations they want to test, and

comparing them to American students (Caucasian sophomores) is dangerously misleading (this is certainly true, but not in all instances).

- The tests are unfair, and biased to middle-class, white people, hence, white males tend to do better or get a more attractive profile and therefore get selected than, say, black females. They therefore fly in the face of anti-discriminatory legislation.
- Freedom of information legislation may mean that candidates would be able to see and thence challenge either the scores themselves, their interpretation or the decisions made on them. The less objective recorded data, the better for those unprepared to give negative feedback.
- As (ability and personality) tests become well known, people could buy copies and practise so that they know the correct or most desirable answers. This happens extensively with GMAT testing, and results could be seen to do more with preparation and practice than actual ability.

Frequently personality tests are used for selection and appraisal because of: the high number of applicants (particularly in times of unemployment); the high costs (man hours/reimbursement) of interviewing; the poor reliability of interviewing (specifically choosing weak candidates); the necessity for objective comparative data (chosen vs. not chosen); allegations about nepotism and favouritism (in the selection process).

There are at least four types of question that potential test users often ask themselves:

What are the test results to be used for?   Are they to be used to select people in, or select them out? That is, are they best at spotting *high flyers* or those considered too *dangerous or risky* to employ, or both, or neither. Quite different tests (or at least dimensions) should be used for these rather different questions. Are the results to be used in counselling or predicting work performance? The necessity that a test be reliable and valid is less important in counselling where the aim of the test might be to encourage a person to talk about particular areas of strength or weakness. Are the results intended to be correlated with other measures or stand alone? How reliant is one on these test results? That is, are tests used to help make decisions or are they the only or major criteria of selection?

What dimensions of personality or individual differences or intelligence are crucial? Should one buy an off-the-shelf general test that measures the whole person? This may be interesting but does it provide the data one wants? If managers are most concerned with people being careful, scrupulous, correct, it is important to measure impulsivity, obsessionality, and need for arousal not unrelated aspects of personality. It is more time consuming but ultimately more useful and cost-effective to decide beforehand *what* one wants to measure and why and then choose the best test for the job.

What is to be done with the results after initial use?   Many organisations are amnesic, forgetting the very useful data that they have on employees tested earlier. Test results gathered in selection interviews or annual appraisals can be extremely useful in checking the validity of the test in each organisation specifically. They also provide extremely useful data on how people change over time.

What questions should one ask when choosing tests?   What is the object of the test? How is this objective the same or different from existing tests designed to measure the same thing? How will the objective(s) be met? Is there really a need for this test? Are there other tests that purport to measure the same thing? In what ways will the proposed test be better than existing tests? Will it be more reliable? More valid? More comprehensive? How might this not be better than the other tests? Who would use this test and why? Who would need to take this test? Who would need the data derived from an administration of it? Why? What control area should the test cover? How will the test be administered? Will the test be individually administered, or should it be amenable to both individual and group administration? What difference will exist between the individually administered version and the group-administered version? How might differences between the two versions be reflected in test scores? What is the ideal format for this test? Why? Should the test be amenable to computerised administration, scoring, and/or interpretation? Should more than one form of test be developed? What special training will be required of test users in terms of administering or interpreting the test? What background and qualifications will a prospective user of data derived from administration of this test need to have? What restrictions, if any, should be placed on distributors of the test and the test's usage? What type of responses will be required by test takers? What "real-world" behaviours would be anticipated to correlate these responses? Why will scores on this test be important?

Attention needs to be given to *all* of these questions before tests are employed. The use and abuse of tests in applied settings often occurs because many of these questions have not been fully asked or answered.

Conclusion

Interest in assessing individuals for places in education and organisational settings is an important issue for many people. Most attempt an insightful and veridical assessment of an individual's ability, motivation and personality in order to predict how they might function in that institution. Methods available range from the pre-scientific (astrology and graphology) to the futuristic (brain scanning and DNA analysis).

Selectors have first to decide what they want to measure and then how they presume to do so in a manner that is acceptable, accurate and cost-efficient. The former, wisely or not, is usually done through competency analyses (see Chapter 11) and most organisations have little trouble coming up with what they believe to be a comprehensive list of desirable attributes.

There is, however, much more debate concerning the latter – which methods to use. Whilst most organisations use – and candidates like – the formula of application form, references and interview these have not shown themselves to be very reliable or valid under very particular circumstances (Furnham, 2005a). Thus, if the application form uses biodata methods, interviews are planned and structured, and referees are asked direct questions, the methods can achieve modest to good reliability and validity.

Various meta-analyses of the predictive validity of assessment methods have tended to show similar results. Thus, those techniques that have been consistently found to have high predictive validity include intelligence tests (cognitive ability and aptitude tests); assessment centre data, and work samples. Ratings by peers (on previous jobs or in training settings), structured interviews and tests of specific job knowledge are also good predictors. However, academic record, self-assessments and references do not do very well.

Test validity is not, however, the only criterion of interest to assessors. They are inevitably interested in acceptability to senior managers and candidates, cost, legality and practicality. Yet the popularity of tests seems still more dependent on test publisher marketing than those judgements.

There still remains a large gap between what academics interested in individual differences and applied personnel (HR) practitioners recommend. Inevitably they have different agendas and values. Few deny, however, the importance of assessing individual differences to improve their selection decisions and ultimately the success of the organisation. Which facets are assessed remains an issue of debate. Further, changes in the workforce, science and the law have made many of these debates highly salient for both parties.

3 Personality testing in the workplace

Introduction

One way to understand individual differences relationship to work-related behaviour is the *applied literature* on personality testing in the workplace. Psychological tests, attempting to measure individual differences related to occupational behaviours, have been used for over 90 years, and there now exist nearly 80,000 occupational-related tests. Both world wars, particularly the second, were very important for the "testing business" and most armed services are still active users of psychological tests for selection and training. Selectors have to find fighter pilots and bomb disposal experts, as well as cooks, administrators and military police. With conscription they have to reliably and efficiently determine an individual's potential to do these military jobs effectively.

In 1869, Galton expressed an interest in intelligence testing with his book *Hereditary Genius*, which presented a classification scheme based on abilities. Wundt in the first psychological laboratory in the 1870s began using reaction-time measures and tests of visual and auditory acuity as indexes of intelligence. This effort was greatly advanced by Binet at the turn of the century, because he reconceptualised intelligence as consisting of more complex mental processes than had Wundt and, accordingly, developed tests of memory, attention, comprehension, and imagination. Munsterberg in 1913 brought this fledgling movement into the industrial context in general, and employee selection in particular, by using a battery of tests available at the time to help select motormen for the Boston Railway Company.

Psychological testing has blossomed fully since that early era, to gain a place not only in industry, but also in educational, clinical, and counselling settings. Its greatest boost for selection purposes came during World War I. Under the leadership of many of these early pioneers, 1,726,966 men were tested (for selection and classification purposes) as a part of the war effort.

There are now psychological test publishers and innumerable management consultancies that sell and use psychological tests primarily for recruitment and training. In fact the industry has expanded so much, that many are deeply cynical about it (Paul, 2004). Despite this, there has been a noticeable increase in the use of testing in business over the last decade (Furnham, 2003b; Goodstein & Prien, 2006).

A short history of industrial testing

The United States Employment Service provided free aptitude testing, which provided a rich data bank, just after the Second World War. The twelve tests measured nine of the aptitudes thought to be related to the requirements needed in the performance of many jobs. The *General Aptitude Battery*, as it was known, was intended to be used in two ways:

1   As an integral part of counselling where a measure is needed of the applicant's abilities in relation to the various fields of work in which he may have interest but no practical experience.
2   As an approach to the problem of developing specific batteries for the countless occupations for which selection tests may be needed. Those tests in the General Aptitude Battery that measure abilities significant to the successful performance of a given job could be administered as a specific aptitude test battery, and the other tests omitted.

Certain of the tests with their cut-off or minimum scores were recommended for use in the selection of applicants for a wide variety of occupations. For example, the job of all-round mechanical repairing included testing for intelligence, numerical and spatial aptitudes, and finger dexterity. Plumbing included tests for numerical and spatial aptitudes, and motor dexterity. Typewriting requires verbal aptitude, clerical perception, etc.

The battery was administered to a large number of persons employed in a wide range of occupations. Over 500 employers and many schools and colleges cooperated in the development of occupational norms. While the GATB demonstrated its validity in a variety of situations and jobs, it was probably being used in many situations where its value as a predictor was highly questionable.

Traditionally, industrial testing was oriented toward the blue-collar (i.e. manual), sales, and clerical workers, since it was felt that this was where the largest increase in efficiency could be achieved. These individuals usually presented the bulk of the labour force employed by a company, and by improving the average quality (as defined by one or more criterion dimensions) large benefits should accrue to that company. In the 1950s the emphasis shifted to an intensified concern for selection of individuals higher up in the managerial hierarchy. It moved essentially from blue- to white-collar workers. Indeed, now most testing is on graduate trainees and potential "high flyers".

The major problem in predicting executive success is in establishing a valid multidimensional and sensitive criterion against which to validate the test. Attempts to use tests to predict success, once success has been arbitrarily defined for research purposes, have been less successful – particularly tests of ability. Fifty years ago, Gaudet and Carli (1957) estimated that seven times as many executives failed due to personality problems rather than from lack of technical competence. Hogan (2006) would certainly agree with this. Taylor and Nevis (1957) noted that this is not really too surprising; the executive job is a very complex one. Thus, to isolate specific abilities may not be sufficient; the abilities required are generally cognitive rather than physical; intelligence measures are probably not good predictors because to get into management requires a fairly bright person in the first place.

An example of the use of tests with supervisory-level personnel was given by Neel and Dunn (1960) who used the How to Supervise test, the F Scale measure of authoritarian personality, and the Wonderlic test to predict the degree of success that 32 supervisors would have in a supervisory training programme. The Wonderlic (intelligence) test correlated ($r = .69$) with the How to Supervise test.

Wagner (1960) attempted to predict ratings of on-the-job success of 150 executives using a total of 31 different variables. These variables included measures of both intelligence and personality. The only correlation that was found to be high enough to be of any value was the correlation between ratings and amount of education (r = .39). However, the pure chance likelihood of this correlation is substantial.

In all this research, the criterion problem immediately raises its ugly head. What is a "successful" scientist, salesman, manager? How does one measure success? How efficient are tests in separating good scientists from poor scientists? One of the more elaborate research projects has been conducted by Taylor et al. (1961), who carried out extensive interviews with over 200 physical scientists concerning the nature of scientific productivity and the characteristics of effective scientists. Using the interview suggestions as a base, data were obtained on 52 different criteria. These measures were then factored into 14 relatively independent dimensions by which the performance of scientists could be evaluated. A number of tests were then used to predict how well a scientist would score on each of the 14 dimensions. In addition to the 14 dimensions obtained in the factor analysis, three other criteria based upon supervisor and peer judgements were included, since these were the most frequently used methods of performance evaluation. Thus, the criteria used were:

1 Productivity in written work (effectiveness in completing paperwork).
2 Recent quantity of research reports (number of articles and research reports, in a two-year period).
3 Quality (without originality) of research reports.
4 Originality of written work.
5 Scientific and professional society membership.
6 Actual quantity of work output as judged by peers, supervisors, and laboratory chiefs (higher-level supervisors).
7 Creativity rating by laboratory chiefs (higher-level supervisors).
8 Overall performance (quality ratings by supervisors on ten different scales).
9 Likableness as an effective member of the research group.
10 Visibility of the scientist (well known by person or by name).
11 Recognition for organisation contributions (organisational awards).
12 Status-seeking, "organisational-man" tendencies.
13 Current organisational status.
14 Contract monitoring load (numbers of research contracts supervised).
15 Peer ranking on productivity as a scientist.
16 Supervisory rating of drive resourcefulness.
17 Supervisory rating of creativity.

A total of 130 different predictors were validated against *each* of the 17 different criteria. Many of these predictors were simply different a priori scores, which could be applied to the same questionnaire or test instrument. For example, the Personality Research Inventory was given to all scientists in the validation sample for purposes of prediction. However, this single test yielded a total of 23 subscores, each of which was separately validated. The validation sample consisted of 197 scientists. By relating the 130 predictors to the 17 criteria, 2210 validity coefficients were obtained – a testimony to the computer technology of time! Of these, 568 were significant.

The different predictors varied considerably in their efficiency as Table 3.1 shows.

Table 3.1 The percentage of valid scores obtained from each of the major categories of predictor information

Type of test	Percent of scores valid
Biographical Information (BI), with empirically keyed scores	47
Biographical Information Blank (BIB), a priori keyed scores only	34
Self-ratings (SR)	33
Grade-point average	24
Minimum Satisfactory Level (MSL)	22
Profile matching	20
Motivated Analysis Test (MAT)	8
Personality Research Inventory (PRI)	8
Creative process check list	6
Aptitude tests	4

Source: Taylor et al. 1961

Table 3.2 Weighted mean validity coefficients of personality inventories for various occupation groups

Mean r	Total number of cases	Total number of rs	Occupation
.14	518	8	General supervision
.18	6433	44	Foremen
.25	1069	22	Clerks
.36	1069	8	Sales clerks
.36	927	12	Salesmen
.24	536	5	Protective workers
.16	385	6	Service workers
.29	511	8	Trade and crafts workers

Source: Ghisselli and Barthol (1953)

This result certainly would suggest the importance of biographical factors as predictors of occupational success.

Earlier, Ghiselli and Barthol (1953) reviewed 113 studies dealing with the validity of personality inventories in employee selection. This has become a very famous study quoted many times. The results are summarised in Table 3.2. They conclude that under certain circumstances scores on personality inventories correlate better with proficiency on a wider variety of jobs than might have been expected. The authors recognise both the potential value of personality testing in industry and the need for a vast increase and improvement in research and development.

Ghiselli and Brown (1955) reported on the efficiency of testing for various types of industrial jobs. They examined large numbers of validation studies and classified them in terms of the type of test being used and the type of criterion involved. All validities within a particular category were then averaged to give the figures shown in Table 3.3. Note that only three of the values in Table 3.3 exceed .40 in size, and that two variables are *not* tests but are personal-history items. While the process of averaging used by Ghiselli definitely masks some very substantial validities, it should be sufficiently clear that testing is not a complete solution to the selection problem.

The work of Ghiselli and Brown (1955) is among the most celebrated in "the literature". They examined intelligence, interests and personality, and looked at how they

Table 3.3 Average validity coefficients for various types of tests

Type of test	Type of criterion	
	Training	*Job proficiency*
Intellectual abilities		
Intelligence	.38	.19
Immediate memory	.29	.19
Substitution	.26	.21
Arithmetic	.41	.21
Spatial abilities		
Spatial relations	.31	.14
Location	.24	.15
Perception of details		
Number comparison	.26	.21
Name comparison	.25	.21
Cancellation	.29	.20
Pursuit	.19	.17
Perceptual speed	.39	.27
Mechanical comprehension		
Mechanical principles	.34	.26
Motor abilities		
Tracing	.16	.16
Tapping	.12	.14
Dotting	.14	.15
Finger dexterity	.22	.19
Hand dexterity	.38[a]	.14
Arm dexterity	.30[b]	.17
Personality traits		
Personality	.16[a]	.21
Interest	.14[a]	.27
Personal data	.44	.41

Notes: N ≥ 1000 for all tests, except [a]*N* = 100–499 cases or [b]*N* = 500–999 cases.
Source: Ghisselli and Brown (1955)

related to job performance in a variety of occupations. Their results showed considerable differences in size of correlations between the different jobs. Further, correlations were never strikingly high being around $r = .30$. Their work is critical, comprehensive and their conclusions cautious.

Ghiselli and Barthol (1953) showed that intelligence tests are more likely to be helpful in selecting skilled workers, supervisors, clerical workers, and salesmen, but likely to be of little or no value in selecting unskilled workers and sales clerks. One early study of the selection of clerical workers in a life insurance company showed a tendency for applicants scoring high on intelligence tests to leave the job after a few months (Kriedt & Gadel, 1953). However, the authors stated that irrespective of the results of their study, they felt it desirable to hire some applicants demonstrating a high level of intelligence in order to have individuals on hand that could be promoted to supervisory positions.

In general, the more the amount of preparation and training required for a job and the more complex the job, the more likely intelligence is to be the factor in job success. Indeed, one of the most defensible arguments in favour of including intelligence tests in selection batteries is the need to train the applicants, in that the longer and more complex the training required for the job, the more likely intelligence is to be an important factor.

Randle (1956) provided another excellent illustration of the use of the method of the period. This study involved 1427 executives from 25 different companies. It involved four phases: First, very extensive appraisals were carried out on each executive to provide a complete dossier on each person. In phase two, each executive's dossier was examined to determine the "degree of promotability". They were classed into three groups as shown below: promotable (35%), satisfactory (34%), and inadequate (11%). In the third phase, all appraisals were content analysed to determine what identifiable characteristics were possessed by the 1427 people in the sample. These analyses reveal over 100 different characteristics or traits. However, only 30 occurred with sufficient frequency to be regarded as "common denominator" characteristics. The final phase was to determine which of these 30 characteristics were related to promotability. To be considered a predictor of promotability, a characteristic had to be either significantly more or significantly less present in those judged inadequate. The results indicated that the "composite executive" was a person who was distinguished by eight qualities shown in Table 3.4

In addition to these general "traits" for successful executives, Randle also found that there was a tendency for certain traits to gain in importance as one goes up in the managerial hierarchy. This was particularly true of the *motivation* characteristic, which was judged outstanding in 84% of top executives considered promotable and in only 14% of top executives considered inadequate. There were a number of other important studies in the 1950s and 1960s (Borislow, 1958; Bridgman & Hollenbeck, 1961; Kirchner, 1961, 1962).

Most of the above studies were conducted by academics interested in occupational behaviour before the mid-1960s (i.e. 40 years ago). There have also been studies by practitioners – human relations and personnel officers – in which they have tested the validity of personality tests in their organisation. Miller (1975) has edited a useful volume in which personnel managers write about their experiences of tests. For instance, Wilson (1975) used tests (the 16PF and AH5, a British intelligence test) along with an interview, case study and peer rating to judge graduate recruitment. In order to determine the efficiency of the 16PF they (at United Biscuits) compared high- and low-rated managers on the 16PF. These results are shown in Table 3.5

Table 3.4 Qualities of the "composite executive"

Characteristics	Percentage present	
	Promotable executives	Inadequate executives
Position performance	50	5
Drive	47	14
Intellectual ability	44	8
Leadership	41	6
Administration	40	6
Initiative	38	7
Motivation	34	8
Creativeness	30	6

Source: Randle (1956)

Table 3.5 16PF and AH5 results for 50 middle managers attending company assessment centres (average age 35)

Test	Max. score	Raw score means (standard deviations)		
		Low-rated managers (N = 20)	Middle-rated managers (N = 14)	High-rated managers (N = 16)
16PF				
A	(20)	10.9 (3.7)	10.5 (2.4)	12.4 (3.3)
B	(13)	9.0 (1.5)	10.3 (2.4)	12.4 (3.3)
C	(26)	16.7 (3.5)	18.9 (3.5)	18.1 (3.2)
E	(26)	14.8 (5.9)	14.2 (4.8)	16.1 (3.6)
F	(26)	13.1 (3.0)	13.7 (4.1)	15.4 (4.6)
G	(20)	14.9 (3.3)	13.7 (4.4)	11.6 (3.7)
H	(26)	16.2 (5.2)	15.4 (4.1)	16.6 (5.7)
I	(20)	7.3 (3.7)	11.1 (3.0)	8.6 (3.9)
L	(20)	5.9 (3.5)	7.1 (2.8)	6.9 (3.3)
M	(26)	15.2 (3.3)	15.3 (3.6)	16.6 (3.6)
N	(20)	9.9 (3.2)	9.3 (3.3)	8.3 (3.3)
O	(26)	7.5 (4.6)	6.9 (3.3)	7.1 (3.3)
Q1	(20)	10.5 (3.3)	10.4 (3.0)	11.7 (2.8)
Q2	(20)	10.8 (3.2)	10.8 (4.2)	9.4 (2.8)
Q3	(20)	15.0 (3.3)	13.7 (2.2)	12.5 (2.8)
Q4	(26)	11.1 (5.6)	9.4 (3.0)	8.2 (4.5)
AH5	PT1	14.4 (3.6)	18.1 (4.4)	19.5 (3.6)
	PT2	13.6 (4.2)	14.7 (6.7)	18.5 (4.5)
Total		28.0 (7.1)	32.8 (6.7)	38.1 (6.7)

Source: Wilson (1975)

High-rated managers were more intelligent, relaxed, outgoing, self-assured, sensitive, and group oriented, less rule bound, concerned over procedure, and shrewd. Twelve of the 16 factors showed significant differences, suggesting the usefulness of the test for selection and promotion decisions.

Ingleton (1975) described the use of tests in an oil-marketing organisation in Great Britain. They used intelligence tests (Raven's Progressive Matrices), the Thurston Interest Inventory and the 16PF. Among the initial difficulties reported were preparing a report in a format helpful to the interviewing panel, and gaining the confidence of bright but sceptical student applicants. Although they met initial resistance from interviewers things did improve. They appeared to use the 16PF to determine, if offered, whether the applicant accepted or declined the offer.

Randell (1975) was concerned with the selection of salesmen and notes the number (well over 200) of references concerning salesmen selection. Using the 16PF, Allport–Vernon–Linzey Study of Values, and Thurstone Interest Schedule tests, as well as the EP1, Strong Vocational Interest Blank (SVIB), and many others, together with biographical criteria, he looked at people in the gas, tyre, and oil industries. Although the tests were predictive there was no general trait of salesmanship across organisations and thus, it was concluded:

The search for the use of any general traits of "salesmanship" would seem to be less useful to selling organisations than attempts at matching people to specific sales jobs.

From this, the general implication emerges that organisations should be cautious about appointing salesmen just on the grounds of their previous sales experience.

(p. 89)

Copeland (1975) reported on the selection of engineers using the Morrisly Differential Test Battery – an ability/intelligence test that provides 12 separate tests. Starting from a position of scepticism, the organisation appeared to have embraced testing as an extremely useful selection device, through evidence of test validity.

Miller (1975), on the other hand, was concerned with clerical selection and used a large battery of ability, aptitude, and personal value tests. Using four groups in four locations (to check replicability and generalisability) he found the ability tests (verbal, arithmetic, and clerical) predicted training grades. Beaton (1975) used a variety of tests in a retail business for a variety of reasons: to improve selection; to create an impression among potential applicants; to reduce turnover; and to identify potential. This work used intelligence and mechanical reasoning tests as well as Cattell's 16PF, all of which proved to have predictive validity.

Bentz (1985) reported on a remarkable programme, where executives were given an extensive battery of personality and ability tests (called the Sears Executive Battery). They were used mainly in selection but have other obvious uses. Using sensitive robust criteria, various attempts have been made to validate the scale. These results were summarised:

> Persuasive and socially assured, the person moves aggressively into a central role whenever a part of a social or business group (Sociability, Social Ascendancy, Persuasive Interests). Confident to initiate and act without external support (Self-Confidence), the individual catches on rapidly (Mental Ability) and moves into action with energy and flexibility (General Activity and Serious versus Carefree). With heightened personal concern for status, power, and money (Political and Economic Values), the person will work hard to achieve positions that yield such rewards.

(pp. 109–112)

He also reported various longitudinal, follow-up studies which demonstrated both the stability of personality *and* the stability of personality–occupational behaviour relationships. He argued from his findings that the bias against paper-and-pencil personality tests is unjustified. The correlations, he reports, were frequently between .3 and .5 accounting for between a tenth and a quarter of the variance. But the results are consistent, replicated, robust and generalisable – surely a tribute to the measures used.

Yet despite evidence extending over 40 years showing evidence of the validity of some psychological tests there remain critics. In their review of the validity of personality measures in personnel selection, Guion and Gottier (1965) concluded that: "it is difficult, in the face of this summary to advocate with a clear conscience, the use of employment decision about people" (p. 160). The low validity and utility of personality measures become particularly salient when compared to the validity and utility of other available selection methods, such as ability tests. It was probably this review that stopped, or certainly inhibited, research in this area for 20 years. Just as Mischel's (1968) book on *Personality and Assessment* set that field back for two decades so the Guion and Gottier paper published in the mid-1960s effectively meant both academics and practitioners lost faith in the possibility of measuring individual differences that could be demonstrated to be, even modestly, predictive of behaviour at work. Hence the relative paucity of research studies published in the period 1970–1990.

However, Hollenbeck and Whitener (1988) have argued that the dismal evidence currently available on personality traits as predictors can largely be traced to: (a) theoretical inadequacies; and (b) methodological problems associated with past research dealing with statistical power and contaminated measurement. They argue that personality traits, which as a whole reflect individual differences in values, performances, needs or beliefs, would seem to be more strongly related to one's motivation to perform than one's capacity (i.e. ability) to perform. Indeed, a dozen or so exhaustive meta-analyses over the past decade have concluded conclusively that the early scepticism and cynicism that arose from the work between the 1950s and the 1970s was inappropriate (Hough & Furnham, 2003; Ones et al., 2005).

Research on the relationship between personality traits and work-related behaviours in the years from 1950 to 1980 was fragmented, piecemeal and not very sophisticated. This was partly due to a lack of agreement about what traits to measure by which instrument as well as the small amount of theoretical development by either personality or organisational psychologists concerning the process that might explain the relationship. The situation over the past decade, however, has changed rapidly. Extensive reviews and studies by researchers like Hough, Hogan, Judge and Ones with colleagues have shown that personality traits do predict behaviour at work; that these relationships are consistent over jobs; that the processes are explicable; and most importantly that traits account for important non-trivial amounts of variance in predicting such things as job productivity and satisfaction.

Testing in Europe today

Within Europe the use (and abuse) of personality tests and psychometric testing remains a hot and continually debated topic (Barrett, 1998; Brown, 1999; Jones & Poppleton, 1998; Warr, 1987). Some commentators are concerned specifically with test validity (Barrett, 1998; Warr, 1987) and others with the trends of (inappropriate) use of tests in business. It has been argued that European data provide clear evidence that personality is logically, consistently, and powerfully related to work behaviours. However, practitioners should note specifically that: the unfocused (i.e. unthought-out) use of tests is not likely to be of value; only psychometrically valid instruments should be used; candidates do "fake good" in selection assessment testing; personality factors interact and, hence, one needs to look at the overall profile of individuals; work-related behaviour is determined by both person(ality) and situational (contextual) factors; personality data has clear diagnostic value; but personality data alone is insufficient for most human-resource decisions.

Inevitably I/O psychologists interested in individual differences turn to their local personality specialists who seem to prefer theories and measures developed, tested and marketed locally. "Home-grown" theories and specialists are equally favoured over "foreign imports". There are, thus, national differences in what is the preferred outcome or dependent measure used to validate the instrument. Thus, in America it seems organisations have long collected supervisor evaluations on staff, occasionally along with other ratings such as self-ratings, direct report (subordinate ratings) and peer ratings, all on work performance. This has meant that the multi-rater (360°) feedback literature has been dominated by Americans though there are signs that the Europeans are now taking an interest (Furnham & Stringfield, 1993a, 1993b).

It is also apparent that some issues, and the academic literature which accompanies them, is nation specific. For instance, the concern with integrity testing (honesty, integrity, consciousness, dependability, trustworthiness, reliability) seems almost exclusively an American obsession (Hogan & Brinkmeyer, 1997; Hough, 1996a). On the other hand the Europeans have been very concerned with employment status (De Fruyt & Mervielde, 1999).

It is not clear why integrity testing is so much more popular in America because it is unlikely that the incidence of workplace deviance is very different in Europe and America. Cook (1998) has suggested that honesty tests have become popular in America since 1988 when the general use of the polygraph was restricted. Furthermore, the implementation of fair-employment law has meant that some American organisations have stopped using tests that measure things like conscientiousness, which give reasonably indexes of honesty, integrity and morality. Hence, they have felt the need to use specific tests to measure this phenomenon. It is often local employment law that affects selection procedures and which in turn, some years later, influences academic interests. Furthermore, high-profile litigation cases have had a sudden and dramatic influence on companies, often dissuading them from using particular tests.

Choice of personality instrument is often more a function of "marketing science" than "psychometric science". There is nearly always a supply–demand function for personality tests. In Britain, one consultancy/test publisher showed enormous growth in their sales of their test (the OPQ) loosely based on other tests at the time. It has been carefully examined by psychometricians who have found it wanting (Barrett et al., 1996), though it has predictable conceptual overlaps with the Big Five (Stanton et al., 1991). American test publishers have certainly been more active in Europe than the other way round, though primarily in Northern Europe, where English is better understood.

Often I/O psychologists are dependent on HR specialists to provide their data and it is the latter's rather than the former's decision about which tests to use. Certainly tests that appeal to organisations (e.g. MBTI; FIRO-B) are often those with serious psychometric shortcomings and hence they never reach the academic literature. Europeans have also taken an active part in the debate about the Big Five.

Some of the European research has done little more than take well-known and currently popular American tests, translate them into major European languages, and demonstrate their comparative psychometric qualities. Thus, according to Rolland et al. (1998) who translated it into French, the famous five-factor measure, the NEO-PI-R, has also been translated into eight other European languages (Croatian, Dutch, German, Hebrew, Italian, Portuguese, Spanish, Russian). Further, the longer versions of the same instrument have also been translated (Silva et al. 1994).

Europeans, probably more so than outsiders, are highly conscious of their differences rather than similarities. With many different languages, histories and economies it is not by accident that organisational practices are so different (Hodgkinson & Payne, 1998). These inevitably impact on how organisations are structured and run, and, more importantly for I/O psychologists, on what individual differences are measured, when and why. The use of tests in selection provides an excellent example.

Various studies have focused on national differences in selection processes. Smith and Abrahamson (1992) looked at 10 studies done in European countries to compare their method of selection. The authors concluded, after calculating correlations, that the

Table 3.6 National differences in the use of selection methods

Methods of selection	Country						
	GB	F	D	IS	N	NL	All
Interviews	92	97	95	84	93	93	93
CV/application letter	86	89	92	72		63*	80*
Medical examination			50			71	61
Experience			40			63	52
References/recommendations	74	39	23	30		49	43
Diplomas and certificates				44		28	36
Cognitive tests	11	33	21		25	21	22
Performance evaluation			19				19
Preliminary test						19	19
Personality tests	13	38	6		16		18
Discussion groups			15				15
Trainability tests	14						14
Graphology	3	52	2	16	2	4	13
Work sample	18	16	13			5	13
Assessment centres	14	8	10		3		8
Biodata	4	1	8		1		4
Astrology	0	6			1		2

Notes: GB = Great Britain, F = France, D = Germany, Is = Israel, N = Norway, NL = Netherlands.
Source: Smith and Abrahamson (1992).

results indicated far more similarities than differences (Table 3.6). The much higher use of graphology in France and references in Great Britain are the only factors that seem to stand out.

A more recent and robust survey covered 12 Western European countries (Dany & Torchy, 1994). The work of Smith and Abrahamson (1992), shown in Table 3.7, indicates various interesting features:

- The French favour graphology but no other country does.
- Application forms are widely used everywhere except Sweden.
- References are widely used everywhere, but are less popular in Spain, Portugal and The Netherlands.
- Psychometric testing is most popular in Finland, Spain and Portugal, and least popular in West Germany and Turkey.
- Aptitude testing is most popular in Spain and The Netherlands, and least popular in West Germany and Sweden.
- Assessment centres are not used much, but are most popular in The Netherlands, and least popular in Portugal.

Cook (1998) speculates:

What the USA does today, Britain does tomorrow. "Today" and "tomorrow" are years apart – but how many? Suppose Britain is 20–30 years "behind" the USA.

The future in Britain will see mental ability tests being used very widely in all organisations at all levels. The future will see personality tests used quite widely at supervisory level and above, and Weighted Application Blanks used quite widely below. The future will see the demise of the unstructured interview and the free-form reference, and a proliferation of rating systems.

But the future could turn out quite differently. In one important respect, Britain is only 10 years "behind" the USA – equal employment legislation. British personnel managers might now be belatedly adopting methods the law will shortly force them to abandon. By 2002, mental ability tests could be virtually outlawed, personality tests suspected, and biographical methods unthinkable. Selectors might be forced back onto the classic trip, or forced out of business all together.

(p. 25)

Table 3.7 shows variability in the use of psychometric (nearly all personality) and aptitude tests. Over half the companies in Finland, Spain and Portugal use psychometric tests in selection, whereas under a third use them in Germany, France, Ireland, Norway, The Netherlands, Sweden and Turkey. This may reflect either scepticism or legal restraints on the part of the latter countries. Certainly the use of tests in general (personality and aptitude) seems to be similar, though far fewer countries use assessment centres, no doubt due to cost.

Another review (see Table 3.8) attempted an equally comprehensive cross-European study. Two things are striking from this table: first, the considerable within-Europe differences, second, the variability between meta-analyses of the same country data by different researchers, suggesting the importance of sampling.

Tables 3.6 to 3.8 illustrate considerable within-content variability. Enthusiasm for personality and ability tests in different countries differs widely as indeed does the use of tests of development and training and reasons for development. It is, however, probably true to say that at least in Northern (Protestant) Europe (Britain, Holland, Germany, Scandinavia) there is a renewed interest in, and preference for, testing. This

Table 3.7 The Price-Waterhouse-Cranfield survey of selection methods in 12 Western European countries

Countries	Methods							
	AF	IV	Psy	Gph	Ref	Apt	AC	Grp
D	96	86	6	6	66	8	13	4
DK	48	99	38	2	79	17	4	8
E	87	85	60	8	54	72	18	22
F	95	92	22	57	73	28	9	10
FIN	82	99	74	2	63	42	16	8
IRL	91	87	28	1	91	41	7	8
N	59	78	11	0	92	19	5	1
NL	94	69	31	2	47	53	27	2
P	83	97	58	2	55	17	2	18
S	Na	69	24	0	96	14	5	3
T	95	64	8	0	69	33	4	23
UK	97	71	46	1	92	45	18	13

Notes: AF = application form; IV = interview panel; Psy = psychometric testing; Gph = graphology; Ref = reference; Apt = aptitude test; AC = assessment centre; Grp = group selection methods. D = West Germany; DK = Denmark; E = Spain; F = France; FIN = Finland; IRL = Ireland; N = Norway; NL = Netherlands; P = Portugal; S = Sweden; T = Turkey; UK = United Kingdom. From Dany and Torchy (1994). Used with permission of Routledge.

Table 3.8 Management selection practices in Europe

Methods	Surveys								
	Bruchon-Schweitzer (1989) France N = 102	Smith (1990) United Kingdom N = 40	Beavan & Fryatt (1987) United Kingdom N = 293	Schuler (1990) Germany N = 88	Abramsen (1990) Norway N = 61	Lievens (1989) Belgium N = 89	De Witte et al. (1991) Flanders N = 53	Mabey SHL (1989) United Kingdom N = 300	SHE (1992) France N = 48
Interviews	99	100	95	37	93	100	98	100	90
References	–	–	78	9	–	73	59	–	–
CVs/application forms	–	–	91	90	–	91	–	–	86
Situational tests, work samples	7	–	32	16	–	51	37	37	8
Personality questionnaires	35	10	9	6	16	42	63	47	39
Cognitive and aptitude tests	31	5	5	15	25	71	74	66	31
Projective techniques	12	–	–	–	–	42	6	–	6
Assessment centres	–	10	–	9	3	31	–	–	9
Biodata	–	3	–	6	1	–	–	–	–
Graphology	93	2	5	6	2	36	7	3	46
Other methods*	15	0	–	–	1	2	–	–	–

Notes: Figures represent the percentage of respondents who say they use the method. – Indicates the question was not used in the survey. *Other methods include astrology and morphopsychology. Dates indicate when the survey was conducted, not published.

Source: Modified and reproduced by special permission of the Publisher, Consulting Psychologists Press Inc, Palo Alto, CA 94303 from Handbook of Industrial and Organizational Psychology, Volume 4, by Harry C. Triandis, Marvin D. Dunnette, and Leaetta M. Hough. Copyright 1994 by Consulting Psychologists Press, Inc. All rights reserved. Permission also received from Leaetta Hough. Further reproduction is prohibited without the publisher's written consent.

considerably increases the database available to I/O psychologists to investigate the ever-salient issue of how individual differences impact on work-related behaviour. It is no accident that British, German, Scandinavian and Benelux psychologists seem to dominate European research, doing empirical work on personality and organisation.

The occupational application of major tests

Perhaps the most useful way to review this highly scattered and varying literature is to examine research concerning a number of specific instruments. Few will be examined in detail. Most work these days, however, uses the NEO set of instruments, developed by Costa and McCrae and covered in Chapter 4. An increasing number use the Hogan Personality Inventory (Hogan & Hogan, 1992), which will be discussed. A cursory review of both the academic "pure" and applied literature, as well as a poll of the test usage and familiarity in occupational settings, seems to suggest that a fairly limited number of tests have been used to predict occupational behaviour. These will be reviewed systematically.

The Myers-Briggs Type Indicator (MTBI)

The theoretical background to the measure of personality is derived from the theoretical work of Jung (1953). The test was devised by a mother and daughter team – Myers and Myers-Briggs – over 30 years ago and has been extensively and aggressively marketed ever since. According to McCrae and Costa (1989), the MBTI is unusual among personality assessment devices for three reasons: it is based on a classic theory; it purports to measure types rather than traits of continuous variables; and it is widely used to explain individuals' personality characteristics not only to professionals but also to the individuals themselves, and their co-workers, friends, and families. But they also point out its limitations: the original Jungian concepts are distorted even contradicted; there is no bi-model distribution of preference scores; studies using the MTBI have not always confirmed either the theory or the measure. Yet, Devito (1985) has described the MBTI as: "probably the most widely used instrument for non-psychiatric populations in the area of clinical, counselling, and personality testing" (p. 1030).

The criticism of the typology theory is also cogently put by Hicks (1984). He points out that even the manual provides less evidence for type than for continuous trait-like measurement, which is against the spirit of the test. However, after careful evaluation he argues that the MBTI merits serious consideration by psychologists.

In an extensive, much-quoted early review of the instrument, Carlson (1985) pointed out that the MBTI has been used somewhat unsystematically over a very wide range of areas, but generally with favourable validity assessment. The limited reliability research shows satisfactory internal (alpha) and test–retest reliability, but is limited by student samples and short test–retest intervals. Carlson reviewed criterion-related studies in treatment and research settings and noted that "it is to the credit of MBTI that the instrument successfully predicted behaviours as far apart as personal problems to imagery and group conformity" (p. 364).

However, he does note that the introversion–extraversion dimension of the scale has shown most validational evidence, which is perhaps not surprising given that this dimension is perhaps the most well-established one in all personality testing.

Relatively few of the empirical studies in this area have been addressed to the relationship between MBTI variables and occupational behaviour. Most of the better studies have been addressed to clinical- or counselling-dependent variables. Some studies have yielded impressive evidence. For instance, Carlson (1985) was able to conclude: "Results of all three studies gave unambiguous support for hypotheses discussed from Jungian type theory. Type differences in memorial and perceptual processes, previously identified in laboratory set-ups also operate in the personal world, where individuals remember, construe, and imagine their significant moments and relationships" (p. 358).

In an early and much quoted study, Stricker and Ross (1964) looked at personality, ability, and interest correlates of MBTI. Many of the findings, such as the relationship between the E/I scale and vocational interests, showed somewhat contradictory results. They concluded: "the empirical support for the alternative interpretation does suggest that the indicator's scales are strongly subject to influences other than the typological variables . . . the E–I and J–P scales seem to reflect something quite different from their postulated dimensions, and the S–N and T–F scales at best, seem to reflect restricted aspects of them" (p. 642).

Although there has been a vast amount of work on the MBTI, little of this has examined the relationship between types and occupational behaviour, such as productivity or satisfaction. Yet, this literature has increased rather than decreased over the past fifteen years. Some of these studies have shown few predicted differences. For instance, Slocum (1978) examined changes in cognitive style (MBTI scores) and the tactics subjects would most likely use to bring about organisational and individual change. He found only limited evidence that different types use different amounts of information in the diagnosis of the client/organisation problems, and may use different tactics to bring out organisational change, not all studies have been empirical. Also, Blaylock and Winkofsky (1983) used MBTI concepts to explain the problem-solving differences between scientists and managers. They pointed out that most scientists are STs or NTs, while many R&D managers are SFs and NFs and their given preferences for seeing the world lead to various conflicts.

But most of the studies in this area have been empirical. Rahim (1981) tested the hypothesis that there would be congruences between MBTI type and occupational type (technical, intellectual, and social) as measured by a job-satisfaction index. The results did not confirm the person–job first hypothesis but did show Extraverts were more satisfied than Introverts, and Judging types more satisfied than Perceiving types, irrespective of their occupation. Other results have also shown evidence of the main effects of personality on job satisfaction (Furnham & Zacherl, 1986). A good example is the work of Nutt (Henderson & Nutt, 1980; Nutt, 1986a, 1986b, 1989), who has completed a number of very competent simulated decision-making studies. Nutt (1986a) described how MBTI type was related to managers' decisions concerning leadership, team building, control, and future orientation.

Nutt (1989) used the MBTI to define various organisational decision-making styles: ST (analytical), NF (charismatic), SF (conservative) and NT (speculative), and showed how items affected decision making. In a later study, Nutt (1990) showed that the organisational culture was more powerful than the person's individual style in determining decision making. Nutt (1990) showed that top-executive and middle-management decision style was a key factor in explaining the likelihood of taking strategic action and the risk associated with this action. He concluded: "The decisions of top executives were more *style* dependent than those of middle managers. The judicial (SF) top executives were action-averse, with the speculative and charismatic (NT and NF) top executives taking nearly identical and neutral positions. Using the extended definition of decision style and its categories, top executives with a sensate (S) style were found to be much like top executives with pure (narrowly defined) systematic or analytic style (ST), and top executives with a feeling (F) style similar to top executives with a pure judicial (SP) style. Top executives with a pure ST style were much more conservative than the traditional STs, and the pure SFs far more action-orientated than the trad-itionally defined SF" (p. 192).

In a similar simulated study Haley and Stumpf (1989) tested real managers in groups of 12. The simulation revolving around a hypothetical commercial bank with 12 senior management posts across three hierarchical levels and two product areas. After select-ing managerial roles, participants received information on the financial issues and then they ran the bank as they saw fit. Trained observers rated the information-gathering methods that the participants used, which were then related to their MBTI scores. The hypotheses, derived from the work of Tversky and Kahneman (1982), which all received support, revolved around the idea that managers' information input biases have subsequent output biases, which may lead to operational biases. For instance, STs succumb to functional-fixedness and regularity-and-structure biases, while NFs succumb to reasoning-by-analogy and illusory-correlation biases. They argued that this research indicated the choices that different personality types usually make under the various environmental conditions. Thus, managers' predominant styles may lead to good or poor strategies. This information could help managers sensitise themselves to sequential biases in decision making by identifying appropriate and erroneous tactics.

Researchers are aware of the criticism that simulated decisions, as in these studies, may not replicate the decisions that executives would make when faced with a real deci-sion but argue that the strength of the findings overcomes this problem. Other empirical studies have, however, overcome these problems of ecological validity by looking at actual occupational behaviour. For instance, Rice and Lindecamp (1989) correlated MBTI types with gross personal income of small business managers to return on assets. Although extraverts tended to do better than introverts, and thinking types better than judging types, the authors concluded: "The study found no convincing support for any link between Jungian personality types and performance of small businessmen, and this included failure to support the expectations of Myers" (pp. 181–182).

Yet, other studies have found significant and predictable relationships. For instance, Marcia et al. (1989) compared the MBTI, self-esteem and job satisfaction scores of 102 American Managers with their organisation's "normative" personality type. It was hypothesised that managers whose personality type was the norm of their particular organisation, should show higher self-esteem, greater job satisfaction, and a lower turnover rate. The results were confirmed for self-esteem but not for job satisfaction. They argue that those with high fit tend to be more rewarded by the organisation, which tends to increase their self-esteem.

Many studies using students, have demonstrated behavioural correlates of the MBTI that are clearly related to the world of work. For instance, Danziger et al. (1989) found a relationship between MBTI types and time keeping and appointments for an experi-ment on problem solving. Also Schurr et al. (1985) found MBTI types were significantly related to self-reported academic problems, skills and scholastic aptitude. For instance, personality type scores could explain 21% of verbal score variance, and 8% of the mathematics scores variance.

More recently Moore (1987) has noted that the use of personality tests in industry is widespread, and Haley and Stumpf (1989) have pointed out, quite correctly, that the popularity of the MBTI in executive circles affords researchers tremendous opportunities for research. Moore (1987) noted that most companies use the MBTI to help managers better understand how they come across to others who may see things differently. Other applications include team building, improving customer service, smoothing out group differences, working on projects, adapting to change, analysing troubles, behaviour between employees, and between employees and their jobs, and facilitating competitive strategic thinking.

In a fairly large representative study of American managers, Campbell and Van Velsor (1985) found 46% with ST preferences and 37% with NT preferences with few SF or NF types. Thus, according to Haley and Stumpf (1989): "Organisations may adopt conservative recommendations or those based on patterned data more often than people-oriented or innovative recommendations. These biases may account in part for organisational difficulties in adapting to environmental changes. Ideally, decision tasks should dictate cognitive styles managers use. Good managers should at least be able to apply and to understand conclusions drawn from different decision models and processes, or to understand when their specific skills should come into play and when they prove counter-productive. However, these ideal decision making approaches may not be possible . . . Only about 17% of American managers see things in personal and interpersonal dimensions: 83% tend to see things in technical and structural dimensions" (p. 493).

Work psychology–MBTI links do occasionally appear in the literature. However, because the MBTI is not favoured by psychometric researchers, these studies appear on a very ad hoc basis.

Criticisms of the MBTI

Over the years, there have been academic and practitioner assessments and critiques of the MBTI and the Jungian theory upon which it is based. Some of these critiques have been more disinterested and objective than others. A typical objection by practitioners is that the test measures preferences not competencies. Thus, one can have a competent or incompetent ENTJ. Many object that "labelling is disabling" and that "pigeonholing" inhibits rather than facilitates career development. Others point out the poor test–retest reliability with fewer than a quarter of individuals being assigned the same categorisation when tested a second time.

A recent debate in a business magazine has been instructive. Case and Phillipson (2004) argued that it is (loosely) based on Jung's theory, which is informed rather bizarrely by pre-modern cosmology and symbolism, namely astrology and alchemy. Dawes (2004), however, argues that this is not really important as many great ideas and breakthroughs have come through intuition, inspiration and other non-rational sources.

In a number of studies Saggino and colleagues tested the Italian version of the MBTI (Saggino & Kline, 1996). They used a large database and sophisticated analyses and found evidence of five not four factors, so confirming the McCrae and Costa (1989) analysis. Bets and Blank (1992), on the other hand, developed a German translation of the scale that seemed reasonably reliable.

Assessments and critiques of the MBTI have been published for over 40 years (Mendelsohn, 1965). Carlyn (1977) concluded that the MBTI is "adequately reliable" and that the scales seem to be "relatively independent" of each other. She noted that the test seemed to be measuring dimensions of personality "quite similar" to those postulated by Jung. She concluded after examining the modes studies up to that point in time that the content, predictive and construct validity of the scale suggest it is "a reasonably valid instrument which is potentially useful for a variety of purposes" (p. 471). Murray (1990) was equally positive, concluding that the test "has been extensively investigated and has met successfully most challenges to its rationale, test procedures and test results" (p. 1201). Looking at many psychometric studies published in the 1980s he concluded: "Reliability and validity of the inventory have been estimated and generally have been acceptable. Four scales have won approval but the test structure, test evidence, and scoring system do not support 16 different types. The scales probably do not measure adequately what Jung intended but the four dimensions have reasonable validity. Jungian type theory is probably too complicated to be captured on an objective personality test but the Myers–Briggs Indicator has been praised as a practical assessment instrument whose constructs have been clarified by extensive research" (p. 1195).

Various researchers have attempted to test the structure of the MBTI. Thompson and Borrello (1986) found good evidence for four clear factors using factor analysis, claiming this provided evidence of the test's construct validity. Lorr (1991) used a cluster analysis and found weak negligible agreement between his test-derived clusters and the 16 categories in the manual. He suggested that this was due to the poor empirical base for partitioning or sectioning the scales (KI–VSE) depending on which preference score is higher. Second, preference scores are very sensitive to the unreliability of the subject response. Further the categorisation ignores the level (mean), scatter (score variations) or shape (pattern of high and low scores). Profile patterns are complex and varied but this information is largely ignored.

Indeed, the attacks on the categorical classification of the MBTI strike at the very heart of a type measure (Cowan, 1989). Arnau et al. (2003) investigated three Jungian personality measures, including the MBTI. They noted that an individual with just slight preferences is classified in the same category as one with strong preferences. They did their boot-strapping taxometric study to determine whether the Jungian preferences actually exist as dichotomies or whether they are really continua and so valuable information is lost when they are artificially dichotomised. Their analysis was clear: the analysis does not support the categorical (strictly Jungian) position. It is more appropriate and informative to give people a score on a dimension. The MBTI does not do this even though the other Jungian instruments investigated do.

Because of its popularity – it has been argued that an MBTI is completed every second of the day somewhere in the world – it has been the focus of a great deal of psychometric scrutiny. Some academics are concerned with its poor predictive validity and low reliability and others unhappy about the pigeonholing of a four-letter code. The test has shown to be fakeable. Furthermore, it has various forced-choice responses with paired dichotomies, which have serious measurement implications. McCrae and Costa (1989) made a number of damning critiques of the MBTI, where their data suggest "that Jung's theory is either incorrect or inadequately operationalised by the MBTI and cannot provide a sound basis for interpreting it" (p. 17). Their criticisms are:

- That if you read Jung you find many of his descriptions concern the unconscious life of an individual, not directly accessible to self-report. Indeed "real" Jungians often question the whole enterprise.

- That his descriptions of the types include traits that we know empirically do not covary.
- The MBTI includes a scale (the JP scale) that is not part of Jung's theory.
- The measurement identifies people in terms of dominant function and hence dichotomises preference scores. People are assumed to fit into mutually exclusive groups yet the scores, when plotted out, are not bimodally distributed.
- Empirical evidence that there are interactions, as well as main effects, for the types is lacking.
- Essentially the questionnaire fails to measure neuroticism.

They argue from their results that people who use the MBTI should "seriously consider abandoning Jungian theory and some of the associated language" (p. 32). The classification system often misclassifies people at or near the cutting point and, more importantly, fails to note the large differences within each type.

Others have come up with similar criticisms, especially differences between Jungian theory and the theory behind the test. Thus, as Garden (1991) notes, Jung had as a basic premise that everyone should not be considered or treated as a type. She also questions whether the MBTI should be used outside the context of Jungian theory. She notes the disparity and divorce between orthodox Jungian theory and the many writings about the MBTI. She also notes that "empirical support for the distinctive typological features of Jung's theory is equivocal at best" (p. 14).

Querk (2000) in a review of the latest literature attempts a fair evaluation of various strengths and weaknesses. Two are worth noting (Table 3.9).

Various studies have looked at the location of the MBTI in personality factor space (Saggino & Kline, 1996) as well as the relationship between the MBTI and the Big Five factors. Saggino and Kline (1996) also looked at correlations between the MBTI and Cattell's 16PF as well as Eysenck's EPQ. Their factor analysis of the MBTI yielded five not four factors. They argued the EI dimension is clear, but the T–F dimension is "not sufficiently pure" because it loads on to different factors. Overall, apart from correlations with EI, the size of the correlations was modest. They concluded: "According to the available data, it could be argued that the MBTI is invalid, because it does not measure the Jungian typology as it is supposed to do (McCrae & Costa, 1989). In fact, its scales seem to measure three of the 'Big Five' factors and in particular those corresponding to Eysenck's three factor theory (Eysenck, 1992). However, the MBTI is an important test owing to its widespread utilisation and the extensive normative data we possess particularly in the fields of organisational psychology and vocational counselling. Thus, we think the MBTI is not to be abandoned, even if it needs to be substantially modified. However, before programming such a revision, the Italian version of the MBTI should be subjected to a confirmatory factor analysis to confirm the results of the exploratory factor analyses already performed and to better understand the meaning of its factors" (p. 596).

McCrae and Costa (1989) found that the four MBTI indices measured aspects of four of the Big Five dimensions of personality. More specifically, they found that EI was correlated with Extraversion, SN with Openness, TF with Agreeableness and JP with Conscientiousness. These results were replicated by McDonald et al. (1994). Furnham (1996a) also provided evidence supporting these results, but further found Neuroticism to be correlated to both EI and TF. Furnham looked at the correlations between the MBTI scales and the 30 subfactors of the FFM. The highest correlations were between

Table 3.9 5.1. Strengths and weaknesses of the MBTI (Querk, 2000, p. 90).

Strengths	Weaknesses
• The comprehensive theory provides a context for understanding individual complexity.	• Adequate understanding of the theory is needed to administer and interpret the instrument.
• Clients recognise the types as real and the typology as a useful way of describing themselves and others.	• Clients and professionals ascribe trait qualities to type preferences, leading to inappropriate interpretations of type.
• Non-normative basis of preferences and types identifies and affirms client individual differences as normal.	• From a normative perspective, positive type descriptions too easily gloss over real psychological problems.
• Questions about simple surface behaviours adequately identify the complex constructs that interact, as specified in the theory.	• Simplicity of questions encourages the idea that the typology itself is simple and static rather than complex and dynamic.
• Test yields four largely psychometrically independent scales that are relatively unambiguous in what they measure.	• The scales look like familiar trait measures, and can easily be interpreted as four independent traits.
• The test is parsimonious. It requires only four measured constructs to yield rich personality descriptions with broad applicability.	• The 16 types are not measured directly; knowledge of theoretical assumptions regarding how the four scales interact dynamically is needed to identify types.

5.5. Strengths and weaknesses of the MBTI Form M Reliability and Validity (Querk, 2000, p. 94).

Strengths	Weaknesses
• There is improved internal consistency and test–retest reliabilities on all scales.	• Test–retest data are necessarily based on small samples and brief time periods.
• There is improved accuracy relative to best fit type estimates.	• Larger samples to assess best fit type with Form M would be desirable.
• Manual validity information emphasises research that studies the validity of whole types.	• Research on the 16 whole types requires larger samples and an accurate understanding of the theory.
• Data presented throughout the manual provide strong support for type dynamics and the distinctiveness of the 16 types.	• Dynamics-oriented research techniques and results are more difficult to comprehend than simple correlational studies of the four dichotomies.
–	• The Form M database available for research is limited.

EI and Gregariousness, Warmth, and Positive emotions (Extraversion), between SN and Ideas, Fantasy and Aesthetics (Openness), between TF and Tender-mindedness, Trust and Altruism (Agreeableness), between JP and Order, Deliberation and Self-discipline (Conscientiousness) and between EI and Self-consciousness, Depression and Vulnerability (Neuroticism). Furnham et al. (2003) found similar results.

There is no doubt that the MBTI has stimulated a great research output, from studies on the MBTI profiles of accounting students (Wolk & Nikolai, 1997) or software engineers (Capretz, 2003), to those of suicidality in affective disorder patients (Janowsky et al., 2002). Indeed in the 25th anniversary issue of the *Journal of Psychological Type*, the abstracts of 400 papers using the MBTI were published. There does remain, however, serious criticism of its psychometric properties, especially reliability and validity.

Eysenckian theory: extraversion, neuroticism and psychoticism

Without doubt the most sophisticated trait personality theory is that of H. J. Eysenck, which has been likened to finding St Pancras railway station (i.e. an elaborate Victorian structure) in the jungle of personality theories. In a recent review of the Eysenck Personality measures (EPI, EPQ, EPP) Furnham et al. (2007a) noted five positive features of the measures: parsimony; explanation of processes; evidence based on experimentation; wide application; and continuous improvement and development. The theory has spawned the Maudsley Personality Inventory (MPI), the Eysenck Personality Inventory (EPI), and the Eysenck Personality Questionnaire (EPQ), which has been recently revised. These questionnaires have been subjected to extensive investigation and have proved robust (Helmes, 1989). The theory, which has undergone various changes over a 30-year period, argues for the psychophysiological basis of personality, and locates 3 major factors that relate to social behaviour: extraversion, neuroticism, and psychoticism. Although the theory has been applied to a wide range of activities including criminality, sex, smoking, health and learning, less work has been done on the Eysenckian dimension correlates of occupational behaviour. However, over the last 25 years there has been evidence not only of the application of Eysenck's theory but its predictive usefulness in the occupational sphere.

In one study of telephone sales employees, Furnham and Miller (1997) related EPI measures of Neuroticism and Extraversion to sickness and absenteeism as well as performance data. They found young extraverts had most periods of sick leave and stable extraverts received highest potential and performance ratings. In another study of sales staff, Furnham et al. (1999b) found that introverts got higher ratings than extraverts. Clearly the size and specific relationship of personality variables to work factors depends strongly on the nature of the job considered.

In an early study, Rim (1961) looked at personality determinants of job incentives. He found students scoring low on extraversion and neuroticism ranked "opportunity to learn new skills", as more important than high scorers, while high neuroticism scorers ranked "good salary" as more important than low scorers.

Bendig (1963) used the Strong Vocational Interest Blank with the MPI and discovered that introverts preferred scientific and theoretical jobs such as journalism, architecture, and the teaching of mathematics, whereas extraverts expressed more interest in occupations involving more social contact (e.g. selling life insurance and social work). Extraversion was consistently and negatively correlated with preferences to become an architect, dentist, mathematician, physicist, engineer, or chemist, while neuroticism was negatively correlated with accountant, office manager, banker, sales manager, and teacher. Overall the results showed social extraversion was negatively correlated with SVIB scales in Strong's areas I (General Professional), II (Science and Engineering), and IV (Practical) for both sex groups. Stable extraversion (SE) was positively correlated with area V (Social Service) and negatively correlated with areas VIII (Business) and III (Production Manager) for men, while SE was positively correlated with interests in area IX (Sales) for women. SE was also negatively related to the Author–Journalist interest scale for both sexes. The "Emotionality" (EM) trait, as measured by the Neuroticism scale, was negatively correlated with SVIB scales in area III (Production Manager) and VIII (Business) for both men and women, and with areas IV (Practical) and V (Social Service) for women.

In a study more useful for its norms than theory, Eysenck (1967) collected EPI data on 1504 businessmen. His results are shown in Table 3.10.

Table 3.10 Personality scores of businessmen in different areas of business

Area of business	N	Neuroticism		Extraversion		Lie scale	
		M	SD	M	SD	M	SD
General management	165	7.04	4.03	11.13	3.58	2.80	2.12
Production	135	6.90	3.77	11.05	3.72	3.08	1.69
Research & development	574	7.42	4.05	9.98	3.88	2.76	1.49
Finance	132	7.53	4.49	10.12	3.40	2.93	1.97
Sales	168	7.04	3.64	11.33	3.98	2.93	1.92
Personnel	88	7.11	4.04	11.34	4.36	2.95	1.72
Consultancy	218	7.32	3.93	10.09	3.93	2.91	1.66
More than one of above	24	7.70	5.16	11.91	3.26	2.66	1.49
Total	1504						
Standardised data							
Normal population	2000	9.06	4.78	12.07	4.37	–	–
Salesmen	37	8.38	4.72	13.63	3.76	–	–
Professional	23	7.95	5.11	11.40	4.91	–	–
Normal population	651	–	–	–	–	2.26	1.57

Source: Eysenck (1967).

On the E scale the business groups are relatively introverted, but significantly different between themselves, with Finance, R&D, and Consultants being the most introverted, and those belonging to more than one group being the most extraverted. Eysenck (1967) noted:

> [S]uccessful businessmen are on the whole stable introverts; they are stable regardless of what type of work they do within business, but their degree of extraversion may be related to type of work. The data are probably reasonably reliable because relatively few respondents failed to answer, and because scores on the lie scale did not indicate any market tendency to "fake good". The results suggest that the EPI may have some modest role to play in furthering research into the personality patterns of persons engaged in business and industry.
>
> (p. 250)

Martin and Kirkcaldy (1998) later found predictable EPQ correlates of work attitudes, which suggests that it is unwise to hire those with high Psychoticism (or indeed Neuroticism) scores. The notion that introverted workers are better able than extraverted ones to handle routine work activities was investigated by Cooper and Payne (1967) in a study carried out in the packing department of a tobacco factory, where the work was repetitive and light. Job adjustment, as assessed by two supervisors, was negatively related to extraversion, and those workers who left the job in the 12 months following testing were significantly more extraverted than those who remained. Neuroticism was also implicated, being related to poor job adjustment and to frequency of non-permitted absence. They note:

> Beginning with the withdrawal indices, we find that the only appreciable correlations are with Length of Service and Non-Permitted Absences. The more extraverted workers in this study have shorter periods of service to their credit than

the less extraverted (more introverted); this finding may be taken as evidence that the more extraverted individuals will withdraw permanently from work of a routine nature. Non-Permitted Absence offers further interesting support for the withdrawal assumption. The correlation between Extraversion and Surgery Attendance, although in the expected direction, is probably too small to merit serious attention. Surprisingly, Certified Sickness Absence is almost completely unrelated to Extraversion; it would be tempting to account for this non-relationship on the basis of Certified Sickness requiring a visit to a doctor and subsequent submission of a medical certificate to the employer, all of which may not be considered worth the effort when there exists the alternative of taking one or two days' Uncertified Absence (i.e. Non-Permitted Absence) with virtually no trouble at all. However, such an explanation is not in keeping with an unpublished finding of Taylor that Extraversion scores for 194 male oil refinery workers correlated .22 with Sickness Absence.

(p. 55)

The use of both conditioning and arousal theory is evident in Cooper and Payne's (1967) thinking: Because extraverts condition poorly and introverts readily, extraverts are less able to tolerate tasks of routine nature since inhibition accumulates and inhibits sustained task performance; Because extraverts are under-aroused they seek arousal and do not function as well as introverts with a minimal or moderate sensory variation input. Eysenck's (1981) theory states that extraverts function better cognitively when in a state of high neurophysiological arousal, whereas introverts function more effectively when they are less aroused. If the optimum range of functioning for an extravert is, as is suggested, higher than that of an introvert, then any distraction that brings the mood further outside of the respective optimal ranges may result in differential performances.

This has led to a number of studies on distraction at work. Various studies have demonstrated that music at work has a differential impact on introverts, who are overaroused, than extraverts, who are under-aroused (Furnham & Bradley, 1997; Furnham & Stephenson, 2007). Furnham and Strbac (2002) found that music was almost as impactful as noise in lowering the work efficiency of workers but particularly introverts.

Indeed the literature suggests that introverts choose and thrive in quieter, less-distracting work environments than extraverts. Therefore they might be likely to be much less favourably disposed to open-plan work environments than extraverts.

Savage and Stewart (1972) also found that 100 female card-punch operators in training showed negative correlations between extraversion and supervisor ratings of output per month, although there was no relationship between this personality variable and dropouts from the program.

In another relevant paper Hill (1975) compared the behaviour of introverts and extraverts on a monotonous task. He found, as predicted, that extraverts tend to build more variety into their responses on a monotonous task compared to introverts. Wankowski (1973) investigated a random sample of students at Birmingham University and extraverted students tended to choose practical or people-oriented courses, whereas introverted students preferred more theoretical subjects. Introverts had greater examination success than extraverts in the physical sciences. Low-neuroticism scorers opted for practically biased courses, whereas high-neuroticism scorers preferred people-oriented courses. In terms of examination success, low neuroticism was associated with success in the applied sciences. Wilson et al. (1972) used various ability and personality tests (including the EPI) to predict three criteria among gas fitters: examination results, supervisor ratings, college attendance. Neuroticism was a much better predictor than extraversion and results showed high scores were negatively associated with both exam results and absenteeism.

Morgenstern et al. (1974) demonstrated that introverted subjects function less efficiently in the presence of distractions, while extraverts show actual improvement in the presence of distractions. They concluded: "It would seem that the extraverted subjects do not merely prefer to be in the company of others, but that their work efficiency actually improves in the face of distractions, while the solitary preference of the introverts are reflected in their reduced efficiency of work when distracted. Paying heed to such preferences, as measured by the Eysenck Personality Inventory, is therefore not only a method of increasing contentment at work by means of personnel selection, but should also result in improved efficiency of output" (p. 220).

Rim (1977) got several job applicants to complete the Eysenck Personality Inventory and rated statements according to how well they described their ideal job. Among the male subjects, the neurotic extraverts had the most distinctive ratings, valuing social contact, economic, social position, patterning of time, and power functions of work more than neurotic introverts, stable extraverts, or stable introverts. There were only modest and uninterpretable effects of personality on the description of the ideal job among female subjects.

Since neurotic individuals in general and neurotic introverts in particular are especially susceptible to stress, it might be thought that such people would prefer jobs that involve minimal stress. However, Rim (1977) did not find any large differences in the ideal job as a function of either neuroticism or neurotic introversion, while Bendig (1963) reported only that high neuroticism was associated with a dislike of business-type occupations such as banking, office management, and accountancy.

Organ (1975) examined personality correlates of conditionability in organisations as operationalised by students getting bonus points for performance on random quizzes. Introverts did better than extraverts, who presumably got diverted from the routine discipline of the daily preparation for classes regardless of contingencies.

Extraverts are more likely than introverts to prefer occupations that involve social contact. There is, therefore, a danger that introverted workers may become over-aroused if their jobs involve considerable extra-organisational contact and a relative absence of routine. Blunt (1978) argued that introverted managers would, thus, tend to choose positions involving relatively routine duties (finance, production, or technical managers), whereas extraverted managers would be more likely to select jobs in sales, marketing, or transport. The results were broadly as hypothesised, except that transport managers were less extraverted and production managers more extraverted than predicted.

The relationship between personality and occupational success has been frequently examined. Fairly impressive findings were obtained among trainee pilots by Jessup and Jessup (1971). They tested would-be pilots with the Eysenck Personality Inventory early in their course and discovered that the subsequent failure rate varied considerably as a function of personality. Specifically, 60% of the neurotic introverts failed, against 37% of the neurotic extraverts, 32% of the stable extraverts, and only 14% of the stable introverts. Thus, high levels of neuroticism had a much greater adverse effect on introverts than on extraverts. They note that they expect the introverted cadet to learn better both in the aircraft and lecture room more than extraverts. Jessup and Jessup (1971) concluded: "The comparative failure of the specifically neurotic introvert may be tentatively explained as follows. High arousal in the visceral system is associated with high N; high cortical arousal with low E. Given that there is an optimal level of arousal for learning to fly and that this is a particularly stressful experience, it seems likely that the neurotic introvert will be aroused beyond the optimum; the learning of the stable introvert on the other hand profits from cortical arousal while suffering from additional visceral arousal" (p. 120).

Similar findings were reported by Reinhardt (1970), who carried out a battery of personality tests on a sample of the United States Navy's best pilots. Their mean score on the neuroticism scale of the Maudsley Personality Inventory was only 11, compared with a mean of 20 among American college students. Okakue et al. (1977) divided the extraversion and neuroticism scores of military pilots into three categories (high, average, and low) on each dimension. Of the sample of 75 pilots, 38 fell into the stable extravert category, with the highest frequency in any of the other eight categories being only 8. In more recent research with military pilots in the United Kingdom, Bartram and Dale (1982) found a tendency for successful pilots to be more stable and more extraverted than those who failed flying training. They had data on over 600 pilots from the Army Air Corps and the Royal Air Force. The consistent finding that neuroticism is negatively related to flying success makes intuitive sense. Flying can obviously be stressful, with a single mistake proving fatal. In such circumstances, pilots who are especially susceptible to stress are likely to perform less well than those who are more stable.

Looking at more common jobs, Kirton and Mulligan (1973) found attitudes towards organisational change to be related to a combination of neuroticism and extraversion among 258 managers from eight companies with at least 1000 employees each. The four extraversion-by-neuroticism groupings were compared and the finding was that the two personality variables interacted, although there was no effect of either taken separately. Subjects scoring high on both the neuroticism and extraversion, and subjects scoring low on both scales (neurotic extraverts and stable introverts) had more positive attitudes toward change in managerial practices in general, more positive attitudes toward specific, innovative appraisal schemes or promotional policies being introduced, and the lowest level of discontent with the institution and with superiors.

Yet Turnbull (1976) found that among more than 100 male college students involved in a summer of book sales, neither Eysenck Personality Inventory extraversion scores alone nor in combination with other personality scales predicted sales success. Sales success was determined on the basis of total wholesale business and a sales index indicating amount of business per call made. In the global studies presented earlier, the sales vocations were only weakly related to extraversion. Turnbull noted a wide range of scores on the extraversion–introversion dimension among the individuals applying for the job and no personality differences between those who completed the summer of sales and those who dropped out. It was found, as predicted, that extraversion scores increased from the beginning of the summer to the end of the summer as a result of the summer of sales experience, an increase that was equal for more successful and less successful salesmen.

Studies of personality correlates of mood have revealed interesting results. Christie and Venables (1973) asked 80 volunteers whose jobs ranged from office clerks to heads of academic departments in the various schools to complete the Mood Adjective Check List on Monday and Friday mornings and afternoons for four successive weeks. They combined the scales of concentration, activation, and deactivation to form an efficiency index, for which there was a significant four-way interaction effect involving day of week, time of day, extraversion, and neuroticism. The authors described a pattern of high arousal and low euphoria experienced by neurotic introverts on Monday morning, absenteeism and a pattern of high arousal and high euphoria experienced by stable extraverts on Friday afternoon, with premature departures from work at that time. Bishop and Jean Renaud (1976) related end-of-day moods to amount of change in daily activities and personality. Choosing people at random in a community, representing a number of different vocations, they asked subjects to keep a diary in which entries were made each 15 minutes during both a workday and a leisure day. Mood ratings were taken from the last hour before bedtime, and again there was a four-way interaction effect. Activity variation was not related to mood on workdays but it was on leisure days. The fact that activity variation was related to pleasantness of mood for stable extraverts and neurotic introverts but related to unpleasantness of mood for neurotic extraverts and stable introverts indicates how increased variation and stimulation (and its opposite, monotony) has different value for different individuals.

Kim (1980) using undergraduates on a simulated work task found, as predicted, that introverts were less dissatisfied on a non-stimulating task than extraverts who were more satisfied on a stimulating task, though there was a difference in their actual performance. They also found that introverts and extraverts differed in their perception of expectancy and motivating characteristics of objective tasks.

More recently, in a study of personality correlates of job preference and satisfaction, Sterns et al. (1983) found that extraverts preferred jobs with higher levels of cognitive task demands, pace of task demands, cognitive closure, extrinsic rewards, and intrinsic rewards. Neuroticism on the other hand was negatively related to each of the above preferences except for extrinsic rewards. Extraverts were less satisfied with the clerical work itself, supervision, and co-workers than introverts. It should be pointed out that subjects were non-managerial civil service clerical employees in a job that would suit stable introverts more than extraverts.

The Eysenckian trait dimensions have also found to predict "negative" occupational variables. There has been some interest in the relevance of personality to performance under rather monotonous conditions. It might be predicted that under-aroused extraverts would find it more difficult than introverts to maintain performance over time. Extraverts showed a greater deterioration than introverts in driving performance over a four-hour period (Fagerström & Lisper, 1977). However, their performance improved more than that of introverts when someone talked to them or the car radio was turned on.

Shaw and Sichel (1970) compared the personality characteristics of accident-prone and safe South African bus drivers. Most of the accident-prone drivers were neurotic extraverts, whereas the safe drivers were predominantly stable introverts. As might have been expected, it is the impulsiveness component of extraversion rather than the sociability component that is more closely related to poor driving and accident proneness (Loo, 1979; see Chapter 8).

Eysenck and Eysenck (1975a) have concluded: "In sum, it appears that preferences for different kinds of occupation and occupational success are both determined to some extent by personality. The research to date mostly suffers from the disadvantage that job characteristics are discussed in an ad hoc fashion. A major dimension along which jobs can be ordered is the extent to which the behaviour of an individual doing that job is constrained by external factors. For example, a car worker on an assembly line has minimal control over his work activities, whereas a university lecturer has greater control. It seems likely that personality will be a more consequential determinant of job satisfaction and success when severe constraints exist. It may be coincidence that two of the occupations wherein personality has been found to be relevant (flying and driving) both involve considerable constraints. In other words, the fit of a worker to his job is especially important when the worker has little scope for tailoring the work environment to his needs" (p. 329).

However, it is possible to argue the precise opposite. That is, where there are few external demands, personality (and ability) factors may be primary causes of success and failure. Thus, it may be argued that personality factors are more relevant and crucial under these conditions.

Finally, what happens if an individual finds himself in a job that is ill-suited to his personality? If he remains in that job, then the obvious answer is that his job performance will tend to be relatively poor. An alternative possibility that has rarely been considered is that his personality may alter as a result of being exposed to a particular job environment. Turnbull (1976) found that there was no tendency for success among male student salesmen to be related to extraversion. However, the experience of selling and making numerous contacts with strangers produced a highly significant increase in the average level of extraversion.

Most of the Eysenckian studies were based on the three (EPI) or four (EPQ) dimension scales. However recent research has involved the longer EPP. The long version of the EPP consists of 440 items (questions) yielding 21 scores (7 for each of the three factors) plus, if administered by questionnaire, three other measures: Dissimulation (i.e. lie), time taken (to complete the whole test) and the number of "can't decides". The 21 traits are:

- Extraversion: Activity, Sociability, Expressiveness, Assertiveness, Ambition, Dogmatism and Aggressiveness.
- Neuroticism: Inferiority, Unhappiness, Anxiety, Dependence, Hypochondria, Guilt and Obsessiveness.
- Psychoticism: Risk-taking, Impulsivity, Irresponsibility, Manipulativeness, Sensation-seeking, Tough-minded and Practicality.
- A Lie Scale is also included.

Furnham et al. (2001) explored various test correlates of the EPP. This was treated as a concurrent validity study. The factor structure of the EPP has been the object of several psychometric investigations, most of which involved various forms of exploratory factor analysis (EFA; Costa & McCrae, 1995a; Jackson et al., 2000). These studies have suggested that some EPP scales either measure more than one superfactor (i.e. they are "factorially complex") or do not fit well into the Eysenckian personality hierarchy (but may fit into other hierarchies such as the Big Five; see Costa & McCrae, 1995a).

The EPP was constructed for use in work-related settings and most of its applications focus on organisational psychology issues (e.g. job satisfaction; Furnham et al., 2002) or are based on employee samples (e.g. Jackson et al., 2000). However, the inventory can also be used in non-occupational settings (e.g. Francis et al., 2001; Wilson & Jackson, 1994).

However, perhaps the most interesting Eysenckian-inspired research on the relationship between personality and work-related behaviour is Reinforcement Sensitivity

Theory, which is essentially Jeffrey Gray's modification of Hans Eysenck's personality theory (Corr, 2004). It is based on two dimensions of systems called BIS (the Behavioural Inhibition System) and BAS (the Behavioural Activation System).

As Furnham and Jackson (2007) have noted, the practical application of Gray's theory to occupational settings is obvious particularly with respect to motivation. It should be a waste of time to try to motivate an extravert (high on BAS) with threats of dire punishment (such as sacking, no pay rise) and it would prove equally unsuccessful to attempt to entice an introvert (high on BIS) with promise of pay or benefits. However, because the theory clearly stipulates that introverts have some BAS activity and extraverts some BIS activity, everyone is sensitive to both reward and punishment but to varying degrees. The stronger the reward or the punishment the less differentiating its effect. To exact the highest level of performance from individuals, motivators must encourage the BAS extravert with potential reward and prompt the BIS introvert with judicial use of punitive threats. Further, they need to get the optimal reward/punishment right for their particular employees. Thus, BAS-extraverted organisations, like those involved in selling, could best motivate and satisfy their staff by providing regular, but varied, rewards. Equally a primarily BIS-introverted organisation, as in many bureaucracies, can best shape or motivate staff by the suggestion of imposed sanctions.

The degree of neuroticism heightens an individual's sensitivity to reward or punishment. The introvert, sensitive to punishment, who displays high neuroticism becomes, and indeed is, more sensitive to reward and punishment with the greatest increase being toward punishment. That is, the neurotic introvert becomes more concerned with reward but is even more anxious about punishment than the low neurotic introvert. As neuroticism increases, the extravert (sensitive to reward) becomes more sensitive to both reward and punishment, with high increases in reward sensitivity. Although extraverts and introverts increase in sensitivity to that trait commonly attributed to extraversion of introversion.

Thus, an extraverted neurotic, being highly sensitive to reward, is less socialisable in terms of legal and organisational norms and more likely to become maladaptive or difficult. Given moderate levels of extraversion, high (neurotic) individuals are usually more responsive to control techniques than low (stable) individuals. Whether reward or punishment is the controlling factor, the over-socialised individual will respond readily and may tend to become over-controlled, while under-socialised individuals may show little or no response to control measures. Consequently, the low Neuroticism (stable) individual may necessitate the use of rigid control and severe disciplinary measures (Wakefield, 1979).

According to Gray's reinforcement sensitivity theory (RST) theory, once the BAS has been activated it should produce motor activity, overall motivation and feelings of desire, elation and hope: optimistic, reward-sensitive, motivated behaviour. On the other hand BIS arouses anxiety (avoidance), and inhibition (the later theory suggests avoidance tendencies are inhibited). Whilst a cursory glance over the literature suggests that high BAS, but low BIS levels may be beneficial for work this is clearly an oversimplification. Thus studies have shown, as predicted, that whilst BIS is clearly a vulnerability factor of anxiety and depression so BAS may be related to drug and alcohol use. Thus the impulsive BAS individual may be particularly prone to accidents, mishaps and mistakes while the anxiety-sensitive BIS related to absenteeism, perfectionism and difficult task avoidance. However, there are adaptive levels of both BIS and BAS where they can be beneficial. Indeed, Perkins and Corr (2005) argued that anxiety at work can be good in situations that require caution, self-discipline and anticipa-tion of threat. They found that (only) for cognitively able individuals, worrying was positively correlated with performance but as ability declined the relationship disap-peared. Recently Van der Linden et al. (2007) found that BIS/BAS predicted various indices of occupational health. Reinforcement sensitivity was linked to job satisfaction and involvement while punishment sensitivity related to stress and fatigue.

Clearly, different jobs call for different abilities and temperaments. Optimistic, fun-seeking, reward-sensitive drive associated with high BAS levels is clearly an asset in jobs associated with the service sector, sales and entertainment, even the military. Equally it is possible to see situations where moderate BIS scores may be useful in research or safety-related occupations. Research in this area continues to grow.

Cattell's 16PF

Perhaps the most famous of all personality tests applied to industrial, organisation, and occupation settings is R. B. Cattell's 16PF, published initially over 40 years ago. Per-haps predictively, because of their similar approach and methods but relatively subtle differences, such as the fact that Eysenck stresses superfactors and orthogonal factor rotations, and Cattell stresses simple factors and oblique rotations, these two figures have occasionally taken swipes at each other. For instance, Eysenck (1985a) has claimed that Cattell's 16 factors are unstable: "When results are thus completely unreplicable, it would seem that the theory based on the original analysis is unacceptable, and that such scales should not be used in theoretical or practical scientific work" (p. 9).

Cattell (1986), in reply, quotes 41 published studies that replicated his system. He notes: "Eysenck's resort to 3 factors is shown to be theoretically faulty and unable to equal the criterion predictions obtainable from the 16PF primaries" (p. 153), and later: "Eysenck's attack on the continuing lack of clear paradigms in current personality discussion is well merited, but he does not need to criticise one of the most scientifically established maps of human personality structures because it is not quite as simple as his own idea of things" (p. 158).

Yet both men, graduates of London University, have developed questionnaires useful in the world of occupational testing.

For Cattell the test has a number of advantages: It is unusually *comprehensive* in its coverage of personality dimensions; it is based on the *functional* measurement of previ-ously located natural personality structures; the measurements are relatable to an *organisational* and *integrated* body of practice and theoretical knowledge in clinical education and industrial psychology.

The test measures 16 dimensions of personality (and 6–9 second-order factors), which are supposedly independent and identifiable; reliably and validly measurable. The psy-chometric properties of the scale are well documented as well as the problem of decep-tion. The very fact that the test has been around so long, very shrewdly and aggressively marketed in a variety of countries, and that Cattell himself has been such an active researcher and zealous advocate of the test for so long – means it has attracted incredible attention. For instance, if one consults the handbook printed 40 years ago (Cattell et al., 1970) one finds incredible evidence of the application of the test. The data are in fact divided into two sections. The first concerns available specification equations against cri-teria – here various weights are given (per dimension), derived from multiple regressions – against specific measurable criteria. Policemen to school counsellors are considered.

Consider for instance the following:

Salesmen: Retail. Two studies, the larger by Industrial Psychology Inc., have related actual sales volume in comparable situations (retail bakery route salesmen, soft-drink salesmen) with the following average equation:

Salesmanship = $.44A - .11B + .11C - .22E + .11F - .11G + .22H - .33L - .11M + .11N + .11O + .44Q_3 + .22Q_3 - .22Q_4 + 1.87$.
[Group mean = 5.56]

In this case, even the smaller weights have been retained because the sign was the same in the two studies. It will be clear from this, as from some other instances, that the popular stereotypes and impressions on which occupational selections are still often based can be erroneous. Thus, dominance, E+, is actually not effective in face-to-face selling, and the view of the successful salesman as an "extravert" has to be modified. For although gains are shown through exviant deviations (the temperament source traits of A, F, and H), self-sufficiency. Q_2, is actually oppositely weighted to the extravert direction; i.e. the inviant endowment is required.

Salesmen: Wholesale. On wholesale (grain) salesmen, personality has similarly been correlated with *actual sales income*, resulting in the following equation:

Wholesale Sales Success = $.21A + .10B + .10C + .10E + .21F + .10G - .10L - .31M + .21N - .31Q_2 + .21Q_3 - .21Q_4 + 3.80$.
[Group mean = 5.09]

It will be noted that intelligence shifts to a positive effect here, autism (M) is more of a drawback than it was in the retail field, and so on, but otherwise there is a "family similarity" between the two types of sales activity."

(pp. 166–167)

Second, equations indirectly calculated – here equations are derived and cross-validated on samples. Occupations as varied as accountants to athletes; military cadets to musicians; and sales personnel to social workers are considered.

Some of these findings have received moderate corroboration by replicative studies. For instance, Cattell et al. (1970) report on 139 cabin crew: "The most noteworthy features of the primaries are high ego strength, parmia (insusceptibility to sympathetic-system upset by stress), high self-sentiment (control), low pretension (tolerance of 'difficult' passengers!), low inadequacy–guilt proneness and, especially, low ergic tension. With this high general strength of character and self-control, there is, however, only average dominance. Such an unusual degree of deviation toward character and control (along with sociability), and away from neuroticism, suggests (along with rather small standard deviations) that the air line is doing an excellent job" (p. 189).

Twenty years later, using cabin crew from a British airline, Furnham (1991b) showed the Spearman rank–order correlation between the two to be $r = .63$, which is significant at .01. Yet he found that the 16PF did not discriminate between good, average, and poor employees. One hundred and thirty-six crew members completed the Cattell 16PF at the beginning of their training as the personnel department wanted to determine the effectiveness of the test in predicting occupational success. Over the course of a six-month period detailed daily reports were kept on their in-flight behaviour. These reports were later used to categorise the subjects into above average, average, below average, and to note those who left the airline. Pearson correlations and one-way ANOVAs across various groups (i.e. above vs. below average; stayed vs. left) failed to yield significant differences, though some clear trends were apparent.

Yet it is not only the relationship between personality and vocational/occupational variables that has interested Cattell and his colleagues. For instance, Cattell and Butcher (1968) looked at the relationship between personality and clinical and educational outcomes. In fact, the occupational correlates of personality seem to have excited Cattell least, though many followers have pursued this path.

There have been very many studies looking at cross-cultural differences in personality as measured by the 16PF. These have important implications because there are notable and significant personality differences between different countries; these may be reflected in the organisational structures that occur in that country. For instance, if country A tends to be more extraverted than B one might expect organisations in country A to have more open-planned offices; to have a more explicit performance reward structure; to have many more social events than country B.

Studies have, however, shown some pretty clear patterns. For instance, Cattell and Warburton (1961) found, in comparable student groups, that the British were more conservative, less emotionally sensitive, with higher ego-strength and self-sentiment, but lower super-ego development and self-sentiment than Americans. Similar subject studies have shown them to be consistent but relatively minor.

As regards an occupational application, Cattell has outlined two approaches to deciding a person's suitability for a specific occupation or a particular job. First is the effectiveness estimate approach in which goodness of performance is estimated by a quantitive value. Second is the adjustment approach, whereby a person is allocated to a specific group – for example a group of "successful" salesmen. This is usually done by computing a similarity coefficient relating that person's profile to the mean profile of that group.

The first approach assumes a linear relationship between the various factors and the criterion, and is usually expressed as a linear regression equation with weights attaching to each factor. The second approach assumes a curvilinear relationship as there is an "optimum" value for each factor, that "optimum" value being the mean score of the successful group in that factor. Most of the research in this area, under Cattell's guidance has adopted the first route.

A review of the occupational literature has shown that Cattell's 16PF has also worked well in a variety of practical situations. Bernardin (1977) studied absenteeism and turnover in a sample of 51 sales personnel; he found correlations between the 16PF Conscientiousness and Anxiety scales and absenteeism and turnover varying between .21 and .40. Karson and O'Dell (1970) studied 568 air traffic controllers and found a number of low but significant correlations with peer and supervisory ratings. Toole et al. (1972) used the 16PF to study the relationship between personality and job performance in minority and non-minority employees; they found zero-order correlations less than .30, but a multiple r of .41 between scale scores and performance ratings. Topp and Kardash (1986) found that the 16PF predicted performance in a police academy. There is also considerable concurrent validity of the 16PF. Jones et al.

(1976) found the 16PF correlated, significantly and predictably, with the Work Motivation Inventory, a measure of Maslow's needs.

Rather than look at correlates (predictors) of success some researchers have looked specifically at personality predictors of failure. McLoughlin et al. (1983) compared 49 "terminated" male executives to an employed sample on the 16PF. Compared to those not sacked, the terminated group were less warm hearted (A); more emotionally stable (C); more assertive (E); more conscientious (G); more imaginative (M); more unperturbed (O); more self-sufficient (Q_3) and more controlled (Q_4). Curiously, then, the sacked executives appeared on the whole healthier and happier than the employed executives, but neither scores were outside the average range. The authors noted that the personality characteristics of the sacked may have been less contributory factors in their dismissal, yet they show the pattern of the driven, self-absorbed, and successful executive. However, it is crucial to know *why* people were dismissed to make sense of this data. Similarly, Moore and Stewart (1989) found various 16PF correlates of employee honesty and integrity. Although the study did not show a consistent pattern of 16PF correlates of four quite different measures, the size and number of the correlations indicated effects well above chance level.

More recently Fraboni and Saltstone (1990) used the 16PF to see if it could distinguish between first-generation entrepreneurs, who had established their own businesses, and second-generation entrepreneurs in businesses established by their parents. The results showed that compared to second-generation entrepreneurs, the first generation were *more* suspicious (L), assertive (E), imaginative (M); controlled (Q_3), and reserved (A) but *less* trusting, humble, practical, undisciplined, and outgoing. First-generation entrepreneurs are more innovatively oriented and second-generation ones more administratively oriented. No doubt because it has been around for a very long time, and it is still aggressively marketed, the 16PF is still used widely in organisational contexts. Thus Davidson and Etherington (1995) looked at the 16PF profile of accountants while Arnold (1999) compared high- and low-performing radiographers on the 16PF. Similarly, Csoka (1993) looked at the 16PF formula for high- and low-performing military leaders. More recently Hartung et al. (2005) showed that 16PF profiles of medical students could predict their specialty choice at a later stage. Cattell's contribution to all aspects of psychology has been immense (see Chapter 6), even without having taken a special interest in trait predictors of work behaviours.

Hogan personality questionnaires

Since the early 1990s Robert and Joyce Hogan have made a major contribution to our understanding of personality at work. They have done so predominantly through the development of three different measures: one of normal functioning, or the bright side (Hogan Personality Inventory), one of abnormal functioning, or the dark side (Hogan Developmental Surveyor), and one of values.

Socioanalytic theory (Hogan, 2006) is a model of personality that tries to integrate the best insights of psychoanalysis, symbolic interactionism and evolutionary psychology. The model suggests that at a deep (and perhaps unconscious) level people are motivated by needs for social acceptance, social status, and meaning and purpose in their lives. They attempt to both *get along with* and *get ahead of* others while bringing meaning to their everyday lives. The model also suggests that for many people, if not most, these needs are met (or frustrated) by their occupational pursuits; work is, indeed, a primary venue for people to find friends, status, and meaning (Hogan & Hogan, 1992).

Hogan (2006) distinguishes three further aspects of personality, referred to as "the bright side", "the dark side" and "the inside". The *bright side* reflects people's performance when they are acting normally in day-to-day situations; inventories of normal personality concern the bright side. The Big Five model is an accepted taxonomy of the bright side. The *dark side* reflects people's performance when they are tired, stressed or otherwise not paying attention. The spectrum hypotheses suggest that dark-side behaviours are manifestations of extreme (high or low) scores on normal personality traits. Dark-side tendencies derail careers; the DSM-IV, Asiz 2 personality disorders provides a taxonomy of these tendencies (Hogan, 2006). The *inside* reflects people's core values.

The relevance of the dark side, the Hogan Developmental Survey, will be discussed in Chapter 5. Most of the salient work related to behaviour has been based on the Hogan Personality Questionnaire, which has seven scales:

1   The *Adjustment Scale* reflects the degree to which a person is calm and self-accepting, or conversely, tense and self-critical. Individuals with high scores are not introspective, rarely take things personally, and generally handle pressure well. Individuals with low scores are more self-reflective; they tend to take things more personally and do not enjoy pressure.

2   The *Ambition Scale* evaluates the degree to which a person is confident, seeks status, and values achievement. Individuals with high scores are competitive and concerned with success. Individuals with low scores are cautious, uncertain and possibly lack focus about where their lives are leading.

3   The *Sociability Scale* assesses the degree to which a person needs and enjoys social interaction. Individuals with high scores are extroverted, uninhibited, and impulsive; they can also be exhibitionists, and they create a strong social impression. Individuals with low scores are more predictable, quiet and reserved; they prefer to keep a low social profile.

4   The *Likeability Scale* reflects social sensitivity, tact, and perceptiveness. Individuals with high scores tend to be warm, friendly and considerate; individuals with low scores are often unconcerned with how they are regarded by others.

5   The *Prudence Scale* concerns self-control and conscientiousness. Individuals with high scores tend to be orderly and dependable; they may also be conservative and over-controlled. Individuals with low scores tend to be impulsive and disorderly, but they may be flexible and innovative.

6   The *Intellectance Scale* reflects the degree to which a person is interested in intellectual matters – science, art and philosophy. Individuals scoring high on intellectance tend to be original, to be imaginative and to have many interests and hobbies. Individuals scoring low on intellectance tend to be practical, cautious, and not interested in speculative questions.

7   The *School Success Scale* reflects the degree to which a person enjoys academic activities and values education as an end in itself. Individuals with high scores on this scale tend to be good students and high academic achievers. Individuals with low scores regard education as a means to an end and not as something that is intrinsically important.

The manual asserts that the HPI is uniquely designed to forecast performance in real-world settings. Furthermore, and probably uniquely, it has various specific subscales that are made up of primary factors from the different seven domains or superfactor levels. Thus, there are occupational scales that measure things like service orientation, stress tolerance, reliability (honesty, dependability), clerical potential, sales potential, managerial potential, etc.

There have been many validity tests of these measures. Perhaps the most useful summary is Hogan and Holland (2003), where they stipulate the sort of criteria they use to establish the validity of their different measures (Box 3.1).

In that review they demonstrate impressive validity for their measure. Certainly the HPI is a new generation of measures and one which will justifiably attract a good deal of research interest particularly from those who are interested in the relationships between personality traits and work outcomes.

Research on other tests

Over the past 40 years various personality tests have been developed that have been correlated with occupational performance.

Guilford–Zimmerman Temperament Survey

The most recent version of the *Guilford–Zimmerman Temperament Survey Manual* (Guilford et al., 1976) reports 23 separate studies of managerial performance. Harrell and Harrell (1984) tested 336 MBA students who graduated between 1961 and 1964, and the class of 1966, to see if scores predicted earnings 5, 10, and 20 years after graduation. The correlations between compensation, Sociability and Ascendance averaged about .20 across all three follow-up periods and were the most stable coefficients in the study. Harrell and Harrell (1984) noted that personality predicted success better than academic aptitude; they thought this was because "business success is usually . . . dependent upon relating effectively with people, rather than solving a scholastic puzzle" (pp. 29–30).

Sparks (1983) tested 2478 men in a large oil company and found consistent relationships between scale scores and indices of job success, job effectiveness, and managerial potential. Bentz (1985) described 20 years of research designed to identify "general executive competence" using a test battery selected by L. L. Thurston in the early 1940s. Bentz showed that Sociability, Energy, and Ascendance are modestly but steadily and significantly correlated with a surprising variety of criterion data (ratings, nominations, compensation level, promotability) across a large number of samples.

Bentz concluded that: "It has been demonstrated that personality measures are reliable over a considerable time span; tests taken years ago predict both job progress and current performance. From the perspective of this research it is appropriate to conclude that the pervasive academic bias against paper-and-pencil personality assessment is unjustified" (p. 143).

Californian Personality Inventory

The Californian Personality Inventory (CPI) has been used for a very long time in managerial settings. For instance, Goodstein and Schroder (1963) used the CPI to

Box 3.1 Criteria used to establish validity of HPI

Adjustment

Remains even tempered
Manages people, crisis, and stress
Shows resilience
Demonstrates patience

Ambition

Exhibits leadership
Demonstrates effectiveness
Takes initiative
Generates new monthly accounts

Likeability

Shows interpersonal skill
Exhibits capacity to compromise
Demonstrates tactfulness and sensitivity
Shares credit

Prudence

Stays organised
Works with integrity
Abides by rules
Follows safety procedures

Intellectance

Achieves quality with information
Analyses finances/operations
Seems market savvy
Displays good judgement

School Success

Capitalises on training
Exhibits technical skill
Makes progress in training
Possesses job knowledge

develop a reliable and valid "good manager" scale. Gough (1984) later showed the subscale diagnostic of behavioural effectiveness, self-confidence, cognitive clarity, and good orientation. Other measures of the whole scale have been shown to be useful. Orpen (1983) found significant correlations between the CPI and ratings of managerial effectiveness. These accounted for about 10% of the variance. Mills and Bohannon (1980) used the CPI in a study of 49 highway patrol officers; for six scales and two criterion ratings, they found nine significant correlations varying between .26 and .43. There is also interesting CPI literature concerned with forecasting educational performance (Gough, 1968). Gough (1985) developed a work-orientation scale for the CPI and it showed high scores to be dependable, moderate, optimistic, persevering, and conservative. He hypothesised that individuals with strong managerial drive and high Wo scores should be circumspect, judicious, and cautious, while those with strong drive but low Wo scores would be more venturesome, quick, and risk taking. More recently, Gough published CPI scales designed to assess individual differences in devotion to the work ethic and in managerial effectiveness (Gough, 1989).

Rawls and Rawls (1968) used the EPPS and CPI to see if they could discriminate 30 more- and 30 less-successful executives based on salary, title, and appraisal performance ratings. They also administered a biographical information form. In all, 5 of the 15 EPPS scales and 10 of the 18 CPI scales showed significant differences. The more-successful executives made significantly higher scores on the Dominance, Heterosexuality, and Aggression scales of the EPPS and on the Dominance, Capacity for Status, Sociability, Social Presence, Self-acceptance, Intellectual Efficiency, Psychological-mindedness, and Flexibility scales of the CPI. Less-successful executives, on the other hand, scored significantly higher on the Deference and Order scales of the EPPS and on the Self-control and Femininity scales of the CPI.

The biographical items showed that more-successful executives' fathers often had a high-school education, while less-successful executives' fathers frequently had only a junior high-school education. Successful executives had more often belonged to the Boy Scouts. They were younger than less-successful executives when they learned to swim, travelled alone on a trip over 100 miles, started to date, earned their own living in a regular job, and started to drink alcoholic beverages. As youngsters, successful executives were more frequently chosen as leaders in group activities and felt their general athletic ability to be above average. Successful executives belonged to more social organisations and had more close friends. In contrast to less-successful executives, they felt prestige and "coming up with something new" to be major motivations in their lives.

Successful executives read more books, newspapers, and periodicals (better informed), felt more confident in most areas (self-reliant, self-confident), expressed their opinions freely (forward), expected to make more money and attain higher levels in the organisation (ambitious), were at ease in social situations (confident in social interaction), and felt they had been more aggressive and successful in life (aggressive, dominant).

Continued occupational applications of the CPI certainly suggests that it has validity for predicting behaviour at work.

Gordon Personal Profile

Various studies have attested to the usefulness of this measure. Dodd et al. (1970) reported significant correlations between the Gordon Ascendancy Scale and a criterion measure of progress for 396 maintenance technical trainees over 9 years, and 103 sales trainees over 11 years. Spitzer and McNamara (1964) divided a sample of 102 manu-facturing managers into four groups. In three of the four groups, Ascendancy correlated .28, .27, and .31 with peer ratings for managerial potential. Palmer (1974) corroborates these results with both versions of the Gordon in a different sample.

Personality Research Form

In a recent study Tett and Jackson (1990) correlated PRF scores with the in-basket exercise scores derived from 78 Canadian managers. Although many of the correla-tions were significant, a number were contrary to predictions (i.e. PRF autonomy and dominance correlated positively with participative tendency). In a recent study of accountants, Day and Silverman (1989) found, even with cognitive ability taken into consideration, three personality dimensions (orientation to work; degree of ascendancy; degree/quality of interpersonal orientation) significantly related to important aspects of job performance. They concluded: "In summary, it appears that scores on specific, job-relevant personality scales are significantly related to important aspects of job performance in this sample of accountants. One of the three significant predictor scales (viz., interpersonal orientation) also provided a significant increase in validity for the global or overall measure of job performance. It has been argued that this would be expected due to collinearity among the different behavioural dimensions at the true score level. However, relying solely on the global measure would mask the significant relationships found between work orientation and ascendancy and some of the specific performance dimensions. In addition, examining the individual behavioural dimensions is interesting because it reveals that some of the highest correlations are found between those personality–performance links that are theoretically most similar, such as inter-personal orientation and ratings of cooperation. From the results of this study, it also can be concluded that particular, job-relevant aspects of personality are significantly related to ratings of job performance above what can be predicted by cognitive ability measures alone" (p. 34).

Occupational Personality Questionnaire

Commercial organisations, as well as academic researchers, devise personality measures to be sold as diagnostic instruments. One such organisation, which has expanded greatly over the past 20 years all around the world is the consultancy and test publisher Saville & Holdsworth Ltd (SHL), which claims several advantages for its Occupational Personality Questionnaire (OPQ). It is said to be based on a conceptual model provid-ing comprehensive coverage of personality, and to be psychometrically sound. It is designed specifically to be easily used in occupational contexts.

The most comprehensive versions of the OPQ measure 30 scales derived from a conceptual model based on existing personality inventories, repertory grid studies and criteria for occupational success, with an additional social desirability scale. The scales are grouped into three categories, associated with relationships with people, thinking style, and feelings and emotions, respectively. The OPQ manual presents data showing that the 30 "concept model" scales have generally satisfactory internal consistency and test–retest reliability.

Two major issues have exercised researchers. The first is whether the underlying dimensions of this measure (relating, thinking, feeling) are indeed independent of one another. In two studies, Matthews et al. (1990) found that test constructors "understated" the degree of intercorrelation of the 31 concepts. In a later study, Matthews and Stanton (1994) found that the dimensions measured by the OPQ are in fact fairly similar to the "Big Five" model discussed earlier. They suggest that further work may be necessary to establish conclusively that the "Big Five" is the stronger model in psychometric terms. The thrust of much prior work on the "Big Five" has been to show that a three-factor model fails to capture important broad models of personality. Proponents of the "Big Five" have perhaps paid insufficient attention to the possibility that the five factors may be too few. The hypothesis that openness may be split into cognitive and non-cognitive elements may also merit further work. However, it was not supported in the OPQ data, perhaps because the questionnaire does not include scales directly related to self-rated intelligence.

A second, perhaps more important, line of research is the validity of the OPQ – does it really predict occupational behaviour? Robertson and Kinder (1993) carried out a meta-analysis of 21 different populations who had all completed the OPQ. They showed that, if specific hypotheses were tested, there was strong evidence of the criterion-related validity of the OPQ. They noted that personality variables seem most important where the work performance is associated with creativity, analysis, management of others, energy and communication.

Various versions of this British normed measure have been developed. It has shown to be reliable (Budd & Paltiel, 1989), but there are doubts about the dimensional structure (Matthews et al., 1990) and its predictive validity.

Other tests

There are many other tests that are used in selection, training and development. These include the FIRO-B, the Belbin Team Role Inventory, the PAPI and many more. Some have received more empirical validation than others.

Conclusion

Personality tests have been used fairly extensively in management for over 50 years. Robertson and Makin (1986) contacted 304 major British companies in the mid-1980s of which 108 (34%) replied. Whereas just under 10% used personality tests fairly frequently, 65% said they never did. They mainly used interviews and references, though a very small minority (under 5%) used graphology, astrology, biodata or assessment centres. In America the number is probably higher. In a more recent study Furnham (2007b) asked 255 adult professionals concerned with selection, assessment and training to complete a questionnaire that asked their beliefs about the validity, cost, practicality and legality of different assessment techniques (i.e. assessment centres, biodata, interviews), and their knowledge and use of both personality and ability tests. They tended to be positive about the tests themselves, how they were used and about test publishers. They rated assessment centres, cognitive ability tests and work samples as the most valid, while interviews were rated as most practical. Results from knowledge of personality and intelligence tests indicated that only a few tests were widely known, more so in personality/motivation than intelligence.

They were asked if they were familiar with various personality tests. In all 50% (only) of the respondents had claimed to have heard about eight of these tests. Thus, according to their "fame" (for this sample) the following had at least been "heard about": 16PF; Myers Briggs; OPQ; Belbin Team Role; EPI/Q/P; Big Five (NEO-PI-R); FIRO; and OSI. Three had not been heard of by a fifth (< 20%) of the respondents (PRISM, PASAT, Orpheus). More than 50% of the respondents had taken only four of these tests: MBTI, 16FF, Belbin, and OPQ. For over half of the tests (11 in fact) less than a fifth (< 20%) had themselves taken the test. Over half the respondents' organisations used the MBTI; a third the OPQ, FIRO and Belbin. Fewer than 10% used 12 of the tests, suggesting a few frequently used and a number very rarely used.

They were less knowledgeable about intelligence tests. They were also less discriminating between the tests. The tests that were best known were: GMA, Watson–Glazer, Critical Reasoning, Raven's PM, and AMT. However, it should be pointed out that more than 50% of the respondents only knew about only two of these tests. There were only six tests that a third or more of the respondents had themselves completed: Watson–Glazer, Raven's PM, GMA, AMT, MGIB, and CCAS. The results indicated that around a quarter to a third of respondents' companies used these tests. The three most widely used were Watson–Glazer, GMA, and AMT. There was surprisingly little variability in the rating.

There remains considerable scepticism in applied circles as to the usefulness of personality tests. Stone (1988) refers to familiar objections to the use of personality tests: they were designed to identify mental disorders; they are difficult to validate; there is a great deal of vagueness in the trait definitions; they are open to faking and response bias; respondents frequently lack self-awareness; they are not reliable in equal opportunity, legislation prevents them being used anyway; there is a lot of research evidence to support them; etc. He concludes: "All in, then, personality testing is not a very rewarding approach for selecting managers and probably shouldn't be used at all" (p. 54).

There has also been a significant increase in the development of specialist tests for use in personnel selection. For instance, Sackett et al. (1989) survey tests aimed specifically at measuring employee integrity (dishonesty, theft). These have been developed mainly by test publishers but seem to do the job well.

This chapter has attempted a fairly comprehensive review of the early, as well as more recent, literature on personality test score correlates of occupational behaviour. This literature is widely scattered, of uneven quality, and frequently atheoretical but there is sufficient evidence to suggest that there is a place for psychological (particularly personality) testing in the workplace.

Results using the Cattellian measures (16PF) and the Eysenckian measures (EPQ) were most promising as they tended to support theoretically based predictions. However, it was not until the widespread adoption of the five-factor model and the Costa and McCrae measures (NEO-FFI) that research really began to demonstrate the logical, consistent and powerful relationship between individual person ability and their work style, satisfaction and productivity. This will be considered in detail in the next chapter.

4   Types, temperaments and traits at work

Introduction

This chapter will look at three very different approaches to understanding and describing personality and its relation to the world of work. The first is *neo-psychoanalytic* in origin and attempts to describe personality in *types*. The second has a *psychophysical* origin and looks primarily at temperament and the physical functioning of personality. The third is *psychometric* in origin and looks at personality traits.

It has been argued that there are three Ts in the evolution of personality scales. They are temperaments, types and traits. Temperaments have been measured in many ways but types and traits (often using the same language) differ, often because of the nature of the (well-known self-report) tests to measure them. Type measures are more of style than of core traits. They measure observable "outside" behaviour more than inner beliefs and motives. They are often theory driven and more concerned with being loyal to the theory than interested in the psychometric properties of scales.

Applied researchers and human resource professionals often favour type measures as clients like them because they are easy to understand. Thus, people can be given a simple summary of their type. However, psychometricians have long moved on from categorical to dimensional systems noting that they offer much better measurement sensitivity and diagnostic accuracy. All human characteristics (with very few exceptions like handedness) are normally distributed and better measured dimensionally.

Traits and types

It is always important to distinguish between traits and types. Types (e.g. gender), are regarded as categories of membership that are distinct and discontinuous. People are either the one or the other. In trait theories, people differ in amounts on a single continuum. Trait theorists see the difference between individuals *quantitatively* rather than *qualitatively*. Typologies are out of fashion because assignment has often proved to be too arbitrary and unreliable. After all, even gender is not absolutely perfect. Trait theories often talk in typological terms, but think of traits as continuously (often normally) distributed. One way to contrast the two is shown in Table 4.1.

The world of psychiatric diagnosis still seems to use types in the sense that people are either labelled/diagnosed X (depression, anxiety, schizophrenia) or not. Typological theory suggests a discontinuity between similar behaviours, while trait theory does not. Trait theorists believe that on all variables there is a *continuum*, and that cut-off into types is therefore arbitrary, or at least follows a set convention. There remain few

Table 4.1 The differences between traits and types

Trait theory	Type theory
Concerned with universals possessed in different amounts	Concerned with preferences which are perhaps inborn or learnt
Involves measuring	Involves sorting
Extreme scores are important for discrimination	Midpoint is crucial for discrimination
Normally distributed	Skewed distribution
Scores mean amount of trait possessed	Scores indicate confidence that sorting is correct

modern personality psychologists who actively follow the type strategy (Meehl, 1992). Between the 1940s and 1970s, many trait measures were devised to measure single trait concepts as well as multiple traits. They differed enormously in approach, the amount of effort put into questionnaire development, and the sophistication and resulting evidence of their reliability and validity.

Typologies

Most of the personality typologies are Freudian or neo-Freudian in nature. Thus there are, for example, measures of the classic Oral and Anal types. These have, however, excited very little research in psychometric psychology today.

Without doubt the most widely known and used personality test in the world is the Myers–Briggs Type Indicator (MBTI). It is estimated that 3.5 million people take it every year in the USA. It has been translated into two dozen languages. It was developed before the war but became widely known and available after 1975. It is based, very loosely, on Jungian theory and is a four-dimensional model that allows people to be described by four letters (e.g. ENTJ, ISFP) representing their particular type.

Over the years it has been subject to considerable testing with all sorts of variables from MBTI correlates of keeping appointments (Danziger et al., 1989) to organisational performance (Ruble & Cosier, 1990). Various studies have attempted to demonstrate the relationship between the specific types and management practices (Furnham & Stringfield, 1993a, 1993b). Whilst there remain relatively few work construct validity studies using the MBTI they do appear from time to time. For example Berr et al. (2000) were interested in personality correlates of managerial self-awareness as measured by multi-rater (self, reports, peers, subordinates) disparity feedback. Many of the findings confirmed theoretical predictions: extraverts seem optimistic, introverts more ethical; intuitives are innovators, learners are systematic thinkers. For feeling types, the right relationship is everything. Perceivers are seen as innovative, judges are seen as effective. This study, however, was about perceptions not behaviour.

Typologies tend to offer richer descriptions than explanations. Hence, there are many detailed descriptions of particular types. Further, as test publishers see new markets they are eager to interpret or specify type-related behaviour in very specific settings like that of work. For example, Hirsch and Kummerow (1998) specified how the various dimensions "play out" in the world of work (Box 4.1). Note that these could easily serve as highly testable hypotheses.

What is interesting about the MBTI industry is that there are many manuals that

Box 4.1 Effects of preferences in work situations

Extraversion	*Introversion*
• Like participating actively in a variety of tasks	• Like quiet and private space for concentration
• Are often impatient with long, slow jobs.	• Tend to be comfortable working on one project for a long time without interruption
• Are interested in the activities of their work and in how other people do them	• Are interested in the facts and/or ideas behind their work
• Act quickly, sometimes without thinking	• Like to think before they act, sometimes to the point of not acting
• Find phone calls a welcome diversion when working on a task	• Find phone calls intrusive when concentrating on a task
• Develop ideas by discussing them with others	• Develop ideas alone through reflection
• Like having people around and working on teams	• Like working by themselves or occasionally in small groups

Sensing	*Intuition*
• Like using experience and standard ways to solve problems	• Like solving new, complex problems
• Enjoy applying skills already perfected	• Enjoy the challenge of learning something new
• Seldom make errors of fact, but may ignore inspirations	• Seldom ignore insights but may overlook facts
• Like to do things with a practical bent	• Like to do things with an innovative bent
• Like to present the details of their work first	• Like to present an overview of their work first
• Prefer continuation of what is, with fine tuning	• Prefer change, sometimes radical, to continuation of what is
• Proceed step-by-step or piece-by-piece, accurately estimating the time needed	• Proceed in bursts of energy, following their inspirations

Thinking	*Feeling*
• Use logical analysis to reach conclusions	• Use values to reach conclusions
• Can work without harmony, concentrating instead on the task	• Work best in harmony with others, concentrating on the people
• Upset people inadvertently by overlooking their emotions	• Enjoy meeting people's needs, even in small matters
• Decide impersonally, sometimes paying insufficient attention to people's wishes	• Let decisions be influenced by their own and other people's likes and dislikes

• Tend to be firm minded and ready to offer critiques • Look at the principles involved in the situation • Want recognition after task requirements are met or exceeded	• Are sympathetic and dislike, even avoid, telling people unpleasant things • Look at the underlying values in the situation • Want appreciation throughout the process of working on a task
Judging	*Perceiving*
• Work best when they can plan their work and work their plan • Enjoy organisation and finishing tasks • Keep the focus on what needs to be completed, ignoring other things that come up • Feel more comfortable once a decision has been made on a thing, situation or person • Decide quickly in their desire for closure • Seek structure and schedules • Use lists to prompt action on specific tasks	• Want flexibility in their work • Enjoy starting tasks and leaving them open for last-minute changes • Want to include as much as possible, thus deferring needed tasks • Feel comfortable staying open to experiences, not wanting to miss anything • Postpone decisions because of a search for options • Adapt to changing situations and feel restricted with too much structure • Use lists to remind them of possible things to do when time allows

Source: Adapted from Hirsch and Kummerow (1998, p. 3).

describe all the 16 types in detail and particularly how the types behave at work. However, there seems precious little empirical data to support these assertions. Further, different manuals offer rather different interpretations. Consider two descriptions of one of the most common (and successful) types, ENTJ.

Rogers (1997, p. 22) notes:

> The energetic, decisive and clear-sighted approach of the ENTJ often brings them to leadership roles. The directness of their personal style can sometimes cause problems for them with others.
>
> - *Overriding need* to be authoritative.
> - *Seen by others* as energetic, articulate, confident, vivid, funny: can seem overbearing.
> - *Sees self* as always on probation.
> - *Works best* with committed people who deliver what they are asked on time and are prepared to stand up for themselves.
> - *Works least well* with people who seem unenthusiastic, self-indulgent and over-emotional.

- *As team member* contributes insistence on looking at the big picture; rigorous standards; concern for deadlines; enthusiasm; a passion for action.
- *Leads by* sink or swim enthusiasm for long-term trends and selling ideas boldly to others; loves radical overhaul; relishes growth and being entrepreneurial; leads through restlessness and manages by walking about; devoted coach to those who can keep up with the high standards demanded.
- *Ideal organisation* large and stable but now facing major change and needs the energy, commitment to standards; avoids being wet or woolly; enjoys a robust discussion without getting upset.
- *In relationships* gives a lot and expects a lot; regards being liked as less important than being right; wants intimacy and closeness but on own terms. May not always be able to resolve resulting tension. Relationships tend to be colourful, sometimes stormy.
- *Makes enemies* when trying to control everything or getting into tussles about who is right.
- *Decides* confidently by generating many possibilities and coming to a swift, logical conclusion.
- *Sees change* as another part of life's jigsaw; let's make it happen now and worry about the detail later.
- *Thinks* strategically; loves solving complex problems.
- *Communicates* confidently and frequently; inspires with optimism; may get impatient if others don't follow – e.g. interrupting or finishing people's sentences for them; can speak in public fluently without notes.
- *Irritated by* special pleading; bureaucratic detail; people who beat about the bush.
- *Irritates by* not listening; jumping to conclusions without factual evidence; fidgeting.
- *As a parent* wants to do the job well but often finds it difficult to devote sufficient time; may solve problem with a "quality time" approach when children are slotted in for high-energy attention.
- *Relaxation* – rarely relaxes, work is usually too absorbing; "leisure" may involve competing with others, making it as exhausting as work.
- *Under stress* gives way to emotional outbursts; drives too hard; gets caught up with detail; becomes overly self-critical and feels unappreciated; over-does eating and drinking.

ENTJs may become more effective through:

- Showing that they value their staff individually and not just as work machines.
- Praising the positive and playing down the criticisms.
- Improving listening skills.
- Avoiding jumping to action before reflection.
- Becoming more discerning about which deadlines really matter.
- Giving up the struggle to control everything.
- Learning patience with younger, less bright and less experienced people.
- Counting to ten or more before giving way to an emotional explosion.
- Getting in closer touch with the tender and vulnerable sides of their personality.

Hirsch and Kummerow (1998) offer a rather detailed description of the ENTJ on page 25 of their manual:

> ENTJs are logical, organised, structured, objective, and decisive about what they view as conceptually valid. They enjoy working with others, especially when they can take charge and add a strategic plan.

Contributions to the organisation:

- Develop well-thought-out plans.
- Provide structure to the organisation.
- Design strategies that work toward broad goals.
- Take charge quickly and do what it takes.
- Deal directly with problems caused by confusion and inefficiency.

Leadership style:

- Initiate an action-oriented, energetic approach.
- Provide long-range plans to the organisation.
- Manage directly – tough when necessary.
- Enjoy complex problems and are resourceful in managing them.
- Run as much of the organisation as possible.

Preferred learning style:

- Cutting edge and theoretically based, delivered by experts.
- Open to challenges and questions.

Potential pitfalls:

- May overlook people's needs and contributions in their focus on the task.
- May overlook pragmatic considerations and constraints.
- May decide too quickly and appear impatient and domineering.

Order of preferences:

1 Thinking.
2 Intuition.
3 Sensing.
4 Feeling.

Problem-solving approach:

- Want to logically analyse and control situations (T) based on an internal understanding of what could be (N).
- May want to include a realistic determination of the actual facts (S) and to consider the impact on people and themselves (F) for optimal results.

Preferred work environments:

- Contain results-oriented, independent, and competent people focused on solving complex problems.
- Are goal oriented.
- Have efficient systems and people.
- Provide challenges with a direct payoff for effort.

- Reward decisiveness.
- Include tough-minded people.
- Offer structure and focus on use of a master plan.

Suggestions for development:

- May need to factor in the human element and appreciate others' contributions.
- May need to check the practical, personal and situational resources available before plunging ahead.
- May need to take time to reflect and consider all sides before deciding.
- May need to learn to identify and value feelings in both themselves and others.

Criticisms of the MBTI have been covered in Chapter 3. Many of these critiques apply to nearly all typological measures. The central issue is about classification. Whilst we talk in type terms (he is an Introvert, she is an Extravert), we measure dimensionally. Thus, many measures of everything from team role to learning style do classify people by their highest and lowest score but always provide the numerical score on a dimension. In this sense, the cut-off point between one type and another appears rather arbitrary.

Typologies seem popular with business writers and PR professionals. But they have long disappeared from the panoply of the serious academic concerned with understanding the cause and manifestations of individual differences at work.

Temperaments

The concept of temperament, at least in differential psychology, usually, but not exclusively, refers to the Pavlovian or neo-Pavlovian theory of action. The theory is a psychophysiological theory of how individuals attempt to regulate their environment to suit their emotional and physical needs. Thus, behaviour can be described in terms of energetic and temporal concepts. Typical concepts include strength of excitation, strength of inhibition, and mobility of nervous processes (Strelau, 1996, 1997).

Zuckerman (2006), in his attempt to distinguish between temperament and traits, notes six specific features of temperament:

1   Distinguished by basic, relatively stable, personality traits.
2   Expressed in the energetic and temporal (rather than the motivational or goal-directed) aspects of behaviour.
3   Present from early childhood.
4   Known to have behavioural counterparts in other species of animals.
5   Primarily determined by inborn (genetic) biological mechanisms.
6   Subject to changes caused by maturation and the interaction of the genotype with specific life experiences.

Strelau (1983, 1996) has championed this approach with his *regulative theory of temperament* and his well-validated measures that assess temperamental traits. They are:

- *Briskness* (BR): tendency to react quickly, to keep up a high tempo of performing activities, and to shift easily in response to changes in the surroundings from one behaviour (reaction) to another.

- *Perseverance* (PE): tendency to continue and to repeat behaviour after cessation of stimuli (situations) evoking this behaviour.
- *Sensory Sensitivity* (SS): ability to react to sensory stimuli of low stimulative value.
- *Emotional Reactivity* (ER): tendency to react intensively to emotion-generating stimuli, expressed in high emotional sensitivity and in low emotional endurance.
- *Endurance* (EN): ability to react adequately in situations demanding long-lasting or high-stimulative activity and under intensive external stimulation.
- *Activity* (AC): tendency to undertake behaviour without strong stimulation from the surroundings.

Strelau and his colleagues have done a great deal of concurrent validity work examining the relationship between the above traits and those from other systems. Thus, Activity is strongly correlated with Eysenckian measures of Extraversion while Emotional Reactivity and Perseverance are correlated with measures of Neuroticism. The questionnaire he developed has been translated and validated in many different languages (De Pascalis et al., 2000; Newberry et al., 1997). Further, these dimensions have been shown to be modestly related to intelligence. Miklewska et al. (2005) found the mobility of the nervous system was positively related to intelligence, with emotionality negatively correlated with fluid intelligence and activity with crystallised intelligence.

This temperament model makes many and clear predictions about how temperamental traits are related to work behaviour. Michielsen et al. (2004) found that, as predicted, strength of inhibition was negatively correlated with self-reported fatigue at work. In a very different study on the time taken to resume tasks after interruption Van den Berg et al. (1996) found that those secretaries with higher scores on strength of excitation and mobility affect behaviour needed less time to resume tasks after interruption. Given the nature of modern work with its many and frequent interruptions, this is an important finding.

Zuckerman (2006) has reviewed various systems of temperament. There are various other temperament models to complement that of Strelau. There is a significant literature on Cloninger's model (Cloninger, 1986, 1987, 1994; Cloninger & Gilligan, 1987; Cloninger et al., 1993) as well as self-report measures (Clonginer et al., 1991). His revised biosocial model of personality posits seven domains of personality as measured by the Temperament and Character Inventory (TCI; Cloninger, 1994): four temperament (Harm Avoidance, Novelty Seeking, Reward Dependence and Persistence) and three character domains (Self-directedness, Cooperativeness, and Self-transcendence).

Gilliespie et al. (2003), who did an impressive genetic and psychometric evaluation and analysis of the theory, described it thus: "Temperament was conceptualised as corresponding to heritable biases in memory processing involved in pre-semantic perceptual processing and encoding of concrete visuo-spatial structural information and affective valence," These processes were hypothesised to be functionally organised as independently varying brain systems aligned to specific mono-aminergic cell bodies, which in turn are responsible for autonomic responses involved in the activation, maintenance and inhibition of behaviour (such as differences in classical conditioning, operant conditioning and non-associative learning, i.e. sensitisation and habituation).

The model was revised to include three dimensions of character: Self-directedness, Cooperativeness and Self-transcendence. These dimensions were based on a synthesis of information about social and cognitive development and descriptions of personality development in humanistic and transpersonal psychology. Specifically, the scales were designed to measure conceptual memory biases involved in the processing or conversion of sensory input into abstract symbols which translate into concepts of personal, social and universal identity. Self-directedness measures individual self-acceptance, Cooperativeness measures acceptance of other people, while Self-transcendence captures the degree to which an individual feels a part of nature and the universe at large.

(Gillespie et al., 2003, p. 1932)

Not all evaluations of the Temperament and Character Inventory (TCI) have been positive (Gana & Trouillet, 2003) but the theory continues to attract attention. However, it is probably true to say that applications of this theory have been more commonly applied to clinical rather than work situations.

It is, however, not difficult to derive some testable hypotheses from Cloninger's model. Thus, high novelty seeking people seek variety, quick rewards and active avoidance of frustration or punishment. Their impulsive decision making and quick temper would not make them particularly good employees except perhaps in sales. High harm avoidance people on the other hand tend to have classic Neuroticism traits: pessimism, worrying, tense and anxious in unfamiliar environment. Being easily fatigable and shy with strangers would also mean high scores would tend not to be associated with success at work.

Reward dependence reflects greater sensitivity to signals of reward in many forms. Thus, these types would be happiest in environments that gave them lots of feedback in their performance. Persistence refers to the perseverance of behaviour despite fatigue and frustration, which would clearly be advantageous in a whole range of occupations.

There are yet other temperament type theories and measures, often two-dimensional measures. Hence, augmenting–reducing theory, which postulates temperament differences based on difference in the modulation of stimulation (Petrie, 1967). Reducers need more stimulation than augmenters because of cortical attenuation of incoming stimuli. Thus, reducers dampen down incoming stimuli while augmenters amplify them. Once a questionnaire measure of this concept was constructed a new research area emerged.

What all temperament theories appear to have in common are two things. *First* a belief that individual differences are clearly physiologically based. Most have concepts concerned with activation, arousal, inhibition, and speed of response. They all tend to concentrate on the way individuals characteristically react to, and also seek out, specific environmental features and responses. Stimulus hunger and sensitivity are at the heart of these theoretical formulations.

Second, whilst theories are usually derived from psychobiological and experimental theory, research seems to "take-off" once questionnaire measures are devised. Whilst not all show equal validity, they tend to encourage researchers to work in the area. However, most valid studies tend to be in the areas of clinical and psychometric psychology rather than organisational and work psychology. Hence, perhaps, the rather disappointing lack of influence of this approach in work psychology.

Traits at work

Personality measurement has a long history in psychology. However, during the 1960s personality psychology was attacked repeatedly and very effectively by social psychologists and behaviourists. In his book, *Personality and Assessment*, Mischel (1968) argued that traits are an illusion and that behaviour is explained more by differences in social situations than differences in stable, internal traits. This book sparked off the person–situation debate, which set back personality theory nearly 20 years.

There were various reasons why the study of personality went into such a decline. There was no consensus regarding what traits to measure, even if there was some agreement regarding why they should be measured (Hogan & Roberts, 2000). Concurrent with this view, many psychologists thought that personality variables were poor predictors of social and work behaviours. Guion and Gottier (1965), in what later turned out to be a very influential review, considered the criterion-related validity of personality variables. They concluded that the empirical evidence suggested that personality variables have *little or no systematic relationship* to the various important criterion variables relevant to organisational psychologists. Similarly Ghiselli and Barthol (1953) concluded that there was very little evidence to support the use of personality measures in a personnel selection context. This conclusion was based on the fact that validity coefficients for personality measures were so low (most below .30). These factors, in combination, conspired against using personality variables in research or applied settings, resulting in their virtual demise in organisational psychology.

In the last fifteen years, personality measures have been reborn in industrial, work and organisational psychology and much research has focused on the exploration of personality–performance relationships (Barrick & Mount, 2005; Hough, 1992, 1996b; Hough & Furnham, 2003). In particular, organisational psychology rediscovered the utility of personality measures in selection contexts. There were three main reasons for this. *First*, other than an interview (and application form and references), the selection method of choice for organisational psychology was a cognitive test. However, cognitive ability tests almost always result in adverse impact for certain "protected classes" of employees. Meta-analytic evidence suggests that most personality variables have significantly less adverse impact against the protected classes than those of cognitive ability variables do (Hough, 1996b; Ones et al., 1993). *Second*, research has provided a general agreement on the taxonomy of personality variables, enabling psychologists to organise the literature on personality and job performance (Furnham & Heaven, 1999). Exploration of personality performance relationships within, rather than across, personality constructs revealed statistically and practically significant relationships where they had not been revealed before (Hough & Schneider, 1996). *Third*, meta-analytic reviews by Barrick and Mount (2005), Tett et al. (1991) and many others provided further evidence that personality measures were more valid than generally believed. Later meta-analyses since the turn of the millennium have been even more encouraging. The results are clear: if you reliably measure traits and specific behaviour at work that are theoretically related, the data suggest the correlation between the former and the latter is between $r = .20$ and $r = .50$. If you add to this measures of cognitive ability and specific demographic factors you may be able to account for between a half and two thirds of the variance on any work measures.

Nearly all the recent work has been around the five-factor model of personality, which specifies five clear traits (Table 4.2).

The multidimensional conceptualisations of job performance have also been critically important in highlighting the relevance of personality and measurement variables for predicting job performance (Campbell et al., 1993). It is now evident that personality variables correlate differently with many different job-performance constructs (Day &

Table 4.2 The Big Five traits

High	Average	Low
1. Neuroticism		
Sensitive, emotional and prone to experience feelings that are upsetting.	Generally calm and able to deal with stress, but you sometimes experience feelings of guilt, anger or sadness.	Secure, hardy and generally relaxed, even under stressful conditions.
2. Extraversion		
Extraverted, outgoing, active and high-spirited. You prefer to be around people most of the time.	Moderate in activity and enthusiasm. You enjoy the company of others but you also value privacy.	Introverted, reserved and serious. You prefer to be alone or with a few close friends.
3. Openness to Experience		
Open to new experiences. You have broad interests and are very imaginative. Practical but willing to consider new ways of doing things.	You seek a balance.	Down to earth, practical, traditional and pretty much set in your ways.
4. Agreeableness		
Compassionate, good natured and eager to cooperate and avoid conflict.	Generally warm, trusting and agreeable, but you can sometimes be stubborn and competitive.	Hard-headed, sceptical, proud and competitive. You tend to express your anger directly.
5. Conscientiousness		
Conscientious and well organised. You have high standards and always strive to achieve your goals.	Dependable and moderately well organised. You generally have clear goals but are able to set your work aside.	Easy-going, not very well organised and sometimes careless. You prefer not to make plans.

Source: Adapted from Costa and McCrae (1992).

Silverman, 1989; Hough, 1996b). Another factor that has prompted the rebirth of personality variables in organisational psychology is the fact that more than half of the developed economies are considered service economies. This growth in both the service and sales sector has affected how organisational psychologists define and measure job performance (Hough & Schneider, 1996) and has highlighted the importance of investigating the link between personality and job performance.

It has now been recognised that part of the reason for the decline of personality variables in psychology, particularly organisational/work psychology, was due to the fact that no well-accepted taxonomy existed for classifying personality traits (Barrick & Mount, 2005). Taxonomies are critically important to the advancement of science as they facilitate the organisation and accumulation of knowledge, hypothesis generation, efficient communication among scientists, and retrieval of information (Fleishman & Quaintance, 1984). Thus, it is recent personality taxonomies that have provided the organising principles that have enabled researchers to establish relationships between personality constructs and job-related criteria (Hough & Schneider, 1996) and has highlighted the importance of investigating the link between personality and job performance.

In general, the taxonomies used are based upon measures of normal and adult personality. The initial purpose in the construction of these was the accurate description of individual differences in personality, therefore providing a broad description of personality that could be used in a whole range of settings (Ones & Viswesvaran, 2000). Examples of inventories relevant to this study are provided by the five-factor model (FFM). However, it has been argued that the taxonomy the organisational psychologists use makes a difference to the outcome of the analysis. Conclusions about the usefulness of personality and the nature of personality–performance relationships depend upon the taxonomy used. Many respected personality psychologists believe that the FFM is an adequate taxonomy for organisational psychology (Costa & McCrae, 1995b; Digman, 1990b). That is, it provides a sufficient, succinct and parsimonious description of personality functioning. Indeed, the FFM has been shown to be useful as an organising taxonomy for organisational research (Ones et al., 1993). However, some scepticism regarding the adequacy of the FFM has been raised (Block, 1995; Hogan, 2005b; Hough, 1992). Thus, some split the factors into two, while others add new superfactors. There are therefore five-, six-, seven-, eight- and nine-factor models.

Whilst the FFM has, and will continue to have, its critics, it is clear that it has done a great deal to advance differential organisational psychology. Nearly all studies in this area these days are done using FFM models. This, in turn, allows for better meta-analyses to be done, which are now relatively common. Furthermore, they tell an interesting and important, if complex, story with the very clear bottom-line fact that quite evidently personality traits do predict occupational behaviour of many sorts.

Does personality predict job performance?

Research clearly suggests that personality variables correlate differently with different job performance constructs (Day & Silverman, 1989; Hough, 2001). Current research on the relation between personality and job performance has involved the integration of personality measures with the FFM. This method was used in various reviews of criterion validity (Barrick & Mount, 1991; Tett et al., 1991). For years, psychologists tried to establish the mean predictive validity of different assessment methods. Some of these reviews and meta-analyses contained some personality dimensions (e.g. Conscientiousness) and others none at all (see Box 4.2). Further they did not all concur exactly with each other. Consider that of Schmidt and Hunter (1998) and Hogan (2005b). Schmidt and Hunter (1998) rated Conscientiousness traits rather highly, nearly as good as assessment centres. Barrick and Mount rated them less highly.

Barrick and Mount (1991) undertook a large scale meta-analysis using 117 validity studies and a total sample that ranged from 14,236 people for Openness to Experience to 19,721 for Conscientiousness. Performance measures within these groups were classified into three broad criteria that included: job proficiency, training proficiency and personnel data (Box 4.3). Barrick and Mount reported that Conscientiousness was consistently found to be a valid predictor for *all* five occupational groups and for *all* performance criteria. However, the other four personality factors only generalise their validity for some occupations and some criteria. Extraversion was observed to be a valid predictor (across the criterion types) for two occupations, managers and sales. Emotional Stability is a valid predictor for police. Agreeableness was a valid predictor for police and managers while Openness to Experience was found to predict the training proficiency criterion relatively well, as did Emotional Stability and Agreeableness.

Box 4.2 Corrected mean validities	
Predictor: work sample tests	*Overall job performance*
General mental ability tests	.51
Employment interviews (structured)	.51
Peer ratings	.49
Job-knowledge tests	.48
T&E behavioural consistency method	.45
Job tryout procedure	.44
Integrity tests	.41
Employment interviews (unstructured)	.38
Assessment centres	.37
Biographical data measures	.35
Conscientiousness measures	.31
Reference checks	.26
Job experience (years)	.18
T&E point method	.11
Education (years)	.10
Interests	.10
Graphology	.02
Age (years)	.01

Note: T&E = training and experience.
Source: Adpated from Schmidt and Hunter (1998, p. 265).

However, although Openness to Experience was found to be a valid predictor of training proficiency, it was not predictive for the other two criterion categories, job proficiency or personnel data.

In a follow-up study Mount and Barrick (1995) found that overall validity of Conscientiousness had been underestimated and that the overall score and both of its dimensions (dependability and achievement) predicted specific performance criteria better than global criteria (e.g. overall rating of job performance).

Tett et al. (1991) used only confirmatory studies, that is studies based on hypothesis testing or on personality-orientated job analysis. Mean validities derived from confirmatory studies were considerably greater than those derived from exploratory studies. These results generally supported those reported by Barrick and Mount (1991), but are distinctly more positive for the predictive validity of traits. In essence, Tett et al. (1991) found that *all* personality dimensions were valid predictors of job performance. However, Extraversion and Conscientiousness had lower validity coefficients, whereas Neuroticism, Openness to Experience and Agreeableness had higher validities than had been previously shown.

A third review in the 1990s of the relationship between personality measures and performance criteria was reported by Hough et al. (1990), who investigated the relationship of nine personality dimensions and a range of performance criteria specific to military settings. Results indicate that Adjustment (Emotional Stability) and Dependability (Conscientiousness) were valid predictors for the two most used performance

Box 4.3 Corrected average validities

	Personality construct				
	Extraversion	Emotional stability	Agreeableness	Conscientiousness	Openness to experience
Job					
Professionals	-.09	-.13	.02	.20	-.08
Police officers	.09	.10	.10	.22	.00
Managers	.18	.08	.10	.22	.08
Salespeople	.15	.07	.00	.23	-.02
Skilled/semiskilled workers	.01	.12	.06	.21	.01
Criterion					
Job proficiency	.10	.07	.06	.23	-.03
Training proficiency	.26	.07	.10	.23	.25
Personnel data	.11	.09	.14	.20	.01
Mean	.13	.08	.07	.22	.04

Note: Corrected for range restriction, criterion unreliability, and sampling error and between-study differences in test unreliability.

Source: Adapted from Barrick and Mount (1991, pp. 13 and 15).

criteria: training and job proficiency; and that the Big Five are predictors of training criteria. Thus, the findings of Hough et al. (1990) were partly convergent with those of Barrick and Mount (1991) but also provided evidence of some divergence. Further research by Hough (1992) suggested that each of the eight personality constructs correlates with important job and life criteria and that each of the nine constructs has a different pattern of relationships with that criteria (Box 4.4). On the basis of Hough's data it has been suggested that Barrick and Mount overemphasised the broad dimensions of Conscientiousness at the expense of other useful personality traits (Furnham, 2001d).

The fact that other personality variables are not correlated with all occupational categories or criterion types does not necessarily mean that they are unimportant. Different jobs make different demands on employees and may contribute to a pattern of job-dependent validity coefficients (Furnham, 2001d).

In a further European contribution to the debate, Salgado (1997) undertook a meta-analytic review, which differed from previous studies in that it only included studies conducted in the European Community. He found that the overall validity of personality constructs is small, excepting Emotional Stability (Neuroticism) and Conscientiousness even when effects of measurement error in predictors and criteria and range restrictions have been corrected. In this respect the results show a great similarity to Barrick and Mount (1991) and Hough et al. (1990). Again, concurrent with Barrick and Mount (1991) and Hough et al. (1990), but partially divergent from Tett et al. (1991), Conscientiousness showed the highest estimated true validity that could be generalised for all occupations and criteria. A third finding of Salgado (1997) was that the estimated true validity for Emotional Stability was comparable to that for Conscientiousness. Moreover, as with Conscientiousness, Emotional Stability could be generalised across jobs and criteria. This finding is contrary to Barrick and Mount (1991) but is consistent with Hough et al. (1990). Openness to Experience was found to be a valid predictor for training proficiency, thus consistent with Barrick and Mount (1991) and Hough et al. (1990). Other results support the suggestion that individuals with high scores in Openness to Experience may be those who are most likely to benefit from training programs (Dollinger & Orf, 1991). A positive correlation was found between Extraversion and two occupations in which interpersonal characteristics were likely to be important, confirming Barrick and Mount (1991) and Hough et al. (1990). However, contrary to Barrick and Mount (1991), Extraversion did not seem to be a valid predictor for training proficiency (Salgado, 1997). Finally, the results for Agreeableness suggest that this factor may be relevant to predicting training performance. This is consistent with Barrick and Mount (1991) and Hough et al. (1990).

More recently Hogan (2005b) has summarised the validities of his seven-factor model (Table 4.3).

Studies showing the consistent, powerful and predictable relationship between personality traits and work performance/job success continue. Thus Tyler and Newcombe (2006) obtained data from four organisations in Hong Kong that demonstrated many significant and explicable relationships between personality and various measured job competencies like customer service, managing change and time management. Similarly Smithikrai (2007) examined data from seven different occupational groups (e.g. air traffic controller, pharmacist, dentist, teacher) in Thailand. Conscientiousness was consistently positively related to job performance while in many samples Extraversion was a positive predictor and Neuroticism a negative predictor of (self-reported) overall job success.

Box 4.4 Relationships (uncorrected mean validities) between personality constructs and job performance constructs

Criterion type	Job performance construct							
Construct	Job proficiency	Educational success	Irresponsible behaviour	Sales effectiveness	Creativity	Teamwork	Effort	Combat effectiveness
Affiliation	.00	.01	.01	.19	-.25	–	.00	-.02
Potency	.10	.12	-.06	.25	.21	.08	.17	.08
Achievement	.15	.29	-.19	.27	.14	.14	.21	.13
Dependability	.08	.12	-.24	.06	-.07	.17	.14	.08
Adjustment	.09	.20	-.15	.18	-.05	.13	.16	.19
Agreeableness	.05	.01	-.08	–	-.29	.17	.15	-.04
Intellectance	.01	.13	-.15	.15	.07	.11	.11	-.07
Rugged individualism	.08	-.02	.00	–	.01	.08	-.03	.25

Note: Observed validities.

Source: The "Big Five" personality variables–construct confusion: Description versus prediction, by L. M. Hough, 1992, *Human Performance, 5,* pp. 146, 152–153. Copyright 1992 by Lawrence Erlbaum Associates, Inc. Adapted with permission of the author.

Table 4.3 Summary of results from Hogan and Holland (2003)

HPI Scale	k	N	r	p
Adjustment	24	2573	.25	.43
Ambition	28	3698	.20	.34
Sociability	NA	NA	NA	NA
Likeability	17	2500	.18	.36
Prudence	26	3379	.22	.36
Intellectance	7	1190	.20	.34
School success	9	1366	.15	NA

Note: HPI = Hogan Personality Inventory.

Whilst it is true that different meta-analyses have yielded somewhat different results, there are some very clear emerging themes. *First*, specific traits (particularly Conscientiousness and Neuroticism) predict work behaviours. The more reliable the measure of the work behaviour, the stronger the association. *Second*, although the meta-analyses are descriptive it is not difficult to understand the process underlying the association. *Third*, these relationships seem robust and consistent across cultures, measures, populations and sectors. In short, theoretically derived, psychometrised measures of personality trait predict many different work-performance outcomes. They tend to account for between 5 and 30% of the variance.

Whilst there are differences between the different meta-analyses (which is to be expected because they are based on different data banks), what is very clear is that there are logical, predictable and significant (socially and statistically) relationships between trait variables and work outcome measures.

Personality and specific work behaviours

More recent concerns have been around very specific work behaviours like selling, leadership, absenteeism and the like. Since the turn of the millennium there have been many excellent studies and meta-analyses on the relationship between personality and highly specific positive and negative work-related behaviours.

Personality has been shown, much more specifically, to predict *sales performance*. In the past, classic studies investigating personality as a predictor of sales performance have generally found inconsistent and inconclusive results and it was suggested that no significant relationship existed (Matteson et al., 1984). Schmitt et al. (1984) analysed sales validity coefficients and found uncorrected $r = .17$ for all types of predictors and criteria for sales jobs. They found personality factors to have the lowest validity coefficient of any predictor group. Furnham (2001d) suggested that this underestimation of the predictive validity of personality in sales performance was due to lack of understanding of the nature of the sales job itself. Another possible reason why research into personality as a predictor of sales performance has failed to find predictive validity, is that investigations have tried to predict performance across different types of sales people, in different types of sales jobs and in different industries, using the same performance criteria and the same set of predictor variables (Furnham, 2001d). Research suggests that personality may be a more useful predictor when performance is broken down into components and specific work-related personality dimensions are targeted (Robertson & Kinder, 1993).

One study (Hurtz & Donovan, 2000) and one meta-analysis (Barrick et al., 2002), set out in Boxes 4.5 and 4.6, show two things. First, evidence that two of the Big Five traits seem most clearly implicated in sales (Box 4.5). Second, that even within the sales area it is important to make distinctions both with regard to motives and performance (Box 4.6).

An earlier meta-analytic review of predictors of job performance in sales by Vinchur et al. (1998) found more positive results than those noted above. They reported that Extraversion and Conscientiousness predicted sales success in terms of both objective sales volume and managerial ratings. This study confirms previous findings by Barrick and Mount (1991). The subdimensions suggested by Hough and co-workers were particularly strong predictors of sales success. It was found that Potency (which includes assertiveness) appeared to be the key part of Extraversion that predicted sales performance and it was suggested that Achievement was the key part of Conscientiousness that predicted objective sales success (Vinchur et al., 1998). The results from this study indicate that specific personality subdimensions are able to predict specific sales performance criteria more accurately than broad personality dimensions.

In earlier studies Churchill et al. (1985) examined, by meta-analyses, a range of predictors of different types of salesperson's performance. Their results indicated that aptitude and personal characteristics (i.e. personality) account for only 2% of the work

---

Box 4.5 Personality and sales performance

	Status striving	*Accomplishment striving*	*Job performance*
Extraversion	.48	.32	.21
Stability	.18	.15	.14
Conscientiousness	.39	.39	.26
Agreeableness	−.11	.10	−.12
Openness	.12	.09	−.05

Source: Adapted from Barrick et al. (2002).

Box 4.6 Personality and job performance: Meta analysis

	Sales	*Service*	*Management*	*Skilled*
Extraversion	.18	.17	.11	.10
Stability	.09	.08	.08	.06
Conscientiousness	.03	.11	−.03	.06
Agreeableness	.10	.01	.08	.00
Openness	.03	.10	−.02	−.01

Note: Numbers are sample-size weighted mean observed validity.
Source: Adapted from Hurtz and Donovan (2000).

outcome measures, based on self-report, manager and peer-ratings and objective company data. Churchill et al. (1985) postulated that the strength of the relationship between the major determinants and sales performance was affected by the type of products sold, the specific tasks to be performed and the type of customer to be targeted. Furthermore, it has been argued that there are aspects of the sales job that make unique demands on an employee and may contribute to a pattern of validity coefficients different from other jobs (Vinchur et al., 1998). Churchill et al. (1985) suggested that the most prominent of these demands were the degree of autonomy and the degree of rejection experiences by many salespersons. They further reasoned that given this level of autonomy, persons in sales must be self-starters, relying on their own initiative and powers of persuasion to see tasks through to completion.

The literature cited has suggested that personality dimensions or patterns of dimensions are predictive of sales success and job performance in general (Barrick & Mount, 1991; Vinchur et al., 1998). It could be suggested that biographical variables such as gender and age, known to play a role in personality (Costa & McCrae, 1992), can also be used to predict occupational success and failure (Furnham, 1994). However, research has found age to be a poor predictor of both productivity and ratings across a wide cross-section of jobs. Hunter and Hunter (1984) reviewed over 500 validity coefficients and found that age alone has zero validity as a predictor, whether the criterion is supervisor rating or training grade. Similarly, Vinchur et al. (1998) found evidence to partially support this view. They found age to be a valid predictor of the rating criterion but not actual sales. The research into gender differences has mainly focused on issues such as occupational values (Bridges, 1989), preferred rewards (Wheeler, 1981), occupational interest (Block, 1980). The results, however, are equivocal. There has been little investigation into gender differences and sales performance. In terms of personality, it has been suggested that women score more highly than men on Neuroticism and Conscientiousness (Costa & McCrae, 1992). However, from the findings discussed, high scores on Neuroticism (low score HPI adjustment) do not predict high sales performance (Vinchur et al., 1998) but high scores on conscientiousness do (Barrick & Mount, 1991; Salgado, 1997). Therefore, there is conflicting evidence on whether females will show a higher or lower sales performance compared to men and the debate continues on whether gender differences exist in the workplace.

Personality can also predict *absenteeism*. A study by Judge et al. (1997) considered the degree to which dimensions of the FFM and personality are related to absence (Box 4.7). Their results supported the proposition that absenteeism can successfully be predicted by employees' personalities as described by the FFM. Specifically, Judge et al. (1997) reported Extraversion and Conscientiousness as moderately strong predictors of absence. The carefree, excitement-seeking nature of Extraverts and the dutiful, reliable nature of conscientious employees lead the former to be absent more and the latter to be absent less. Previous research by Bernardin (1977) reported the effects of extreme anxiety levels on absence. However, Judge et al. (1997) reported no evidence of such an association. Alloy and Abramson (1979) suggested that neurotic individuals, although impulsive, are more realistic in evaluating contingencies and consequences of their actions. Thus, Neurotic individuals may be more attuned to the potentially negative consequences of absence. Results by Judge et al. (1997) also suggest that absence history (measured by the previous year's level of absence) partly mediated the relationship between the personality variables and absence.

At the turn of millennium there was a new sense of optimism among personality

Box 4.7 Personality and absenteeism

Regression estimates predicting post-survey absence			*Regression estimates predicting post-survey absence: Including prior absence*		
Independent variable	β	R^2	*Independent variable*	β	R^2
Step 1: Control variables			*Step 1: Control variables*		
Hours worked	.04		Hours worked	.04	
Subjective health	−.17		Subjective health	−.17	
Age	−.29*		Age	−.29*	
Number of dependent children	.03		Number of dependent children	.03	
ΔR^2		.12	ΔR^2		.12
R^2		.12	R^2		.12
Step 2: Big Five traits			*Step 2: Prior absence*		
Neuroticism	−.07		Prior absence	.43*	
Extraversion	.38*		ΔR^2		.17
Openness to Experience	−.14		R^2		.29
Agreeableness	−.05		*Step 3: Big Five traits*		
Conscientiousness	−.32*		Extraversion	.21*	
ΔR^2		.18	Conscientiousness	−.21*	
R^2		.30	ΔR^2		.05
			R^2		.34

Note: R^2 values are unadjusted. *$p < .01$.

Source: Adapted from Judge et al. (1997).

theorists. There was broad agreement on the fundamental, higher order, orthogonal superfactors and impressive developments in the construction of measures. Moreover there has been consistent evidence that personality tests do indeed predict behaviour at work.

Since the start of the millennium researchers and reviewers have been looking at the relationship between the Big Five traits and various aspects of organisational behaviour. Judge et al. (2002a) chose *leadership* as the dependent variable. From their data, set out in Table 4.4, it seems clear that leaders are stable Extraverts who are both Open and Conscientious.

Further, the Big Five have been linked to *job satisfaction*. The results seem clear (see Box 4.8). Conscientious, Agreeable, Extraverts seem to experience and express job satisfaction. Neurotics seem consistently dissatisfied while Openness has little impact on satisfaction.

It is not difficult to provide an explanation for these findings, albeit post hoc. Conscientious people work hard: hard work is usually equitably rewarded by salary increases, promotion and other forms of recognition that add to job satisfaction. Extraverts tend to be dispositionally happy, and have good social support networks. They

Table 4.4 Meta-analysis of the relation between Big Five personality dimensions and leadership

Dimension	Average			
	k	*N*	*r*	*p*
Neuroticism	48	8025	−.17	−.24
Extraversion	60	11,705	.22	.31
Openness	37	7221	.16	.24
Agreeableness	42	9801	.06	.08
Conscientiousness	35	7510	.20	.28

Note: k = number of correlations, p = corrected correlation. Data from Judge et al. (2002a).

also tend to have higher emotional intelligence, which helps their interaction with superiors, peers and subordinates. Agreeable people are liked and admired for their cooperativeness, empathy and trustworthiness. They are the sort who tend to be helpful and "happy with their lot".

Neurotics are dispositionally unhappy, gloomy worriers. Prone to anxiety, depression and hypochondriasis they are often very sensitive to, and unhappy about, hygiene factors at work. Many studies have shown this.

So, once again, we have the same factors working in the same way. Of all the Big Five factors, those that seem most logically and consistently related to all aspects of work behaviour are Conscientiousness (positively) and Neuroticism (negatively).

One recent study looked at personality and "job switching", i.e. personal turnover/mobility. Vinson et al. (2007) had a database of 1081 individuals traced over several years. They found Extraversion, Openness to Experience and Conscientiousness modestly related to organisational switching.

Without doubt the most enthusiastic exponents of meta-analysis are Ones and her colleagues, who have made exhaustive attempts to capture and record the data of all relevant studies and evaluate their meaning. Ones et al. (2005) have argued from their data that compound personality variables have substantial validities for predicting job performance. Not all personality traits have equal validity for predicting and explaining every different type of job outcome.

When those that do have predictive validity are combined, however, the results are impressive, pushing validities to over .40. This is a very important and often overlooked point. Most people think of individual trait predictions of job performance rather than profiles combining salient traits. When that combination is done, the validity increases to a significant extent.

It is clear, then, that there is good evidence of the relationship between traits and performance at work. However, recently there has been an interest not only in productivity but also in what has become known as contextual or citizen performance (Borman & Penner, 2001). In some senses this is the re-emergence of the old task vs. socioemotional distinction. Contextual performance has various components: working with enthusiasm and volunteering extra effort; volunteering to carry out tasks not actually part of your job description; being generally helpful and cooperative at work; following, obeying and upholding organisational rules and procedures; and consistently supporting, and where necessary defending, organisational objectives. This is becoming an increasing area of research and there is naturally an interest in personality trait correlates of citizenship performance. It is relatively straightforward to test hypotheses like

Box 4.8 Personality–job satisfaction correlations by measure of job satisfaction

Big Five trait	Brayfield & Rothe measure (1)	Hoppock Job Satisfaction Blank (2)	Job Descriptive Index (3)	Minnesota Satisfaction Questionnaire (4)	Other previously validated (5)	Ad hoc measures (6)
Neuroticism	$-.36_{4,5}$	$-.56$	$-.30$	$-.26_1$	$-.26_1$	$-.30$
Extraversion	$.37_{4,5,6}$	$.33$	$.24$	$.23_1$	$.21_1$	$.25_1$
Openness to Experience	$-.01$	$.02$	$.06$	$.13_5$	$-.01_4$	$.02$
Agreeableness	$.31_{2,5,6}$	$.13_1$	$.22$	$.19$	$.15_1$	$.02_1$
Conscientiousness	$.38_{3,5,6}$	$.45$	$.20_1$	$.30$	$.19_1$	$.23_1$

Note: Table entries are meta-analytic estimates of the average true score correlation (p) between Big Five traits and job satisfaction, corrected for measurement error. Subscripts indicate significant differences in correlations. Across the cells the number of correlations ranged from $k = 4$ ($n = 441$) to $k = 26$ ($n = 4959$).

Source: Adapted from Judge et al. (2002b).

Agreeableness and Conscientiousness are positively correlated with contextual performance. This area of research will, no doubt, continue to grow.

Recent debates

In 2005 the journal *Human Performance* (Vol. 18, Number 4) featured two articles with three commentaries and a response to the issue of "Pro and Cons of Personality Assessment in Work Organisations".

Hogan (2005b) with typical gusto, confidence and bravado offered a succinct defence of personality measurement at work. He based his argument on the simple fact that "there has always been good data supporting the validity of personality measures, but that the critics of personality won't pay attention" (p. 338). He drew four conclusions from his overview:

1   Good research shows single performance work-based criteria of $r = .30$ and multiple criteria of $r = .50$ with personality trait measures.
2   Personality predicts occupational performance almost as well as measures of cognitive ability.
3   Personality tests do not discriminate between groups (Blacks/Whites; males/females).
4   There are solid conceptual accounts of these findings.

"The bottom line is, personality measures work pretty well, especially when compared with all other measures" (p. 340).

Murphy and Dzieweczynski (2005) begged to differ. They explained why the famous review by Guion and Gottier (1965) caused the divorce between work and personality psychologists for 30 years. Their central point is that little has changed and the correlations between personality traits and job performance remain very low (even close to zero). They remain pessimistic about the utility and validity of personality measures in organisations for three reasons:

1   Theories that describe and explain personality–performance relations are weak. They fail to take into consideration context, complexity and non-monotonicity as well as variability across jobs, organisations and settings. Further, bidirectional effects threaten simple causal theories.
2   Difficulties in matching personality attributes to jobs. That is, the conceptual language of job analysis is different from that of trait theorists. It is therefore difficult to specify which traits apply to which jobs, when and why.
3   Poor personality measures. That is, that many of the most popular tests have often poor psychometric properties while those tests (namely Integrity Tests) that do predict well are not strictly speaking personality tests nor is it known why they are so (comparatively) effective.

On the other hand, Murphy and Dzieweczynski (2005) were happy to accept the evidence for the predictive validity of cognitive ability tests. They saw these tests as different from (and superior to) personality tests. They accepted the notion of general intelligence (all cognitive ability tests are highly inter-corrrelated and are reliable). Further, ". . . because most work tasks involve active information processing it is virtually guaranteed that a reliable measure of cognitive ability will be correlated with reliable measures of performance in the workplace" (p. 352).

Cognitive ability tests are performance tests, while personality tests are preference tests. The latter are more dubious because they depend on the ability and willingness of respondents to report accurately on their behaviour. Also, they tend to be less well psychometrically evaluated than ability tests. Cognitive ability tests have also come under stricter legal and predictive scrutiny than personality tests, particularly as they have been used more in high-stake decisions.

Barrick and Mount (2005) argued that personality matters (at work) for seven reasons: (1) managers care about personality; (2) meta-analyses have helped understand the theoretical and empirical personality–performance relations; (3) meta-analyses underestimate the relationships because they are done on a trait, not a complete profile, basis; (4) traits account for additional (incremental) validity (over ability tests) in predicting work performance; (5) personality tests show little race bias; (6) longitudinal data support the predictive validity of trait measures; and (7) personality–performance outcomes are important to organisations.

"In light of the research evidence, it simply is not feasible to suggest that being hard working and persistent doesn't matter, or that being co-operative or considerate is not relevant in team settings, or that being ambitious and sociable is unimportant" (p. 363). Barrick and Mount do note that researchers need to look at "situational strength" and how that shapes the personality–performance link. Equally, it is important to understand mediational and moderating factors. They stress the importance of getting better measures of personality and of using observer ratings as well as self-reports.

Hough and Oswald (2005) accept, in part, the pessimistic view of Murphy and Dzieweczynski (2005) but go on to provide solid reasons for hope in the development and use of personality tests at work. They note that the "low to no" criterion-based validity of personality tests is an unwarranted and untrue summary of the literature. They address various points:

- Personality theorists do not have an agreed agenda.
- Many personality test developers seem unconcerned with measurement validity.
- Too many personality researchers have little regard for practical implications.
- Unfortunately, the quality of research in personality psychology is rather low.
- Often managers and some researchers choose poor quality tests for research.
- Ability tests do predict work behaviours better than personality tests.

At the heart of the matter lies the issue of validity: specifically construct and predictive validity. They conclude that "thoughtfully matching criterion constructs with relevant predictor constructs is critically important, both when conducting meta-analysis and when conducting individual studies that make meaningful contributions to the research literature and to selection projects" (p. 381).

- "Validities for personality variables vary across global, overall criterion variables. For example, Emotional Stability predicts overall job satisfaction in the mid .20s whereas validities for predicting overall job performance are less than .10. Similarly, for the compound variable of Generalised Self-Efficacy, the validity for predicting overall job satisfaction is in the high .30s, whereas the validity for predicting overall job performance is in the high .10s.

- When the criterion is complex, such as overall job performance, validities of compound personality variables are higher than validities of narrower (more homogenous) personality variables. For example, the validities just cited are higher for the compound variable of Generalised Self-Efficacy than for the constituent Big Five variable Emotional Stability. Similarly, personality-based integrity measures tend to have higher validities for predicting overall job performance than does, for example, the Big Five variable Conscientiousness (i.e. a validity in the mid .20s for Integrity versus less than .10 for Conscientiousness).
- Validities for different personality variables vary across the same work-performance constructs. For example, validities of Openness to Experience for predicting creativity are positive, whereas validities of Agreeableness for predicting creativity are negative.
- Validities for the same personality variable fluctuate across different work-performance constructs. For example, the validity of Emotional Stability for predicting counterproductive behaviour is in the mid-to-high .20s, whereas its validity for predicting task performance is less than .10. Similarly, for compound variables, Rugged Individualism predicts combat effectiveness in the mid .20s, but not task performance, contextual performance, or counterproductive behaviour, where correlations are near zero.
- Validities differ for facets within Big Five variables. For example, within Conscientiousness, the facet achievement predicts sales effectiveness in the mid .20s, whereas the validity for dependability predicting sales effectiveness is less than .10.
- Validities for different personality variables fluctuate across global work criteria. For example, whereas Agreeableness does not predict job satisfaction, internal locus of control does predict job satisfaction in the mid .20s, with validity slightly lower for Conscientiousness. Similarly, for overall job performance, personality-based integrity tests predict overall job performance in the mid .20s, locus of control predicts overall job performance in the mid .10s, and Openness to Experience is essentially uncorrelated with overall job performance.
- Validities for different personality variables fluctuate with respect to specific performance constructs. For example, the Extraversion facet dominance predicts leadership in the mid .20s, whereas it is essentially uncorrelated with task performance.
- Validities fluctuate across job types. For example, the compound personality variable, customer service, predicts overall job performance in customer service jobs (validity in the mid .20s), and the compound variable, managerial potential, predicts overall job performance in managerial jobs (validity also in the mid .20s). Big Five variables do display practically useful levels of validity in predicting overall job performance for some specific job types. For example, the validity of Agreeableness is approximately .20 for predicting overall job performance in team settings, whereas the validity is essentially zero in sales jobs. Similarly the validity of Conscientiousness for predicting leadership varies according to the job setting" (pp. 379–381).

They end by calling for the development of better personality constructs, and better criterion constructs, as well as reporting validities within situations according to personality and criterion constructs. They conclude, "In other words, if we 'do good science' not only will we better understand the determinants of work attitudes, behaviour and performance, we can apply the knowledge to predict workplace criteria more appropriately and accurately. In short, better science leads to better practice" (p. 385).

Ones et al. (2005) note that personality traits are hierarchically organised and that there are compound personality traits that are especially useful in the prediction of organisational behaviour. Thus, they describe two higher-order factors: *Alpha*, high N, low A, low C – the negatively emotional, disagreeable, disinhibited, lazy, unconscientious worker; and *Beta* made up of E and O. They note "whenever compound traits have been examined in meta-analyses or large-scale studies, the operational validities associated with scales assessing them have outperformed those obtained from Big Five factor scales" (p. 393). They show impressive operational validities of criterion-focused, occupational personality scales.

Ones et al. (2005) are clear and upbeat in two fundamental assumptions. *First*, that (the Big Five) personality variables have sizeable operational validities for predicting job performance and other criteria at work. *Second*, that there are solid theoretical explanations for how and why personality variables predict job performance and work outcomes.

Thus, they argue: "The operational validities for compound personality variables are in the .40s. Such a level of validity places these personality constructs among our best predictors and best explanatory variables in IWO psychology. Similarly, the Big Five as a set produce operational validities in the .30s and .40s, for a range of important criteria. These conclusions are supported by more than two dozen meta-analyses, incorporating thousands of individual studies, spanning decades of research" (p. 401).

Hogan (2005a), in his reply, notes that critics of the importance of personality at work are clearly not persuadable by the data, so it must be a personality issue! Although a clever and amusing point, it is rarely considered how the ability and personality of researchers affects not only the research questions that they ask but indeed how they go about that individual research.

This debate and evaluation has done much to clarify the state of the art in this area. Recent studies have examined many work-related behaviours and their systematic relationship to personality traits. For instance, Kornor and Nordvik (2004) examined the relationship between personality traits and *leadership behaviour* in a Norwegian sample. They set out to test whether three traits were implicated in three aspects of leadership: Openness with concerns about change and development; Conscientiousness with concerns about production, task and structure; and Agreeableness with concerns about empathic and interpersonal relations with reports. They called the leadership styles more prosaically "looking for new possibilities", and "dealing with people". They found support for their hypotheses using the leaders' subordinate ratings as the criteria variables.

Lounsbury et al. (2004) looked at individual difference predictors of career satisfaction. They measured both job and career satisfaction and used two standard personality measures: 16PF and MBTI. There were no MBTI correlates for either measure, but those 16PF dimensions that did relate to job and career satisfaction tended to show a similar pattern. Outgoingness (A) and Vigilance (L) were positively correlated while Apprehensiveness (O), Openness (Q1) and Tension (Q4) were negatively related. Interestingly, intelligence was negatively correlated with satisfaction in hourly (blue-collar) workers and positively correlated in managers (white-collar workers).

Zweig and Webster (2004) wondered whether the Big Five traits related to goal orientation and, thence, performance. They found strong evidence that all five traits related to how students approached their studies and, thence, actually how they intended to work.

Zhao and Seibert (2006) did a very useful meta-analysis on the relationship between entrepreneurship and the Big Five personality dimension. In their analysis of 23 studies they compared the personality trait scores of identified entrepreneurs and managers. They hypothesised that the entrepreneurs would be lower on Neuroticism and Agreeableness and higher on Extraversion, Openness and Conscientiousness. The results confirmed their hypotheses except that for Extraversion and they noted considerable variability between studies. However, they did find a multiple R of .37 when all five variables were regressed onto entrepreneurial status, which is a moderate effect size by conventional standards. The strongest predictors were Conscientiousness (positive) and Agreeableness (negative).

Debates as to the power and, therefore, usefulness of personality traits to predict work behaviour will no doubt continue. It is healthy to debate but more so to collect good empirical data in favour of one's position.

Why personality traits do not predict behaviour at work

Furnham (2005b) has noted why various studies have shown little relationship between personality tests. There are around ten well-rehearsed reasons why studies fail to show the relevance or importance of personality traits in work-related outcomes:

1   *The personality theory itself is problematic.* There are a large number of personality theories derived from very different traditions (psychoanalytic, psychometric and work-related behaviour). These may have little good theoretical foundation. A good current example may be emotional intelligence, which is not yet based on sound non-ambiguous theoretical foundations (Petrides et al., 2004b). In this sense, hypotheses derived from weak or erroneous theories are rarely confirmed. Some theorists also spurn good tests of the theory.

2   *The personality test has not been sufficiently psychometrised.* To validate any personality test is a long, difficult and expensive business. It is often the case that test producers "cut corners" and end up with a so-called unidimensional scale that is in fact multidimensional (or the other way around); has good face validity but is, therefore, very sensitive to dissimulation and impression management; has scales that are badly skewed or have little evidence of predictive and construct validity.

3   *The specific traits measured are not theoretically related to the particular work behaviour specified.* Too often researchers use multidimensional personality tests that measure traits at the primary – rather than superfactor – level and relate these to a range of often unreliable work measures. The result is a large correlation matrix – often 30 primary traits (Big 5 × 6 Facet) and 10 work-related measures. They are then disappointed that so few correlations are significant. Yet, there is often no reason to suppose that a particular trait (i.e. openness) is related to a particular work-related behaviour (absenteeism). When specific traits are thoughtfully and carefully related to well-measured outcome variables the results are often much clearer.

4   *The measurement of work-related dependent variable is poor.* Getting accurate, reliable, relevant and robust work-related measures is often difficult as organisations may be either loath (or unable) to collect or disclose them. Hence, it is quite often

the case that researchers have only limited and poor quality data – such as supervisor assessment ratings that are skewed, with restricted range, and strong evidence of a halo effect. It is particularly important that work-related behaviour is aggregated to get a reliable measure and that, where possible, systematic errors are eliminated. A major problem lies in using single predictors of single work-outcome measures. It is also important to get behavioural and observational as well as self-report measures.

5 *The work behaviour is shaped and constrained by other power factors.* Unknown restrictions, corporate cultural norms, changes in market conditions, team competence and the power and reliability of new technology mean that work output may be artificially enhanced or restricted, usually the latter. Work output is constrained by a large number of factors, which means if there is a relationship between personality and work outcomes, it may be significantly affected by poor or faulty machinery; a sudden drop in demand for a product, etc. Inevitably other intra- and interpersonal factors are important as well as personality traits in shaping behaviour.

6 *Group norms and the tall-poppy syndrome.* People at work are always sensitive to equity of in- and output and hence, group norms. In Australia they talk of the "tall-poppy syndrome", which are intact group sanctions aimed at curtailing highly effective performance. This leads to a severe restriction of range in the output variable that cannot be easily corrected statistically.

7 *Personality is a moderator variable, and if unmeasured remains unrecorded.* It is quite possible that many "zero order" relationships at work are spurious in the sense that the supposed causal link between them is affected by a personality variable. Thus, it has been argued that the relationship between smoking and cancer is moderated by Extraversion and Neuroticism. Similarly, the same two fundamental personality traits probably moderate the relationship between job satisfaction and productivity (Furnham, 1999).

8 *Personality is a mediator variable.* It is also possible that personality traits are mediator variables in the sense that the relationship between the two variables, say ability and sales, is mediated by personality. Although there may be a modest relationship between the two variables, it soon becomes abundantly clear that this is a strong relationship mediated by a particular trait. Thus, measuring only ability and not personality, and vice versa, does not reveal the true nature of the causal path.

9 *Sampling problems have "washed-out" or suppressed the relationship between the two variables.* The process of recruitment and induction often aims to select a particular type of individual who may or may not be productive in the workplace. As a consequence, organisations tend to show a pretty consistent profile, which equally implies that many "types" are missing. This may mean that it is not possible to test particular hypotheses if, for instance, all introverts or neurotics have been selected out. Equally, the same problem may arise from a volunteer effect as it is well established that the personality profile of volunteers is different to that of non-volunteers.

10 *Through resignation, sacking, and promotion a chronic restriction of range occurs.* Over time, the forces of the corporate culture can easily lead to significant homogeneity of staff. Thus, it is possible that most individuals with a particular personality profile leave or get sacked, while those with a somewhat different profile tend to get promoted. It thus becomes particularly difficult when trying to investigate the relationship between personality traits and outcome measures in any organisation.

This list is more a condemnation of poor research than of personality traits. There is probably now sufficient good evidence from well-known studies for optimistic supporters of personality testing to seriously challenge the sceptics.

Researchers and recruiters are increasingly aware of the usefulness of measuring personality traits both as select-in and select-out decisions. But a knowledge of an individual's personality is also important to help understand preferences and predictions, as well as learning style.

Conclusion

The literature linking personality traits to work-related behaviour goes back over a hundred years. Until the 1950s, the research was piecemeal and the measure of both personality and work-related behaviour fairly doubtful. The area suffered two blows, one at the beginning of the 1950s from early negative reviews (Ghiselli & Barthol, 1953) and later from the behaviourist attack by Mischel (1968).

Type researchers continued to propagate tests and theories largely ignorant of, or simply ignoring, the academic literature on personality. They continue to this day outside of mainstream applied psychology, but, nevertheless, very successfully from a consulting and training point of view.

Temperament theorists, though relatively few in number, have continued to improve on their self-report measures and demonstrate their validity in the work place. They have also demonstrated the logical and consistent relationship between temperament and trait measures.

Since the mid-1980s, thus for almost 20 years, there has been a rapprochement between differential and work psychologists led by people like Judge, Hogan, Hough, and Ones, and the standard of research, meta-analyses and theorising has improved beyond all recognition. Thanks in part to the general acceptance (albeit with many reservations) of the big five factor model researchers have done good work trying to understand, which, when, why and how personality factors relate to work behaviour.

There is healthy debate and dialogue in the area, but it is difficult not to be impressed by the consistent results of the ever growing meta-analyses that are published. They tell a compelling story with three bottom-line findings. *First*, when both personality traits and work-performance data (of all sorts) are reliably measured there are clear, replicable, explicable, meaningful and comparatively large relationships between the two. *Second*, whilst there are differences depending on which personality trait measure is being considered two traits seem consistently to predict work-related behaviour: namely Conscientiousness (positive) and Neuroticism (negative). *Third*, when personality traits are aggregated into profiles, the validities go up considerably.

Type, temperament and trait psychologists neither ignore nor deny the importance of situational factors on work-related behaviours. People who work with poor equipment, in a declining industry with dysfunctional supervision and uncompetitive pay are likely to be poor performers, whatever their profile. Equally, a well-managed company can get the best out of its workers. What trait psychologists do want, however, is the recognition that there are obvious, robust and meaningful differences between workers' attitudes and behaviour, which can be explained and predicted.

5   Personality disorders at work

Introduction

Psychologists are interested in personality *traits*; psychiatrists in personality *disorders*. Both are powerful predictors of behaviour at work. Psychologists argue that each individual has a particular personality profile, which may be accurately assessed and mapped into personality space. Whichever taxonomic system is used, the assumption is that people have a unique personality profile. Just as all people have stable physical characteristics – height, weight, body mass index, eye colour – that may be measured and recorded so it is with personality traits. Psychiatrists interested in abnormal behaviour make similar assumptions.

However, there has been something of a tussle over whether the five-factor trait model of personality can adequately (sufficiently, parsimoniously) describe psychopathy or abnormal behavioural patterns (Lynam & Widiger, 2004). Thus Miller et al. (2001) argued that psychopathy can be understood as an *extreme variant* of the common (five) trait dimensions of personality. Thus, extremely conscientious people may be seen as *obsessive*, or extremely introverted people as *schizoid*. Equally, Trull et al. (2003) have shown that the borderline personality disorder can be seen as a maladaptive variant of the five-factor trait model. There has come to be known as a phenomenon called the *spectrum hypothesis*. This suggests that abnormality is essentially characterisable by people at the ends of the trait dimensions or spectrums. Thus it is *not* adaptive to be too Extraverted or Stable or Conscientious, or even Agreeable. However, it is the clinical psychologists and psychiatrists who have concentrated more on personality abnormality.

Psychiatrists are interested in personality functioning. They talk about personality disorders that are typified by *early onset* (recognisable in children and adolescents), *pervasive effects* (on all aspects of life) and with relatively *poor prognosis* (that is difficult to cure).

Over the years psychiatrists have labelled various disorders: eating disorders, sexual and gender identity disorders, anxiety disorders, mood disorders. They have made great strides in clarifying and specifying diagnostic criteria and these can be found in the various editions of the *Diagnostic and Statistical Manual of Mental Disorders* (called DSM for short) published by the American Psychiatric Association. The manual has changed over the years and it is now in its fifth edition (American Psychiatric Association, 2007).

Psychiatrists and psychologists share some simple assumptions with respect to personality. Both argue for the *stability* of personality. The DSM criteria talk of "enduring pattern", "inflexible and pervasive" or "stable and of long duration". The pattern of behaviour is not a function of drug usage or some other medical condition. The personality pattern furthermore is *not* a manifestation or consequence of another mental disorder. One factor does differentiate the two. Psychiatrists tend to think in categorical terms: "He is, or is not, schizoid; she is, or is not, a psychopath." Psychologists, on the other hand, *talk* in categorical terms but *measure* and research in terms of dimensions. Thus there are ambiverts, mild extraverts and very strong extraverts. They argue that all characteristics are normally distributed and that it is clumsy and inefficient to measure categorically, which throws away important information.

Both argue that the personality factors relate to *cognitive, affective and social aspects of functioning*. In other words, the disorder or trait affects how people think, feel and act. It is where a person's behaviour "deviates markedly" from the expectations of that individual's culture that the disorder is manifest. The psychiatric manual is very clear that "odd behaviour" is not simply an expression of habits, customs, religious or political values professed or shown by people of particular cultural origin.

The DSM manuals note that personality disorders all have a long history and have an onset no later than early adulthood. Moreover, there are some gender differences: thus the antisocial personality disorder is more likely to be diagnosed in men while the borderline, histrionic and dependent personality is more likely to be found in women.

The manuals are at lengths to point out that some of the personality disorders look like other disorders: anxiety, mood, psychotic, substance-related, etc., but have *unique* features. The essence of the argument is: "Personality Disorders must be distinguished from personality traits that do not reach the threshold for a Personality Disorder. Personality traits are diagnosed as a Personality Disorder only when they are inflexible, maladaptive, and persisting and cause significant functional impairment or subjective distress" (American Psychiatric Association, 1994, p. 633).

DSM-IV provides a clear summary of the diagnostic criteria for personality disorders (see Box 5.1).

Box 5.1 General diagnostic criteria for a personality disorder

---

A   An enduring pattern of inner experience and behaviour that deviates markedly from the expectations of the individual's culture. This pattern is manifested in two (or more) of the following areas:

1   cognition (i.e. ways of perceiving and interpreting self, other people, and events);
2   affectivity (i.e. the range, intensity, lability, and appropriateness of emotional response);
3   interpersonal functioning;
4   impulse control.

B   The enduring pattern is inflexible and pervasive across a broad range of personal and social situations.
C   The enduring pattern leads to clinically significant distress or impairment in social, occupational, or other important areas of functioning.

D The pattern is stable and of long duration and its onset can be traced back at least to adolescence or early childhood.

E The enduring pattern is not better accounted for as a manifestation or consequence of another mental disorder.

F The enduring pattern is not due to the direct physiological effects of a substance (e.g. a drug of abuse, a medication) or a general medical condition (e.g. head trauma).

Source: Adapted from the American Psychiatric Association (1994, p. 633).

According to the DSM there are eleven or more defined and distinguishable personality disorders (American Psychiatric Association, 1994, p. 629), which will be considered in due course.

1 *Paranoid Personality Disorder* is a pattern of distrust and suspiciousness such that others' motives are interpreted as malevolent.
2 *Schizoid Personality Disorder* is a pattern of detachment from social relationships and a restricted range of emotional expression.
3 *Schizotypal Personality Disorder* is a pattern of acute discomfort in close relationships, cognitive or perceptual distortions, and eccentricities of behaviour.
4 *Antisocial Personality Disorder* is a pattern of disregard for, and violation of, the rights of others.
5 *Borderline Personality Disorder* is a pattern of instability in interpersonal relationships, self-image, and affects, and marked impulsivity.
6 *Histrionic Personality Disorder* is a pattern of excessive emotionality and attention seeking.
7 *Narcissistic Personality Disorder* is a pattern of grandiosity, need for admiration, and lack of empathy.
8 *Avoidant Personality Disorder* is a pattern of social inhibition, feelings of inadequacy, and hypersensitivity to a negative evaluation.
9 *Dependent Personality Disorder* is a pattern of submissive and clinging behaviour related to an excessive need to be taken care of.
10 *Obsessive-Compulsive Personality Disorder* is a pattern of preoccupation with orderliness, perfectionism, and control.
11 *Personality Disorder Not Otherwise Specified* is a category provided for two situations: (1) the individual's personality pattern meets the general criteria for a Personality Disorder and traits of several different Personality Disorders are present, but the criteria for any specific Personality Disorder are not met; or (2) the individual's personality pattern meets the general criteria for a Personality Disorder, but the individual is considered to have a Personality Disorder that is not included in the classification (e.g. passive-aggressive personality disorder).

One of the most important ways to differentiate personal style from personality disorder is flexibility. There are lots of difficult people at work but relatively few whose rigid, maladaptive behaviours mean they continually have disruptive, troubled lives. It is their *inflexible, repetitive, poor stress-coping responses* that are marks of disorder.

Personality disorders influence the *sense of self* – the way people think and feel about themselves and how other people see them. The disorders often powerfully influence *interpersonal relations at work*. They reveal themselves in how people "complete tasks, take and/or give orders, make decisions, plan, handle external and internal demands, take or give criticism, obey rules, take and delegate responsibility, and cooperate with people" (Oldham & Morris, 1991, p. 24). The antisocial, obsessive-compulsive, passive-aggressive and dependent types are particularly problematic in the workplace.

People with personality disorders have difficulty expressing and understanding emotions. It is the intensity with which they express them and their variability that makes them odd. More importantly they often have serious problems with self-control.

Not surprisingly, at work people with personality disorders are often extremely problematic (Babiak, 1995; Babiak & Hare, 2006). Furnham (2007a), who examined the paradoxical positive influence of personality pathology at work, noted:

> Three categories or types are most commonly implicated in management derailment and they are, in order of frequency: antisocial (psychopath), narcissistic and histrionic. Machiavellianism (which is not strictly a personality disorder) has been considered another dimension. These have been variously described as the dark triad of personality though there is some disagreement about all dimensions. In lay term, psychopaths are selfish, callous, superficially charming, lacking in empathy and remorse; narcissists are attention seeking, vain, self-focused and exploitative, while Machiavellians are deceptive, manipulative and deeply self-interested.
>
> Paradoxically it is often these disorders that proved to be an asset in acquiring and temporarily holding down senior management positions. The charm of the psychopath, the self-confidence of the narcissist, the clever deceptiveness of the Machiavellian and the emotional openness of the histrionic may be, in many instances, useful business traits. When candidates are physically attractive, well-educated, intelligent and with a dark triad profile it is not difficult to see why they are selected for senior positions in management. In this sense, assessors and selectors must bear part of the blame for not selecting out those who so often so spectacularly derail. They do not recognise in the biography of the individual all the crucial indicators of the disorder. Alternatively the biography as portrayed in the CV may easily be a work of fiction.
>
> It is ironic that personality disorders may serve individuals in particular businesses well to climb the ladder of success. If they are bright and intelligent, their disorder profile may at least for a time seem beneficial, even attractive in the business environment. However, it is likely over time to be discovered and to lead to manifold types of business failure.
>
> (p. 3)

It should be pointed out, however, that interesting and important as this area of research may be there is still not much empirical research relating the personality disorders to work-related behaviour. The situation is changing but still a great deal remains speculative rather than proven. This situation will no doubt change over the next couple of years as a number of researchers are working in the area.

Traits and disorders

There have been numerous attempts to relate the two worlds of traits and disorders (Dyce, 1997) from the two disciplines of psychology and psychiatry. Indeed Wiggins and Pincus (1989) noted that the personality disorders are "readily interpretable" (p. 314) within the Big Five framework. Perhaps the most comprehensive comparative attempt has been by Widiger et al. (2001, 2002), who believed that having extreme (high or low) scores on personality traits renders individuals at risk for certain disorders. Further, a recent edited book examined the relationship between personality disorders and the five-factor trait model (Costa & Widiger, 2005).

There are a wide variety of measures of personality disorders, the most common of which was one of the Millon measures (MCMI-I, II, III; 1981). De Clercq and De Fruyt (2003) in their study, however, used the APP-IV measure developed by Schotte and De Doncker (1994). Saulsman and Page (2004) have done an excellent review of the various checklists and questionnaires available to measure personality disorders.

It should be noted that personality traits are traditionally measured at two levels: the superfactor or domain level, as well as primary or facet level. Thus in the Costa and McCrae (1992) measures the Big Five super-factors can also be broken down and interpreted at the primary factor level. Each of the five factors has six facets. Analysing personality at the lower level offers a richer and more detailed description of personality factioning. Widiger et al. (2002) compared the personality disorders with FFM traits at the primary factor facet level. Thus they specified that only one of the six facets of Agreeableness, namely low compliance, was associated with the personality disorders (see Table 5.1).

There remains debate, however, concerning whether personality disorders are qualitatively different from "normal" behaviour or whether the behaviours associated with each specific disorder should be considered simply as an exaggerated or extreme form of normal behaviour (Clark & Watson, 1999). Further, it has been suggested that some forms of personality disorder (histrionic, narcissistic, compulsive) may even be socially acceptable and rewarded in business and society at large (Babiak, 1995; Millon, 1981). Thus, successful business people may be characterised by egocentricism, superficial charm and manipulativeness (histrionic); exploitative, grandiose and unempathic behaviour (narcissistic); and dictatorial, rigid and stubborn (compulsive). There are various self-report measures available to measure personality disorders (Kaye & Shea, 2000; Morey et al., 1985; Widiger & Coker, 2001).

There have been numerous attempts to relate the two worlds of traits and disorders. Perhaps the most comprehensive attempt has been by Widiger et al. (2001) who believed that having extreme (high or low) scores on personality traits renders individuals *at risk* for certain disorders. Their analysis is set out in Table 5.1 but will be described more simply below:

1 *Paranoid.* They score *low on agreeableness* (particularly low trust) and straightforwardness. They also score *high on facets of neuroticism* (particularly angry hostility). They also are cold and antisocial (introverts) and closed rather than open to experience.
2 *Schizoid.* They are *strongly introverted*: loners, isolated, withdrawn with little interest in, or ability to initiate and maintain, social relationships.
3 *Schizotypal.* They, too, are *introverted* but can manifest fairly strong *neuroticism*

Table 5.1 DSM-III-R personality disorders and the five-factor model

Diagnostic criteria	PAR	SZD	SZT	ATS	BDL	HST	NAR	AVD	DEP	OBC	PAG
Neuroticism											
Anxiety	h			h/L				H	H		
Hostility	H	L		H	H	H	H			h	H
Depression		L	h	h	H		H/L	h	H	H	
Self-consciousness			H	L	H	H	H	H	h	h	
Impulsiveness				H	H	H	H				
Vulnerability			h		H			H	H		
Extraversion											
Warmth	l	L	L	l		H		L/H	h	L	
Gregariousness	l	L	L		h	H		L			
Assertiveness					h		H	L	L	H	
Activity		L				H		L			
Excitement Seeking	l	L		H		H				l	
Positive Emotions	l	L			h	H				l	
Openness											
Fantasy	l		H			H	H				
Aesthetics	l					H					
Feelings	l	L	L			L				L	
Actions								L			
Ideas	L		H			H					
Values						H				L	
Agreeableness											
Trust	L		L			H					
Straightforwardness	L			L	L	L			H		L
Altruism	L			L		L			H	L	L
Compliance	l	h		L	L		L		H	L	L
Modesty	l			L			L		h		
Tendermindedness	l			L					h		
Conscientiousness											
Competence	h					L	H			L	L
Order				L						H	
Dutifulness										H	L
Achievement Striving		l		L			H		L	H	L
Self-discipline				L		L				H	
Deliberation				L						H	L

Notes: H = high, L = low, based on DSM-III-R diagnostic criteria (American Psychiatric Association, 1987); h = high, l = low, based on associated features provided in DSM-III-R (American Psychiatric Association, 1987); **H/h** = very high/high, **L/l** = low/very low, based on clinical literature. Personality disorders: PAR = paranoid; SZD = schizoid; SZT = schizotypal; ATS = antisocial; BDL = borderline; HST = histrionic; NAR = narcissistic; AVD = avoidant; DEP = dependent; OBC = obsessive-compulsive; PAG = passive-aggressive.

Source: From Widiger et al. (2001). Used with permission of the American Psychological Association, Washington.

traits. However, they tend to score high on openness, which reflects their association with creativity. This condition is particularly associated with self-consciousness, vulnerability and a rich fantasy life.

4 *Antisocial*. They are *low on agreeableness and conscientiousness*, being exploitative, vengeful and antagonistic. They have a mixed profile on neuroticism, being high on hostility but low on self-consciousness.

5 *Borderline*. They are essentially *unstable*, having high scores on most neuroticism facets particularly hostility, impulsivity, vulnerability, depression and anxiety. They are hot tempered, often apprehensive and easily rattled. They are characterised by vulnerability to stress, impulsivity, dyscontrol and negative emotionality.

6 *Histrionic*. There are extreme *extraverts*: convivial, assertive, energetic, flashy and high spirited. They express emotions with inappropriate exaggeration and display inappropriate affection, intimacy and seductiveness. They may also be low in self-discipline.

7 *Narcissistic*. They tend to score *low on agreeableness and low on neuroticism*. They are suspicious and manipulative, however, despite low self-consciousness, hostility and depression. Their conscientiousness scores can be very low.

8 *Avoidant*. They are clearly *introverted neurotics*. They are anxious, timid and insecure; easily rattled and panicked; apprehensive and prone to feelings of embarrassment and inferiority. They probably also have low openness scores.

9 *Dependent*. They tend to score *high on both agreeable and neuroticism*. Their pathological agreeableness makes them self-effacing, docile, submissive and sacrificial. They may describe themselves as being low in competence and dutifulness, which makes them look low in conscientiousness.

10 *Obsessive-Compulsive*. These perfectionistic, *over-conscientious* people tend to be preoccupied with details and order and often excessively devoted to productive work. But they can be very fearful of making mistakes. They can also be rather antagonistic: low on compliance and altruism, insisting that others follow orders, and stubborn. They are thus *high on conscientiousness and neuroticism but low on agreeableness*.

11 *Passive-Aggressive/Negativistic*. They tend to be *low on both agreeableness and conscientiousness*. They can be said to be sullen, complaining, stubborn, irritable and disgruntled. They may also be high on certain features of neuroticism like hostility.

12 *Self-defeating/Depressive*. These are the *neurotics with low conscientiousness scores*. They feel inadequate, pessimistic and worthless and are, as a result, self-blaming, self-critical and brooding. They fail to finish tasks and choose situations that may lead to failure. May also have low agreeableness.

13 *Sadistic*. They score *very low on agreeableness*, but also high on extraversion and often low on conscientiousness. They are characterised by their tendency to harm, humiliate, intimidate and act aggressively to others. They are ruthless, domineering and brutal with few signs of warm gregariousness or positive emotions.

Another way of marrying classic personality theory with the psychiatric system is by using the three personality trait factors identified by Eysenck (Eysenck & Eysenck, 1989). This would mean that 10 disorders would be classified, thus: *Psychotics*: Paranoid, Schizoid, Schizotypal. *Extraverts*: Antisocial, Borderline, Histrionic, Narcissistic. *Neurotics*: Avoidant, Dependent, Obsessive-Compulsive.

What all this suggests is that there is considerable, logical overlap between the psychologists' categorisation scheme for "normal" personality traits and the psychiatric criteria for personality disorders.

Hogan and Hogan (1997) have "translated" the disorders into ordinary language and devised a test of them (see Table 5.2).

More recently, various empirical studies have looked at personality disorder functioning from a five-factor model perspective. De Clercq and De Fruyt (2003) tested adolescents to see if five-factor facet variables (derived from the NEO-PI-R) could predict personality disorder symptoms. Further, in a recent meta-analysis Saulsman and Page (2004) analysed 15 independent samples to investigate how personality disorders are respectively different from, and similar to, underlying personality traits. Predictably, Neuroticism correlated positively and Agreeableness negatively with many of the disorders. Further, Extraversion was strongly but directionally variably associated with many dimensions. What is particularly interesting about this analysis is that, despite the fact that researchers have used quite different (at least 8) different measures of the personality disorders they seem consistently related to personality traits. Saulsman and Page note:

> Ultimately, this meta-analytic review indicates what personality traits are maladaptive in a personality-disordered population according to the five-factor model. It suggests that neurotic and disagreeable type traits are of primary importance as they are relevant to most personality disorders and that extraverted–introverted type traits are of next importance as they are relevant to some personality disorders. This summary of the five-factor model and personality disorder literature provides purely descriptive information about the trait structure of personality disorders. To have these findings translate into any practical applications, such as generic and specialised personality trait interventions previously mentioned, requires that research now turns to the question of how these traits are disordered. That is, in what ways are Neuroticism, Disagreeableness, and Extraversion–Introversion maladaptive in individuals with a personality disorder? This requires knowledge of the functioning and operation of disordered personality. Modification of maladaptive trait dimensions or the development of appropriate coping strategies to deal with maladaptive trait dimensions will be impossible without knowledge of the nature of this maladaptivity.
>
> (2004, p. 1079)

At least three studies have recently examined the relationship between traits and disorders. Deary et al. (1998) correlated results from the Structural Clinical Interview for the DSM-III-R (SCID-III) with the Revised Eysenck Personality Questionnaire. They found Psychoticism correlated with Passive-Aggressive and Antisocial disorders. Extraversion was negatively correlated with Avoidant but positively correlated with Histrionic and that Neuroticism was positively correlated (> .40) with seven disorders particularly Borderline and Avoidant. They argued that there is substantive overlap between normal and abnormal personality dimension.

Various recent studies have used the Hogan measure. Rolland and De Fruyt (2003) in a study of 130 French military personnel found that personality disorders (labelled maladaptive traits) did not predict negative affect beyond the Big Five personality traits and believe they have no incremental validity in predicting (military) work behaviour.

Table 5.2 Overlapping themes from HDS and DSM-IV, Axis 2 personality disorders

DSM-IV Personality Disorder		HDS themes	
Borderline	Inappropriate anger; unstable and intense relationships alternating between idealisation and devaluation.	Excitable	Moody and hard to please; intense but short-lived enthusiasm for people, projects, or things.
Paranoid	Distrustful and suspicious of others; motives are interpreted as malevolent.	Sceptical	Cynical, distrustful, and doubting others' true intentions.
Avoidant	Social inhibition; feelings of inadequacy, and hypersensitivity to criticism or rejection.	Cautious	Reluctant to take risks for fear of being rejected or negatively evaluated.
Schizoid	Emotional coldness and detachment from social relationships; indifferent to praise and criticism.	Reserved	Aloof, detached, and uncommunicative; lacking interest in or awareness of the feelings of others.
Passive-Aggressive*	Passive resistance to adequate social and occupational performance; irritated when asked to do something he/she does not want to.	Leisurely	Independent; ignoring people's requests and becoming irritated or argumentative if they persist.
Narcissistic	Arrogant and haughty behaviours or attitudes; grandiose sense of self-importance and entitlement.	Bold	Unusually self-confident; feelings of grandiosity and entitlement; over-valuation of one's capabilities.
Antisocial	Disregard for the truth; impulsivity and failure to plan ahead; failure to conform with social norms.	Mischievous	Enjoying risk taking and testing the limits; needing excitement; manipulative, deceitful, cunning, and exploitative.
Histrionic	Excessive emotionality and attention seeking; self-dramatizing, theatrical, and exaggerated emotional expression.	Colourful	Expressive, animated, and dramatic; wanting to be noticed and needing to be the centre of attention.
Schizotypal	Odd beliefs or magical thinking; behaviour or speech that is odd, eccentric, or peculiar.	Imaginative	Acting and thinking in creative and sometimes odd or unusual ways.
Obsessive-Compulsive	Preoccupations with orderliness, rules, perfectionism, and control; over-conscientious and inflexible.	Diligent	Meticulous, precise, and perfectionistic, inflexible about rules and procedures; critical of others' performance.
Dependent	Difficulty making everyday decisions without excessive advice and reassurance; difficulty expressing disagreement out of fear of loss of support or approval.	Dutiful	Eager to please and reliant on others for support and guidance; reluctant to take independent action or go against popular opinion.

Note: *From DSM-III-R (American Psychiatric Association, 1987).

Source: Furnham, A. & Crump, J. (2005). Personality traits, types and disorders. *European Journal of Personality, 19*, 167–184. Copyright © 2005 John Wiley & Sons Limited. Reproduced with permission.

The Hogan Development Survey (HDS) was explicitly based on the DSM-IV Axis 2 personality disorder descriptions, but it was not developed for the assessment of all the DSM disorders (see Table 5.2). The HDS focuses only on the core construct of each disorder from a dimensional perspective (Hogan & Hogan, 2001, p. 41). An overview of the item selection guidelines can be found in Hogan and Hogan (2001). The HDS has been cross-validated with the MMPI Personality Disorder scales. Correlations ($n = 140$) range from .45 for Antisocial to .67 for Borderline (Hogan & Hogan, 2001). Fico et al. (2000) report coefficient alphas between .50 and .70, with an average of .64 and test–retest reliabilities ($n = 60$) over a three-month interval ranging from .50 to .80, with an average of .68. There were no mean-level differences between sexes, racial/ethnic groups or younger versus older persons (Hogan & Hogan, 2001).

Furnham and Crump (2005) tested the relationship between the Big Five and the disorders (Table 5.3). All but two of the correlations with Neuroticism were significant, particularly those associated with Excitable (Borderline) and Cautious (Avoidant). Correlations with Passive Aggressive and Dependent types were also significant at $r > .20$. This mirrors the meta-analysis of Saulsman and Page (2004). Two were significantly negative indicating that Stability, rather than Neuroticism was associated with Bold (Narcissistic) and Colourful (Histrionic) personality types. This does not concur with Widiger et al.'s (2002) hypothesis. Further, the results from Saulsman and Page (2004) show both significant negative and positive correlations with Neuroticism and Narcissistic and Histrionic personality disorders.

Seven of the correlations with Extraversion were significant. Extraverts were more likely to be bold (Narcissistic); Mischievous (Antisocial) and colourful (Histrionic) while Introverts were more likely to be Excitable (Borderline), Cautious (Avoidant), Reserved (Schizoid) and Leisurely (Passive-Aggressive). This partly confirms Widiger et al. (2002) though they expected no significant relationships for either Bold or Excitable. The results, however, do fit in with the pattern established by Saulsman and Page (2004).

Table 5.3 Examination of the overlap between the NEO-PI-R and the HDS

Types	N	E	O	A	C
1 Enthusiastic-Volatile EXCITABLE	.58***	−.27****	−.04	−.26***	−.027***
2 Shrewd-Mistrustful SKEPTICAL	.18**	.00	−.06	−.27***	.02
3 Careful-Cautious CAUTIOUS	.54***	−.50***	−.19***	.10	−.23**
4 Independent-Detached RESERVED	.15**	−.53***	−.26***	−.15**	−.14***
5 Focused-Passive Aggressive RESERVED	.27**	−.19**	−.14**	−.05	−.10*
6 Confident-Arrogant BOLD	−.17**	.34***	.18**	−.26**	.23***
7 Charming-Manipulative MISCHIEVOUS	.09**	.40***	.34***	−.24***	−.05
8 Vivacious-Dramatic COLOURFUL	−.16**	.55***	.34***	−.23***	.01
9 Imaginative-Eccentric Imaginative	.05	.31***	.43***	−.13**	−.09**
10 Diligent-Perfectionist DILIGENT	.06	.00	−.09**	.03	.54***
11 Dutiful-Dependent DUTIFUL	.24**	−.09	−.02	.18**	−.08*
12 Social Desirability	.08*	.03*	.10**	.03	.10**

Notes: ***$p < .001$, **$p < .01$, *$p < .05$. N = Neuroticism; E = Extraversion; O = Openness; A = Agreeableness; C = Conscientiousness.

Source: From Furnham, A. & Crump, J. (2005). Personality traits, types and disorders. *European Journal of Personality*, *19*, 167–184. Copyright © 2005 John Wiley & Sons Limited. Reproduced with permission.

Eight correlations with Openness were significant; four weakly negative and four more strongly positive. Those participants with high Openness scores tended to score higher on Mischievous, Imaginative, Colourful, and Bold, but lower on Independent, Careful, Focused and Diligent. Widiger et al. (2002) predicted that facets of Agreeableness should be positively correlated with Dutiful, but predominantly negatively correlated with Sceptical, Mischievous and Bold. Two disorders showed positive significant correlations with Conscientious (Diligent, Confident), while six significant correlations were negative (Enthusiastic, Careful, Independent, Focused, Imaginative and Dutiful). Widiger et al. (2002) predicted Conscientiousness would be positively related to Diligence and negatively correlated with Mischievous.

More recently, Furnham et al. (2007b) looked at traits, disorders and work values. Correlational and regressional analyses revealed modest but predictable relationships between all personality traits (except Neuroticism) and the values, particularly Recognition, Power and Security – the personality traits accounted for most variance with respect to Aesthetics, Altruism, Security and Power. The values most related to "flawed interpersonal style" were Recognition, Affiliation, Power and Security. Step-wise regressions indicated that the disorders accounted for incremental validity over the traits in predicting core work values.

Disorders at work

Over the last decade various psychologists have noted that the personality disorders may easily account for people having serious problems at work (Oldham & Morris, 1991). Indeed, one psychiatrist at a European business school has made it his life's work to describe the manifestation of personality disorder among business people (Kets de Vries, 1999, 2004). He has concentrated on psychopathic managers who cause great damage. Indeed most researchers in this area believe it is psychopaths that are the most common and dangerous people at work (Babiak & Hare, 2006). However, most of this research is based on case-study observation rather than more traditional empirical research using large studies and validated measures.

Kets de Vries also examined *hypomanic* managers, whose behaviour, with its recurring upswings and downswings, has a larger-than-life quality. On the upswings, hypomanics exhibit abundant energy, unbridled enthusiasm, thirsty gregariousness, intense feeling, a sense of destiny, a strong belief in themselves and their ideas (bordering on the grandiose), persuasiveness in convincing others of their point of view, willingness to go where others dare not go, optimism, heightened alertness and observational ability, courage, a willingness to take risks (bordering on the imprudent), unpredictable and subtle changes in mood, impatience and shortened attention span. During their highs, hypomanics have a feeling of unlimited physical and mental energy, the expansiveness in mood state symptomised by grandiose thoughts and feelings. Hypomanics on the upswing enjoy feelings of ease, strength, buoyancy, financial omnipotence, and euphoria (Kets de Vries, 1999, p. 10).

Equally, Kets de Vries is fascinated by the extremely low *EQ manager* who he describes thus:

> In such people, the normal experience and expression of emotions has been subdued, removed from conscious awareness. These people are, in effect, emotional illiterates. Incapable of reflective self-awareness, they express little interest in their

inner subjective lives. Their tendency to externalise, that is, to steer clear of emotion, is reflected in a cognitive style focused on external processes and activities. They seem to live in a world of concrete operations.

Alexithymics are unable to symbolise their emotions as fantasies, dreams, images or desires. They have marked difficult verbally expressing or describing their feelings. They go to considerable effort, however to mask this deficit, behaving like colour-blind people who have learned to infer, Alexithymics may use the right words to describe certain feelings, that is where the process stops; they cannot develop their personal reactions to emotionally charged issues any further. Their observations remain at a rather vague and general level. True Alexithymics feel neither passion nor enthusiasm; they have no fire in their belly.

(Kets de Vries, 1999, p. 14)

Kets de Vries (2004), like others in this area, recognises the double-edged sword of self-belief, self-confidence or narcissism in the business world. He writes: "A solid dose of narcissism is a prerequisite for anyone who hopes to rise to the top of an organisation. Narcissism offers leaders a foundation for conviction about the righteousness of their cause. The narcissistic leader's conviction that his or her group, organisation, or country has a special mission inspires loyalty and group identification; the strength (and even inflexibility) of a narcissistic leader's worldview gives followers something to identify with and hold on to. Narcissism is a toxic drug, however. Although it is a key ingredient for success, it does not take much before a leader suffers from an overdose" (pp. 188–189).

He distinguished between health-constructive narcissists and reaction-destructive narcissists. He further notes:

Typically, reactive narcissistic leaders become fixated on issues of power, status, prestige, and superiority. To them, life is a zero-sum game; there are winners and losers. They are preoccupied with looking out for number one. They are often driven toward achievement and attainment by the need to get even for perceived slights experienced in childhood. Reactive narcissistic leaders are not prepared to share power. On the contrary, as leaders they surround themselves with "yea-sayers". Unwilling to tolerate disagreement and dealing poorly with criticism, such leaders rarely consult with colleagues, preferring to make all decisions on their own. When they do consult with others, such consultation is little more than ritualistic. They use others as a kind of "Greek chorus", expecting followers to agree to whatever they suggest.

Reactive narcissistic leaders learn little from defeat. When setbacks occur, such leaders don't take any personal responsibility; instead, they scapegoat others in the organisation, passing on the blame. Even when things are going well, they can be cruel and verbally abusive to their subordinates, and they are prone to outbursts of rage when things don't go their way. Likewise, perceiving a personal attack even where none is intended, they may erupt when followers rebel against their distorted view of the world. Such "tantrums", re-enactments of childhood behaviour, originate in earlier feelings of helplessness and humiliation. Given the power that such leaders now hold, the impact of their rage on the immediate environment can be devastating. Furthermore, tantrums intimidate followers, who then themselves regress to more childlike behaviour.

(pp. 189–190)

What Kets de Vries has done is three things. *First*, he has described the personality disorders in everyday language. *Second*, he has shown that much "odd, dangerous and counter productive behaviour" of business people is due to their personality disorders. *Third*, he has alerted people to "tell-tale" signs of those problems. Many people have assumed that those with personality disorders were unlikely to reach managerial level and thus that there was little point in trying to measure the personality disorders for the purpose of *selecting out* individuals who may cause significant damage to an organisation. The work of Kets de Vries and others (Babiak & Hare, 2006; Hogan & Hogan, 1997, 2001) has shown that, indeed, this is not the case. Further, Furnham (2007a) has argued that, at least initially, some of the personality disorders actually increase the possibility of being selected to senior managerial jobs, particularly if individuals are bright and good looking or charming.

To make the somewhat archaic language more intelligible various writers have redefined the types. For example, Oldham and Morris (1991) have provided a set of "translations" (see Box 5.2).

However, perhaps the most insightful and useful approach had been that of Hogan and Hogan (2001) who have developed a self-report questionnaire called the Hogan Development Survey (HDS), which quite specifically measures 11 of the personality disorders but expresses them in accessible language (see Table 5.2).

Hogan and Hogan (2001) said that this "view from the dark side" gives an excellent understanding of the causes of management derailment. They argued that it is probably easier to define incompetence than competence, that there are obviously many "mad" managers in organisations and that helping people identify potentially bad or derailed managers can help alleviate a great deal of suffering. They also noted, from their reading of the literature, that derailment is more about having undesirable qualities than not having desirable ones.

Box 5.2 Modern "translations" of archaic type names

Old	*New*
Obsessive-Compulsive	Conscientious
Narcissistic	Self-Confident
Histrionic	Dramatic
Paranoid	Vigilant
Borderline	Mercurial
Dependent	Devoted
Schizoid	Solitary
Passive-Aggressive	Leisurely
Avoidant	Sensitive
Schizotypal	Idiosyncratic
Antisocial	Adventurous
Self-Defeating	Self-Sacrificing
Sadistic	Aggressive

Source: Adapted from Oldham and Morris (1991).

Their research in the area has led them to seven conclusions:

1   There is substantial (between-study) agreement regarding the dysfunctional dis-
    positions/traits associated with management incompetence and derailment.
2   Many derailed managers have impressive social skills, which is why their disorders
    are not spotted at selection but only later by their subordinates.
3   Bad managers are a major cause of misbehaviour (theft, absenteeism, turnover) by
    staff: it is poor treatment that often makes them resentful.
4   It is important to take the observers view in personality: that is, the descriptions of
    the personality disorders from those that deal with them.
5   The problem for much research is that it can describe what derailed and derailing
    managers do rather than why they do it.
6   Whilst the origin (in terms of learning or biology) is not clear for the personality
    disorders/derailment factors, their consequences are very apparent. And the most
    obvious one is, quite simply, the inability to learn from experience.
7   A second crucial consequence of the disorders is that they erode trust.

The Hogans' highly useful measure has alerted many researchers and managers to the
fact that understanding and looking out for evidence of personality disorders is very
important to try to prevent serious selection errors. They argue that there is a danger
zone for managers in the sense that their personality disorders manifest themselves
when under pressure. Thus there are high- or moderate-risk people whose malfunc-
tioning, personality-disordered behaviour seems to be "under control" most of the time
but "comes out" in times of frustration or stress.

The types

In this section the various types will be described in some detail and speculations made
about their behaviour at work. There is very little research on this topic, however, with
the exception of the work of Babiak and Hare (2006) as well as Hogan and Hogan
(2001).

1. Paranoid (Argumentative, Vigilant)

It is thought that between 0.5 and 2.5% of the population have these disorders, which
must not be confused with the paranoid delusions of schizophrenics, or the behaviour
of refugees and migrants whose personal history leads to widespread mistrust. Paranoids are *super-vigilant*: nothing escapes their notice. They seem tuned into mixed messages, hidden motives, and secret groups. They are particularly sensitive to authority
and power, and obsessed with maintaining their own independence and freedom.

Distrust and suspiciousness of others at work is their abiding characteristic. The
motives of all sorts of colleagues and the boss are interpreted as malevolent, all the time.
The "enemy" is both without and within. Naturally they are often found thriving in
security organisations where their suspiciousness is not only "normal" but often praised.

They suspect, without much evidence that others are exploiting, harming, or deceiv-
ing them about almost everything both at work and at home. They are preoccupied with
unjustified doubts about the loyalty or trustworthiness of subordinates, customers,
bosses, shareholders, etc., on both big and small matters. They are reluctant to confide

in others (peers at work) because of the fear that the information will be used against them: kept on file; used to sack them. They may even be wary of using e-mail. They read hidden or threatening meanings into most benign remarks or events from e-mails to coffee-room gossip, and they remember them. They are certainly *hyper-sensitive* to criticism. They persistently bear grudges against all sorts of people going back many years and can remember even the smallest slight. They perceive attacks on their character or reputation that others do not see and are quick to react angrily or to counter-attack. They seem *hyper-alert and sensitive*. They have recurrent suspicions, without justification, regarding the fidelity of their sexual or business partner and can be pretty obsessed with sex.

Paranoid individuals are slow to commit and trust but once they do so, are loyal friends. They are very interested in others' motives and prefer "watch-dog" jobs. They like being champions of the underdog, whistle-blowers on corruption. They are courageous because they are certain about their position. They are on the side of right: idealists striving for a better world. But they can be overly suspicious or fearful of certain people, which can manifest itself in an irrational hatred of certain races, religions or political groups.

They are not compromisers and often attack attackers. Many of their characteristics make them excellent managers: *alert, careful, observant* and *tactical*. But they can have problems with authority; and in dealing with those who hold different opinions from their own. However, they are more sensitive to the faults in others than the faults in themselves. The business world, they believe (sometimes correctly), is full of danger, dishonest people and those who are untrustworthy and will let them down. Because they believe others are out to harm them they can be over-argumentative, bellicose, belligerent, hostile, secretive, stubborn and consumed with mistrust. They are not disclosive, suspicious of others and experts on projecting blame on to others.

Psychoanalysts believe that the paranoid feel weak and dependent but are sensitive to weakness in others and decry them for it. They yearn for dependency but fear it. Instead of showing personal doubt, they doubt others. Their self-righteousness, morality and punitiveness can be very attractive to some people.

Hogan and Hogan (2001) call this disorder "Argumentative". These types, they argue, expect to be wronged, to be betrayed, to be set up, to be cheated or to be deceived in some way. They see the world as a dangerous place, full of potential enemies, and they enjoy conspiracy theories, they are keenly alert for signs of having been mistreated. When they think they have been unfairly treated they retaliate openly and directly. This may involve physical violence, accusations, retaliation, or litigation. Retaliation is designed to send the signal that they are prepared to defend themselves. They are known for their suspiciousness, their argumentativeness, and their lack of trust in others. They are hard to deal with on a continuing basis because you never know when they are going to get offended by something (unpredictability), and because they are so focused on their own private agenda they don't have much time for others (unrewarding).

> At their best they are very insightful about organisational politics and the motives of their counter players, and they can be the source of good intelligence regarding the real agendas of others, and the real meaning of events. Although they are very insightful about politics, they are often not very good at playing politics. This is because they are true believers, they are deeply committed to their worldview, and they tend to be unwilling to compromise, even on small issues. Nonetheless, with

their passionate commitment to a theory about how the world works, they can be visionary and charismatic, and people may be drawn to them. . . . Because they are unpredictable and not rewarding to deal with, they have trouble maintaining a team over a long period.

(p. 48)

Paranoids mishandle stress by retreating, by withdrawing into their ideology and then attacking that which is threatening them. They are very persistent and tend to accumulate enemies. They are self-centred and ideology centred – all information and experience is filtered through their odd world view and evaluated in terms of the degree to which it fits with, or threatens, that view, which somehow reflects on them.

To work with them reports have no alternative but to agree with them, because they will defeat your objections in a way that makes sense to them. Reports won't be able to persuade them that they are wrong or risk alienating them by challenging them, as once they decide people can't be trusted the relationship will be over. Reports are either for them or against them.

According to Oldham and Morris, the following six traits and behaviours are clues to the presence of what they call the Vigilant style. A person who reveals a strong Vigilant tendency will demonstrate more of these behaviours more intensely than someone with less of this style in his or her personality profile.

1　"*Autonomy*. Vigilant-style individuals possess a resilient independence. They keep their own counsel, they require no outside reassurance or advice, they make decisions easily, and they can take care of themselves.
2　*Caution*. They are careful in their dealings with others, preferring to size up a person before entering into a relationship.
3　*Perceptiveness*. They are good listeners, with an ear for subtlety, tone, and multiple levels of communication.
4　*Self-defence*. Individuals with Vigilant style are feisty and do not hesitate to stand up for themselves, especially when they are under attack.
5　*Alertness to criticism*. They take criticism very seriously, without becoming intimidated.
6　*Fidelity*. They place a high premium on fidelity and loyalty. They work hard to earn it, and they never take it for granted" (1991, pp. 151–152).

Some jobs suit these people well: security, the military, perhaps insurance. But the hyper-vigilant, argumentative, wary manager can be very difficult to live with. Often those with paranoia are not particularly problematic but buckle under stress and it is then that this disorder is noticeable. Scepticism turns into cynicism and then full-blown paranoia.

2. Schizoid (Solitary, Reserved)

These are the *cold fish* of the personality-disordered world: distant, aloof, emotionally flat often preferring the affection of animals to that of people. These are the solitary loners of the personality disorders world. They are very self-contained: they do not need others to admire, entertain, guide or amuse them. And yet they report being free of loneliness. They seem completely dispassionate. They are doers and observers not feelers. They seem stoical in the face of pain and passion. Relationships? They can take them or leave them. They don't really understand emotions.

Here the manager seems detached from social relationships. They often have a restricted range of expression of emotions in interpersonal settings. They seem rather more emotionally flat than necessary. They are thought of as unresponsive, and disparately low in emotional intelligence.

They neither desire nor enjoy close relationships at work, including being part of a family. They are never team players and hate the idea of being so. They almost choose solitary activities, feeling uncomfortable even in informal gatherings. They have little, if any, interest in having sexual contact with others, which is perhaps not a bad thing at work. They take pleasure in few, if any, activities. They seem joyless, passionless, and emotionless. They lack close friends or confidants other than first-degree relatives. They are isolates at work but apparently not unhappy with their friendlessness. They appear indifferent to the praise or criticism of others. Absolutely nothing seems to get them going. They show emotional coldness, detachment, or flattened emotionality.

Schizoid people are not team players; nor are they sensitive or diplomatic. They are not aware of office politics. Hence they may be more successful in solitary careers. They are not antisocial but asocial. They are the "hollow man": empty, flat, emotionally unmovable. They may have a rich fantasy life but a very poor emotional life.

Hogan and Hogan (2001) call these types Reserved: self-absorbed, self-focused, indifferent to the feelings or opinions of others – especially their staff. They are introverted, misanthropic, imperceptive, and lacking in social insight. They appear thick skinned and indifferent to rejection or criticism. They prefer to work alone, and are more interested in data and things than in people. They tend to work in finance, accounting, programming, and information technology where their progress will depend on their technical skills and not their social insight. They are often uncommunicative and insensitive, which makes them unpredictable and unrewarding, and they have trouble building and/or maintaining a team.

They can be very tough in the face of political adversity; they have a hard surface, and they can take criticism and rejection. They can also stay focused and on task, and not be distracted by tumult, emotional upheavals, and stressful meetings; through it all, they will continue to do their jobs. Because they are indifferent to others' needs, moods, or feelings, they can be rude, tactless, insensitive, and gauche. They are, therefore, very poor managers. They are unperturbed by daily stress and heavy workloads; at the same time, they are insensitive or indifferent to the stress levels of their staff. When the pressure is really on, they retreat into their office, begin handling matters themselves, and stop communicating – which leaves others at a loss to know what they want or need. Always extremely self-centred, and self-reliant; they do not need emotional support from others, and they don't provide any to others. They primarily do not want to be bothered by other people's problems, they just want to do their work.

To work with the detached, reports should stay task orientated and keep questions and comments job related. They will ignore requests for more and better communications, and will tend to work by themselves. Reports should observe what they do, so that they do not act that way themselves, and develop lines of communication to other people in the organisation so that they will have a source of advice during times of trouble.

Again, there may be jobs where detached, solitary ways of behaving can be adaptive. The R&D scientists; the meteorologists on an uninhabited island; the artistic craftsperson may work very well alone. It is when they are promoted to the position of managing teams that the problem arises.

3. Schizotypal (Imaginative, Idiosyncratic)

This disorder, more common in males than females, has been estimated to affect about 3% of the population. In a sense they are mild schizophrenics but do not show the gross disorganisation in thinking and feeling or severe symptoms of the latter. However, they all appear to be pretty idiosyncratic and often creatively talented and curious. They often hold very strange beliefs enjoying the occult. They have odd habits and eccentric lifestyles.

Schizotypal people have a rich inner life and often seek emotional experience. Hence they are drawn to religion and pharmacological techniques that promise "testing the limits". They seek rapture and nirvana. Here the schizotypal manager is marked by acute discomfort with, and reduced capacity for, close relationships. They show many eccentricities of behaviour. They may look odd and have a reputation for being "peculiar".

They often have very odd ideas about business: how to succeed, who to hire, what controls what. They can have very odd beliefs or magical thinking that influences their behaviour and is inconsistent with business norms, e.g. superstitiousness, belief in clairvoyance, telepathy. They get into crystals, feng shui, etc., in a very big and serious way. They can have odd thinking and speech styles being very vague or very elaborate. They can seem "other worldly" and may be very difficult to follow. They can have unusual perceptual experiences, seeing things that are not there, and smell and taste things differently. Some are very suspicious or paranoid around the home and office. They show inappropriate or constricted affect: they react oddly emotionally in various contexts. That is they may become very emotional around some trivial issues but strangely and unpredictably cold at others.

Many organisations do not tolerate the odd behaviours of these idiosyncratic types. They dress oddly and work odd hours. They are not very loyal to their companies and do not enjoy the corporate world. They do not "connect" with staff, customers or their bosses. Their quirky quasi-religious beliefs estrange them yet more from the normal world of the other people. They are often loners.

Hogan and Hogan (2001) call these types *Imaginative* and describe them thus: they think about the world in unusual and often quite interesting ways. They may enjoy entertaining others with their unusual perceptions and insights. They are constantly alert to new ways of seeing, thinking, and expressing themselves, unusual forms of self-expression. They often seem bright, colourful, insightful, imaginative, very playful, and innovative, but also eccentric, odd, and flighty.

These people are curiously interesting and maybe fun to be around. But they are distractible and unpredictable and as managers they often leave people confused regarding their directions or intentions. They tend to miscommunicate in idiosyncratic and unusual ways. At their best, these people are imaginative, creative, interesting, and amazingly insightful about the motives of others, but at their worst they can be self-absorbed, single-minded, insensitive to the reactions of others, and indifferent to the social and political consequences of their single-minded focus on their own agendas.

Under stress and heavy workloads, they can become upset, lose focus, lapse into eccentric behaviour, and not communicate clearly. They can be moody and tend to get too excited by success and too despondent over failure. They do want attention, approval, and applause, which explains the lengths that they are willing to go to in order to attract it.

To work with the imaginative, reports need primarily to be a good audience, to appreciate these people's humour, creativity, and spontaneity, and to understand that they do not handle reversals very well. They will not mind suggestions and recommendations regarding important decisions and, in fact, may even appreciate them. Reports should study their problem-solving style, listen to their insights about other people, and model their ability to "think outside the box".

The imaginative, idiosyncratic person is unlikely to reach a very high position in organisations though they may be promoted in advertising or academia. The absent-minded, nutty professor; the creative advertising genius may share many schizotypal behaviours. If talented they may do well but rarely as managers of others.

4. Antisocial (Mischievous, Adventurous)

The term psycho- or sociopath was used to describe antisocial personality types whose behaviour was amoral or asocial, impulsive and lacking in remorse and shame. It is, indeed, perhaps for obvious reasons, the most studied of all the personality disorders and probably the most important for those interested in individual differences at work. Once called "moral insanity" it is found more commonly among lower socioeconomic groups, no doubt because of the "downward drift" of these types. Since the 1940s it has been shown that the characteristics defining this disorder: self-centredness, irresponsibility, impulsivity and insensitivity to the needs of others are found in many professions.

For most people psychopath means "dangerous axe murderer" or "serial killer". They recall the film *Psycho* and associate this disorder with the most fearful of all mental disorders. Yet there is now a small but growing literature on what is called the "successful psychopath" (Babiak & Hare, 2006; Widom & Newman, 1985). Essentially these are non-institutionalised individuals who "fit" the classifiable criteria but who lead apparently successful lives, often holding down good jobs.

These managers show a disregard for, and violation of, the rights of others. They often have a history of being difficult, delinquent or dangerous. They show a failure to conform to social norms with respect to lawful behaviours (repeatedly performing acts that are grounds for arrest, imprisonment and serious detention). This includes lying, stealing and cheating. They are always deceitful, as indicated by repeated lying, use of aliases, or conning others for personal profit or pleasure. They are often nasty, aggressive, con artists, the sort who often get profiled on business crime programmes. They are massively impulsive and fail to plan ahead. They live only in, and for, the present. They show irritability and aggressiveness, as indicated by repeated physical fights or assaults. They manifest a terrifyingly reckless disregard for the physical and psychological safety of self, others or the business in general. They are famous for being consistently irresponsible. Repeated failure to sustain consistent work behaviour or to honour financial obligations are their hallmark. Most frustrating of all they show lack of remorse. They are indifferent to, or rationalise, having hurt, mistreated, or stolen from another. They never learn from their mistakes. It can seem that labelling them as antisocial is a serious understatement.

In his famous book, called *The Mask of Insanity*, Cleckley (1976) set out ten criteria: superficial charm and intelligence; absence of anxiety in stressful situations; insincerity and lack of truthfulness; lack of remorse and shame; inability to experience love or genuine emotion; unreliability and irresponsibility; impulsivity and disregard for socially acceptable behaviour; clear-headedness with an absence of delusions or irrational thinking; inability to profit from experience; and lack of insight.

Antisocial, adventurous, psychopaths are not frightened by risk: indeed they thrive on it. They love the thrill of adventure and are happy to put others' lives at risk as well as their own. They tend to appear self-confident and not overly concerned with the approval of others. They live for the moment: they are neither guilty about the past nor worried about the future. They can be seriously reckless and they tend not to tolerate frustration well. They resist discipline and ignore rules. They have poor self-control and think little about the consequences of their actions.

Antisocial individuals do not hide their feeling and they do not experience stress unless confined or frustrated. They are, in a sense, adolescents all their life: careless, irresponsible, hedonistic, forever sowing wild oats. They need excitement all the time and are very easily bored. They can be successful entrepreneurs, journalists, bouncers, lifeguards and managers. They like outwitting the system; opportunistically exploiting who and what they can. They are rolling stones who gather no moss. They hate routine and administration, which is seen as drudgery.

They make very bad bosses and bad partners because they are egocentric, only continuing a relationship as long as it is good for them. They rarely have long-lasting, meaningful relationships. They have two pretty-crucial human ingredients missing: conscience and compassion. Hence they can be cruel, destructive, malicious and criminal. They are unscrupulous and exploitatively self-interested with little capacity for remorse. They act before they think and are famous for their impulsivity.

Hogan and Hogan (2001) call the antisocial person *Mischievous*. They note that these types expect that others will like them and find them charming; and they expect to be able to extract favours, promises, money, and other resources from other people with relative ease. However, they see others as merely to be exploited, and therefore have problems maintaining commitments, and are unconcerned about violating expectations. They are self-confident to the point of feeling invulnerable, and have an air of daring and *sang-froid* that others often find attractive and even irresistible.

They are highly rewarding to deal with, but unpredictable. They can be charming, fun, engaging, courageous, and seductive, but also they are impulsive, reckless, faithless, remorseless and exploitative. They also have problems with telling the truth. Their self-deception, self-confidence, and recklessness leads to lots of conflicts, but they have almost no ability to learn from experience. According to Hogan and Hogan (2001):

> They tend to be underachievers, relative to their talent and capabilities; this is due to their impulsivity, their recklessness, and their inability to learn from experience. These people handle stress and heavy work loads with great aplomb. They are easily bored, and find stress, danger, and risk to be invigorating – they actively seek it. As a result, many of these people become heroes – they intervene in robberies, they rush into burning buildings, they take apart live bombs, they volunteer for dangerous assignments, and they flourish in times of war and chaos. Conversely, they adapt poorly to the requirements of structured bureaucracies.
>
> (p. 49)

To work with them, employees must be prepared to help them follow through with commitments and pay attention to details, and to encourage them to think through the consequences of their actions. They should not expect a lot of gratitude or even loyalty, but reports can learn a lot by watching how they handle people and how they are able to get what they want through charm and persuasion.

Oldham and Morris (1991) note the traits and behaviours that are clues to the presence of the Adventurous style (Box 5.3).

Box 5.3 Adventurous style

The following eleven traits and behaviours are clues to the presence of the Adventurous style. A person who reveals a strong Adventurous tendency will demonstrate more of these behaviours more intensely than someone with less of this style in his or her personality profile.

1 *Nonconformity*. Men and women who have the Adventurous personality style live by their own internal code of values. They are not strongly influenced by other people or by the norms of society.
2 *Challenge*. To live is to dare. Adventurers love the thrill of risk and routinely engage in high-risk activities.
3 *Mutual independence*. They do not worry too much about others, for they expect each human being to be responsible for him- or herself.
4 *Persuasiveness*. They are silver-tongued, gifted in the gentle art of winning friends and influencing people.
5 *Sexuality*. Adventurers relish sex. They have a strong sex drive and enjoy numerous, varied experiences with different partners.
6 *Wanderlust*. They love to keep moving. They settle down only to have the urge to pick up and go, explore, move out, move on.
7 *Freelance*. Adventurous types avoid the nine-to-five world. They prefer to earn an independent, freelance living, do not worry about finding work, and live well by their talents, skills, ingenuity, and wits.
8 *Open purse*. They are easy and generous with money, believing that money should be spent and that more will turn up somewhere.
9 *Wild oats*. In their childhood and adolescence, people with the Adventurous personality style were usually high-spirited hell-raisers and mischief makers.
10 *True grit*. They are courageous, physically bold, and tough. They will stand up to anyone who dares to take advantage of them.
11 *No regrets*. Adventurers live in the present. They do not feel guilty about the past or anxious about the future. Life is meant to be experienced now.

Source: Adapted from Oldham and Morris (1991, p. 218).

In many ways these types are the most common in the business world because if bright and good looking their pathology may benefit them. They can be found in all sectors but may be most attracted to those jobs that involve persuading others, like the media, politics and religion.

There are some fascinating studies of successful industrial psychopaths. Babiak (1995) found five distinguishing characteristics in many studies of industrial psychopathy and various case studies. He has reported a series of case studies of individuals and described how they succeeded despite their predisposition. From these, he has noted the following:

> Comparison of the behaviour of the three subjects observed to date revealed some similarities: each (a) began by building *a network of one-to-one relationships* with powerful and useful individuals, (b) *avoided virtually all group meetings* where maintaining multiple facades may have been too difficult, and (c) *created conflicts* which kept co-workers from sharing information about them once their power bases were established, (d) *co-workers who were no longer useful* were abandoned, and (e) *detractors were neutralised* by systematically raising doubts about their competence and loyalty. In addition, unstable cultural factors, inadequate measurement systems, and general lack of trust typical of organisations undergoing rapid, chaotic change may have provided an acceptable cover for psychopathic behaviour.
>
> (pp. 184–185)

It is difficult to estimate the number of successful "industrial" psychopaths, or what Babiak and Hare (2006) called "snakes in suits". It is also sometimes difficult to explain why they "get away with it" for so long. However, there is no mystery, when enquiring from those who do or have worked with a successful psychopath, in how much misery or dysfunctionality they can bring to the workplace.

Babiak and Hare (2006) believed that psychopaths are indeed attracted to today's business climate. They devised a questionnaire to help people at work spot them. There are, according to the authors, 10 markers of the problem. The successful, industrial psychopath is characterised by the following. He or she:

1 Comes across as smooth, polished and charming.
2 Turns most conversations around to a discussion of him- or herself.
3 Discredits and puts down others in order to build up his or her own image and reputation.
4 Lies to co-workers, customers, or business associates with a straight face.
5 Considers people he or she has outsmarted or manipulated as dumb or stupid.
6 Is opportunistic; hates to lose, plays ruthlessly to win.
7 Comes across as cold and calculating.
8 Acts in an unethical or dishonest manner.
9 Has created a power network in the organisation and uses it for personal gain.
10 Shows no regret for making decisions that negatively affect the company, shareholders or employees.

Psychopaths can easily look like ideal leaders: smooth, polished, and charming. They can quite easily mask their dark side – bullying, amoral, and manipulative. In the past it used to be politics, policing, law, media and religion that attracted psychopaths but more and more it is the fast-paced, exciting, glamorous, world of business.

5. Borderline (Excitable, Mercurial)

These are people "living on the edge". Around 2% of the population have this disorder, which is more common in women than men. The term borderline originally referred to the border between neuroses and psychoses. There are often signs of other disorders: mood, depression, and histrionic. People like Marilyn Monroe, Adolf Hitler and Lawrence of Arabia have been diagnosed with this disorder, being impulsive, unpredictable, and reckless. Most of all borderline people tend to have problems with their self-image often "splitting" their positive and negative views of themselves. They can vacillate between self-idealisation and self-abhorrence.

These individuals show chronic instability of interpersonal relationships, self-image, and emotion. They are also marked by impulsivity in their daily behaviour.

Sometimes they show frantic efforts to avoid real or imagined abandonment by managers or their staff. They can become dependent and clinging. They often show a pattern of unstable and intense interpersonal relationships characterised by alternating between extremes of love and hate; worship and detestation. Most have identity disturbance: markedly and persistently unstable self-image or sense of self. They are not really sure who they are and their assumed identity can easily change. They are impulsive with money, sex, booze, driving, etc., and accident-prone, in every sense of the word. They might spend lavishly one day and be miserly the next. At extremes they can show recurrent suicidal behaviour, or threats. Most noticeable is their marked change of mood (e.g. intense episodic dysphoria, irritability or anxiety, usually lasting a few hours and only rarely more than a few days). They seem to be on an emotional roller coaster with ups and downs even on the same day. They often talk about chronic feelings of inner emptiness. Unfortunately for their reports and managers they have inappropriate, intense anger or difficulty controlling anger (e.g. frequent displays of temper, constant anger, recurrent physical fights).

These mercurial types are on the roller coaster of life. They are intense and demanding. Their emotional world is geological: full of volcanic explosions and movement of tectonic plates. They can blow hot and cold; fire and ice very quickly. They are driven by emotions and find emotional significance in everything. Hence they are very moody. People can drop from idols to "bad objects" in the space of days. But because they can not control their emotional states they are frequently in torment.

At work they can be passionately involved with others. They can really admire their bosses when praised but this can just be a phase. They insist on being treated well and have a keen sense of entitlement. They can easily see themselves as more important than others do. As managers they get very involved with their staff and expect total dedication. When their unrealistic expectations are not met they can get very moody and churlish. Their sense of who they are, what they believe, what is the meaning of their life is ever changing. They do not like mixed feelings, ambiguity or solitariness. They prefer to see the world in terms of good and bad. They can have great difficulty concentrating.

Some experts believe that the term personality disorganisation is best suited to this disorder because they seem midway between the functional and dysfunctional. Hogan and Hogan (2001) call these types *Excitable* as they expect to be disappointed in relationships; they anticipate being rejected, ignored, criticised, or treated unfairly. They are on guard for signs that others have treated, or will treat, them badly. They erupt in emotional displays that may involve yelling, throwing things, and slamming doors.

Because they are so alert for signs of mistreatment, they find them everywhere, even when others can't see them. They are neither predictable nor rewarding to deal with. As a result they have a lot of trouble building and maintaining a team – the fundamental task of leadership.

They can be sensitive to the plight of others; they have some capacity for empathy; because they know that life is not always fair, they can genuinely feels others' pain. They sometimes tend to be enthusiastic about, and to work very hard on, new projects. But, they are seriously high maintenance – they require a lot of handholding and reassurance, and they are exceptionally hard to please.

They do not handle stress or heavy workloads very well, and they tend to explode rather easily. Also, they are hard people to talk to and to maintain a relationship with. Consequently they change jobs frequently and they have a large number of failed relationships. They are so easily disappointed in working relationships that their first instinct is to withdraw and leave. They are all self-centred – all information and experience is evaluated in terms of what it means for them personally – and they take the reactions of others personally. They personalise everything, but they do so privately, what others see are the emotional outbursts and the tendency to withdraw. To work with excitable managers, reports must be prepared to provide them with a lot of reassurance, keep them well informed so as to minimise surprises, and give them a lot of preview so that they know what is coming. Think of trying to soothe a fretful child.

The borderline manager is unlikely to be very senior but if they are bright and have frequently left jobs they may be appointed to leadership roles that they are very unsuited to fulfil. They certainly are relatively easy to spot but really unpleasant to work for.

6. Histrionic (Colourful, Dramatic)

The term is derived from the Latin to mean actor, but the original term was hysterical from the Latin root meaning uterus. This disorder is found more frequently in women. They are attracted to "limelight" jobs and strive for attention and praise but setbacks can lead easily to serious inner doubts and depression.

Histrionics are certainly emotionally literate: they are open with all their emotions. But these emotions can change very quickly. These managers have excessive emotionality and are attention seeking. They are the "drama queens" of the business world.

Most are uncomfortable in situations in which they are not the centre of attention, and always try to be so. They delight in making a drama out of a crisis. Their interaction with others is often characterised by inappropriate sexually seductive or provocative behaviour. Needless to say this causes more of a reaction in women than men. They display rapidly shifting and shallow expressions of emotion. They are difficult to read. Most use physical appearance (clothes) to draw attention to self but this may include body piercing or tattooing. They certainly get a reputation in the office for their "unique apparel". Many have a style of speech that is excessively impressionistic and lacking in detail. They always show self-dramatisation, theatricality, and exaggerated expressions of emotion, usually negative. Even the dullest topic is imbued with drama. They are easily influenced by other people or circumstances and therefore are both unpredictable and persuadable. Many consider relationships to be more intimate than they actually are. Being rather dramatic they feel humdrum working relationships more intensely than others.

Histrionics do not make good managers. They get impatient with, and anxious about, details and routine administrative functions. They prefer gossip to analysis, and tend not to be good at detail. They are highly sociable and have intense relationships. They live to win friends and influence people and can do so by being very generous with compliments, flattery and appreciation. They hate being bored: life with them is never staid and dull. They do not like being alone.

Interestingly, the definition of themselves comes from the outside: they see themselves as others say they see them. They therefore lack a consistent sense of who they are. They need constant reassurance and positive feedback from others. Because their heart rules their head they can be impulsive, impetuous and impatient. They live not in the real world but in a story-book world.

At work they can be persuasive and insightful. They enjoy the world of advertising, PR, sales and marketing but need strong back-up for things like plans, budgets and details. At work they are volatile and are known for being moody. They can be effusive with both praise and blame. But everything is an emotional drama and emotionally they can be both childlike and childish. They don't do stable relationships. At work they need to be the star, the centre of attention or else they can feel powerless or desperately unworthy. They are not introspective.

Hogan and Hogan (2001) call these types *Colourful* and seem persuaded that others will find them interesting, engaging and worthy of attention. They are good at calling attention to themselves – they know how to make dramatic entrances and exits, they carry themselves with flair, self-consciously pay attention to their clothes and to the way that others react to them.

Histrionics are marked by their stage presence or persona, their self-conscious and distinctive aura – they perform extremely well in interviews, in assessment centres, and other public settings. According to Hogan and Hogan (2001, p. 49): "They are great fun to watch, but they are also quite impulsive and unpredictable; everything that makes them good at sales (and selling themselves) makes them poor managers – they are noisy, distractible, over-committed, and love to be the centre of attention. They are not necessarily extraverted, they are just good at calling attention to themselves. At their best, they are bright, colourful, entertaining, fun, flirtatious, and the life of the party. At their worst, they don't listen, they don't plan, they self-nominate and self-promote, and they ignore negative feedback."

Histrionics deal with stress and heavy workloads by becoming very busy; enjoying high-pressure situations when they can then be the star. Breathless with excitement, they confuse activity with productivity and evaluate themselves in terms of how many meetings they attend rather than how much they actually get done. A key feature of these people that others may not appreciate is how much they need and feed off approval, and how hard they are willing to work for it. And this explains why they persist in trying to be a star after their lustre has faded. To work with them, reports have to be prepared to put up with missed appointments, bad organisation, rapid change of direction, and indecisiveness. This will never change, although it can be planned for. Yet, by watching reports can learn how to read social clues, learn how to present your views effectively, forcefully, dramatically, and learn how to flatter and quite simple dazzle other people.

There are drama-queens in all sectors though they are likely to be found in the more human-resource-orientated world. They can do very well in PR, marketing and training particularly if they are talented. They certainly remain hard work for their ever-suffering reports.

7. Narcissistic (Arrogant, Self-Confident)

It may surprise some to learn that this disorder only apparently occurs in 1% of the population. There are a lot of narcissists in business, striving for adulation and power. There is, of course, a fine line between healthy self-esteem and serious self-defeating narcissism. The latter is characterised by an insatiable craving for adoration, feeling special entitlement and right to be insensitive to others but at the same time either enraged or crushed by criticism. It is a feeling that one deserves special treatment followed by extreme annoyance if one is treated like the ordinary other person.

They have a grandiose sense of self-importance (e.g. exaggerated achievements and talents, expect to be recognised as superior without commensurate achievements). Most are preoccupied with fantasies of unlimited success, power, brilliance and money. They believe that they are "special" and unique and can only be understood by, or should associate with, other special or high-status people (or institutions). They may try to "buy" themselves into exclusive circles. They always require excessive admiration and respect from everyone at work. Bizarrely, they often have a sense of entitlement, i.e. unreasonable expectations of especially favourable treatment or automatic compliance with their manifest needs. Worse still, they take advantage of others to achieve their own ends, which makes them terrible managers. They lack empathy. All are unwilling to recognise or identify with the feelings and needs of others. They have desperately low emotional intelligence. Curiously they are often envious of others and believe that others are envious of them. They show arrogant, haughty behaviours or attitudes all the time and everywhere at work (and home). At times this can be pretty amusing but is mostly simply frustrating.

Narcissists are super self-confident: they express considerable self-certainty. They are "self-people" – self-asserting, self-possessed, self-aggrandising, self-preoccupied, self-loving and ultimately self-destructive. They really believe in themselves: they were born lucky. At work they are out-going, high-energy, competitive and very "political". They can make good leaders as long as they are not criticised, or made to share glory. They seem to have an insatiable need to be admired, loved and needed. They are often a model of ambitious, driven, high self-esteem, self-disciplined, socially successful people. The world is their stage.

But narcissism is a disorder of self-esteem: it is, in a sense, a cover-up. They self-destruct because their self-aggrandisement blinds their personal and business judgement and perception. At work they exploit others to get ahead, yet they demand special treatment. But their reaction to any sort of criticism is extreme: shame, rage, tantrums. They aim to destroy that criticism, however well intentioned and useful it may be. They are poor empathisers and thus have low emotional intelligence. They can be consumed with envy and disdain of others and prone to depression. Manipulative, demanding and self-centred, even therapists don't like them.

Hogan and Hogan (2001) call these types *Arrogant*. Narcissists expect to be liked, admired, respected, attended to, praised, complimented, and indulged. Their most important and obvious characteristic is a sense of entitlement, excessive self-esteem, and quite often an expectation of success that often leads to real success. They expect to be successful at everything they undertake, believe that people are so interested in them, that books will be written about them, and when their needs and expectations are frustrated, they explode with "narcissistic rage".

What is most distinctive about the narcissists is their self-assurance, which often, paradoxically gives them charisma. Hogan and Hogan (2001) noted that they are the first to speak in a group, and that they hold forth with great confidence, even when they are wrong. They so completely expect to succeed, and take more credit for success than is warranted or fair, that they refuse to acknowledge failure, errors or mistakes. When things go right, it is because of their efforts, when things go wrong, it is someone else's fault. This is a classic attribution error. This leads to some problems with truth telling because they always rationalise, and reinterpret their failures and mistakes, usually by blaming them on others.

Narcissists can be energetic, charismatic, leader-like, and willing to take the initiative to get projects moving. They can be successful in management, sales, and entrepreneurship. However, they are arrogant, vain, overbearing, demanding, self-deceived, and pompous. They are so colourful and engaging that they often attract followers.

Narcissists handle stress and heavy workloads with ease, they are also quite persistent under pressure and they refuse to acknowledge failure. As a result of their inability to acknowledge failures or even mistakes and the way that they resist coaching and ignore negative feedback they are unable to earn from experience.

Oldham and Morris (1991) noted nine characteristics of these types called Self-Confident (see Box 5.4).

Box 5.4 Self-Confident personality style

1   *Self-regard.* Self-Confident individuals believe in themselves and in their abilities. They have no doubt that they are unique and special and that there is a reason for their being on this planet.
2   *The red carpet.* They expect others to treat them well at all times.
3   *Self-propulsion.* Self-Confident people are open about their ambitions and achievements. They energetically and effectively sell themselves, their goals, their projects, and their ideas.
4   *Politics.* They are able to take advantage of the strengths and abilities of other people in order to achieve their goals, and they are shrewd in their dealings with others.
5   *Competition.* They are able competitors, they love getting to the top, and they enjoy staying there.
6   *Dreams.* Self-Confident individuals are able to visualise themselves as the hero, the star, the best in their role, or the most accomplished in their field.
7   *Self-awareness.* These individuals have a keen awareness of their thoughts and feelings and their overall inner state of being.
8   *Poise.* People with the Self-Confident personality style accept compliments, praise, and admiration gracefully and with self-possession.
9   *Sensitivity to criticism.* The Self-Confident style confers an emotional vulnerability to the negative feelings and assessments of others, which are deeply felt, although they may be handled with this style's customary grace.

Source: Adapted from Oldham and Morris (1991, p. 80).

The business world often calls for and rewards arrogant, self-confident, self-important people. They seek out power and abuse it. They thrive in selling jobs and those where they have to work with or in the media. But, as anyone who works with and for them knows, they can destabilise and destroy working groups by their deeply inconsiderate behaviour.

8. Avoidant (Cautious, Sensitive)

This disorder is equally common in men and women and is believed to affect between 0.5 and 1% of the population. People with this disorder appear to be social phobics in that they are socially isolated and withdrawn. Feelings of possible rejection drive them to situations where they are likely to be shunned. They seek acceptance, approval, and affection.

These individuals show social inhibition, feelings of inadequacy, and hypersensitivity to negative evaluation. They are supersensitive, delicate flowers. They are therefore unlikely to reach high levels in the management hierarchy or to be particularly successful at work. They avoid occupational activities that involve significant interpersonal contact, because of fears of criticism, disapproval, or rejection. Any chance of negative feedback is to be avoided. They are unwilling to get involved with people unless certain of being liked, which is pretty difficult at work, or indeed anywhere. They show restraint within intimate relationships because of the fear of being shamed or ridiculed. They are cold fish and always seem to be preoccupied with being criticised or rejected in work situations. They are inhibited in new interpersonal situations because of feelings of inadequacy. They see themselves as socially inept, personally unappealing, or inferior to others. It can be puzzling to imagine how they ever became managers in the first place. Certainly, low self-esteem people rarely make it to the top in business.

These rather sensitive types seek safety: in people and environments that they know and trust. But they can easily become anxious, guarded and worried. Beneath a polite and cool facade they can feel very uneasy. They cope with their anxiety by being prepared for everything. They like life, their friends and work to be safe, secure and predictable. They do not like the new: strangers, unfamiliar people or ways of working. They prefer what they know and they try to make work a home away from home. They can be effective, reliable and steady and show little need for variety and challenge. They like routine and are pleased to help their seniors. But they are not political in organisations and can take refuge in their professionalism. They do well in technical fields that require routine, repetition and habit.

But the avoidants are so afraid of rejection that they live impoverished social lives. The paradox is that they avoid close relationships that could bring them exactly what they want: acceptance and approval. Because they feel isolated, unwanted, and incompetent, they are sure that others will reject them and often, because of their cold, detached behaviour, that is what happens. They are supersensitive to negative feedback and want unconditional love. Yet they believe that one cannot really be loveable unless one is without imperfections. They are often very self-conscious and can feel strong self-contempt and anger towards others; allergic to social anxiety they routinise themselves in a safe world.

Hogan and Hogan (2001, p. 43) call this type *Cautious* and they stress the fear of being criticised, shamed, blamed, humiliated, or somehow disgraced.

They do not handle failure, rejection, or criticism well; as a result, they are constantly on guard against the possibilities of making errors, mistakes, or blunders, that might cause them to be publicly embarrassed. Because they are so alert to possible criticism, they see hazards and threats everywhere, even when others cannot see them. They respond to the possibility of being criticised by hand wringing, perseverance, freezing, becoming very cautious, and by taking no action at all. When they are threatened they will also forbid their staff from taking any initiative. These people are unpopular managers because they are so cautious, indecisive, and controlling.

Avoidant types can be prudent, careful, and meticulous about evaluating risk. They rarely make rash or ill-advised moves, and they can provide sound, prudent advice about intended future courses of action. However, they avoid innovation and resist change, even when it is apparent that something needs to be done. They seem particularly threatened by the new, the different, and the strange, and they vastly prefer to react rather than to take the initiative. If their working world is stable they can thrive: if not their behaviour may be maladaptive.

Under stress, avoidants begin to adhere to established procedures, and will rely on the tried and true rather than on any new technology or other procedures. They may try to control their staff, in fear that someone on the staff will make a mistake and embarrass them, especially with their seniors. They do exactly what their seniors tell them and they enforce standard rules and procedures on their staff and others over whom they have any power. They hate to be criticised; what others will see is cautiousness, rigidity, adherence to standardised procedures, and resistance to innovation and change.

To work with the cautious type, reports need to keep them well informed about activities that concern them where negative outcomes could reflect on them, and to consult them about intended future actions. When rapid action is needed, or when some form of innovation needs to be implemented, it is best to avoid them or put in writing the fact that you recommend action or innovation, then be prepared for nothing to happen.

9. Dependent (Dutiful, Devoted)

People with this disorder are more heavily reliant on other people for support or guidance than most. Like young children, they can be clinging, submissive, and subservient in all relationships and fear separation. Dependents are carers – most happy helping others to be happy. Others give meaning to their lives. They worry about others and need others. They find contentment in attachment and define themselves by others. They are not good at giving (or receiving) criticism and negative feedback. At work they are cooperative, supportive, caring and encouraging. They do brilliantly in jobs like nursing, social work and voluntary organisations, but rarely take on senior positions that require managerial duties. As managers they have a pervasive and excessive need to be taken care of by others. This leads to submissive and clinging behaviour and fears of separation.

As managers they suffer analysis paralysis. They cannot make decisions on their own without continual advice and reassurance from others. They need to assume responsibility for most major areas of their lives. Inevitably they are good at delegating, but they seem always to need help and reassurance. Most have difficulty expressing disagreement with others because of the fear of loss of support or approval. They publicly agree while privately disagreeing. This, of course, makes them difficult to read. They all have difficulty initiating projects or doing things on their own (because of a lack of self-confidence in judgement or abilities rather than a lack of motivation or energy). So, they resist change, particularly where it leads to them being isolated or threatened. Some go to excessive lengths to obtain nurturance and support from others often humiliating themselves in the process. All feel uncomfortable or helpless when alone because of exaggerated fears of being unable to care for themselves at work (and home).

Dependent people do not make good managers because they are too quick to be apologetic, submissive and self-depreciating. They attach themselves to others who may all too easily take advantage of them. Kind, gentle, generous and full of humility they do not believe in themselves. They have very low self-confidence in all aspects of life and acquire self-esteem through their attachments to others. Despite their smiling exterior they often feel depression and dejection. Further, they can doom the relationships they value so much because they are too clinging and eager to please.

Hogan and Hogan (2001) noted that they are deeply concerned about being accepted, being liked and getting along, especially with authority figures. They are hyper-alert for signs of disapproval, and for opportunities to ingratiate themselves, to be of service, to demonstrate their fealty and loyalty to the organisation. When they think they have given offence, they redouble their efforts to be model citizens. People notice their good nature, their politeness, their cordiality, and their indecisiveness. As managers, they will do anything their boss requires, which means that they are reluctant to stick up for their staff or challenge authority, and this inevitably erodes their legitimacy as leaders.

They are polite, conforming, and eager to please. They rarely make enemies and they tend to rise in organisations. But they have problems making decisions, taking initiative, or taking stands on tough issues. Thus their sections tend to drift, and they can have trouble maintaining a team.

They respond to stress by freezing and becoming passive, and by hoping that someone else will take the initiative, step up, make a decision, assign responsibility and get things moving. They are too reliant on the initiative of others and can become a bottleneck for productivity and a source of delay and lost time.

They are deeply concerned with pleasing authority, which, in turn, is pleasing to authority, but they provide little leadership for those who must work for them. To work with them, reports must be prepared for indecisiveness, inaction, and lack of leadership. Reports must also be prepared to take the initiative when processes get stalled, but accept the fact that they won't be supported should their initiative fail or backfire. Hogan and Hogan (2001) believed that to work with these people, you must be prepared to flatter them, to agree with them, to be exploited, to allow them to take credit for your accomplishments, and allow them to blame you for their failures.

This personality disorder is nearly always associated with being a number two rather than a number one in any relationship. Even so, they may have a staff that they inevitably do not manage well.

10. Passive-Aggressive (Leisurely)

This personality type is very concerned about "doing their own thing". They demand the "right to be me". They have a right to do their thing in their way and no one has the right to deprive them of it. They believe at work and in private relationships nobody has the right to own them. They like the companionship of others but need strong defences against being ill-used. They are particularly sensitive to fairness.

They do not find the workplace of great importance. They can be good managers and workers. But they do not work overtime, take it home or worry much about it. They certainly will not do any more than their contract specifies. They do not work to please their boss or feel better about themselves. They are often heard saying, "It's not my job", and they tend to be suspicious of workplace authority. If their boss asks them to work harder, faster, or more accurately they feel unfairly treated, even abused. They are supersensitive to their rights, fairness and exploitation avoidance. They seem leisurely; they believe success is not everything. They tend not to be found above middle-management levels because they are not ambitious or thrusting enough. For them the game is not worth the candle.

Passive-Aggressive types are not usually stressed. They sulk, procrastinate and forget when asked to do things they think are not fair. They are called Passive-Aggressive because they are rarely openly defiant; yet they are often angry. They snipe rather than confront, and they are often furious. They can be needy but resentful about those moods. They are, in essence, oppositional: not assertive. They often have downward job mobility.

Hogan and Hogan (2001) called these people *Leisurely*. They argued that these types march to the sound of their own drum, they are confident about their skills and abilities, cynical about the talents and intentions of others – especially superiors, and they insist on working at their own pace. They tend to get angry and slow down even more when asked to speed up. They tend to feel mistreated, unappreciated and put upon and when they sense that they have been cheated, they retaliate, but always under conditions of high deniability. Curiously, they are quite skilled at hiding their annoyance and pretending to be cooperative, and their peevishness and foot dragging are often very hard to detect.

They are often late for meetings, they procrastinate, they work at around 80% of their capacity, and they are very stubborn and hard to coach. They will rarely directly confront others. Their prickly sensitivity, subtle uncooperativeness, stubbornness, and deep absorption make them both unpredictable and unrewarding to deal with. As a result, they have trouble building and maintaining a team.

Passive-Aggressives handle stress and heavy work loads by slowing down, by simply ignoring requests for greater output, and by finding ways to get out of work. Because they seem overtly cooperative and agreeable, it takes a long time to realise how unproductive and refractory they actually can be. They are self-centred, they focus on their own agendas, and they deeply believe in their own superior natural talent and their right to leisure. They believe they have nothing to prove to themselves, are quite indifferent to feedback from others, and therefore become annoyed and resentful when criticised or asked for extra effort.

People need to be aware that they are not nearly as cooperative as they seem, and that they are only pretending to agree with you about work and performance issues. Also, they need to get them to commit to performance goals in public, in front of witnesses, so that a community of people can hold them accountable. Social pressure won't change their views of the world, but it will serve to make their performance deficits less easily deniable.

Oldham and Morris (1991) claim that five traits and behaviours are clues to the presence of what they call the Leisurely style (Box 5.5). A person who reveals a strong Leisurely tendency will demonstrate more of these behaviours more intensely than someone with less of this style in his or her personality profile.

Box 5.5 The Leisurely style

1   *Inalienable rights.* Leisurely men and women believe in their right to enjoy themselves on their own terms in their own time. They value and protect their comfort, their free time, and their individual pursuit of happiness.
2   *Enough is enough.* They agree to play by the rules. They deliver what is expected of them and no more. They expect others to recognise and respect that limit.
3   *The right to resist.* Leisurely individuals cannot be exploited. They can comfortably resist acceding to demands that they deem unreasonable or above and beyond the call of duty.
4   *Mañana.* Leisurely men and women are relaxed about time. Unlike Type A individuals, they are not obsessed by time urgency or the demands of the clock. To these individuals, haste makes waste and unnecessary anxiety. They are easygoing and optimistic that whatever needs to get done will get done, eventually.
5   *I'm okay.* They are not overawed by authority. They accept themselves and their approach to life. They are content with their place in the universe.

Source: Adapted from Oldham and Morris (1991, pp. 194–195).

There are many senior managers with this rather unattractive profile. Their "pathology" may have served them well even if the burden of it has been "picked-up" by their long-suffering staff. This personality disorder is so pervasive, however, that it has disappeared from some categorisations of the disorders.

11. Obsessive-Compulsive (Diligent, Conscientious)

This disorder is more common in men and around 1% of the population exhibit the symptoms. They are often known for their zealous perfectionism, for their attention to detail, for their rigidity and for their formality. They are also often the workaholics; those who really "live" the work ethic. They are competent, organised, thorough, and loyal. They enjoy, even in their holidays, leisure time being intense, detailed, goal-orientated activity.

These managers show a preoccupation with orderliness, perfectionism, and mental and interpersonal control, at the expense of flexibility, openness, and efficiency. They are the most anal of bureaucrats. They are always preoccupied with details, rules, lists, order, organisation, or schedules to the extent that the major point of the business activity is lost and forgotten. All show perfectionism that interferes with task completion (e.g. he or she is unable to complete a project because his or her own overly strict standards are not met). And, of course, they demand it in others however unproductive it makes them. These managers are often seriously driven workaholics who exclude leisure activities and friendships. They have a well-deserved reputation for being over-conscientious, scrupulous, and inflexible about matters of morality, ethics, or values.

They are (often amazingly) unable to discard worn-out or worthless objects even when they have no sentimental value. They hoard rubbish at home and in the work-place. They are reluctant to delegate tasks or to work with others unless they submit exactly to their way of doing things. They do not let go and pay the price. They are misers towards both self and others; money is viewed as something to be hoarded for future catastrophes. Because they never fully spend their budget they never get it increased. In short they show rigidity and stubbornness and are thus very unpleasant to work for.

Conscientious, obsessive-compulsives rise through the ranks through hard work. But at certain levels they start to derail because they have problems in making quick decisions, setting priorities and delegating. They tend to want to check the details again and again. They function best as right-hand men to leaders with strong conceptual skills and visions. They are very self-disciplined and put work first. They are often not very emotionally literate and can be fanatical and fundamentalist about moral, political and religious issues. They can find it difficult to relax and difficult to throw things away. Their relationships are marked by conventionality and coolness. They are faithful and responsible but unromantic and unemotional. They can be seen as mean and over-cautious.

The obsessive-compulsive manager *must* have everything done *perfectly*. They get wrapped up in details and lose any sense of directions and priorities. They can be tyrannical bosses who are super-attentive to time, orderliness and cleanliness. They are driven by "oughts" and "shoulds" and expect others to be likewise. They make rules for themselves and others and are rigid, perfectionistic and controlling. They are the over-bearing, fault-finders of the business world. They are driven to achieve respect and approval and control their, and others', dangerous impulses, desires and feelings.

Hogan and Hogan (2001) called these types *Diligent* because they are concerned with doing a good job, being a good citizen, and pleasing authority. They noted that the Diligent type is hard working, careful, planful, meticulous, and has very high standards of performance both for themselves and other people. They live by these rules and expect others to do so too, and they become irritable and erratic when others do not follow their rules. What is most distinctive is their conservatism, their detail orientation, and their risk aversion, but they are also thought of as reliable, dependable, and pre-dictable. They are often desirable organisational citizens who can always be relied upon to maintain standards, do their work competently and professionally, and treat their colleagues with respect.

Hogan and Hogan suggest that they are good role models who uphold the highest standards of professionalism in performance and comportment. They are popular with their bosses because they are so completely reliable, but not necessarily those who report to them. However, they are fussy, particularly nit-picking, micro-managers who deprive their subordinates of any choice or control over their work. This alienates their staff who soon refuse to take any initiative and simply wait to be told what to do and how to do it. Diligent, conscientious, obsessive-compulsives also cause stress for them-selves; their obsessive concern for quality and high performance makes it difficult for them to delegate. It also makes it difficult for them to prioritise their tasks. They also have problems with vision and the big picture. Consequently, they have a kind of ambivalent status as managers and can function in some environments at certain levels.

Diligent obsessionals tend to become stressed by heavy workloads. They respond to increased workloads by working longer and harder (not smarter) and they fall further and further behind, and they find this intolerable. They often become a bottleneck to productivity – because everything must pass through them, be checked and revised by them or be approved by them, and they will not let anything go that is not completed according to their standards. They closely supervise their staff. It can help to make suggestions regarding prioritising work, and by putting tasks into context by reflecting on the big picture.

The diligent, conscientious type *can* do *very well* in business. Certain jobs demand obsessive-compulsive checking such as health and safety and quality control. But like all the other disorders it is too much of this trait that leads to serious problems both for the individual and his or her staff. It often leads to phobia, and other stress-related illnesses. Just as in all the other disorders there is a curvilinear relationship between the disorder and success at work. Too little diligence and dutifulness is as detrimental as too much.

12. Self-Defeating (Self-sacrificing)

These are the self-sacrificing altruists of the personality-disordered world. They achieve meaning in life and satisfaction through serving others and sacrificing for them. They may feel undeserving of attention and pleasure and unworthy of love, and therefore they have to earn it. They work long and hard for others and give their all in relationships. But they do not want thanks or attention and feel discomfort with positive compliments or praise. They seem guilty but they can be seriously neglected and under-recognised, which does cause pain and confusion. They tend not to have their own needs met. They see life as tough, unfair and uncompromising and their job is to help those less fortunate than themselves. They are good under stress but can get resentful if consistently ignored.

To a large extent the self-defeating personality is ideal at work. Hard-working, respectful and adaptable, they are, however, very concerned about the value and meaning of the work. They make reliable, loyal, undemanding, non-assertive workers. However, they rarely realise their potential: they turn down promotion for others.

Self-defeatists rarely end up as managers. But their dedication and loyalty may mean that they end up in middle-management positions. However, inevitably they have problems with delegation and discipline and take on too much themselves. They may feel, quite rightly, that their staff are ungrateful and underperform. Some, but a minority, may demand that staff expect their subordinates to adopt similar self-sacrificial behaviour as themselves.

Because they have problems with success they may suffer the imposter's syndrome and consciously or unconsciously self-destruct. And, of course, they are immensely vulnerable to exploitation by others. Their generosity makes them masochists, which was the term previously used for this disorder.

13. Sadistic (Aggressive)

The sadistic personality-disordered individual is aggressive. They are strong, forceful, courageous, pugilistic and confident. They want to be leader, "top dog". They have a need to dominate and organise others. Hence they are autocratic, dictatorial and can be immoral. They give orders, make rules, and run the show.

At work they are ambitious and purposeful. They have the drive for power. They thrive in the win–lose, dog-eat-dog, rough-and-tumble of the business world. They are not squeamish or sentimental and can be very tough. They thrive when they have clear goals and directions. And the end justifies the means: which is where the problem can begin.

They can make brilliant managers: goal orientated, organised, disciplined. But they focus on results not feelings. They demand total loyalty and hard work and have little patience with errors, inefficiency, waste or failure of any type. They also do not like being bored. The most serious source of stress for them is losing power. They need to know power and how to manipulate it.

They have strong emotions but strong control over them. They tend to be more crafty and shrewd than physically aggressive, but they do bully, hurt and humiliate others who are subordinate to, and dependent on, them. They are disciplinarians who can easily inflict pain. Hence they can be very malevolent.

Oldham and Morris (1991) specified six criteria of the Aggressive style, as they called it (Box 5.6).

Box 5.6 The Aggressive style

The following six traits and behaviours are clues to the presence of the Aggressive style. A person who reveals a strong Self-Sacrificing tendency will demonstrate more of these behaviours more intensely than someone with less of this style in his or her personality profile.

1 *Command.* Aggressive individuals take charge. They are comfortable with power, authority, and responsibility.
2 *Hierarchy.* They operate best within a traditional power structure where everyone knows his or her place and the lines of authority are clear.
3 *Tight ship.* They are highly disciplined and impose rules of order that they expect others in their charge to follow.
4 *Expedience.* Aggressive men and women are highly goal directed. They take a practical, pragmatic approach to accomplishing their objectives. They do what is necessary to get the job done.
5 *Guts.* They are neither squeamish nor fainthearted. They can function well and bravely in difficult and dangerous situations without being distracted by fear or horror.
6 *The rough and tumble.* Aggressive people like action and adventure. They are physically assertive and often participate in or enjoy playing competitive sports, especially contact sports.

Source: Adapted from Oldham and Morris (1991, pp. 336–337).

The bullying, aggressive, sadist has often punched, clawed and scratched their way to the top. They are very difficult to work with and soon derail established working groups.

Pathological organisations

Kets de Vries and Miller (1985) have suggested that the language of personality disorders can actually be used to describe and explain the often bizarre processes that occur in organisations. They argued that senior managers influence the organisational style in their image. Their disorders influence (create and sustain) corporate cultures. Strategy, process, structure, selection, even advertising, reflect their personal pathology. Powerful but disturbed leaders create businesses in their image in order to deal, often unsuccessfully, with their personal pathologies. Thus the whole organisation takes on the pathology of the single manager. What Kets de Vries and Miller (1985) do is to take selective categories of personality disorder and show how powerful leaders with these psychiatric disorders actually form companies in their own image sharing similar pathologies. They identified five neurotic styles, although, to be accurate, some are actually psychotic.

1. The paranoid organisation

When power is highly centralised in a leader with paranoid tendencies ("everybody is out to get me"), there will tend to be a great deal of vigilance caused by distrust of subordinates and competitors alike. This may lead to the development of many control and information systems and a conspiratorial fascination with gathering intelligence from inside and outside the firm. Paranoid thinking will also lead to a centralisation of power as the top executive tries to control everything himself (no one can be completely trusted). The strategy is likely to emphasise "protection" and reduce dependency on particular consultants, sources of data, markets or customers. There is likely to be a good deal of diversification, with tight control over divisions and much analytical activity. A leader who is obsessed with fantasies concerning distrust can set a very distinctive tone for the strategy, structure and culture of an organisation.

The characteristics of these paranoid organisations are easy to describe. Suspiciousness and mistrust of others; hyper-sensitivity and hyper-alertness; readiness to combat perceived threats; excessive concern with hidden motives and special meanings; intense attention span; cold, rational, unemotional, interpersonal relations. The paranoid organisation is defensive and hyper-vigilant. It is pervaded by an atmosphere of distrust. But this can have benefits – certainly such organisations will be alert to threats and opportunities inside and outside the organisation. A small advantage, perhaps, and at a great cost.

2. The compulsive organisation

An *obsessive-compulsive* manager leads to the development of a *compulsive organisation*. A compulsive organisation emphasises ritual; it plans every detail in advance and carries out its activities in a routine, pre-programmed style. Thoroughness and conformity are valued. Such organisations are hierarchical and generally have elaborate policies, rules and procedures. The strategies of compulsive firms reflect their preoccupation with detail and established rituals. Each compulsive organisation has a distinctive area of competence and specialises in this area, whether or not the area is related to the marketplace.

For Kets de Vries and Miller (1985) these organisations are characterised by: perfectionism; preoccupation with trivial details; insistence that others submit to an established way of doing things; relationships defined in terms of dominance and submission; lack of spontaneity; inability to relax; meticulousness, dogmatism and obstinacy. This is the military organisation that Dixon (1981) talks about so eloquently. Compulsive managers are inward looking, indecisive, cautious and fearful about making mistakes. They are deeply involved in the minutiae of facts and figures and love promulgating rules and regulations to make their lives easier. They are often inflexible, oriented to the past and unwilling to change. They typically have excellent internal control and audit mechanisms and well-integrated procedures. But all too often they are anachronistic bureaucracies that seem out of touch with the flexible and adaptive companies of today. The faster the world changes, the more incompetent they are – change is an enemy not an opportunity.

3. The dramatic organisation

The *impulsive, creative, intuitive* manager will also stamp his or her organisation in characteristic ways. The *dramatic organisation* is hyperactive, impulsive and uninhibited. In such an organisation, decision makers prefer to act on hunches and impressions, and take on widely diverse projects. Top managers reserve the right to start bold ventures independently; subordinates have limited power.

Such organisations are characterised by: self-dramatisation and excessive emotional displays; incessant self-displays organised around crises; a need for activity and excitement; an alternation between idealisation and devaluation of others; exploitativeness; inability to concentrate or sharply focus attention. This is not only the world of "Ad-land" but increasingly that of e-commerce.

Dramatic managers are not risk averse. They often make rash, intuitive decisions, swinging company policy in radically different directions. They are impulsive and unpredictable. At their best they can revitalise tired companies and provide the necessary momentum at crucial periods in a company's history (merger and acquisition or start-up). But most of the time they simply create instability, chaos and distress. A major task of any manager is to bring order and predictability to business issues, not the opposite.

4. The depressive organisation

Many people are prone to depression or may experience periods of depression caused by stress or trauma. But some managers seem always to have depressive symptoms, and this can lead to *depressive organisations*. The depressive organisation lacks confidence, is inactive, conservative and insular, and has an entrenched bureaucracy. The only things that get done are routine activities. Depressive organisations are well established and often serve a single, mature market.

The characteristics of a depressive manager and the organisation he or she creates in his or her own image are feelings of guilt, worthlessness, self-reproach, inadequacy and a sense of helplessness and hopelessness – of being at the mercy of events; there is also a diminished ability to experience pleasure. Depressives are negative, pessimistic and inhibited. Apathetic, inactive, hopeless managers are prevalent in these organisations. The gloom pervades all.

5. *The schizoid organisation*

The fifth type of *neurotic* organisation according to Kets de Vries and Miller (1985) is called schizoid. The *schizoid organisation* lacks leadership. Its top executive discourages interaction. Sometimes the second level of executives makes up for the leader's lack of involvement, but often they simply fight to fill the leadership vacuum. In such organisations strategy often reflects individuals' goals and internal politics rather than the external threats or opportunities the organisation needs to take into account.

These organisations are characterised by: detachment, non-involvement and withdrawal; a sense of estrangement; a lack of excitement or enthusiasm; an indifference to praise or criticism; a lack of interest in present or future; and a cold and unemotional climate. These organisations are quite political and the resulting climate of distrust inhibits normal collaboration.

Kets de Vries and Miller (1985) suggested that the unconscious and neurotic needs of the key people in an organisation lead them to do things to the organisation that create incompetence. Observations suggested that neurotic managers choose, create and maintain dysfunctional work groups that have shared organisational myths, and that these myths often distract them from primary tasks. Their neuroticism means that they transfer their anxieties and odd imaginings on to their staff (superiors, subordinates, peers and even shareholders and customers) and this frustrates and angers staff who may be somehow bound to or curiously abandoned by their neurotic managers.

Conclusion

Academics interested in the personality disorders have disagreements and debates over three issues: classification, origin of the disorders and treatment for them. The issue of classification is that there may be, quite simply, too much *overlap* among the diagnoses to really justify so many categories. Thus, although some personality disorders have quite unique and distinctive features they appear to share common traits. The *line or divide* between normal, rational, healthy behaviour and abnormal, self-defeating behaviour is often a fine one. It is where behaviours (suspiciousness in the paranoid; exaggerating importance in the narcissistic) are pervasive, inflexible and maladaptive causing chronic and acute personal distress that means they probably should be diagnosed as having a fully-blown personality disorder. There are also suggestions and, indeed, evidence of *sex bias* – women are more likely to be diagnosed borderline, histrionic and males schizoid.

Most importantly, perhaps diagnosticians should not *confuse labels with explanations*. Such labelling also causes attribution errors by ignoring social, cultural and environmental factors that may play a part.

No approach does very well in accounting for the origin of all the disorders. Psychoanalysts believe they can in part explain the borderline and narcissistic disorders, while those with a more physiological bent believe they are good at explaining the aetiology of the antisocial personality.

Personality-disordered people are more likely to be referred to treatment by others than to seek it themselves. What do they find? Interestingly, many therapists do not like dealing with patients who can be demanding, manipulative and fickle. Some even believe that people with certain disorders are really beyond the reach of therapy.

Some therapies attempt to teach acceptable interpersonal behaviours; others actively confront a person's defences. Some try to work on a person's beliefs about themselves, trying the correct distortions that suggest that they are either all good or all bad. Personality-disordered patients need social and problem-solving skills, which can be taught. Incarcerated patients (in prisons, residential homes) may be put on a token economy schedule such that they get rewarded (in tokens) for good behaviour (only), which can be exchanged for all sorts of privileges. Interestingly drug therapies are very seldom used for this disorder.

The implications for those interested in individual differences at work is this. One can think of disorders as extreme traits. The line between pathology and normality is unclear. Under stress those prone to disorder processes often show their dark side. This is not unusual and the distribution of the disorders in the population means they are probably quite common at work. There is, however, one other more important implication noted by Furnham (2007a). Some disorders, in the short-run, actually appear to benefit business careers.

As McCall (1998) pointed out, often when talented people are promoted in organisations their obvious abilities and strengths mean that selectors ignore or downplay weaknesses and problems, which then return to haunt them in the form of the derailed senior manager. Many people assume that these pathological disorders will easily be diagnosed and that it is virtually impossible for such individuals to rise to important positions in business. That is simply not true and there is increasing evidence that well-known and initially respected politicians, religious leaders, lawyers and businessmen have turned out to be clearly diagnosable as having a disorder.

Paradoxically, perhaps, three personality disorders (psychopath, narcissist, histrionic) may indeed help people in many business settings. The willingness to take risks on the part of the psychopath, the confidence of the narcissist; the emotional maverickness of the histrionic may make them particularly attractive to certain people in certain businesses.

The data on the prognosis for the personality disorders are not hopeful. They are unlikely to be changed much, though they can be managed. There is no very clear cut-off point on the continua that make up these three disorders. People may be on the borderline rather than in the "dangerous" area, which clearly makes them less of a risk than if they were at more extreme points on the continuum.

The intelligent, educated, middle-class individual with one (or more) of these disorders no doubt fares better. They can even be seen as an asset at certain times in the business cycle. But over the long term they are likely to reap problems for themselves, their direct reports, their colleagues and their company. They can, as a single individual, turn the happy, efficient and functional workplace into one where people distrust each other, sabotage work and under-perform. As powerful individuals they can often be seen as the root cause of the shift from a functional to a dysfunctional workplace.

As noted earlier, this area of study is based more on case studies than large-scale psychometric studies. Further, some of the idea are strictly speculative and thus essentially hypotheses. However, it does remain an important new area of research: organisational psychiatry. It has very important implications for management derailment, stress and failure, which is a seriously unresearched area.

6   Cognitive ability at work

Introduction

It takes a clever, but also a courageous, academic to research the topic of intelligence – or general mental ability (GMA) these days. One perhaps has to be even more confident and certain as a human resource manager to suggest, and then use, intelligence (cognitive ability) tests in selection, appraisal, assessment and development centres. The topic has become highly politically loaded and cries by researchers to be left alone to do disinterested scientific enquiry fall on deaf ears.

Certainly intelligence testing has had a chequered and controversial history in psychology. Yet research from *many scholars* over *many areas* in *many countries* and *over a century* has demonstrated the pervasive influence of intelligence in *all walks* of life from health and happiness to wealth and welfare. It is a basic building block for the differential psychologist. It is, quite simply, the most easily and reliably measured individual difference variable with the best reliability and validity.

The last 10–20 years have seen different attempts to expand the concept of intelligence (social, practical; see Chapter 7), to devise tests of greater face validity and acceptability, to monitor group (sex, race) differences carefully, and to provide incontrovertible evidence of the predictive validity of tests.

Those investigating the relationship between cognitive ability and job performance have agreed on the basis of the data numerous times. *First*, validities are around the .3 to .5 mark, and higher for training than job performance. *Second*, validity increases with job complexity but also the validity generalises well across countries, criteria, jobs, settings and industries. *Third*, intelligence is, quite simply, the *best predictor of overall job and training* (and specific task) performance. *Fourth*, the predictive validity of tests increases as job complexity increases. *Fifth*, measuring very specific abilities (like verbal or numerical ability) does not give much incremental advantage over general IQ or mental ability scores.

There are many fundamental psychometric questions about intelligence which get asked again and again:

- Do intelligence tests have good reliability? Yes. Only high anxiety or situationally induced low motivation causes test–retest correlations to drop below $r = .90$.
- Are IQ scores stable over (lifetime)? Yes. By late childhood tests reasonably accurately predict adult scores as many as fifty years later.
- Do intelligence tests have adequate validity? Yes. They predict school success

(around $r = .50$) and how long people remain in school ($r = .70$), and many other educational, or organisational and social variables.

- Do intelligence tests predict job performance and academic success? Yes. There are various caveats to this question, which is central to this chapter and this book, which will be discussed later in detail.
- But are there not multiple intelligences? No. Not in the sense that most people are very good at some cognitive tasks and very bad at others. Generally we find that scores on all sorts of (good) IQ tests correlate positively and significantly with one another. That is, people perform at a broadly similar level across all tasks (vocabulary, maths, etc.).
- Are all IQ tests equally good? No. It takes quite some effort to develop, refine and produce a test that gives an all-round picture of a person's cognitive functioning.

Other questions include:

- The psychometric properties of tests, specifically reliability and validity. Nearly always the most interesting type of validity sought is predictive validity, which asks the fundamental question asked in this chapter: Do test scores predict later behavioural outcomes? There is now considerable evidence that good IQ test scores do correlate with all sorts of issues like academic achievement, occupational performance and status.
- One intelligence (general intelligence) or many (multiple intelligences)?
- How much is intelligence shaped by environment vs. heredity?
- How much can intelligence be enhanced?

Most people are familiar with the many and frequent objections to tests. Consider the following *all of which are erroneous*:

- All IQ tests are timed but the ability to think fast is not necessarily the ability to think well.
- All tests are culture bound – devised for, and by, white middle class (males) to their advantage.
- All they measure is how rich a person's parents are/were and how much education they had.
- There are many very different types of intelligence and no one test (or even battery) can properly measure them all.
- The more you practise the higher your score. They therefore measure only effort not ability.
- We all know seriously bright people who never excel at school or in jobs. Test scores predict nothing.
- Test scores change. You can increase your intelligence. Scores should measure potential not how well you do today.

In this chapter different issues will be discussed. *First*, a brief overview of the issues of intelligence research will be covered. *Second*, the current state of the art will be reviewed with an emphasis on what researchers agree about, and what they find to be important questions to try to answer. *Third*, and most importantly, the research on intelligence in the workplace will be covered. This essentially aims to examine the empirical literature on the data and explanation for intelligence test scores and measured work output. As noted above, the world of intelligence testing is one where passion and prejudice surpass disinterested evaluation. Eysenck (1998), in his last book, lists five widely held and false beliefs about intelligence:

1   Psychologists disagree about the nature and definition of intelligence. He points out that debates about certain aspects of intelligence have little to do with fundamental agreement on the basics. Also, with few exceptions, all experts in the area largely agree with one another.
2   IQ tests measure nothing important; merely the ability to do IQ tests. "Nobody who has even the most passing acquaintance with IQ testing would ever make such an outrageous statement" (p. 8).
3   The notion that differences in IQ are largely determined by heredity has been disproved. "Quite the contrary is true." Indeed the pendulum has swung dramatically against the environmentalist position, not only in the world of intelligence but also everywhere else in psychological research.
4   IQ testing was invented to maintain the "status quo" and strengthened the ruling class. He argues that IQ testing leads to meritocracy and social mobility. In other words it has the precise opposite effect, by identifying a person's potential, whatever their background, and giving them a chance to realise that potential.
5   IQ testing was introduced to bolster the claims of the white race to superiority. Eysenck points out that the data in fact suggest that the Japanese and Chinese score higher than White Americans or Europeans.

It is these myths that frustrate researchers as well as selectors who are trying to select the best candidate.

The publication of a highly controversial book on intelligence (*The Bell Curve*; Herrnstein & Murray, 1994) and passionate, although not necessarily well-informed, debate led over 50 of the world's experts on intelligence to write to the *Wall Street Journal* on 15 December 1994. Their 25-point summary (see Box 6.1) is an excellent and clear statement on what psychologists think about intelligence.

Box 6.1 Psychologists' thoughts on intelligence

The meaning and measurement of intelligence

1   Intelligence is a very general mental capability that, among other things, involves the ability to reason, plan, solve problems, think abstractly, comprehend complex ideas, learn quickly and learn from experience. It is not merely book learning, a narrow academic skill, or descriptive of test-taking smarts. Rather, it reflects a broader and deeper capability for comprehending our surroundings – "catching on", "making sense" of things, or "figuring out" what to do.
2   Intelligence, so defined, can be measured, and intelligence tests measure it well. They are among the most accurate (in technical terms, reliable and

valid) of all psychological tests and assessments. They do not measure creativity, character, personality or other important differences among individuals, nor are they intended to.

3   While there are different types of intelligence tests, they all measure the same intelligence. Some use words or numbers and require specific cultural knowledge (such as vocabulary). Others do not, and instead use shapes or designs and require knowledge of only simple, universal concepts (many/few, open/closed, up/down).

4   The spread of people along the IQ continuum, from low to high, can be represented well by the bell curve (in statistical jargon, the "normal curve"). Most people cluster around the average (IQ 100). Few are either very bright or very dull: About 3% of Americans score above IQ 130 (often considered the threshold for "giftedness"), with about the same percentage below IQ 70 (IQ 70–75 often being considered the threshold for mental retardation).

5   Intelligence tests are not culturally biased against African American or other native-born, English-speaking people in the USA. Rather, IQ scores predict equally accurately for all such Americans, regardless of race and social class. Individuals who do not understand English well can be given either a non-verbal test or one in their native language.

6   The brain processes underlying intelligence are still little understood. Current research looks, for example, at speed of neural transmission, glucose (energy) uptake and electrical activity of the brain.

Group differences

7   Members of all racial-ethnic groups can be found at every IQ level. The bell curves of different groups overlap considerably, but groups often differ in where their members tend to cluster along the IQ line. The bell curves for some groups (Jews and East Asians) are centered somewhat higher than for Whites in general. Other groups (Blacks and Hispanics) are centered somewhat lower than non-Hispanic Whites.

8   The bell curve for Whites is centered roughly around IQ 100; the bell curve for American Blacks roughly around IQ 85; and those for different subgroups of Hispanics roughly mid way between those for Whites and Blacks. The evidence is less definitive for exactly where above IQ 100 the bell curves for Jews and Asian are centered.

Practical importance

9   IQ is strongly related, probably more so than any other single measurable human trait, to many important educational, occupational, economic and social outcomes. Its relation to the welfare and performance of individuals is very strong in some arenas in life (education, military training), moderate but robust in others (social competence), and modest but consistent in others (law-abidingness). Whatever IQ tests measure, it is of great practical and social importance.

10   A high IQ is an advantage in life because virtually all activities require some reasoning and decision making. Conversely, a low IQ is often a disadvantage, especially in disorganized environments. Of course, a high IQ no more guarantees success than a low IQ guarantees failure in life. There are many exceptions, but the odds for success in our society greatly favor individuals with higher IQs.

11   The practical advantages of having a higher IQ increase as life settings become more complex (novel, ambiguous, changing, unpredictable or multi-faceted). For example, a high IQ is generally necessary to perform well in highly complex or fluid jobs (the professions, management); it is a considerable advantage in moderately complex jobs (crafts, clerical and police work); but it provides less advantage in settings that require only routine decision making or simple problem solving (unskilled work).

12   Differences in intelligence certainly are not the only factor affecting performance in education, training and highly complex jobs (no one claims they are), but intelligence is often the most important. When individuals have already been selected for high (or low) intelligence and so do not differ as much in IQ, as in graduate school (or special education), other influences on performance loom larger in comparison.

13   Certain personality traits, special talents, aptitudes, physical capabilities, experience and the like are important (sometimes essential) for successful performance in many jobs, but they have narrower (or unknown) applicability or "transferability" across tasks and settings compared with general intelligence. Some scholars choose to refer to these other human traits as other "intelligences".

Source and stability of within-group differences

14   Individuals differ in intelligence due to differences in both their environments and genetic heritage. Heritability estimates range from 0.4 to 0.8 (on a scale from 0 to 1), most thereby indicating that genetics plays a bigger role than does environment in creating IQ differences among individuals. (Heritability is the squared correlation of phenotype with genotype.) If all environments were to become equal for everyone, heritability would rise to 100% because nearly all remaining differences in IQ would necessarily be genetic in origin.

15   Members of the same family also tend to differ substantially in intelligence (by an average of about 12 IQ points) for both genetic and environmental reasons. They differ genetically because biological brothers and sisters share exactly half their genes with each parent and, on average, only half with each other. They also differ in IQ because they experience different environments within the same family.

16   That IQ may be highly heritable does not mean that it is not affected by the environment. Individuals are not born with fixed, unchangeable levels of intelligence (no one claims they are). IQs do gradually stabilize during childhood, however, and generally change little thereafter.

17   Although the environment is important in creating IQ differences, we do not know yet how to manipulate it to raise low IQs permanently. Whether recent attempts show promise is still a matter of considerable scientific debate.

18 Genetically caused differences are not irremediable (consider diabetes, poor vision and phenylketonuria), nor are environmentally caused ones necessarily remediable (consider injuries, poisons, neglect and some diseases). Both may be preventable to some extent.

Source and stability of between-group differences

19 There is no persuasive evidence that the IQ bell curves for different racial-ethnic groups are converging. Surveys in some years show that gaps in academic achievement have narrowed a bit for some races, ages, school subjects and skill levels, but this picture seems too mixed to reflect a general shift in IQ levels themselves.

20 Racial-ethnic differences in IQ bell curves are essentially the same when youngsters leave high school as when they enter first grade. However, because bright youngsters learn faster than slow learners, these same IQ differences lead to growing disparities in amount learned as youngsters progress from grades one to twelve. As large national surveys in the USA continue to show, Black 17-year-olds perform, on average, more like White 13-year-olds in reading, maths and science, with Hispanics in between.

21 The reasons that Blacks differ among themselves in intelligence appear to be basically the same as those for why Whites (or Asians or Hispanics) differ among themselves. Both environment and genetic heredity are involved.

22 There is no definitive answer to why IQ bell curves differ across racial-ethnic groups. The reasons for these IQ differences between groups may be markedly different from the reasons why individuals differ among themselves within any particular group (Whites or Blacks or Asians). In fact, it is wrong to assume, as many do, that the reason why some individuals in a population have high IQs but others have low IQs must be the same reason why some populations contain more such high (or low) IQ individuals than others. Most experts believe that environment is important in pushing the bell curves apart, but that genetics could be involved too.

23 Racial-ethnic differences are somewhat smaller but still substantial for individuals from the same socioeconomic backgrounds. To illustrate, Black students from prosperous families tend to score higher in IQ than Blacks from poor families, but they score no higher, on average, than Whites from poor families.

24 Almost all Americans who identify themselves as Black have White ancestors – the White admixture is about 20%, on average – and many self-designated Whites, Hispanics and others likewise have mixed ancestry. Because research on intelligence relies on self-classification into distinct racial categories, as does most other social science research, its findings likewise relate to some unclear mixture of social and biological distinctions among groups (no one claims otherwise).

Implications for social policy

25 The research findings neither dictate nor preclude any particular social policy, because they can never determine our goals. They can, however, help

us estimate the likely success and side effects of pursuing those goals via different means.

Source: Wall Street Journal, 15 December 1994.

Those favourable to the idea of using cognitive ability/intelligence tests at work in assessment, promotion and selection note test scores are the *best single predictor* of job performance (efficiency, productivity, profit; Hulsheger et al., 2007). Those unfavourable stress racial/ethnic minority discrimination, inequity and unfairness. This represents a severe and perhaps irreconcilable clash of values (Murphy, 2002).

Cognitive ability tests do show adverse impact. But racial differences in test scores are larger than in measures of job performance. Thus, a workforce based on actual performance would be less racially segregated than one based on ability tests. Yet there remains a powerful applied quandary:

> If you emphasise efficiency criteria, and are willing to live with adverse impact, your choice is easy – that is, rely heavily on cognitive ability tests. If you emphasise equity criteria and are willing to live with lower levels of performance, longer training time, more errors, and so forth, your choice is also easy – that is, remove cognitive tests and other selection devices that have strong cognitive components (e.g. scores on cognitive ability test are correlated with scores on structured interviews and on assessment centres). Many decision makers care about both efficiency and equity, and the choice faced by these decision makers is necessarily more complex.
>
> (Murphy, 2002, p. 178)

One solution is to try to find non-cognitive, non-discriminatory tests that predict work performance. Indeed the problem seems so intractable that, as Murphy (2002) argues, one cannot avoid *value trade-offs* but one has to learn how to make value-based, trade-off decisions. He cautions against values distorting the evidence and suggests that when organisations choose either to, or not to, use tests they should make the values underlying this decision explicit and public.

Hough et al. (2001), in an important and extensive review, looked at all the issues, evidence and lessons learned around the matter of adverse impact. They noted that the setting, the sample, and the construct measured often individually or in combination moderate the magnitude of differences between groups. The more specifically the nature of work is specified and the more salient and valid instruments are chosen the better. The data looking at both crystallised intelligence (namely verbal ability, quantitative ability, science achievement) as well as fluid ability (spatial ability, memory, mental processing speed) reveal systematic and replicable race, gender and age differences. There are also personality and physiological differences between these groups. They suggested various possible ways of reducing negative impact including test coaching for applicants; improving test-taking motivation of applicants; using different criteria for different groups distinguishing between task and contextual performance. They also consider in detail statistical methods for detecting and reducing adverse impact like test score banding and predictor/criterion weighting.

Indeed, it is these applied and practical quandaries, rather than the science behind intelligence testing, that has led it to be such a controversial topic in organisational psychology.

Distinctions, differences and disagreements

There are very different approaches to intelligence. Sternberg (1990) identified seven academic metaphors of intelligence, their central questions and typical theorists taking each position. He argued that specific models or metaphors generate specific questions about intelligence, which theories and research seek to address. Scientists may be unaware of these metaphors, which can both limit but also expand views on intelligence. The metaphors are:

1 *Geographic*, which seeks to map the mind and understand the structure of intelligence.
2 *Computational*, which seeks to understand information-processing programmes and processes underlying intelligence.
3 *Biological*, which attempts to understand how the anatomy, physiology and chemistry of the brain and CNS account for intelligence through hemispheric localisation and neural transmission.
4 *Epistemological*, which attempts to answer the fundamental question of what are the structures of the mind through which all knowledge and mental processes are organised.
5 *Anthropological*, which asks what form intelligence takes as a cultural invention and may be comparative and relativistic.
6 *Sociological*, which examines how social pressure (mediated learning experiences) in development are internalised.
7 *Systems*, which is concerned with how we understand the mind as a system that crosscuts metaphors.

According to Sternberg, researchers in the controversial field of intelligence tend either to be *lumpers* or *splitters*. The former emphasises that people who tend to do well on one sort of IQ test do well on practically all others. They talk of general intelligence (*g*) and see the IQ score (derived, of course, from a good test) as highly predictive of educational, business and life success.

Splitters, on the other hand, are advocates of multiple intelligence. Sternberg himself is a splitter and a well-known advocate of practical or successful intelligence (Sternberg, 1997a). Claims and evidence for the theory, however, have been exhaustively and analytically investigated and found wanting (Gottfredson, 2003a). Some of these issues will be discussed in Chapter 7.

However, another, more important and widely accepted distinction has been made between *fluid* and *crystallised* intelligence by Cattell (1987). The analogy is to water – fluid water can take any shape, whereas ice crystals are rigid. Fluid intelligence is effectively the power of reasoning, and processing information. It includes the ability to perceive relationships, deal with unfamiliar problems and gain new types of knowledge. Crystallised intelligence consists of acquired skills and specific knowledge in a person's experience. Crystallised intelligence thus includes the skills of an accountant or a lawyer, as well as a mechanic and a salesperson.

Fluid intelligence peaks before 20 and remains constant, with some decline in later years. Crystallised intelligence, on the other hand, continues to increase as long as the person remains active. Thus, a schoolchild is quicker than a retired citizen at solving a problem that is unfamiliar to both of them, but even the most average older person will excel at solving problems in his/her previous area of occupational specialisation.

In some cases, people try to solve problems by thinking about them in familiar terms – that is by using crystallised intelligence. Most intelligence tests use both types of intelligence, though there is a clear preference for fluid intelligence tests. Thus, consider the following:

(a) Underline which of these numbers does not belong with the others:
625, 361, 256, 193, 144

(b) Underline which of the following towns is the odd one out:
Oslo, London, New York, Cairo, Bombay, Caracas, Madrid

The former is a measure of fluid, the latter of crystallised intelligence.

These two types of intelligence are highly correlated, although they are conceptually different. Usually *what* you have learned (crystallised intelligence) is determined by *how well* you learn (fluid intelligence). Other factors, like personality, do play a part – introverts like to read, study and learn, while equally bright extroverts like to socialise, have fun and experiment (see Chapter 4). Introverts who like learning thus often do better at tests of crystallised intelligence. And, self-evidently, motivation is important – a highly motivated adult will learn more efficiently and effectively than an adult less interested in learning.

Thus, one good reason to have a measure of crystallised ability is that a tendency to work hard is a good measure of scholastic and business success – and hard work results in better scores in tests of crystallised ability. Another reason is that even short *vocabulary tests* give very reliable scores.

With changing technology, the value of crystallised intelligence may be dropping. Crystallised intelligence comes with age and experience. It is a repository of knowledge. Yet, if that knowledge can be cheaply, accurately and efficiently stored and accessed on computers by high fluid intelligence "Young Turks", whence the usefulness of the years of experience?

Sceptics may argue that computers could also assist in fluid intelligence problems thus making that sort of intelligence equally less valuable. Yet, in the business world, it seems to be less and less the case.

Furnham (2001b) has argued that it is business CEOs' fluid intelligence, personality and motivation that appear to be the key to success. In a different age, when education came through the apprenticeship system, the value of crystallised intelligence was particularly great. It still is in some sectors. Being a wine-buff, an antiques expert or a skilled musical performer all mean long hours of attempts to accumulate wisdom. Skills need to be practical and knowledge always increased. In the cut and thrust of a quick-changing business, crystallised intelligence is of less use, save, of course, a good memory for how things did not work out in the past. Tomorrow belongs to the quick-witted, agile, fluid thinkers and less to the salty old stalactites and stalagmites, who cling to the cave walls, gradually getting bigger.

What is, however, very clearly apparent is that despite problems that need to be overcome, like potential litigation over test bias, organisational psychology can add a great deal by carefully assessing employer and employee intelligence.

Over the years, in a systematic and research programmatic way, Ackerman and colleagues have tried to map out and explain the relationship between concepts like intelligence, interests, knowledge and personality. In a very important historical and conceptual overview Ackerman and Heggestad (1997) found evidence of what they called *trait complexes*. These are clusters of personality and ability traits and interests that have striking overlaps or commonalities. These were labelled social, clerical, conventional, science/maths and intellectual/cultural. They argued that it is possible that abilities, interests and personality develop *in tandem* because ability and personality predict success (and failure) in a particular task domain and interests determine the motivation to attempt the task. Success thus leads to increased motivation and interest and vice versa.

Ackerman and colleagues (Ackerman & Rolfhus, 1999; Beier & Ackerman, 2001; Rolfhus & Ackerman, 1999) have looked at academic and occupational knowledge as a way of conceptually understanding how ability and non-ability traits interact. They proposed PPIK theory, which sees intelligence as process, personality, interests and knowledge. Knowledge is accumulated only through expanded effort over time. Personality traits influence the process of acquiring knowledge. Ackerman and Rolfhus (1999) found that knowledge in 20 areas (from astronomy and biology through to physics and world literature) was predicted by a combination of general intelligence, crystallised abilities, personality, interests and self-concept. Rolfhus and Ackerman (1999) found further evidence for PPIK theory. Domain knowledge (i.e. of biology or business management; music or physics) is logically and statistically related to general intelligence, verbal abilities, trait Openness, Typical Intellectual Engagement and specific vocational interests.

Beier and Ackerman (2001) added further evidence to the call for expansion of the type of knowledge included in adult intelligence assessment, especially the type of knowledge important for success in work and adult life. It is essentially as *investment theory*, which suggests that knowledge represents an individual's choice to invest cognitive resources, effort and time in acquiring knowledge about the world.

In one sense, controversy has been good for intelligence researchers because it has given them an opportunity to articulate in straight-forward language what the research data reveal.

Intelligence and IQ: What managers should know?

Nettlebeck and Wilson (2005) have recently written a clear, helpful paper on what teachers should know about intelligence. The issues are identical for managers and represent a sensible overview in everyday language.

They acknowledge that IQ tests have been, are, and no doubt will be, misused and misinterpreted. But, they argue, that for little more than an investment of an hour or two's testing one can gain insights that are unlikely to be achieved even with long periods of detailed observations. Further, they remain happy with the definition of the intelligence as the "ability to understand complex ideas, to adapt effectively to the environment, to learn from experience and to engage in various forms of reasoning to overcome obstacles by taking thought" (Neisser, 1967, p. 7).

Their bottom line is the same for all researchers: IQ test scores tap a general ability that predicts life success in all cultures at all times. IQ tests are as valid as medical tests like mammograms or home-pregnancy tests. Further, it is also widely accepted that there is some, as yet not fully identified, universal biological substratum that underpins intelligence meaning that "being clever" is cross-situational, cross-temporal and cross-cultural. IQ scores account for about 25% of the variance in school and work performance. There is no single better predictor of this stable individual characteristic, which is measurable very accurately at age 10 years.

Nettlebeck and Wilson (2005) argued that IQ scores are not the same as intelligence: "Intelligence is best defined in terms of multiple domains configured within a hierarchical structure that accounts for different degrees of commonality among, and specificity between, those domains. IQ, on the other hand, has until fairly recently amounted to little more than an average outcome from an abridged range of those domains" (p. 613).

Individual IQ remains stable over the lifetime but there is evidence that IQ in the population as a whole is rising (the Flynn effect – see later). This is probably due to a combination of factors like improved educational opportunities, increased competition and work demands, technological advances, better health care, better nutrition, improvements in child-rearing practices. Flynn believes people now invest more of their mental capacities in better abstract problem solving and take up and enjoy more intellectual challenges. Thus tests will need to be, and have been, recalibrated as long as IQ appears to rise.

They also addressed the general vs. multiple intelligence theory, which goes back to the 1920s with all the great names in the area like Spearman, Thorndike and Thurlstone. They are scathingly dismissive of Gardner's (1999) theory – "A person doing well in one domain tends to do well in others" (p. 615) – but accept the Carroll (1993) model with a strong general intelligence factor but also eight or nine additional broad forms of intelligence. Thus, they believed that any really adequate psychometric description of intelligence was dependent on a large array of tests for all differentiated cognitive abilities. One criterion for inclusion should be tests that definitely strengthen the general factor (are highly correlated), but also add specificity. At the heart of this research endeavour is the attempt to expand the definition, measurement and theory of intelligence beyond that which simply predicts academic achievement and which admits numerous environmental influences. Few of those in applied fields would have problems with this concept.

Their take on emotional intelligence (see Chapter 7) is that it is important and useful only to the extent that it adds something to explaining and predicting real-life outcomes over and above that of IQ and personality traits. That has yet to be proven.

One interest of all applied researchers is the question of whether the new electronic and neurological technologies can provide new and improved ways of assessing intelligence, namely the biological indices of brain function and structure. This remains both a hope and a goal but progress is slow. At this stage most progress appears to be more in the improvement of current tests even of an "elementary" nature than the invention of robust tests with predictive validity.

Can IQ be enhanced or improved by formal education and training as well as work experience? There is now ample strong evidence that IQ is stable over the life span. Yet this does not mean that IQ is fixed and unchangeable from a very early age and resistant to improvement via education. Certainly, duration of education correlates with adult IQ, income and organisational level but thus could simply mean brighter children stay in school longer. Yet, there is evidence that education has noticeable and measurable beneficial effects on IQ. What education and training does, is to provide IQ-relevant knowledge, and inculcate specific modes of thought and self-discipline.

Nettlebeck and Wilson (2005) ended their review by addressing the uses for IQ tests. *First*, they argued that tests can be used to clarify the existence of some "exceptionality"; which presumably could be positive or negative. *Second*, they can diagnose the source of certain difficulties. They do, however, warn that assessment should always involve other activities such as may be found in assessment centres. They concluded: "Our support for these tests is contingent on two provisos. First, they must be consistent with current hierarchical, multifaceted theory that includes a general ability. Second, the child's cultural background must be the same as that within which the tests were developed" (p. 626). This is good advice for testing adults in workplace settings as well.

Intelligence research and testing at work

Most people understand intelligence to be about learning, adaptation and problem solving. It is about being good at abstract reasoning, decision making, and speed of uptake. Fundamental differences in definitions revolve around how wide or inclusive it should be. Thus, some researchers want social competence, creativity, and practical solving all to be included in the definition. Some even favour dropping the term altogether and introducing something that is less "hot" or more politically correct, i.e. cognitive ability, capacity, etc.

Lay people use the term to describe people, though they do not always understand the mechanism or process by which it is possible to deduce or measure that one person is significantly more intelligent than another. A lot of attention has been focused on the use of tests and the meaning of the scores. However, it is difficult to deny the accumulated evidence that intelligence scores do have predictive significance: that is when administered and scored at time 1; they predict behaviour, educational and work achievement at time 2 (Deary, 2000, 2001; Mackintosh, 1998).

There are at least half a dozen hotly debated issues in the area, many of which have been around since tests were first constructed 100 years ago.

Harrell and Harrell (1945) showed that individuals with low IQs were unlikely to be found in higher status, "white-collar" jobs, which appeared to require high levels of education as a condition of entry to them. They found more variability at the bottom than the top: that is, there is a greater range in the IQs of people in less prestigious, skilled and unskilled professions than those in higher professions. However, studies and reviews by Ghiselli (1966) suggested that IQ scores were modest (even mediocre) predictors of job performance over time in a particular occupation.

The armed services have always been a good source of data on intelligence and job performance. Indeed, many have developed their own intelligence tests like the American Armed Services Vocational Aptitude Battery (ASVAB). Because of the number of recruits into the army and because of the necessity of technical training it has been relatively easy for psychologists to relate test to job performance on large numbers of recruits (Campbell et al., 1990).

Thus, Jones (1988) looked at an overall *g* score and training outcomes for various courses (mechanical, administrative, technical and electronics) for nearly 25,000 soldiers. The correlation was $r = .75$. Ree and Earles (1994) did a similar analysis across 89 military jobs with big samples (between 274 and 3939) and found a correlation of $r = .76$. McHenry et al. (1990) looked at nine army jobs and found correlations of around $r = .64$ between IQ test scores and "core technical proficiency" and "general soldiering proficiency".

Ree et al. (1994) looked at seven army jobs: air traffic controller; laboratory scientist; armouries communication specialist; ground equipment mechanic; jet engine mechanic; radio operator; and personnel specialist. In each case they were given the IQ subtest ASVAB. When the overall g score was correlated with good criteria measure, the r varied between .21 (air traffic) and .72 with an average of .44. In accordance with previous research the study showed quite simply that general (rather than specific) intelligence was the best predictor of all the work outcomes.

Reviewers have pointed out that there are many correlates of IQ scores. Ree and Earles (1994) listed 10 categories of psychological outcomes:

1   Abilities: reaction time, analytic style, eminence.
2   Creativity/artistic: craftwork, musical ability.
3   Health and fitness: infant mortality, dietary preference, longevity.
4   Interests/choice: marital partner, sports participation, breadth and depth of interest.
5   Moral: delinquency (–), racial prejudice (–) values.
6   Occupational: SES, occupational status, income.
7   Perceptual: myopia, field-independence, ability to perceive brief stimuli.
8   Personality: achievement motivation, altruism, dogmatism (–).
9   Practical: (social skills, practical knowledge) and other (motor skills).
10 Everyday: talking speed, accident proneness (–).

Various reviews published in the 1960s and 1970s suggested that intelligence (and personality) tests did not predict organisational outcomes very well. Further the socio-political zeitgeist of those times discouraged many business people from trying to measure intelligence. Major controversies about intelligence and race suggested that tests were significantly biased as well as lacking in predictive validity.

However, things were to change dramatically with the paper by Hunter and Hunter (1984) who presented a re-analysis of earlier studies plus other databases. In their analysis they took into account various statistical factors that impact on the size of correlations: size of sample, restriction of range and reliability of data. Based on data from 30,000 people and 425 correlations their "bottom-line" figure for the correlation between supervisor-rated job performance and IQ was $r = .53$. They broke this down for various job families. The highest correlation was for salespeople ($r = .62$) and nearly all were over $r = .40$. Thus, for service workers it was $r = .49$, trades and crafts workers $r = .50$ and vehicle operators $r = .46$.

As Brody (1992) noted, despite some criticisms of their methods Hunter and Hunter (1984) demonstrated quite clearly that IQ scores related logically and consistently with many kinds of job performance. By the end of the century, reviewers like Ree and Carretta (1998) felt able to conclude: "Occupational performance begins with learning the knowledge and skills required for the job and continues into on-the-job performance and beyond. We and other investigators have demonstrated that g predicts training performance, job performance, lifetime productivity, and finally, early mortality"

(p. 179). More recent reviews (see next section) are even more positive about the role of intelligence in all aspects of life.

Intelligence and occupational performance

Do tests predict behaviour at work? If they do, how do we explain this? And what else predicts work-related behaviour and success? There is a very long and important literature on IQ and education, which of course informs the concept of training at work. The efficiency, speed and generalisability of learning via training is indeed related to intelligence. Estimates differ between about $r = .30$ and $r = .60$ (Ree & Carretta, 1998).

Researchers have been interested in this question since at least the First World War. There have been various studies and meta-analyses of various sorts, which can probably be divided logically into three time periods. From the 1920s to the 1970s; the 1980s and 1990s; and post-millennium work. The amount of work, the quality of the data and the sophistication of the analyses have all systematically improved.

A central, often unanswered, question is *how* intelligence predicts overall or specific job performance. This, in the first instance, can best be done via path analysis. Hunter (1986) showed that intelligence strongly predicted job knowledge, which predicted both "objective" job performance and supervisors' ratings.

Borman et al. (1993) tested a model that went thus: IQ (ability) results in a person having an opportunity to acquire job experience as a supervisor. It also predicts an increase in job knowledge. Experience in turn leads to a further increase in job knowledge. Experience, ability and knowledge predict proficiency. Thus intelligence predicts job performance. Ree et al. (1995) also argued that intelligence predicts job knowledge prior to training as well as job knowledge acquired during training.

Thus, it seems that intelligence predicts learning, knowledge and proficiency, which in turn usually predicts learning from experience. That is, bright people learn faster, demonstrate salient skills and get promoted. This adds to their knowledge and experience, all of which influence supervisor ratings or any other measure of job performance.

Ree and Carretta (1998) noted that intelligence predicts performance and promotion. That is, longitudinal studies have shown that brighter individuals attain higher occupational status. Thus, intelligence predicts job knowledge, which predicts job performance.

After some important early work that, because of both poor measurement and poor meta-analytic techniques, seemed to suggest both personality and intelligence tests had poor predictive validity in predicting behaviour at work, the situation has changed. Over the last 20 years there have been around a dozen good large meta-analyses looking at the validity of cognitive ability tests.

Whilst these analyses used different tests they were all reliable and highly intercorrelated (Hulsheger et al., 2007). However, it is possible to divide the tests essentially into those that measure general mental ability (GMA) compared to specific cognitive abilities.

The best known meta-analyses from the 1980s were those by Hunter and Hunter (1984) and Hunter (1986), though there were others before. Although there were some trends, what was noticeable was the variability in the correlations between IQ test scores and job performance: some very high, others very low. This led to the "doctrine of situational specificity", which argued that the relationship was dependent on the particular job, job performance criteria and IQ test itself. However, in turn, this led to the development of meta-analysis, which through various statistical and "corrective" techniques aims to show the true operational validity between GMA and work outcomes (Hunter, 1986; Hunter & Hunter 1984; Hunter & Schmidt, 1976, 1990; Schmidt & Hunter, 1977, 1984, 1998).

Ones et al. (2006), in an excellent, comprehensive and up-to-date review of the meta-analyses, were concerned with cognitive ability, selection decisions and success at work. In doing this they examined many different areas and came to clear conclusions:

- Based on data of well over a million students they noted that GMA was a strong, valid predictor of exam success, learning and outcome at school and university regardless of the speciality or subject considered.
- Training success at work, as measured by such things as supervisor ratings or job knowledge acquired, is predicted by GMA and the more complex the job, the more powerfully it predicts.
- Regarding job performance, cognitive-ability tests predict outcomes across jobs, situations and outcomes – i.e. validity is transportable across occupational group and is cross-culturally generalisable.
- Tests of specific ability do *not* have incremental validity over general measures and although they may be more acceptable to job applicants the relative importance of these abilities alters over time.
- Intelligence predicts job performance well because it is linked to the speed and quality of learning, adaptability and problem-solving ability.
- Cognitive-ability tests are predictively fair to minority groups but can have an adverse impact, which is a sensitive political issue.
- In short, GMA is one of the best, if not the best predictor of success in applied settings.

Various meta-analyses have been done over the last five years that have attempted a critical, comprehensive overview of the role of intelligence (often called general mental ability or cognitive ability test results) in predicting work-related outcomes.

Some reviewers have tended to concentrate on data from one country, like America (Schmidt & Hunter, 2004), Britain (Bertua et al., 2005), Germany (Hulsheger et al., 2007) or from wider areas like the European Community (Salgado et al., 2003). Despite these differences the results were essentially the same and all reviewers argued for the practical use of cognitive ability tests which are quite clearly good predictors of both overall job performance as well as training success.

Salgado et al. (2003) looked at the predictive validity of GMA as well as specific cognitive abilities like verbal, numerical, spatial-mechanical, perceptual and memory to predict measurable job performance and training success (Table 6.1). Different selection and personnel practices could, they argued, lead to difference when comparing American and European data. Following the rigorous demands of meta-analysis found over 250 studies that tested over 25,000 Europeans. They found an operational validity of .62, which they noted "means GMA is an excellent predictor of job performance" (p. 585) and that "GMA is the best predictor of job performance" (p. 585). The validity of the five specific measures varied from .35 for verbal to .56 for memory. The data on training ratings was broadly similar if slightly lower (.54 for GMA; .44 for verbal and .34 for memory).

Their conclusion was that, internationally, GMA measures are the *best predictors* of work performance. That is, despite differences in tests used; measures/conceptualisations of job performance and training; differences in unemployment rates, cultural values,

Table 6.1 The meta-analytic results of operational validity of overall and specific measures

	Performance	*Training*
GMA	.62	.54
Verbal	.35	.44
Numerical	.52	.48
Spatial/Mechanical	.51	.40
Perceptual	.52	.25
Memory	.56	.43

Source: Derived from Salgado et al. (2003).

Table 6.2 Correlations between overall and specific IQ measures and job performance and training

	Performance	*Training*
GMA	.48	.50
Verbal	.39	.49
Numerical	.42	.54
Perceptual	.50	.50
Spatial	.35	.42
Average	.42	.49

Source: Derived from Bertua et al. (2005).

demographics, still GMA wins out as the best individual difference psychometric measure. Indeed, the results were strikingly similar to earlier data coming out of America (Hunter, 1986; Hunter & Hunter, 1984; Kuncel et al., 2001; Viswevaran et al., 1996). They concluded that because of the predictive validity of GMA at work across cultures one can easily conceive of a scientifically feasible general theory of personnel selection. They also pointed out that: "tests of specific abilities such as verbal, numerical, spatial-mechanical, perceptual and memory failed to demonstrate higher validity than GMA measures. It is thus prudent to reiterate the main practical implications of this finding that GMA tests predicted these two criteria most successfully" (p. 594).

Another meta-analysis focused exclusively on British data. This had 283 samples of over 13,000 people in total (Bertua et al., 2005). This analysis looked at the predictive validity of specific abilities (i.e. verbal, numerical, etc.) as well as GMA over seven main groups (clerical, engineer, professional, driver, operator, manager, sales). As in all meta-analyses they found GMA and abilities valid predictors of job performance and training success (performance rho = .48; training rho = .50; see Table 6.2).

They also found, as one may predict, that the greater the job complexity, the higher the operational validities between the different cognitive tests and job performance and training success (Table 6.3).

Thus these results were broadly in line with those from both Europe and America. Once again the conclusion is that GMA measures may be the best single predictor for personnel selection for all occupations. Bertua et al. recommended the use of psychometrically proven measures of GMA for use in selection "regardless of job type, hierarchical seniority, potential future changes in job role composition or whether the tests are principally for general or specific cognitive ability" (p. 403).

Table 6.3 The meta-analytic results for GMA over the eight occupational groups

	Performance	Training
Clerical	.32	.55
Engineer	.70	.64
Professional	.74	.59
Driver	.37	.47
Operator	.53	.34
Manager	.69	
Sales	.55	
Miscellaneous	.40	.55

Source: Based on Bertua et al. (2005).

In their meta-analysis of German data examining both training success (of 11,969 people) and job performance (746 people) Hulgsheger et al. (2007) found validities of .47 for training success and .53 for job performance. They found also, as they suspected they would, that job complexity did moderate that relationship. Their results were therefore strikingly similar to those shown in other countries.

Thus, over the past quarter century there has accumulated a "large and compelling literature" showing that intelligence is a good predictor of both job performance and training proficiency at work (Dragow, 2002). Extensive meta-analytic reviews have shown that intelligence is a good predictor of job performance, particularly in complex jobs. Although debatable, researchers suggest the correlation between intelligence and job performance is around $r = .50$ (Schmidt & Hunter, 1998). The central question is what other factors like personality or social/emotional intelligence (sometimes called "social skills") account for the rest of the variance. But referring to g or general intelligence Dragow (2002) is forced to conclude: ". . . for understanding performance in the workplace, and especially task performance and training performance, g is the key . . . g accounts for an overwhelming proportion of the explained variance when predicting training and job performance" (p. 126).

A recent survey of over 700 American applied psychologists showed considerable consensus that cognitive ability (intelligence) tests are valid and fair; that they provide good but incomplete measures that different abilities are necessary for different jobs, and that diversity is valuable.

Ree and Carretta (1998), in another careful review of their own and others' work, as well as criticisms of it, concluded thus: "Occupational performance begins with learning the knowledge and skills required for the job and continues into on-the-job performance and beyond. We and other investigators have demonstrated that g predicts training performance, job performance, lifetime productivity, and finally, early mortality" (p. 179).

One hundred years after Spearman (1904) published his paper "General Intelligence: Objectively Determined and Measured" in the *American Journal of Psychology* there were various celebrations, conferences and special issues to celebrate the fact. One paper entitled "Academic Performance, Career Potential, Creativity and Job Performance: Can One Construct Predict Them All?" concluded, *yes*! (Kuncel et al., 2004). Further, as Lubinski (2004) notes it is no surprise that intelligence test scores have such predictive validity over so many areas like education, health, interpersonal relationships and job performance. He concludes:

> As modern societies move to create more information and to make this information readily available, more opportunities become available for differential development. In addition, tasks important at school, at work, and in life are becoming less concrete and less well defined. The dimensions of educational, occupational and social niches are becoming more abstract and fluid. An examination of phrases used to characterise skills needed in today's most complex learning and work environments quickly reveals that the current need is for abilities for "coping with change", "dealing with novelty", "quickly grasping" the relevance of innovative ideas for staying "ahead of the curve" and "anticipating change". The skills needed in modern society require dealing with complexity and with change and more than ever before, these changes are relatively content free. At work as in life in general, people are required to respond to situations for which they have not practised.
>
> The specific content is not fundamental, because the specific content of life is ever changing. Coping with life requires the continuous development of new skills, so abilities useful for mastering new content – and new relationships – are what is needed.
>
> Assessment designed to index individual differences in prespecified domains (e.g. mastery of prescribed content in educational and occupational contexts) will always be important, but, increasingly, skills in coping with novelty, generalising and discriminating dynamic relationships, and making inferences that anticipate distal events are what modern society demands."
>
> (p. 108)

Leading researchers in the area, Schmidt and Hunter (2004) also came to a clear conclusion based on 100 years of work. It is:

> The research evidence shows that GMA predicts both occupational level attained and performance within one's chosen occupation and does so better than any other ability, trait, or disposition and better than job experience. The sizes of these relationships with GMA are also larger than most found in psychological research. Evidence is presented that weighted combinations of specific aptitudes tailored to individual jobs do not predict job performance better than GMA alone, disconfirming specific aptitude theory. A theory of job performance is described that explicates the central role of GMA in the world of work. These findings support Spearman's proposition that GMA is of critical importance in human affairs.
>
> (p. 162)

Thus, for complex, senior jobs the correlation between GMA and job performance is around .50. Further, intelligence is a more powerful predictor than personality. It is because people with higher GMA acquire job knowledge more efficiently (faster and more) that it is such a good marker of career success. Job experience does relate to job performance but it declines over time, unlike the intelligence–performance relationship, which increases.

Since the turn of the millennium there have been some excellent reviews on the subject of intelligence at work. Below are quotes from those reviews:

There is abundant evidence that general cognitive ability is highly relevant in a wide range of jobs and settings and that measures of general cognitive ability represent perhaps the best predictors of performance. Ability–performance relations are essentially linear and the correlation between general cognitive ability and performance appears similar across jobs that differ considerably in content. There is some evidence that ability–performance correlations tend to increase as jobs become more complex but few other consistent moderators of the ability–performance correlation have been reported. Finally, the incremental contribution of specific abilities (defined as ability factors unrelated to the general factor) to the prediction of performance or training outcomes may very well be minimal.

(Murphy, 2002, p. 175)

Given the overwhelming research evidence showing the strong link between general cognitive ability (GCA) and job performance, it is not logically possible for industrial–organisational (I/O) psychologists to have a serious debate over whether GCA is important for job performance. However, even if none of this evidence existed in I/O psychology, research findings in differential psychology on the nature and correlates of GCA provide a sufficient basis for the conclusion that GCA is strongly related to job performance. From the viewpoint of the kind of world we would like to live in – and would like to believe we live in – the research findings on GCA are not what most people would hope for and are not welcome. However, if we want to remain a science-based field, we cannot reject what we know to be true in favour of what we would like to be true.

(Schmidt, 2002, p. 187)

[T]he utility of g, is that g (i.e. possessing a higher level of g) has value across all kinds of work and levels of job-specific experience, but that its value rises with (a) the complexity of work, (b) the more "core" the performance criterion being considered (good performance of technical duties rather than "citizenship"), (c) the more objectively performance is measured (e.g. job samples rather than supervisor ratings). Predictive validities, when corrected for various statistical artefacts, range from about .2 to .8 in civilian jobs, with an average near .5. In mid-level military jobs, uncorrected validities tend to range between .3 and .6. These are substantial. To illustrate, tests with these levels of predictive validity would provide 30% to 60% of the gain in aggregate levels of worker performance that would be realised from using tests with perfect validity (there is no such thing) rather than hiring randomly.

(Gottfredson, 2003b, p. 293)

The strong case for measuring intelligence

Gottfredson (2003b) argues that *life is a mental test battery*. By this she means that the business of living involves solving various problems and completing various tasks. Jobs like good psychometric IQ tests have a variety of performance tasks, which are judged against an accepted standard. The more demanding the job, the brighter people have to be. Jobs operate like "differentially *g* loaded mental tests" because workers' differences in job performance simultaneously measure their differences in intelligence. Being more intelligent gives one a competitive edge for performing the job's core technical duties. Superior knowledge and extensive job experience, she argues, may sometimes hide a lower intelligence level, but never nullify or compensate for it. Brighter workers apply past knowledge more effectively, and deal with novel problems more effectively and efficiently.

In a series of extremely important, critical and comprehensive papers Gottfredson (1997, 1998, 2002, 2003b, 2003c) has made an overwhelming case to measure general (*g*) intelligence and to take it into consideration in everyday management decisions.

Intelligence, she notes, has pervasive functional importance in people's lives. This is particularly true at work: "Intelligence turns out to be more important in predicting job performance than even personnel psychologists thought just two decades ago" (Gottfredson, 1997, p. 81). Interestingly, it was civil rights laws and regulations aimed at reducing discrimination that encouraged researchers to look very closely at this area. Looking at this research she came to various very important conclusions:

1 The prediction validity of intelligence is ubiquitous. Across all jobs and all ratings of success intelligence is very important.
2 The predictive power of intelligence rises with job complexity. The more intellectually and technically demanding the job, the more important is intelligence for success.
3 The validity of intelligence is high compared to other factors like personality, particular aptitudes or vocational interests.
4 Intelligence is important in a casual sense. More surprising differences between individuals do not decrease with training (the less good become better and the good remain much the same) but can increase. Intelligence is a major source of enduring, consequential differences in job performance.
5 Higher levels of intelligence are required as people rise up the occupational ladder. Occupations both attract and accommodate individuals from a wide range of IQ levels but job incumbents are more homogeneous than applicants. But there do appear to be minimum IQ thresholds that rise steadily with job level.
6 Higher intelligence reflects higher trainability. That is, intelligence predicts a person's capacity to learn, i.e. trainability.
7 The essence of intelligence at work is the ability to deal with complexity, which is an individual's ability to acquire, apply, organise, recognise, select and update salient work-related information. In other words to mentally manipulate information.
8 Complexity is the key feature in the workplace. It is the major distinguishing factor between jobs. It is all about information processing.
9 As social, cultural and work life becomes more complex the role of intelligence inevitably increases.
10 Where people have little time and ability to learn and be trained it is best to focus on specific training for specific skills.

Gottfredson (2002) believed it was vitally important for personnel psychologists and managers to understand the role of intelligence at work. In a wonderfully clear and important synthesis, she outlines the real importance of *g* (or general intelligence) at work (Gottfredson, 2002, pp. 44–46). This is well-worth repeating in full (Box 6.2).

Quite simply for Gottfredson (2003a, 2003b) all of life is a mental test battery. In this sense a higher intelligence is related to most advantages in life. The better paid, more demanding, more socially desirable jobs recruit workers from the higher reaches of the IQ distribution. Intelligence provides the competitive edge for a job performance

---

Box 6.2 Gottfredson's synthesis of the importance of *g* at work

---

Major findings on g's impact on job performance: A utility of g

1   Higher levels of *g* lead to higher levels of performance in all jobs and along all dimensions of performance. The average correlation of mental tests with overall rated job performance is around .5 (corrected for statistical artefacts).

2   There is no ability threshold above which more *g* does not enhance perform- ance. The effects of *g* are linear: successive increments in *g* lead to successive increments of job performance.

3   (a) The value of higher levels of *g* does not fade with longer experience on the job. Criterion validities remain high even among highly experienced workers. (b) That they sometimes even appear to rise with experience may be due to the confounding effect of the least experienced groups tending to be more variable in relative level of experience, which obscures the advantages of higher *g*.

4   *g* predicts job performance better in more complex jobs. Its (corrected) cri- terion validities range from about .2 in the simplest jobs to .8 in the most complex.

5   *g* predicts the core technical dimensions of performance better than it does the non-core "citizenship" dimension of performance.

6   Perhaps as a consequence, *g* predicts objectively measured performance (either job knowledge or job sample performance) better than it does subject- ively measured performance (such as supervisor ratings).

Utility of g relative to other "can do" components of performance

7   Specific mental abilities (such as spatial, mechanical or verbal ability) add very little, beyond *g*, to the prediction of job performance. *g* generally accounts for at least 85–95% of a full mental test battery's (cross-validated) ability to predict performance in training or on the job.

8   Specific mental abilities (such as clerical ability) sometimes add usefully to prediction, net of *g*, but only in certain classes of jobs. They do not have general utility.

9   General psychomotor ability is often useful, but primarily in less complex work. Its predictive validities fall with complexity while those for *g* rise.

Utility of g relative to the "will do" component of job performance

10   *g* predicts core performance much better than do "non-cognitive" (less *g*-loaded) traits, such as vocational interests and different personality traits. The latter add virtually nothing to the prediction of core performance, net of *g*.

11   *g* predicts most dimensions of non-core performance (such as personal discipline and soldier bearing) much less well than do "non-cognitive" traits

of personality and temperament. When a performance dimension reflects both core and non-core performance (effort and leadership), *g* predicts to about the same modest degree as do non-cognitive (less *g*-loaded) traits.

12 Different non-cognitive traits appear to usefully supplement *g* in different jobs, just as specific abilities sometimes add to the prediction of performance in certain classes of jobs. Only one such non-cognitive trait appears to be as generalisable as *g*: the personality trait of Conscientiousness/integrity. Its effect sizes for core performance are substantially smaller than *g*'s, however.

Utility of g relative to the job knowledge

13 *g* affects job performance primarily indirectly through its effect on job-specific knowledge.

14 *g*'s direct effects on job performance increase when jobs are less routinised, training is less complete, and workers retain more discretion.

15 Job-specific knowledge generally predicts job performance as well as does *g* among experienced workers. However, job knowledge is not generalisable (net of its *g* component), even among experienced workers. The value of job knowledge is highly job specific: *g*'s value is unrestricted.

Utility of g relative to the "have done" (experience) component of job performance

16 Like job knowledge, the effect sizes of job-specific experience are sometimes high, but they are not generalisable.

17 In fact, experience predicts performance less well as all workers become more experienced. In contrast, higher levels of *g* remain an asset regardless of length of experience.

18 Experience predicts job performance less well as job complexity rises, which is opposite the trend for *g*. Like general psychomotor ability, experience matters least where *g* matters most to individuals and their organisations.

Source: Adapted from Gottfredson (2002, pp. 44–46).

particularly in high-level, more technically demanding jobs. Being intelligent provides a big, but not decisive, advantage. Intelligence has a large causal effect on one's career.

Gottfredson (2003a, 2003b) believed that jobs act as a template for understanding the role of intelligence in all daily life. Intelligence relates to functional literacy, which has many educational, health and social relationship concomitants. Indeed Gottfredson and Deary (2004) showed that intelligence is a good predictor of health and longevity. The central question, of course, is why this is true. It seems that less intelligent people adhere less often to treatment regimens; learn and understand less about how to protect their health; seek less preventative care, even when free; and less often practise healthy behaviours for slowing and preventing chronic disease.

Applications and implications of testing at work

Is it advisable to use cognitive tests to make selection, training and promotion decisions? If so, what tests should be administered to whom and for what purpose? Are the potential negative consequences greater than the benefits? Could one make a good economic, as opposed to legal, argument for testing in the workplace?

Viswesvaran and Ones (2002) examined in detail eight issues surrounding the use of ability testing in the workplace. It was a summary of 11 excellent articles published in *Human Performance*, 2002, Volume 15, including many important papers (i.e. Murphy, 2002; Reeve & Hakel, 2002; Schmidt, 2002; Tenopyr, 2002). They were even-handed in their approach, happy to point out areas of agreement and disagreement.

A. What is the predictive value of intelligence (general mental ability) tests for real-life outcomes and work behaviour?

Results show consistently that intelligence is positively related to educational level, income and positive health behaviours, and negatively related to delinquency, disciplinary problems and health issues. People need a level of ability to thrive in a particular work environment: more cognitive demands, more ability required. To many this is self-evident.

But there are three criticisms. The *first* is the size of correlation between intelligence and job outcome – in other words the strength of that relationship and the amount of variance being accounted for. Some argue that the relationship is too weak or too small and may only account for 25% of the variance. Thus, hard work, honesty and training could all easily compensate for relatively low intelligence in a competitive working environment.

A *second* criticism concerns the relationships looked at. If you examine the relationship between intelligence and work outcomes of job incumbents and find them small, that should be no surprise, because if they have been well selected there should be little variance. That is, they should all be within the appropriate intelligence range. On the other hand, if all job applicants were tested that would yield a far better index. Equally, we need to consider how reliable the measurement of the criterion work outcome/ variable is. Critics argue, then, that if we correct for range restriction (of those in the job) and the unreliability of the outcome measure we will see a much stronger relationship between IQ and work. The *third* criticism, quickly dismissed by Viswesvaran and Ones (2002), is that intelligent behaviour at work is the result of more than just what intelligence tests measure.

B. Do overall IQ test scores predict better than measures of specific abilities?

This question is whether very specific tests of verbal, or mathematical or spatial ability will relate to work outcomes, more strongly and logically than general IQ test results. It is agreed that there are non-cognitive factors that do predict job performance in addition to GMA. But are there very specific abilities that predict success in all jobs (rather than very specific jobs).

Whilst there may be good reason to use very specific ability measures like those of verbal reasoning or mathematical ability (for face validity, legal reasons) that give incremental validity over a GMA the evidence suggests that it is small. This could be for many reasons: restriction of range in certain occupational samples; a limited number of criteria. Nevertheless, based on the current data, it is fairly difficult to provide evidence to justify the use of tests of specific ability over those of GMA.

C. How good are the criteria (job or training performance)?

The central question here is how reliable, representative and parsimonious are the traditional outcome measures? There have always been doubts about the narrowness of these measures that neglect, for instance, both team and organisational effectiveness. Few researchers are completely happy with the criteria but find it difficult to find better ones.

D. Is the utility evidence for GMA convincing?

Is it possible to place monetary values on the consequence for an organisation choosing people of high, average or low intelligence based on the provided predictive validity of IQ test/job performance links. This is not a methodological issue but one of focusing only on organisational productivity as opposed to health or harmony. Utility evidence is therefore a value statement. However, it is frequently done and yields some startling results usually showing the great economic benefits of testing.

E. Are the negative reactions to GMA tests a result of group differences?

That is, is the debate about black/white differences and the association of such concepts as "adverse impact", "bias", "discrimination" and "fairness" the real cause of public cynicism, and scepticism about tests? In other words, would the controversies about intelligence be less intense and passionate if there were no evidence of group differences?

The problem is of logic: GMA predicts work performance better than specific ability measures but there are recognised, replicable group differences in IQ not due (solely) to measurement bias. Yet it seems that negative attitudes to testing go beyond the race (and sex) issue. They may be caused by historically recorded abuses of testing as well as the philosophy of equality and equal opportunity that eschews selection on ability. Another reason is that most people believe that IQ is not the only important predictor of educational, job, and life success. Indeed, it is not even the most important predictor.

F. Is the theoretical knowledge of GMA adequate?

At the heart of the problem is the very meaning of the concept of GMA. That is, researchers seem not to understand the process or mechanism that leads to GMA or indeed its association with job success. There may be interesting statistical evidence of behavioural and biological correlates of GMA scores but how it operates remains unclear. Defenders say we know as much about the construct as many others in psychology while critics detect a theoretical dark hole at the centre of all this research.

G. Is there promise in various new methods of testing for GMA?

That is, using different technologies – biological, computational, video based – will we be able to measure intelligence more reliably, and presumably understand GMA? The question is whether changing the measurement changes what is measured. Some had hoped that tests using different media would reduce group differences, whereas others believe that all they have done is increase measurement error. However, as Viswesvaran and Ones (2002) have noted: "Whether these potentially more invasive assessments are developed and become available for use depends on how society decides to balance the privacy rights of individuals against the needs of organisations" (p. 224).

H. What is the current status of non-GMA predictors and substitutes or supplements to GMA?

The search for other good predictors has been long and hard. Thus, can personality variables, work samples or some measured motivational variable act as a substitute or supplement to GMA as an accurate predictor? Can we find factors that both increase predictive validity and reduce group differences? Many have been suggested from tacit knowledge, through working memory capacity to psychomotor ability. The problem is that few (good) studies attempt to compare the predictive validity of alternative tests with GMA. Two issues are important here according to Viswesvaran and Ones (2002). *First*, not to confuse constructs and methods and, *second*, to examine predictor inter-correlations. Further, there are important consequences of choosing people on the basis of the supplementary predictor. Thus, Conscientiousness is thought to be a better predictor of GMA. However, one would have an organisation full of ambitious, hard-working, persistent, dutiful and perhaps dependent people rather than fast, accurate, effective problem solvers.

Controversies in intelligence research

Using psychometrically valid intelligence tests in selection and promotion may seem a logical consequence of reading the academic literature. However, this is far from the case as there are numerous controversies around the fair use of tests in selection. Controversies revolve around group differences (especially sex and race) and the Flynn effect. Group differences refer to the collective property of a group as distinct from the individual property of an individual.

Sex differences

Few dispute that there are consistent, replicable and significant differences in cognitive test scores (Halpern, 1992). Females do better at tasks that require rapid access to, and use of, phonological, semantic and other information in long-term memory. Females are better at speed articulation, production and comprehension of complex prose and tend to get higher grades in school (for most subjects). Males do better on tasks that require transformations in visual working memory, i.e. those involving moving objects and aiming. However, differences are small and reviewers tend to argue five things. *First*, gender differences in general intellectual ability are small and virtually nonexistent. *Second*, secular changes in society have diminished gender differences in special ability scores. *Third*, mean differences in verbal ability and mathematical ability in the general population have virtually disappeared – though this is not true of spatial ability. *Fourth*, males appeared to be more variable in a number of ability measures and this difference in variability, particularly at the high end of the distribution of ability, may contribute to an excess number of males above relatively high cut-off scores. *Fifth*, there are gender differences on tests of spatial ability. The magnitude of the difference appears to vary with the type of test and may be as high as .75 standard deviation units in favour of males over females for tests of mental rotation.

Brody (1992) notes that meta-analyses point to the smallest effect sizes (.10 to .20) relating to gender differences in IQ scores. Sex differences in IQ scores appear to be declining due to a reduction in sex stereotyping of activities, interests and curricular choices. Sex differences are more likely to be present in samples that are above average in abilities.

Mackintosh (1998) argued that it is not true that tests were designed and defined to show sex differences. Most early test constructions were not very interested in sex differences and tended not to find much evidence for them. There are sex differences on particular WAIS tests that are robust and reliable but small (2 IQ points). The sexes do not differ on measures of general reasoning ability. There are various biological (sex-linked recessive gene hypothesis) and environmental (early socialisation) explanations for sex differences but they remain unclear.

However, Lynn and colleagues (Lynn, 1999; Lynn & Irwing, 2004) have argued and demonstrated the small (around .3 of an *SD*) sex differences in favour of males. Through a developmental theory they argued that the male advantage is most notice-able after the age of 16. This may be more particularly true of spatial tasks. The argument is logical: it is known that brain size is correlated with intelligence; males have bigger brains than females; therefore males are more intelligent. Females mature more rapidly than males in terms of neurological development and brain size up to the age of 15 years. This "compensates" for their smaller brain size with the result that there are negligible differences, but from the age of 16 years the growth rate of girls decelerates relative to that of boys. Thus by (early) adulthood there is a discernable 4 IQ point difference (almost one third of an *SD*) in favour of males that is consistent with their brain size difference.

The theory was confirmed in a 57 study meta-analysis of sex differences in the general population using Raven's progressive matrices (Lynn & Irwing, 2004). It showed that after the age of 15, but not before, the male advantage occurred. Interestingly they found little cross-cultural variation in sex differences, despite some marked cultural differences in adult sex roles. Further, they found no evidence of generational change, i.e. the reduction is sex differences over time. However, they felt obliged to try to explain the anomalous finding that (at least in Great Britain) suggest that in secondary schools and at universities females tend to perform as well as, or better than, males. Their suggestion is that females' greater achievement motivation is the primary explanation for these findings.

Support for Lynn's position has recently been provided by Jackson and Rushton (2006) who had data from 100,000 17- to 18-year-olds. They found males averaged 3.63 IQ points above females (effect size of .12). they found these male–female differences throughout the entire distribution of scores, at every socioeconomic level and in every group: "We conclude that while the magnitude of the male–female difference in *g* is not large, it is real and non-trivial" (p. 479).

Asserting sex differences causes considerable debate in the popular press based more on ideology than a cool and disinterested evaluation of the evidence. However, if indeed there are sex differences in intelligence they are very small. There may well be gender differences in self-estimated intelligence or indeed the way males and females attempt intelligence tests but there is very little evidence to suggest that testing at work would be advantageous or disadvantageous to either males or females.

Race differences

Since he published a paper in 1969, Jensen has continued to argue for there being systematic and replicable differences in IQ between different racial (and national) groups. He has been supported by many working in the area (Herrnstein & Murray, 1994; Rushton, 1995). Few who have done research on the topic of IQ believe that there are not race differences but they do argue, quite passionately, about the *cause* of race differences in IQ scores.

The predictive validity of IQ (for education and job) is comparable for Black and White samples. Tests, even subtests of knowledge, are not particularly race biased in favour of WASPs. There is little difference between culture-bound and non-culture-bound tests. Further, test administration (i.e. race of examiner) is a small and not very important source of difference. Class and status of examiner have little effect and English dialect of test or tester has little effect.

Brody (1992) argued that: "More generally, one can conclude from this review of research on bias in mental testing that the Black–White difference in performance on tests of intelligence is not substantially attributable to differences in the construct validity of the tests for Black and White samples. The factor analytic studies, item analysis research, and research on the predictive validity of tests suggests that the Black–White difference in test scores is substantially attributable to differences in the construct that is assessed by the test" (p. 217).

Mackintosh (1998), however, is less impressed by the universal validity of IQ tests. He notes: "We need to remember that standard IQ tests were designed to measure the knowledge, intellectual skills, and cognitive abilities valued in Western industrial societies, especially by the education systems of these societies. They may do a reasonable job of that. But there is no reason to assume that other cultures and societies share the same values. Administering such tests to people of other cultures may tell us whether they do or do not share the same values. But it will not necessarily tell us much about their 'intelligence' " (p. 366).

Despite some doubt as to the cultural fairness of some tests the real argument lies between the genetic vs. environment camps. Certainly, while everybody accepts the role of certain environmental factors, even singly or together, they cannot account for the observable, empirically derived differences in IQ. Mackintosh (1998) makes the following points:

- The established Black–White difference debate/research has a major social and political impact.
- There are three strong positions: genetic; environmental; test bias.
- Interbreeding means geneticists/anthropologists do not find "race" a useful concept. There are no clear single markers.
- Adoptive studies (of Black children by White parents) are problematic and yield contradictory evidence.
- The acid test of the environment argument is to manipulate (enrich) the environment and see its effects on IQ. But enriched and compensatory environments have limited and short-term effects.

- Poverty and discrimination cannot be sufficient explanations, so the environmental factors that do affect IQ remain unclear.
- Chinese/Japanese superiority also remains a challenging issue.
- All IQ tests are imperfect measures aimed to provide a true (unbiased, valid) measure of intellectual functioning. But valid tests should predict/correlate with educational and occupational attainment.

The debate continues and is likely to do so. A whole issue of the journal *Psychology, Public Policy and Law* (June 2005, Volume 11, No. 2) was dedicated to the thorny issue of race differences in cognitive ability with those on all sides of the argument making their case (Gottfredson, 2005; Rushton & Jensen, 2005; Sternberg, 2005).

There are, it seems, three types of explanations. *First*, there is evidence of biological, genetic differences between the races. *Second*, there is evidence of sociocultural, economic and political forces that are quite distinct from racial characteristics though confounded with them. *Third*, race differences are essentially artefacts of test design, administration or measurement. In other words there are no real differences.

Brody (1992) noted that the study of race differences in intelligence goes back to the beginning of research. Substantial research shows that Black Americans score 15 points (1 *SD*) lower than White Americans. It is clear that variations *within* race are larger than variations *between* races. This means 16% of the Black population have scores above the White mean; at a cut-off of 70 points for special education there will be 1 White for every 7 Blacks. Black–White differences appear to be constant over time and over the life span. Further, racial differences are present prior to school entry. Racial differences are, however, not constant for different types of measures of intelligence.

Brody argues that those who reject race differences as a function of test measurement are wrong:

> Research on Black–White differences in intelligence fails to provide answers to three critical questions. (1) what are the reasons for the difference? (2) Can we eliminate it? (3) If we cannot eliminate the difference, can we design an environment in which the effects of individual differences in intelligence are mitigated such that they are not determinative to the extent they are now of racial differences in performance in the schools and in other socially relevant contexts? If we could make progress on the third question, the answers to the first two questions would appear to be less pressing. It is possible that the answer to the first question might enable us to eliminate the difference or to design ways to mitigate the difference. If so, the study of the reasons for Black–White differences would be socially useful.
>
> (Brody, 1992, p. 310)

Gottfredson (2002) provides a clear example from America:

> To take some more specific examples, about 22% of Whites and 59% of Blacks have IQs below 90, which makes considerably fewer Blacks competitive for mid-level jobs, such as fire fighting, the skilled trades and many clerical jobs. The average IQ of incumbents in such jobs is nearer IQ 100, one standard deviation above the Black average of roughly IQ = 85. IQ = 80 seems to be the threshold for competitiveness in even the lowest level jobs, and four times as many Blacks (30%) as Whites (7%) fall below that threshold. Looking toward the other tail of the IQ

distribution, IQ = 125 is about average for professionals (e.g. lawyers, physicians, engineers, professors) and high-level executives. The Black–White ratio of availability is only 1 : 30 at this level. Disparate impact, and therefore political and legal tension, is thus particularly acute in the most complex, most socially desirable jobs.

(p. 41)

Gottfredson notes that many hoped psychologists would "invent" better tests that would reduce the racial disparity. This did not happen and tests were blamed for the problem: that is, for some, if tests showed a race difference, they did not want or expect this and blamed the test. Some turned away from testing. She concludes cautiously thus:

Reducing disparate impact is a worthy goal to which probably all selection professionals subscribe. What is troubling are the new means being promulgated: minimising or eliminating the best overall predictor of job performance. They amount to a call for reducing test validity and thereby violating personnel psychology's primary testing standard. Reducing the role of g in selection may be legally and politically expedient in the short term, but it delays more effective responses to the huge racial gaps in job-relevant skills, abilities and knowledge.

(p. 43)

Generational effects

For over 20 since the papers of Flynn (1984, 1987) psychologists have debated the possible causes of the established phenomenon concerning the rise of intelligence over each generation. Looking at 20 countries over a 50-year period there has been an increase of 2.9 points per decade on non-verbal IQ (specifically abstract problem-solving ability) and 3.7 points on verbal IQ. This rapid increase cannot be due to genetic factors. The likely causes are:

- Increases in the number of years of education.
- Greater access to information (e.g. television, Internet).
- The increased cognitive complexity of the average person's job now compared to several decades ago.
- More generally, a large increase in the number of middle-class families.

Flynn's data have been replicated but still have no clear explanation. Various ideas have been put forward: improved nutrition, educational innovation, television, experience of speeded tests. Yet he had received stern and cogent criticism for his methods and conclusions. Most reviews have inferred longitudinal explanation from cross-sectional data. Rodgers (1999) points out that population IQ gains do not operate within the individual. In fact IQ declines with age. Similarly the Flynn effect does not operate within the family. IQ declines with birth order. It is not clear whether the Flynn effect is a period effect (i.e. changes over time because of improved education) or a cohort effect (i.e. changes over time in one group would carry on with it).

Further, Rodgers (1999) points out that it is unclear whether the Flynn effect operates across all races and ability distributions or whether it operates on only certain abilities (like problem solving or vocabulary). Rodgers (1999) has noted that the Flynn effect is an inference from data. He proposed an alternative model based on the variability of scores. Thus, if over the population as a whole certain changes (better diet, education, etc.) reduced variability of scores (fewer people scored low) this would result very clearly in the Flynn effect.

What remains clear is that the Flynn effect is a phenomenon still in search of a cogent explanation. It certainly has important implications for everyone interested in age and group differences in intelligence.

Conclusion

Few areas of psychology attract as much discussion and debate as the topic of intelligence. More academic researchers have been attacked (physically), hounded, sacked and vilified for what they have written about intelligence. The area that inevitably causes most passion is that of sex and race differences in intelligence. There is also still considerable debate about the role of intelligence testing in educational settings.

There are essentially two issues: an empirical one and a social policy one. Most of the debate is about the latter not the former though there remains still considerable controversy about the predictive power of intelligence tests.

The data on general intelligence as a predictor of work-related behaviours are, however, very clear. There are very few researchers who have inspected recent meta-analyses who could not but be impressed by the fact that without doubt the best single predictor of success at work (particularly in senior complex jobs) is intelligence. This is not to deny that there are other important factors nor that it is patently obvious that not all intelligent people do particularly well in the workplace. Intelligence is relatively easy to measure reliably and accurately. Intelligence test scores are influenced by other factors (like personality) but not to any great extent. Intelligence is cognitive capacity and refers to both efficient problem solving but also accumulated knowledge.

However, the science and the practice of intelligence testing remain far apart because of the history of misunderstanding, misapplications and political differences. The signs are hopeful for the future where differential psychologists and people at work could benefit from some of the most valid and predictive of all measures in the workplace.

7 The social intelligences at work

Introduction

Since first coined by Thorndike (1920) and echoed later by Guilford (1967) psychologists have been interested in the "social intelligences". These are nearly always put in "inverted commas" because, strictly speaking, they are not intelligences but conceived of as social skills, even dispositions, that have both multiple causes and multiple consequences. As Locke (2005) has noted for the most famous of the multiple intelligences, notably emotional intelligence, "the concept of emotional intelligence is invalid because it is not a form of intelligence and because it is defined so broadly and inclusively that it has no intelligible meaning" (p. 425).

There are many explanations for the interest in the "social intelligences". One is, of course, that cognitive ability rarely explains more than one third to one half of the variance in any outcome measure, be it academic achievement, job performance or health. The question is, do the social intelligences account for incremental variance over IQ test results? A second reason is that it has been recognised and demonstrated that it is difficult to improve or teach cognitive ability. Third, for over twenty years new advocates of "multiple intelligence" have been enormously successful in persuading people both of their existence and importance, despite the quality of their empirical evidence.

The question is, what is social intelligence? Eysenck (1985b) conceived of a useful model that differentiated three types of intelligence – biological, psychometric and social – and the factors that influenced it (Figure 7.1).

Mackintosh (1998) suggested that social intelligence – that is the aspect of intelligence not measured by IQ tests – was an intelligence "defined in a sufficiently liberal manner" (p. 367). He saw it as social competence and success in social interactions. He argued that social intelligence was adaptive and could be seen in other animal species. It allows individuals to understand others' hopes, fears, beliefs and wishes. Indeed he linked it to the "Theory of Mind" literature from developmental and clinical psychology.

Mackintosh (1998) believed that was not too difficult to define social intelligence (mainly in terms of social skills) or indeed to devise tests to measure it. But he doubted two things: *first*, if these many social and interpersonal skills actually load on a single dimension, and, *second*, whether they are uncorrelated with, and therefore related to, standard IQ measures of cognitive ability.

Various researchers have reviewed the concept of social intelligence including its discriminant validity, relationship to personality and classic cognitive ability, its role in "life tasks" and how it develops over time. Their belief was that it is multifactional,

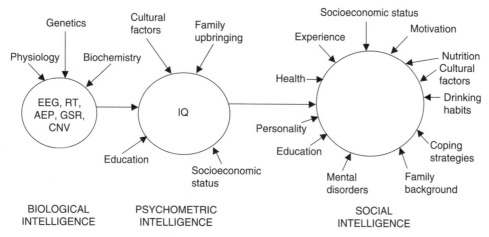

Figure 7.1 Eysenck's (1985b) representation of three different conceptions of "intelligence". In this model many things, like cognitive ability, predict social intelligence. Reproduced with kind permission of Springer Science and Business Media.

Table 7.1 The many identified multiple intelligences

	"Multiple intelligence"	*Author*	*Year*
1.	Analytical	Sternberg	1997a
2.	Bodily-kinaesthetic	Gardner	1999
3.	Creative	Sternberg	1997a
4.	Emotional	Salovey and Mayer	1990
5.	Interpersonal	Gardner	1999
6.	Intrapersonal	Gardner	1999
7.	Mathematical	Gardner	1999
8.	Musical	Gardner	1999
9.	Naturalistic	Gardner	1999
10.	Practical	Sternberg	1997a
11.	Sexual	Conrad and Milburn	2001
12.	Spatial	Gardner	1999
13.	Spiritual	Emmons	2000
14.	Verbal	Gardner	1999

relating to such issues as social sensitivity, social insight and social communication. In other words, it is much more of a social or personality variable than a cognitive variable, which is more about information processing and accumulation. Hence trait emotional intelligence (Petrides & Furnham, 2001, 2003, 2006). Others, like Landy (2006), were much more circumspect about the concept. This was nicely described in the title of his chapter heading: "The Long, Frustrating and Fruitless Search for Social Intelligence".

Over the past decade or so there has been an explosion in the number of "multiple intelligences" discovered. Hardly a year goes by before yet another is discovered. Table 7.1 shows 14 "different intelligences".

Among academic researchers social intelligences are not usually considered part of cognitive ability and "intelligences" is always put in inverted commas. There are two reasons for this: *first*, there is very little good, empirical evidence supporting the idea that these are separate factors, distinguishable from each other; *second*, they seem unrelated to traditional measures of intelligence. More interestingly, in a variety of studies, Furnham (2001a) has shown that lay people believe that many of the multiple intelligences (i.e. musical, bodily-kinaesthetic, emotions) are *not* linked to traditional ideas of intelligence.

The two figures most powerfully involved with multiple intelligence world are Sternberg (1997a) and Gardner (1983, 1999). Gardner (1983) defined intelligence as: "the ability to solve problems or to create products that are valued within one or more cultural settings" (p. 11), and specified seven intelligences. He argued that *linguistic or verbal* and *logical or mathematical intelligences* are those typically valued in educational settings. Linguistic intelligence involves sensitivity to the spoken and written language and the ability to learn languages. Logical or mathematical intelligence involves the capacity to analyse problems logically, solve maths problems and investigate issues scientifically. These two types of intelligence dominate intelligence tests. Three other multiple intelligences are arts based: *musical intelligence*, which refers to skill in the performance, composition and appreciation of musical patterns; *bodily-kinaesthetic intelligence*, which is based on the use of the whole or parts of the body to solve problems or to fashion products; and *spatial intelligence*, which is the ability to recognise and manipulate patterns in space. There are also two personal intelligences: *interpersonal intelligence*, which is the capacity to understand the intentions, motivations and desires of other people and to work effectively with them; and *intra-personal intelligence*, which is the capacity to understand oneself and to use this information effectively in regulating one's life.

However, in his later book, Gardner (1999) defines intelligence as a "biopsychologi-cal potential to process information that can be activated in a cultural setting to solve problems or create products that are of value in a culture" (pp. 33–34). In this work, he introduces three possible new intelligences, although he notes: "The strength of the evidence for these varies, and whether or not to declare a certain human capacity another type of intelligence is certainly a judgement call" (p. 47). However, he only adds one new intelligence, namely *naturalistic intelligence*, which is "expertise in the recogni-tion and classification of the numerous species – the flora and fauna – of his or her environment" (p. 43). It is the capacity to taxonomise: to recognise members of a group, to distinguish among members of a species and to chart out the relations, formally or informally, among several species. The other two were spiritual and existential intelli-gences. *Spiritual intelligence* is the ability to master a set of diffuse and abstract concepts about being, but also mastering the craft of altering one's consciousness in attaining a certain state of being. This has recently become an issue of considerable debate (Emmons, 2000). *Existential intelligence* is yet more difficult to define: "the capacity to locate oneself with respect to the furthest reaches of the cosmos – the infinite and infinitesimal – and the related capacity to locate oneself with respect to such existential features of the human condition as the significance of life, the meaning of death, the ultimate fate of the physical and the psychological worlds and such profound experi-ences as love of another person or total immersion in a work of art" (p. 61).

It should be pointed out, however, that despite its popularity in educational circles, Gardner's theory has been consistently attacked and criticised by those working empirically in the area (Allix, 2000; Klein, 1997; Morgan, 1996). White (2005), like other educationalists, has questioned the veridicality of the basic assumption that Gardner makes. Almost none of the researchers attempting to understand the structure of intelligence believe that the "social intelligences" are real intelligences (Furnham & Bunclark, 2006), but rather broad, possibly learnt abilities, which some people like to label intelligences.

Until comparatively recently there had been no real attempt to provide empirical evidence for multiple intelligence theory. However, Visser et al. (2006) tested 200 participants giving them eight tests of the Gardner intelligences. Factor analysis revealed, against the Gardner theory, a large *g* factor. The highest loading tests on this *g* factor were Linguistic (Verbal), Logical-Mathematical, Spatial, Naturalistic and Interpersonal intelligences. The authors concluded: "Results support previous findings that highly diverse tests of purely cognitive abilities share strong loadings on a factor of general intelligence and that abilities involving sensory, motor or personality influences are less strongly *g*-loaded" (p. 487). Later they conclude:

> The substantial *g*-loadings of all purely cognitive tests in the current study contra-dict Gardner's assertion that there are at least eight independent intelligence domains. Although Gardner has acknowledged the existence of *g* and has con-ceded that the eight intelligences might not be entirely independent, his contention that positive correlations between various cognitive tasks are largely due to verbal demands was clearly not supported in this study, in which those verbal demands were minimised. Instead, measures of Linguistic, Spatial, Logical-Mathematical, Naturalistic, and Interpersonal intelligences showed a positive manifold of correl-ations, substantial loadings on a *g* factor, and substantial correlations with an outside measure of general intelligence. The common element that saturated the highly *g*-loaded tests most strongly was their demand on reasoning abilities, not their specifically verbal content.
>
> The finding that several of the partly non-cognitive tests in this study were very weakly *g*-loaded is unsurprising, and suggests that Gardner is likely correct in claiming that Bodily-Kinesthetic ability is quite different from the various cognitive abilities. Given the important contribution of non-cognitive as well as cognitive abilities to performance in the Bodily-Kinesthetic, Musical and Intrapersonal domains, "talents" might be a more appropriate label than "intelligences".
>
> Finally, some of the ability domains proposed by Gardner were not supported by the present data, as the within-domain correlations were either very weak (Bodily-Kinesthetic, Intrapersonal) or attributable entirely to *g* (Naturalistic). The coher-ence of some of the other ability domains (e.g. Linguistic, Spatial), as shown by significant residual correlations after the extraction of *g*, is consistent with multiple intelligences theory. However, this result is explained equally well by the much older hierarchical models of intelligence, which postulate several group factors in addition to an important *g* factor.
>
> (p. 501)

Sternberg (1997a) has developed a multidimensional model, also known as the "triar-chic" theory of "successful" intelligence. This posits that human intelligence comprises three aspects, that is, componential, experiential and contextual. The *componential* aspect refers to a person's ability to learn new things, to think analytically and to solve problems. This aspect of intelligence is manifested through better performance on standard intelligence tests, which require general knowledge and ability in areas such as arithmetic and vocabulary. The *experiential* aspect refers to a person's ability to combine different experiences in unique and creative ways. It concerns original thinking and creativity in both the arts and the sciences. Finally, the *contextual* aspect refers to a person's ability to deal with practical aspects of the environment and to adapt to new and changing contexts. This aspect of intelligence resembles what lay people sometimes refer to as "street smarts". Sternberg (1997a) popularised these concepts and referred to them as analytic, creative and practical intelligence.

Whilst this model has attracted some independent research (Furnham & Petrides, 2004), practical intelligence theory, however, has also attracted very serious criticism. Gottfredson (2003a), in an extremely exhaustive review of all the work in the area, disputes Sternberg's central claim that there exists a general factor of practical intelligence (made up of the three intelligences), that is distinct from academic intelligence as usually conceived. She concludes:

> It is true that *g* provides only a partial explanation of "intelligent behaviour", and that its role in everyday affairs is yet poorly understood. But there is a solid, century-long evidentiary base upon which researchers are busily building. Simply positing a new and independent intelligence to explain much of what remains unexplained (and much of what has *already* been explained), while simultaneously ignoring the ever-growing evidentiary base, does not promise to advance knowledge. The concept of tacit knowledge does, I suspect, point to a form of experience and knowledge that lends itself to the development of what might be called wisdom – a gradual understanding of the probabilities and possibilities in human behaviour (and in individual persons) that we generally develop only by experiencing or observing them first-hand over the course of our lives. This is not a new form of intelligence, however, but perhaps only the motivated and sensitive application of whatever level of *g* we individually possess. Sternberg et al. could better advance scientific knowledge on this issue by probing more deeply and analytically into the role of tacit knowledge in our lives rather than continuing to spin gauzy illusions of a wholly new intelligence that defies the laws of evidence.
>
> (p. 392)

Neisser (1976) was one of the first researchers to distinguish between academic and practical intelligence, but saw them as closely related. Yet, many psychometricians are against the whole concept of multiple intelligence, arguing for the "*g*" factor (Eysenck, 1998; Jensen, 1998). This is essentially the idea that all valid tests of intelligence correlate highly with each other. That is, when individuals take a range of tests, they tend to score in the same range on all of them. One has *general*, unitary not multiple intelligences. Yet the concept of multiple, unique, unrelated intelligences has been so popular that authors from a variety of backgrounds have "discovered" or distinguished between various other multiple intelligences.

The idea of multiple intelligences seems to have been warmly embraced in the business world (Nardi, 2001). Riggio et al. (2002) noted that the multiple intelligence idea was intuitively appealing because it is self-evident that people require various areas of competence, other than only academic intelligence, to succeed at business leadership. Most organisations have used competency framework in selection, assessment and appraisal, including all specific multiple (often between six and eight) competencies that are desirable/required to do the job (see Chapter 11). They nearly always involve cognitive ability and other skills.

The reason for human resource specialists and others favouring the idea of multiple and social intelligences is partly due to their caution in using traditional tests (see Chapter 4). With litigation issues concerning test bias and a general dislike of cognitive ability tests, despite their proven validity, many have turned to multiple intelligence tests, such as they exist.

The concept of multiple intelligences, particularly emotional intelligence, has become extremely popular. Academic research has begun to "catch up" with this wave of interest by trying to define and measure it. More importantly for the topic of this book, researchers have begun to test the central claim that it adds incremental validity over conventional intelligence tests in predicting success at work, however measured.

Business or managerial intelligence

In a study of impatriate managers, Harvey et al. (2002) listed eight "managerial intelligences". They took as their starting point Sternberg's (1985) triarchic theory of intelligence, but split the three intelligences further. Thus *analytic* intelligence was split into cognitive and emotional intelligence; *practical* intelligence into political, sociocultural, organisational and network intelligence; and *creative* intelligence into innovative and intuitive intelligence. Clearly this classification is controversial: for many researchers in the field, emotional intelligence is not part of general or cognitive intelligence.

The authors argued that cognitive IQ is the "*g*" factor of general intelligence that measures problem-solving abilities. They categorise emotional intelligence within the analytic category because "emotional development and maturity are viewed as necessary to allow managers to effectively utilise their cognitive abilities. The importance of emotional intelligence increases with the level of authority in an organisation" (Harvey et al., 2002, p. 504).

The four practical intelligences are, inevitably, more controversial. *Political IQ* is defined as "the ability to gain resources through exercising political power in situations where ambiguity and accountability levels allow for a shaping (i.e. spin) of attitudes and images among those being influenced. . . . A high political IQ refers to having a sense about the social infrastructure and the individuals that occupy key positions that can be instrumental in exercising influence to change resource, allocation or direction of the decision making" (p. 506).

Sociocultural IQ is really cultural knowledge and the ability to translate or integrate specific cues about culture. *Organisational intelligence* is knowledge of how things are done via policies, procedures, planning processes and audits. It is, in effect, an understanding of the official formal rules of the organisation and the ability to get things done in a specific organisational context. *Network intelligence* is essentially about inter-organisational management, while *organisational IQ* is about intra-organisational IQ. *Management IQ* is based on the size, structure and centrality of a person's personal relationships crossing organisations.

According to Harvey et al. (2002), the two creative intelligences are innovating and intuitive intelligences. *Innovative intelligence* is defined quite specifically as: "the ability to think in abstract terms, to develop business ideas and concepts that have not been conceptualised by others, constitutes business innovation. The embodiment of ideas/concepts into new processes, products, services and technologies is a valuable outcome of innovation" (p. 511). *Intuitive intelligence* seems harder to define, and the authors talk about its "subconscious origin", "tacit nature", "street smarts", "sixth sense" and "gut knowledge". The concept of intuitive intelligence does seem close to Sternberg's (1997a) and Neisser's (1976) work on tacit knowledge and practical intelligence.

The authors provided a profile that would allow somebody to score individuals on their eight intelligences. They did *not*, however, provide any data for their theory that supported the threefold classification. More importantly, they made little attempt to distinguish between abilities and traits or to consider whether it was possible to train or develop these intelligences. Interestingly, nearly all the measures they proposed for each of the IQs, save cognitive intelligence, are measured by self-report tests of preference, rather than power-based ability tests. Nevertheless, people recognise these different abilities/skills and traits.

One of the advantages of Harvey et al.'s (2002) description of managerial intelligences was that they used psychological and psychometric concepts in the language of business.

The concept of business IQ, at least as outlined by Harvey et al. (2002), has not, as yet, attracted much attention. Certainly there remains little evidence of the separate "unique" existence of these intelligences or indeed evidence that they predict anything.

However, Furnham (2005c) asked working adults to rate themselves, their boss, and their boss's boss on these eight intelligences. He found males rated their overall IQ as well as their cognitive, creative and political intelligence as significantly higher than females. Females rated their boss's overall, emotional and organisational IQ significantly higher than did male participants. Participants believed they had higher emotional, but lower political, organisational and network intelligence than their boss. Regressions indicated that only one of the eight estimated business intelligences (cognitive intelligence) was related to overall (total, general) estimated intelligence in self, boss or boss's boss.

Table 7.2 shows the results of the self-estimates. Once again, although this idea is immensely appealing to consultants and managers themselves, it is essentially misleading to label these "intelligences". It would be more sensible, however, to call them competencies (see Chapter 11). The question, rarely asked, but nevertheless very important is the origin of such "intelligences"/competencies. How and when are they acquired? Can they easily be taught? Are there systematic (i.e. gender) differences in these competencies? How are they measured? Are people accurate at self-assessment? Are they linked in any systematic way, i.e. is there an underlying structure to these beliefs. And, most importantly, what is their relationship with cognitive ability as measured by conventional power tests of intelligence? It seems now that to attract attention the word intelligence is put after any skill or competency to give it respectability.

Emotional intelligence

However, of all the "hot" intelligences it was, and is, the idea of *Emotional Intelligence* that has most captivated people's imagination. Just as history is told by the victors so the "story" of EI is told rather differently by different groups. Some claim EI was part of the "multiple intelligence" movement dating back to the social intelligences of the 1920s (Petrides et al., 2004b) or the mischievous muddling of McClelland responsible for other similar concepts like competency (see Chapter 11).

Certainly there are two dates that mark the start of academic research and popular interest. It is Salovey and Mayer's (1990) paper, published in a relatively obscure journal, that most academics refer to as the beginning of academic and conceptual research

Table 7.2 The questionnaire showing mean scores and standard deviations for self-estimates

	Type of IQ	Description	You
1.	Cognitive	The traditional measure of intellectual ability. This IQ measures the ability to reason, learn and think analytically.	116.7 (13.7)
2.	Emotional	The ability to use one's own affective state to tap the affective state of others to accomplish objectives. The ability to display an appropriate emotional state and to respond to others' emotions in an effective manner.	115.3 (14.8)
3.	Political	The ability to use the formal and informal power in the company to accomplish objectives. The ability to know how to prudently, judiciously and artfully use power in the organisation.	107.2 (13.8)
4.	Social/Cultural	The extent to which one is adequately socialised in a society, an organisation, or a subculture. Recognition and understanding of roles, norms, routines and taboos, in various setting.	112.9 (11.5)
5.	Organisational	Having a detailed and accurate understanding of how the organisation operates both functionally and the time that is needed to accomplish certain tasks in the company. The detailed knowledge of how to "get things done" in the company.	111.3 (14.0)
6.	Network	The ability to get things done with multiple organisational units. Accomplishing the goals of the company effectively by recognising, understanding and managing inter-organisational relations.	110.2 (12.9)
7.	Creative	The ability to diverge/innovate in thinking and create fresh novel ideas and solutions to problems. The ability to address problems/issues with insight and resourcefulness and to find unique solutions.	114.7 (14.4)
8.	Intuitive	The ability to have quick insights into how to solve problems or to address situations without past experience of the problem, and without formally processing information (e.g. street smart).	113.8 (12.8)

Source: Adapted from Furnham (2005c).

on the topic. But it was definitely Goleman's (1995) blockbuster book that spurred massive popularity of the concept.

The term "emotional intelligence" was probably first used in a German paper by Leuner (1966). However, the first formal "definition" of EI, along with the first model, appeared in Salovey and Mayer (1990), who also carried out the first empirical studies. Goleman's (1995) international best-seller and "follow-up" (Goleman, 1998) propelled EI into the limelight and influenced most subsequent conceptualisations of EI. Towards the latter half of the 1990s, the first EI measures started to appear (Bar-On, 1997; Mayer et al., 2000; Salovey et al., 1995; Schutte et al., 1998).

The operationalisation of individual difference constructs hinges essentially on two issues. The first concerns the *sampling domain* of the construct (or "universe of items"), which refers to the elements or facets that a particular construct is hypothesised to encompass. For example, the basic or primary elements that largely define the personality dimension of Neuroticism are "inferiority", "unhappiness", "anxiety," "dependence" and "guilt". While for Extraversion they are such things as "sociability", "optimism", "assertiveness" and "activity".

The problem can be seen with many established questionnaires. Thus the EPP (Eysenck's Big 3, with 21 scales) and the NEO-PI-R (Costa & McCrae's long measure) both have primary factors or facets of both extraversion and neuroticism, but they are clearly different in length and label. What is important, however, is to recognise that two superfactor scores correlate very highly, suggesting that there is more overlap and agreement at the item and primary factor/facet level.

A difficulty arises, however, with deciding exactly which are the "facets" or primary factors that a construct encompasses. As Petrides and Furnham (2001, p. 428) put it, "asking what precisely should be part of a construct is like asking what sports should be in the Olympics; neither question can be answered objectively". Petrides et al. (2004b) have, however, listed facets of EQ that appear in different conceptualisations of the concept (Table 7.3).

However, Perez et al. (2005) have found eight other models (see Table 7.4) of different dimensions of EI showing much disagreement there is still in the area.

Petrides et al. (2004b) noted that the second fundamental issue in the operationalisation of a construct concerns *the procedures by which it is measured*. More specifically, there is a basic distinction between measures of *maximum* performance (e.g. IQ tests) and measures of *typical* response (e.g. personality questionnaires) with far-reaching implications for construct operationalisation. Self-report measurement leads to the operationalisation of the construct as a personality trait ("trait EI" or "emotional self-efficacy"), whereas potential maximum-performance measurement would lead to the operationalisation of the construct as a cognitive ability ("ability EI" or "cognitive-emotional ability"). It must be understood that trait EI and ability EI are two *different*

Table 7.3 Common facets in salient models of EI

Facets	High scorers perceive themselves as . . .
Adaptability	Flexible and willing to adapt to new conditions
Assertiveness	Forthright, frank, and willing to stand up for their rights
Emotion expression	Capable of communicating their feelings to others
Emotion management (others)	Capable of influencing others people's feelings
Emotion perception (self and others)	Clear about their own and other people's feelings
Emotion regulation	Capable of controlling their emotions
Impulsiveness (low)	Reflective and less likely to give in to their urges
Relationship skills	Capable of having fulfilling personal relationships
Self-esteem	Successful and self-confident
Self-motivation	Driven and unlikely to give up in the face of adversity
Social competence	Accomplished networkers with excellent social skills
Stress management	Capable of withstanding pressure and regulating stress
Trait empathy	Capable of taking someone else's perspective
Trait happiness	Cheerful and satisfied with their lives
Trait optimism	Confident and likely to "look on the bright side" of life.

Source: Petrides et al. (2004b). Taken from The Psychologist, October 2004. See www.bps.org.uk/7zxj.

Table 7.4 Summary of EI models

Salovey & Mayer (1990)		• Appraisal and expression of emotion • Utilisation of emotion • Regulation of emotion
Goleman (1995)		• Self-awareness • Self-regulation • Self-motivation • Empathy • Handling relationships
Mayer & Salovey (1997)		• Perception, appraisal, and expression of emotion • Emotional facilitation of thinking • Understanding and analysing emotions; employing emotional knowledge • Reflective regulation of emotions to promote emotional and intellectual growth
Bar-On (1997)	Intrapersonal	• Emotional self-awareness • Assertiveness • Self-regard • Self-actualisation • Independence
	Interpersonal	• Empathy • Interpersonal relationship • Social responsibility
	General	• Happiness • Optimism
	Adaptation	• Problem solving • Reality testing • Flexibility
	Stress management	• Stress tolerance • Impulse control
Cooper & Sawaf (1997)	Emotional literacy	• Emotional fitness • Emotional depth • Emotional alchemy
Goleman (1998)	Self-awareness	• Emotional self-awareness • Accurate self-assessment • Self-confidence
	Self-regulation	• Self-control • Trustworthiness • Conscientiousness • Adaptability • Innovation
	Self-motivation	• Achievement orientation • Commitment • Initiative • Optimism
	Empathy	• Empathy • Organisational awareness • Service orientation • Developing others • Leveraging diversity
	Social skills	• Leadership • Communication • Influence

		• Change catalyst
		• Conflict management
		• Building bonds
		• Collaboration and cooperation
		• Team capabilities
Weisinger (1998)	Self-awareness	• Emotional management
		• Self-motivation
		• Effective communication skills
		• Interpersonal expertise
		• Emotional coaching
Higgs & Dulewicz (1999)	Drivers	• Motivation
		• Intuitiveness
	Constrainers	• Conscientiousness
		• Emotional resilience
	Enablers	• Self-awareness
		• Interpersonal sensitivity
		• Influence
		• Trait

Source: From Perez et al. (2005). Copyright © 2005 by Hogrefe & Huber Publishers. Reproduced with permission.

Table 7.5 Trait EI versus ability EI

	Trait EI	*Ability EI*
Measurement	Self-report	Performance based
Conceptualisation	Personality trait	Cognitive ability
Expected relationship to g	Orthogonal (i.e. uncorrelated)	Moderate to strong correlations
Construct validity evidence[a]	Good discriminant and incremental validity vis à vis personality	Limited concurrent and predictive validity
	Good concurrent and predictive validity with many criteria	Lower than expected correlations with IQ measures
Example measures	EQ-I SEIS TEIQue	MSCEIT
Properties of measures[a]	Easy to administer Susceptible to faking Standard scoring procedures Good psychometric properties	Difficult to administer Resistant to faking Atypical scoring procedures Weak psychometric properties

Notes: g = general cognitive ability; EQ-I = Emotional Quotient Inventory (Bar-On, 1997); SEIS = Schutte Emotional Intelligence Scale (Schutte et al., 1998); TEIQue = Trait Emotional Intelligence (e.g. Petrides & Furnham, 2003); MSCEIT = Mayer–Salovey–Caruso Emotional Intelligence Test (Mayer et al., 2002).
[a]Entries in these rows are generalisations and do not apply equally to all measures.
Source: Petrides et al. (2004b). Taken from The Psychologist, October 2004. See www.bps.org.uk/7zxj.

constructs because the procedures used in their operational definitions are fundamentally different, even though their theoretical domains might overlap. The primary basis for discriminating between trait EI and ability EI is to be found in the type of measurement approach one chooses to employ and not in the elements of the sampling domains of the various conceptualisations (Table 7.5). Many dispute the more fundamental point that EI could ever be actually measured by cognitive ability tests. That is, that EI concepts, like emotional regulation, can never be reliably and validly measured by an objective ability test because of the subjective nature of emotional experience.

There now exists a large number of measures of EI, many of which are poorly constructed and validated. Perez et al. (2005) in an exhaustive review found, described and evaluated 5 ability EQ tests and 15 trait measures.

Petrides et al. (2004b) argued that because trait EI encompasses behavioural tendencies and *self-perceived* abilities, as opposed to *actual* cognitive abilities, it belongs in the realm of personality. In contrast, ability EI, which encompasses actual abilities, belongs primarily in the domain of cognitive ability. While trait EI is hypothesised to be orthogonal to cognitive ability (Furnham & Petrides, 2003, 2004; Petrides et al., 2004a) ability EI should be related mainly to general intelligence (g), but also to specific personality dimensions that reflect basic individual differences in emotionality (especially Neuroticism).

Traditionally psychologists have argued and demonstrated that personality and intelligence are effectively unrelated to one another. It seems that normal dimensions of personality are essentially not related to ability tests even when the former are measured by objective tests. Yet recent models have attempted to integrate these two basic dimensions of differential psychology (Chamorro-Premuzic & Furnham, 2005).

A major difficulty with the operationalisation of ability EI is that emotional experiences are *inherently subjective* and, consequently, lack the objectivity required to make them amenable to robust, valid and reliable maximum performance measurement. There is no simple way of applying truly veridical criteria in the objective scoring of items relating to the intrapersonal component of ability EI (e.g. "I am aware of my emotions as I experience them") simply because the application of such scoring procedures would require direct access to privileged information, such as inner feelings and private cognitions, that is available only to the individual who is being assessed. Attempts to get around this problem (e.g. Mayer et al., 2002) are predicated on scoring procedures that had been tried in the past with limited success. In addition to conceptual limitations, these procedures produce test scores with undesirable psychometric properties (see Roberts et al., 2001, for a review).

Brody (2005) has delivered a cogent attack on the single ability measure of EQ: the Mayer–Salovey–Caruso Emotional Intelligence Test (MSCEIT). He objected to the scoring method because he noted that the test measured emotional knowledge not emotional management as claimed. "A person who has expert knowledge of emotions may or may not be expert in the actual ability that is allegedly assessed by the test" (p. 234). The test defines correct answers as those defined by experts but does not indicate the extent to which experts agree (i.e. their consensus).

He also doubted that there was sufficient evidence that EI might really be conceived of as a latent trait like that of intelligence: "owing, in part, to the relatively brief history of research on this topic, it is not possible to document a nomological network of laws and relations defining the conceptual and empirical relations that obtain between tests of EI and the latent trait of which they are alleged manifestations" (p. 234).

Third, he argued from a characteristically careful analysis of all the supposed evidence available that he remained deeply sceptical of the evidence for the predictive validity of the MSCEIT.

At the moment two "schools" exist that are mutually hostile: The *ability* school vs. the *trait* school. They measure, write and proselytise differently. Researchers from the "trait school" complain that their papers are regularly and "unconditionally" rejected by those from the "ability school" who refuse to accept that EI is just another second-order trait. The ability school frequently write papers that systematically ignore the, now many, papers there are from the trait tradition. Even conference symposia tend to be homogeneous. Mutual contempt is not unusual among researchers but not usually as early on in the development of a concept.

What of the lay person? Many talk of EQ as a skill; some of it being like intuition. Lay people seem as divided on the issue as the academics. However, commercially the trait camp has won. There are dozens of poor or non-psychometrised instruments on the market. A web search soon confirms this. Nearly all are questionnaires: self-report measures that have high face validity; and possibly high fakeability. They look like older measures of assertiveness, social skill or interpersonal style. Ability measures are difficult to devise and take time to administer. Also, they may not always appear to be relevant to people in business who may be interested in training EQ or selecting those with high scores.

Lay people, even hard-headed business people, are surprisingly unimpressed by, or worse uninterested in, psychometric evidence. Either because they do not understand or care about concepts like test–retest reliability, Cronbach's alpha, predictive validity or orthogonal dimensionality, they appear to buy questionnaire products on packaging and promise much more than on evidence. This partly explains the popularity of EI. Demand is quickly met by supply but not by many reputable test publishers because validation is too time consuming. This does not, however, prevent others from aggressively marketing their essentially "not proven" products.

Emotional intelligence at work

It was no doubt Goleman's book that electrified the public and popularised the term. He has retried to capture attention more recently with *Social Intelligence* (Goleman, 2006). In his *second* book he extended his ideas to the workplace. Now he has over 25 facets subsumed under five domains. Any one inspecting this system (see Box 7.1) would be astounded by the conceptual muddle at both levels. Thus personality traits, like Conscientiousness, are subsumed under the domain of self-regulation. Equally, unrelated psychological concepts like initiative and optimism are classified under motivation. It seems difficult, in fact, to specify what is *not* a facet of EQ. That is: does it have any divergent validity?

The book argued (usually without good, direct evidence) that, at work, relationship building is more important than technical skills. Further, Goleman argued that technical training, in the essential job knowledge of any career, from accounting to zoology, is easy compared to teaching EQ skills. That is, as an adult it is comparatively more straightforward to teach a person the technical aspects of the job than the soft skills. The idea seems to be that there is a critical period to acquire the bases of EI, which is probably during early to late adolescence. The young person, often a male, may experience social anxiety, discomfort and rejection while attempting to interact with and influence others (specifically those they are attracted to, which is most often people of the opposite sex).

Box 7.1 The emotional intelligences at work

Personal competence

Competencies that determine how we manage ourselves

Self-awareness: *Knowing one's internal states, preferences, resources and intuitions*

- *Emotional awareness*: recognising emotions and their effects
- *Accurate self-assessment*: knowing own strengths and limits
- *Self-confidence*: strong sense of self-worth and capabilities

Self-regulation: *managing one's internal states, impulses and resources*

- *Self-control*: keeping disruptive emotions and impulses in check
- *Trustworthiness*: maintaining standards of honesty and integrity
- *Conscientiousness*: taking responsibility for personal performance
- *Adaptability*: flexibility in handling change
- *Innovation*: being comfortable with novel ideas, approaches and new information

Motivation: *Emotional tendencies that guide or facilitate reaching goals*

- *Achievement drive*: striving to improve or meet a standard of excellence
- *Commitment*: aligning with the goals of the group or organisation
- *Initiative*: readiness to act on opportunities
- *Optimism*: persistence in pursuing goals despite obstacles or setbacks

Personal competence

Competencies that determine how we manage relationships

Empathy: *Awareness of others' feelings, needs and concerns*

- *Understanding others*: sensing others' feelings and perspectives and taking an active interest in their concerns
- *Developing others*: sensing others' development needs and bolstering their abilities
- *Service orientation*: anticipating, recognising and meeting customer needs
- *Leveraging diversity*: cultivating opportunities through different kinds of people
- *Political awareness*: reading a group's emotional currents and power relationships

Social skills: *Adeptness at inducing desirable responses in others*

- *Influence*: wielding effective tactics for persuasion
- *Communication*: listening openly and sending convincing messages
- *Conflict management*: negotiating and resolving disagreements
- *Leadership*: inspiring and guiding individuals and groups
- *Change catalyst*: initiating or managing change
- *Building bonds*: nurturing instrumental relationships
- *Collaboration and cooperation*: working with others toward shared goals
- *Team capabilities*: creating group synergy in pursuing collective goals

Source: Goleman (2006). Permission sought from Bantam Dell Publishing.

Hence, over time, they may find solace in computers and other activities with a high skills and low contact basis. Thus, in early adulthood, they appear to be technically very competent in certain areas (IT, engineering) but still rather undeveloped in people skills and more specifically emotional awareness and regulation. They may even be "phobic" about emotional issues and resistant to (social skills) training. It is also assumed that people are less able to pick up EI "skills" as well as less willing to try. To acquire technical skills often requires considerable dedication and opportunities to acquire social skills (EQ) are, therefore, reduced. Then the low EQ person chooses technology rather than people for fun, comfort and as a source of ideas because they do not understand emotions.

The argument goes, according to Goleman, that failed and derailed managers tend to be rigid, with poor self-control, poor social skills and are weak at building bonds. And, yet, understanding and using emotions and feelings are at the heart of business and indeed being human. It is, says Goleman (1998), no accident that motive and emotion share the same Latin root meaning to move . . . great work starts with great feeling.

But the book seems to have an over-inclusive view of what EQ is. There are lists of facets and features, some derivative of each other, some quite unrelated to any-thing about emotion (see Box 7.1). It does echo themes in the zeitgeist . . . hence its popularity. The book is also easy to dip into; with many summaries and précis. Hence, there were, and indeed still are, a rash of magazine and newspaper articles that popularised the book and the concept. This is not "trickle down" economics but a waterfall of publicity. The sheer amount of positive publicity given to the book must be one of the factors involved in its success and the popularity of the concept at the heart of it.

In his 1995 book Goleman, claimed that cognitive ability (i.e. intelligence) contri-buted around 20% toward life success but the remaining 80% is directly attributable to emotional intelligence. In a later book, Goleman (1998) listed 25 social competencies from conflict management to self-control all of which make up social competencies that lead to success at work.

Equally in their book entitled *Executive EQ*, Cooper and Sawaf (1997) put forth the four cornerstones of emotional intelligence at the executive level: *emotional literacy* (involves the knowledge and understanding of one's own emotions and how they function), *emotional fitness* (involves trustworthiness and emotional hardiness and flexibility), *emotional depth* (involves emotional growth and intensity), and *emotional alchemy* (involves using emotions to discover creative opportunities).

Since the start of the millennium there have been a veritable stream of empirical papers on EQ (Lopes et al., 2003; Petrides & Furnham, 2000a, 2000b, 2001, 2003; Petrides et al., 2004a, 2004b). Some have focused very specifically on *EQ at work*. Thus Jordan et al. (2002) developed a workgroup EQ scale to test hypotheses about the relationship between EQ, team process effectiveness and team goal focus. They did, indeed, find some evidence that low EQ teams did perform at lower levels than high EQ teams. Critics, however, would probably simply want to relabel EQ as social skills or emotional awareness.

Quebbeman and Rozell (2002) defined emotional intelligence in terms of self-awareness, self-regulation, motivation, empathy and social skills. They tested a model that suggested that work experiences trigger responses that are mediated by EQ and Neuroticism to produce affective outcomes and thence behavioural outcomes. Similarly Petrides and Furnham (2006) looked at the relationship between EQ, job stress, control and satisfaction as well as organisational commitment. EQ predicted perceived job control, which predicted job satisfaction and thence commitment. However, they found significant sex differences in the whole process.

Many have subsequently discussed and tested the idea that emotional intelligence is related to work success. Some papers have been theoretical, others empirical. Thus Quebbeman and Rozell (2002) propose a model that posited how emotional intelligence is related to workplace aggression. Despite not having any empirical evidence they feel able to conclude:

> As shown by the model, individuals with higher emotional intelligence and high positive affect are more likely to react to perceived injustices with adaptive/constructive behaviours. Because these individuals are less likely to engage in aggression in the face of conflict, organisations should seek to hire and retain employees with high emotional intelligence and high positive affect. Incorporating emotional intelligence and positive dispositional affectivity into daily organisational life will include training for emotional intelligence, revising selection and placement practices, counselling, training for attributional style, encouraging constructive behaviours through the organisation's performance appraisal and reward structure, and incorporating organisational strategies to reduce triggering events.
>
> (p. 137)

Equally Dulewicz and Higgs (2001) have developed, and part tested, a model that puts EQ at the centre of the predictors of job performance. Thus, they believe that cognitive ability and specified management competencies contribute to a person's EQ (self-awareness, interpersonal sensitivity, etc.). EQ is modified by other factors called drivers (decisiveness) and constrainers (lack of emotional resilience) but directly predicts performance. They argued that they had evidence to suggest that EQ was directly related to leadership through specific leadership competencies like creating the case for change and engaging others, as well as implementing and sustaining change.

There have also been various empirical studies. Thus Jordan et al. (2002) looked at the work-related performance of low vs. high EQ work groups. They found that high emotional intelligence teams operated at high levels of performance throughout the study period while low emotional intelligence teams, on the other hand, initially performed at a low level, but equalled the performance of the high emotional intelligence teams by the end of the study period. This suggested that the power of EQ is rather limited.

Similarly, Petrides and Furnham, in a study of British working adults, found that emotional intelligence was related to perceived job control, which predicted job satisfaction. They found, however, evidence of sex differences such that in males EQ was negatively predictive of perceived job stress while there was no significant relationship in females.

There will no doubt continue to be many more papers on the role of emotional intelligence at work even long after the "fad" has passed in the management consultancy world. Further, it is likely that most papers will indeed show that EQ is a significant predictor and correlate of IQ. However, this is not to show that EQ and IQ are related. Most measurement devices still employ trait measures of intelligence. Thus, what this enterprise is more about is the demonstrably true assertion that personality traits (however labelled) predict work performance.

More recently Zeidner et al. (2004) provided a useful critical overview of the role of EQ in the workplace. As they noted, often business people prefer to talk about emotional competencies (rather than traits or abilities), which are essentially learned capabilities. In this sense, EQ is "the potential to become skilled at learning certain emotional responses" (p. 377). It does not ensure, therefore, that individuals will (as opposed to can) manifest competent behaviours at work. Thus, EQ is an index of potential. However, emotional competence does, it is argued, assist in learning (soft) interpersonal skills.

Zeidner et al. (2004) tried to specify these emotional competencies. They include: emotional self-awareness, emotional self-regulation, social-emotional awareness, regulating emotions in others, understanding emotions, etc. If one is to include older related concepts like social skills or interpersonal competencies then it is possible to find a literature dating back thirty years showing that these skills predict occupational effectiveness and success. Further, there is a convincing empirical literature that suggests that these skills can be improved and learnt.

However Zeidner et al. (2004) were quite rightly eager to squash the IQ vs. EQ myth. They note (my italics) "*several unsubstantiated claims* have appeared in the popular literature and the media about the significance of EI in the workplace. Thus, EI has been claimed to validly predict a variety of successful behaviours at work, at a level exceeding that of intelligence. . . . Of note, however, Goleman is unable to cite empirical data supporting any causal link between EI and any of its supposed, positive effects" (p. 380).

The authors quite rightly pointed out that EQ measures must demonstrate criterion, discriminant, incremental and predictive validity to be cost effective in business and scientifically sound. We know that general ability (IQ) predicts around 20–30% of the variance in (higher) job performance across all jobs, all criteria, but more for complex jobs.

They reviewed studies that provide positive, mixed and negative results. Quite rightly they offered critiques of the studies that purport to show EQ linked to work success. Typical problems include: the psychometric properties of the EQ measure; not controlling for intelligence (cognitive ability) or personality factors; not having very robust measures of work-related behaviour; not being able to disentangle the direction of causality through using longitudinal studies; and having too many impressionistic, anecdotal studies and few published in peer-review journals.

The authors were also interested in the explanation for the process. Thus *if* EQ does predict satisfaction, productivity, team work, etc., the question is what is the *process* or *mechanism* that accounts for this? It seems, in the literature, that there are various speculations to account for this:

- High EQ people are better at communicating their ideas, intentions and goals. They are more articulate, assertive and sensitive.
- EQ is closely associated with team-work social skills, which are very important at work.
- Business leaders, high in EQ, build supportive climates, which increase organisational commitment, which in turn leads to success.
- High EQ leaders are perceptive and know their own and their teams' strengths and weaknesses, which enables them to leverage the former and compensate for the latter.
- EQ is related to effective and efficient coping skills, which enable people to deal with demands, pressure and stress better.
- High EQ leaders can accurately identify what followers feel and need, as well as being more inspiring and supportive. They generate more excitement, enthusiasm and optimism.
- High EQ managers, unlike their low EQ companions, are less prone to negative, defensive and destructive coping and decision-making styles.

Zeidner et al. (2004) ended with an evaluative summary and guidelines to do good research in the area:

> Overall, this section of our review suggests that the current excitement surrounding the potential benefits from the use of EI in the workplace may be premature or even misplaced. Whereas EI appears related to performance and affective outcomes, the evidence for performance is very limited and often contradictory. Much of the predictive validity of questionnaire measures of EI may be a product of their overlap with standard personality factors. Furthermore, the literature is replete with unsubstantiated generalisations, with much of the existing evidence bearing on the role of EI in occupational success either anecdotal or impressionistic and/or based on unpublished or in-house research. Thus, a number of basic questions still loom large: Do emotionally intelligent employees produce greater profits for the organisation? Does EI enhance well-being at the workplace? Are the affects of training in EI likely to result in increases in job performance and/or work satisfaction?
>
> (p. 380)

In order to provide both good theory and evidence to support the use of EQ in organisational settings, Zeidner et al. (2004) recommended the following:

- The measure of EQ used needs to have reliability and validity and be clearly differentiated from related constructs. "A science of EI requires specifying the definition, number, type and range of primary emotional abilities within a formal psychometric model" (p. 390).
- Researchers need to match the test to the job and specify precisely the context and

process by which it works. They recommended an emotional task analysis to understand how EQ works in different jobs.

- Researchers need good measures of the criterion job behaviour; they need to look at facets or components of EQ and they need to measure other variables like IQ or personality traits.

And their final conclusion was this:

> Despite the important role attributed to a wide array of emotional competencies in the workplace, there is currently only a modicum of research supporting the meaningful role attributed to EI (and nested emotional competencies) in determining occupational success. Many of the popular claims presented in the literature regarding the role of EI in determining work success and well-being are rather misleading in that they seem to present scientific studies supporting their claims, while in fact failing to do so. In short, despite some rather fantastic claims to the contrary, the guiding principle appears presently as "caveat emptor".
>
> (p. 393)

Management fads

The application of EI in the work place seems the virtual prototype of a fad. Furnham (2006) suggested that all management fads have a similar natural history, which has seven separate identifiable phases: One question is whether EQ will follow this trajectory and if so, where is it now?

1. Academic discovery

Faddish ideas can often be traced to the distinctly unfaddish world of academia. A modest discovery may result in a pretty indigestible paper in a specialist journal. These papers show the causal link between two factors relevant to work situations. These papers are not only dry, complicated and heavily statistical but they are cautious and preliminary. Academics often call for replications, more research, they are hesitant and underline the complexity of all the actual and possible factors involved. Few are interested in immediate application. Their job is understanding the process, not changing the world. The early social and emotional intelligence papers are a little like this. However, it is difficult to trace the concept to one study or paper.

2. Description of the study

This process can last a long time, and usually involves a lot of elaboration and distortion in the process. Someone reads the paper and provides a summary. The summary may be verbal and if so may end a little like Chinese whispers. Others hear it and repeat it. But with every repetition, the findings become stronger and the complexity weaker. In this sense effect size estimates go up and criticisms about experimental technique go down. Selective memory ensures that the crucial findings are recorded and embellished. At this stage, it is unlikely that the researchers would recognise the findings as they were in the first place. This phase is difficult to document, but it is often trainers, consultants and I/O psychologists who are primarily responsible for it.

3. Popularisation in a best seller

The next stage is when a business writer/guru takes up the call, hears about the findings, gives them a catchy title and before you know it the fad is about to begin. That one single and simple idea/finding/process soon becomes a book. This is where the Goleman (1998) book played such an important role. It was very widely reviewed in the media around the world. Quizzes began to appear and it soon entered both common consciousness and the language. The best seller with a snappy title and publisher hype, means that the average manager at least reads a few reviews of the book. He or she may even buy it, but many are content to hear the gist from reviewers. They are frequently envious of seemingly powerful results that occur when the great idea is followed. It is at this stage that the fad becomes a *buzzword*.

4. Consultant hype and universalisation

It is not the academic or the author that really powers the fad but an army of management consultants trying to look as if they are at the cutting edge of management theory. Because the concepts are easy to understand and are said to have wide application, the consultants seek to apply them everywhere. Those who don't climb aboard are made to feel left out, "fuddy-duddy", even bad for their shareholders. What made the EQ phenomenon different were two things. First, the web, which now has a very big impact on the rapid and universal popularisation of ideas. The second factor was the rapid development of measures of EQ. The concept not only struck home, but it could be very easily (supposedly) efficiently and validly measured. It was the measurement of EQ that really appealed to the management consultants.

5. Total commitment by true believers

At this point, the evangelists move from the consultant to the managers. For a small number of companies, the technique *seems* to have brought quick, massive benefits. They become happy and willing product champions, which only serves to sell more books and fan the fires of faddishness. EQ champions are paraded at conferences. EQ awareness, courses and training improve performance and make people into better managers. The Total Quality Management movement seems an excellent exemplar of the process.

With hindsight, it is sometimes difficult to explain why the concept had such an impact on the lay public or why people seemed to believe it worked. This is somewhere between the Hawthorne effect and the placebo effect. The former refers to the way people react positively when they are treated differently (irrespective of what the treatment consists of) while the latter refers to the sugar pill effect, where simply believing that it will do you good is enough.

In fact, years after the TQM fad has passed, there are little outstations of believers who continue to be the faithful. In time, they are quiet reminders of the past as they cling on. The Amish of Management, they resolutely cling on to their old ways.

6. Doubt, scepticism and defection

After pride comes the fall. After a few years of heavy product selling, the appetite for the fad becomes diminished. The market is saturated. Various "new and improved" or just as likely "shorter and simpler" versions of the fad are introduced. But it is apparent that the enthusiasm is gone. And then the avalanche or mudslide begins. It begins with managerial doubt and then academic scepticism, followed by journalistic cynicism, and finally consultant defection. It may be that the whole process starts with people pointing out the poor cost–benefit analysis of introducing the fad. Or it may occur because someone goes back to the original finding and shows that the gap has widened so much between what was initially demonstrated and what is now done that the two are different species.

Then management journalists smell blood. It is easy to find disaffected managers happy to squeal. They point out the thousands spent for little reward and the incredible consultant rip-off the whole thing has become. A trickle becomes a stream and then a river. And the consultants who were so eager to pick up the fad are the first to drop it. What gave them both credibility and massive invoicing ability now makes them look like con-artists as they distance themselves from the fad. But this phase may be some time away with EQ. After all the fad – at least in the market-place terms – is only 3–5 years old. No alternative is on the horizon. Many organisations are still in the early part of their infatuation with the idea. But nemesis may not be too far behind.

7. New discoveries

The end of one fad is an ideal time for trainers, writers and consultant to spot a gap in the market. They know there is an incurable thirst for magic-bullet, fix-all solutions, so the whole process starts again. The really clever people begin to sense when the previous fad is reaching its sell by date, so that they have only enough time to write their new best seller to get the market just right.

Is EI a management or educational fad? Has it passed through the above phases? And if so where is it now? Certainly the academics are only now beginning to respond with careful, considered research that attempts to unpick the concept. Suddenly the academic journals, particularly in differential psychology, are bursting with papers that take (hopefully) a disinterested scientific and measured look at EI (Austin, 2004; Chan, 2004; Roberts et al., 2001). There has also appeared a serious, thoughtful and balanced review of work in the area to date (Matthews et al., 2002). Academic researchers are not immune to fad and fashion. However, the lag time is longer and thus what interests the two worlds of science and practice may easily be out of synchrony.

Conclusion

There is no doubt that the social skills and emotional sensitivity of managers at work are very important. Emotional perceptiveness, sensitivity and management are more important in some jobs rather than others. More than 20 years ago after a study of airline steward staff, Hochschild (1983) wrote a book, *The Managed Heart: Commercialisation of Human Feeling*. In it she argued for a new concept: *emotional labour*. She said many jobs require physical and mental labour but some, uniquely, require emotional labour.

The idea is that service staff are required to express emotions they do not necessarily feel. They are required to smile, be positive and to appear relaxed whatever they are actually experiencing. Hochschild called this *surface acting*. However, in some jobs you are almost required to feel these emotions. This is called *deep acting*. The idea is that (canny) customers can spot the false display of emotion so you have to learn the "inside-out smile".

Service staff have to learn to become method actors. Karl Marx said workers were alienated from the products of their labour. Equally, Hochschild believed service workers, whose emotions are "managed and controlled" by their employers become alienated from their real feelings. Hochschild argued that this cost too much, in that it caused psychological damage in the long term. Yet there remains controversy, not so much about the concept but whether it is essentially damaging in the way it alienates workers from their true feelings (Seymore, 2000).

As for emotional intelligence, despite being advocated and used extensively in the business world for training and selection, it has not been until comparatively recently that organisational psychologists have begun to look at the issue to test the many assertions of popular writers in the field. Hence a special issue of the *Journal of Organisational Behaviour* (Volume 26) in 2005. This included a review of measures (Conte, 2005), but also a conceptual critique by Locke (2005), who concluded robustly thus:

> EI's extension into the field of leadership is even more unfortunate. By asserting that leadership is an emotional process, Goleman denigrates the very critical role played by rational thinking and actual intelligence in the leadership process. Given all the add-ons to the concept proposed by Goleman (1995), any associations between leadership effectiveness and an EI scale that included these add-ons would be meaningless.
>
> What, then, are we to conclude about EI?
>
> 1 The definition of the concept is constantly changing.
> 2 Most definitions are so all-inclusive as to make the concept unintelligible.
> 3 One definition (e.g. reasoning with emotion) involves a contradiction.
> 4 There is no such thing as actual emotional intelligence, although intelligence can be applied to emotions as well as to other life domains.
>
> A more productive approach to the EI concept might be to replace it with the concept of introspective skill. (This would be a prerequisite to emotional self-regulation.) Alternatively, it might be asked whether EI could be relabelled and redefined as a personality trait – possibly, provided it was (re)defined intelligibly and that it was differentiated from skills and from traits that have already been identified (e.g. empathy). However, it is not at all clear at this point what such a trait would be called.
>
> (p. 430)

However, Ashkanasy and Daus (2005) argue the concept and its measurement is sound and worthy of attention. They assert four things:

1 Emotional intelligence is distinct from, but positively related to, other intelligences.
2 Emotional intelligence is an individual difference, where some people are more endowed, and others are less so.
3 Emotional intelligence develops over a person's life span and can be enhanced through training.

4   Emotional intelligence involves, at least in part, a person's abilities effectively to identify and to perceive emotion (in self and others), as well as possession of the skills to understand and to manage those emotions successfully (p. 449).

Daus and Ashkanasy (2005) also identified and refuted three claims by their critics namely:

1   Emotional intelligence is dominated by opportunistic "academics-turned-consultants" who have amassed much fame and fortune based on a concept that is shabby science at best.
2   The measurement of emotional intelligence is grounded in unstable, psychometrically flawed instruments, which have not demonstrated appropriate discriminant and predictive validity to warrant/justify their use.
3   There is weak empirical evidence that emotional intelligence is related to anything of importance in organisations.

The area is thus alive and well with vigorous debate about concepts, measurement and usefulness. From an academic perspective it seems very important to establish the independence of either trait or ability emotional intelligence from related concepts and provide robust measures of it. More importantly there remains a great deal of work to be done on demonstrating how, when and why emotional intelligence impacts on work-related behaviour. If the area has done nothing else, it has succeeded in making emotions at work a topic worthy of investigation.

8   Creativity at work

Introduction

Most organisations say they value creativity because creativity is the *father of innovation*, which is the *engine of change*. Organisations all recognise the fact that those who are best at developing new (and desirable) products and processes are those that are likely to endure and succeed. Some spend billions on *Research and Development*, which is usually a creative process that looks to find different, better, cheaper, stronger, etc., products and work processes.

Some have argued creativity is an individual's, an organisation's, a society's, indeed even a species' greatest resource. Creativity means adaptation and innovation (Runco, 2004). People have been studying creativity since the beginning of psychology but it was probably Guilford's (1950) address to the *American Psychological Association* that acted as a stimulus to research in the area.

Some organisations have innovation or innovativeness as a measurable core competency for senior staff. They attempt to select for, encourage and manage innovation, believing it to be a core competency. Some appear to believe that innovation is best achieved through the selection and management of creative individuals. Hence they attempt to recruit those with trait creativity, which is usually conceived of as an ability to come up with new ideas.

As a result there is an important literature on innovation at work (Anderson & West, 1998). West and Farr (1990) defined innovation as "the intentional introduction and application within a role, group or organisation of ideas, processes, products or procedures, new to the relevant unit of adoption, designed to significantly benefit role performance, the group, the organisation or the wider society" (p. 239).

West and Farr (1990) developed a four factor theory to describe and explain the process of innovation in organisations. The factors are:

1   *Vision*: A higher-order goal, which acts as a motivating force. It helps establish goals that are clear, valued, attainable and shared.
2   *Participant safety*: The fact that the environment is interpersonally non-threatening because people can influence decisions and fully share information.
3   *Task orientation*: An emphasis on accountability, evaluating and modifying performance, on feedback, cooperation, monitoring, improving.
4   *Support for innovation*: Support is both articulated and enacted.

West and Farr (1990) suggested that if these four factors are in place it means the group is likely to seek for, accept and implement innovative ideas and practices.

People like to believe they are all (particularly, especially) creative. Organisations like to believe they need creative ideas, which come from creative people. Managers might or might not be wrong depending on the organisation they come from. Others believe that creativity can be relatively easily taught. Many researchers have been sceptical of the many courses available that supposedly teach creativity.

Furnham (2005b) argued that there seemed to be five related "models" in inspired creativity programmes. *First*, there is the *muesli* model. People need to unblock their creativity. They are in some curious way constipated and unable to let go and express themselves. In this sense creativity course may be seen as cognitive laxatives. *Second*, there is the *dominatrix* model. Here we are told to unleash our creativity. Somehow one has been bound up, tied down, physically constrained from that most natural and normal of tasks, namely, being creative. So courses are liberators.

Third, there is the *arsonist* model. Creative consultants and trainers aim to spark ideas and light fires. They see people as dry tinder just waiting for the right moment. Their job is to find ways of facilitating fire-setting ideas. *Fourth*, there is the *kindergarten* model. The problem appears to be that we have all forgotten how to be playful. Playfulness is apparently not only a lot of fun but it is also very productive. Thus creativity trainers help delegates regress to a time when they were happy and quite unabashed to draw pictures, sing songs, and so on.

Fifth, there is the *jail-liberator* model. The problem is that we have all been boxed in a sort of cognitive jail that has stopped us thinking outside the box. The trainer throws open the doors of our prison and out pops our creative jack-in-the-box. "Note that all the models assume that somewhere and somehow our natural creativity is suppressed. Quite contrary to all that we know about individual differences and human abilities, the assumption is that creativity is not normally distributed: everybody is (potentially) very creative" (p. 57).

This chapter will examine individual difference correlates of creativity. Inevitably, in doing so, it is important to attempt both a definition of creativity and a description of the measures used to try to obtain reliable and valid measures of it. The intelligence, personality, trait and other individual difference correlates of creativity will be discussed. Finally, the role of creativity in organisations will be discussed.

Defining creativity

Creativity has been, and no doubt will continue to be, variously defined. At the heart of most definitions, however, is the concept of creativity leading to, or being manifest in, the production of ideas and/or products that are both *novel and useful*. That is, an idea might be new, but not at all useful, or practical but not new. The essence of the idea is that real, genuine creativity is marked by new thinking that has real applications.

However, there is something of a process versus product debate in the literature, which concerns the issue of whether creativity can ever be studied just in terms of a process (as may be done in a laboratory) or whether it has to be understood in relation to some particular product. That is, having novel ideas is not enough: they have to be used to produce a useful product.

Batey and Furnham (2007) obtained nearly 18 definitions of creativity, which they grouped under four headings: New and Useful; Part of a Process; Componential Conceptions and Product-Oriented (Table 8.1). Whilst there is fairly good consistency within some areas, particularly the first, the complexity and difference between some of the later definitions gives a good indication of why research in this area remains a problem. "What creativity is, and what it is not, hangs as the mythical albatross around the neck of scientific research on creativity" (Prentky, 2001, p. 97).

Table 8.1 Definitions of creativity

A. New and useful	
Boden (2004)	"Creativity is the ability to come up with ideas or artefacts that are *new, surprising and valuable.* 'Ideas' here include concepts, poems, musical compositions, scientific theories, cookery recipes, choreography, jokes – and so on. 'Artefacts' include paintings, sculptures, steam engines, vacuum cleaners, pottery, origami, penny whistles – and many other things you can name."
Mumford (2003a)	"Over the course of the last decade, however, we seem to have reached a general agreement that creativity involves the production of novel, useful products."
Sternberg & Lubart (1999)	"Creativity is the ability to produce work that is both novel (i.e. original, unexpected) and appropriate (i.e. useful, adaptive concerning task constraints)."
Simonton (1999)	"Psychologists have reached the conclusion that creativity must entail the following two separate components. First, a creative idea or product must be original. . . . However, to provide a meaningful criterion, originality must be defined with respect to a particular sociocultural group. What may be original with respect to one culture may be old news to the members of some other culture. . . . Second, the original idea or product must prove adaptive in some sense. The exact nature of this criterion depends on the type of creativity being displayed."
Feist (1998)	"*Creative thought or behaviour* must be both novel-original and useful-adaptive."
Csikszentmihalyi (1996)	"Creativity is any act, idea, or product that changes an existing domain, or that transforms an existing domain into a new one. . . . What counts is whether the novelty he or she produces is accepted for inclusion in the domain."
Ochse (1990)	"*Bringing something into being* that is *Original* (new, unusual, novel, unexpected) and also *Valuable* (useful, good, adaptive, appropriate)."
B. Part of process	
Runco (2004)	"Creativity is a useful and effective response to evolutionary changes. In addition to what may be its most obvious function, namely as part of the problem-solving process."
Feist & Barron (2003)	"Creativity is a specific capacity to not only solve problems but to solve them originally and adaptively."
Finke, Ward, & Smith (1992)	"We conceive of creativity not as a single unitary process but as a product of many types of mental processes, each of which helps to set the stage for creative insight and discovery. . . . In particular, we distinguish between processes used in the generation of cognitive structures and those used to explore the creative implications of those structures."

(*continued*)

Table 8.1 continued

Mednick (1962)	"We may proceed to define the creative thinking process as the forming of associative elements into new combinations, which either meet specified requirements or are in some way useful."
C. Componential conceptions of creativity	
Csikszentmihalyi (1996)	"The systems model of creativity, where creativity 'exists' in the juncture between domain, person and field:
	1. The creative *domain*, which is nested in culture – the symbolic knowledge shared by a particular society or by humanity as a whole (e.g. visual arts);
	2. The *field*, which includes all the gatekeepers of the domain (e.g. art critics, art teachers, curators of museums, etc.);
	3. The individual *person*, who using the symbols of the given domain (such as music, engineering, business, mathematics) has a new idea or sees a new pattern, and when this novelty is selected by the appropriate field for inclusion into the relevant domain."
Eysenck (1993)	"I argue that creative achievement in any sphere depends on many different factors: (a) cognitive abilities – for example, intelligence, acquired knowledge, technical skills, and special talents (e.g. musical, verbal, numerical); (b) environmental variables – such as political-religious, cultural, socioeconomic, and educational factors; and (c) a personality trait – such as internal motivation, confidence, nonconformity, and originality. All or most of these, in greater or lesser degree, are needed to produce a truly creative achievement, and many of these variables are likely to act in a multiplicative (synergistic) rather than additive manner."
Mumford & Gustafson (1988)	"Creativity appears to be best conceptualised as a syndrome involving a number of elements: (a) the processes underlying the individual's capacity to generate new ideas or understandings; (b) the characteristics of the individual facilitating process operation; (c) the characteristics of the individual facilitating the translation of those ideas into action; (d) the attributes of the situation conditioning the individual's willingness to engage in creative behaviour; and (e) the attributes of the situation influencing evaluation of the individual's productive efforts."
Torrance (1966, 1974)	"A process of becoming sensitive to problems, deficiencies, gaps in knowledge, missing elements, disharmonies, and so on; identifying the difficulty; searching for solutions, making guesses, or formulating hypotheses about the deficiencies: testing and retesting these hypotheses and possibly modifying and retesting them; and finally communicating the results."
Guilford (1950)	"In its narrow sense, creativity refers to the abilities that are most characteristic of creative people. Creative abilities determine whether the individual has the power to exhibit creative behaviour to a noteworthy degree. Whether or not the individual who has the requisite abilities will actually produce results of a creative nature will depend upon his motivational and temperamental traits."

D. Product-oriented

Amabile (1982)	"Creativity can be regarded as the quality of products or responses judged to be creative by appropriate observers, and it can also be regarded as the process by which something so judged is produced."
Rogers (1954)	"There must be something observable, some product of creation. Though my fantasies may be extremely novel, they cannot be usefully defined as creative unless they eventuate in some observable product. . . . These products must be novel constructions . . . the creativity has the stamp of the individual upon its product, but the product is not the individual, nor his materials, but partakes of the relationship between the two. . . . The action of the child inventing a new game with his playmates; Einstein formulating a theory of relativity; a housewife devising a new sauce for the meat; a young author writing his first novel; all of these are, in terms of our definition, creative, and there is no attempt to set them in some order of more or less creative."

Source: Adapted from Prentky (2001).

One issue that does seem important is to decide on whether the determinants of, and the process involved in, creativity are different in different areas like arts, business, commerce or science (Baer, 1998). Another is whether creativity as an ability or trait is *normally distributed* in the population as a whole, or highly skewed such that only a very few are highly creative.

Yet, creativity remains an academic backwater, mainly because of how to decide whether a person, invention, work of art or science is *truly* creative. The question is *who makes the judgement* and the extent to which they have to agree before one can say "it" is a real manifestation of creativity. Criteria could be based on patent awards, judgements made by professionals, social recognition or even sales. Different groups have different criteria and different levels of reliability. For the scientist the whole enterprise hardly gets off the starting blocks. If one cannot adequately, robustly and reliably describe the criteria or label the product it remains particularly difficult to understand the process.

Essentially, it seems that researchers have adopted one of four approaches to the problem:

1 *The creative person*: differential psychologists have attempted to delineate the particular and peculiar set of abilities, motives and traits that together describe the creative individual (Eysenck, 1993, 1994).
2 *The creative process*: this is an attempt to understand the thought (cognitive) processes that go on in the process of creativity. It is not so much an attempt at the "who", but the "how" question (Finke et al., 1992).
3 *The creative situation*: social and business psychologists are particularly interested in cultural, environmental and organisational factors that inhibit or facilitate creativity. The idea is that one can therefore construct situations that induce creativity even in the not particularly creative (Csikszentmihalyi, 1999).
4 *The creative product*: this approach attempts to study all aspects of creativity by looking at those products that are clearly defined as creative (Amabile, 1996).

To make matters even more complicated Sternberg and Lubart (1999) have delineated seven very different approaches to the study of creativity.

1   *Mystical*: perhaps even divine intervention and clearly not a subject for science.
2   *Pragmatic*: which is about teaching or developing creativity in the style of De Bono (1985, 1992) rather than trying to describe or understand the process.
3   *Psychodynamic*: or the classic Freudian perspective seeing creativity as arising from tensions between conscious and unconscious forces.
4   *Psychometric*: which is the attempt to investigate the issue by devising tests that assess it.
5   *Cognitive*: which tries to understand the mental processes involved in the whole business of creative endeavours.
6   *Social psychological*: which looks at the fit or misfit between individuals and their environment that sparks creativity.
7   *Synthesis/confluence*: which attempts to model the different components (person, environment) combined to produce the process and product.

This is where the problems begin because the field is so obviously fractured. Diversity of conception inevitably leads to diversity of measures. Lubart (1994) described eight different measures from attitude inventories and biographical surveys to divergent thinking tests and ratings by all sorts of individuals. Without consensus even at the elementary level, however, the field has not greatly developed. There are few grand theories in this area and few recognised or well psychometrised tests.

Creativity and intelligence

Is creativity a subcomponent of intelligence? Can one be intelligent without being creative? Both creativity and intelligence researchers refer to each others' concepts. Many intelligence researchers (Feist & Barron, 2003; Snyderman & Rothman, 1987) made direct references to creativity though others are more likely to use terms like problem solving. Certainly, although there are both definitional and measurement problems in the intelligence literature, this is not as bad as in the creativity area.

Early researchers used the terms *imagination* (Andrews, 1930; Dearborn, 1898) and others *inventiveness* (Colvin, 1902) and correlated some relatively crude tests of this construct with IQ tests of the day. Correlations were positive but low, nearly always below $r = .30$. This may be seen to be the result of unreliable tests or the fact that the two concepts are indeed unrelated. This problem still dogs the literature today.

There has also been an active research tradition looking at the concept of giftedness, genius and eminence (Simonton, 1976; Terman, 1925, 1973). Between the wars, gifted children were targeted, measured on other variables and followed-up over time. The results of these studies found that superior intellect (defined as an IQ greater than 140) alone was clearly insufficient to determine eminent achievement. Some researchers identified persistence (Cox, 1926) and others social adjustment, emotional stability and drive as crucial factors leading to adult achievement (Terman & Oden, 1940).

A problem with many of the early studies lay in their measure of intelligence, which yielded a culture-unfair measure only of general intelligence rather than working at a different domain-specific level. Later work showed that eminent scientists differed in the patterns of their clearly superior verbal, spatial and mathematical intelligence.

Guilford's divergent thinking model

Guilford's structure-of-intellect (SI) model postulated that there are three fundamental dimensions of intelligence (Guilford, 1967): (1) *Operations* (cognition, memory, divergent production, convergent production, evaluation); (2) *Content* (figural, symbolic, semantic, behavioural); and (3) *Products* (units, classes, relations, systems, transformations, implications). These dimensions can be represented as a cube. With 5 operations, 4 contents and 6 products, the model yields 120 factors, which allows specific components of cognition to be related to creativity. Guilford originally postulated there to be 24 intellectual abilities related to creative thinking. These included:

1   Fluency of thinking: consisting of word, ideational, expressional and associational fluency.
2   Flexibility of thinking: consisting of spontaneous and adaptive flexibility.
3   Originality.
4   Sensitivity to problems.
5   Figural and semantic elaboration.

Collectively these factors were called Divergent Thinking (DT). This still remains one of the more influential models in the whole area.

Lowenfeld and Beittel (1959) examined highly creative art students and found evidence for the role of five attributes: fluency, flexibility, redefinition, sensitivity to problems and originality, seemingly lending weight to Guilford's model. Earlier, Drevdahl (1956) studied arts and science students and found ratings of creativity correlated with Guilford's DT tests to the magnitude of $r = .33$.

Tests of DT similar to those utilised by Guilford were administered to high-school students and then related to teacher ratings of creativity (Piers et al., 1960; Torrance, 1962), the correlations were positive, but low, generally in the order of $r = .20$. In a test of a large sample of fifth-grade schoolchildren Lauritzen (1963) found that a score for originality predicted teacher ratings of originality with a correlation of $r = .48$.

It seems, then, that among school and university students the sort of correlation one may expect between various different measures of DT and creativity was around $r = .30$, which means accounting for around 10% of the variance. It should also be noted that DT measures have been shown to be stable over time suggesting that they are linked to stable, biologically based phenomena like personality and intelligence (Magnusson & Backteman, 1978).

Various other groups have been tested. For instance Wallace (1961) used the DT tests with saleswomen. The key finding was that the saleswomen, assigned to the "high customer service" group, obtained significantly higher mean scores on the DT tests than the saleswomen allocated to the "low customer service" group. Elliot (1964) found that creative public relations personnel could be differentiated from their less-creative peers on the basis of five out of eight of Guilford-type tests.

However, MacKinnon (1961) found creative architects, judged to be creative by their peers, could *not* be identified on the basis of their DT scores. Gough (1961) noted that creativity among research scientists correlated with Guilford's unusual uses, consequences and transformations at the $r = -.05, -.27$ and $.27$ levels, respectively.

The results of the DT investigations seem to suggest that DT skills contribute towards creativity in students and in occupational groups, but do not help differentiate highly creative individuals (Batey & Furnham, 2007). DT tests are primarily a measure of *ideational fluency*. In "normal" samples the rapid production of ideas may make for the difference between those considered creative versus those rated as uncreative. In eminent samples, fluency alone is not sufficient to be considered creative. This indicates that DT skills are part of creativity as a normally distributed trait, but do not help to explain the difference between moderately and highly creative individuals. Not all experimental studies have been supportive of Guilford's model, it has also received theoretical criticisms.

Guilford assumed that the different factors that comprise the SI model were orthogonal. He used orthogonal, rather than oblique rotation, procedures to "isolate" the different factors. However, critics fundamentally disagreed with the factorial statistical procedures that Guilford advocated (Cattell, 1971; Horn & Knapp, 1973; Sternberg & Grigorenko, 2001).

Guilford treated creativity as a subset of overall intelligence, with DT one of the intellectual factors that constituted the structure of intellect. Later researchers began to question this idea and suggested that there was a clear distinction between the traditional concept of intelligence and the cognitive function of "creativity" identified by Guilford.

Divergent thinking as a criterion of creativity

Until around the 1960s, DT had been seen as a cognitive ability that was *necessary*, but not *sufficient* for creative achievement. The next generation of research started to use "creativity tests". These creativity tests were practically identical to the tests used by Guilford to measure divergent thinking; according to Guilford, a factor of intelligence. However, many researchers made the fundamental error of equating divergent thinking with creativity (Batey & Furnham, 2007). That is, that creativity was essentially nothing more than divergent thinking.

In an early and celebrated study Getzels and Jackson (1962) administered five "creativity" measures to approximately 500 schoolchildren, which were then correlated with IQ test results. The main aim of the studies was to identify two types of students and examine the differences between them. The first group were those children who had high IQ scores and low creativity scores (the High-IQ group). The second group were children who had obtained low scores on the IQ tests, but high scores on the "creativity" test (the High-C group).

Batey and Furnham (2007) have pointed out five important features of this study. *First*, the mean IQ of the students tested was 132. *Second*, the authors wished to compare high IQ with high creativity. This meant that those children who scored high or low on both tests were excluded from the final analysis. *Third*, the authors did not report many of the intercorrelations between measures. *Fourth*, the tests were administered in a classroom setting in a manner similar to the administration of IQ tests. *Fifth*, the "creativity" tests could not be said to measure creativity per se, but divergent thinking.

The average correlation between the creativity measures and IQ was around $r = .26$. When comparing the high-IQ group (mean IQ of 150) with the high-C group (mean IQ of 127) there were *no differences* in the scores of school achievement or achievement motive. Getzels and Jackson also found that teachers preferred to instruct high-IQ students. High-IQ students wished to possess the attributes they thought contributed toward adult success, whereas the high-C group did not desire these attributes, even though they also agreed that they were liable to lead to adult success. The most striking differences were observed in the attitudes of the two groups, with the high-C group prone to unconventionality.

Following the study by Getzels and Jackson, Wallach and Kogan (1965) conducted another investigation into IQ and DT, with the aim of correcting some of the errors found in the celebrated 1962 investigation. Their study of schoolchildren was careful to induce a game-like quality to the administration of DT "creativity" measures. They utilised five creativity measures not dissimilar to the Guilford tests, each scored for uniqueness and productivity, i.e. originality and fluency to yield ten scores for "creativity". Ten different tests of intelligence were used to assess IQ. The average correlation among the ten DT scores was around $r = .40$; the average correlation among the ten IQ measures was $r = .05$, whilst the average correlation between the creativity and intelligence scores was only around $r = .10$. The authors noted that this finding was especially surprising, given that the creativity measures relied in part on verbal intellectual skills.

Cropley (1968) used the same tests as Wallach and Kogan (1965) and was able to replicate their findings in a group-administration setting. These findings suggested that creativity (as operationalised in DT tests) and intelligence are essentially independent concepts.

The studies also indicated that earlier studies into the relationship between creativity and intelligence may have been compromised because of test conditions. Before Wallach and Kogan's study, creativity assessments were typically conducted in examination-like conditions. They concluded that the inability to produce an environment conducive to creation led to poor convergent and discriminant validity of creativity tests. However, as Batey and Furnham (2007) have noted, the criticisms that were applied to Getzels and Jackson (1962) regarding the use of DT tests as a criterion are just as relevant for these investigations.

A review of the evidence of the importance of "game-like conditions" has concluded that there are no differences in the correlations between creativity and intelligence relating to the conditions of measurement (Hattie, 1977). Hattie (1980) administered five creativity tests and a measure of IQ to 11-year-old students under both untimed, game-like conditions and timed, test-like conditions. The average correlation among the creativity variables was $r = .24$, and the average between the creativity and intelligence measures was $r = .14$. The results of these two studies indicated that the social psychological environment may not matter as much as Wallach and Kogan supposed. This also suggests that creativity is more trait-like than state-like. This has implications for social psychologists who stress the importance of situational variables in the stimulation of creativity at work.

Wade (1968) studied tenth-grade students from selective schools. She reported a correlation between IQ and creativity, measured using Guilford DT tests, in the order of $r = .37$. A combination of intelligence and creativity was able to explain twice the variance in scores of achievement, than intelligence alone. This again suggested that DT and intelligence work independently to affect academic output.

Torrance (1967), one of the most celebrated creativity researchers, conducted a meta-analysis of 388 correlations between intelligence measures and the Torrance Tests of Creative Thinking, and found a median correlation between the verbal DT tests and IQ in the order of $r = .21$, and a median correlation of $r = .06$ for the figural DT tests. Guilford (1967) reported average correlations of $r = .22$ for verbal DT tests; $r = .40$ for symbolic DT tests; and $r = .37$ for semantic DT tests with measures of IQ.

Batey and Furnham (2007) do not find these results surprising. Guilford originally designed the tests of DT as measures of a subset of intelligence. Therefore correlations between DT and IQ in the order of $r = .20$ to $.40$ are to be expected irrespective of the measures of either used. Batey and Furnham (2007) noted that one of the principal problems with research into the relationship between creativity and intelligence has been the confusion and variability over the choice of a criterion for creativity. The experiments conducted using DT tests as a measure of creativity (e.g. Cropley, 1968; Getzels & Jackson, 1962; Guilford, 1967; Torrance, 1967; Wallach & Kogan, 1965) have been criticised (Amabile, 1996; Lubart, 2003). Critics have suggested that DT tests measure aspects of creative intelligence, as such; they cannot also be a measure of creativity. This is especially true if it is argued that creativity involves the production of socially valuable products.

More recent research by Gilhooly et al. (2004) has further questioned the validity of DT tests as criteria for creativity. They suggested that subjects involved in a DT test might rely on memory far more than they rely on the generation of novel concepts. The studies indicated that DT tests, and especially DT tests that are administered over short periods of time, are primarily measures of long-term memory (LTM) retrieval. While most researchers would agree that LTM has a role to play in the production of creative ideas, they would be unlikely to suppose LTM alone to be sufficient. However, studies that have utilised Guilford-like tests of DT may have measured exactly those traits.

The failure to clearly differentiate between intelligence, creative thinking skills and creative achievement made the vast bulk of the psychometric investigations of creativity problematic. Indeed, it remains a problem to this day with no set of instruments agreed to be a good (valid and reliable) measure of trait creativity.

Ratings of creativity

An alternative to the use of DT tests as a criterion of creativity are ratings for creativity. Such measures are open to far greater bias than the scores produced by an individual on a DT test, but they possess far greater ecological validity.

Researchers at the Institute of Personality Assessment and Research (IPAR), in California, found further evidence to suggest that creativity and intelligence were different. The IPAR studies used eminent people and socially constructed ratings of creative potential and achievement. Among artists, the correlation between rated quality of work and IQ was zero or slightly negative (Barron, 1963). For MacKinnon's (1961) studies of architects, the correlation between the Terman Concept Mastery Test and rated creativity was $r = - .08$. Among mathematicians and scientists the correlation between rated creativity and IQ was $r = .07$ (Gough, 1961). In a later study Gough (1976) reported a correlation between the Concept Mastery Test and creative achievement, for research scientists and engineers of $r = -.05$. In a historiometric study, Simonton (1976) found that IQ and ranked eminence did not correlate. Again, then, it would appear that when the criterion of creativity is socially or ecologically valid (as opposed to a DT test) there is little or no relation between IQ and creativity.

Barron (1963) and MacKinnon (1978) summarised the IPAR research. Across the total range of intelligence and creativity, both found a moderate positive correlation in the order of $r = .40$. Above an IQ of 120, intelligence seems to explain little of the variance in creative achievement. This has become known as the threshold theory of IQ (Guilford, 1967; Torrance, 1962). The *threshold theory* of intelligence and creativity posits that at low IQ levels there is little variation in the levels of creativity, with low IQ usually corresponding to low levels of creativity. At high levels of IQ, there is considerable variance in the range of creativity scores (Torrance, 1962).

Yamamoto (1964), in a replication of Torrance (1962), divided a sample of students into high and low creativity groups. The results demonstrated that, irrespective of the subject matter, highly creative students performed at a higher level than less creative students when the effects of intelligence were controlled.

In a summary of some of his earlier work, Guilford (1981) suggested a non-linear relationship between creativity and intelligence, with a high correlation between IQ and creativity below an IQ of 120, and a low correlation with IQ scores over 120. Guilford explained this discrepancy on the basis of the levels of convergent and divergent thinking that might be employed by problem solvers. At IQs of less than 120, problem solvers might make great use of their DT skills. Above 120, problem solvers might rely on their strong convergent thinking skills to reach an acceptable answer (Guilford, 1968).

Comparisons between MacKinnon's (1961) architect sample, who were of above average intelligence, and Barron's (1963) military officer sample, who were of average intelligence, have yielded interesting findings. For the architects the correlation between IQ and creativity was $r = -.08$, for the military officers the correlation was $r = .33$. From this perspective, intelligence can be seen as necessary for creative achievement, but not sufficient. In addition, attention must be paid to the domain of the endeavour, that is trait creativity may be more important in some worlds (i.e. visual arts) than others (i.e. civil engineering).

As Torrance (1962) noted: "No matter what measure of IQ is chosen, we would exclude about 70% of our most creative children if IQ alone were used in identifying giftedness." This has very important implications for the identification of creative individuals.

The role of knowledge

In the 1960s there were the beginnings of theoretical work that tried to model and explain the complex relationship between intelligence and creativity. Mednick's (1962) *associative basis of creative thinking* suggested that creativity arose from the combination of associative elements and that mental elements that are conceptually distant will be the most likely, upon combination, to yield creative results.

Mednick contended that creative people could be distinguished from their less creative peers on the basis of their "response hierarchies". Less creative people are believed to have a steep hierarchy of responses. Thus, when a situation demands the combination of ideas, the pool from which ideas may be drawn and combined is limited. It was postulated that individuals with a steep hierarchy are those for whom few associates are extremely probable. As a consequence, the combinations of ideas are not likely to be novel and will be exhausted quickly. Alternatively, the creative person's response hierarchy is considered to be flat. Flat associative hierarchies are those in which the probability of the evocation of a large number of associates is high. Thus, when new combinations are called for, the diversity of potential ideas is great, making the potential for creative combination more likely.

Less creative people are thus thought to be able to provide stereotyped answers quickly, because of the relative ease of association of highly related but limited associates. This has an effect on long-term fluency as the "potential" pool of ideas is soon exhausted. Creative people are thought to produce ideas much more slowly (because they are combining ideas that are conceptually distant and therefore take longer to be associated), but will produce ideas for longer and with greater potential for novelty.

Mednick (1962) proposed that remote ideas may be brought together through *serendipity, similarity* or *mediation*. Serendipitous ideas would occur as a result of unguided contiguity. The combination of ideas based upon similarity occurs when associative elements are combined, because they share similar features. Mednick felt the most important means of combining elements to be mediation. In mediation, idea X and idea Y would be combined, because they were both associated with idea Z. Further, the probability and speed of creative solutions would depend on the condition of the problem solver. Individuals with a vast array of knowledge, with good cognitive organisation/structure would be better able to combine new elements.

The Remote Associates Test (RAT; Mednick & Mednick, 1967) was designed to be an easily administered paper-and-pencil measure of creativity. Test takers are required to provide a remote associate to three presented words. Mednick and Andrews (1967) demonstrated correlations between the RAT; and the Wechsler Intelligence Scale for Children (WISC) in the order of $r = .55$; with the SAT verbal in the order of $r = .43$ and with the Lorge–Thorndike Verbal intelligence measure in the order of $r = .41$.

Batey and Furnham (2007) have offered four criticisms of this test. *First*, the test items require the production of one correct answer, making the RAT essentially a test of convergent thinking. *Second*, the test is unable to distinguish between people with flat or steep response hierarchies, because respondents need find only one answer. *Third*, the test does not require the combination of ideas in any new ways. The testees are asked to find traditional associations to stimulus words. *Fourth*, the RAT items seem to require high levels of crystallised verbal knowledge (Mednick & Andrews, 1967). The relationship between the RAT and intelligence seems to be high.

Mednick saw creativity as an extension of ordinary intelligence. Mednick's theories also depend on the quality and quantity of the information encoded by the individual. An individual with little stored knowledge (i.e. crystallised intelligence) would not be able to produce creative combinations, even with an extremely flat response hierarchy.

There is an important distinction between Mednick and Guilford. As Batey and Furnham (2007) have noted, Guilford's theories suggested that DT was sufficient for creative thinking; because a problem solver has the mental machinery to think divergently, they could be creative. Mednick's theory is that people may have the cognitive mechanisms and processes to combine ideas in ways that could be creative, but creativity will only occur if the quality of the ideas to be associated is high.

Cattell (1943, 1971) also drew a distinction between mental processing and accumulated knowledge in his theory of fluid (Gf) and crystallised (Gc) intelligence. Fluid intelligence comprised information processing and reasoning ability; crystallised intelligence the ability to gain, retain, structure and conceptualise information. Crystallised intelligence is measured by tests of general knowledge and verbal comprehension, while fluid intelligence is assessed by tests of abstract reasoning. In addition to the three factors of general, crystallised and fluid intelligence, Cattell hypothesised there to be a number of primary abilities. The list of abilities is extensive, but more applicable than Guilford's 120, 150 or 180 factors (Guilford, 1983). The primary abilities that Cattell thought particularly important for creativity were Originality and Ideational Fluency.

Cattell suggested that real-life creative endeavour was determined primarily by general intelligence, followed by fluid intelligence. Crystallised intelligence was deemed less important. Cattell did not distinguish between eminent and everyday creativity, and the relationship of *g*, *Gf* and *Gc* to specific domains. In "everyday" creativity crystallised knowledge is probably not particularly important. However, great creators in knowledge-intensive domains (e.g. science) will, by necessity, require a certain level of knowledge if they are to advance a field. Hence the "ninety-nine per cent perspiration and one per cent inspiration" idea. It may well be that fluid and crystallised intelligence have different roles to play during the life span of a great creator. In early-period career, once a certain level of competence has been attained, *Gf* is likely to be particularly important. In late-period career, when attention often turns to consolidation, *Gc* would be essential.

Confluence model studies

Early studies examined unitary concepts of intelligence and creativity. The studies of the 1980s and beyond are both scientifically and theoretically more sophisticated. For instance, Hocevar (1980) examined the relative importance of a traditional measure of intelligence (Concept Mastery Test; Terman, 1973) and three DT measures of Ideational Fluency, in relation to creative achievement in the fields of arts, crafts, performing arts, maths–science, literature and music, for a sample of undergraduate students. In this experiment the ratings of creativity were drawn from behavioural inventories of creative abilities and achievements, and then compared to DT abilities. The mean "creativity" score was the aggregate fluency score for the three DT tests used. The correlation between the mean creativity and mean intelligence score was in the order of $r = .26$. The total score for Ideational Fluency correlated with an aggregate creativity achievement score in the order of $r = .25$.

Batey and Furnham (2007) have pointed out that fluency is distinct since the correlations *within* the traits are high, while the correlation *between* the traits is low. Also, the criterion of creativity – ratings on an inventory of creative behaviours, rely upon self-reported incidents of creative ability and achievement, which leaves the inventory open to bias effects. Further, the creative behaviours and abilities that each participant listed are independent of quality. An ability or an achievement that a participant listed has not been assessed for quality or utility (e.g. The Consensual Assessment Technique; Amabile, 1982).

Kershner and Ledger (1985) compared 30 highly gifted children with matched controls, on measures of intelligence and DT. They tested Wallach's (1970) suggestion that Flexibility, Originality and Elaboration are largely measures of IQ. The supposition was that only Fluency provides an accurate measure of DT. The results indicated that the scores for verbal originality were heavily influenced by IQ. The gifted children held no advantage over the average children when it came to the scores for figural Flexibility and Fluency. The main finding of the study was that "there was a consistent female advantage over males across every creativity subset".

Batey and Furnham (2007) believed that this study raised two important questions for the study of creativity. *First*, fluency and flexibility, as measured by DT tests, would appear to be relatively independent of IQ. Kershner and Ledger's (1985) study indicated that scores of originality are highly dependent upon intellectual endowment. This calls into question the validity and utility of Torrance's (1974) scoring system for DT type tests, especially if the DT tests are to be used as measures of creative intelligence. *Second*, their results indicate that females have an advantage over males in their ability to produce ideas divergently. This, has important implications for the scoring and inter-pretation of DT tests. Also, it would appear important for researchers in future to ensure that the gender composition of participant populations is clearly presented. The apparent advantage of females, over males, on divergent thinking tests was not explained. It may be that the observed differences were a result of motivational individual differences. However, the explanation for the differences in the DT performance between males and females may lie at the neuroanatomical level.

Multiple "intelligence"

Both the well-known advocates of multiple intelligence have written about creativity (see Chapter 7). Gardner (1999) suggested eight multiple intelligences (MI); a position not dissimilar to that adopted by Thurstone (1938). Each intelligence is thought to occupy a different module in the brain. The eight MIs are: (1) Linguistic; (2) Logical-Mathematical; (3) Spatial; (4) Bodily-Kinesthetic; (5) Musical; (6) Interpersonal; (7) Intrapersonal; and (8) Naturalistic.

Creativity can be understood to emanate from these intelligences in two ways. *First*, great creators may have an overabundance of talent in one of the eight intelligences, for example Mozart was hugely talented in the domain of musical intelligence. However, insofar as a great talent might be observed, in almost every case great creators will also have weaknesses or deficits in one or more of the other intelligences. For example, Mozart was reported to be weak in Linguistic intelligence (Ochse, 1990). Darwin whilst possessing an overabundance of Naturalistic intelligence, was known for his poor math-ematical skills (Hudson, 1970). *Second*, Gardner (1999) suggested that attempting to qualify which specific MI component makes a creator eminent is misleading. Rather, great creators often show strengths on two or more MI components. Gardner cites Einstein, who had high ability in both Logical-Mathematical and Spatial intelligences.

Gardner (1983, 1999) sees creativity arising from the constellation of MI com-ponents. As such, creators do not possess any special intellectual capacity or ability, rather the configuration of their intellectual traits predisposes them to creative endeavour. It would appear that Gardner views creativity as the outcome of "ordinary" intelligence. Importantly, Gardner insists that intellectual traits alone will not be suf-ficient for eminence. However, Gardner's work has inspired no empirical research and his ideas remain speculative. He appears to be satisfied with case studies rather than experimental evidence.

Another psychologist attracted to the unconventional world of multiple intelligences is Sternberg. The *investment theory of creativity* of Sternberg and Lubart (1991, 1992, 1995) is an example of how intelligence can be placed as one of the components of creativity. The authors propose that creativity relies upon the confluence of six main factors. These are intelligence, knowledge, thinking styles, personality, motivation and the environment.

The intelligence component of the theory consists of synthetic (creative), analytic and practical abilities. These are drawn from Sternberg's (1985, 1988, 1996) *triarchic theory of human intelligence*. The three components are seen as interactive and as working together in creative endeavours. Synthetic ability "is the ability to generate ideas that are novel, high in quality and task appropriate" (Sternberg & O'Hara, 1999). Synthetic ability relies, in part, upon a metacognitive component (Sternberg, 1985), which is similar in nature to the concept of problem finding. Tetewsky and Sternberg

(1986) utilised tests of problem definition and their experiments showed that creative thinkers could be differentiated on the basis of their flexibility in the use of different conceptual systems.

Sternberg (2003) suggested that in addition to the role of recognising the existence of a problem, the metacomponents are also used to: define the nature of the problem; allocate resources for solving the problem; mentally represent the problem; formulate a strategy to solve the problem; monitor the solution of the problem while problem solving is ongoing; *and* evaluate the solution to the problem after problem solving is completed.

In addition to the metacomponents, the *synthetic* part of intelligence also involves three knowledge-acquisition components or processes. These are: (1) selective encoding, selecting relevant from irrelevant information; (2) selective combination, combining relevant encoded information in new ways; and (3) selective comparison, comparing new information to old information in novel ways.

The *analytical* part of intelligence is the component that most closely resembles traditional tests of intelligence. Analytical ability is viewed as essential to the creative process, because it is the component that is used to evaluate the validity of ideas produced synthetically. The *practical* part of intelligence is the component that relates to a person's ability to apply their intellectual skills in everyday scenarios.

There is, however, no accepted validated measure. For Sternberg's triarchic conceptualisation of intelligence, tests have been devised – Sternberg Triarchic Abilities Test (STAT; Sternberg, 1985). Sternberg et al. (1996) examined STAT in relation to four other tests of intelligence in a sample of gifted nominees involved in a summer-school programme. Three of the tests were well-known IQ measures, the fourth was a test of creative insight constructed by Sternberg and his colleagues. Sternberg et al. (1996) reported correlations between the Cattell Culture–Fair test of *g* of $r = .68, .78$ and .51 for analytical, creative and practical subtests, respectively. This appears to indicate that Sternberg's creativity measure is little more than a measure of general intelligence.

Later, Sternberg et al. (1999) used STAT and tested approximately 300 American high-school students. Students were assessed for their analytical, creative and practical abilities. Assessment in ability was by three multiple-choice tests and an essay. Confirmatory factor analysis was deemed to be supportive of the triarchic theory. They found uncorrelated analytical, creative and practical factors. They believed the lack of correlation "was due to the inclusion of essay as well as multiple-choice subtests".

In another study, Sternberg and colleagues tested almost 3500 students in the USA, Finland and Spain (Sternberg et al., 2001). In this study only the multiple-choice sections of STAT were used in a confirmatory factor analysis to test five alternative models of intelligence. A model with a general factor of intelligence (*g*), fitted the data relatively poorly. The application of a triarchic model that allowed for intercorrelations between analytic, creative and practical factors was considered to provide the best fit to the data.

Grigorenko and Sternberg (2001) looked at the relative importance of creative, analytical and practical intelligence for healthy adaptive functioning in 745 Russian adults. Of the three kinds of intelligence, practical intelligence was the best predictor of adaptive functioning. Analytical intelligence also predicted adaptive functioning. The relationship between creative intelligence and adaptive functioning was not so clear. There was a marginal relationship between creative intelligence and poor physical health.

There have been serious misgivings about the interpretation and analysis of Sternberg's data (Gottfredson, 2003a, 2003c). Some critics have suggested that triarchic theory is "more a comforting envelopment in jargon than a carefully thought-through functional model" (Rabbitt, 1988).

Brody (2003) conducted a construct validation of STAT. He analysed the data from Sternberg et al. (1996, 1999) and also Sternberg et al. (2001). Brody proposed to critically evaluate the interpretation taken by Sternberg and colleagues with regard to data collected in these studies. He was particularly interested in three issues: (1) the relationship between the three abilities assessed by STAT and *g*; (2) the relationship between STAT abilities and measures of academic achievement; and (3) the inter-relationships between the STAT abilities. Brody's reanalysis found all three STAT abilities were substantially related to measures of *g*. The correlation between creative abilities and *g* was of greater magnitude than that between analytical ability and *g*. It is therefore hard to see how Sternberg and his colleagues can assert that conventional measures of intelligence are predominantly measures of analytical abilities, or that the STAT measures abilities distinct from *g*. These findings seriously cast doubt on the validity of a three-factor model of intelligence that does not incorporate a general factor of intelligence. It is clear that there is little statistical evidence for the validity of triarchic theory (Brody, 2003; Gottfredson, 2003a; Koke & Vernon, 2003).

Leadership, expertise and creativity

Are more-successful leaders creative? If so, should we select for creativity; or should we attempt to train it? Vincent et al. (2002) assessed the relationship between DT and other cognitive capacities in military leaders. Intelligence was assessed psychometrically. Expertise was assessed with special reference to the domain of organisational leadership. DT was measured using five items from Guilford's Consequences test. Responses were scored using a variation of Hennessey and Amabile's (1988) consensual assessment technique. Assessments were also made regarding the participants' problem-solving skills and leadership performance. Problem-solving skills were assessed using an ill-defined, novel task in the form of a complex military problem. Participants were required to answer short questions about what they would do in the prescribed hypothetical scenario. The questions focused on both idea generation and idea implementation. Idea generation was postulated to be an early-cycle problem-solving activity, while idea implementation was postulated to be a late-cycle problem-solving activity (Basadur, 1997). Four observers rated the effectiveness of solutions.

A measure of leadership performance was also obtained. For this, participants were required to list the number of medals, citations received, prior performance evaluations, promotions ahead of schedule and admission to special training programmes, though these measures do not constitute an accurate assessment of leadership performance or potential.

Vincent et al. found intelligence and expertise were correlated. Both intelligence *and* expertise had a direct effect on DT. These results suggested that both a general factor of intelligence and specifically crystallised intelligence (expertise) had an effect on the production of socially meaningful consequences. This provides evidence to support Mednick's (1962) theory that creativity relies upon a rich set of stored information.

Batey and Furnham (2007) noted that an important finding was that DT had a direct effect on idea generation, but not on idea implementation. Expertise also produced a moderate effect on idea generation. This suggests that people are able to make viable problem-solutions when they use both DT skills and acquired expertise. The generation of good solutions had a direct effect on the effective implementation of solutions. This finding is not surprising, given that an implemented idea would be unlikely to be awarded favourable ratings if it was based on a poor-quality generated idea. The path from idea implementation to organisational recognition (leadership performance) was confirmed. The authors suggested that DT was most important for early-cycle creative problem solving. A more important finding was that DT had a stronger direct effect on idea generation than intelligence. This suggests that "divergent thinking measures capture unique variance and do not simply represent a surrogate for intelligence or expertise. These findings, moreover, suggest that divergent thinking cannot be viewed as simply a subset of intelligence" (Vincent et al., 2002, p. 175). They continued to suggest that intelligence cannot be viewed as a primary cause of idea generation.

A tabulated summary

Table 8.2 presents the data from many studies dating over 80 years. This is not a meta-analysis, although one is long overdue. The results seem to indicate that intelligence and creativity, however defined and measured, are only marginally related. Corrrelations between the two are in the range of $r = .20$ to $r = .40$ suggesting that around 10% of the variance (only) is accounted for. Even if a good deal of noise in the system is masking the relationship it is unlikely that these two "latent" traits will ever be thought of as synonymous, though they are clearly related.

The results of all this work still leave many unanswered questions such as the genetics, mechanisms and processes underlying both factors; how they interact; what it is like to be highly intelligent but only modestly creative, and vice versa.

There also remain many interesting and important applied questions. These include: to what extent creativity is useful and important at work, specifically at what type of job and at what levels? Further, the vexed question of whether creativity can be trained remains very important. It is certainly believed by most researchers in the area that intelligence cannot be taught, though one can be trained to "do better" in intelligence tests. However, if creativity is essentially independent of intelligence, it may be that certain facets of it may be taught.

Personality and creativity

Feist (1998) suggested that personality research with regard to creativity had taken two forms. The first is the *between-groups* comparison, e.g. artists compared with scientists. The second form of creativity research with regard to personality has sought to analyse *within-group* differences. In these cases highly creative individuals from a domain are compared with their less creative peers. Such analyses are essential, because the within-group variance in creativity will be markedly different for artists and scientists (MacKinnon, 1965). Scientists were posited to have more pronounced variation in ratings of creativity, because they may be involved in "very routine, rote, and prescribed" research (Feist, 1998), in addition to the few scientists engaged in "revolutionary" work (Kuhn, 1970). Alternatively, while artists can be employed in routine work "anyone who makes a living at Art has to be more than one step above a technician" (Feist, 1998, p. 291).

Table 8.2 IQ and creativity

Author(s)	Sample	Measure used	Key finding
Cox (1926)	Eminent creative geniuses	Historiometric	Correlation between IQ and ranked eminence of .16
Simonton (1976)		Reanalysis of Cox's data	No correlation between IQ and ranked eminence
Andrews (1930)	Pre-school children	Three tests of imagination and IQ	Mean correlation of .07
McCloy & Meier (1931)	School children	Quality of response to abstract symbolism and IQ	Correlation of .22
Welch (1946)	Adults (artists and students)	Tests of ideational combination and IQ	Correlation of .27
Drevdahl (1956)	Art and science students	Guilford DT tests and ratings of creativity	Correlation of .33
Gough (1961)	Research scientists	Guilford DT tests and ratings of creativity	Mean correlation of – .02
MacKinnon (1961)	Architects	Rated creativity and IQ	Correlation of – .08
Getzels & Jackson (1962)	School children	DT tests and IQ tests	Mean correlation of .26
Barron (1963)	Aggregated IPAR findings	DT scores and ratings of creativity	Correlation of .4
Barron (1963)	Air-force officers	Aggregate DT score and ratings of creativity	Correlation of .55
Cline et al. (1963)	High-school children	Aggregate DT score and IQ	Mean correlation of .34
Wallach & Kogan (1965)	Fifth-grade school children	DT tests and IQ tests	Correlation between mean of creativity scores and mean of IQ scores was .1
Torrance (1967)	Meta-analysis	TTCT and IQ measures	Correlations between IQ and verbal DT were .21 Correlations between IQ and figural DT were .06
Guilford (1967)	Meta-analysis	DT tests and IQ	Mean correlation between IQ and verbal DT was .22 Mean correlation between IQ and symbolic DT was .40 Mean correlation between IQ and semantic DT was .37
Mednick & Andrews (1967)	College students	RAT and IQ	Correlation between RAT and WISC was .55 Correlation between RAT and SAT verbal was .43 Correlation between RAT and Lorge–Thorndike verbal was .41
Wade (1968)	School children	DT and IQ tests	Mean correlation of .37
Richards (1976)	Naval officers	DT and IQ tests	Mean correlation of .27

Author(s)	Sample	Measure used	Key finding
Hocevar (1980)	Undergraduates	DT, IQ and Creative Behaviours Checklist	Correlation between mean creativity and mean IQ score of .26 Correlation between ideational fluency and mean creativity score was .25
Kershner & Ledger (1985)	Gifted children vs. matched controls	DT measures and IQ	Fluency is best measure of DT ability Girls outperform boys on DT subscales
Rushton (1990)	Psychology professors	Creativity score (number of citations, works published, etc.) and composite rating of IQ	Correlations between the measures of .4
	Researchers	Composite measures of research effectiveness and IQ	Correlations between the measures of .05
	Undergraduates	DT measures and Multidimensional Aptitude Battery	Correlations between the measures of .24
Ai (1999)	School children	Teacher ratings of creativity and academic performance	For boys: teacher ratings of flexibility and elaboration correlated with achievement in six academic areas For girls: teacher ratings of fluency, flexibility, originality and elaboration were correlated with academic achievement
Kuncel et al. (2004)	Meta-analysis	Miller Analogy Test (MAT) and ratings of creativity and potential	Correlation between MAT and creativity of .36 Correlation between MAT and potential of .37

The early studies of creativity and personality were characterised by the diversity and dubiousness of the personality measures used. Similar to the study of creativity and intelligence, researchers have employed different definitions of personality, and have sought to assess the construct using different measures. This makes the interpretation of the results particularly difficult.

Early research using pre-Eysenckian Gigantic 3 and Costa and McCrae's Big 5 measures

MacKinnon (1965) used expert ratings and the California Personality Inventory (CPI) to investigate the creativity of architects (Table 8.3). In order to ascertain within-group differences, creative architects were compared with their less creative peers. The key finding was that the highly creative architects, in comparison with the non-creative architects, were less deferent and team-oriented; more aggressive, dominant and

Table 8.3 Creativity and non-Gigantic 3 or Big 5 measures

Authors	Sample	Personality measures used	Criterion of creativity	Key finding
MacKinnon (1965)	Architects	California Personality Inventory (CPI)	Ratings	In comparison with "normal" architects, creative architects were: (a) More aggressive, dominant, autonomous (b) Less deferent and team oriented (c) Less socialised
Domino (1974)	Cinematographers	CPI	Occupation	In comparison with matched controls, cinematographers were: (a) More concerned with status, achievement and change (b) More self-accepting (c) Less deferent and less concerned with order

autonomous; and less socialised (responsible, self-controlled, tolerant, concerned with good impressions and communal in attitude).

Domino (1974) also utilised the CPI (Table 8.3), in addition to the Edwards Personal Preference Schedule, the ACL scored for creativity (Domino, 1970), the Barron–Welsh Art Scale and the RAT to assess the creativity of cinematographers versus matched controls. Cinematographers, in comparison with matched controls, exhibited a greater desire for status, need for achievement, self-acceptance and need for change, but lower on the scales for need for deference and need for order. The ACL, when scored for creativity, differentiated the two groups, with the cinematographers scoring higher. There were no differences revealed between the two groups on the Barron–Welsh Art Scale or the RAT.

Early research utilising the CPI and other measures indicated that creative individuals tend to prefer autonomy and independence, that they are often less socialised than their less creative brethren with tendencies towards aggression, or what might be termed low agreeableness, and, lastly, that they appear less concerned with convention.

Eysenckian-inspired research

Studies of the personality characteristics of West German artists were performed by Gotz and Gotz (1973, 1979a, 1979b). These investigations revealed that in the domain of the visual arts, Neuroticism (N) as measured by the Maudsley Personality Inventory (MPI; Eysenck, 1960) and the Eysenck Personality Questionnaire (EPQ; Eysenck & Eysenck, 1975b) is an important variable for consideration. The 1973 Gotz study indicated that gifted art students scored higher on N and Introversion (I) scales than 50 less gifted art students. Gotz and Gotz (1979a) studied professional artists and found them to have higher scores on Psychoticism than a group of controls. In a follow-up study, Gotz and Gotz (1979b) compared the personality scores of highly successful and less successful professional artists. They found that successful artists scored significantly higher on the P (Psychoticism) scale than less successful artists. No differences were found between the two groups on the E, N or Lie (L) scales.

Woody and Claridge (1977) demonstrated the link between P and trait creativity. In all 100 undergraduates were administered the EPQ and slightly modified versions of the five tests that constituted the Wallach–Kogan (1965) "creativity tests". The "creativity tests" yielded scores for fluency and originality. Fluency scores for the five tests were all significantly correlated with P, with a range of correlation coefficients between $r = .32$ and $r = .45$. Originality scores were also significantly correlated with P, with a range of correlation coefficients between $r = .61$ and $r = .68$. There were no significant correlations between the scores for the creativity tests and E or N.

Kline and Cooper (1986) cast doubt on the generality of the link between creativity and P. They argued that P was more predictive of originality than fluency scores on DT tests (Eysenck & Eysenck, 1976; Woody & Claridge, 1977). Undergraduates were given the EPQ and the Comprehensive Ability Battery (CAB; Hakstian & Cattell, 1976). The CAB consisted of several measures of primary-ability factors, including several used to measure creativity; Flexibility of Closure, Spontaneous Flexibility, Ideational Fluency, Word Fluency and Originality. Only one significant correlation was revealed between the CAB and P, this was for males only on the Word Fluency measure. There were no significant correlations between P scores and CAB measures for the females sampled ($n = 96$).

In order to explain why the results from this study were incongruent with the findings of Woody and Claridge (1977), the authors suggested that, unlike the untimed tests of creativity used by Woody and Claridge, the CAB was timed. Wallach and Kogan's (1965) assertion that *timed tests produce less creative responses* may be at the heart of these discrepant findings on the nature of P and creativity. It was also noted that the variance in IQ scores for the Kline and Cooper sample was greater than the students used in the Woody and Claridge experiment.

Eysenck and Furnham (1993) tested the relationship between personality and creativity using the EPQ and The Barron–Welsh Art Scale. However, the total score for the Barron–Welsh Art Scale did not significantly correlate with P.

In a study of adolescents Sen and Hagtvet (1993) administered a battery of tests that included measures of personality (MPI; Eysenck, 1960), divergent thinking (Torrance, 1966), intelligence (Raven, 1963), and a study of values (Allport et al., 1960). Examination marks were also taken as a measure of academic achievement. Of the personality variables, only E correlated significantly with the composite creativity score ($r = .14$). When the sample was split to compare the scores of high scorers and low scorers on the creativity tests, the "high creatives" were significantly more extraverted.

Following the increasing interest in the relationship between creativity and P, Eysenck (1993, 1994, 1995) produced a model to explain how P and creativity were related. Eysenck suggested there to be three major variables, which interactively relate to creativity as an achievement. These are cognitive variables (intelligence, knowledge, technical skills, special talents), environmental factors and personality variables (internal motivation, confidence, non-conformity and trait creativity).

For Eysenck (1995), it is the process of over-inclusive or allusive thinking that characterises both psychotic and creative thinking:

Creativity is indexed by certain cognitive styles (overinclusiveness, allusive thinking, looseness or "slippage" of ideation), which increase fluency and originality. This type of cognitive style is closely related to psychoticism, and accounts for the many links between psychosis and creativity. Psychosis as such is, of course, likely to *prevent* creative achievement, in spite of being related to the trait of creativity; it constitutes a negative factor in the multiplicative relationship between the factors making for creative achievement. Psychoticism is linked directly with both trait creativity and achievement creativity, the link being overinclusiveness.

(p. 232)

Studies have examined the relationship between creativity and psychopathology (Carson et al., 2003; Cattell & Drevdahl, 1955; Dellas & Gaier, 1970; Goertzel et al., 1978; Heston, 1966; Jamison, 1989, 1993; Lloyd-Evans et al., 2006; MacKinnon, 1965; Peterson et al., 2002; Prentky, 1980, 1989, 2001; Sass, 2001) and many of them have found evidence to support Eysenck's hypothesis that there are similarities between creatives and schizophrenics or sufferers of bipolar disorder. Schizotypy is postulated to contribute toward a creative thinking style, while bipolar disorder is postulated to contribute toward creativity by predisposing sufferers to experience the extremes of affect.

Most of these studies concluded that there are signs of psychopathology (especially psychoses) among famous creators, and they pointed to a link between creativity and psychopathology. However, historiometric analysis of eminent individuals may reveal that they suffered from psychoses, but it does not indicate whether it is the thought disorder, the social anhedonia or both that contribute to creativity (Batey & Furnham, 2007).

Eysenck (1993) pointed out that much of the debate about whether or not creative geniuses are psychotic could be resolved by disregarding the assumption that psychiatric abnormality is categorical rather than dimensional. According to Eysenck and Eysenck (1976), psychopathology can be conceptualised as an exaggeration/extension of underlying personality traits. Accordingly, psychosis lies at the extreme end of the distribution of "psychoticism", a hypothetical dispositional personality trait, which is conceived of as a continuum "ranging from normal to psychotic". Psychoticism has been described as consisting of several characteristics, one of which is creativity. Other characteristics include aggressiveness, impersonal and antisocial behaviour, coldness, egocentricity, impulsivity, unempathic behaviour and tough-mindedness.

The assumption of Eysenck (1993), therefore, is that creative people possess the personality characteristics of psychoticism at a higher level than the mean normal individual and that, if adequate control is missing or if they experience stressful situations, then they may develop psychosis. Equally the personality characteristics of the high P scorer makes them predisposed toward creativity. The coexistence of both dominant/independent attitudes with a cognitive style that allows for greater flexibility would ensure that high P scorers could be creative, providing they also possessed the necessary motivational traits, cognitive variables and an environment conducive to creative expression.

Eysenck's (1993) position can be summarised as follows. Provided that there is a link between psychosis and creativity *and* psychoticism taps a unitary dimension underlying susceptibility to psychotic illness, then it is postulated that the important personality factor that acts synergistically with trait creativity (DT) and that may, under favourable environmental conditions, lead to real-life creative achievement, is psychoticism. In fact, studies have found a correlation between psychoticism and trait creativity (e.g. Aguilar-Alonso, 1996; Merten & Fischer, 1999; Woody & Claridge, 1977), and also between psychoticism and achievement–creativity (Gotz & Gotz, 1979a, 1979b; Rushton, 1990). However, studies have also failed to find significant relationships between creativity and P (Eysenck & Furnham, 1993; Kline & Cooper, 1986; Martindale & Dailey, 1996).

What explains this relationship between psychoticism and the creative process? It could be argued that common *information-processing patterns* can be found in both creative people and psychotics. Close examination of the theories developed in order to explain the cognitive deficits in psychotics (Hemsley, 1991) and those relating to the cognitive aspects of creativity (Martindale, 1981, 1989, 1999) reveals many similarities.

Batey and Furnham (2007) have suggested that most of the theories relating to the cognitive deficit in schizophrenia seem to propose that there is a deficit in selective attention mechanisms, which results in schizophrenics being unable to inhibit irrelevant information from entering consciousness (Hemsley, 1991). Consequently, many unrelated ideas become interconnected, resulting in a "widening of the associative horizons" (Eysenck, 1993) of schizophrenics. Evidence that schizophrenics, as well as normals who obtain high scores on psychoticism scales, are characterised by "wide associative horizons", i.e. they produce more unusual associations between words and ideas compared to normals and low-psychoticism scorers, comes from a number of studies. (Merten & Fischer, 1999; Miller & Chapman, 1983; Upmanyu et al., 1996).

Many studies have directly examined the hypothesis that a mechanism of reduced cognitive inhibition occurring during selective attention is responsible for the "widening" of associative connections. Most of these studies have used a "negative priming" (Tipper, 1985) paradigm to measure inhibition. Negative priming refers to the delay in responding to a current target object when this object has been a distracter to be inhibited on a previous display. In other words, if an ignored object on a prime display is the same as the object to be named on a subsequent probe display, naming latencies are impaired.

Bullen and Hemsley (1984), using a negative-priming word task and the EPQ as a measure of psychotic tendencies, found a significant negative correlation between P and the magnitude of the inhibitory negative-priming effect. High P scorers showed reduced cognitive inhibition compared to low P scorers. No other correlations between the negative-priming task and the other personality scales of the EPQ were obtained.

Beech et al. (1989) studied the effect of chlorpromazine (a drug routinely administered to reduce schizophrenic symptomatology) on negative priming. They found that, although negative priming was observed in both the drug and placebo conditions, the effect was stronger in the drug condition.

Theories developed to explain the creative process share many similarities with theoretical views about schizophrenia. A number of authors have suggested that the creative process is an associative one. Mednick (1962) proposed that individuals who demonstrate low creativity have a small number of strong, stereotyped associative responses to a given stimulus, compared to highly creative individuals. Wallach (1970) suggested that what is important in creativity is the generating of associates, and that attention deployment is the process underlying this generation. Kasof (1997) has shown that breadth of attention correlated positively with creative performance on a poetry writing task, thereby demonstrating that part of an individual's performance on a creativity task can be explained by attentional abilities.

Martindale (1981, 1989, 1999) has shown that creative people have a high resting level of activation, and that they are oversensitive to stimuli. However, they also have a low level of inhibition, so that the more they are stimulated, the more their level of arousal drops, favouring creative performance. Again, the notions of reduced inhibition and mood fluctuation (arousal levels rising and falling) are common notions in the literature on schizophrenia.

A small number of studies has contrasted the attentional and information-processing strategies of schizophrenics (and high-P scorers) and creative individuals. Rawlings (1985) used the EPQ, two subscales of the Wallach–Kogan (1965) DT test and a dichotic shadowing task (as a measure of cognitive inhibition) on a group of undergraduate students. The author found that performance on the shadowing task was positively correlated with DT scores and with psychoticism scores on the "divided attention" condition. However, the pattern of results was reversed in the focused attention condition and, moreover, the correlation between psychoticism and DT was not statistically significant.

Recent experimental research has indicated that those rated as superior in creative ability, also demonstrate low levels of latent inhibition in comparison with people not rated creative (Carson et al., 2003; Peterson & Carson, 2000). This evidence is supportive of Eysenck's (1994) theory of creativity.

Upmanyu et al. (1996) tested male graduate students in India. They found that extremely unique word associations were positively associated with verbal "creativity". However, atypical or moderately unusual responses were substantially related to verbal "creativity". Extremely unique word associations were positively associated with P and psychopathic deviation. The authors suggested that the P scale contributes toward creativity, in that it predisposes individuals to social anhedonia, social deviance, unconventionality and mild antisocial behaviour.

Using a battery of creativity tests, Aguilar-Alonso (1996) found that P and E were significant predictors of DT measures of creativity. High-P scorers were more verbally creative and flexible than low-P scorers. Moreover, extraverts were more original, fluent and flexible than introverts, but the neuroticism factor was uncorrelated.

Merten and Fischer (1999) selected "creatives" on the basis of occupation. A group of 40 actors and writers were compared with 40 schizophrenics and 40 unselected subjects. A word association test requiring common and uncommon responses (Merten, 1993, 1995), Two tests of verbal creativity (Schoppe, 1975) and two story-writing tasks were used as measures of creativity. The EPQ was utilised as a measure of personality. Participants were also given a vocabulary test, Raven's Standard Progressive Matrices and a measure of basic cognitive functioning (Reitan, 1992). The "creatives" sample scored higher on the P scale than the non-patient group controls. The "creatives" also produced the most original word associations of the three groups. The creatives did not produce any response repetitions in the common or unusual response conditions. This was taken to be an indication of the mental health of the creative group.

However, Batey and Furnham (2007) noted that caution should be exercised when interpreting the results of this study. The criterion of creativity was inadequate. The "creatives" group consisted of actors and writers. *First*, actors and writers may have different approaches to creativity. Therefore the study may have failed to take domain specificity into account. *Second*, there was no measure of the quality of the work of the actors or writers, making it difficult to ascertain whether they deserved the moniker "creative".

This body of Eysenckian-inspired research is summarised in Table 8.4.

Table 8.4 Creativity and the Gigantic 3

Authors	Sample	Personality measures used	Criterion of creativity	Key finding
Gotz & Gotz (1973)	Gifted art students	Maudsley Personality Inventory (MPI)	Ratings	In comparison with less-gifted art students, gifted art students scored: (a) Higher on the Neuroticism (N) scale (b) Lower on the Extraversion (E) scale (Introverted)
Gotz & Gotz (1979a)	Professional artists	Eysenck Personality Questionnaire (EPQ)	Occupation	In comparison with controls, professional artists scored higher on the Psychoticism (P) scale
Gotz & Gotz (1979b)	Professional artists	EPQ	Ratings	In comparison with less successful professional artists, successful professional artists scored higher on the P scale
Woody & Claridge (1977)	Undergraduate students	EPQ	DT tests	Fluency correlated with P Originality correlated with P
Kline & Cooper (1986)	Undergraduate students	EPQ	Comprehensive Ability Battery (contained DT-like tests)	No correlations between P and: (a) Flexibility of Closure (b) Spontaneous Flexibility (c) Ideational Fluency (d) Originality Correlation between Word Fluency and P (males only)
Eysenck & Furnham (1993)	Undergraduate students	EPQ	Barron–Welsh Art Scale (BW)	No significant correlation between P and BW total score
Sen & Hagtvet (1993)	Adolescents	MPI	DT test	Correlation between composite creativity score and E
Aguilar-Alonso (1996)	Mixed adult volunteers	EPQ	DT-like tests	Correlation between creativity scores and E and P
Martindale & Dailey (1996)	Undergraduate students	EPQ	(a) DT tests; (b) fantasy story; and (c) remoteness of association	Correlation between creativity measures and E
Merten & Fischer (1999)	(a) Actors and writers; (b) unselected participants; and (c) schizophrenics	EPQ	DT tests	Creatives scored higher on P scale against controls

Research using Big 5

During the 1980s and 1990s popularity began to form around a new conceptualisation of personality, namely the Big Five. McCrae (1987) found that DT was consistently associated with self-reports and peer ratings of Openness to Experience, but not with Extraversion, Neuroticism, Agreeableness or Conscientiousness. However, he noted:

> Creative ability does not inevitably lead to recognised creativity, and a variety of personality traits may be involved in being conceived as creative. Conscientious individuals may complete their creative projects more often; extraverts may exhibit them more readily; adjusted individuals may be less distracted from creative work by personal problems ... smart extraverts make intelligent conversation, smart introverts read difficult books; conscientious individuals use their intellectual gifts, lackadaisical individuals do not. Openness to experience and divergent thinking abilities may also interact as mutually necessary conditions for creativity, the former providing the inclination and the latter providing the aptitude for original thinking.
>
> (p. 1264)

An innovative study by Dollinger and Clancy (1993) required participants to create autobiographical story-essays using twelve photographs (Ziller, 1990). The instructions were that the "photographs should describe who you are as you see yourself". Participants were also given the NEO Personality Inventory (NEO-PI). The pictorial autobiographical stories were extensively coded, with a main rating of "richness of self-depiction". A multiple regression to predict richness rating revealed that O was significant while N and E fell just short of significance. When analyses were conducted to investigate gender differences, the richness of men's essays was predicted by O ($r = .28$), with the only significant facet being aesthetic openness ($r = .42$). These results were also replicated for women. However, the O facet of ideas was also a significant predictor. The richness ratings for women were significantly correlated with the N (positive) and I domains.

King et al. (1996) examined the relations between creative ability, creative accomplishments and a five-factor model of personality. Participants were given verbal DT tests, asked to list their creative accomplishments over the previous two years. The correlations indicated that verbal creativity was significantly correlated with E and O. There were significant correlations between creative accomplishments and O and negative A. Regressions with all five personality factors using verbal DT scores, and then creative accomplishments, revealed a significant prediction for O alone.

Gelade (1997) gave the NEO-PI to a group of advertising and design creatives, and to a comparable group of professionals and managers in occupations that were not apparently creative. Compared to the "non-creatives", the "commercial creatives" were more neurotic (particularly in terms of angry hostility, depression, self-consciousness, impulsivity and vulnerability), more extraverted (especially in terms of gregariousness and excitement seeking), more open to experiences (particularly fantasy, aesthetics and feelings) and less conscientious (particularly in terms of overall competence, order, self-discipline and deliberation).

Martindale and Dailey (1996) failed to find correlations between scores on the openness subscale from the NEO-PI and creativity as measured by DT tests or fantasy story writing. They did find correlations between DT performance and extraversion.

Furnham (1999) administered the Barron–Welsh Art Scale and the NEO-PI. Participants were also requested to provide three self-ratings of creativity (estimate of Barron–Welsh score, a rating of how creative they thought they were and a rating of the frequency of creative hobbies). Openness to Experience was a significant predictor of the participant's estimate of their Barron–Welsh score, the self-rating of how creative they thought they were and the rating of creative hobbies.

George and Zhou (2001) demonstrated that the application of creative potential depends upon several factors. They found that rated creative behaviour was highest when individuals with high Openness were set tasks that had unclear demands or unclear means of achieving ends and were given positive feedback. Their analyses of the role of Conscientiousness also yielded clear findings. They found that if an individual's supervisor monitored their work closely and their co-workers were unsupportive of creative endeavour, then high Conscientiousness inhibited creative behaviour: "Importantly it is not conscientiousness per se that appears to be detrimental. Rather, it is combination of high conscientiousness and a situation that simultaneously encourages conformity, being self-controlled, meeting predetermined expectations, and lacks support for creative behaviour" (p. 521).

Batey and Furnham (2007) noted that if the findings of this study were generalised from the workplace to the laboratory, then it may explain why some studies have produced contradictory findings. It may be that participants in laboratory studies have been influenced by the environment (experimenter attitude, exam-like conditions, etc.) and that these unaccounted-for variables have influenced the expression of creative potential. It may be that Wallach and Kogan (1965) were indeed correct; the conditions of testing can affect creativity.

More recently Wolfradt and Pretz (2001) investigated the relationship between creativity and personality. The measures of creativity deployed were the CPS for the ACL, a story-writing exercise for which the stimulus was a picture, and a list of hobbies. The story exercise and the list of hobbies were rated using the consensual assessment technique. Participants were students from diverse academic fields. The CPS was predicted by high scores on O and E. The best predictor for hobby creativity was Openness. Creative story writing was predicted by O and low scores on C. The results were also analysed by field of study, with "scientists" scoring significantly lower on the three measures of creativity and O than participants studying psychology or art and design. There were also gender effects, with females scoring higher on story and hobby creativity.

Wuthrich and Bates (2001) gave 54 participants the NEO-PI-R (Costa & McCrae, 1992) and the P scale of the EPQ-R (Eysenck et al., 1985), in addition to DT tests. Tests of Latent Inhibition (LI) were administered as well as a priming test involving a word-stem completion and recognition task. The results of the experiment indicated that the measures of creativity were related to N, E and O, but were not related to P, LI or priming.

Peterson et al. (2002) administered an LI task, the NEO-PI-R, the CPS and two tests of intelligence. The results indicated that "decreased LI is associated with creative personality". The study also confirmed an earlier finding, that decreased LI is correlated with O and E (Peterson & Carson, 2000). These results seem to contradict the findings of Wuthrich and Bates (2001). Batey and Furnham (2007) believed that one explanation was that quite different measures of creativity were used. A methodological issue to afflict both the Peterson et al. (2002) and Wuthrich and Bates (2001) studies

Table 8.5 Creativity and the Big 5

Authors	Sample	Personality measures used	Criterion of creativity	Key finding
McCrae (1987)	Adult male volunteers	NEO-PI	DT tests	Divergent thinking correlated with self-reported and rated Openness to Experience (O)
Dollinger & Clancy (1993)	College students	NEO-PI	Autobiographical photographic essays – scored for "richness"	O predicted "richness of self-depiction" (a) Males – O (b) Females – O, high N and low E
King et al. (1996)	Undergraduate students	Big Five Inventory (BFI)	(a) DT tests; (b) self-reported creative accomplishments	Verbal creativity correlated with E and O. Creative accomplishments correlated with O and low A
Martindale & Dailey (1996)	Undergraduate students	NEO-PI	(a) DT tests; (b) fantasy story; (c) remoteness of association	Correlation between DT scores and E
Gelade (1997)	(a) Advertising and design "creatives"; (b) matched controls	NEO-PI	Occupation	In comparison with controls, advertising and design creatives scored: (a) High on N (b) High on E (c) High on O (d) Low on C
Furnham (1999)	Undergraduates	NEO-PI	(a) BW; (b) self-rating of estimated BW score; (c) self-rating of personal creativity; (d) self-rating of creative hobbies	Openness predicted: (a) Self-rated estimated BW score (b) Self-rated creativity (c) Self-rating of creative hobbies
Wolfradt & Pretz (2001)	Undergraduate students	German version of NEO	(a) Creative Personality Scale (CPS) for the Adjective Check List (ACL); (b) story writing; (c) list of hobbies	(a) CPS predicted by high O and E (b) Story creativity predicted by high O and low C (c) Hobby creativity predicted by high O "Scientists" scored lower on the 3 measures of creativity and on O than students studying art and design or psychology
Wuthrich & Bates (2001)	Mixed adult volunteers and undergraduate students	NEO-PI-R	DT tests	Divergent thinking correlated with high N, E and O

concerns the employment of inadequate criteria of creativity. They utilised DT tests in isolation (without measures of achievement creativity or creative personality) while Peterson et al. (2002) utilised a measure of creative personality alone.

This body of research utilising the Big 5 is summarised in Table 8.5.

Longitudinal and meta-analytical research

In order to separate cause and correlation, longitudinal research is preferable. Further, meta-analysis provides a powerful way of seeing patterns in the results. Feist (1998), in an important meta-analysis, investigated creative personality in the arts and sciences. In order to analyse the disparate collection of personality data, the data from 83 experiments were converted so that the different personality scores were all in the FFM format, effect sizes were measured using Cohen's *d*. Subsequent analyses were conducted investigating three main comparisons: (1) scientists vs. non-scientists; (2) creative vs. less-creative scientists; and (3) artists vs. non-artists.

For the scientists vs. non-scientists, 26 studies were meta-analysed. The results indicated that O, E and C differentiated scientists from non-scientists. The confidence–dominance subcomponent was found to be more important than the sociability sub-component. With regards to C, "it is clear that relative to non-scientists, scientists are roughly half a standard deviation higher on conscientiousness and controlling of impulses".

For creative scientists vs. less-creative scientists 28 studies were meta-analysed. The traits that most strongly distinguished the creative from less creative scientists were E and O. Similar to the results from the comparison of scientists vs. non-scientists the confidence–dominant subcomponent of E contributed to the effect size, with no effect derived from the sociability subcomponent. A moderate effect size was noted for the direct expression of needs and psychopathic deviance subcomponents of C.

For the artists vs. non-artists sample, 29 studies were meta-analysed. The traits that most clearly differentiated artists from non-artists were C and O; where artists were roughly half a standard deviation lower on C and half a standard deviation higher on O.

Feist (1999) summarised the influence of personality on creative achievement in the arts and in science. Creative scientists and artists were found to be open to new experiences, less conventional, less conscientious, self-confident, self-accepting, driven, ambitious, dominant, hostile and impulsive. Artists were found to be more affective, emotionally unstable, less socialised and less accepting of group norms than scientists. Scientists were found to be more conscientious than artists. These findings seem to suggest why it is has proved difficult to produce a comprehensive list of the personality characteristics of creative people.

Soldz and Vaillant (1999) reported the results of a 45-year longitudinal study of 163 males. Participants were regularly assessed to measure factors as diverse as health, career functioning, social relations, mental health, political attitudes, childhood characteristics and creative achievement. Participants were given the NEO-PI at a mean age of 67. NEO scores were then calculated for the men at the end of their college careers. The results of the study confirmed that O was significantly positively related to the ratings of creativity. Interestingly, O also demonstrated significant relation to psychiatric usage and depression. Caution should be exercised in the interpretation of these results, because the personality scores for the college years were estimated and the participants were males alone.

The results of a 55-year longitudinal study were reported in Feist and Barron (2003). The sample consisted of 80 male graduates from 14 different academic departments. Data were collected for the subjects at age 27 (1950) and age 72. The nature of the longitudinal data-collation procedures meant that complete sets of data for all of the different measures were unavailable. The primary interest of the study was to report on the prediction of creativity from early to late adulthood utilising measures of intellect, potential and personality. At age 27, intellect was measured by observer-rating and measures from Thurstone's Primary Mental Abilities test (PMA; Thurstone, 1938). Observer ratings of potential were taken from at least nine raters and from the subjects themselves.

Observer ratings of personality were taken using early versions of the ACL and trait ratings of the following characteristics: Role Flexibility, Dominance, Poise and Balance, Ingenuity, Positive Character Integration, Deceitfulness and Vitality. Participants also completed parts of the CPI (Tolerance and Capacity for Status). Nine other CPI scales were retroactively pro-rated in 1953. The MMPI was administered and self-ratings of personality were taken using the ACL.

At age 72, data were collected for creative achievement and personality. Creativity data were drawn from *American Men and Women of Science* and/or from the subject's curriculum vitae. In order to allow comparisons across academic disciplines, awards and achievements for the sample were sent to full professors ($n = 95$) at major research universities. The professors rated on a 10-point scale the magnitude of achievement. The mean value for the most prestigious honour received, plus the total number of fellowships, honours and awards received were taken, z-scored and summed. This produced the "Awards" score.

Personality measures were also taken at age 72. These were the CPI, the MMPI-2 (Hathaway & McKinley, 1967) and the ACL. Observer-rated intellect at 27 was related to originality at age 27 and also to lifetime creativity at age 72. Tested intelligence was not so predictive, with only the spatial element demonstrating a significant correlation with creativity, in this case with creativity at age 27. The measures of *potential* taken at age 27 strongly covaried with *originality* at age 27 and were moderately predictive of lifetime creative achievement.

Hierarchical regression analyses revealed that once intellect and potential had been accounted for and held constant, personality was able to add further predictive power. At age 27 personality variables predicted an additional 8% of the variance in concurrent creativity over that contributed by intellect and potential. Age 27 measures of personality predicted an additional 20% of the variance in lifetime creative achievement over that contributed by intellect and potential.

This body of research utilising meta-analytical and longitudinal research is summarised in Table 8.6.

Woodman and Schoenfeldt (1989) have pointed out that studies of personality characteristics associated with creativity have waxed and waned in popularity over the years. Sternberg and Lubart (1999) have suggested that this is because concentration has begun to focus on confluence approaches. Attempts have been made to delineate the core characteristics of the creative personality, yet, despite the convergence of results, it has proved difficult to generalise the findings across various creative fields of endeavour.

Baer (1998) has argued that the continued inability to find the core characteristics of creative people is because creativity is not a general, domain-transcending phenomenon.

Table 8.6 Creativity and meta-analytical and longitudinal research

Authors	Sample	Personality measures used	Criterion of creativity	Key finding
Feist (1998)	Meta-analysis of: (a) Scientists vs. non-scientists (b) Creative vs. less creative scientists (c) Artists vs. non-artists	Converted to five-factor model (FFM) format	Mixed	(a) Scientists compared with non-scientists were high on O, E and C (b) Creative scientists compared with less creative scientists were high on O and E (c) Artists compared with non-artists were high on O and low on C
Soldz & Valliant (1999)	Longitudinal study of males	Estimated NEO college scores and NEO scores at age 67	Ratings	Creative accomplishment predicted by high O

However, psychologists have sought to find a general model for creativity, because large, all-encompassing models would prove more satisfying (Batey & Furnham, 2007).

Meta-analytical studies, i.e. Feist (1998), will hold the key to determining which personality variables are important for creative achievement, and in what domains. However, they will not aid in the discovery of the underlying processes.

Batey and Furnham (2007) argued that different personality measures have been utilised alongside various conceptualisations of creativity. When the criterion of creativity employed is a DT test, the results tend to suggest that Extraversion is predictive (e.g. Aguilar-Alonso, 1996; King et al., 1996; Sen & Hagtvet, 1993, Wuthrich & Bates, 2001). This finding holds true whether the instrument is from the Gigantic 3 or the Big 5 (Martindale & Dailey, 1996). Possible explanations for this are that DT tests are often administered in group settings, which is a more conducive setting for an extravert. Second, extraverts may perform better at DT tests, because they seek stimulation (Eysenck & Eysenck, 1975a) and the DT test environment provides the perfect opportunity to do just that. McCrae (1987) suggested that extraverts may be happier to exhibit their work. Some investigators have demonstrated relationships between DT and the P scale of the EPQ (Aguilar-Alonso, 1996; Merten & Fischer, 1999; Woody & Claridge, 1977), but others have failed to note such a correlation (Kline & Cooper, 1986; Martindale & Dailey, 1996; Rawlings, 1985). Researchers who have examined DT and the Big 5 have found evidence for the role of Openness to Experience (King et al., 1996; McCrae, 1987; Wuthrich & Bates, 2001).

When the criterion of creativity employed has been ratings of a product (e.g. story writing or quality of work) the picture is even less clear. Some studies have found creatives to score higher on the Neuroticism scale, on the EPQ (Gotz & Gotz, 1973) and the NEO (Dollinger & Clancy, 1993). The P scale of the EPQ has been shown to differentiate between successful and less successful artists (Gotz & Gotz, 1979b).

Clearer findings have come from studies that have employed the NEO in conjunction with creativity measures that utilise ratings, where the quality of rated products or work has been predicted by O (Dollinger & Clancy, 1993; Furnham, 1999; Soldz & Valliant, 1999; Wolfradt & Pretz, 2001).

Batey and Furnham (2007) have suggested that the greatest limiting factor in attempting to assess the relative importance and influence of different personality variables on creativity has been the failure to consider the domain of endeavour. There are three separate issues here. The *first* concerns the difficulty of producing categories of domains, e.g. art vs. science vs. leadership. Rarely are occupations solely focused on one domain (e.g. what domain does a scientist running a research programme inhabit?). The *second* issue concerns the notion of domain specificity itself. Within one domain there may be several levels. Thus, within the domain of the arts, is it sensible to consider an abstract sculptor to be the same as a poet or choreographer? The *third* issue concerns the allocation of students to specific domains when they have yet to start a profession. When assessing an adolescent or schoolchild, who has yet to "achieve", how is it possible to ascertain which categorical distinction to employ?

There is a potential explanation of why O may be implicated in rated products, but not DT tests. The products of DT tests are rarely qualitatively judged. It is most common to take measures of fluency (number of responses) or originality (statistical infrequency). As there is no judgement of quality in these measures, then an individual high in openness to new experiences will not be discernable from an individual who is not, rather the test will select an individual with high ideational fluency. When the quality or ingenuity of a product is rated, qualitative judgements are performed regarding the novelty or utility of the product. In this scenario, a preference for new and surprising behaviours (as measured by O) will be rated (Batey & Furnham, 2007).

It seems, therefore, that there is no doubt that *certain* personality traits are important for explaining and predicting *certain* types of creativity. This may account for as much as one quarter to one third of the variance in explaining the causes of creative work. However, most personality studies have assumed that underlying personality traits are domain general. This approach has resulted in mixed evidence concerning which personality traits are important in what circumstances. As suggested, possessing certain traits, such as openness to experience or tough-mindedness (psychoticism), is probably necessary, but not sufficient for creativity as achievement. To ensure that a person fulfils his or her potential, other requisite cognitive and situational variables will need to be present.

Creativity in business

Brilliant ideas are clearly not enough in the business world. They need to be translated into practical actions, processes or products. Thus, being creative and the innovation of creativity are not the same. Innovation is all about risk assessment, the identification, understanding, monitoring and management of risk. It can be about new products, processes, structures, relationships or strategies. Most people think of business creativity as new product development, but equally important is process innovation and structural change. It may be equally important to innovate one's relationships with clients, suppliers, etc., or how the organisation goes about strategic planning. Sherwood (2001) has identified 12 differences:

1 Creativity is about bright ideas; innovation is about the wisdom in identifying the commercially viable ones and bringing them to fruition.
2 Innovation applies to all aspects of business activity, including how one manages.
3 Everybody, irrespective of their level of creativity, can contribute to the business of innovation.
4 People can learn the tools and techniques that enhance the process of creativity and innovation.
5 People innovate better in groups. Innovation requires the coordination of many organisational resources.
6 Some organisational cultures are better suited to innovation than others, being better at the deployment of teams and the promotional process.
7 The heart of business creativity is searching for new patterns in existing patterns and components.
8 Innovation never (or very rarely) starts from a greenfield/blank-sheet start.
9 Paradoxically the core of much innovation is not learning new habits but rather unlearning familiar habits.
10 The innovative, unlearning organisation adopts a slow, deliberate process involving a great deal of time, energy, leadership and effort.
11 Innovation organisations make time for, and work at, innovative processes.
12 Innovative, unlearning organisations, really do have unassailable, ultimate, competitive advantages.

Many of these points may be disputed. What is beyond dispute, however, is that all organisations have to adapt and innovate and that being the first with a really good idea very clearly offers considerable benefits.

Sherwood (2001) contended that innovation was a four stage process. *First*, the generation of ideas; *then* their critical evaluation; *then* the development from abstract concept to working reality; and *finally* the implementation of the idea. The generation of ideas – the creativity bit – takes aptitude, effort and motivation. He conceived of a virtuous cycle thus: level of proficiency (talent), level of enjoyment (motivation), and amount of time spent (effort). Premature evaluation is often done unwisely. Personal and group factors all play a part related to previous histories of success or failure and attitudes to risk. Development is about the appropriate and judicious allocation and expenditure of money, time and people to get the show on the road. But implementation is also very important. Often it follows a careful, and hopefully, accurate, sensible and objective plan.

In the business world the innovator has to learn to educate, manage and persuade the ignorant and reluctant boss and/or board. They need to think about innovation as an individual and/or organisational competency be it hard or soft (i.e. technical vs. people). Sherwood (2001) recommended thinking of creativity as a stage process: first define the focus of interest, then define what you know, third share your understanding with others, then ask the question as to how things might be different. The latter may be categorised into size and scale, sequence and flow, roles and responsibilities, function and purpose.

Sherwood (2001) believed that business innovation was all about corporate culture. Some organisations welcome innovation: they have the time, money and will to do it. They know they need to revisit all sorts of issues on a regular basis: rewards and recognition, performance management, funding and budgeting arrangements. They understand about managing innovation products and embedding the process. They certainly know about the crucial role of senior management and how to reward innovation. However, most organisations are the opposite. Their problem is not so much the introduction of new ideas as the unlearning of old ones. They are reactive not proactive, full of hubris rather than humility; risk and failure averse; against things new; quick to judge and punish innovations.

Over the years, people have come up with many tricks/methods or processes that supposedly improve creativity. Indeed there are "bumper books" that list techniques that help generate new ideas. Foster (1991) suggests 101 methods, Jay (2006) a mere 36; and Van Grundy (1988) an impressive 250. Essentially, each attempts the same goals – to create new patterns out of the familiar: To recombine, rearrange, reduce, enlarge or synthesise products, components or processes that are probably very familiar. These include word associations; attempting to use similes, metaphors and analogies to describe things; using proverbs to spark ideas; doing role plays, and the like. The ideas, once generated, then need to be evaluated. This can be done according to various criteria like cost and radicalness.

De Bono (1992) coined the term "lateral thinking" among others. The idea was to provoke new thoughts and ideas; to think quite differently; to ask obvious "naïve" questions that provoke very different answers. These ideas have then to be evaluated looking at issues like benefits (Who benefits? For how long?); what issues need to be managed in implementation (risk); what constituencies (people, groups) will be affected and what their feelings might be; what data do we have/need to proceed (How good is it? Where do I get it?); what solutions have we identified; and what actions should we take?

Furnham (2004) made a similar distinction between what he called *fixers* and *inventors*. Every organisation needs its fixers: those diplomatic, behind-the-scenes operators who through stealth, charm, cajoling or even threat, make things happen. They are more wily, shrewd and courageous than creative. But there are also those technical people who mend the unmendable, adapt things quite successfully to be used for something quite different and generally "keep the lights on".

Traditionally fixers are good with their hands, but they have to have the ideas in the first place. They really understand "efficient and effective" and can often work out how to do things better with what they have. Fixers are practical realists. They are often surprisingly conventional. Paradoxically they can be seen by others as inflexible and change averse mainly because they are interested in things working better not differently.

Inventors are very different animals. They do not so much think outside the box – they throw it away. They are interested in doing things (very) differently. They do not solve problems: but they can cause them. Inventors are the real creatives. They are usually seen as difficult, low on charm, high on egocentricity, totally impractical, completely unrealistic. They are full of ideas but not interested in how to finance them or turn them into action.

It is known that really creative people have an unusual thinking pattern. They report that they cannot inhibit or repress seemingly irrelevant information from reaching consciousness. But what inventors do is see the relevance of interconnected ideas. It is from this bizarre and often uncomfortable process that really original ideas arise.

Creative inventors cannot *not* think this way. Indeed, it often gets them into trouble. Certainly they are often at loggerheads with the status quo. Many have a reputation for being poorly organised, unreliable, irresponsible, callous and self-centred (in Eysenckian terms high P scorers). They can also be fickle, egocentric and rather too laid back. But if they are bright, fairly technically competent and well managed they are very valuable indeed. It is the last, *but* the really hard task. Organisations need to find and nurture these people who are self-confessedly odd. They do not advertise their creativity and often have a very patchy educational and employment record. They don't interview well and don't do skilful impression management. They can have poor references or none at all, and often a reputation for being unmanageable. But never underestimate the potential of the real creative.

Conclusion

Creativity is a deeply frustrating concept for social scientists and applied researchers. It is clearly an interesting and very important facet of human beings. Some clearly have more talent than others. Further, it seems that it is not particularly prone to "development".

This chapter has considered first the problems with how to define and thence measure creativity. To an extent this is where all the problems remain. There is still no agreed robust, parsimonious, psychometrically valid measure of creativity used in research or applied settings. Every method available is not so much flawed by being unreliable and invalid as inadequate, because it seems to measure only part of the complex concept.

A related problem is that there remain few good descriptions of the mechanisms or processes by which some latent creative individuals produce new and useful products or ideas. We have few powerful theories that describe, let alone explain, that process.

This chapter reviewed the century-long literature on the relationship between two abstract concepts, at one time equally troubled by definition and measurement. Whilst intelligence research has come a long way in the past 100 years, the same cannot be said for creativity. Yet the concepts are linked and the available data indeed illustrate the point. Correlations between reasonably good tests of the two concepts suggest correlations in the $r = .30$ range. Clearly the two "traits" are related but not that closely. The same can be said of personality. Some traits like Openness to Experience and Psychoticism seem clearly related to creativity and offer an explanation by which the process may be understood.

Surprisingly, few studies have tried to look at the incremental validity of personality over intelligence in trying to explain creativity. No doubt this is due to the simplest but most important reason: there remains no psychometrically acceptable test of creativity to warrant such a useful research investment.

The business world, however, seems less concerned with psychological theory and measurement than the academics. Various popular books and assertions are mooted and accepted often with little or no proof. Perhaps the most important contention is that creativity may be relatively easily and quickly taught, as if it were a simple skill. The second is that all organisations want and need creative individuals in order for them to thrive. Whilst this may well be true of some it is by no means true for all. Thus, creativity research remains one of the most beguiling and interesting fields in the whole area.

9 Attitudes, beliefs, styles and values at work

Introduction

Whilst personality psychologists have been particularly interested in fundamental, probably biologically based, certainly enduring, traits and abilities, social psychologists have been more interested in attitudes, beliefs and values and how they shape a worker's behaviour. Whilst the former have spent considerable effort "mapping the territory" to come up with the definitive classificatory system for personality (see Chapter 3) and ability (see Chapter 6), social psychologists seem more content to explore a whole range of seemingly unrelated belief and value systems. This makes it equally problematic for the academic reviewer and the practising manager. It is unclear what to focus on, and what is most important in the sense of having work behaviour predictive validity.

This chapter will also look at research in a number of these areas. The focus will be on how, when and why these attitudes, beliefs and value systems predict behaviour at work. This chapter will also explore the concept of style. There is a vast literature on style – cognitive style, learning style, attribution style, and coping style. For some, the concept of style is a nice bridge between traits and abilities while for others it is a poor muddled compromise. Some attitudinal variables are extremely well researched and ignored. Thus, there is a great interest in job satisfaction, which has been variously conceived as work commitment, or engagement or centrality (Hirschfeld & Field, 2000). Most studies on these topics have tried to identify the causes, correlates and consequences of these beliefs.

Before proceeding, however, it is important to answer two fundamental questions:

1. What is the essential difference between the concepts of attitudes, beliefs and values?

Beliefs are thoughts about concepts, events, objects or people; or about the relationship between these things. Beliefs do not have an evaluative (good/bad, like/dislike) component. One can have beliefs about the functions of marketing or the movement of the stock market. Traditionally, social psychologists are interested in *attitudes* to things like work, one's boss, or the organisation. They are usually defined as relatively stable, affective or evaluative dispositions towards a particular person, situation or thing. They have three components: cognitive, evaluative and behavioural. They form into bundles, constellations or theories. Thus, job satisfaction is essentially an attitude to the job. People also have very specific attitudes like those toward work schedules, or the labour unions or physical working conditions.

People have attitudes to, at and about work. There have been literally dozens of studies about attitudes to appraisal, flexitime, pay, promotion, retirement, tenure and work–life balance. Some are theory driven, others are not. How they measure attitudes differs, and comparatively few examine how personality traits and cognitive abilities are related to these attitudes. Even fewer examine the relationship between attitudes to, and specific behaviour concerning, a particular issue at work.

Attitudes are functional and they guide behaviour. Because work is such an import-ant part of people's lives, they quite naturally have strong, complex and diverse atti-tudes to it. However, attitudes to (and indeed behaviour at) work may be shaped by strongly held *social values*. Everyone has certain implicit and explicit values that reflect their unique upbringing, their education and the wider culture within which they live. Some of their values are overtly materialistic, others completely spiritual. These values about freedom, equality and altruism are very relevant in the workplace. For instance, they are partly responsible for *where* people choose to work. We often hear of people boycotting organisations and products that are associated with specific values anti-thetical to their own. They would clearly never work for these organisations. Many people seek out organisations whose values (expressed in their mission statement, or known by reputation) fit their own.

Values are related to belief systems, that is values are groups of beliefs about a particular object or process. Thus, people may have a fairly elaborate gender belief system about such issues as discrimination against women, biological differences between the sexes, attitudes to homosexuals and lesbians, and the problems associated with people of one gender working in a job commonly associated with the opposite gender (a man as a midwife, a woman as a soldier). These belief systems are, in turn, related to highly specific attitudes to issues at work. Attitudes towards pay and absen-teeism may be part of a reward belief system shaped by values about equity.

2. Do attitudes predict behaviour?

Whilst it is interesting to know about attitudes at work, if they are weak predictors of work behaviour they are of considerably less interest. One explanation is the *level of specificity* at which we usually measure attitudes and behaviour. Often, attitudes are measured at a very general *abstract* level and behaviour at a highly *specific* level. The more the two are in alignment, the better the one predicts the other. To predict a particular work-related behaviour, one needs to measure specific related attitudes to that behaviour. Second, there is the problem of *single versus multiple act* measurement. If people are interested in attitudes to migrant workers, it is better to look at a series of possible behaviours associated with them. Attitudes are much better predictors when a series of behaviours (multiple acts) is taken into account. "One-shot" measures of behaviour are often unreliable and do not give us much information about the relation-ships between attitudes and behaviour. One needs to *aggregate* observed or recorded behaviour to make certain the measure is robust and reliable before attempting to see if it is logically related to any particular attitude pattern.

Third, *situational factors* may strongly influence attitudes as well as behaviours. Where situational pressures are strong, such as at the scene of an industrial accident or in a religious building, people of widely different attitudes may act in a similar way. Thus, external factors may constrain behaviour and reduce or even change the relation-ship between attitudes and behaviour. Fourth, it is possible that a given behaviour might relate to a *range of attitudes*. For instance, imagine we are interested in predicting, in general, how likely people are to go on strike and, specifically, how likely to go on strike in support of a sacked disabled colleague. A person might be unfavourably disposed to disabled people, very positive about management and very strongly against any form of sacking. It is difficult to know which of these attitudes would best predict behaviour.

Other factors, too, mediate between attitudes and behaviour, many of which are known and appear to have a systematic relationship. Thus, rather than despair, it may be possible to show a strong relationship depending on how one measures both attitude and behaviour. For instance, Ajzen and Fishbein (1980) have concluded from their extensive research that: "A person's attitude has a consistently strong relation with his or her behaviour when it is directed at the same target and when it involves the same action" (p. 912). Work attitudes *can* predict work behaviour when both are appropriately measured *and* relevant confounding factors are taken into consideration.

Where do particular attitudes come from and how are they maintained? Three important issues mean that the answer to this question (as with the others) is complex. *First*, factors that lead to the *adoption* of an attitude often differ from those that *maintain* it. (We know, for instance, that social factors are important in determining when and why certain young people begin to smoke, but that *personality* factors are much more important in explaining why some continue.) *Second*, each set or group of attitudes may be maintained by different factors. Thus, personality factors may relate to racial attitudes, whereas social-class factors relate to attitudes towards health. *Third*, these different factors are themselves interrelated and confounded and, hence, are difficult to tease apart.

The attitude–behaviour link has been most effectively spelt out by Fishbein and Ajzen (1975) in their theory of reasoned action (TRA; Figure 9.1) and their later, improved theory of planned behaviour (TPB; Ajzen, 1988). *Intentions*, in turn, are determined by two conceptually independent components – attitudes and subjective norms. Attitudes are conceptualised as overall positive or negative evaluations of the behaviour. Attitudes, in turn, are assumed to be a function of an individual's salient behavioural beliefs about the consequences of performing the behaviour. An individual who believes that a particular behaviour will lead to a positive outcome will hold a favourable attitude to that behaviour, whereas an individual who believes that the behaviour will lead to a negative outcome will hold an unfavourable attitude. Based on expectancy-value conceptualisations, attitudes are also based on the evaluation of these beliefs. Hence, attitudes are the multiplicative combination of behavioural beliefs and the evaluation of these beliefs.

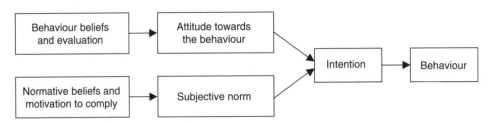

Figure 9.1 Schematic representation of the theory of reasoned action. Adapted from Fishbein and Ajzen (1975).

The second determinant of intention is a social factor termed subjective norms. Subjective norms refer to the perceived pressure from significant others to perform or not perform the behaviour. Subjective norms, in turn, are assumed to be a function of normative beliefs. Normative beliefs are an individual's perceptions of whether salient others (individuals or groups whose beliefs about an individual's behaviour are important to them) think they should or should not engage in the behaviour. Subjective norms are also determined by the individual's motivation to comply with that referent's expectation. Hence, subjective norms are the multiplicative combination of normative beliefs and the motivation to comply.

However, Ajzen (1988) himself conceded: "The theory of reasoned action was developed explicitly to deal with purely volitional behaviours" (p. 127), and he acknowledged that the enactment of behaviour is not always under complete volitional control, in that there may be internal obstacles (e.g. skills, ability, knowledge) or external obstacles (e.g. time, money, opportunity) that may limit performance. To accommodate such factors, Ajzen (1991) included a third conceptually independent component in the model termed "perceived behavioural control" (PBC), which resulted in the formulation of the TPB (see Figure 9.2). PBC is a measure of the amount of control the individual has over the behaviour in question.

As can be seen from Figure 9.2, the PBC component can have both a direct impact on behaviour and an indirect impact through behavioural intention. The proposed relationship between PBC and behaviour is based upon two rationales. *First*, holding intention constant, the enactment of a behaviour will increase as PBC increases. *Second*, PBC will influence behaviour directly to the extent that perceived control reflects actual control.

In addition, levels of PBC should also influence behavioural intentions, in that if an individual perceives that he or she has little control over the performance of a behaviour, their motivation to do so is likely to be weak. Perceived behavioural control works in parallel with attitudes and subjective norms as determinants of intentions: thus, a stronger intention to enact a behaviour is therefore dependent upon positive attitudes, perceived social acquiescence and perceived ease of behavioural performance.

Just as behavioural beliefs and normative beliefs are assumed to influence attitudes and subjective norms respectively, control beliefs are assumed to influence PBC. Control beliefs are judgements about whether one has access to the necessary resources and opportunities to perform the behaviour, and include both internal control factors (e.g. skills) and external control factors (e.g. opportunities). Perceived behavioural control is

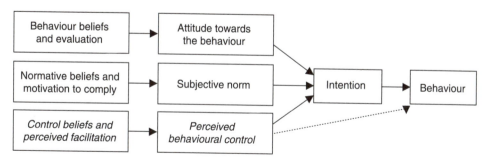

Figure 9.2 Schematic representation of the theory of planned behaviour. Adapted from Ajzen (1988, 1991).

also determined by the perceived power of the control of belief to facilitate or inhibit performance of the behaviour. Hence, PBC is the multiplicative combination of control beliefs and the perceived power of the control belief.

However, Ajzen (1991) argued that the inability of the TRA to account for the influence of past behaviour on subsequent behaviour might be attributed to the absence of the perceived control component. Ajzen proposed that the effect of past behaviour is primarily mediated by the PBC component, which is consistent with Bandura's (1982) claim that past behaviour provides important information about an individual's sense of control. Hence, when perceived control is taken into account, past behaviour should no longer contribute to the prediction of intention and behaviour.

Figure 9.3 is a schematic representation of the complex relationship between the components of the TRA, the TPB and the additional contribution of past behaviour to intentions and actual behaviour. *The "bottom line" is that attitudes (alone) are poor predictors of behaviour at work.* However, if various other beliefs are measured (such as those shown in Figure 9.3) plus past behaviour, it is quite possible to be reasonably good at predicting behaviour in the workplace.

Do attitudes predict behaviour at work, such as absenteeism, measured productivity or accidents? The two theories outlined above would suggest they do, but only under certain circumstances and in conjunction with the measurement of other variables. Thus, in addition to attitudes, one needs to consider, and measure, subjective norms or beliefs about how others in the organisation behave; personal beliefs about self-efficacy – the extent to which the individual believes he or she has personal control over the behaviour; as well as their history of this specific behaviour in the past. Next, one has to measure, as accurately as possible, their actual behavioural intentions. Once these factors have been carefully measured and considered, it becomes possible to show when, where, why and how attitudes *do* predict behaviour at work.

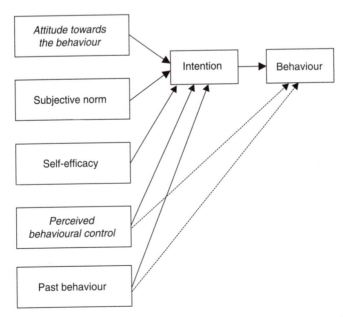

Figure 9.3 Schematic representation of the proposed relationship between the TRA and extended TPB variables.

Beliefs about work

Some researchers have attempted quite specifically to look at work-related attitudes and beliefs. One of the first published accounts of the "beliefs about work" questionnaire is that provided by Buchholz (1976). The measure contained five indices, as follows:

1 The work ethic – the belief that work is good in itself, offers dignity to a person and that success is a result of personal effort.
2 The organisation belief system – the view that work takes on meaning only as it affects the organisation and contributes to one's position at work.
3 Marxist-related beliefs – the opinion that work is fundamental to human fulfilment but as currently organised represents exploitation of the worker and consequent alienation.
4 The humanistic belief system – the view that individual growth and development in the job are more important than the output.
5 The leisure ethic – which regards work as a means to personal fulfilment, through its provision of the means to pursue leisure activities.

Buchholz (1978) looked at the relationship between age, sex, race, education and job status with work beliefs and values in the general population. Whereas humanistic work beliefs did not differentiate between people of different backgrounds, Marxist-related beliefs did. Younger rather than older, female rather than male, poorly rather than better educated, Black more than White, and workers more than management, tended to support "Marxist ideas". The work ethic was related only to age (young people showed a stronger work ethic orientation than older people), whereas the leisure ethic was related to occupation (top management indicated that they liked their work and were not willing to accept leisure as a substitute for the benefit of work). It was concluded that, in general, the work ethic is not held very strongly but that no other belief system emerges as a clear preference to it. Dickson and Buchholz (1977) actually compared these same work beliefs among three working groups in Scotland and the USA. Overall, the Marxist-related and leisure belief systems most differentiated the workers from the different cultures. They also examined the effects of company size, occupation, age, education and religion on work belief and found very much the same as Buchholz (1978).

Because this measure has the advantage of being sphere-specific, in the sense that it is actually trying to measure different, unrelated work beliefs, it has been shown to be fairly predictive of the behaviours of managers. Certainly, work ethic beliefs are positively, and Marxist-related beliefs are negatively, related to personal satisfaction and productivity (Furnham, 1990, 1994). These two systems are opposed on many issues such as pay, promotion and how people are managed. The measure is also related to how people manage others, as well as more general social and political beliefs.

Various other researchers have used this measure in their research. Thus, Guastello et al. (1992) showed cynical students endorsed Marxist-related beliefs. More recently Puffer et al. (1997) looked at 292 Russian managers' beliefs about work, many of which disconfirmed previous stereotypes.

The advantage of looking at these beliefs is that they have high face validity. Despite the usefulness of the measure, however, there seems to be little research on individual difference (i.e. personality) correlates of these beliefs or, more importantly, how, whether, when and why these beliefs actually predict work-related behaviour.

Belief in a just world

The "belief in a just world" (BJW) pattern was identified over 25 years ago and concentrates on the tendency of people to blame victims of misfortunes for their own fate (Lerner, 1980). The essence of this hypothesis or theory was succinctly summarised by Lerner and Miller (1978):

> Individuals have a need to believe that they live in a world where people generally get what they deserve. The belief that the world is just enables the individual to confront his physical and social environment as though they were stable and orderly. Without such a belief it would be difficult for the individual to commit himself to the pursuit of long-range goals or even to the socially regulated behaviour of day-to-day life. Since the belief that the world is just serves such an important adaptive function for the individual, people are very reluctant to give up this belief, and they can be greatly troubled if they encounter evidence that suggests that the world is not really just or orderly after all.
>
> (pp. 1030–1031)

Many studies have used this scale to examine further the relationship between "just world" and other beliefs and behaviours (Furnham & Proctor, 1989). The measure is not without its difficulties. For instance, Furnham and Proctor considered the validity of the unidimensionality of the concept of a just world. They suggested that there might well be three worlds: a *just* world where people get what they deserve (the good and virtuous are rewarded and the bad punished); the *unjust* world where the opposite occurs (the good go unrewarded and may even be punished, but the wicked win out in the end); and the *random* or *a-just* world where neither occurs consistently, in that some good deeds are rewarded, others ignored, and still others punished. Furthermore, it is possible that people believe that some aspects of their life are just (e.g. interpersonal relations) and others unjust or a-just (socio-political happenings).

Nevertheless, the "belief in a just world" measure has been shown to correlate significantly with demographic variables such as age, income and religion, but also such personality factors as attitudes to authority, conservatism and locus of control. People with strong needs to believe in a just world find it difficult to deal with others' misfortunes, such as illness. Hence, they may be particularly unsympathetic to colleagues going absent with serious illnesses, because they find it difficult to accept the idea that some illnesses and diseases seem to strike people randomly.

The second major development has been to view the "belief in a just world" as a healthy coping mechanism rather than being the manifestation of antisocial beliefs and prejudice (Dalbert, 2001). There has been a subtle movement from focusing on victim derogation to positive coping. Recent studies have portrayed BJW beliefs as a personal resource or coping strategy, which buffers against stress and enhances achievement behaviour. For the first time, BJW beliefs have been seen as an indicator of mental health and planning. This does not contradict the more extensive literature on BJW and victim derogation. Rather, it helps to explain why people are so eager to maintain their beliefs, which may be their major coping strategy. BJW is clearly functional for the individual. One important issue for future research is how BJW relates to other coping strategies, and which are favoured by healthy individuals who have low BJW beliefs.

Again, the focus is on how BJW relates to personal experiences rather than that of others (Furnham, 2003a).

In an important review, Hafer and Begue (2005) noted that there are many individual differences associated with the BJW. They also reviewed the many studies that showed how these beliefs relate to ideas and beliefs about justice in many different settings.

There is a vast and important literature on distributive and procedural justice in psychology that pays scant attention to personality and ability. However, it does seem the case that BJW would relate logically and strongly to many issues at work, like pay equity and equality, discipline and sacking, as well as appraisal. BJW predicts how people react to perceived injustice against both themselves and others, as well as how they might attempt restitution.

One of the most pervasive issues in the workplace is workers' perceptions of being dealt with fairly. That is, that they are fairly appraised, paid, trained and rewarded relative to their peers. These are essentially beliefs about justice and they considerably influence behaviour at work, particularly "negative" counterproductive work behaviours, when workers feel they are unjustly managed. Hence, the potential importance of measuring and understanding their BJW.

The Protestant work ethic

The concept of the Protestant work ethic (PWE) was devised by the German sociologist Max Weber (1905), who saw it as part explanation for the origin of capitalism. People who believe in the PWE tend to be achievement- and success-orientated, stress the need for efficacy and practicality, tend to be anti-leisure, and are conservative and conscious about wasting time, energy, and money (see Chapter 2).

Nearly all the social-science disciplines have been interested in the PWE. Psychologists have tried to define it in psychological terms. Thus, Jones (1997) noted that PWE was related to strong beliefs about five issues: hard work, use of time, saving, innovation and honesty. Psychologists have also spent a great deal of effort in devising valid and reliable measures of the PWE. Perhaps the most comprehensive is that of Miller et al. (2002), whose measure tapped into seven dimensions: (1) belief in work for its own sake; (2) striving for independence in one's daily work; (3) belief in the virtues of hard work; (4) pro-leisure attitudes and belief in the importance of non-work activities; (5) believing in a just and moral existence; (6) orientation toward the future and postponement of rewards; and, finally, (7) attitudes and beliefs reflecting active and productive use of time.

It has been argued that PWE-believing parents socialise their children by rewarding them for success, independent rational behaviour and postponement of gratification. They, therefore, become economically successful and, thus, explain the relationship between the PWE and economic growth.

Experimental studies on the PWE, reviewed by Furnham (1990), have shown believers to be competitive, very eager to have equitable rather than equal rewards, to have a tendency towards workaholism, and to be able to tolerate tedious jobs. PWE beliefs have also been shown to be good predictors of leisure-time and retirement activity, as well as vocational preference and the saving of money.

Research on the work ethic is alive and well. Evidence of this comes from Miller et al. (2002), who recently developed a new (and improved) multidimensional Work Ethic Profile. This 65-item questionnaire measures seven conceptually and empirically distinct facets of the work ethic, including such things as self-reliance, delay of gratification and attitudes to wasted time. They argued that this measure is not only conceptually grounded in the original Weberian construct, but is appropriate for use today and across different religions.

Cherrington (1980) listed eight attributes of the PWE. The broader meaning of the work ethic typically refers to one or more of the following beliefs:

1   People have a normal and religious work obligation to fill their lives with heavy physical toil. For some, this means that hard work, effort and drudgery are to be valued for their own sake; physical pleasures and enjoyments are to be shunned; and an ascetic existence of methodological rigour is the only acceptable way to live.
2   Men and women are expected to spend long hours at work, with little or no time for personal recreation and leisure.
3   A worker should have a dependable attendance record, with low absenteeism and tardiness.
4   Workers should be highly productive, and produce a large quantity of goods or service.
5   Workers should take pride in their work and do their jobs well.
6   Employees should have feelings of commitment and loyalty to their profession, their company, and their work group.
7   Workers should be achievement-orientated and should constantly strive for promotion and advancement. High-status jobs with prestige and the respect of others are important indicators of a "good" person.
8   People should acquire wealth through honest labour and retain it through thrift and wise investments. Frugality is desirable; extravagance and waste should be avoided.

At the centre of the concept of the PWE is the idea that the values and beliefs underlying the PWE (morality, control, postponement of gratification, asceticism, hard work) actually lead to economic success on both an individual and a national level. In this sense, the PWE can be conceived as a personally held belief system that is predictive of economic success (Furnham, 1990). Economists have attempted to translate or apply Weberian ideas into the language and concepts of today. Ditz (1980), in an interesting essay on the PWE and the market economy, described the PWE idea of profit making as a calling as "the sacramentalisation of acquisition". He explained, in lay economic terms, how the PWE had affected the market economy (what Marx called capitalism) over the last few hundred years. His key concepts were:

- Inputs to productivity – because pessimistic Calvinists were so concerned with scarcity, they stressed the need for productive work to bring about surpluses.
- Propensity to save – because maximisation of productivity and minimisation of consumption were ethically important, saving seemed the most useful solution.
- Risk-taking investments – saving was more acceptable than spending, and investing more acceptable than saving because charging interest was taboo.
- A calculating orientation – effective efficiency means knowledge of, and ability in, making calculations of input and output, demand and supply, cost, price and profits. Quantitative skills became professionalised.
- Profit-making as a calling – profit maximisation was the prime objective. The acquisition instinct became a Utopian ideal.

- From labour costs to profits – anything that increases net profit is good and anything that lowers it is bad. Labour per se is only good when it becomes efficient, cost reducing and effective.
- Encouragement of marketing – marketing helped the consumer consume more effectively and, hence, the producer produce more efficiently, hence, marketing empathy with the consumer.
- Emergence of new elites – the new "would-be saints" were successful entrepreneurs, captains of industry, elected political leaders, certified men of knowledge and accepted opinion leaders.
- Creation of new democracies – all organisations were turned into meritocratic democracies. Liberty and equality were promoted as was work, psychologically democratised social structure, etc.
- Resolution of organised conflict – the PWE philosophy was individualistic against government interference, noncomformist and against conflict and militant behaviour. It tended to retreat from conflict and be anti-authoritarian.
- Middle class and mass market – PWE endorsers were upward moving, middle-class oriented and tried to resolve conflicting claims of meritocratic elitism and egalitarianism.
- The manipulation of consumers – promotion of products through advertising, etc., was given ethical support because self and other material improvement was thought of as morally desirable.

Of all the "belief systems" investigated jointly by social and organisational psychologists certainly the PWE seems most relevant to understanding behaviour at work. Clearly, of all the personality variables related to the concept conscientiousness seems the most relevant. Indeed the facets of conscientiousness, like need for achievement, dutifulness and diligence, seem at the very heart of the PWE. In this sense, one would expect the two to be very highly correlated.

Perceived control

The perceived control personality variable or dimension relates to beliefs about *internal versus external control of reinforcement*, that is the cause of behavioural outcomes. It assumes that individuals develop a general expectancy regarding their ability to control their lives. People who believe that the events that occur in their lives are the result of their own behaviour and/or ability, personality, and effort are said to have the *expectancy of internal control*, whereas those who believe events in their lives to be a function of luck, chance, fate, God(s), powerful others or powers *beyond their* control, comprehension or manipulation are said to have an *expectancy of external control*. Managers with internal locus of control tend to see threatening events at work as less stressful and they cope with it better than managers with external locus of control. Locus of control is related to *desire for control*, conceived of as a trait reflecting the extent to which individuals are generally motivated to control the events in their lives. People with high desire for control tend to have internal control, to have higher aspirations, to be more persistent and respond more to challenge, and to see themselves as the source of their own success.

The concept of locus of control, has been applied to *behaviour in organisations*. Spector (1982), in a review paper, noted that locus of control is related to motivation, effort, performance, satisfaction, perception of the job, compliance with authority, and supervisory style, as well as being an important moderator between incentives and motivation, satisfaction and turnover. For instance, internals tend to prefer piece-rate systems, whereas externals tend to be more satisfied with direct supervision, to comply more with demands of coercive supervisors, and to be more compliant with social demands than internals. Spector concluded that much more organisational theory may be applicable to internals. Similar studies on employment, unemployment and labour market discrimination have demonstrated different levels of internality and externality as a function of work experience.

In a large study of nearly 3000 employed people, Andrisani and Nestle (1976) examined the influence of internal/external control on success in the world of work. Locus of control was significantly related to occupational attainment, hourly earnings, job satisfaction, annual earnings and perceived financial progress.

> More specifically, the cross-sectional data suggest that internals are in the better and higher status occupations, earn more money, and tend to be more highly satisfied in their work than comparable externals. The longitudinal data further suggest that internals experience more favourable employment circumstances than their external counterparts, namely greater earning and job satisfaction.
>
> (p. 460)

Franz (1980) looked at the effect of work (labour market experience) upon the internal locus of control of a large group of young American people. He found, as predicted, that increases in hourly earnings, additional labour market experience, and more years of formal schooling increase feelings of internal control. However, public sector employment was associated with increasing external locus of control as a result of bureaucratic structures tending to restrict opportunities for developing abilities. More recently, studies have related locus of control beliefs to economic crisis, and others have attempted to develop a measure specifically of economic locus of control, which was demonstrated to be related to the PWE (Furnham, 1990).

Studies since the mid-1960s have revealed refreshingly unequivocal results supporting the fact that instrumentalism (internal locus of control) is a cause and consequence of success, and fatalism a cause and consequence of failure. Results show the following:

- *Motivation.* Instrumentalists are more likely to believe that their efforts will result in good performance, and they exhibit stronger belief in their own competence.
- *Job performance.* Instrumentalists perform better because of their greater effort, seeking more information in complex task situations, and exhibiting greater personal career effectiveness.
- *Job satisfaction.* Instrumentalists should be more satisfied than fatalists (externals), generally, as well as in the job, partly because of their success.
- *Leadership.* Instrumentalists prefer participative approaches from their supervisors, rely more on personal persuasion with their subordinates, and seem more task orientated and less socially orientated.
- *Job perception.* Instrumentalists perceive more personal control over their environment, request more feedback on the job and perceive less role strain.
- *Turnover.* Highly job-satisfied instrumentalists exhibit the same rate of turnover (presumably low) as fatalists, but for highly dissatisfying jobs instrumentalists exhibit more turnover than fatalists.

Spector (1982) devised a very simple locus of control measure. This simple measure has been shown to be closely related to work motivation and satisfaction (Furnham & Drakeley, 1993). Certainly, there is now ample evidence that high, although not extremely high, internal scores are good predictors of occupational success.

There is also considerable evidence to suggest that personality traits and cognitive abilities are significantly and logically related to general as well as work-specific locus of control beliefs. Thus, these beliefs may moderate or mediate the relationship between traits, abilities and work-related outcomes.

Social values and work

Researchers on the topic of social values have conceived of them as a system of beliefs, concerned with such issues as competence and morality, that are derived, in large part, from societal demands. Value systems are organised summaries of experience that capture the focal, abstracted qualities of past encounters; have an oughtness (specifying prescribed and proscribed behaviours) quality about them and that function as criteria or as a framework against which present experience can be tested. Values act as general motives.

A value is considered an enduring belief that a specific instrumental mode of conduct and/or a terminal end state of existence is preferable. Once a value is internalised, it consciously or unconsciously becomes a *standard criterion* for guiding action: for developing and *maintaining attitudes* towards relevant objects and situations, for justifying one's own and others' actions and attitudes, for *morally judging* self and others, and for comparing oneself with others. There continues to be a great interest in the origins, malleability and possible consequences of individuals holding particular world values (De Vos et al., 2005; Rentsch & McEwan, 2002).

Research by Feather (1975) and others has demonstrated that these value systems are systematically linked to culture of origin, religion, chosen university discipline, political persuasion, generations within a family, age, sex, personality and educational background. These values in time may determine vocational choice and occupational behaviour. Feather (1975) argued that social attitudes precede values, which emerge as abstractions from personal experience of one's own and others' behaviour. These values in time become organised into coherent *value systems*, which serve as frames of reference that guide beliefs and behaviour in many situations, such as work. Feather has argued that values, attitudes and attributions are linked into a cognitive–affective (thinking–feeling) system. It may be expected that there are coherent and predictable links between one's general value system and specific work-related beliefs.

What are the things people want and consider important in their lives? Research by Schwartz (1992) and his collaborators showed that people's values can be organised into ten types. They are:

1 Benevolence – active protection of others' welfare.
2 Universalism – equality and justice.
3 Self-direction – independence in thought and action.
4 Stimulation – excitement.
5 Hedonism – sensuous and emotional gratification.
6 Achievement – personal success through competence.
7 Power – status and respect.

8   Security – safety and harmony of self and social groups.
9   Conformity – restraint of actions and impulses likely to harm others or violate norms.
10   Tradition.

Personal values can be reflected in the values at work, which may be categorised into two facets. One is an *outcome* of work (e.g. recognition, pay) or a *resource* that one shares merely by being associated with the work organisation (e.g. working conditions, company reputation). The second facet categorises work outcomes into *instrumental* (e.g. benefits), *affective* (e.g. relationship with co-workers) and *cognitive* (e.g. achievement, contribution to society). Some values are associated with the work ethic – achievement and hard working – whereas others are related to interpersonal relationships at work.

Employees who score highly on these work values focus on the *content* of their work. They are intrinsically motivated, achievement orientated and hardworking, striving to move upwards, and seek challenges. They usually have higher education and occupy senior positions in organisations and tend to be higher in organisational commitment.

Other values are associated with the *context* of work: high salary, job security, pleasant physical working environment and many fringe benefits. These are more related to a person's basic survival needs than are the content-orientated values. People who have strong context-orientated, and thus extrinsic, work values ascribe much importance to social status, comfort, salary and benefits. They view work not as an end in itself, but as a means to attain other, more desirable, ends.

A person's values can be assessed by means of self-report questionnaires. Rokeach's (1975) value survey is one of the most widely known instruments. Respondents are required to rank, in order, 18 terminal values and 18 instrumental values. *Terminal values* are "desirable end-states of existence", such as salvation, peace of mind, true friendship and world peace. *Instrumental values* are "desirable modes of conduct", such as being ambitious, clean, honest and loving. These modes of conduct are instrumental to attaining the desired end-state. Researchers have made modifications to the response format of Rokeach's value survey (see Schwartz, 1992). Others have either added more, or changed the list of values presented to the person.

Hogan and Hogan (2001) argued that a person's core values are part of the individual's identity and key drivers in what they both desire and strive to attain at work. Further, as many vocational psychologists have noted, people prefer to work with others who share their values and are happiest in environments that are consistent with their values. Equally, people find it stressful and disagreeable to act contrary to their values.

There are several measures of work values, such as the nine-item Survey of Work Values (Wollack et al., 1971), which measures five types of values (activity preference, attitude toward earning, job involvement, pride in work and upward striving; Young & Parker, 1999). One of the earliest measures was the Allport et al. (1960) study of values, which measured six basic values: theoretical, economic, aesthetic, social, political and religious. Another questionnaire used mainly in the area of vocational choice is Super's (1970) Work Values Inventory, which consists of 15 scales measuring extrinsic values in the form of rewards such as money and prestige (way of life, security, prestige, economic returns), extrinsic social and environmental concomitants of work (surroundings, associates, supervisory relationships, and variety), and intrinsic rewards derived from activity pleasure and goal accomplishment (creativity, management, achievement, altruism, independence, intellectual stimulation, and aesthetics; Ben-Shem & Avi-Itzhak, 1991). There is also the Work Values Questionnaire (Elizhur, 1984), which comprises 24 different values to be rated on a 6-point scale. In a large international study, Elizhur et al. (1991) found three dimensions for this questionnaire, which they labelled cognitive (advancement, feedback, status), affective (recognition, esteem, interaction), and instrumental (pay, benefits, security).

Other measures of work values include the Minnesota Importance Questionnaire (Gay et al., 1975), which measures six types of values (achievement, altruism, autonomy, comfort, safety and status; Keller et al., 1992). Manhardt (1972) developed the Work Values Inventory, which measures 25 values that factor into three broad dimensions (comfort and security, competence and growth, status and independence; Meyer et al., 1998). Occasionally, authors appear to develop measures specifically for the purposes of one study. For example, Johnson (2001) devised a 14-item questionnaire to measure four types of work values (extrinsic, intrinsic, altruistic and social) and subsequently to investigate how they changed over time. There have also been a number of studies using the Work Values Questionnaire (Furnham et al., 2002, 2005), which has undergone various changes over time. This is shown in Table 9.1.

Table 9.1 The revised Work Value Questionnaire

		Unimportant					*Important*
1	**Balance** – a job that allows me to lead a balanced life.	1	2	3	4	5	6
2	**Benefits** – a job that provides many features additional to pay (e.g., pension top-ups, extra holidays).	1	2	3	4	5	6
3	**Bonuses** – a job that provides many opportunities for topping up the basic salary.	1	2	3	4	5	6
4	**Clarity** – a job with clear and well-defined roles and responsibilities.	1	2	3	4	5	6
5	**Comfort** – a job that can be carried out in physically comfortable conditions.	1	2	3	4	5	6
6	**Competition** – a job that provides me with opportunities to compete with others.	1	2	3	4	5	6
7	**Conditions** – a job that can be carried out in conditions, that are safe, modern, and clean.	1	2	3	4	5	6
8	**Contribution to society** – a job that allows me to work for a good cause.	1	2	3	4	5	6
9	**Effortlessness** – a job that is relatively easy and does not require excessive effort.	1	2	3	4	5	6
10	**Equipment** – a job that can be carried out with up-to-date equipment and technology.	1	2	3	4	5	6
11	**Flexibility** – a job that allows me to work flexible hours to suit my personal needs.	1	2	3	4	5	6
12	**Independence** – a job that allows me to work autonomously without much supervision.	1	2	3	4	5	6
13	**Insurance** – a job that provides health and life insurance.	1	2	3	4	5	6
14	**Intellectuality** – a job that is challenging and involves a lot of thinking and analysis.	1	2	3	4	5	6

15 **Location** – a job that is conveniently located and easily accessible.	1	2	3	4	5	6
16 **Organisational image** – a job within an organisation that is widely recognised and respected.	1	2	3	4	5	6
17 **Pay** – a job that is very well paid.	1	2	3	4	5	6
18 **Perks** – a job that provides many extras (e.g. company car, discounts on goods, etc.)	1	2	3	4	5	6
19 **Personal growth** – a job that provides opportunities for self-improvement.	1	2	3	4	5	6
20 **Personal relevance** – a job that provides me with opportunities to use my personal talents, education, and training.	1	2	3	4	5	6
21 **Power** – a job that allows me to control my destiny and be influential.	1	2	3	4	5	6
22 **Promotion** – a job that provides opportunities for rapid advancement.	1	2	3	4	5	6
23 **Recognition** – a job that leads to clear and wide recognition of my achievements.	1	2	3	4	5	6
24 **Regularity** – a job that can be performed in a standard, stable and controlled manner.	1	2	3	4	5	6
25 **Responsibility** – a job with many appropriate responsibilities.	1	2	3	4	5	6
26 **Safety** – a job that can be carried out in safe and secure conditions.	1	2	3	4	5	6
27 **Security** – a job that is secure and permanent.	1	2	3	4	5	6
28 **Simplicity** – a job that is not overly complicated.	1	2	3	4	5	6
29 **Social interaction** – a job that provides many good opportunities for social contact with others.	1	2	3	4	5	6
30 **Status** – a job that is generally recognised as "high-status" in our society.	1	2	3	4	5	6
31 **Stimulation** – a job that I personally find very interesting.	1	2	3	4	5	6
32 **Supervision** – a boss who is fair and considerate.	1	2	3	4	5	6
33 **Teaching** – a job that allows me to train others and to pass on my expertise.	1	2	3	4	5	6
34 **Teamwork** – a job that provides me with opportunities to cooperate with others.	1	2	3	4	5	6
35 **Tranquillity** – a job that is not particularly stressful.	1	2	3	4	5	6
36 **Variety** – a job that allows me to get involved in many different kinds of activities.	1	2	3	4	5	6
37 **Visibility** – a job that gives me a fair amount of publicity.	1	2	3	4	5	6

Reiss and Havercamp (1998) developed and tested a 16-dimension fundamental motive inventory that included some better-known dimensions like status, power, independence and tranquillity, but some rather less-well-known dimensions like saving, eating and vengeance. Olson and Weber (2004) looked at the relationship between the

Big Five and these motives in a population of 138 university students. When the Big Five traits were regressed onto each motive seven showed that personality traits accounted for a fifth of the variance. Stable neurotics valued social contact, conscientious, closed neurotics valued order, and disagreeable extraverts valued vengeance. The authors suggested that the relationship between traits and motives may be curvilinear and that extremely high- or low-motive desires were associated with adjustment problems, noticeably neuroticism.

Most value instruments are used to help make decisions on vocational choice and change. Perhaps the one theory of vocational preferences that has attracted most attention is Holland's theory of vocational choice (Holland, 1966, 1973, 1985). Whilst there have been changes in the development of measures to assess choice fit (VPI = Vocational Preference Inventory; SDS = Self Directed Search), the sixfold personality/job typology (RIASEC) has remained the same. It remains one of the most fecund and tested theories in vocational psychology (Furnham, 2001c). It has also served to inspire other instruments. Further, because of the long standing use of this measure it has been correlated with measures of the Big Five.

Hogan and Hogan (1997) have developed a psychometrically valid measure with impressive adult norms, the Motives, Values, Preferences Inventory (MVPI). It measures 10 values (set out in Table 9.2). It has been heavily informed by Holland's work and ideas (Hogan & Blake, 1999). It has also been shown to be correlated with measures of the Big Five.

Inevitably there have been various attempts to examine the relationship between personality measures and values mainly using the Holland measure (Goh & Leong, 1993; Tokar & Swanson, 1995). Indeed, there have been a number of attempts to look at the "overlap" between different NEO measures and different Holland measures. Costa et al. (1984) found Neuroticism correlated weakly with the Artistic type in men, and negatively with the Social type in women. Extraversion was strongly positively correlated with the Enterprising type and negatively correlated with the Conventional type. Openness was strongly positively correlated with the Artistic type and negatively correlated with the Conventional type. The authors pointed out that one dimension missing from the Holland typology is Neuroticism, which is, of course, directly relevant to occupational behaviour (Furnham, 1994).

Gottfredson et al. (1993) found Social and Enterprising vocational preference were positively correlated with Extraversion; Investigative and Artistic preferences were correlated with Openness; and Conventional preferences were correlated with Conscientiousness. They concluded: "despite their regularity, the vocational personality correlations were too low to suggest that either form of assessment is a dependable substitute for the other" (p. 524).

Tokar and Swanson (1995) found Openness, Extraversion and Agreeableness in females discriminated Holland's groups. They concluded that Holland's SDS measure typology corresponds with a position of the five-factor model, particularly Openness and Extraversion. They noted, however, that the five-factor model cannot account for Holland's model in its entirety.

Schinka et al. (1997) established high correlations between Extraversion, Openness and Agreeableness traits and the Enterprising, Artistic and Social scales from the RIASEC system. They believed that the five-factor model ignored the Realistic dimension and "provides coverage" of the Investigative and Conventional dimensions in women only (p. 366). They noted that: "Although RIASEC measures may provide valid

Table 9.2 Correlations between the trait and values measure

		N	E	O	A	C
		67.20	126.42	120.40	114.40	130.10
		23.86	26.92	17.79	23.05	16.56
Recognition	Desire to be known, seen, visible and famous, which leads to a lifestyle guided by a search for opportunities to be noticed and dreams of fame and high achievement, whether or not they are fulfilled.	.02	.22**	.19**	−.28**	.05
Power	Desire to succeed, make things happen, make a difference and outperform the competition.	−.02	.24**	.13	−.30**	.14*
Hedonistic	Pursuit of fun, excitement, pleasure and a lifestyle organised around eating, drinking and entertainment.	.14	.16*	.11	−.11	−.13*
Altruistic	Desire to help others, a concern for the welfare of the less fortunate in life, and a lifestyle organised around public service and the betterment of humanity.	.00	.12	.25**	.31**	.02
Affiliation	Needing and enjoying frequent and varied social contact and a lifestyle organised around social interaction.	−.02	.31**	.28**	−.04	.03
Tradition	A belief in and dedication to old-fashioned virtues such as family, church, thrift, hard work, appropriate social behaviour, and a lifestyle that reflects these values.	.06	.10	.09	.07	.17*
Security	A need for predictability, structure and efforts to avoid risk and uncertainty – especially in the employment area – and a lifestyle organised around minimising errors and mistakes.	.01	−.20**	−.29**	.15*	.27**
Commerce	Interest in earning money, realising profits, finding new business opportunities, and a lifestyle organised around investments and financial planning.	−.03	.04	−.02	−.18*	.30**
Aesthetics	Need for self-expression, a dedication to quality and excellence, an interest in how things look, feel and sound and close attention to the appearance of things.	.15*	.01	.49**	−.06	−.19**
Science	Being interested in science, comfortable with technology, preferring data-based – as opposed to intuitive – decisions, and spending time learning how things work.	.00	−.12	.07	.02	.04

Note: **$p < .001$; *$p < .01$. N = Neuroticism; E = Extraversion; O = Openness; A = Agreeableness; C = Conscientiousness.

measures of occupational interests, the results of this study raise questions about their adequacy in measuring the major domains of personality" (p. 366).

De Fruyt and Mervielde (1997) found the pattern of correlations showed clearly that few of the Big Five facets (six per trait) were related to the Realistic and Investigative type, while many were related to the Social and Enterprising type. Using regression, the five factors were able to account for 40% of the variance in the Enterprising types, showing them to be stable, conscientious, extraverts but low on Conscientiousness. The five factors accounted for 32% of the variance for artistic occupations though this was primarily due to a very high beta-weight for Openness. The third highest r square (22%) was for the Social occupations and this showed that Neurotic, Extraverted, Agreeable individuals who were open to experience were attracted to this particular type. Thus, they concluded, as have nearly all others in the area, that there is some overlap in the models but that they account for unique variance. Hence, they recommend that both instruments are used for educational and vocational counselling.

There have been various excellent reviews of the relationship between the Big Five and Holland's Occupational Types. Larson et al. (2002) reviewed 12 studies with 24 samples. They looked at sex differences and moderator variables and concluded that there were five very robust correlations: Artistic–Openness (r = .48); Enterprising–Extraversion (r = .28); Social–Extraversion (r = .31); Investigative–Openness (r = .28) and Social–Agreeableness (r = .19). They concluded:

> For the researcher, the implications of these meta-analytic results may suggest new conceptualisations of our understanding of both personality and interest. Can the theoretical convergence be pushed further? For example, the hexagonal calculus of interests predicts how interests are similar and different. Does this have implications for the interest–personality linkages? Does it suggest that the calculus principles might be applied to the Big Five personality dimensions? Can we actually say that some of the Big Five dimensions – especially Openness and Extraversion – are perhaps interest dimensions? Does personality precede vocational interests, as espoused by the social cognitive model of career development, or are both present at birth, as some genetic studies seem to suggest with the expression of both determined by life experiences?
>
> (p. 226)

In a different analysis but of the same area, Barrick et al. (2003b) had 39 samples and nearly 11,000 participants. They found Extraversion correlated with Enterprising (r = .4) and Social (r = .29); Agreeableness correlated with Social (r = .15); Conscientiousness correlated with Conventional (r = .17); Neuroticism correlated with Investigative (r = .11) and Openness correlated with Artistic (r = .39) and Investigative (r = .25). Using regressions they found the Big Five could account for 47% of the variance in explaining Enterprising, 42% for Artistic, 31% for Social, 27% for Conventional, 26% for Investigative but only 11% for Realistic. They concluded:

> From a theoretical perspective, the preceding discussion suggests that the motivational processes associated with the joint relationship between personality and vocational interests most likely proceeds along one or both of the following paths. One path pertains to Extraversion, Agreeableness and Openness. For these traits, motivation levels are contingent upon the degree of congruence between personal-

ity traits, individuals' preferences for certain activities, and the demands of the job. Thus, an extraverted person with congruent interests will be motivated when the job also emphasises competitive demands and advancement through a hierarchy. For example, an extraverted person is more likely than an introverted person to be motivated in a door-to-door sales job that requires frequent interactions with others and involves persuasion.

The other path pertains to Conscientiousness and Emotional Stability. For these traits, motivation levels are derived from self-regulatory processes associated with goal setting, expectancy beliefs, and self-efficacy. Thus, motivation levels are not contingent on whether there is congruence between the personality traits and preferences for different types of work environments.

Practically, these results suggest that higher performance can be obtained across all jobs if one hires employees who are highly conscientious and emotionally stable. Whether other personality traits (Extraversion, Agreeableness and Openness to Experience) result in higher performance depends on whether these traits are congruent with the person's interests and actual job activities. The role of personality and vocational interests is more complex in such situations, however, as the effect obtained from the "contingent" traits and interests are dependent on the personality and interests of other employees in the work environment. This is a fundamentally different approach to selection than that typically conducted.

(p. 70)

Various researchers have looked at the relationship between personality traits and both work satisfaction and work values. Most, but not all, have looked at either the three- or five-dimensional model. Researchers have argued that personality dispositions influence work values. Thus, extraverts seek jobs with variety, and neurotics seek jobs with stability.

Furnham et al. (1999a) obtained data from 92 job applicants who completed the Eysenck Personality Profiler and also rated 24 work values (e.g. convenient hours of work, opportunities for personal growth, job security). They classified 18 of these into a hygiene/extrinsic or a motivator/intrinsic composite on the basis of the Herzberg et al. (1959) two-factor theory. Furnham et al. (1999a) found that Extraversion was associated with the motivator/intrinsic composite, whereas Neuroticism was associated with the hygiene/extrinsic composite. Psychoticism was also related to the hygiene/extrinsic composite, albeit marginally. However, Furnham et al. constructed their two composites on an a priori rather than on an empirical basis, and therefore they did not provide a test of the validity of the two-factor theory. Furnham et al. (2002) found Conscientiousness the best predictor of work values.

More recently, Furnham et al. (2005) undertook a two-study cross-cultural investigation of the relationship between the Big Five and the Works Value Questionnaire (WVQ; Mantech, 1983). The authors observed a similar factor structure for the WVQ items in both studies. Personality traits, age, and gender explained between 5% and 13% of the variance in the WVQ subscales. As a result of the two studies, the authors concluded that there are robust associations between certain personality traits and work values, although they do not clearly follow the intrinsic vs. extrinsic distinction.

Personality and intelligence do relate to work values. Together they can account for as much as 50% of the variance in understanding work motivation, productivity and satisfaction. However, values are less biologically based than traits and abilities, and more open to moderation. Certainly, as Furnham et al. (2007b) have concluded, given what we know about predictors of success at work, it remains important to measure work values as well as other things such as personality traits and disorders.

Style at work

The concept of style in psychology can be traced back over 80 years (Wulf, 1922). It seems that the concept of *cognitive* style preceded others, like *learning* style. The concept of style is particularly attractive to many people, more so than trait, at least in popular and applied rather than academic circles, partly because it implies ease of change. One adopts a style, which is easy to modify. Applied psychologists in educational, clinical and work settings have embraced the concept and this has led in turn to a profusion of concepts and measures.

One of the most alluring features of the style literature is the idea of match or fit. Thus, it is recognised that individual difference in (educational, social, work) performance is a function of the person and the situation (institution, organisation, system, work) routines (Riding, 2005). It is then asserted that if one can find a match between styles performance will improve. There is a vast, but ambiguous and very unsatisfactory, literature on student–teacher style, which hopes to show that the better the match the better the result. However, numerous other variables moderate and mediate this relationship, which is often weak (Zhang, 2004b). As Price (2004) concluded from a recent study "on the whole the studies showed that the value of learning style tests may be limited" (p. 681).

Messick (1976) listed 19 cognitive style variables alone. The idea of style is for many people intuitively appealing. Style seems to imply choice, preference and therefore change. One can *choose* a learning style, *adopt* a cognitive style and *moderate* an attributional style. It seems much easier and more natural to change style than personality, let alone ability. The traditional view of styles is that they are stable dispositions to behave in a certain way (Baron, 1985). According to Baron, this does not mean that individuals always behave in the same way: "styles, like other traits may be somewhat situation specific" (p. 380). Thus, although each person has a modal style of walking, people will walk faster when in a hurry or swing their arms more when in a carefree mood. This property of styles is shared by learning styles and cognitive styles. Inherent in the notion of style, individuals tend to exhibit consistent patterns of behaviour across situations and over time. However, they can *choose* to change those styles and learn other forms of behaviour. It is supposedly relatively easy to develop another style.

Learning, teaching and even "personality" style, as well as the later styles (attribution, coping), were more broadly based, linking cognition and affect, but tending to be focused on specific areas of social behaviour. Yet, many personality and cognitive theorists and psychometricians have given up on stylistic concepts and measures. The field is fragmented, idiosyncratic and egocentric. There are dozens of style instruments, many with poor or no psychometric data in their support. A central concern of differentiated psychologists is whether they have incremental validity over measures of traits and abilities. If they can be demonstrated, along with predictive validity, there is a clear case for using them in all sorts of assessment at work. If not, it remains unclear as to their functional utility. There even remains confusion about the two major style concepts, namely cognitive and learning style.

Cassidy (2004) has attempted an overview of the many theories, models and measures, just in the learning style area. He noted that learning style was essentially the application of a cognitive style in a learning situation. That is, a cognitive style is the way an individual characteristically approaches a cognitive task, while a learning style is the way they approach a learning task. Styles are more automatic than strategic. They are thought to be stable over time but modifiable, responsive to experience and the demands of the situation. Some researchers have concentrated on preference for instruction type (i.e. teacher style), others on information processing and still others on social interaction. Some are cognitive centred, others activity centred and still others personality centred in their approach. The area remains terribly fragmented.

As well as cognitive and leaning styles, certain researchers have talked about thinking styles (Sternberg, 1997b) and intellectual styles (Zhang, 2004a). Some of these have stimulated a considerable research effort to see how these styles are related to and differentiated from (convergent and divergent validity) other concepts, measures, traits, etc. (Zhang, 2004a). The results always show predictable, modest correlations but it remains unclear as to what to do with that information.

Cognitive styles are essentially thought to determine the amount and organisation of information available to the individual at the moment. They mediate the influence of personality tests on motivation and intellectual functioning. However, different "style" researchers have used very different concepts. Thus, we have cognitive *controls*; cognitive *attitudes*; cognitive *system principles*; cognitive *strategies*; intellectual executive functions; and preferences in information processing (Furnham, 2002).

Cognitive styles have three distinct research origins: *Perceptual* factors – speed and strength of closure; *Ego adaptation* – maintaining harmony and equilibrium of feelings/impulses; *Developing cognitive systems* – Gestaltism. Compared to cognitive styles, *learning styles* are both broader and more focused; include cognitive, affective, sociological, and physiological preferences *specifically in relation to the learning situation*; are stable but innate or learned; and tend to confound ability with style.

Messick (1976) noted that cognitive styles: "have their roots in the study of perception and thus have had close ties since their inception with the laboratory and the clinic psychologists . . . have tended to utilise measures derived from laboratory apparatus or clinical tools" (p. 10). Cognitive-style instruments examine accuracy and correctness of performance. In contrast, most learning-style instruments have been designed for easy administration in a classroom context by teachers. They are generally self-report inventories that measure typical or usual ways of behaving and preferences. The concept of preference is an important one in learning-style measurement. While style refers to the processes a learner is likely to use, preference refers to the choices a learner makes. The notion that people choose one learning situation or condition over another is termed learning preference. Thus, learning-style instruments are not measuring the accuracy or correctness of responses but merely gathering information on how a student "likes", "tends" or "prefers" to learn. It is often difficult to differentiate between learning-style instruments and personality tests. Indeed, they often correlate very highly (Furnham, 1992, 1996b).

Learning style is often characterised as the composite of characteristic cognitive, affective and physiological factors that serve as relatively stable indicators of how a learner perceives, interacts with, and responds to the learning environment. It is demonstrated by the pattern of behaviour and performance with which an individual approaches educational experiences (Keefe, 1988, p. 3). Messick (1984), on the other hand, defines cognitive styles as "'characteristic self-consistencies' in information processing that develop in congenial ways around the underlying personality trends" (p. 61). According to Messick: "They are conceptualised as stable attitudes, preferences, or habitual strategies determining a person's typical modes of perceiving, remembering, thinking, and problem solving. As such, their influence extends to almost all human activities that implicate cognition, including social and interpersonal functioning" (Messick, 1976, p. 5).

It has always been easier to distinguish ability from style, compared to personality and style (Messick, 1984; Tiedemann, 1989). Ability questions refer to *how much* and *what*; style questions to *how*. Ability refers to what kind of information is being processed, by what operation, in what form, and more importantly how efficiently. Style refers to the manner or mode of cognition. Ability implies *maximal* performance; style implies *typical* propensities. Ability is measured in terms of accuracy, correctness and speed of response, whereas style emphasises the predominant or customary processing model. Again, style looks like personality simply using a different name.

There are, however, other differences: *Abilities are unipolar – style is bipolar*. Ability levels range from none to a great deal, whereas styles usually have two different poles with quite different implications for cognitive functioning. *Abilities are value directional – styles are value differentiated*. Usually, having more of an ability is considered better than having less, whereas supposed stylistic extreme poles have adaptive value but in different circumstances. *Abilities are often domain specific – styles cut across domains*. Abilities are often specific to various domains (e.g. verbal, numerical, or spatial areas), whereas styles often serve as high-level heuristics. Abilities are *enabling* variables because they facilitate task performance; styles are *organising* and controlling variables. Abilities dictate level of performance, whereas styles contribute to the selection, combination and sequencing of both topic and process.

The difference between traits and styles is, however, much less clear. Studies in the area suggest correlations between established traits (i.e. Extraversion/Neuroticism) and well-measured styles (i.e. learning styles) to be in the $r = .20$ to $r = .40$ range (Furnham, 1992, 1996b). Indeed, most styles are measured and thought about in trait-like terms (Furnham & Steele, 1993). Several researchers have attempted to integrate personality traits and style theory. However, as Messick (1994) noted, these efforts do not fulfil the aspiration of style theorists, who believe styles embrace personality *and* cognition. It is, of course, a moot point to argue that trait theorists themselves do not take cognisance of cognitive variables. Further, there are numerous and often radical differences between the assumptions of different learning style theorists and test constructors. Some seem much less concerned with marrying trait and cognitive variables, as Messick implied.

Furnham (1995) has pointed out a number of unsatisfactorily answered problems for the issue of style:

- *Aetiology of a cognitive/learning style*. The question arises as to their origin: are they biologically based, the result of early learning, neither, or both? This is a fundamental question that must be answered to avoid tautology. Aetiology determines how much a style may be changed.
- *Variance accounted for*. Even if styles exist and determine in part the learning that takes place in social behaviour, few would argue that they are the only – or even the most important – factor that determines learning. The question then needs to be

asked whether the amount of variance accounted for by this factor is so small as to be trivial, or, indeed, a major and central feature. Do styles have incremental validity over ability, personality or value measures?

- *The nature of style as a variable.* If cognitive/learning style is a moderator variable between intelligence, personality and performance, the precise nature of this relationship needs to be spelt out. Indeed, it is necessary to list all relevant variables that relate to learning and specify how they interact.
- *The processes underlying style.* So far, a great deal of the research in this field has been descriptive and taxonomic, aimed at identifying various styles and their consequences. Less work has gone into describing the mechanism or process whereby the individual styles operate.

Furnham concludes:

> A pessimist might argue that despite fifty years of research into cognitive/learning style, we still know precious little if the above questions have not been answered or even attempted. An optimist, though, might be impressed by the research effort that has gone into this topic, by the proliferation of ideas, and by the evidence already accumulated. Nevertheless, pessimists sound more profound that optimists, and hence, most recent reviewers in the field tend to be highly critical of developments in this area.
>
> (p. 411)

Messick (1994) likewise notes: "The literature of cognitive and learning styles is peppered with unstable and inconsistent findings, whereas style theory seems either of value in glossing over inconsistencies or confused in stressing differentiated features selectively" (p. 131).

But the style concept has its defenders and detractors. Sternberg and Grigorenko (1997) remain in favour of the style concept. They argue that thinking style is a subset of cognitive style, which itself is a subset of style (a distinctive/characteristic method/ manner of acting/performing). They provide three explanations of why psychologists would be interested in cognitive styles. Style bridges the concept of cognition and personality, though they overlook the extensive work on the relationship between cognitive processing and personality traits, especially Neuroticism (Furnham & Cheng, 1996). Cognitive style added to measures of ability improves the predictability of school behaviour, yet very little evidence is brought to bear supporting this assertion. Third, cognitive styles help explain occupational choice and performance. Yet again, any reviewer of this literature may be equally impressed by the poor predictive power of cognitive styles in the work place (Furnham, 1992, 1994).

Sternberg and Grigorenko (1997) then set out the five criteria for the evaluation of theories of style:

1 *Theoretical specification*: the positing of a reasonably complete, well-specified, and internally consistent theory of styles that makes connection with extant psychological theory.
2 *Internal validity*: a demonstration by factor analysis or some other method of inter-analysis that the underlying structure of the item or subset data is as predicted by the theory.

3 *Convergent external validity*: a demonstration that the measures of styles correlate with other measures with which, in theory, they should correlate.
4 *Discriminant external validity*: a demonstration that the measures of styles do not correlate with other measures with which, in theory, they should not correlate.
5 *Heuristic generativity*: the extent to which the theory has spawned, and continues to spawn, psychological research and, ideally, practical application (p. 703).

They argue:

> We believe that styles have a great deal of promise for the future. First, they have provided and continue to provide a much-needed interface between research on cognition and personality. Second, unlike some psychological constructs, they have lent themselves to operationalisation and direct empirical tests. Third, they show promise for helping psychologists understand some of the variation in school and job performance that cannot be accounted for by individual differences in abilities. For example they predict school performance significantly and add to the prediction provided by ability tests. Finally, they can truly tell something about environments as well as individuals' interactions with these environments, as shown by the fact that correlations of styles with performance that are significantly positive in one environment are significantly negative in another environment.
>
> (p. 710)

Suffice it to say that the concept of style in psychological theory and measurement remains problematic. Indeed, it could be argued that because style affects many forms of social behaviour – particularly in applied settings like work and leisure – certain behaviours in the testing situation may themselves be indices of style. That is, how people complete tests, be they behavioural or self-report, may be a good individual difference measure, be it trait or style. There have been various recent attempts to investigate whether a specified learning or cognitive style does add incremental validity over classic measures of personality and ability in the prediction of work-related behaviour.

Conclusion

Individual difference psychologists interested in understanding and predicting work-related behaviour cannot afford to neglect attitudes, beliefs and values. It is abundantly clear that many factors help shape and change attitudes, beliefs and values, including personality and abilities.

The most important issue for both practitioner and theorist is whether attitude/beliefs/values act as powerful and important, moderating or mediating variables between personality and intelligence and work behaviour. Unfortunately, trait psychologists and social psychologists have not really had a long history of collaborative work showing how traits relate to attitudes, which then relate to behaviour.

The second issue, related to the above, is the issue of incremental validity: that is the extent to which belief/attitudes/values consistently and logically account for additional variance over and above that accounted for by personality traits and intelligence. This is certainly the issue for differential psychologists. Social psychologists on the other hand are interested in whether traits and abilities account for more variance over and above attitudinal variables. A problem for all researchers is which attitude, belief and value variables to choose.

The choice may be made on many different grounds. Thus, one option is to choose self-report inventories that attempt a comprehensive measure of beliefs (Buchholz, 1976) or values (Hogan & Hogan, 1997) or those attempting to measure one feature only, like attitudes to computers or work–life balance. A second decision may be based on the theoretical foundation, and psychometric evidence, of a particular test. It is quite clear some concepts like belief in a just world, personal control, and the work ethic have attracted a good deal of research and have been shown to be useful in predicting behaviour. Yet, compared to the world of individual differences, the literature in this area appears highly fragmented.

The concept of style is different from attitudes and beliefs, and values are often conceived as a moderator variable between personality and ability (see Chapter 1). Despite a massive research effort into cognitive and learning style by applied, cognitive and educational psychologists, the theory has never lived up to its expectations as a useful concept or measure.

10 Integrity and dishonesty at work

Introduction

People steal money, goods and time at work. They also steal secrets. This is not about shop-lifting or thieves who break in at night. It is about people who work for an organisation stealing money, equipment or produce in one form or another. It is a serious problem. *Counterproductive behaviours at work* are manifold and have attracted an ever-growing applied and research literature (Fox & Spector, 2005; Griffin & O'Leary-Kelly, 2004).

A number of different topics come under the rubric of counterproductive work behaviours (CWBs), including aggression, bullying, alcohol and drug use, emotional abuse, incivility, mobbing and sexual harassment and violence. Also included are "under-the-table deals" (Rousseau, 2004), "extreme careerism" (Bratton & Kacmar, 2004) and breaking organisational contracts (Robinson & Brown, 2004). There are dark-side behaviours that harm others (violence, harassment, unsafe work practices), behaviours that hurt individuals (drug abuse, unsafe work practices) and those that harm the organisation financially (absenteeism, theft, destruction, tardiness, violation of rules) and reputatively.

Fox and Spector (2005) have provided a very useful taxonomy of different types of these CWBs (Table 10.1).

Table 10.1 Characteristics of different counterproductive work behaviour (CWB) concepts

Term	Person target	Organisation target	Physical acts included	Intent to harm	Violates norms or standards	Pattern of behaviour
Aggression	Yes	Indirectly	Yes	Yes	No	No
Bullying	Yes	No	Yes	Yes	No	Yes
Counterproductive work behaviour	No	No	Yes	Yes	Yes	No
Deviance	Yes	Yes	Yes	Yes	Yes	No
Emotional abuse	Yes	No	No	Yes	Yes	Yes
Incivility	Yes	No	No	Ambiguous	Yes	No
Mobbing	Yes	No	Yes	No	No	Yes
Retaliation	Indirectly	Yes	Yes	Yes	No	No
Revenge	Yes	No	Yes	Yes	No	No
Violence	Yes	No	Yes	No	No	No

Source: From Fox and Spector (2005). Used with permission of the American Psychological Association, Washington DC.

A central issue is why some individuals do, or do not, get involved in these activities, and how to prevent or minimise the problem. The central issue for a differential psychologist is to what extent one can explain the behaviour in terms of individual differences in integrity beliefs and behaviours, as well as how the latter are related to established personality, value or belief differences.

We know that stealing and deceit are more common in some jobs compared to others. The following generalisations seem to hold:

- The more skilled the job holder, the less he/she will be likely to cheat/steal.
- Flexibility in time keeping will be negatively associated with lying.
- Higher performance expectations on the part of the boss or company will be associated with more lying, stealing and cheating.
- People having more than one formal role will be more likely to try to deceive.
- People with considerable demands (i.e. parental) outside the organisations are likely to be more deceitful.
- People reporting to more than one boss are more likely to be deceitful.

There are a number of important questions here. They include: Why do people steal? How and what do they steal? How do they feel after stealing? How do they justify their stealing? And what can de done to prevent it? There is a growing and important literature on this topic of organisational justice and deviant behaviour at work (Kidwell & Martin, 2005; Skarlicki & Folger, 1997).

Why do people steal? People have tended to focus on two different, but interrelated reasons.

1. Person theories

These are concerned with the essentially psychological problem of explaining why some individuals (and not others) are involved with pilfering and theft. Various explanations have been suggested:

1   *Financial needs.* Here it is suggested that stealing occurs as a function of financial need. Needs are complicated, such as social or belongingness needs, because people may steal in order to obtain goods/money that allow them to become a "club member". However, this explanation does not distinguish the origin or type of need (for example drug addition, gambling, sick relatives).

2   *Deviant personality/background.* The concept here is that there is a person type who is more vulnerable to opportunities to steal, as well as personally more likely to rationalise stealing behaviour. The theory is weak and tautological – people who steal are the stealing type.

3   *Greed/tempted opportunities.* The idea is that people are inherently greedy and steal when they can: they are inherently untrustworthy. However, it fails to explain why there are systematic individual differences in greed.

4   *Moral laxity.* Here the theme is that some groups (especially young people) do not possess the same ethical standards or trustworthy equalities as other groups. Again the argument is poor: it is tautological and does not explain individual differences.

5   *Marginality.* People who are marginal have less static jobs with no tenure or social

standing and steal as a way of expressing grievances. Because they have had no opportunities to develop commitment – they steal.

These are essentially all "bad-person theories". They suggest that it is individual demography, morality, personality or psychopathology that explains why individuals steal either at a specific time for a specific purpose or in general.

2. Workplace theories

These, on the other hand, emphasise rather different factors:

1   *Organisational climate.* In effect this refers to a moral atmosphere that can even endorse dishonesty (i.e. even encourage theft) or at least turn a blind eye to it. The idea is that the prevailing climate sends clear messages to employees about whether, what, which and when thieving and thefts are acceptable or not.
2   *Deterrence doctrine.* This refers to the existence, explicitness and retributive nature of company anti-theft policies and the perceived certainty and severity of punishment, as well as the visibility of that punishment. The idea is simple: get tough with deterrence and theft will be reduced.
3   *Perceived organisational fairness.* This "theory" suggests that it is exploitation by the employer that causes pilfering. Note that exploitation is the crucial factor. Pay cuts in particular lead to this activity.

A major workplace theory that attempts to explain the origin or maintenance of things like theft at work is *social exchange theory*. The theory (sometimes called *equity theory*) suggests that all employees are in a social exchange relationship at work: they give and they get. They "sell" their time, expertise, labour and loyalty and, in return, get a salary, pension, paid holidays, etc. Where the "equation" is balanced all is well. Where not, people are motivated to balance it. Thus people can ask for a pay rise, or leave, or work less hard, or go absent or steal.

People who feel frustrated, cheated, humiliated or undervalued often steal as revenge and to right a perceived wrong. This is not to say that *all* dissatisfied people thieve. But there is evidence that thieving is often a restitution and retaliatory response to perceived unfairness. People steal partly because of the way they are treated. People strike back with *reciprocal deviance* if they feel poorly or unfairly treated.

There is an extensive and important social and organisational psychology literature on this topic, much of it pioneering, by Greenberg with his interests in justice in the workplace (Giacalone & Greenberg, 1997; Greenberg, 2006; Robinson & Greenberg, 1998). This literature looks at various categories of counterproductive work behaviours like interpersonal (bullying), production (absenteeism), property (theft, vandalism) and political (whistle-blowing, deception) misbehaviours. With ingenious laboratory and field experiments Greenberg has tested equity theory, showing how through restitution and retaliation employees "even the score", as the theory suggests. However, this is not an individual difference theory and tends not to focus on individual difference variables and factors, which are the primary concern of this book.

There seems to be evidence of employee theft acceptance based on three factors: (1) people's willingness to harm (particularly big) organisations; (2) organisations too infrequently prosecute employees caught thieving; and (3) many employees feel complete lack of guilt over stealing.

Often many large organisations are seen as very rich abusers of power, bullies of their workforce and competitors and, hence, just "victims" or targets of "Robin Hood" restitutional thieving. Companies do not prosecute, however, because of the cost, the nature of the evidence they have, the poor publicity and the effect on the other staff. Thus, employees do not see the activity as necessarily wrong and hence steal happily and without guilt.

Equally, supervisors may condone or even encourage theft! This may occur because of *parallel deviance* or *passive imitation*, which simply means that people follow the lead of their bosses who they notice abusing the system and thieving. If the supervisor calls theft "a perk" so do the staff. There is also the *invisible wage* structure or system of *controlled larceny*, which effectively means that supervisors allow, help and even organise employee theft. They often say they do this to enrich jobs and motivate staff more efficiently.

Even more common are work-group norms that support and regulate employee theft. Becoming part of a group may involve being taught how, when and where to steal. Indeed, work-group thieving may ritualistically and symbolically be linked to becoming a successful employee. Thieving norms involve how people divide the spoils/outcomes of theft. The group helps "neutralise" its acts with a raft of excuses/explanations such as denials of responsibility, injury, the company being a victim, appeals to higher authority and a condemnation of the condemner. Group norms often spell out the parameters of thieving behaviour – that is, what is and is not stolen, and the worth of what has been stolen.

Mars (1984) has done a brilliant and fascinating analysis of how people steal, lie and cheat in various jobs. He specified four types of people. These are not based on individual difference factors so much as the opportunities various jobs provide for individuals.

Type A: Hawks

This type relates to occupations that emphasise individuality, autonomy and competition. That is, the control that members have over others is greater than the controls exercised over themselves. They emphasise entrepreneurship: individual flair (i.e. optimism) is at a premium. Success is indicated by the number of followers a person controls. Rewards go to those who find new and better ways of doing things and here the drive for successful innovation is paramount. They are individualists, inventors, small businessmen: typically entrepreneurial managers, waiters, taxi-drivers, owner businessmen, successful academics, pundits, the prima donnas among salesmen and the more independent professionals and journalists. Alliances among *hawks* tend to shift with expediency and a climate of suspicion is more common than one of trust. Usually they work on their own. They are experts in beating the system's inherent rigidities, and dealing principally in information. They are, paradoxically, vital to the system, though the system tries to ignore them.

Type B: Donkeys

These are characterised by both isolation and subordination. An example today may be a "live-in" nanny to a wealthy household with many children or an "indispensable" PA to a senior executive. *Donkeys* are in the paradoxical position of being either powerless or powerful or both. They are powerless if they passively accept the constraints they face, but they can also be extremely disruptive. Resentment at the impositions caused by such jobs is common and the most typical response is to change jobs. Other forms of "withdrawal from work", such as sickness and absenteeism, are also higher than normal. Where constraints are at their strongest, sabotage is possible, particularly where constraints are mechanised. People dislike being treated like a programmed robot and "fiddling" makes a job much more interesting; it provides new targets and a sense of challenge, as well as hitting the boss where it hurts.

Type C: Wolves

This is the home of those "traditional", rapidly disappearing, working-class manual occupations such as miners. These are occupations based on groups with interdependent and stratified roles (garbage collection crews, aeroplane crews) and stratified groups who both live and work in "total institutions" such as prisons, hospitals, oil rigs and hotels. Where workers do live in or close to the premises in which they work, group activities are reinforced by cohesion in others. Such groups then come to possess considerable control over the resources of their individual members. Once they join such groups, individuals tend to stay as members. There is no place here for the independent individualist; teamwork is vital and highly valued both for success and for security.

Type D: Vultures

Vulture jobs include sales representatives and travellers of various kinds, like driver deliveries, linked collectively by their common employer, common work-base and common task, but who have considerable freedom and discretion during their working day. These are jobs that offer autonomy and freedom to transact but where this freedom is subject to an overarching bureaucratic control that treats workers collectively and employs them in units. Workers are members of a group of co-workers for some purposes only and they can and do act individually and competitively for others. They are not as free from constraint as are hawks, but neither are they as constrained as donkeys; the group is not as intrusive or controlling as are wolf packs.

Mars (1984) was not concerned with why certain individuals within these occupational groups indulged more or less in counterproductive behaviours at work. However, his anthropological work, as well as that of social and organisational researchers like Greenberg (2006), makes a very salient point. This is that social factors, perhaps more than individual difference factors, are the best predictors of workplace deviance and dishonesty. However, it would be equally unwise to neglect the obvious fact that there are consistent, robust and important individual difference correlates of counterproductive behaviour at work.

Personality, integrity and dishonesty

This chapter focuses on all aspects of dishonesty at work and the use of integrity tests in selection. It focuses on individual difference correlates of these topics: Essentially, when two or more individual in identical jobs behave quite differently with respect to matters of honesty and integrity, these are individual difference correlates of counter-productive work behaviours (CWBs).

Hogan and Hogan (1989), for instance, described the design and validation of a personality questionnaire that predicted individuals who engaged in counterproductive behaviours at work. It also predicted the opposite, i.e. persons who were trusted by co-workers and supervisors. Murphy and Lee (1994) showed, as one may expect, that the trait of conscientiousness was powerfully correlated with integrity. Conscientiousness is associated with dependability, perseverance and achievement orientation while integrity is about honesty, so these are not interchangeable measures but they are logically related. Marcus et al. (2006) found integrity tests related to three personality variables: agreeableness, conscientiousness and emotional stability.

From an Eysenckian (1964) perspective CWBs are forms of criminal or delinquent behaviour. Therefore, according to the controversial theory of crime and personality, he argued that criminals are more extraverted and neurotic than non-criminals. The argument for extraversion is essentially that the inhibitory features of extraverts, coupled with their low arousability and low arousal levels, means that they require higher levels of stimulation. They take more risks in their attempt to get more excitement. Introverts by contrast, show less inhibition and have high arousability and high arousal levels and thus, prefer lower levels of stimulation. Thus extraverts show stimulus hunger and will seek excitement to increase their too low arousal and may be more readily temped to seek arousal in manners that may not be socially acceptable (and/or legal). The opposite is true for introverts, who display a stimulus avoidance.

Eysenck (1964) suggested that neuroticism acts as an amplifying device by virtue of its drive properties. This drive multiplies with the learned behavioural patterns based on the biological foundation. This increases the antisocial behaviour exhibited, especially when combined with extraversion traits. Eysenck and Gudjonsson (1989) have argued that criminals should also be relatively high on psychoticism. High scorers on psychoticism tend to be uncaring with respect to people and are unlikely to feel guilt, empathy or sensitivity to the feelings of others. It seems reasonable to assume that individuals with these characteristics would experience relatively few qualms about behaving anti-socially. Indeed, it seems almost tautological to say that psychoticism is linked to crim-inality because the measurement of the former includes items that look very much like the latter.

Thus, Eysenckians would argue that those most likely to partake of deviancy at work of any sort would be high E, N and P scorers. Certainly the literature on delinquency would support this view (Furnham & Thompson, 1991). Results from a Big Five per-spective are similar. Heaven (1996) has shown that young people, low on Conscien-tiousness and Agreeableness (as well as excitement seeking) are those prone most to vandalism, theft, violence, etc. Thus, it seems that if individuals have a particular personality profile, as well as an opportunity and motive to behave dishonestly, then CWB is much more likely to occur.

Interestingly, integrity testing is now part of a greater interest in CWBs that cost organisations billions. Key CWBs include deviance, aggression, antisocial behaviour and violence. Most are dysfunctional behaviours where an employee, or group at work, engages in motivated behaviour aimed to have specific and general negative consequences for another individual, group or the organisation as a whole.

There are beginning to emerge some specific CWB theories such as the causal reasoning perspective of Martinko et al. (2002). Nearly all of these theories stress the interaction of both personality (internal) and situational (external) factors leading to cognitive and affective states that trigger CWBs.

Inevitably, however, some researchers have adopted a clearly intra- and interpersonal perspective. Murphy and Lee (1994) found Conscientiousness (or prudence) by far the most powerful predictor of an integrity test. They argued that the constructs (Conscientiousness and Integrity) are distinct and that correlations are modest. They also found modest but significant relationships that indicated that Openness (intellect) and Extraversion (sociability) are negatively, but Neuroticism (adjustment), Agreeableness (likeability) and Ambition positively correlated with integrity. Ones and Viswesvaran (2001) reported correlations between seven personality traits and a measure of CWB. In rank order they were: Achievement Orientation ($r = .51$); Conscientiousness ($r = .47$); Dependability ($r = .47$); Neuroticism ($r = -.39$); Openness ($r = -.28$); Extraversion ($r = .15$); and Agreeableness ($r = .09$).

Penny and Spector (2002) hypothesised and demonstrated a relationship between CWBs and trait narcissism. Narcissism, they argued, led to ego-threat and anger and increased CWB aggression. Further, when job constraints were high, narcissists tended to greater CWBs.

In a study of 267 Korean employees and using the Big Six personality inventory, Lee et al. (2005) distinguished between antisocial behaviour *targeted at individuals* and that *targeted at organisations*. The results showed that disagreeable Extraverts, low on honesty–humility were more likely to indulge in individually targeted antisocial behaviour, while Extraverts low on both Conscientiousness and honesty–humility were more like to indulge in organisationally targeted antisocial behaviour.

A German study of both personality trait and disorder correlates of white-collar crime, Blickle et al. (2006), found that business white-collar crime was associated with being low on behavioural control, but high on hedonism, narcissism and Conscientiousness. Interestingly, white-collar criminals in business have a combination of low integrity with high Conscientiousness. This is an important finding because it shows that personality (and other factors) correlates of CWBs depend very specifically on what crime/behaviour is being considered.

Connelly et al. (2006) also found the personality disorders to be most closely related to integrity and dishonesty. Five personality disorders were all associated with low scores on an integrity test. They were (in order of power): Machiavellian Egocentricity, Blame Externalisation, Impulsive non-Conformity, Fearlessness and Carefree non-Planfulness.

A good example of a study that tried to combine individual and situational predictors of integrity-test performance was the study by Mumford et al. (2001). Among the individual predictive factors were narcissism and power motives, while the most predictive of the situational variables were alienation and exposure to negative peer groups. Interestingly, they found the situational variables more predictive than the individual variables. The things they measured included alienation, non-supportive family, negative role models, life stressors, competition pressure, exposure to negative peer groups and financial need.

There have just recently been two important studies and reviews on the relationship between personality and integrity tests. Marcus et al. (2006) used structural equation modelling to test two models. The first was that integrity was essentially a *super-factor* made up of high Agreeableness and Conscientiousness and low Neuroticism. The second was the several-facet model, which suggested that it would be better to think of integrity as a constellation of narrow personality traits. Using data from 213 German undergraduates they found strong support for the second position though they found that results varied according to precisely what measure of integrity was used. Thus, facets that seemed particularly related to an overt integrity test score including: N1 (Angry Hostility), N5 (Impulsiveness), N6 (Vulnerability), E5 (Excitement Seeking), A1 (Trust), A2 (Straightforwardness), C3 (Dutifulness), and C5 (Self-Discipline).

An important review and meta-analysis by Berry et al. (2006) concluded that although interpersonal deviance (gossip, violence) and organisational deviance (theft, sabotage) are highly correlated they are differentially related to personality traits. Their results showed the following: the factors most closely related to CWB (both interpersonal and organisational deviance) are Agreeableness, Conscientiousness and Neuroticism in that order. The more agreeable, conscientious and stable the individual the less likely they were to be deviant. Whilst results for individual and organisational deviance were similar for Neuroticism there was a reverse pattern for the other traits. Thus, it was low Conscientiousness first and Agreeableness second that related to organisational deviance but the reverse pattern to interpersonal deviance.

Further, when these authors compared their results with the meta-analysis by Salgado (2002) they found stronger evidence for the role of personality variables, particularly Agreeableness. These results are not particularly surprising but they are important. They indicate that comparatively Openness and Extraversion are not particularly related to CWB and therefore integrity. Some researchers have concentrated on personality correlations of very particular CWBs like Extreme Careerism defined by Bratton and Kacmar (2004) as "the propensity to pursue career advancement, power or prestige through any positive or negative non-performance-based activity that is deemed necessary" (p. 291). They developed a self-explanatory model of the various factors involved and the process (Figure 10.1).

They argued that extreme careerists have a propensity to behave politically and to further their (excessive) ambitions through a series of negative, manipulative, impression-management strategies.

The literature on personality suggests that personality factors are implicated in many sorts of crime. The question is how much variance do they account for? Certainly it should come as no surprise to either researchers or managers to find that personality traits are clearly linked to dishonesty at work.

Integrity testing

Every organisation would prefer to have honest, dependable and trustworthy employees. In some organisations, like police forces, banks and the military, it is essential. Hence they often invest a lot in techniques that attempt to assess individual honesty and integrity. Equally, these techniques can be used to "vet" people in the organisation or to attempt to establish guilt after the event. However, it is in the area of pre-employment screening that they are most used.

Integrity testing techniques vary greatly in technology, if not in purpose (Miner & Capps, 1996). They can probably be broken down into three types:

1   Physiologically based assessments like the polygraph/lie detector or those methods that seek to analyse voice stress patterns.

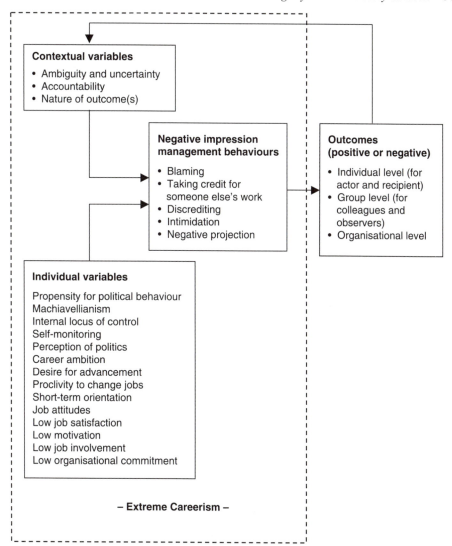

Figure 10.1 Bratton and Kacmar's (2004) model of the factors and process involved in Extreme Careerism. Copyright © 2004 John Wiley & Sons Ltd. Reproduced with permission.

2 Behaviourally based assessments that look at visual and vocal concomitants of stress and deception like stuttering, nose touching, etc.

3 Self-report methods based on an analysis of interviews (tape-recorded and transcribed) as well as questionnaires.

They are all, however, based on the premise that responses to questions about *past* attitudes, behaviours and values can be validly used to infer *future* levels of honesty. That is, the score on a test (of whatever type) is able to predict a wide range of dishonest, illegal or unacceptable behaviours.

A decade ago Iacono and Patrick (1997) reviewed the literature on integrity testing. Then, as now, the critical questions were the same: what is the evidence of reliability and validity (criterion-related construct)? They also considered typical controversial issues like false-positive misclassification, fakeability, adverse impact, privacy and informed consent, and the current legal status of integrity testing.

Integrity tests, also called honesty tests, are pencil-and-paper questionnaires designed to assess a very wide variety of work-related behaviours. These include:

- *Dishonesty and general untrustworthiness* – unauthorised use of company information, forgery;
- *Alcohol/drug abuse* – selling, using on the job, coming to work with a hangover/intoxicated;
- *Deception and deliberate misrepresentation* – tax fraud and cheating, bribery;
- *Violent behaviour* – physical assault on others at work;
- *"Maladjustment"* – blackmail;
- *Job instability/excessive absenteeism* – turnover/time theft; coming late to work; using sick leave when not sick;
- *Theft* – of cash, merchandise and property, misuse of discount privileges, embezzlement;
- *Poor conscientiousness/prudence* – no work ethic, intentionally going slow or producing sloppy work, failure to implement company policy;
- *Alienation attitudes* – the opposite of commitment and engagement;
- *Inattention to safety rules* – causing preventable accidents, Ludditism and damage to property, wilful damage and waste, vandalism;
- *Poor time keeping* – having unauthorised work breaks;
- *Sabotage*; and
- *Sexual harassment*.

Various studies have shown that scores on integrity type variables tend to correlate with each other (Posthuma & Maertz, 2003).

These tests have been in existence for some time but they appear to be used more and more by employers eager to select out various potentially problem candidates. Some tests attempt to measure all aspects of what Hogan and Hogan (1989) call unreliability and include among other features excessive grievances, bogus worker compensation claims and even temper tantrums. They note:

> We have argued that antisocial behaviour is a syndrome whose components include hostility toward authority, impulsiveness, social insensitivity, and feelings of alienation. These characteristics predispose people to defy rules, ignore social expectations, and avoid commitments to other people and organisations. These tendencies are normally distributed in the general population. Persons who are unusually hostile, insensitive and alienated quickly (and usually permanently) run foul of public authority. Persons who are only moderately hostile, impulsive, insensitive, and alienated have careers marked by frequent job change, job dissatisfaction and limited achievement.
>
> We also argued that persons who are only moderately antisocial engage in a wide variety of delinquent behaviours on the job ranging from insubordination and tardiness through frequent absenteeism to theft, sabotage, and even arson. This argument suggests that it is useful to consider alternatives to theft as an index of dishonesty, in part because theft has a low base rate in normal organisations and in

part because it is only one element of the larger behavioural syndrome that we call organisational delinquency.

(pp. 277–278)

Historically self-reported honesty tests contain items of four different types. *First*, confessions – admissions of illegal, disapproved, prohibitive or antisocial behaviour. *Second*, attitudes/opinions – about the above type of behaviours. *Third*, self-descriptions of personality and thought patterns around illegal activities and moral issues. *Finally*, reactions to hypothetical situations.

Some tests try to veil or disguise their purpose. Others assumed low integrity is associated with thrill-seeking, non-conformity and low conscientiousness. Many tests have traditionally been used either to screen out undesirable applicants; to investigate crimes by current employees; to vet those being considered for promotion or transfer; or just to assess the current moral beliefs of people within the organisation. Integrity tests were typically used with supervisory-level personnel, especially in retail and financial companies.

There has been a great growth and interest in, as well as use of, integrity tests. However, personality and other similar tests have been used since the 1930s to identify "agitators, malcontents and thugs" (Zichar, 2001). Recent American data suggest that as many as 6000 companies employ one of the 50 or so tests on the market using five to twenty-five million tests per annum (Miner & Capps, 1996). There seems to be both demand and supply for integrity tests – the test publishers responding to the market need. Popularity is put down to various specific but predictable issues:

1 *Increase in theft*. Though initially it was lower-level blue-collar workers, typically in supermarkets, that were considered for testing, more interest has been given to white-collar employees. Surveys in America have suggested that arrests for fraud have doubled. Also, a reasonable estimate of the value of theft stand at $100 billion (£70 billion). More surprisingly, a quarter to a third of employees (depending on sector) gets involved in theft every year.

2 *Alcohol and drug problems*. Relative reduction in the cost of alcohol, and its acceptance in society, has no doubt affected consumption in and out of work. The same applies to a range of illegal "recreational" and hard drugs. It is estimated that random drug testing with younger people would reveal that about 10% were taking drugs.

3 *Workplace violence and bullying*. Frustration due to stress and other factors, including a corporate culture that condones it, means that violence in the workplace, especially serious physical assault as well as psychological bullying, appears to be on the increase.

4 *Legal liabilities*. The cost of dishonesty, especially law suits brought against a company, means companies see honesty as a good investment. Where a company is found negligent the compensation fee to aggrieved workers can be astronomical.

5 *The difficulty of sacking*. Most employers will describe how difficult it is to "discharge" a poor or problematic employee. More and more seriously problematic employees find it convenient to argue that their dismissal is based on sex, age, race, religion, handicap, sexual orientation, etc.

Estimates of the use and growth of integrity tests come almost exclusively from America. The following are typical estimates from the 1980s and 1990s:

1   Around 5000 companies use pre-employment integrity tests to screen around 5,000,000 applicants.
2   Somewhere between 5 and 20% of all American companies use some form of testing for some forms of job (high sensitive).
3   There are 40–50 commercially available tests in the market, as well as various in-house measures developed for very specific purposes.

Another reason for the growth in integrity testing is quite simply the fact that the use of the lie detector/polygraph has become more problematic. So, with a favoured method less available and no longer respectable and with evidence of increasing counterproductive behaviours at work it seems natural to resort to any integrity tests on the market.

Reviews of integrity tests

Between 1990 and 2000 a large number of papers appeared in the literature each of which attempted a state-of-the-art and disinterested review. The following five are good examples. In a very important and ground-breaking meta-analysis in this field Ones et al. (1993) reviewed 25 different tests of integrity. In their first study with a sample of more than 68,000 people they found a correlation of $r = .21$ between integrity test scores and job performance. With over half a million participants in the meta-analysis they found a correlation of $r = .33$ between integrity test scores and CWBs. In this analysis they took into consideration the effects of possible moderator factors like job complexity, and job-performance measures like supervisory ratings vs. actual production records. Overall the estimated mean predictive validity of integrity tests for predicting supervisor ratings of job performance was $r = .41$. They concluded:

> One question we have repeatedly pondered since beginning our research on integrity tests has been the issue of potential response distortion by test takers, including the possibility of faking, responding in a socially desirable manner, or otherwise responding inaccurately. The conclusion we inferred from our meta-analytic results was that response distortion, to the extent that it exists, does not seem to destroy the criterion-related validities of these tests. We found substantial validities for studies conducted on applicants. Applicants in these studies experienced all the usual inducements for response distortion, yet, nevertheless, we observed substantial estimated mean validities.
>
> (p. 696)

And finally they noted:

> When we started our research on integrity tests, we, like many other industrial psychologists, were sceptical of integrity tests used in industry. Now, on the basis of analyses of a large database consisting of more than 600 validity coefficients, we conclude that integrity tests have substantial evidence of generalisable validity. Our findings indicate that both overt and personality-based measures of integrity correlate substantially with supervisory ratings of job performance and with both

externally measured and self-reported counterproductive behaviours. Our meta-analyses confirmed many of our moderator hypotheses. However, perhaps the most significant conclusion of this research is that integrity test validities are positive across situation and settings despite moderating influences on their exact magnitudes.

(p. 697)

One of the results of this article is that it led to the development of many attempts to establish criterion-focused occupational personality scores. Examples include integrity tests (which aim to predict dishonest behaviours at work), violence scales (which aim to predict violent behaviours at work), drug and alcohol avoidance scales (which aim to predict substance abuse at work), stress tolerance scales (which aim to predict handling work pressures well) and customer service scales (which aim to predict serving customers well). Ones and Viswesvaran (2001) first reviewed the criterion-related validity, construct validity and incremental validity evidence for integrity tests, violence scales, stress tolerance scales, and customer service scales.

Hough (1996a) asked the question: "Can integrity tests be trusted?" She concluded:

Intentional distortion on self-report measures is often assumed to be a serious threat to criterion-related validity of such measures. The preponderance of evidence to date suggests that it may not be as serious a problem as is often thought. Indeed, the evidence suggests that validity, if it is affected at all, is affected only modestly. Though more research is needed, this conclusion may be more accurate for moderately subtle tests than for overt, obvious tests. In general, however, the evidence indicates that integrity test scores can be trusted.

(p. 103)

Waneck (1999) asked two questions about integrity and honesty tests: What do we know and how do we use them? He concluded thus:

To summarise what we know, integrity tests exhibit internal and temporal stability, and have respectable levels of criterion-related validity across a wide variety of counterproductive and productive criteria, including absenteeism, turnover, disciplinary actions taken and global measures of job performance, across jobs and settings. The underlying integrity construct shows relationships with the general personality dimensions of Conscientiousness, Agreeableness and Emotional Stability and near zero correlations with measures of cognitive ability, suggesting useful incremental validity in selection systems. There are differences between overt and personality oriented integrity tests in spite of a shared underlying construct and differences between the same kinds of tests.

In practical application, using what we know, an integrity test score should never be the sole basis for an employment decision. However, when used as a final assessment in a multiple-assessment system, employers can "play the odds". Between otherwise equal final candidates, choosing the candidate with the highest integrity test score will lead, over the long run, to a work force comprised of employees who are less likely to engage in counterproductive activities at work, and more likely to engage in productive work behaviours.

(p. 193)

Camara and Schneider (1994) reported on two independent reports (APA; US Congress Office) on integrity tests. Their conclusion was:

> Researchers have generally agreed that there is insufficient evidence to reach definitive conclusions on some aspects of integrity testing and that the underlying construct of integrity itself is poorly understood. However, there is also general agreement that integrity tests can predict a number of outcomes of interest to employers and that they have levels of validity comparable to many other kinds of tests used in employment settings.
>
> Integrity testing would benefit if publishers encouraged more research on potential moderators of the validity of integrity tests, on divergent and convergent validity, and on comparisons with other measures. Integrity testing could benefit from the growing body of research on personality constructs by establishing empirical linkages to the Big Five personality constructs. Test publishers could benefit from greater openness in encouraging independent researchers to evaluate their tests. Employers could benefit from more skepticism of marketing claims and from independent and professional expertise in measurement and selection before purchasing tests and establishing comprehensive selection systems that evaluate all relevant aspects of job performance, rather than focusing solely on risk of internal theft. Finally, the public and the profession of psychology could benefit from increased screening and training for test users, who could take a more proactive role in ensuring that tests are used appropriately by organizations. Increased scrutiny of test use and test users can minimize misuse of assessments, increase the validity and utility of tests, and deter further regulation of employment testing at the local, state, and federal levels.
>
> Although technical and scientific questions about integrity tests (e.g. how well they work, what they measure, and why they work) may not be answered to the complete satisfaction of behavioral scientists, a general consensus on their validity and utility has emerged. This approval is, of course, limited to properly documented tests. The fate of integrity testing and perhaps all personality tests and preemployment tests may eventually be decided by legislatures and the courts. We psychologists should willingly participate in such public policy debates.
>
> (p. 117)

Murphy (1994) in a very scholarly and measured review aimed at the police concluded thus:

> Integrity tests have been the focus of a great deal of controversy. On the whole, the available research suggests that these tests can be useful, and that they are likely to be preferable to most available alternatives. These tests do provide some information about an individual's trustworthiness, and if properly used, can contribute to the quality of personnel decisions. It is important, however, to keep in mind the known limitations of such tests. These tests do not necessarily measure honesty, they do not tell you with any degree of certainty whether an individual will commit or has committed a dishonest act, and they are not the solution to the problems of employee theft and counterproductivity. If used thoughtlessly, these tests can do more harm (in terms of the negative reactions they might invoke) than good, but if used with care, skepticism and caution,

they can provide a worthwhile tool for decreasing negative behaviors in the workplace.

Integrity testing may be especially attractive to police departments, because of the strong emphasis placed on personal integrity. The available evidence suggests that applicants for positions in police departments who receive low scores on integrity tests are likely to present larger risks of dishonest behavior than those who do not receive low scores. Considerable caution should be used in selecting and implementing integrity tests; there are a large number of tests and testing firms and the quality of these tests varies considerably. However, if used with appropriate caution, these tests can be a useful adjunct in the selection of police officers.

(p. 225)

Whilst there are slight differences between these reviewers it does seem that they are cautiously positive about the validity of integrity tests.

Reaction to tests

How do people react when asked to do an integrity test? Jones (1991) found the following reactions to the idea of doing tests:

- 90% felt it was appropriate for an employer to administer such a test.
- 4% would refuse to take such a test.
- 63% would enjoy being asked to take such a test.
- 11% felt this type of test was an invasion of privacy.
- 2% said if they had two comparable job offers, they would reject the company using such a test.
- 3% would resent being asked to take such a test.
- 82% felt that a test such as this is sometimes an appropriate selection procedure.
- 5% believe that administering a test such as this reflects negatively on the organisation.
- 80% indicated that being asked to take such a test would not affect their view of the organisation.
- 80% indicated that tests such as this are routinely used in industry.

One recent study looking at seasonal student employees found, as predicted, that those who were given clear advance notification of work monitoring and thought it fair were much more likely to return to the organisation the following year compared to those with no warning or who thought it unfair (Hovorka-Mead et al., 2002).

Zweig and Webster (2003) found that employees' acceptance of monitoring systems was a function of their perceived usefulness, fairness and privacy invasion, which in turn was dependent on the precise characteristics of the monitoring system involved and the justification for its use.

What would be particularly interesting would be to compare these results with those from other tests. Would people be happier to complete ability or personality tests than honesty tests? Are people simply wary of tests in general? It seems that many people tend to accept tests as job relevant and many even find them enjoyable.

Much, no doubt, depends on the type of test used, the way it is presented, the candidate's previous experience of testing as well as their personality and values.

Certainly, results appear to indicate that neither extreme view is correct: people neither happily embrace the idea of being tested, nor do they find the whole idea irrelevant, immoral and offensive. There have been pencil-and-paper tests for over 50 years that have attempted to measure integrity. Those have tended to grow over the past decade or so as issues with integrity appear to have increased.

The tests themselves

Tests of all sorts are still being enthusiastically developed. Thus, Becker (2005) has attempted to devise a situational integrity test. He found that test scores were related to measures of career potential, leadership activities and job performance but not ratings of the quality of interpersonal relationships. Three examples of questions in this test (plus the scoring) are shown below:

> Your work team is in a meeting discussing how to sell a new product. Everyone seems to agree that the product should be offered to customers within the month. Your boss is all for this, and you know he does not like public disagreements. However, you have concerns because a recent report from the research departments points to several potential safety problems with the product. Which of the following do you think you would be most likely to do?
>
> A　Try to understand why everyone else wants to offer the product to customers this month. Maybe your concerns are misplaced. (– 1)
> B　Voice your concerns with the product and explain why you believe the safety issues need to be addressed. (1)
> C　Go along with what others want to do so that everyone feels good about the team. (– 1)
> D　Afterwards, talk with several other members of the team to see if they share your concerns. (0)
>
> (p. 229)

> It is a beautiful day outside – sunny warm, and inviting. You are scheduled to work, but you are tempted to take the day off and go to the beach with some friends. In all honesty, which of the following would you most likely do?
>
> A　Call in sick and go to the beach. (0)
> B　Go into work and work as hard as you usually do. (1)
> C　Call your boss and tell him or her that you'd like to go to the beach, and see if your boss can find someone else to work for you. (– 1)
> D　Go into work but do not work as hard as normal. (0)
>
> (p. 234)

> You're a new clerk in a clothing store and are being trained by Angie, a veteran employee. She quietly tells you that because employees are paid minimum wage, most people take home clothes for themselves. Employees who don't are considered dumb and arrogant. At closing time, Angie hands you a scarf to take home. Which of the following would you most likely do?

A   Take home the scarf and keep your mouth shut. (− 1)
B   Take home the scarf, but return it to the shelf later without letting other employees see you. (− 1)
C   Politely tell Angie that you don't need any more scarves. (0)
D   Tell Angie that you don't want to take home any clothes, now or ever. (1)

(p. 230)

Clearly a good deal of work needs to be done assessing the validity of these type of tests but they do look promising. Integrity tests are fairly varied but appear to concentrate on the following areas:

1   Direct, explicit admissions of dishonest behaviour (lying, cheating, stealing, whistle-blowing).
2   Opinions/attitudes about the acceptability of dishonest behaviour (prevalence in society, justification of causes).
3   Traits, value systems and biographical factors thought to be associated with dishonesty.
4   Reactions to hypothetical situations that do or do not feature dishonest behaviour.

Often these self-report measures can be distinguished in terms of whether they are overt, explicit, "clear-purpose" tests or personality-based, "veiled-purpose" tests. The sort of issues that an overt test examines includes: honesty attitudes/admission of previous dishonesty; substance abuse, drug avoidance; personal past achievements; service orientation, customer relations; work values; clerical, mathematical, verbal skills, abilities and aptitudes.

On the other hand, the "veiled-purpose" tests are more likely to try to measure: conscientiousness, dependability, prudence; hostility to rules and regulations; impulsivity, thrill seeking, disinhibition; alienation and lack of commitment.

Recently, Bennett and Robinson (2000) developed a measure of workplace deviance. This inevitably involved defining specific items that make up deviance. Table 10.2 shows 28 items from their measure.

In the end Bennett and Robinson developed a two-part questionnaire: one part measuring organisational deviance (behaviours directly harmful to the organisation) and the other interpersonal deviance (behaviours directly harmful to individuals). They also provided validity data for their instrument.

Clearly, one obvious advantage of the so-called veiled-purpose test is that it is less open to faking or not admitting wrongdoing. Faking threatens test reliability. However, it has been shown to be significantly reduced when people are aware that the investigators (potential employers) have (many) other sources of information about their honesty.

There are different themes tapped into by self-report integrity tests. Further, there is an assumption that the honest, reliable person with integrity acts somewhat differently from the dishonest person on this dimension:

1   *Report incidences of explicit dishonesty.* Honest people will honestly report that they have been dishonest in the past.
2   *Leniency towards dishonesty.* Honest people are likely to excuse, forgive or explain away dishonesty in others and themselves.

Table 10.2 Deviant workplace behaviour

Item	Participation rate[a]
1 Worked on a personal matter instead of work for your employer	84.3
2 Taken property from work without permission	51.8
3 Spent too much time fantasising or daydreaming instead of working	77.4
4 Made fun of someone at work	77.8
5 Falsified a receipt to get reimbursed for more money than you spent on business expenses	24.6
6 Said something hurtful to someone at work	55.2
7 Taken an additional or a longer break than is acceptable at your workplace	78.5
8 Repeated a rumour or gossip about your company	72.5
9 Made an ethnic, religious, or racial remark or joke at work	52.5
10 Come in late to work without permission	70.0
11 Littered your work environment	28.5
12 Cursed someone at work	50.5
13 Called in sick when you were not	57.8
14 Told someone about the lousy place where you work	58.9
15 Lost temper while at work	78.8
16 Neglected to follow your boss's instructions	60.6
17 Intentionally worked slower than you could have worked	54.1
18 Discussed confidential company information with an unauthorised person	33.3
19 Left work early without permission	51.9
20 Played a mean prank on someone at work	35.7
21 Left your work for someone else to finish	48.6
22 Acted rudely toward someone at work	53.0
23 Repeated a rumour or gossip about your boss or co-workers	69.1
24 Made an obscene comment at work	48.4
25 Used an illegal drug or consumed alcohol on the job	25.9
26 Put little effort into your work	64.0
27 Publicly embarrassed someone at work	33.9
28 Dragged out work in order to get overtime	26.0

Notes: Responses ranged from 1 (*never*) to 7 (*daily*). N = 226. [a]Percentage of respondents who indicated that they had participated in the behaviour at least once in the last year. (Adapted from Bennett & Robinson, 2000.)

3   *Rationalisation for thieving.* Honest people are less likely to try to excuse or provide rationalisation for theft in organisations.

4   *Brooding and rumination about theft.* Honest people are less likely to even think (plan, plot, fantasise) about thieving from their organisation.

5   *Rejecting dishonest norms.* Honest people are likely to question or reject dishonest behaviour of all sorts accepted within the organisation as acceptable.

6   *Impulse control.* Honest people are less likely to act on their impulses, preferring to think through an issue before acting.

7   *Punitive attitude.* Honest people have less punitive attitudes to themselves and others.

Certainly, tests have been validated against very different criteria: theft, faking credentials, "counterproductive" behaviour, and they do tend to produce rather different results. Working on company time and taking over-long lunch breaks are called "time theft". Stealing office stationery (pens, paper) is strictly theft. But both of these could be considered trivial, certainly quite different from the theft of company secrets, or of valuable products used for production or the products themselves.

Integrity tests today

What is the latest thinking around these tests? *First*, it is agreed that these tests are certainly useful. They are valid enough to help prevent various problems. *Second*, testing alone will not stop theft, dishonesty, sabotage as many other factors (other than dishonest individuals) cause them. *Third*, integrity tests may be measuring aspects of human personality that are stable over time though it is not certain which. *Fourth*, there are problems in testing because some testing codes and standards insist that testees give informed consent on details about the test such as what it measures; hardly the best thing to hand to the dishonest person. *Fifth*, there may be legal issues concerning how "cut-off" scores are used and labelled. One could classify people as pass/fail or very, highly, moderately dangerous. How this information is used or recorded can cause expensive legal action. *Sixth*, integrity tests are used to "select-out", not "select-in". They are designed to help people screen out high-risk applicants not identify "angels".

These tests naturally cause a great deal of interest and discussion. Some reject the idea of using them at all. Various arguments are put forward. Others object that they are of limited worth (validity). The *first* objection is that they frequently mislabel people. If tests were totally valid people would be neatly and accurately categorised as honest or dishonest (given some cut-off score). But it is inevitable (as with our entire legal system) that guilty people are judged honest and vice versa. Some organisations argue that, even if the validity is not perfect, it may be better to reject a candidate who is in fact honest than let a dishonest person (or, indeed, many people) join the organisation. Most of the debate concerns the innocent labelled guilty rather than the equally (or more) worrying situation of the dishonest being admitted to the workforce.

A *second* objection lies in the assumption that dishonesty is a stable characteristic of individuals. The one side argues that dishonesty is primarily a function of the individual – their personality, values, conscience – and, therefore, that integrity tests are useful in principle. Others argue that honesty is much less stable and is a function of situational factors like poor security, seeing others steal, or being offered bribes. In this sense, people may be very honest in one situation and quite dishonest in another. In this sense, some situations provoke dishonesty, others not. Equally, it could be argued that people are honest about some issues (their childhood, their leisure activities) but not others (tax and money issues, relationships and sex).

Over 70 years ago, psychologists found that children seemed particularly variable in their honesty behaviour and a situational view presided. But later research and analysis of the data have shown stable individual differences in honesty. However, there remains sufficient substantial evidence to suggest that certain external and situational factors can serve to influence honesty. This means that there are inevitably limits that one can achieve with any integrity test no matter of what kind.

A *third* objection is that, paradoxically, it is more-honest people that admit to dishonesty in the past. In this sense tests are better at detecting "goodies" rather than "baddies". Tests assume that those who more freely admit dishonesty in the past are more likely to do so in the future, or that individuals who have relatively lenient attitudes toward wrongdoing may be more likely to violate laws and policies. Indeed, the opposite may apply.

A *fourth* objection is that cultural factors determine the meaning of honesty and dishonesty. A gift in one culture is a bribe in another. Traditional employment patterns in one society represent nepotism in a second. The argument is that honesty and integrity are socially defined with no absolutes. Hence it is wrong and unjust to judge a person by the dictates of a different national or, indeed, corporate culture. In short, integrity tests are culture dependent.

A *fifth* objection is that some people do not know the difference between right and wrong. The law makes allowance for children and certain types of mental illness. The psychopath or sociopath is, in Victorian terminology, a moral imbecile in the sense that they do not (and cannot) distinguish between right and wrong. Tests – even the polygraph – will not detect them because they feel no guilt. The implication is that there are personality factors that are associated with wrongdoing.

In America, where these tests are most widely used, the issue of the violation of civil rights is now discussed. But tests are now becoming broader to include everything from emotional instability, through drug taking to potential for violence. Thus, integrity testing is controversial. However, there is comparatively little evidence that either job applicants or incumbents find them objectionable in practice or principle.

Certainly some people do indicate "principled dissent" to integrity testing that is seen as non-job-related and an invasion of privacy. However, one study showed that, compared to non-drug users, drug users had stronger negative reactions to personality tests, overt integrity tests and urine analysis (Rosse et al., 1996). One may be tempted to conclude that those who "protesteth too much" may be doing so for a good reason.

All forms of integrity testing are controversial. This is partly because of problems of misclassification. Thus, even if a test is 95% accurate (which is extremely unlikely) then 5000 in every 100,000 would be misclassified. Further, the stigma of being classified dishonest (correctly or incorrectly) may have very enduring and negative consequences quite out of proportion with the initial "crime". The punishment (rejection) therefore does not fit the crime.

However, at the heart of the issue is another more important and more pervasive factor. It is this: research has shown that *honesty* is the single most important quality that we rate in others. It is also (almost uniquely) one characteristic nobody rates themselves on as below average. It is therefore a very hot topic that has to be dealt with very sensitively. To accuse someone of trait (that is stable) dishonesty is, therefore, a very serious accusation that needs to be correct.

Reviewers (Sackett, 1994) have noted that several millions of integrity tests are administered to low-pay job entrants where people have access to money or merchandise (financial services, retailing).

Integrity test validity

Is there evidence that these relatively simple questionnaires mean that people are more or less likely to engage in dishonest, counterproductive behaviours? Can they predict who will be honest or dishonest?

There are various ways of checking the validity of tests. They include:

1　*The "known" or contrast groups method.* People who are known to be both honest and dishonest are given the test and the quantity and quality of the difference in response are recorded.

2   *Background, biographical check.* A thorough background check (number of convictions) using police, school and organisations' records are related to test scores.

3   *Admissions and confessions.* Separate (perhaps confidential) admissions to a wide range of dishonest behaviours in tests, from the trivial to the very serious, are correlated with test scores.

4   *Predictive or future method.* People are tested at organisational entry and scores are related to documented (proven) dishonest behaviours over their career.

5   *Time series or historic method.* Before honesty tests are used in selection, all sorts of indices are collected: loss, shrinkage. The same data are collected after tests are used in selection to see if there is a noticeable difference

6   *Correlations.* With polygraph or anonymous admissions of theft or absenteeism.

Studies have shown individual differences on integrity-test faking. For instance, it seems that brighter people fake better than less intelligent people (Brown & Colthern, 2000). Each method has its limitations and failings. For instance, background checks won't show working on company time. Predictive methods can take a decade. A reduction in stealing may have as much to do with the installation of a new security system as it does the use of tests.

The issue of the validity of integrity tests and interpreting the evidence is technical. Four issues are relevant:

1   What is the criterion (or criteria) against which test scores are measured? How specific or serious is it? Is it global like job performance or specific like absenteeism or stealing?

2   What type of measure is it? Is it subjective or objective? Is it recorded electronically (on camera), by others' disinterested observations or is it done by a person's own self-report?

3   What is the validation strategy? That is, is it concurrent – are things compared at the same time (test scores and cheating data) or is it predictive when scores are seen to predict behaviour forward in time?

4   Who is the validation sample of people on whom to do the study? Is it job applicants or job incumbents?

Researchers argue that studies using objective data predictively and job incumbents rather than applicants are best. Objective data are better than subjective data because of distortion. Predictive studies are best because that is how integrity tests are used: to attempt to predict behaviour ahead of time. Job applicants are the best sample precisely because they are motivated to present themselves in the best possible light.

Miner and Capps (1996) provided a masterful review of reviews that was more positive than negative. They concluded, as others have done, that it is quite possible to construct honesty/integrity tests and this has been done but it is essential to examine the validity evidence for each test. Yet the controversy has not and probably will never go away because the issue of using tests "goes beyond science into values: the very use of these tests infringes certain values and beliefs". Yet, they conclude: "we foresee a prosperous future for honesty testing. These tests serve a significant need. It is important that they be permitted to continue to serve that need, and we believe that society will have the good sense to let that happen" (p. 241).

The most obvious and fundamental questions about honesty testing must be about *validity*. What is the evidence that they measure (only) honesty and can differentiate between the honest and dishonest? Over the past decade there have been various studies and excellent reviews. Those who are positive conclude that integrity tests are often as good at detecting counterproductive behaviours as supervisors' ratings of good/poor performance. Others believe that the "jury is out" and that we need more high-quality, disinterested and sceptical research before making a judgement. Whatever the evidence and however it is reviewed, it is apparent that the debate for and against tests is driven by strong emotions.

1   "There is now a reasonable body of evidence showing that integrity tests have some validity for predicting a variety of criteria that are relevant to organisations. This research does not say that tests of this sort will eliminate theft or dishonesty at work, but it does suggest that individuals who receive poor scores on these tests tend to be less-desirable employees" (Murphy, 1994, p. 215).
2   "Thus, a large body of validity evidence consistently shows scores on integrity tests to be positively related to both a range of counterproductive behaviours and supervisory ratings of overall performance. However, virtually all the research has been done by test publishers, leading sceptics to question whether only successes are publicised" (Sackett, 1994, p. 74).
3   "Intentional distortion on self-report measures is often assumed to be a serious threat to criterion-related validity of such measures. The preponderance of evidence to date suggests that it may not be as serious a problem as is often thought. Indeed the evidence suggests that validity, if it is affected at all, is affected only modestly. Though more research is needed, this conclusion may be more accurate for moderately subtle tests, than for overt, obvious tests. In general, however, the evidence indicates that integrity test scores can be trusted" (Hough, 1996a, p. 103).

Whilst validity is always the single, and simply most important, criterion of any test, there are others, some of which have a direct effect on validity. These include reliability, dimensionality, etc., but perhaps the most important is *fakeability*. Can clever (and dishonest) people "beat the test" and come out looking virtuous when they are not? This problem applies to all tests but particularly to honesty tests. Results suggest that one can catch dissimulators but that there is a general, and quite understandable, trend to over emphasise honesty.

Of course, the issue with testing is the problem of false positives and negatives, that is classifying the honest as dishonest and vice versa. Both are equally undesirable but they do have quite different consequences.

Whilst it is not difficult to make a case for the use of integrity tests it seems ironic that test publishers seem to make possibly fraudulent claims for the efficacy of their tests in detecting dishonest people and thence reducing theft and stealing problems. Honesty testing is a competitive business. It is possible that honesty testing in the future will attempt to measure very specific, rather than general, types of honesty. Further, it is likely that the tests will be computer administered.

In America in the 1980s there were both inquiries and legislation concerning the lie detector. In the 1990s the public, the media and the politicians started to become interested in self-report integrity tests. By the early 1990s, 46 publishers and developers were identified, with products that measured constructs like counterproductivity, honesty, job performance, integrity and reliability. Paradoxically, the integrity of integrity testers was questioned.

In 1994 the American Psychological Association listed various recommendations based on their task force investigation of test publishers. After the American Psychological Society published its report many psychologists commented on it. Their reactions can be considered under various headings.

1. *The jury is not out: Tests are valid*

Three researchers from different universities published a report that examined studies that were done on over half a million participants (Ones et al., 1995). They noted:

> First, integrity tests predict supervisory ratings of overall job performance with a mean operational validity of .41. This is the predictive validity that is relevant when applicants are being selected. The operational validity of .41 for integrity tests for predicting overall job performance implies that integrity tests have higher validity than some of the more accepted forms of personnel selection, including assessment centre ratings, biodata, and even mainstream personality inventories. In fact, integrity test validities for overall job performance are second only to the validities of ability tests, work sample tests, and job knowledge tests used in personnel selection.
>
> Second, integrity tests predict non-self-report broad composites of counterproductive behaviours with operational validities of .39 and .29 (depending on the type of test).
>
> Third, integrity test validities generalise across tests, jobs, organisations, and settings.
>
> (p. 456)

They also believed that integrity tests being broad based was desirable. Further, they believed it was disingenuous to believe that test publishers' data was questionable.

2. *Classification errors are not random*

Some researchers claim that integrity tests do not mention morality but more likely conventionality, conformity and traditionalism (Lilienfeld et al., 1995). In this sense, rather old-fashioned, honest people can get systematically misclassified. Equally true, these tests have been shown to be highly susceptible to faking or work "coaching instructions".

3. *Integrity, unlike ability, is changeable/mutable*

Just as criminals and delinquents can "go straight" and even make up for past sins, so those who score low on integrity can reform. But to penalise people for admissions of past misbehaviours condemns them to be "locked in" to their past (Lilienfeld et al., 1995). Dim people cannot go smart but dishonest people can go straight and, of course, the honest can easily wander off "the straight and narrow".

4. Ability and personality tests do not confer value judgements or labels whereas integrity tests do

Rieke and Guastello (1994) believed, because the evidence for honesty tests is not compelling, that they need to be particularly carefully regulated.

Researchers have done very extensive, critical and exhaustive reviews of integrity testing in organisations. Through a range of state-of-the-art statistical measures they have concluded the following (Ones & Viswesvaran, 1998). They found them internally reliable and that they had very similar results (test–retest $r = .80$) on different occasions. They also looked at their validity for predicting job performance, counterproductive behaviours, training success, accidents on the job and property damage. They noted that although integrity tests were developed to predict theft they could be used to predict much more widely. The following are quotes from their review:

1 "Even for high complexity jobs integrity tests display high levels of operation validity . . . Those meta-analytic results lead us to conclude that integrity tests can profitably be used at all levels in organisations" (p. 252).
2 "[O]verall job performance and job training success are both determined by similar individual differences variables, and the personality related variable of integrity is one of them" (p. 254).
3 "Organisations that suffer from high accident rates are likely to benefit from using integrity tests in their selection systems" (p. 255).
4 "In general, the results from these studies indicate that integrity tests are useful in predicting absenteeism, incidents of violent behaviours on the job, and both alcohol and drug abuse" (pp. 256–257).
5 "Hence, we conclude that integrity test operational validities are not moderated by social desirability" (p. 260).
6 "Overall, the research reviewed above leads to the conclusion that although overt and personality based integrity tests appear to be quite different from each other, the construct of integrity that is relevant for personnel selection is captured well by both types of tests" (p. 261).
7 "To the extent that structural interview scores correlate with integrity tests, the incremental validity of structured interviews are likely to be diminished in a selection system including ability measures, integrity tests, and structured interviews" (pp. 266–267).

They concluded thus:

> It is counterproductive to argue whether individual difference predictors are more potent or whether situational predictors are more potent for predicting counter-productivity and for explaining variance in overall job performance. For a healthy and successful human resource system to operate, both situational variables and individual differences variables could be used. However, as empirically shown in this paper, a successful human resource management strategy to combat counter-productivity at work and predicting job performance starts with rigorous personnel selection using integrity tests.
>
> (p. 271)

Conclusion

There are individual different correlates of the dark side of behaviour at work, namely sabotage, theft, vandalism and whistle-blowing. The extensive literature on the relationship between personality and crime and delinquency suggests that those involved in CWBs are likely to have a specific profile. Whilst there is general agreement as to what those trait are (excitement-seeking, impulsive, disagreeable, tough-minded, low conscientiousness) little research has been done on cognitive ability correlates of crime. Certainly, the evidence suggests that high vs. low intelligence, delinquent, criminals and recidivists are likely to take part in very different types of criminal or deviant activity and have differential rates of being caught.

What is clear, however, is that it is both opportunity and feelings of injustice (real or imagined) that are most likely to provide CWBs. That is, it is the interaction of person and situation factors that provokes and maintains CWBs. Applied psychologists have therefore become interested in selecting in and out those whose levels of integrity or dishonesty are thought healthy or harmful for the organisation. This research endeavour has provoked a great interest in the development and assessment of integrity tests.

There is a healthy supply and demand equation for all types of integrity tests. Whilst there remains considerable scepticism about the validity of integrity tests as well as the wisdom of using them in selection, the empirical literature points clearly to their usefulness. Over the past twenty years integrity testing literature has blossomed and it is probably time to say that this has proved to be an important new area in both differential and work psychology. The wide spread of new electronic technology, reduced employee loyalty because of new job contracts, and competitiveness in the workplace mean that all businesses are eager to ensure that their staff are honest, trustworthy and ethical in all their behaviours. This involves not only recruiting and selecting those who know robust and acceptable ethical codes of behaviour but also ensuring through good management that they are not provoked into any form of revenge on their employer.

Integrity testing is where ethics, morality and psychometric testing meet. It remains a very interesting and important topic that will, no doubt, increase research and debate in years to come.

11 Competence at work

Introduction

Psychologists tend to think about individuals in term of ability, motives and traits. Differential psychology is supported by the twin pillars of those interested in power and preference tests (see Chapter 1). Human resource specialists, on the other hand, talk about individual differences in terms of capability, competency, experience, know-how, potential and proficiency. Most organisations now have *competency frameworks* that are used to help human resource specialists make decisions about appraisal, recruitment, selection and training. They often spend years trying to decide on a definitive and parsimonious list of competencies that apply to their *specific* organisation. Though these are often described in great detail, it is unclear how the individual difference competencies originate, how trainable/malleable they are, and whether they change over time. Organisations spend a great deal of effort deciding on their "unique" competencies though the list from one organisation looks very much like that from another. Indeed, trait theorists might argue that these lists are *intuitive taxonomies in modern business language* that represent the Big Five personality factors lexically. On the other hand, many claim that well-designed, behaviourally anchored competencies relating to certain families of jobs provide very useful data for practitioners trying to both understand and select for certain jobs.

Psychological, as opposed to business, journals rarely use the concept of competency. It is considered by many to be both a "fudged" and an unhelpful concept (Furnham, 2000a, 2000b). However, because it is so widely used to describe and define individual difference behaviour at work it is considered in this chapter.

Jacobs (1989) noted that the term competence, with its allusion to *mere* sufficiency and adequacy, sounds dated in a world that demands excellence and outstanding performance. Some have argued that people can only infer competence from *seeing incompetence* (Waibel & Wicklund, 1994). On the other hand, dictionary definitions do stress that competence is an ability, skill, or know-how: something done in an efficient and effective or adequate way. Interestingly, English dictionaries are more likely than American dictionaries to define the word as synonymous with merely adequate. Many organisations still use it as the way to describe salient individual differences that define salient behaviours at work. For all sorts of reasons they seem to prefer not to talk about cognitive ability or personality traits.

Defining competence

Although there may be difficulties with the technical definition of competence, there are even more when it comes to incompetence. Furnham (2000a, 2000b) considered the following half dozen alternative or opposite meanings:

1 *Not having the competencies*: this involves not having the abilities, traits, or motivation to behave competently. Whether these are learned or inherited is, of course, crucially important but the salient point for the definition is that the crucial, specified (core) competencies are missing.
2 *Not applying the competencies*: the definition suggests that a person has the necessary skills, abilities and traits needed for competence but chooses not to exercise them. This may be an individual or collective act. For instance, "work-to-rule" is a possible sign of volitional incompetence. On the other hand it is possible, but unlikely, that people have latent competencies but do not "apply" them through lack of awareness, or lack of self-confidence, or lack of opportunity.
3 *Having irrelevant or redundant competencies*: people may have been recruited and selected for a particular set of competencies that are now redundant. Jobs change as do the skills and attitudes required to do them. It is therefore possible that a person who was once competent becomes less so over time.
4 *Being too competent for a job*: most people have experienced being "over-qualified" for a job. Jobs that are dull, routine, tedious, or repetitive can wear down talented and skilled individuals who then perform them badly.
5 *Being deliberately incompetent*: there are reasons why individuals or groups choose to behave in ways that are less than competent. There are often feelings of anger, vengeance or inadequacy resulting from some perceived inequality at work. They may perform poorly in order to demonstrate the importance of their job (when competently executed) to customers, colleagues, or superiors.
6 *Not practising the competencies*: because competencies are related to abilities and skills, they require practice. If not exercised, they can become rusty and hence a competency becomes an incompetency.

The English-speaking management world has been concerned with defining, delineating, and selecting for management competencies for almost 20 years. The popularity of the concept of competency is usually attributed to Richard Boyatzis' (1982) book, *The Competent Manager*. The concept of competency seemed to offer a new way to think about performance by getting away from the literal mindedness of behaviourism – e.g. what competencies are needed vs. what behaviours are displayed. It also seemed to offer a *neutral* term to evaluate work-related performance. Despite the popularity of the idea, there are various problems in defining it, or indeed in distinguishing it from other concepts. However, it seems arguable that the term has, in fact, made the job for the manager *more*, rather than *less*, difficult because it has confused the various characteristics that are necessary for efficient management.

The confusion was partly created by Boyatzis himself. He defined a competency as "an underlying characteristic of a person". It could be a "motive, trait, skill, aspect of one's self-image or social role, or a body of knowledge which he or she uses". This definition covers almost anything, but it does not define the common denominator of all these things and raises the question of whether the term is simply a piece of jargon.

In an interview with Boyatzis, Adams (1997) noted that the competency movement is a fad with too many people putting old wine in new bottles, simply repackaging their materials in a "competency surround". Adams noted that competency had been trivialised and had become in effect "proficiency". He disapproved of using competencies in selection or pay because they are broader than the capabilities that can be reasonably specified for a job. Further, many people never use their competencies. Competency assessment often ignores the capacity for change and a person's potential for self-development. Boyatzis believed that competencies, like skills, could be developed, though the usual questions about which, how and how much, were ignored.

All researchers have acknowledged, however, that it was probably McClelland's (1973) paper that really popularised the concept of competency. Like many others before (Mischel, 1968) and after (Sternberg, 1997a), McClelland was dissatisfied with the ability of personality and ability tests to predict job success. He hoped to develop tests to measure competencies primarily through the *behavioural event interviews* and *critical incident method*. These techniques compare above-average, average and below-average managers to understand how they do their job (based on critical incidents of good and poor performance) and then use these comparisons to detect competencies. There is, therefore, a dictionary of behaviours behind each competency. A decade later, McClelland and his colleagues tried to find generic competencies – this resulted in Boyatzis' (1982) fundamental nine competencies – and allowed them to be motives, traits, skills, self-image, knowledge set, or whatever. McClelland seemed ambivalent about traits. He rejected the usefulness of single traits (conscientiousness) or abilities (general intelligence) to predict performance in all or most jobs; yet he almost always found achievement motivation (his favourite trait) to be a major determinant of managerial performance.

McClelland (1973) argued that the term competency should replace the term skill, which was too narrow. Thus, one may have the skill to drive a bus, but lack the competency to deal with passengers. He argued that the only comprehensive way to identify competencies was through behavioural event interviews. Further, standard job analysis methods, which focus on minimum competencies, leave things out, particularly how outstanding individuals work. Thus, strategic planning, as a competency, needs to be backed by a competence for influencing so that plans can be "sold" to others.

According to McClelland, the core competencies of an organisation are embedded in the organisation's systems, motives, mechanisms and processes. Core competencies may, he argued, represent unique sources of an organisation's competitive advantage.

McClelland's ideas have been criticised for various reasons. Competencies concern past, not future, behaviour and they concern success in the past, not necessarily the future, which may be quite different. Also, behavioural interview methods are often unfair to minorities or women who have not had the same developmental experiences as White males. It is also very expensive to transcribe long interviews for what may be a poor epistemic or practical yield.

There seem to be as many definitions of competency as there are people who talk about them. The British define competencies in terms of something that managers can do – a demonstrable behaviour or an outcome. Some American writers believe a competency is a "higher order" trait, skill, motive or disposition that distinguishes between average or superior managers. Competency has been used as an *adjective* and a *noun*. Thus, one can be a competent strategic planner or have marketing competency.

Supposedly, one can also draw up a definitive list of required competencies – a discrete and definitive set of knowledge, values and skills. One may have areas of competence – that is parts of a job (or skills) – that one does well.

Mansfield (1999) defined the term as meaning "people who are *suitable for work, sufficiently skilled* for the work they do, *fit* for work and *efficient* in their work!" He suggested that the term implies a barely acceptable level, or threshold, of ability (suitable, sufficient) but also rather more than that (fit, efficient). In short, competent people are efficient and effective: incompetent people are not.

Yet there is confusion over the term for various reasons. Consider the following three issues:

1. Singular or plural

Nouns are divisible into counted nouns and uncounted nouns. The former have simple plurals: manager – managers; article – articles. But the latter do not have simple plurals: asparagus and furniture have to have other nouns to make them plural like head and piece, hence four pieces of furniture. Competence is an uncounted noun. Thus we have *the* competence of managers not a competence, which confuses a task performed or any underlying trait or ability. It does not mean a set standard of behaviour. At present, competence is taken to mean what a person is like, how they do things, and what they can do – all of which are conceptually distinct. Thus, some, supposedly competency-based assessments, look at the *former* two factors to decide whether people have the "competencies" needed to do the job well, while others use the *latter* two factors to decide whether they have the ability or potential to do the job.

2. Adequate or excellent

There is some confusion about whether the term refers to barely capable or extremely good. One approach focuses on abilities and characteristics that may have good comparative norms; hence, it is easy to talk about levels of excellence. A second approach looks at what people should be able to do in order to execute the job competently, not what they are like. A good manager has the skills/knowledge to complete the job and characteristics for a particular team. Having particular characteristics will not ensure success nor will a job analysis say much about personal characteristics. Thus, the adequate/excellent debate needs to be dropped.

3. Inputs and outputs

Most competency approaches have focused on how things are done; on outcomes of activities rather than on the underlying state or disposition that determines the activity. The emphasis is on the resultant behaviour, not on traits or processes.

> To *have* a degree is still taken to be an important signal of general capacity. To *be* experienced is a valued characteristic in selection for employment. In some cultures, to be White or male – or both – is taken to be sufficient evidence of capability. The competency movement seeks to change the tradition by asking a simple question. People may have degrees, they may be experienced, they may be thought

reliable – but what can they actually do? How they learned to do it, how long they have been doing it, and what kind of person they are, are seen as subordinate.

(Mansfield, 1999, p. 14)

The latter point illustrates a major problem with the entire competency discussion – it focuses on consequences not causes. Unless one knows *why* a particular person can or cannot do a job, one has no idea what else that person may be able to do or *whether* he/she can ever be taught. And it illustrates a great deal about the incompetent manager who, for one reason or another, simply cannot do those tasks that are fundamental to the job.

Matthewman (1997) surveyed 50 British organisations and found that, of the companies who used the competency approach, about 50% specified between 10 and 20 essential competencies. Over half used the original McClelland behavioural approach to define competencies; less than 10% defined them in strictly functional terms, and the remainder were in-between. Competencies appeared to be used fairly extensively in recruitment, selection, training, and development. However, only a fifth of those surveyed used competencies as a major factor in calculating compensation.

The term competency appears to have been readily embraced in the world of work in such fields as medicine, law and business. Thus, we have proposals for competency-based training in neurosurgery (Long, 2004), general health (Knox & Spivak, 2004) as well as paediatrics (Tallett & O'Brodovich, 2004). One paper in nursing seemed able to specify 21 competencies clustered into three basic groups: basic-level patient-care skills, intermediate-level patient care and fundamental management skills (Tseng & Streltzer, 2004). The same is true of law, though naturally lawyers seem very interested in the precise meaning of the concept (Coles, 2004).

The nature of competence

Furnham (2000b) set out to ask a dozen questions of the competency literature:

1 *So what are competencies?* Are they just traits or aptitudes, or are they skills that decay if they are not practised?
2 *How are competencies related to each other?* A list of competencies is nearly always just that – a list; but human abilities are related. Depending on intelligence, thinking styles (e.g. convergent or divergent thinking) and temperament, certain human factors are clearly related.
3 *Are competencies learned or inherited – or both?* This question has important implications; if they are primarily learned, then they can be taught; if they are inherited, then they have to be selected. If they are learned, are they best learned at a particular age and in a particular way? Do some simply learn competencies more effectively than others? Are some teaching methods more appropriate than others?
4 *It is also possible that some competencies are found more often among certain demographic, racial, linguistic or religious groups than among others?* Certainly some groups excel at sports and others at science; so it may reasonably be supposed that organisational competencies are unevenly distributed. What is the effect of this? And how can organisations square a competency-based selection policy with equal opportunities?
5 *Are competencies an all-or-nothing phenomenon, under which people can be*

categorised into types, or are they dimensional with a continuum from high to low competence? Most organisations talk about types of people but measure people along dimensions. The very concept of a competence certainly implies that people fall into types, with an implicit idea that someone is either competent or not.

6 *Is there a finite, exhaustive, universal list of competencies from which subsets can be devised, or are competencies so varied and subtle that no such list could ever be derived?* In our experience, every organisation thinks it is unique, but organisations then specify that they need the same competencies. If competencies are organisation-specific, they cannot be compared.

7 The whole point of establishing competencies is to be able to assess people, compare them, track them over time, rate them before and after they go on training courses, and so on. *But how are they measured?* What sort of test should be used: behavioural observation, questionnaire, rating (and, if so, by whom)?

8 Each assessment method has problems associated with it, and they lead to systematic bias and error. Furthermore, not all competencies are likely to be measured in an equally valid way. *Is it easier to measure some traits, such as linguistic skills, than others, such as intelligence?* There are valid tests available to measure certain abilities, traits, and beliefs, but competencies such as "forward planning" and "coping with change" are very difficult to measure.

9 Some people assume that competencies are the major determinant of behaviour in an organisation. Presumably organisations value competencies because they represent the fundamental abilities and capabilities needed to do a job well. *But does having a competency mean that it will be used?* Impersonal factors may prevent competent people from performing and allow incompetent people to perform adequately. Organisational factors can clearly override the contribution of individuals, irrespective of their level of competency. Anxiety, obsessionality, phobias and poor ability to cope with everyday stress may prevent competencies from ever manifesting themselves in behaviour.

10 *Is it possible to compensate for the lack of a particular competence?* Can people function well in an organisation when they do not have a particular competence or set of competencies? This may be possible through hard work, delegation, or redefinition of their job. People with specific handicaps have been able to triumph over considerable difficulties, so it is possible that the absence of some competencies is not necessarily a problem.

11 *Is the opposite of competency no competency or incompetency?* What tasks can be done effectively if a particular competency does not exist or is insufficient? There is quite a difference between knowing how to do a job and doing it badly, which is incompetence, and not knowing how to do it, which is no competence.

12 People-related competencies are different from "thing-related" competencies, such as computing or finance skills. Some people are attracted to computers or accounting systems because they are logical and predictable, while others shun them because they prefer to deal with people using their intuition and sensitivity. *Managerial jobs usually demand both kinds of competencies, but is it possible to find both in equal measure?* It is perfectly possible for personnel managers to have more of the former and engineering managers more of the latter.

Organisational competencies necessarily change over time. All organisations live in volatile environments that demand adaptation and innovation. Does the selection of a homogeneous workforce (in terms of salient and non-salient competencies) mean an organisation will be better able to handle change, because there are bound to be people in the organisation who have the competencies needed to deal with the new environment. From this point of view, the most salient competency may be the ability to deal with change or even seek it out, and the one competency to avoid is resistance to change.

Furnham's (2000b) report showed that these all-important, even fundamental, questions seemed neither asked nor answered by the many consultants and writers in the area. Yet, from a differential and organisational psychological perspective they seem absolutely fundamental.

Competency lists

Boyatzis (1982) listed 10 different competencies, and described a programme of research conducted in a variety of different private and public sector organisations to discover the competencies related to managerial effectiveness. One method used to identify competencies was the "behavioural event interview" (similar to the critical incident technique). Incidents of effective and ineffective behaviour were obtained in interviews with managers who were pre-selected on the basis of their effectiveness. The sample included 253 managers from all levels, some rated low in effectiveness, some rated medium, and some rated high. Incidents were classed into competency categories, and traits and skills were inferred from an analysis of behaviour in relation to the manager's intentions and the situation. A statistical analysis defined nine competencies with a significant trend, such that the average competency score was highest for effective managers and lowest for ineffective managers. These nine competencies were as follows:

1   *Efficiency orientation.* Demonstrating concern for task objectives, high inner work standards, and high achievement motivation, with behaviour such as setting challenging but realistic goals and deadlines, developing specific action plans, determining ways to overcome obstacles, organising the work efficiently, and emphasising performance when talking to others.
2   *Concern with impact.* Demonstrating high need for power and concern for power symbols, with behaviour such as acting assertively, attempting to influence others, seeking high-status positions, and expressing concern about the reputation of the organisation's products and services.
3   *Proactivity.* Demonstrating a strong belief in self-efficacy and internal locus of control, with behaviour such as initiating action rather than waiting for things to happen, taking steps to circumvent obstacles, seeking information from a variety of sources, and accepting responsibility for success or failure.
4   *Self-confidence.* Demonstrating belief in one's own ideas and ability by behaviour such as taking decisive action rather than hesitating or vacillating, and making proposals in a firm, unhesitating manner, with appropriate pose, bearing and gestures.
5   *Oral presentation skill.* Ability to use symbolic, verbal and nonverbal behaviour and visual aids to make clear and convincing presentations to others.
6   *Conceptualisation.* Ability to identify patterns or relationships in information and events (inductive reasoning), and to convey the meaning of developing a concept,

model, or theme, or by using appropriate metaphor and analogy; also the ability to develop creative solutions and new insights into problems.

7   *Diagnostic use of concepts.* Deductive reasoning, using a concept or model to interpret events, analyse situations, distinguish between relevant and irrelevant information, and detect deviations from plans.

8   *Use of socialised power.* Ability to develop networks and coalitions, gain cooperation from others, resolve conflicts in a constructive manner, and use role modelling to influence others.

9   *Managing group process.* Ability to manage group processes to build member identification and team spirit by creating symbols of group identity, emphasising common interests and need for collaboration, encouraging successful teamwork, and providing public recognition of member contributions.

In summary, Boyatzis inferred competencies from descriptions of effective and ineffective behaviour, based on incidents distinguishing more effective from less effective managers. The competencies included motives, personality traits, cognitive skills, and interpersonal skills. In general, his findings were quite similar to those from earlier trait studies using different research methods.

The quest for the definitive, comprehensive, universal "periodic table" of competencies has continued. For instance, Dulewicz (1989, 1992, 1994) was convinced that there were 12 "totally independent" dimensions of performance or key supra-competencies derived from 49 primary competencies. He argued:

> The Supra-Competencies constitute 12 independent dimensions of middle management performance, based on self and boss ratings from a wide range of organisations, which account for more of the total variance in performance. They could, therefore, form the basis of generic personnel selection specifications, dimensions for performance, appraisal systems and as a development needs analysis tool. At a minimum, the model could be used as a template against which to check if company systems are exhaustive and, if not, where possible gaps exist.

Supra-Competencies

Short definitions of 12 independent performance factors:

Intellectual

1   *Strategic perspective.* Rises above the detail to see the broader issues and implications; takes account of wide-ranging influences and situations both inside and outside the organization before planning and acting.

2   *Analysis and judgement.* Seeks all relevant information; identifies problems, relates relevant data, and identifies causes; assimilates numerical data accurately and makes sensible interpretations; work is precise and methodical, and relevant detail is not overlooked. Makes decisions based on logical assumptions that reflect factual information.

3   *Planning and organisation.* Plans priorities, assignments and the allocation of resources; organises resources efficiently and effectively, delegating work to the appropriate staff.

Interpersonal

4   *Managing staff.* Adopts appropriate styles for achieving group objectives, monitors and evaluates their work; shows vision and inspiration; develops the skills and competencies of staff.

5   *Persuasiveness.* Influences and persuades others to give their agreement and commitment; in face of conflict, uses personal influence to communicate proposals, to reach bases for compromise and to reach an agreement.

6   *Assertiveness and decisiveness.* Ascendant, forceful dealing with others; can take charge; is willing to take risks and seek new experiences; is decisive, ready to take decisions, even on limited information.

7   *Interpersonal.* Shows consideration for the needs and feelings and takes account of them; is flexible when dealing with others.

8   *Oral communication.* Fluent, speaks clearly and audibly, with good audience levels of understanding.

Adaptability

9   *Adaptability and resilience.* Adapts behaviour to new situations; resilient, maintains effectiveness in face of adversity or unfairness. Performance remains stable when under pressure or opposition; does not become irritable and anxious, retains composure.

Results-orientation

10   *Energy and initiative.* Makes a strong, positive impression, has authority and credibility; is a self-starter and originator, actively influences events to achieve goals; has energy and vitality, maintains high level of activity and produces a high level of output.

11   *Achievement-motivation.* Sets demanding goals for self and for others, and is dissatisfied with average performance; makes full use of own time and resources; sees a task through to completion, irrespective of obstacles and setbacks.

12   *Business sense.* Identifies opportunities that will increase sales or profits; selects and exploits those activities that will result in the largest return.

Source: V. Dulewicz (1989). Assessment centres as the route to competence. *Personnel Management, 11,* 56–59.

However, Woodruffe (1993) pointed out the similarities between the exclusive and "unique" competencies of various companies. He drew up a table of the competencies used by five major British companies and showed how similar they were (Table 11.1). The fact that different organisations end up with very similar wish-list competencies implies either that competencies are universal or that the companies that actually specify them have almost identical models.

However, other quite different systems exist. Thus, Evers and Rush (1996) listed 18 skills (sort of primary competencies), which they categorised into "four base competencies." They were:

Table 11.1 Woodruffe's comparisons

Cadbury Schweppes	W H Smith	BP	Manchester Airport	National Westminster Bank
Strategy	Written communication	Personal drive	Critical reasoning	Information search
Drive	Oral communication	Organisational drive	Strategic visioning	Concept information
Relationships	Leadership	Impact	Business know-how	Conceptual flexibility
Persuasion	Team membership	Communication	Achievement drive	Interpersonal search
Leadership	Planning and organising skills	Awareness of others	Proactivity	Managing interaction
Followership	Decision making	Team management	Confidence	Developmental orientation
Analysis	Motivation	Persuasiveness	Control	Impact
Implementation	Personal strength	Analytical power	Flexibility	Achievement orientation
Personal factors	Analytical reasoning skills	Strategic thinking Commercial judgement Adaptive orientation	Concern for effectiveness Direction Motivation Interpersonal skills Concern for impact Persuasion Influence	Self-confidence Presentation Proactive orientation

Source: Woodruffe (1993, p. 81). Used with the permission of CIPD Publishing.

1 *Mobilising innovation and change*. Ability to conceptualise, creativity, risk-taking, visioning.
2 *Managing people and tasks*. Coordinating, decision making, leadership/influence, managing conflict, planning and organising.
3 *Communicating*. Interpersonal, listing, oral communication, written communication.
4 *Managing self*. Learning, time management, personal strategies, problem solving.

Despite the fact that so many lists and "models" exist, they are characterised more by their similarity than their differences. This implies that there is a set of traits, abilities and motivations that are related to *success in all jobs*. Personality psychologists believe these can be summed up in terms of a set number (3–7) of specific, clear, unrelated personality traits (like stability) and general intelligence (see Chapters 3 and 4).

Methods for deciding on competencies

According to Adams (1998), there are three key methods for identifying competencies, though they share many common features and only one of these methods was specifically designed to be used in competency analysis.

1. Critical Incident Techniques (CIT)

The idea is to identify how employees behaved during complex, sudden, unforeseen difficult events. Questions include: the specific nature of the problem/situation; who was involved; what were the objectives; what the person actually did and with what effect – therefore, which behaviours were least and most effective. The focus is on behaviours that were successful; these are then grouped into categories, dimensions, or "competencies". This is an expensive method that depends on the insight and honesty of the employee and the skill of the interviewer, both in the "chat" and writing up the data. Further, the method overlooks the many tedious, humdrum, but important tasks that have to be done.

2. Behavioural Event Interviews (BEI)

This is similar to the CITs but focuses more on the person – his/her thoughts, feelings and motivation. The method also seeks to compare the responses of good, average and weak employees in an attempt to find discriminating and predictive behaviours. Again, interviews are analysed and coded for competencies. The interview also considers "folklore" values, namely job incumbents' ideas about the things needed to do the job effectively. Reliability is evaluated by having two coders rate the taped interviews. Validity is evaluated by determining whether the competencies differentiate between known groups in the organisation and predict superior future performance. The method inevitably generates a huge amount of data. However, like biodata, it may be too historically focused. Further, if known groups – high flyers/average performers/weak performers – can't be clearly identified, then the whole system may fail.

3. Repertory Grid (RG)

Derived from clinical psychology, this method uses people to generate constructs. Thus, people (managers, employees) are given the names of three colleagues and asked to specify a dimension (construct) that differentiates one from two others (i.e. confident vs. nervous). Once a list of constructs is generated, they are put into an array, which is a process of explaining who is more effective, confident, or nervous, and why. Finally, experts are asked to describe the typical behaviours of confident people that differentiate them from nervous or anxious employees. This last step yields the competencies. The analysis also yields insights into personal values. However, the people who complete the REP grid may not fully understand the demands, pressures, and role requirements of others at work.

Berman (1997) compared the way competencies are conceived in America, Britain, and France. In America three issues seem unresolved: (1) there is no single agreed-upon method of assessing managerial competency; (2) there is uncertainty as to whether competencies encompass the actual responsibilities of managers; and (3) there is doubt about whether competencies even define the role of managers in a useful way. In France, according to Berman (1997), competency is a cognitive concept – know-how, not performance. Work is defined in terms of acquired knowledge. Yet many French companies still believe formal qualifications are the best criteria for selection and development. The British either follow the American tradition or follow the functional route, which focuses on acceptable performance and adequate knowledge rather than excellent performance. A major problem is that once people have been "certified competent" there is little motivation to check if their subsequent performance is competent.

Moloney (1997) argued that one needs to distinguish between capability and performance when considering competencies. The former refers to skills, knowledge and understanding while the latter refers to achieving targets. The application of capability leads to performance. Competency consultants try to identify clusters of behaviours that are specific, observable and verifiable, and can be theoretically or empirically classified together. Note the emphasis on observable behaviours, which suggests those skills/abilities (like creative thinking) that are hard to observe, may be ignored.

Ziyal (1997) pointed out that most competency specifications and ratings are categorical not continuous. By that she means one can determine that people either do or do not have them; or that they could be judged to have (or not have) the potential to acquire them. But competency analyses typically say nothing about the level and range of competencies needed or whether different business contexts demand different competencies. Her solution is not new, though it is expressed in the language of competencies: identify critical performance (competency) demands of the typical situations associated with a job and then select and train for them.

Drakeley and White (1999) argued that the term competency was an all-purpose umbrella word that meant all things to all people. The two most commonly confused issues are "things" at which people are competent vs. "things" competent people possess. Drakeley and White further argued that: "the evidence strongly suggests that whatever assessment centres measure, they are not measuring competencies with any degree of precision. If anything they measure exercise performance rather than enduring traits or competencies" (p. 7). Rather cynically they point out than organisations have competency lists, frameworks, models or architecture – and the term they use depends on how much they paid their consultants!

They argue it is crucial to distinguish between:

- *Competence* – an individual's capacity to perform a task competently
- *Competency* – a particular skill, ability, knowledge quality possessed by an individual.

Further, it is relevant to distinguish between the task people need to perform and the qualities that they need to perform it and which competencies are needed in order to carry out a task with competence. Thus, a competence task is preparing a budget while conscientiousness is a competency.

Roberts (1998) attempted to introduce personality measures into a system using four categories of competencies. These include a *natural* cluster (essentially four big personality traits), an acquired cluster (experience, professional/technical education), an *"adapting"* cluster, which includes motivational variables, and a *"performing"* output cluster, which includes the observable behaviours resulting from the other two.

To complicate matters further, Losey (1999) provides the following "equation":

intelligence + education + experience + ethics + interest = competency

It is precisely these sorts of "equations" that have given competencies a bad name. This equation does not specify *what* type of intelligence (verbal, spatial, mathematical, crystallised/fluid) nor does it specify *how many* there might be. It is even possible to have too much or too little intelligence. The equation does not weight intelligence or the other four factors; nor does it distinguish between education and experience. In being "all things to all men", competence ends up being a hopeless concept.

Research questions

What are the characteristics of a good, competent framework? In essence, they need to be:

- *Simple*. Parsimonious, not overcomplex, more understandable than fully comprehensive competency frameworks.
- *Salient*. They must be relevant to line mangers, staff, senior managers, and the business objectives and plan.
- *Supported*. They have to be fully supported in terms of staff and money, and, most importantly, morally championed consistently from the top.
- *Flexible*. It must be recognised that all systems are temporary and in need of updating regularly, based on changed circumstances.
- *Rewarding*. The application of the system must be rewarded, particularly for line managers and staff. The former need to see it helps the process of good management and the latter need feedback, qualifications, etc.
- *Developmental*. The idea that the system needs to be initially linked into developmental opportunities for senior managers.
- *Communicated*. The aims, deadlines and benefits of the project need to be spelt out clearly, regularly and simply – and best not oversold.
- *Adaptable*. The system must allow for certain individual departments to add specific or technical competencies. Having both unique and shared competencies.

Furnham (2000b) reached several conclusions from a research and review project on the topic. He suggested dispensing with the concept of competency because of its associations and ambiguities. He also proposed that seven plus or minus two, were enough individual difference factors for any organisation.

He also noted six interesting omissions in the literature:

1. Succession management and manpower planning

Though it is easy to see that competencies are useful for succession planning, they tend not to be used exclusively to drive the process. It seems as if the competency framework "informed" persons responsible for succession planning but did not constrain or limit them to this. Part of the problem appeared to be that the competencies did not take sufficiently into account specialist competencies. Other reasons included not having a succession management strategy; but perhaps the most important problem is that few companies have good databases on the current competencies of their staff.

2. Filling critical jobs

It is always nice to show how useful a system/framework is to solve particular problems, such as filling critical jobs. Inevitably those tend to be either highly specialist jobs or very senior middle-management jobs. Ironically most companies' frameworks seemed unsuited for either, particularly the former. Again, the language of competencies helped clarify discussions when such posts were filled but seemed not to drive the process.

3. Predict future competencies

Some organisations became aware that frameworks were either too static or too backward looking to be useful. Hence, some focused on the issue of potential and the competencies that seemed to predict it. This was not the same as attempting to predict how the competency might have to change to respond to new and different organisations. Thus, for instance, very few organisations attempted to do future-oriented strategic planning and link the anticipated future needs and structure of the company to future frameworks. There seemed little evidence that any one competency would become more or less important over time, let alone which would disappear altogether and which others would emerge over time.

4. Competencies and leadership

The success of introducing a competency framework depended heavily on it being championed by high-profile organisational leaders, preferably the CEO and the members of the board. However, few talked about the leadership style in the organisation (e.g. authoritarian, democratic) and how this itself may have helped or hindered the whole process of introducing a competency framework. Moreover, leadership styles differ in different parts of an organisation, and this may have accounted for the fact that the competency framework approach was embedded so easily and quickly in some parts but resisted so much in others. Further, it was never clear whether leadership (as opposed to management) was one of many competencies or "super-competencies" or the sum of all (or most) of the competencies put together. The competency movement has in some senses usurped the concept of leadership. There was, for instance, no talk of the different competencies required for transactional versus transformational leaders.

5. Corporate culture

In the 1990s there was a great deal of interest in the concept of corporate culture and there were many attempts made to assess or categorise culture. It was argued that corporate culture had a very powerful and often "subliminal effect" on organisations that influenced all aspects of the business such as structure, systems and processes. Thus, one could use various corporate culture models to predict which organisations would embrace and which resist the introduction of competency frameworks. The idea of corporate culture was, however, hardly ever mentioned to describe organisational processes or attempt to explain why they succeeded or failed.

6. The link between the business plan and the competencies

Although the "text books" point to the idea that competencies must be derived and driven from the business plan, this seemed more rhetoric than reality. When competency frameworks were being planned, there seemed to be some concern with the linkage, but after that the idea seemed to have been dropped. It is obviously difficult to translate business/strategic plans and concepts into the language of competency. The former is about strategy and process and the latter about people. Not only is the linkage difficult but also business plans can change radically over the course of a year and from year to year. Thus, even if the link was well established in the first place, it would have to be reforged at least on an annual basis. Because it took companies 2–3 years to put their initial competency frameworks in place, the process of subsequently updating the plan seemed to slip.

The competent organisation

Some writers have talked about competent organisations, rather than individuals. Burn and Dearlove (1995) argued that the effectiveness of a competency approach depended on its ability to raise the performance of an organisation by improving the performance of everyone in it. They believed that a competent organisation would measure and then manage the "hard" and "soft" competencies for each job as they followed from the business plan. Burn and Dearlove described organisational competencies and associated critical competence indicators and stated (1995, p. 37):

> We can now pull together the measurement model for the competent organisation into six basic steps as follows:
>
> 1   The senior management team identifies the organisational competencies required to support the business strategy and the crucial competence indicators that determine the measurements necessary to validate the competency programme.
> 2   The competency task force translates what is required and cascades this information to managers.
> 3   Changes in individual behaviour and competence are measured by managers and reported to the competency task force.
> 4   Components of the competency development programme are monitored by feedback from participants and task force assessments.
> 5   Results of each of the measures are fed into the competency programme to improve the quality of content and delivery.
> 6   The process is audited continuously at each stage to improve standards of assessment.

One important cause of organisational incompetence is that organisations select managers for particular skills and characteristics that they believe are needed to meet current business demands. But when these demands change, and they can do so very quickly, the skills and characteristics of managers must change. Thus, it is not uncommon for senior managers to discover that they are not as well suited to the new conditions as they were the old. Some individuals are ideally suited to start-up operations, others to maintaining existing operations, and still others to rebuilding.

Gerstein and Reisman (1983) argued that managerial selection should be linked to business strategy. They defined various different business situations – start-up, turn-around, rationalising existing business, divesting people (downsizing), maintaining existing business, and making new acquisitions – then they specified the major job thrusts. Following this, they specified the traits or ideal characteristics of managers for each particular phase. Thus, for the situation of liquidation they suggested that managers needed the following characteristics: callous, highly analytic, risk-taking, low glory seeking, and wanting to be respected but not necessarily liked.

Strategic selection, according to Gerstein and Reisman (1983), involves six steps: (1) specifying business conditions and strategic direction; (2) getting an appropriate organisation structure; (3) developing a description for each key managerial job in the structure; (4) assessing key personnel; (5) matching individuals with positions; and (6) implementing the plan.

In this strategic staffing model, incompetent managers are essentially misfits. They have been retained and rewarded by people who believe in the concept of the universal manager – the notion that a good manager can handle any problem, regardless of its peculiar demands. The assumption is that really good managers can adapt to any conditions. Although this may be true of a few, talented, younger managers, the evidence suggests that it is less true of most managers.

The lesson here is that some managerial incompetence is caused either by poor selection – i.e. not getting a good fit in the first place – or by changing circumstances – as a result of which a different mix of dispositions and attitudes becomes necessary.

Conclusion

The competence concept brought both advantages and disadvantages to human relations practitioners. It brought a common, shared descriptive language to talk about individuals at work and their unique performance. However, it also brought a lot of meaningless psychobabble like "take the helicopter view" or "think outside the box", which are conceived of as individual difference variables but resist clear definition or operationalisation. That is, various competencies were extremely ill defined and therefore very problematic to operationalise or measure.

The concept also stressed the need for the measurement of performance and the benefits of giving people regular and specific feedback on that performance.

However, Watson-Wyatt (1998), an international consultancy, noted six benefits of the competency system: (1) articulating what the organisation values; (2) providing a common language for employees and managers to describe value creation; (3) establishing a new paradigm for human resources programmes (organisational levers); (4) focusing on the development of the individual instead of on the organisation structure; (5) linking pay, promotions and growth directly to what the organisation values to be successful; and (6) guiding employees and managers as to what is expected and how value is defined even in times of dramatic change and restructuring.

Other researchers have also come to interesting conclusions. Strebler et al.'s (1997) findings had clear implications for best practices:

1   Introducing competencies without a clear business purpose raises staff suspicion.
2   The perceived job fit and relevance of competency frameworks influences users' satisfaction.

3   Competencies have made the process of performance review more open.
4   Interpersonal skills are perceived to be the most difficult to assess and develop.
5   Competencies are perceived to improve the consistency and fairness of the assessment and measurement process, but not the outcome (e.g. competency measures).
6   The outcomes of the performance review (e.g. link to pay and/or training) impact on users' confidence with their use of competencies.
7   Competencies raise the expectations that improved performance will be rewarded.

Reviews in this area tend to be more from a human resource and practical perspective than that of a differential psychologist. Further, many writers assert things based on a few case studies rather than good empirical studies, which are clearly missing from this literature.

If HR specialists used "competence frameworks" that were simple, salient, flexible, rewarding, adaptable and that stressed the need for personal development, they were usually successful. However, they often failed. The most common reasons were:

- Not having enough or the right "champion(s)" to introduce the competency framework from the start. That is, senior managers, did not really believe in it.
- The development phase was too long and drawn out, and out of date by the time it was introduced.
- The framework itself was too complicated and inclusive to be easily understandable and usable. Some companies would have 35 competencies, which is far too many when we know people only have 5–7 clearly identifiable unique traits.
- Line managers received confused messages about the use and purpose of the system, they felt they were "oversold" on it early on, then experienced it as a bureaucratic burden.
- Not understanding the need for flexibility, in that frameworks require constant updating. As organisations and jobs change so do the competencies of the people within.
- Not allowing for a distinction between general vs. specific/technical frameworks and not ensuring that the business plan and the competency framework remain aligned as the former changes over time.

The world of competencies and the world of personality and ability do still not overlap. Despite the fact that human resource practitioners are some of the heaviest users of psychometric tests, it remains a mystery as to why those two conceptually closely aligned worlds remain so far apart. This may be explained by the fact that the competencies movement has in fact served the useful and important function of job analysis. That is, by understanding what people do and how they do it efficiently. Competencies have served to describe in detail the types of skills and temperaments successful job holders need to have.

12 The future of differential psychology and assessment and selection

Introduction

How will selection and assessment in 2050 or even 2020 be different from how it is today (Anderson, 2003; Barrick et al., 2001; Salgado & Moscoso, 2003; Truxillo et al., 2006)? How will our knowledge of, and ability to measure, personality and intelligence be reflected in new assessment methods and techniques? It is easy to both over- and underestimate the changes at work that have occurred in the last 50 years. Some would argue, looking at selection in certain sectors like the military or the law, that there has been surprisingly *little change* over the past 50 years. After all, assessment centres were being used in World War II. Further, intelligence tests were being used in the World War I. Yet, economic, legal and technological changes have had a high impact on selection by dictating modern organisations' particular practices.

Still, today most organisations are heavily reliant on the "big three" – application form, interview, references. In some sectors there seems to have been little change, nor is there likely to be. This occurs for many reasons. Some organisations do not invest the time and money to ensure that their selection experts (often human resource specialists) know much about specific technique issues or the latest thinking about selection. They can be poorly informed, often misinformed, or out of date. Others believe that selection is less important than development: that is, one can train, mould, shape and motivate people to whatever criterion, whoever one is given. In this sense, getting selection "right" is less important than doing appropriate training.

On the other hand, some futurologists see vast and fundamental changes happening with respect to how, when, why and of whom assessment and selection takes place. For some these changes and developments are *immanent*; for others they are still in a sort of *science-fiction* future. For some most of these changes are welcome. They are positive and desirable. For others they represent the opposite: an infringement on their freedom; high additional and unnecessary costs; or a sort of bio-determinism that makes biology destiny.

For those who speculate about the future, based on either a wise or wild extrapolation of what they see in the present, various developments are portended as a result of five changes:

1. Biological markers

It can be hypothesised that with tremendous developments in the brain (and neuro) sciences we will be able to detect, measure and assess crucially important select-in and select-out factor by using biological markers. Thus, fMRI scans, mouth swabs, and blood samples will replace psychometric tests, interviews and the like. Our DNA will be on file everywhere and in it will be the information selectors need. These are seen to be accurate, cheap and valid predictors of individual factors that predict job success. Just as pupilometry will replace passports so physiology will replace psychology as the primary method to evaluate and assess individuals. This, then, may herald the end of self-report questionnaires of personality and even timed ability tests.

2. *Demographic changes*

Sudden, but dramatic, changes in the profile of the jobforce means that no longer will certain jobs be traditionally staffed by particular groups. Thus, young White males are not plentiful in certain countries in Europe to take up certain positions. Assessing people from different ages, cultural and linguistic traditions is, indeed, an important challenge. New assessment devices will need to be found to measure people accurately and fairly. There may have to be a lot less reliance on verbal measures (i.e. interview and questionnaire) and more on other simpler but equally sensitive and valid measures.

3. *The Internet*

Computerisation and the Internet are offering new opportunities and new problems at the same time. It can make remote testing of people possible. It can mean that reports can be computerised and feedback immediate. It is also difficult to regulate. This means that it is difficult to "patrol" or regulate the web. All sorts of people can post tests of dubious validity on the net. People are concerned that it is not always easy to validate who is actually completing the test. Nevertheless, the Internet has influenced the whole business of selection and assessment, and will continue to do so.

4. *Legal changes*

Legal pre- and proscriptions have already had a big impact on testing. Thus, test data may or may not be legally used to make decisions. Countries and states can ban certain types of test such as the "lie detector". Governments listen to professional bodies (i.e. psychological associations), to patient groups, to minority groups and their specialist advisors. They may try to control the spread of assessors and testees through various techniques such a being a registered test user or a licensed provider. This can have considerable consequences on the assessment industry and partly already accounts for national differences in assessment.

5. *Popular, political, press reactions*

Whatever tests are used, applicants are naturally very interested in the methods by which they are selected. People say that they want them to be accurate, open and fair. They worry about being inappropriately discriminated against. As a result, many are now interested in, and in fact rewarded for, litigation against potential employers who they believe rejected them for unjust reasons. They go to the press, and lobby their local politicians and others to plead their case. Their aim is to embarrass the organisations and bring them into disrepute. Organisations are very sensitive to their methods and have to trade off clear evidence of psychometric validity for popular acceptance of the technique or strategy. Hence, the possibility arises that highly valid methods are not used while highly dubious ones are.

These five societal and scientific changes will no doubt influence how we assess individual differences in the workplace. Some of these changes are already very apparent; others are on the horizon.

In an interesting, important and theory-derived paper, Klehe (2004) has speculated on *institutional pressures* affecting the adoption of personnel-selection procedures. Based on her theoretical model, she has derived 16 propositions that seem a good starting point for research. They are:

Proposition 1

The smaller the long-term financial gain perceived to be attainable from the adoption of a selection procedure, the less likely the organisation is to adopt this procedure.

Proposition 2

The greater the short-term costs expected from the adoption of a specific selection procedure, the less likely the organisation is to adopt this procedure: (a) The higher the initial investment for development and validation expected from the adoption of a selection procedure, the less likely the organisation is to adopt this procedure; (b) The higher the ongoing investment for administration expected from the adoption of a selection procedure, the less likely the organisation is to adopt this procedure.

Proposition 3

The more dependent the organisation is on the approval by owners focusing on short-term benefits, and the greater financial expenditures expected from the adoption of a specific selection procedure, the less likely the organisation is to adopt this procedure: Publicly traded organisations will be less likely to invest heavily in personnel selection than organisations owned privately or by the public sector.

Proposition 4

The more a selection procedure is perceived to contradict the legal regulations of the country the organisation is located in, the less likely the organisation is to adopt this procedure.

Proposition 5

The more dependent the organisation is on fulfilling legal regulations, and the less legally defensive the adoption of a specific selection procedure is perceived to be, the less likely the organisation is to adopt this procedure: The more dependent the organisation is on governmental contracts, and the less legally defensive the adoption of a specific selection procedure is perceived to be, the less likely the organisation is to adopt this procedure.

Proposition 6

The more severe the legal coercion behind the request to use legally defensible selection procedures is perceived to be, and the less legally defensive the adoption of a specific selection procedure is perceived to be, the less likely the organisation is to adopt this procedure: (a) The more legal charges an organisation has faced concerning its selection procedures, and the less legally defensive the adoption of a specific selection procedure is perceived to be, the less likely the organisation is to adopt this procedure; (b) The larger the organisation and the less legally defensive the adoption of a specific selection procedure is perceived to be, the less likely the organisation is to adopt this procedure.

Proposition 7

The more adversely the organisation believes applicants to evaluate a certain selection procedure, the less likely the organisation is to adopt this procedure.

Proposition 8

The fewer applicants the organisation has to choose from, the more dependent it is on filling its vacant posts, and the more adversely applicants are believed to evaluate a certain selection procedure, the less likely the organisation is to adopt this procedure.

Proposition 9

The more the adoption of a selection procedure defies multiple conflicting pressures (even though it may have been developed to satisfy one of them), the less likely the organisation is to adopt this procedure.

Proposition 10

The more an organisation has an internal labour market, and the less valid a selection procedure is, the less likely the organisation is to adopt this procedure.

Proposition 11

The smaller the financial resources the organisation has for selecting new employees (e.g. small firms), and the greater financial expenditures expected from the adoption of a specific selection procedure, the less likely the organisation is to adopt this procedure.

Proposition 12

(a) The less a selection procedure is perceived to permit the reproduction of the organisation's status quo, and the more the organisation is interested in maintaining that status quo, the less likely the organisation is to adopt this procedure; (b) The less a selection procedure is perceived to allow for a change of the organisation's status quo, and the less the organisation is interested in maintaining that status quo, the less likely the organisation is to adopt this procedure.

Proposition 13

The more constraining administrators perceive a selection procedure to be on the selection processes and decisions, the less likely the organisation is to adopt this procedure.

Proposition 14

The fewer other organisations in an organisation's industry and local labour market have adopted a kind of selection procedure, the less likely the organisation is to adopt this procedure.

Proposition 15

The more the organisation maintains relations with other organisations in its field, and the less these other organisations use a specific selection procedure, the less likely the organisation is to adopt this procedure.

Proposition 16

The less uncertain the future appears, the less likely the organisation is to adopt other organisations' procedures.

Future trends only in part follow from previous practices. Futurology is an exciting, albeit imprecise, discipline. However, there are enough technical, demographic, socio-cultural and economic, clearly decipherable, trends to make it reasonably certain that specific changes will occur in the world of assessment and selection.

The politics of assessment

The assessment of a person's abilities, aptitudes, personality and values is never a simple scientific process because nearly always the assessment has important repercussions. One is assessed or evaluated for something, against criteria and compared to other candidates.

Scientists want assessment to be valid, reliable and differentiating. Others, however, are concerned with issues like fairness, bias and discrimination. Even where assessment is made strictly for "developmental purposes" there are issues around why people are treated differently. Most countries have laws pertaining to assessment: which issues, questions and procedures are unacceptable and which acceptable. Second, there are learned bodies and professional associations that always pre- and proscribe particular processes. Third, organisations have histories of test use and procedure that set particular precedents. Finally, individuals have their own experience and values, which dictate how they choose to assess and evaluate.

There are, and will always be, people who object to the very notion of any sort of psychological assessment because of its consequences. The issue is essentially political although it may be discussed in ethical or psychometric terminology. There are, however, various specific sorts of issues that one may distinguish. The first refers to *group differences* (age, gender, race): whether they exist and what to do about them. The second refers to *change*: whether, how or how easily observed individual differences are open to change. The third refers to *socio-legal practices* and the existence of interested and concerned bodies like professional bodies and how the assessment challenges their assumptions. The fourth refers to *crypto-political pressure groups* whose aim is to further a political cause with respect to staffing organisations. Each can put political pressure on assessors and evaluators.

1. Group differences

Those involved in test development and evaluations have inevitably to be concerned with group differences, particularly sex and race differences, in both ability and personality. Once a difference has been consistently established, say that males are superior to females or Whites to Blacks, *or vice versa*, there remain two issues: first, is this a result of test procedure? (rather than veridical evidence of a difference) and, second, if there is a real difference, how does one explain that difference? Next, most people want to know how to eradicate that difference or at least compensate for it.

Many people want to believe that we are all born equal: with equivalent abilities, aptitudes, skills, even personality. This is patently not true, so others redefine this as born with equal potentialities suggesting that with differential encouragement, education and training we can all attain equal or equivalent (superior) status. This too seems fanciful – but this is about ideology not science.

Many academics have backed away from intelligence research because they both find and acknowledge group differences, including age differences. No matter what explanations (genetic, psychological, and sociological) they provide they are vilified.

Others demand that before tests are used they are demonstrated to *be* fair and that when they are used this is *done* fairly. The former involves testing large samples to "prove" that they do not show group differences. Alternatively, a selection criterion is set such that equal proportions from different groups are chosen. This may involve normalising the data or else having different cut-off scores for different groups.

The group differences agenda has moved from gender and race to religion and age. There are quite clearly both cohort and ageing difference correlates of test scores. Thus, IQ test scores, particularly of fluid intelligence, peak and then decline quite noticeably and quickly after the age of 50 years. This would mean that such tests would "unfairly" discriminate against the middle aged. The same issue arises with handicapped people over a wide range of handicaps, be they physical or mental. As a result, the area soon becomes a minefield for the selector interested in choosing the ideal or best person for the particular job.

2. Personality and ability change

The training departments of most organisations are in the business of change. They attempt to improve or increase the competencies and skills of staff so that they are more efficient and productive. However, what is less clear is whether more fundamental features of individuals can be changed. Whilst many acknowledge that one can improve IQ test scores (by say one third of an *SD*) by practice, one can not substantially increase intelligence after the teenage years.

Equally, if personality is essentially hard wired it is virtually impossible to train an extravert to become an introvert. It is possible to train behaviours so that, for example, introverts "look" more extraverted. Hence, the concept of the socialised extravert. The same is true for all the other personality traits.

For many, it is seen to be *pessimistic defeatism* not to believe that people can be taught to radically change so that at work they become both happier and more satisfied. Those who doubt the changeability assertion threaten much training enterprise and place more stress and pressure on those who do selection and assessment.

The possibility of permanent change and development is also an ideological issue. Though the debate can be informed by good empirical studies it rarely is. Hence, it becomes a political assertion regarding how much money and effort should be put on finding (i.e. selecting) the best people as opposed to developing (i.e. training) individuals.

3. Social and professional practices

Different professionals get involved in the process of selection and assessment. In many countries those professionals are tightly regulated. Thus, human resource practitioners may be required, or encouraged, to belong to various professional bodies. Equally, to practise as a clinical or organisational psychologist in many countries one may have to acquire very specific qualifications and show evidence of continuing professional development.

Countries differ in who is regulated and how. There are also interesting cultural factors, which result in certain groups of individuals, like graphologists or *feng shui* experts, having considerable power and influence without regulation.

There is an extensive sociological literature on the issue of professionalisation, which points always to issues around power as dominant groups seek to retain power. Thus, in some countries, psychologists of all sorts are regulated by medical councils, or human resource specialists report to lawyers.

Thus, who is "licensed" to do assessment becomes a socio-legal issue, not simply one of competence and expertise. Further, the licensed may have to follow particular procedures, which may or may not have rigorous scientific evidence to support them.

4. Crypto-political influences

Many groups have considerable interests in who gets particular jobs. People in some jobs exercise considerable power either openly or less obviously. Thus, police selection, civil-service selection, and the selection of teachers and lecturers becomes controversial. Trade unions, political parties, think tanks and other groups see the relevance of getting "their people" into top jobs.

Many of the "political" forces at work in selection and assessment are not obvious. They are, nevertheless, present and surface from time to time, often having considerable impact. Clearly, all this goes to show that recruitment, assessment and selection is far from a dispassionate, empirically based, social science. It can be fairly easily held hostage to fortune.

Changes that are with us

Some themes or activities are already noticeable with respect to changes in the world of selection and recruitment. The following are noticeable.

The development of job-specific psychometric profiles

This is a client-led, test-publisher type of innovation where employers want to select people for very particular jobs like being a salesperson or a submariner. Thus, one may have an accountants' or an air-traffic controllers' personality test. They often use both power and/or preference measures that assess the particular attributes or qualities that make up a successful person in that particular field. Whilst this is no doubt attractive to the client, the whole enterprise is heavily dependent on the current predictive validity data on that particular job. Further, it is possible that what people sell (cars vs. computers) could make a considerable difference. A good example of this is the "pro-active" personality that is defined as a disposition toward taking action to influence one's environment and is said to relate to many positive career outcomes like salary, promotion and career satisfaction (Thompson, 2003).

More interest on the select-out, dark-side factors

An interest in managerial incompetence and derailment has led researchers, test publishers and human-resource experts to focus in on variables, like the personality disorders, which are valid predictors of failure rather than success. This means, rather than rejecting people because they did not have "enough" of some quality, they are rejected because of too much of a relevant trait. Because of concerns with fraud, theft and sabotage at work, as well as management derailment, there is now a significant interest in the "dark side" of behaviour at work and how to prevent it (Furnham & Taylor, 2004).

The return and rebranding of assessment centres

Although considerable time and money has to be spent on well-devised assessment centres it remains clearly true that they have impressive construct and predictive validity. Hence, there remains an interest in rebranding and updating them in order to ensure that they provide an efficient, effective, multi-source data set on individuals. However, they are expensive and time consuming and there is a serious concern about how to ensure that each exercise plays a relevant role and has predictive validity.

Emphasis on ability, capacity and intelligence

The use of intelligence or ability tests in the workplace remains highly contentious, at least among candidates or practitioners. However, we know that, certainly among senior (complex) jobs, they remain the best predictor of work success. More selectors are beginning to recognise this and are attempting to devise face-valid, yet robust, measures of ability, such as proofreading or business problem-solving tasks. Despite various litigation threats, selectors are now realising the importance of using intelligence tests even if they come under new guises such as "proofreading" tests (Furnham et al., 2006).

In most western countries the changing demography has had a big impact on selection and assessment

There is an ageing native workforce and a new less-skilled migrant workforce. This has led to questions about the employability of older people as well as how to fairly assess people from different cultures who speak different languages. In essence, this is about cross-cultural assessment issues. In the workplace, it is human resource specialists who "shoulder most of the burden" for selection and assessment. Until relatively recently, many seemed poorly informed, or even uninformed, about developments in differential psychology. As a result, they seemed to be at the mercy of consultants and test publishers because they were not able to ask salient and penetrating questions about the tools and processes that they were being sold. This situation is changing dramatically, with well-educated HR managers using the latest methods in selection and assessment.

Whilst it seems self-evident that work-sampling test results are a good predictor of work itself, the probationary period has apparently fallen out of favour in many organisations

To a great extent the probationary period is a work-sample test that assesses a person's ability to do the job. It measures typical rather than maximal performance. Organisations are increasingly seeing the value of it. It seems pretty self-evident that actual ability to do the job for a short, albeit extended, period is the *best predictor* of doing the job. In short, the ability to do the job is best predicted by a job "try out". Further, the length of the try out – a day, a week, a month – is no doubt important because it reveals more clearly the difference between typical and maximal performance. Although an expensive method, it may nonetheless be one of the best. The question remains, however, as to who to choose to take part in the try out.

In many countries there is still a great concern with the lack of diversity in the workforce

This has to be seen as the result of direct and indirect discrimination against specific groups, notably women, people of Afro-Caribbean origin and specific Asians. Some countries and organisations are now attempting to impose a quota to ensure that organisations more accurately reflect the population as a whole. These are socio-political not psychometric questions, though they inevitably have an impact on the whole business of assessment and selection. There will no doubt be other sociological, political and economic changes that influence selection. Certainly, the world of work is changing and finding the right people for new jobs, or old jobs done differently, will always remain problematic.

Alternative approaches

As well as trait approaches to personality and intelligence there are biological, cognitive and psychoanalytic approaches, all of which have been considered in different sections of this book.

It is, however, important to briefly note alternatives or challenges to trait psychology (Haslam, 2007). These attacks have been led by philosophers, but have mainly been from social psychologists who launched situational then interactional critiques in the 1970s and 1980s. In essence this approach, which remains alive and well within certain branches of social psychology, doubts the existence of traits at all and suggests that there is little evidence of behavioural consistency. Whilst some acknowledge the existence of traits, they argue that they are far less important than situational variables in explaining behaviour at work.

For both situationists and interactionists social-situational variables at a macro level like corporate culture or at a lower level like group morale are the really powerful determinants of hard and soft outcome variables like productivity, absenteeism or satisfaction.

Whilst the extreme situational critique of the late 1960s has in effect been successfully rebutted, social psychologists continue to emphasise the power of situational factors in shaping behaviour. Many are deeply critical of the idea of a universally applicable coding system for categorising traits.

At the heart of their criticism is the power of traits to explain behaviour. Haslam (2007) believes that their critique has three essential prongs to it. *First*, many trait explanations are circular tautologies. *Second*, traits are either latent variables or inferred hypothetical entities, which are in essence unobserved and unobservable forces. *Third*, trait descriptions provide weak, poor, inadequate descriptions of process.

Whilst it is not difficult to rebut these objections, which has been done, often it is the case that the critique can be, and is, appropriate in certain circumstances. The issue, however, can perhaps be better thought of as the necessary–sufficient distinction (Haslam, 2007). Thus one may argue that traits are necessary for describing behaviour at work but not sufficient. This, of course, begs the question as to what other factors to take into account.

There are various alternatives to traits. These include motives, values and interest. Whilst there is a long-standing interest in the concept of motivation it remains highly problematic. There is no agreed upon taxonomy of motives, nor any psychometrically robust instrument to measure them. More importantly, some doubt whether people could ever accurately report on their motives even if they wanted to.

There is a richer literature on vocational interests (which was covered in Chapter 9). However, it has been suggested that the overlap between taxonomic systems of vocational interests and that of the Big Five trait descriptions is such that they add very little.

There is a long-standing literature on values, which are closer to attitudes and beliefs and have been shown to relate systematically to behaviour at work (and elsewhere). Whilst only a few studies have examined the relationship between traits and values it does seem that they do add some thing over and above traits in their descriptive and explanatory power (Haslam, 2007).

Other factors might include character strengths, derived in large part from new work on positive psychology, as well as goals and personal projects.

For many the necessary–sufficient question and the person–situation debate are empirical questions. There is abundant evidence that traits and abilities predict behaviour at work and can account for a good deal of the variance, often between one and two thirds. Apart from error variance in the measurement of both the independent and the dependent variables, everyone concedes that there are situational and possibly other individual variables that account for the remaining variance. This is indisputable. However, traits supporters may just as easily turn critiques of themselves by social psychologists back on to the latter group themselves to provide descriptions and explanations as to how these social factors and beliefs explain behaviour at work.

State-of-the-art conclusions

Since the beginning of the millennium a number of books with the title *Personality at Work* have appeared. Fontana (2000) placed more emphasis on different approaches to personality. Howard and Howard (2001), on the other hand, have as their subtitle "*How the Big Five Personality Traits Affect Performance, Communication, Teamwork, Leadership and Sales*". They are clearly huge, and perhaps slightly uncritical, fans of the Big Five model, which suggested that people need to be low on N to cope with stress, high on E to be sociable, high on O to encourage curiosity, high on A to be good at negotiation and high on C for focus. Howard and Howard (2001) aim their book at practitioners and do a very persuasive job for the Big Five. Perhaps they go beyond the available data in their interpretation, but they attempt to integrate much material in their "pen-picture" of personality at work.

Nevertheless, what they have attempted to do for the interested person is provide a rich behavioural description of individuals along all Big Five factor dimensions (Table 12.1). Of course, description is not explanation but it certainly is a most lucid way of introducing the non-specialist to the Big Five personality types.

More recently Barrick and Ryan (2003) published a book with the same title, which is subtitled "*Reconsidering the Role of Personality in Organisations*". The chapters cover both familiar and new ground. Lucas and Diener (2003) reviewed the recent positive psychology literature on personality determinants of happiness, seeing the latter as a moderator or mediator variable between the individual and productivity. This seems to be a new individual difference version of the old satisfaction–productivity hypothesis. However, the authors stress that the impact of trait happiness on productivity is very much a function of the task.

The same theme is discussed by Weiss and Kurek (2003), who focus on how personality traits relate to affective or emotional states or moods, which can have a chronic and acute impact on organisational variables. Personality influences emotional regulation, which impacts on outcomes. Indeed the switch in focus from cognitive to affective variables in psychology as a whole has now begun to influence the personality at work literature.

Most of the contributors to the volume are at pains to point out situational, organisational or task constraints that affect the (personality) trait–(work) behaviour relationships. Thus, Barrick et al. (2003a) highlight being cooperative as a competitive demand of the job, as well as personal autonomy and crucial features. Essentially, competitive demands are the vertical, authority-system demands to comply and produce while cooperative demands are the lateral, informal, peer-system demands to cooperate. Extraversion and agreeableness seem particularly relevant to cooperative demands. Barrick et al. see personality variables being related to personal goals, strivings and projects, which are the motivational variables that drive performance outcomes. They separate Accomplishment, Communication and Status Striving.

Johnson (2003) proposed a rather different model, where ability and personality variables predict three sorts of mediator variables: knowledge (declarative, procedural), work habits and motivational processes, which in turn influence job performance and technical proficiency.

Another relatively new area of endeavour is the role of personality in teamwork and "personality of teams". Stewart (2003) explored the idea that personality traits (particularly Agreeableness and Extraversion) impact on teamwork processes, which in

Table 12.1 Clues for estimating a subject's position on the Big Five continuum

Dimension/continuum	Behaviour	Language	Values	Environment (office, car, dress, person)
More reactive (N+)	Is a smoker Is quick to anger Is excitable Is anxious Is extreme in eye contact (gazers and averters) Is somewhat uncomfortable in front of others Is more easily embarrassed, shy Shows signs of discouragement	Tempo changes Makes comments about bodily discomforts Has a tendency to interrupt Finds it harder to say no and resist urges	Tranquillity Universalism, social justice, welfare of all	Sits or stands at a greater distance Easily slips into road rage Is more likely to be and/or appear to be physically out of condition
More resilient (N−)	Remains calm throughout meetings Recovers quickly from crises Has a normal amount of eye contact Is slow to anger Is comfortable in front of others Is less easily embarrassed Doesn't show signs of discouragement	Speaks with a controlled pace and vocabulary Finds it easier to say no and resist urges	Rationality; keeping emotions subdued	Sits or stands at a closer distance Is unfazed by other drivers' idiocies Wears more subdued clothing Is more likely to be physically fit
More extraverted (E+)	Is good at greeting people Is warm and friendly Is less inhibited Makes more eye contact Is an initiator and responder Takes longer strides Uses more caffeine in the morning Is optimistic and cheerful Has a vigorous pace, likes excitement	Talks louder, faster, longer Is impatient with slower speech Is likely to talk "on top of" someone else Responds better to more aggressive humour	Achievement, ambition, success, competence* Power, wealth, authority, social status Self-direction, creativity, independent thought Stimulation, variety in life, novelty, excitement Universalism, social justice, welfare of all	Is more active; doesn't remain at desk or station Keeps the door open Office is "busier", more colourful Sits facing the door Tends to sit opposite people Dresses for the occasion

More introverted (E−)	Is comfortable reading while you wait Is more sedentary Has less eye contact Is more inhibited Is an observer Tends to sit at right angles Takes shorter strides Uses less caffeine in the morning	Pauses and thinks before speaking Is hard to read; is less assertive Talks less and more briefly than most Is unlikely to talk "on top of" someone else Enjoys more subtle humour	Tradition, humility, respect, commitment Privacy	Is more sedentary Keeps the door closed Sits back to the door Office environment is quiet, subdued Is leisurely, reserved, stays in the background Is an independent dresser
More exploring (O+)	Is curious about a wide range of topics Is easily bored Is more likely to have pursued multiple careers throughout life Is less bound by rules and more playful Responds to more unusual humour	Speech is more colourful and entertaining Uses more gestures when talking Language and thinking are more future-oriented Talks and thinks in terms of concepts Emphasises the uniqueness of products and services	Hedonism, pleasure, enjoyment, sensuousness Achievement, ambition, success, competence Power, wealth, authority, social status Self-direction, creativity, independent thought* Stimulation, variety in life, novelty, excitement	Has more unusual furniture and décor Appears busy; has many stacks and books Frequently changes and redecorates the work space Prefers a variety of projects Tends to prefer modern and abstract art Wears more colourful and festive clothing
More preserving (O−)	Is punctual Tends to go by the rules Has a narrow range of interests Is committed to only one career Is more serious Shows little or no interest in the arts Prefers the familiar, the tried and true	Responds to more mainstream humour Expresses more conservative views; prefers the status quo and resists change Talks about today, not tomorrow; is not a futurist	Tradition, humility, respect, commitment* Conformity, obedience, restraint in action	Prefers standard furniture and equipment Uses patriotic paraphernalia Uses neutral colour; décor is often ordinary Wall hangings depict action, plants, products Wears conservative clothing
More adaptive (A+)	Enjoys being helpful Is concerned about others' opinions and reactions Is warm and friendly	Tends to agree, or at least not disagree with most assertions Appears to take you at your word, without checking for proof or detail	Security, reciprocity, safety, harmony Universalism, social justice, welfare of all	Has family memorabilia in evidence Observes traffic rules and laws such as speed limits and no-parking zones

(Continued overleaf)

Table 12.1 continued

Dimension/continuum	Behaviour	Language	Values	Environment (office, car, dress, person)
		Wants to know who else is using or doing the same thing Talks about how people will react	Benevolence, loyalty, welfare of those who are close* Conformity, obedience, restraint in actions Tradition, humility respect, commitment	Clothing tends to follow the local code
More challenging (A−)	Is tough-minded; shows little sympathy Prefers conventional gender roles Is brash, is sensitive only to get something	Is an aggressive asker of questions Is sceptical; doesn't take things at face value Uses expressive language, including expletives and vulgarities Is argumentative	Hedonism, pleasure, enjoyment, sensuousness Power, wealth, authority, social status Self-direction, creativity, independent thought	Is willing to decorate in a daring way; doesn't seek approval Displays evidence of pride in accomplishments, such as trophies, degrees, awards, and certificates Slips into road rage Disregards traffic rules such as speed limits and no-parking zones Clothing makes a statement and is daring
More focused (C+)	Is punctual Tends to go by the rules Always acts professionally Consistently uses personal organiser Is reliable; follows through on promises Allots time for meetings with people and adjourns when the time has run out Sees life as consisting of tasks to accomplish; is goal oriented	Pushes for clarity and closure: "What's next?" Clarifies the agenda up front: "Here's what we're going to discuss and accomplish in this meeting" Talks about alternatives and consequences	Tradition, humility, respect, commitment Achievement, ambition, success, competence Security, reciprocity, safety, harmony Universalism, social justice, welfare of all Conformity, obedience, restraint in actions	Is neat; has everything in its place (sometimes in stacks) Lets others screen calls; lets voice mail pick up calls Car is typically free of any clutter Always looks professional Has better health habits

	Prefers to finish one task or project before starting another; is a serial processor Focuses on the details			
More flexible (C−)	Takes work home Sees life as a series of processes; is role oriented Sees life as consisting of pleasure to be experienced Is comfortable switching from one task or activity to another; is a parallel processor Is content to "wing it" without an agenda Is prone to neglect follow-through Is spontaneous, even knee-jerk, in responding to people	Is easily interrupted and isn't bothered by it Is happy to reopen old issues	Hedonism, pleasure, enjoyment, sensuousness Stimulation, variety in life, novelty, excitement	Shows evidence of disorganisation; may hide clutter in desk or car boot before meetings Is easily distracted by competing events Will take calls and allow interruptions while meeting with people Car is likely to be strewn with papers, pencils, food, cups Is casual about clothing Has poorer health habits

Note: *Clues that are strongly associated with a particular trait.

Source: Howard and Howard (2001, pp. 135–137). Permission sought from Bard Press.

turn influence team outcomes. He argued that it might be useful to think of teams in trait terms.

Yet another emerging issue refers to trying to understand the role of personality traits in understanding dynamic leaders. This goes back over 60 years but Ford and Oswald (2003) updated it by emphasising person-by-situation effects. Related to this is the enduring problem of personality–organisation fit. The essential assumption is that if there is a congruence of fit between an individual's personality-based preferences and behaviours, he or she will be more happy, healthy and productive at work. Ryan and Kristof-Brown (2003) argued that the literature supports the idea that complementarity is better than congruence in terms of outcomes. They also pointed out that a bad fit may have positive consequences in that it can encourage individual adaptiveness, development and flexibility. They noted that some traits are more visible than others (i.e. Extraversion) and hence are easier to assess accurately by recruiters and co-workers.

Inevitably various authors have speculated about the future (Barrick et al., 2003a; Hough, 2003). They include:

- Having better measures of work outcomes (the dependent variable). Thus, we need to distinguish between individual-level variables (i.e. goal setting, workplace aggression), where personality variables have a major impact, and group-level performance variables (task execution, group stability), where personality variables have a less direct influence. Further, it is important to recognise dynamic change in performance over time. Equally, more researchers are pointing to measuring the difference between typical and maximal performance criteria at work.
- Considering carefully the nature of the personality measures (the independent variable). This includes creating "compound" personality predictor variables like the prosocial or proactive personality or the concept of core self-evaluations. Next, it is important to search for other non-"Big Five" personality variables like interests and values, and emotional variables.
- Researchers need to be able to describe and measure work-related situational variables like type of job, task and team more accurately, as well as corporate culture. Everyone agrees that situational variables moderate the relationship between personality and task outcomes but these need to be carefully measured.
- Personality and outcome variables need to be measured at the appropriate level. Often, the more specific the better, because that reveals findings that help spell out the nature of the process.
- It remains extremely important to understand the mediating influences of motivational variables and the moderating influences of situations variables on the direct relationship between personality traits and workplace behaviour and emotion.
- As always, it remains a crucially important research task to specify closely, aggregate always, and measure accurately the work-related criteria. Aggregation helps rehability.

There are also many journal articles and special journal issues concerned with personality at work. Many note the complexity and dynamic nature of the relationship between these variables. Thus, Van den Berg and Feij (2003) proposed a model showing how personality variables predicted factors like work self-efficiency or work stress, which then predicted job satisfaction and the propensity to leave the job. Thus, work stress was seen as a mediator between neuroticism and job satisfaction. Personality variables, they showed, predicted both job attitudes and work behaviours.

More importantly, there are now comprehensive, critical and clear textbooks specifically on trait psychology, such as that by Matthews et al. (2003). In their last chapter they deal with such issues as the achievements of trait psychology and they highlight psychometric issues (like structural equation modelling) and understanding the biology of personality. Next, they see trait psychology as being now much better integrated with mainstream (pure and applied) psychology. Third, they see the widespread application of trait psychology, which must signal its coming of age. Most importantly, perhaps, they sketch out a multi-component and cognitive adaptive theory for understanding the functioning of traits, which looks at information processing, neural systems and behavioural adaptation.

At the end of this important book they draw two wide conclusions:

1. The psychological science of personality traits has made major advances in recent years. Psychometric models of traits such as the five-factor model provide robust constructs with considerable consensual support. The heritability of traits is firmly established and further understanding of the biological bases of personality is expected from studies of molecular genetics and psychophysiology (especially brain imaging). The constructs used by trait psychologists are increasingly well integrated with those of the mainstream psychology of neuroscience, cognitive science and social psychology. The applied relevance of assessment of personality traits is increasingly accepted, especially in organisational and clinical psychology. Many empirical and theoretical issues remain to be resolved, but the strong foundation provided by existing research allows us to anticipate that normal scientific progress will address these issues successfully.

2. Trait psychology has sometimes been criticised for being atheoretical and overly empirical. This criticism has always been rather misinformed, but contemporary trait research is making rapid theoretical progress, as a consequence of integration with mainstream psychology. It is suggested that further progress requires a multi-levelled account of personality data that accepts that observed linkages between traits and external criteria may require a variety of types of explanation. Different types of explanation refer to neuroscience, information-processing and high-level motivations and self-beliefs. We explored a cognitive–adaptive framework for personality that may serve to integrate the different levels at which traits are expressed. Thus, the various correlates of extraversion cohere around adaptation to demanding social environments, and the neuroticism seems to be linked to adaptation to threat.

(pp. 409–410)

The new interest in this area is more than apparent in the number of books and journal articles appearing since the start of the millennium. It may even be time to recognise the beginning of a new subdiscipline called, perhaps, Applied Differential Psychology or Differential Work Psychology.

The fate of organisations

With typical insight and clarity, Hogan (2006) has argued that the personality of senior managers in organisations is inextricably linked with the performance and, hence, fate of those organisations. He reviewed and evaluated studies that clearly demonstrate the relationship between the ability, personality and style of (business) leaders and the (monetary) performance of their organisations. The influence of leaders is inexorable and powerful and they influence the top management team who effectively run organisations. Good leaders have the ability *and* will to influence key processes like the recruiting, training and supervision of staff, the choosing of strategy and the monitoring of outcomes.

Hogan (2006) argued that the value and importance of personality psychology in work settings has never been fully realised because personality psychologists have never really agreed on their agenda or developed commercial, available and viable tests to measure personality. Academic personality theorists and researchers have all been "out of fashion" for the last 50 years of battling romantics, behaviourists, etc.

Hogan's argument was that personality traits are closely linked to leadership and both good and bad leaders have to form productive teams. They have to resist temptations (personal gain, being dictatorial), deal with risk, pursue justice and set an example. That is, personality is closely linked with important leadership behaviours and competencies like maintaining self-control, treating others with respect, building and maintaining a team and exercising optimal control over others. Personality traits and disorders are related to moral competencies or virtues in a leader, setting an example, pursuing a moral mandate, ensuring justice and avoiding the many temptations of personal gain. Leaders need to be versatile and flexible so that they can deal effectively with both task and socioemotional issues, strategic and operational problems as well as being both (when appropriate) forceful and enabling. Hogan (2006) argued that all managers are by definition in leadership positions. Further, who you are as described by personality traits and abilities determines largely *how you lead*. Those led by others want them to be competent, decisive, humble, persistent, visionary and to have clear integrity.

Hogan (2006) noted that a leader's personality inevitably influences the performance of the teams that they lead. Leaders shape team culture through the development of norms, morale and "buy-in". It is the interpersonal styles that equip people to work well in certain teams, to do well in very specific roles, and to be able to integrate their personal values with those of the team.

Leaders have to acquire and maintain power, whether it is based on inheritance, charisma or position. Management failure has many causes: Attractive, articulate, super-confident, just-out-of-business-school types with no real-world experience; those eager to make their fortune and "duck out" later for a quiet life; conventional, meritocrats who don't understand the politics of influence; confrontation-averse peacekeepers unwilling to ruffle feathers; attention-seeking rebels, who are consistently and unwisely always anti-conformist; "pointy headed techies", who can't sell the (often wise) decisions they make; those with an impostor syndrome, who suddenly feel they do not deserve the success they have achieved.

All of these share certain characteristics: lack of self-awareness; an exaggerated sense of self-worth and concomitant entitlement; insensitivity, or indifference, to the needs of those around them; an ever hungry and seemingly unfulfillable need for approbation and approval; and, sometimes, a heavily disguised and hidden insecurity.

It is not that failed leaders are not sufficiently articulate, dedicated and intelligent because they cannot (sometimes will not) do what has to be done. This may be because they have chosen the wrong people around them; maybe because they can't make timely decisions or can't delegate authority and accountability. Some lose the plot: they drift, unfocused and unhappy. Worse, they take their eye off the ball – market realities.

Studies of failed, derailed, incompetent senior managers have yielded rich checklists. They:

- Fail to administer through simple processes of prioritisation, delegation, record keeping – so are over- or under-managing.
- Are reactive not proactive for major events.
- Have poor judgement due to lack of intelligence, being too emotionally involved, too late, or too unclear.
- Show low social unawareness, insensitivity, egotism: unable to build teams, persuade, charm, influence.
- Lack adaptability, flexibility, to change when the situation requires it.
- Are not sufficiently well-adjusted to "take the heat": emotionally unstable, unpredictable, fragile.
- Are lacking in integrity, loyalty: dishonest, betrayers of trust.
- Are, often, overly personally ambitious.

Finally, Hogan (2006) considered how to fix incompetence. He maintained that one needs to be clear about what does and does not change. Some things – skills, competencies can be trained: intrapersonal skills (patience, courage, the work ethic), interpersonal skills (communication, compassion), technical skills (decision making, process management), and leadership (delegating, directing, hiring). However, personality factors play a part in executive learning. They include *self-discipline* and *self-control*, which are linked to Conscientiousness. Second, there is *self-confidence*, which has a double-edged benefit: it may be related to resistance to coaching, poor at acknowledging mistakes but positively related to the ability to withstand criticism. This is related to Stability and Neuroticism. Third, there is the issue of insightfulness. This is perceptiveness, insight and social sensitivity. No doubt this is partly related to Agreeableness and Extraversion. Fourth, there is the ever present issue of rationality: the ability to evaluate data and make good decisions on the basis of this.

Hogan in his research, writing and consultancy has done much for organisational personality theorists. He has championed good research and been able to demonstrate in theory and research the fundamental importance of personality traits in the workplace.

Evolutionary perspectives

Few people could have missed the socio-biological and evolutionary revolution in the social sciences. Various writers have sought to understand the implications of an evolutionary psychology perspective for behaviour at work.

Nettle (2006) has recently attempted an evolutionary perspective on personality theory. The issue is how we explain the existence of the fitness–relevant variability in personality traits. His aim was to examine the ultimate evolutionary origins of the five-factor model through a cost–benefit analysis perspective. He argued that human variability (in traits, abilities, etc.) is normal and ubiquitous. Further, he noted that behavioural alternatives could be considered as trade-offs, with a particular trait producing not unalloyed advantage, but a mixture of costs and benefits such that the optimal value for fitness may depend on very specific local circumstances (p. 625).

Extraversion

Extraverts have more sexual partners, more social behaviour and attract more social support, all of which are good for fitness. They also are more physically active (which may relate to health) and explore their environment more regularly and thoroughly. However, in doing so they also expose themselves to risk and are more likely to be involved in accidents, crime and divorce, which are clearly bad both for themselves and their offspring.

Neuroticism

Neuroticism is clearly undesirable: associated with mental illness, impaired physical health, relationship failure and social isolation. However, their vigilance and wariness may be beneficial as is their avoidance of potentially acute dangers. Anxiety increases the detection of threatening stimuli. Neurotics can also be competitive, which can have its advantages.

Openness

Openness is related to creativity which is attractive to potential mates – hence its survival fitness. Openness is related to cognitive novelty seeking and complexity, which is clearly beneficial, but also to schizotypy and psychosis. Openness has also been associated with increased paranormal beliefs, paranoia and delusions and depression. Non-extreme openness in a benign environment accompanied by specific talents has clear benefits.

Agreeableness

Agreeable people are empathic, cooperative, kind and trustworthy. Hence, they have many friends, coalition partners and harmonious interpersonal relations. But unless their helpfulness and trust are selective they can be abused or "out competed" by others. Further, being too attentive to the needs of others can make them insufficiently aware of their own needs and, hence, lead to a decline in personal fitness.

Conscientiousness

Conscientious people are orderly, self-controlled, hard-working planners. They follow orders, are healthier and live longer. They do well at work. Yet, others can get ahead by opportunistic free-riding, breaking rules and cheating. Conscientious people can overwork and be too ruled and routine bound such that they miss or ignore opportunities. They may forgo exploiting opportunities that offer immediate returns.

Nettle (2006) admitted that his ideas were essentially hypotheses generating and could be wrong. His ideas are not dissimilar from the theories of Hogan (2006), who also had an optimal thesis that could be seen as a trade-off idea. This analysis makes it clear why successful managers tend to be Stable, Extraverted, Open, Agreeable and Conscientious. But as we saw earlier with the *spectrum hypothesis*, extremes of any trait can indicate specific problems. The part of evolutionary psychology is to point to the situations and circumstances in which the expression of traits is more relevant.

Changes in the workplace

Looking back 30 or 50 years to any industry or organisation be it in the administrative, production or service sector, reminds one of the huge changes that have occurred in how, when and where we work. There have been changes in the demographic profile of the workforce, in customer expectations, in technical and legal developments, which have substantially altered how people think about themselves, their boss, their colleagues, their customers and the shareholders at work. People use their time differently.

The reduced cost and size and increased shelf-life and portability of technology has meant that people have more autonomy as to how and where they work. As a result organisations have continually restructured and reorganised to attempt to streamline and rationalise their processes. For many individuals there are new and quite different challenges. These include:

- The idea of no more "jobs for life".
- A change of emphasis from being employed to being employable.
- Job security, such as it is, being based on performance not length of service.
- Of having to face continuous and increasing global competition to be faster, more productive and more innovative.

As a result, organisations have come up with many solutions and strategies to deal with the recent challenges. These include: continual reorganisation of various divisions; sub-contracting non-core services and operations; developing good relationships with key constituencies; streamlining and rationalising processes; subscribing to continuous improvement of processes; creating flatter structures; creating more team working; developing core competencies; recognising workforce diversity; creating a flexible workforce; empowering people at work; promoting the concept of the manager as a facilitator and coordinator; and recognising a need for employees to continually update their knowledge and skills.

Changes have occurred in many areas of business from the era of one's grandfathers (up to the 1950s) and fathers (up to 1980s/1990s), are occurring in one's own, and will occur in the future. Furnham (2003b) attempted to define the changes, albeit rather stereotypically.

The boss's office

Grandfather's The foreman has a functional office with tea-making facilities, personnel files and all the valuable equipment.

Father's office A dark-panelled sober office dominated by a huge desk, which has executive toys and an ashtray on it.

Your open-planned work environment   The boss's glass-panelled enclosure is always open. A coffee table dominates.

Your child's virtual organisation   Nobody has an office. But the building has a "meeting station" for stand-up meetings and mass-visual-display areas.

Incentive systems

Grandfather's   Knowing that after 40 years of dedicated service you were least likely to be laid off.

Father's office   Meet your pre-set goals (management by objectives) and you keep your job.

Your open-planned work environment   Training courses to upskill yourself and performance-related pay.

Your child's virtual organisation   Equity in the company. Total freedom to plan own career; go part time, etc.

Appraisal systems

Grandfather's   If your boss never shouted at you or demanded you to see him in his office you were OK.

Father's office   Annual, staff-department-driven bureaucratic process of no consequence (Appraisal System).

Your open-planned work environment   Mandatory, three-times-a-year progress reviews that bosses have been trained to give.

Your child's virtual organisation   360-degree feedback data, fed into development and assessment-centre data and biannual 20-page report delivered.

Skills valued

Grandfather's   Manual and engineering skills.

Father's office   Knowledge of systems.

Your open-planned work environment   Computing.

Your child's virtual organisation   Knowledge and know-how at the cutting edge of biotechnology.

Working hours

Grandfather's   0700–1800 with a short dinner (lunch) break and the odd tea break.

Father's office   0800–1700 with fixed, negotiated breaks.

Your open-planned work environment   Half an hour before the boss, and an hour after he/she leaves. Sandwiches or desk lunch.

Your child's virtual organisation   Personal circadian rhythms (i.e. morningness and eveningness) dictate flexitime pattern chosen.

Contract

Grandfather's   Nothing formal, easily sacked.

Father's office   Career for life, expected and contracted.

Your open-planned work environment   Contract revised in the 1990s.
Your child's virtual organisation   Short-term, possibly renewable, contract. Restricted pension rights.

Career opportunities

Grandfather's   None, unless you married the boss's daughter.
Father's office   In the service-based system loyalty was rewarded by the "Buggins turn" system.
Your open-planned work environment   Performance-based but liable to erratic but enthusiastic restructuring, downsizing and reappraising.
Your child's virtual organisation   The word career went out of fashion. Workers each carry and compose portfolios of work experience and skills.

As noted before, the world of work is changing, mainly due to the development of technology. Futurologists have made fanciful claims regarding some changes. Yet how people are selected, managed, monitored and rewarded is changing. This inevitably means the personality– and ability–performance relationship will have to be re-examined in the light of these changes.

The value of differential psychology

Few dispute the fact that human capital is important. Not all agree that people are their greatest asset, because they recognise that organisation longevity and profit are dependent on many things including customer demand.

Yet, an understanding of the role of individual differences implies that the effect is, or should be, felt all the way down the value chain. Consider the following:

Sales   Most sales forces suffer considerable staff turnover, which can be very costly to manage. Differential psychology can help in identifying and supporting those who are likely to succeed and fail at this task, reduce turnover and increase profit.
Manufacturing and engineering   The identification, training and motivation of highly technical people remains a crucial issue. This is particularly problematic for organisations when they need to promote highly technical people to managerial positions, which requires a different skill set and temperamental dispositions. Understanding how to train highly intelligent, introverted, technically able people into competent managers is a major issue for organisational psychologists.
Research and development   Many organisations stand or fall by the creativity and innovativeness of their R&D department. The question is how to find and select research scientist who fulfil the basic criteria of creating both new/novel and useful products. Differential psychology can play, and has played, a significant role here, in finding and managing highly creative people.
Finance and accounts   Like R&D scientists, finance specialists tend to have a particular profile. It is comparatively easy to measure numerical ability but senior finance people inevitably require more than that. To succeed as a CFO, people need a range of skills and traits that differential psychology can identify.
Information technology   Differential psychologists have expressed an interest in individual differences in the use of technology, as well as the profile of successful and less

successful IT experts. Together with ergonomists and cognitive psychologists, personality psychologists have helped design IT systems that maximise people's strengths and preferences in the access, processing and storage of information.

Human resources   All HR people express an interest in individual differences in abilities, traits and motivation. They are often the repository of psychological knowledge in the company. Many appreciate the fact that having an up-to-date knowledge of assessment techniques gives them considerable advantage over their competitors.

Support staff   Whether they perform administrative, health and safety or security duties, support staff can fundamentally enable, as well as disable, an organisation. They can be seen as an expensive overhead or a crucially important aspect of the entire business. Selecting and managing competent, motivated, energetic support staff can be facilitated by a knowledge of differential psychology.

Differential and experimental psychologies are the twin bastions of the discipline. Work psychologists correctly and appropriately seek to understand how contextual and situational factors (like experimental conditions) systematically and powerfully influence employees' attitudes and behaviours. Yet, it is painfully obvious that individual difference variables – notably ability and personality – interact with situational factors to predict work outcomes. Understanding this process enriches theories in both differential and work psychology.

Conclusion

Scientific progress in technology, measurement and theory building has recently furthered, and will continued to further, our understanding of the development structure and functioning of individual differences. More importantly, the pendulum has swung back from an environmentalist and behavioural perspective to a developmental and biological one. Hardly a day goes by without press coverage of a new biological discovery relating to individual differences in major areas like education, health and work. We are, it seems, on the very edge of a major breakthrough that will greatly impact the whole of differential psychology.

There are also numerous social, political and economic changes in how, when and on what we work. Whilst our parents may have had various technical skills, most people now are knowledge workers glued to computers. Many work at home; others in open-planned offices. The working day has changed beyond recognition, as have the particular attributes required to thrive in it. These changes have led inevitably to different manpower requirements and the necessity of finding, training and maintaining new skills and work attitudes.

Further, organisational structures, processes and procedures have changed. People can be assessed on line. Some factors crucial for selection and assessment have been chopped for legal or other reasons (age), while other factors have become important. Organisations try to be more socially acceptable by hiring a heterogenous workforce with people of mixed age, ability and ethnicity.

The changes can lead to tension. Thus, while the science might suggest some particular procedure, organisational practice might forbid it. The latter often changing slower than the former. But one thing is certain: It is a good time to be alive for a differential psychologist interested in the world of work.

References

Ackerman, P. (1994). Intelligence, attention and learning: Maximal and typical performance. In D. Detterman (Ed.), *Current topics in human intelligence* (pp. 1–17). Norwood, OH: Ablex.

Ackerman, P., & Goff, M. (1994). Typical intellectual engagement and personality. *Journal of Educational Psychology, 86*, 150–153.

Ackerman, P., & Heggestad, E. (1997). Intelligence, personality, and interests. *Psychological Bulletin, 121*, 219–225.

Ackerman, P., & Rolfhus, E. (1999). The locus of adult intelligence. *Psychology and Aging, 14*, 314–330.

Adams, K. (1997). Understanding and applying competencies: The views and experience of competencies' founding father, David McClelland. *Competency, 4*, 18–23.

Adams, K. (1998). Three key methods of identifying competencies. *Competency, 5*, 37–44.

Adler, S., & Weiss, H. (1988). Recent developments in the study of personality and organisational behaviour. In C. Cooper & I. Robertson (Eds.), *International Review of Industrial and Organisational Psychology* (Vol. 3, pp. 307–325). Chichester, UK: Wiley.

Aguilar-Alonso, A. (1996). Personality and creativity. *Personality and Individual Differences, 21*, 959–969.

Ai, X. (1999). Creativity and academic achievement. *Creative Research Journal, 12*, 329–337.

Ajzen, I. (1988). *Attitudes, personality and behaviour*. Milton Keynes, UK: Open University Press.

Ajzen, I. (1991). The theory of planned behaviour. *Organisational Behaviour and Human Decision Processes, 50*, 179–211.

Ajzen, I., & Fishbein, M. (1980). *Understanding attitudes and predicting social behavior*. Englewood Cliffs, NJ: Prentice Hall.

Allix, N. (2000). The theory of multiple intelligences: A case of missing cognitive matter. *Australian Journal of Education, 44*, 272–293.

Alloy, L., & Abramson, L. (1979). Judgements of contingency in depressed and non-depressed students: Sadder but wiser? *Journal of Experimental Psychology: General, 108*, 441–489.

Allport, G. W., Vernon, E. E., & Lindzey, G. (1960). *Study of values*. Boston: Houghton Mifflin.

Amabile, T. M. (1982). Social psychology of creativity: A consensual assessment technique. *Journal of Personality and Social Psychology, 43*, 997–1013.

Amabile, T. M. (1996). *Creativity in context*. New York: Westview.

American Psychiatric Association. (1987). *Diagnostic and statistical manual of mental disorders* (3rd ed. revised). Washington, DC: APA.

American Psychiatric Association. (1994). *Diagnostic and statistical manual of mental disorders* (4th ed.). Washington, DC: APA.

American Psychiatric Association. (2007). *Diagnostic and statistical manual of mental disorders* (5th ed.). Washington, DC: APA.

Anastasi, A. (2004). *Psychological testing*. New York: Macmillan.

Anderson, C. (1977). Locus of control, coping behaviours and performance in a stress setting: A longitudinal study. *Journal of Applied Psychology, 62*, 446–451.

Anderson, N. (2003). Applicant and recruiter reactions to new technology and selection. *International Journal of Selection and Assessment, 11,* 121–136.

Anderson, N., & Cunningham-Snell, N. (2000). Personnel selection. In N. Chmiel (Ed.), *Introduction to work and organizational psychology* (pp. 69–99). Oxford, UK: Blackwell.

Anderson, N., & West, M. (1998). Measuring climate for work group innovation. *Journal of Organisational Behaviour, 19,* 235–258.

Anderson, N., Lievens, F., van Dam, K., & Ryan, A. (2004). Future perspectives on employee selection: Key directions for future research and practice. *Applied Psychology, 53,* 487–501.

Andrews, E. G. (1930). The development of imagination in the pre-school child. *University of Iowa studies in character, 3*(4).

Andrisani, P., & Nestle, G. (1976). Internal/external control as contributor to, and outcome of, work experience. *Journal of Applied Psychology, 22,* 453–474.

Arnau, R., Green, B., Rosen, D., Gleaves, D., & Melancon, J. (2003). Are Jungian preferences really categorical? An empirical investigation using taxometrical analysis. *Personality and Individual Differences, 34,* 233–251.

Arnold, J., Silvester, J., Patterson, F., Robertson, I., Cooper, C., & Burnes, B. (2005). *Work psychology: Understanding human behaviour in the workplace.* Harlow, UK: Prentice Hall.

Arnold, M. (1999). The importance of personality in the performance of diagnostic radiographers. *Radiography, 3,* 83–98.

Ashkanasy, N., & Daus, C. (2005). Rumours of the death of emotional intelligence in organisational behaviour are vastly exaggerated. *Journal of Organisational Behaviour, 26,* 441–452.

Austin, E. (2004). An investigation of the relationship between trait emotional intelligence and emotional task performance. *Personality and Individual Differences, 36,* 1855–1864.

Babiak, P. (1995). When psychopaths go to work: A case study of an industrial psychopath. *Applied Psychology, 44,* 171–188.

Babiak, P., & Hare, R. (2006). *Snakes in suits.* New York: Regan Books.

Baer, J. (1998). The case for domain specificity of creativity. *Creativity Research Journal, 11,* 173–177.

Bandura, A. (1982). Self-efficacy mechanism in human agency. *American Psychologist, 37,* 122–147.

Bar-On, R. (1997). *Bar-On Emotional Quotient Inventory (EQ-i): Technical manual.* Toronto, Canada: Multi-Health Systems.

Baron, J. (1985). What kinds of intelligence components are fundamental? In J. W. Segal, S. F. Chipman, & R. Glaser (Eds.), *Thinking and learning skills. Vol. 2: Research and open questions* (chap. 16). London: Lawrence Erlbaum Associates Ltd.

Barrett, P. (1998). Science, fundamental measurement and psychometric testing. *Selection and Development Review, 14,* 3–10.

Barrett, P. (2003). Beyond psychometrics: Measurement, non-quantitative structure and applied numerics. *Journal of Managerial Psychology, 18,* 421–439.

Barrett, P., Kline, P., Paltiel, L., & Eysenck, H. (1996). An evaluation of the psychometric properties of the concept 5.2 Occupational Personality Questionnaire. *Journal of Occupational and Organisational Psychology, 69,* 1–19.

Barrick, M., & Mount, M. (1991). The "Big Five" personality dimensions and job performance: A meta-analysis. *Personnel Psychology, 44,* 1–25.

Barrick, M., & Mount, M. (2005). Yes, personality matters: Moving on to more important matters. *Human Performance, 18,* 359–371.

Barrick, M., & Ryan, A. (Eds.). (2003). *Personality and work.* San Francisco: Jossey-Bass.

Barrick, M., Mount, M., & Judge, T. (2001). Personality and performance at the beginning of the new millennium. *International Journal of Selection and Assessment, 9,* 9–30.

Barrick, M., Steward, G., & Piotrowski, M. (2002). Personality and job performance. *Journal of Applied Psychology, 87,* 43–51.

Barrick, M., Mitchell, T., & Stewart, G. (2003a). Situational and motivational influences on trait behaviour relationships. In M. Barrick & A Ryan (Eds.), *Personality and work* (pp. 60–82). San Francisco, Jossey-Bass.

Barrick, M., Mount, M., & Gupta, R. (2003b). Meta-analysis of the relationship between the five-factor model of personality and Holland's occupational types. *Personnel Psychology, 56*, 45–74.

Barron, F. X. (1963). *Creativity and psychological health: Origins of personality and creative freedom*. Princeton, NJ: Van Nostrand.

Bartram, D. (2004). Assessment in organisations. *Applied Psychology, 53*, 237–259.

Bartram, D., & Dale, H. (1982). The Eysenck Personality Inventory as a selection test for military pilots. *Journal of Occupational Psychology, 55*, 287–296.

Basadur, M. (1997). Organizational development interventions for enhancing creativity in the workplace. *Journal of Creative Behavior, 31*, 59–72.

Batey, M., & Furnham, A. (2007). *Creativity, intelligence and personality*. Unpublished paper, University College, London.

Beaton, R. (1975). Use of tests in a national retail company. In K. Miller (Ed.), *Psychological testing in personnel assessment* (pp. 137–148). New York: Wiley.

Becker, T. (2005). Development and validation of situational judgement test of employee integrity. *International Journal of Selection and Assessment, 13*, 225–323.

Beech, A., Baylis, C., Smithson, P., & Claridge, G. (1989). Individual differences in schizotypy as reflected in measures of cognitive inhibition. *British Journal of Clinical Psychology, 28*, 117–129.

Beier, M., & Ackerman, P. (2001). Current-events knowledge in adults. *Psychology and Aging, 16*, 615–628.

Ben-Shem, I., & Avi-Itzhak, T. (1991). On work values and career choices in freshmen students. *Journal of Vocational Behaviour, 39*, 369–379.

Bendig, A. (1963). The relationship of temperament traits of social extraversion and emotionality to vocational interests. *Journal of General Psychology, 69*, 311–318.

Bennett, R., & Robinson, S. (2000). Development of a measure of work-place deviance. *Journal of Applied Psychology, 85*, 349–360.

Bentz, V. (1985). *A view from the top: A 30 year perspective of research devoted to the discovery, description, and prediction of executive behaviour*. Los Angeles: APA Annual Meeting.

Berman, J. (1997). Competency as a management practice in Europe and North America. *Competency, 4*, 24–28.

Bernadin, J., & Beatty, R. (1984). *Performance appraisal*. Boston: Kent.

Bernardin, H. (1977). The relationship of personality variables to organisational withdrawal. *Personnel Psychology, 30*, 17–27.

Berr, S., Church, A., & Waclawski, J. (2000). The right relationship is everything: Linking personality preferences to managerial behaviours. *Human Resource Development Quarterly, 11*, 133–157.

Berry, C., Ones, D., & Sackett, P. (2006). Interpersonal deviance, organisational deviance and their common correlates. *Journal of Applied Psychology, 91*, 653–668.

Bertua, C., Anderson, N., & Salgado, J. (2005). The predictive validity of cognitive ability tests. A UK meta-analysis. *Journal of Occupational and Organisational Psychology, 78*, 387–409.

Bets, R., & Blank, K. (1992). The development of a personality assessment tool. *European Review of Applied Psychology, 42*, 1–8.

Bishop, D., & Jean Renaud, G. (1976). End-of-day mood on work and leisure days in relation to extraversion, neuroticism, and amount of change in daily activities. *Canadian Journal of Behavioural Science, 8*, 388–400.

Blaylock, B., & Winkofsky, E. (1983). An explanation of R&D decision processes through individual information processing preferences. *R&D Management, 13*, 129–141.

Blickle, G., Schlegel, A., Fassbender, O., & Klein, U. (2006). Some personality correlates of business white-collar crime. *Applied Psychology, 55*, 220–233.

Block, J. (1980). Sex differences in interest measurement. *Journal of Occupational Psychology*, *53*, 181–186.

Block, J. (1995). A contrarian view of the five-factor approach to personality description. *Psychological Bulletin*, *117*, 185–215.

Blunt, P. (1978). Personality characteristics of a group of White South African managers. *International Journal of Psychology*, *13*, 139–146.

Boden, M. A. (2004). *The creative mind: Myths and mechanisms* (2nd ed.). London: Routledge.

Borislow, B. (1958). The Edwards Personal Preference Schedule and fakability. *Journal of Applied Psychology*, *42*, 22–27.

Borman, W., & Penner, L. (2001). Citizenship performance: Its nature, antecedents and motives. In B. Roberts & R. Hogan (Eds.), *Personality psychology in the workplace*. Washington, DC: APA.

Borman, W., Hanson, M., Oppler, S., Pulakis, E., & White, L. (1993). Role of early supervisory experience in supervisor performance. *Journal of Applied Psychology*, *78*, 443–449.

Boyatzis, R. (1982). *The competent manager: A model for effective performance*. New York: Wiley.

Brand, C. (1994). Open to experience – Closed to intelligence. *European Journal of Personality*, *8*, 299–310.

Bratton, V., & Kacmar, M. (2004). Extreme careerism: The dark side of impression management. In R. Griffin & A. O'Leary-Kelly (Eds.), *The dark side of organisational behaviour* (pp. 291–307). New York: Jossey-Bass.

Bridges, J. (1989). Sex differences in occupational variables. *Sex Roles*, *20*, 205–211.

Bridgman, C., & Hollenbeck, G. (1961). Effect of simulated applicant status on Kinder Form D occupational interest scores. *Journal of Applied Psychology*, *45*, 237–239.

Brody, N. (1992). *Intelligence*. London: Academic Press.

Brody, N. (2003). Construct validation of the Sternberg Triarchic Abilities test: Comment and reanalysis. *Intelligence*, *31*, 319–329.

Brody, N. (2005). What cognitive intelligence is and what emotional intelligence is not. *Psychological Inquiry*, *15*, 234–238.

Brousseau, K. (1978). Personality and job experience. *Organisational Behaviour and Human Performance*, *22*, 235–257.

Brown, R. (1999). The use of personality tests: A survey of usage and practice in the UK. *Selection and Development Review*, *15*, 3–8.

Brown, R., & Colthern, C. (2000). Individual differences in faking integrity tests. *Psychological Reports*, *91*, 691–702.

Buchholz, R. (1976). Measurement of beliefs. *Human Relations*, *29*, 1177–1188.

Buchholz, R. (1978). An empirical study of contemporary belief about work in American society. *Journal of Applied Psychology*, *63*, 219–221.

Budd, R., & Paltiel, R.L. (1989). A review of the Occupational Personality Questionnaire. *Guidance and Assessment Review*, *5*, 5–7.

Bullen, J., & Hemsley, D. (1984). Psychoticism and visual recognition threshold. *Personality and Individual Differences*, *5*, 633–648.

Burn, D., & Dearlove, D. (1995). The competent organisation. *Competency*, *2*, 37–41.

Bywater, J., & Thompson, D. (2005). Personality questionnaires in a redundancy/restructuring setting – What do we know now? *Selection and Development Review*, *21*, 7–13.

Camara, W., & Schneider, D. (1994). Integrity tests. *American Psychologists*, *49*, 112–119.

Campbell, D., & Van Velsor, E. (1985). The use of personality measures in a management development programme. In H. Bernardin & D. Bownas (Eds.), *Personality assessment in organisations* (pp. 193–214). New York: Praeger.

Campbell, J., McCloy, R., Oppler, S., & Sager, L. (1993). A theory of performance. In N. Schmitt & W. Borman (Eds.), *Personnel selection in organisations* (pp. 35–70). San Diego, CA: Jossey-Bass.

Campbell, P., McHenry, J., & Wise, L. (1990). Modeling job performance in a population of jobs. *Personnel Psychology*, *43*, 313–333.

Capretz, L. (2003). Personality types in software engineering. *International Journal of Human Computer Studies*, *58*, 207–214.

Carlson, J. (1985). Recent assessment of the Myers–Briggs Type Indicator. *Journal of Personality Assessment*, *49*, 356–365.

Carlyn, M. (1977). An assessment of the Myers–Briggs Type Indicator. *Journal of Personality Assessment*, *41*, 461–473.

Carroll, J. (1993). *Human cognitive abilities*. Cambridge, UK: Cambridge University Press.

Carson, S. H., Peterson, J. B., & Higgins, D. M. (2003). Decreased latent inhibition is associated with increased creative achievement in high-functioning individuals. *Journal of Personality and Social Psychology*, *85*, 499–506.

Case, P., & Phillipson, E. (2004). Astrology and alchemy: The occult roots of the MBTI. *European Business Forum*, *17*, 61–66.

Caspi, A. (2000). The child is the father of the man: Personality continuities from childhood to adulthood. *Journal of Personality and Social Psychology*, *78*, 158–172.

Caspi, A., & Roberts, B. (2001). Personality development across the life course: The argument for change and continuity. *Psychological Inquiry*, *12*, 49–66.

Cassidy, S. (2004). Learning styles: An overview of theories, models and measures. *Educational Psychology*, *24*, 419–440.

Cattell, R. (1957). *Personality, motivation, structure and measurement*. Yonkers, NY: World Book Company.

Cattell, R. (1986). The 16PF personality structure and Dr Eysenck. *Journal of Social Behaviour and Personality*, *1*, 153–160.

Cattell, R. (1987). *Intelligence: Its structure, growth and action*. New York: Springer.

Cattell, R., & Butcher, H. (1968). *The prediction of achievement and creativity*. New York: Bobbs-Merrill.

Cattell, R., & Warburton, F. (1961). A cross-cultural comparison of patterns of extraversion and anxiety. *British Journal of Psychology*, *52*, 3–15.

Cattell, R., & Warburton, F. (1967). *Objective personality and motivation tests*. Champaign, IL: University of Illinois Press.

Cattell, R., Eber, H., & Tatsuoka, N. (1970). *Handbook for the 16 Personality Factor Questionnaire (16PF)*. Champagne, IL: IPAT.

Cattell, R. B. (1943). The measurement of adult intelligence. *Psychological Bulletin*, *40*, 153–193.

Cattell, R. B. (1971). *Abilities: Their structure, growth and action*. Boston: Houghton Mifflin.

Cattell, R. B., & Drevdahl, J. E. (1955). A comparison of the personality profile (16PF) of eminent researchers with that of eminent teachers and administrators, and of the general population. *British Journal of Psychology*, *46*, 248–261.

Chamorro-Premuzic, T., & Furnham, A. (2005). *Personality and intellectual competence*. Mahwah, NJ: Lawrence Erlbaum Associates Inc.

Chamorro-Premuzic, T., & Furnham, A. (2006). Intellectual competence and the intelligent personality. *Review of General Psychology*, *10*, 251–267.

Chan, D. (2004). Perceived emotional intelligence and self-efficacy among Chinese secondary school teachers in Hong Kong. *Personality and Individual Differences*, *36*, 1781–1795.

Chapman, D., & Webster, J. (2003). The use of technologies in the recruiting, screening, and selection process for job candidates. *International Journal of Selection and Assessment*, *11*, 113–120.

Cherrington, D. (1980). *The work ethic: Working values and values that work*. New York: Amacon.

Christie, M., & Venables, P. (1973). Mood changes in reaction to age, EPI, scores, time and day. *British Journal of Social and Clinical Psychology*, *12*, 61–72.

Churchill, G., Ford, N., Hartley, S., & Walker, O. (1985). The determinants of sales person performance: A meta-analysis. *Journal of Marketing Research*, *22*, 103–118.

Cimbolic, P., Wise, R., Rossetti, S., & Safer, M. (1999). Development of a combined objective ephebophile scale. *Sexual Addiction and Compulsivity, 6*, 253–266.

Clark, L., & Watson, D. (1999). Personality, disorder and personality disorder: Towards a more rational conceptualisation. *Journal of Personality Disorders, 13*, 142–151.

Cleckley, H. (1976). *The mask of sanity*. St Louis, MO: Mosley.

Cline, V., Richards, J., & Needham, W. (1963). Creativity tests and achievement in high school science. *Journal of Applied Psychology, 47*, 184–189.

Cloninger, C. R. (1986). A unified biosocial theory of personality and its role in the development of anxiety states. *Psychiatric Developments, 4*, 167–226.

Cloninger, C. R. (1987). A systematic method for clinical description and classification of personality variants. A proposal. *Archives of General Psychiatry, 44*, 573–588.

Cloninger, C. R. (1994). *The Temperament and Character Inventory (TCI): A guide to its development and use*. St Louis, MO: Washington University, Centre for Psychobiology of Personality.

Cloninger, C. R., & Gilligan, S. B. (1987). Neurogenetic mechanisms of learning: A phylogenetic perspective. *Journal of Psychiatric Research, 21*, 457–472.

Cloninger, C. R., Przybeck, T. R., & Svrakic, D. M. (1991). The Tridimensional Personality Questionnaire: US normative data. *Psychological Reports, 69*, 1047–1057.

Cloninger, C. R., Svrakic, D. M., & Przybeck, T. R. (1993). A psychobiological model of temperament and character. *Archives of General Psychiatry, 50*, 975–990.

Cohen, R., Montague, P., Nathanson, L., & Swerdlek, M. (1988). *Psychological testing*. Mountain View, AR: Manfield.

Coles, F. (2004). Psychological support for the concept of psychological competencies. *International Journal of Law and Psychiatry, 21*, 223–232.

Collis, J., & Messick, S. (2001). *Intelligence and personality*. Hove, UK: Lawrence Erlbaum Associates Ltd.

Colvin, S. S. (1902). Invention versus form in English composition. *Pedagogical Seminar, 9*, 393–421.

Conley, J. (1985). The hierarchy of consistency. *Personality and Individual Differences, 5*, 11–20.

Connelly, D., Lilienfeld, S., & Schmeelk, K. (2006). Integrity tests and morality. *International Journal of Selection and Assessment, 14*, 82–86.

Conrad, S., & Milburn, M. (2001). *Sexual intelligence*. New York: Crown Publishers.

Conte, J. (2005). A review and critique of emotional measures. *Journal of Organisational Behaviour, 26*, 433–440.

Cook, M. (1998). *Personnel selection and productivity*. Chichester, UK: Wiley.

Cook, M. (2004). *Personnel selection: Adding value through people*. Chichester, UK: Wiley.

Cooper, R., & Payne, R. (1967). Extraversion and some aspects of work behaviour. *Personnel Psychology, 20*, 45–57.

Cooper, R. K., & Sawaf, A. (1997). *Executive EQ: Emotional intelligence in leadership and organisations*. New York: Grosset, Putnam.

Copeland, J. (1975). Selecting engineers in an electronics firm. In K. Miller (Ed.), *Psychological testing in personnel assessment* (pp. 91–107). New York: Wiley.

Corcoran, D. (1964). The relation between introversion and salivation. *American Journal of Psychology, 11*, 289–300.

Corr, R. (2004). Reinforcement sensitivity theory and personality. *Neuroscience and Biobehavioural Reviews, 28*, 317–333.

Costa, P., & McCrae, R. (1992). *Revised NEO Personality Inventory (NEO-PI-R) and NEO Five-Factor Inventory (NEO-FFI): Professional manual*. Odessa, FL: Psychological Assessment Resources.

Costa, P., & McCrae, R. (1995a). Primary traits of the Eysenck P-E-N system. *Journal of Personality and Social Psychology, 69*, 308–317.

Costa, P., & McCrae, R. (1995b). Solid ground in the wetlands of personality: A reply to Block. *Psychological Bulletin, 117*, 216–220.

Costa, P., & Widiger, T. (Eds.). (2005). *Personality disorders and the five-factor model of personality* (2nd ed.). Washington, DC: APA.

Costa, P., McCrae, R., & Holland, J. (1984). Personality and vocational interests in an adult sample. *Journal of Applied Psychology, 69,* 390–400.

Cowan, D. (1989). An alternative to the dichotomous interpretation of Jung's psychological functions. *Journal of Personality Assessment, 53,* 459–472.

Cox, C. M. (1926). *Genetic studies of genius II: The early mental traits of three hundred geniuses.* Stanford, CA: Stanford University Press.

Cronbach, L. (1957). The two disciples of scientific psychology. *American Psychologist, 12,* 671–684.

Cropley, A. J. (1968). A note on the Wallach–Kogan test of creativity. *British Journal of Educational Psychology, 38,* 197–201.

Csikszentmihalyi, M. (1996). *Creativity: Flow and the psychology of discovery and invention.* New York: HarperCollins.

Csikszentmihalyi, M. (1999). Implications of a systems perspective for the study of creativity. In R. J. Sternberg (Ed.), *Creativity research handbook.* Cambridge, UK: Cambridge University Press.

Csoka, L. (1993). Psychological profiles for predicting leader performance. *Human Resource Management Review, 3,* 255–270.

Dalbert, C. (2001). *The justice motive as a personal resource.* New York: Plenum.

Dany, F., & Torchy, V. (1994). Recruitment and selection in Europe: Policies, practices and methods. In C. Brewster & A. Hegewisch (Eds.), *Policy and practice in European human resources management: The Price Waterhouse Cranfield survey.* London: Routledge.

Danziger, P., Larsen, J., & Connors, J. (1989). Myers–Briggs Type and keeping appointments for an experiment on problem solving. *Psychological Reports, 65,* 322.

Daus, C., & Ashkanasy, N. (2005). The case for the ability-based model of emotional intelligence in organisational behaviour. *Journal of Organisational Behaviour, 26,* 453–466.

Davidson, R., & Etherington, L. (1995). Personalities of accounting students and public accountants. *Journal of Accounting Education, 13,* 425–444.

Dawes, R. (2004). Time for a critical empirical investigation of the MBTI. *European Business Forum, 18,* 88–89.

Day, D. V., & Silverman, S. B. (1989). Personality and job performance: Evidence of incremental validity. *Personnel Psychology, 42,* 25–36.

De Bono, E. (1985). *Six thinking hats.* Boston: Little, Brown.

De Bono, E. (1992). *Serious creativity: Using the power of lateral thinking to create new ideas.* New York: HarperCollins.

De Clercq, B., & De Fruyt, F. (2003). Personality disorder symptoms in adolescence: A five-factor model perspective. *Journal of Personality Disorders, 17,* 269–292.

De Fruyt, F., & Mervielde, I. (1997). The five-factor model of personality and Holland's RIASEC interest types. *Personality and Individual Differences, 23,* 87–103.

De Fruyt, F., & Mervielde, I. (1999). RIASEC types and Big Five traits as predictors of employment status and nature of employment. *Personnel Psychology, 52,* 701–727.

De Pascalis, V., Zawadzki, B., & Strelau, J. (2000). The Formal Characteristics of Behaviour–Temperament Inventory (FCB-TI): Preliminary results of the Italian version. *Personality and Individual Differences, 28,* 287–298.

De Vos, A., Buijen, D., & Schalk, R. (2005). Making sense of a new employment relationship. *International Journal of Selection and Assessment, 13,* 41–52.

Dearborn, G. V. (1898). A study of imagination. *American Journal of Psychology, 5,* 183–190.

Deary, I. (2000). *Looking down on human intelligence.* Oxford, UK: Oxford University Press.

Deary, I. (2001). *Intelligence: A very short introduction.* Oxford, UK: Oxford University Press.

Deary, I. (2004). *Looking down on intelligence.* Oxford, UK: Oxford University Press.

Deary, I., & Matthews, G. (1993). Personality traits are alive and well. *The Psychologist, 6,* 299–300.

Deary, I., Ramsay, H., Wilson, J., & Riad, M. (1988). Simulated salivation: Correlations with personality and time of day effects. *Personality and Individual Differences, 4,* 903–909.

Deary, I., Peter, A., Austin, E., & Gibson, G. (1998). Personality traits and personality disorders. *British Journal of Psychology, 89,* 647–661.

Dellas, M., & Gaier, E. L. (1970). Identification of creativity: The individual. *Psychological Bulletin, 73,* 55–73.

Devito, A. (1985). A review of the Myers–Briggs Type Indicator. In J. Mitchell (Ed.), *Ninth mental measurements yearbook* (pp. 1030–1032). Lincoln, NE: University of Nebraska Press.

Dickson, J., & Buchholz, R. (1977). Management and belief about work in Scotland and the USA. *Journal of Management Studies, 14,* 80–101.

Diener, E. (1996). Traits can be powerful, but are not enough. *Journal of Research in Personality, 41,* 417–440.

Digman, J. (1990a). Personality structure. *Annual Review of Psychology, 41,* 303–336.

Digman, J. (1990b). Personality structure: Emergence of the five-factor model. *Annual Review of Psychology, 41,* 417–440.

Dilchert, S., Ones, D., Viswesvaran, C., & Deller, J. (2006). Response distortion in personality measurement. *Psychology Science, 48,* 209–225.

Dilchert, S., Ones, D., Davis, R., & Roslow, R. (2007). Cognitive ability predicts objectively measured counterproductive work behaviours. *Journal of Applied Psychology, 92,* 616–627.

Ditz, G. (1980). The Protestant ethic and the market economy. *Kyklos, 33,* 623–657.

Dixon, N. (1981). *The psychology of military incompetence.* London: Jonathan Cape.

Dobson, P. (2000). An investigation into the relationship between neuroticism, extraversion and cognitive test performance. *International Journal of Selection and Assessment, 8,* 99–109.

Dodd, W., Wollowick, H., & McNamara, W. (1970). Task difficulty as a moderator of long-term prediction. *Journal of Applied Psychology, 54,* 265–270.

Dollinger, S. J., & Clancy, S. M. (1993). Identity self, and personality: II. Glimpses through the autophotographic eye. *Journal of Personality and Social Psychology, 64,* 1064–1071.

Dollinger, S. J., & Orf, L. A. (1991). Personality and performance in "personality": Conscientiousness and Openness. *Journal of Research in Personality, 25,* 276–284.

Domino, G. (1970). Identification of potentially creative persons from the Adjective Check List. *Journal of Consulting and Clinical Psychology, 35,* 48–51.

Domino, G. (1974). Assessment of cinematographic creativity. *Journal of Personality and Social Psychology, 64,* 1064–1071.

Doyle, C. (2003). *Work and organisational psychology.* Hove, UK: Psychology Press.

Dragow, F. (2002). Intelligence and the workplace. In W. Borman, D. Ilgen, & R. Klimozki (Eds.), *Handbook of psychology* (Vol. 12, pp. 107–130). New York: Wiley.

Drakeley, R., & White, A. (1999). Competencies: Foundation garments or emperor's clothes? *Selection and Development Review, 15,* 7–13.

Drevdahl, J. E. (1956). Factors of importance for creativity. *Journal of Clinical Psychology, 12,* 21–26.

Dulewicz, S. V., & Higgs, M. J. (2001). *EI general and general 360 user guide.* Windsor, UK: NFER.

Dulewicz, V. (1989). Assessment centres as the route to competence. *Personnel Management, 11,* 56–59.

Dulewicz, V. (1992). Assessment of management competencies by personality questionnaires. *Selection and Development Review, 8,* 1–4.

Dulewicz, V. (1994). Personal competencies, personality and responsibility of middle managers. *Competency, 1,* 20–29.

Dyce, J. (1997). The Big Five factors of personality and their relationship to personality disorders. *Journal of Clinical Psychology, 53,* 587–593.

Elizhur, D. (1984). Facets of work values: A structural analysis of work outcomes. *Journal of Applied Psychology, 69,* 379–389.

Elizhur, D., Borg, I., Hunt, R., & Beck, I. (1991). The structure of work values: A cross-cultural comparison. *Journal of Organisational Behaviour*, *12*, 21–38.

Elliot, J. M. (1964). Measuring creative abilities in public relations and in advertising work. In C. W. Taylor (Ed.), *Widening horizons in creativity*. New York: Wiley.

Elliott, S., Lawty-Jones, M., & Jackson, C. (1996). Effect of dissimulation on self-report and objective measures of personality. *Personality and Individual Differences*, *21*, 335–343.

Emmons, R. (2000). Is spirituality an intelligence? *International Journal for the Psychology of Religion*, *10*, 3–26.

Evers, F., & Rush, J. (1996). The basis of competence. *Management Learning*, *27*, 275–300.

Eysenck, H. (1967). *The biological basis of personality*. Springfield, IL: Thomas.

Eysenck, H. (1981). Aim and scope. *Personality and Individual Differences*, *1*(1), 1.

Eysenck, H. (1985a). Can personality study ever be scientific. *Journal of Social Behaviour and Personality*, *1*, 3–19.

Eysenck, H. (Ed.). (1985b). *A model for intelligence*. Berlin, Germany: Springer-Verlag.

Eysenck, H. (1992). Four ways five factors are *not* basic. *Personality and Individual Differences*, *13*, 667–673.

Eysenck, H. (1998). *Intelligence: A new look*. New Brunswick, NJ. Transaction Publishers.

Eysenck, H., & Eysenck, M. (1975a). *Personality and individual differences: A natural science approach*. London: Plenum.

Eysenck, H., & Eysenck, M. (1985). *Personality and individual differences*. New York: Plenum.

Eysenck, H., & Eysenck, M. (1989). *Personality and individual differences*. New York: Plenum.

Eysenck, H., & Gudjonsson, G. (1989). *The causes and consequences of crime*. New York: Plenum.

Eysenck, H. J. (1960). *Maudsley Personality Inventory*. London: Maudsley Hospital.

Eysenck, H. J. (1993). Creativity and personality: Suggestions for a theory. *Psychological Inquiry*, *4*, 147–178.

Eysenck, H. J. (1994). Creativity and personality: Word association, origence, and psychoticism. *Creativity Research Journal*, *7*, 209–216.

Eysenck, H. J. (1995). *Genius: The natural history of creativity*. New York: Cambridge University Press.

Eysenck, H. J., & Eysenck, S. B. G. (1975b). *Manual of the Eysenck Personality Questionnaire*. London: Hodder & Stoughton.

Eysenck, H. J., & Eysenck, S. B. G. (1976). *Psychoticism as a dimension of personality*. London: Hodder & Stoughton.

Eysenck, H. J., & Furnham, A. (1993). Personality and the Barron–Welsh Art Scale. *Perceptual and Motor Skills*, *76*, 837–838.

Eysenck, H. J. (1964). *Crime and personality*. London: Routledge & Kegan Paul.

Eysenck, S., Eysenck, H., & Barrett, P. (1985). A revised version of the Psychoticism Scale. *Personality and Individual Differences*, *6*, 21–29.

Fagerström, K., & Lisper, H. (1977). Effects of listening to car radio, experience and personality of the driver on subsidiary reaction time and heart rate in a long-term driving task. In R. Machie (Ed.), *Vigilance* (pp. 73–86). New York: Plenum.

Feather, N. (1975). *Values in education and society*. New York: Free Press.

Feist, G. J. (1998). A meta-analysis of the impact of personality on scientific and artistic creativity. *Personality and Social Psychological Review*, *2*, 290–309.

Feist, G. J. (1999). Influence of personality on artistic and scientific creativity. In R. J. Sternberg (Ed.), *Handbook of creativity* (pp. 273–296). Cambridge, UK: Cambridge University Press.

Feist, G. J., & Barron, F. X. (2003). Predicting creativity from early to late adulthood: Intellect, potential, and personality. *Journal of Research in Personality*, *37*, 62–88.

Fico, J., Hogan, R., & Hogan, J. (2000). *Interpersonal compass manual and interpretation guide*. Tulsa, OK: Hogan Assessment System.

Finke, R. A., Ward, T. B., & Smith, S. M. (1992). *Creative cognition: Theory, research and applications*. Cambridge, MA: MIT Press.

Fishbein, M., & Ajzen, I. (1975). *Belief, attitude, intention and behaviour*. New York: Wiley.

Fleishman, E., & Quaintance, M. (1984). *Taxonomies of human performance*. Orlando, FL: Academic Press.

Fletcher, C., & Bailey, C. (2003). Assessing self-awareness. *Journal of Managerial Psychology, 18*, 395–404.

Flynn, J. (1984). The mean IQ of Americans: Massive gains 1932 to 1978. *Psychological Bulletin, 95*, 29–51.

Flynn, J. (1987). Massive IQ gains in 14 nations: What IQ tests really measure. *Psychological Bulletin, 101*, 171–191.

Fontana, D. (2000). *Personality at work*. Basingstoke, UK: Macmillan.

Ford, J., & Oswald, F. (2003). Understanding the dynamic leader. In M. Barrick & A. Ryan (Eds.), *Personality and work* (pp. 229–261). San Francisco: Jossey-Bass.

Foster, J. (2000). Motivation in the workplace. In N. Chmiel (Ed.), *Introduction to work and organisational psychology* (pp. 302–326). Oxford, UK: Blackwell.

Foster, T. (1991). *101 ways to generate great ideas*. London: Kogan Page.

Fox, A., & Spector, P. (2005). *Counterproductive work behaviour*. Washington, DC: APA.

Fraboni, M., & Saltstone, R. (1990). First and second generation entrepreneur typologies: Dimensions of personality. *Journal of Social Behaviour and Personality, 5*, 105–113.

Francis, L., Jones, S. H., Jackson, C. J., & Robbins, M. (2001). The feminine personality profile of male Anglican clergy in Britain and Ireland: A study employing the Eysenck Personality Profiler. *Review of Religious Research, 43*, 14–23.

Franz, R. (1980). Internal/external locus of control and labour market performance. *Psychology Quarterly Journal of Human Behaviour, 17*, 23–29.

Furnham, A. (1986). Response bias, social desirability and dissimulation. *Personality and Individual Differences, 7*, 385–400.

Furnham, A. (1990). *The Protestant work ethic*. London: Routledge.

Furnham, A. (1991a). *Personality at work*. London: Routledge.

Furnham, A. (1991b). Personality and occupational success: 16PF correlates of cabin crew performance. *Personality and Individual Differences, 12*, 87–90.

Furnham, A. (1992). Personality and learning style: A study of three instruments. *Personality and Individual Differences, 13*, 429–430.

Furnham, A. (1994). *Personality at work*. London: Routledge.

Furnham, A. (1995). The relationship of personality and intelligence to cognitive learning styles and achievement. In O. Saklofske & M. Zeidner (Eds.), *International handbook of personality and intelligence* (pp. 397–413). New York: Plenum.

Furnham, A. (1996a). The Big Five versus the Big Four: The relationship between the Myers–Briggs Type Indicator and the NEO-PI five factor model of personality. *Personality and Individual Differences, 21*, 303–307.

Furnham, A. (1996b). The FIRO-B, the Learning Style questionnaire, and the five-factor model. *Journal of Social Behaviour and Personality, 11*, 285–299.

Furnham, A. (1999). Personality and creativity. *Perceptual and Motor Skills, 88*, 407–408.

Furnham, A. (2000a). *The hopeless, hapless and helpless manager*. London: Whurr.

Furnham, A. (2000b). *Managerial competency frameworks*. London: Career Research Forum.

Furnham, A. (2001a). Self-estimates of intelligence: Culture and gender differences in self and other estimates of both general (*g*) and multiple intelligences. *Personality and Individual Differences, 31*, 1381–1405.

Furnham, A. (2001b). *The 3D manager*. London: Whurr.

Furnham, A. (2001c). Vocational preference and P–O fit. *Applied Psychology, 50*, 5–29.

Furnham, A. (2001d). Personality and individual differences in the workplace. In B. Roberts & R. Hogan (Eds.), *Personality psychology in the workplace* (pp. 223–252). Washington, DC: APA.

Furnham, A. (2002). Personality, style, preference and individual development. In M. Pearn (Ed.), *Individual differences in development in organisations* (pp. 89–105). New York: Wiley.

Furnham, A. (2003a). Belief in a just world: Research progress over the past decade. *Personality and Behavioural Differences*, *34*, 795–817.

Furnham, A. (2003b). *The incompetent manager*. London: Whurr.

Furnham, A. (2004). *Management and Myths*. Basingstoke, UK: Palgrave Macmillan.

Furnham, A. (2005a). *The people business*. Basingstoke, UK: Palgrave Macmillan.

Furnham, A. (2005b). *The psychology of behaviour at work*. Hove, UK: Psychology Press.

Furnham, A. (2005c). Gender and personality difference in self and other ratings of business intelligence. *British Journal of Management*, *16*, 91–103.

Furnham, A. (2006). Explaining the popularity of emotional intelligence. In K. Murphy (Ed.), *A critique of emotional intelligence* (pp. 141–159). Mahwah, NJ: Lawrence Erlbaum Associates, Inc.

Furnham, A. (2007a). Personality disorders and derailment at work. In J. Langan-Fox, C. Cooper, & R. Klimoski (Eds.), *Management challenges and symptoms of the dysfunctional workplace*. Cheltenham, UK: Edward Elgar.

Furnham, A. (2007b). HR professionals' beliefs about, and knowledge of, assessment techniques and psychometric tests. *International Journal of Selection and Assessment*, in press.

Furnham, A., & Bradley, A. (1997). Music while you work. *Applied Cognitive Psychology*, *11*, 445–455.

Furnham, A., & Bunclark, K. (2006). Sex differences in parents' estimations of their own and their children's intelligences. *Intelligences*, *39*, 1–14.

Furnham, A., & Cheng, H. (1996). Psychiatric symptomology on the recall of positive and negative personality information. *Behaviour Research and Therapy*, *34*, 731–733.

Furnham, A., & Crump, J. (2005). Personality traits, types and disorders. *European Journal of Personality*, *19*, 167–184.

Furnham, A., & Drakeley, R. (1993). Work locus of control and perceived organisational climate. *European Work and Organisational Psychologist*, *3*, 1–9.

Furnham, A., & Heaven, P. (1999). *Personality and social behaviour*. London: Arnold.

Furnham, A., & Jackson, C. (2007). Reinforcement sensitivity in the workplace. In P. Corr (Ed.), *The reinforcement sensitivity theory of personality*. Chichester, UK: Wiley.

Furnham, A., & Lambert, A. (2005). *Assessment and selection: Raising the standards*. London: Corporate Research Forum.

Furnham, A., & Miller, T. (1997). Personality, absenteeism and productivity. *Personality and Individual Differences*, *23*, 705–707.

Furnham, A., & Petrides, K. V. (2003). Trait emotional intelligence and happiness. *Social Behaviour and Personality*, *31*, 815–823.

Furnham, A., & Petrides, K. V. (2004). Parental estimates of five types of intelligence. *Australian Journal of Psychology*, *56*, 10–17.

Furnham, A., & Proctor, E. (1989). Belief in a just world. *British Journal of Social Psychology*, *28*, 365–389.

Furnham, A., & Steele, H. (1993). Measuring locus of control. *British Journal of Psychology*, *84*, 443–479.

Furnham, A., & Stephenson, R. (2007). Musical distractors, personality type and cognitive performance in school children. *Psychology of Music*, *35*, 401–418.

Furnham, A., & Strbac, L. (2002). Music is as distracting as noise. *Ergonomics*, *45*, 203–217.

Furnham, A., & Stringfield, P. (1993a). Personality and occupational behaviour: Myers–Briggs Type Indicator correlates of managerial practices in two cultures. *Human Relations*, *46*, 827–848.

Furnham, A., & Stringfield, P. (1993b). Personality and work performance: Myers–Briggs Type Indicator correlates of managerial performance in two cultures. *Personality and Individual Differences*, *14*, 145–153.

Furnham, A., & Taylor, J. (2004). *The dark side of behaviour at work*. Basingstoke: Palgrave Macmillan.

Furnham, A., & Thompson, J. (1991). Personality and self-reported delinquency. *Personality and Individual Differences, 12*, 585–593.

Furnham, A., & Zacherl, M. (1986). Personality and job satisfaction. *Personality and Individual Differences, 7*, 453–459.

Furnham, A., Sadka, V., & Brewin, C. (1994). The development of an occupational attribution style questionnaire. *Journal of Occupational Behaviour, 13*, 27–39.

Furnham, A., Forde, L., & Ferrari, K. (1999a). Personality and work motivation. *Personality and Individual Differences, 26*, 1035–1040.

Furnham, A., Jackson, C., & Miller, T. (1999b). Personality, learning style and work performances. *Personality and Individual Differences, 27*, 1113–1122.

Furnham, A., Jackson, C., Forde, L., & Cotter, T. (2001). Correlates of the Eysenck Personality Profiler. *Personality and Individual Differences, 30*, 587–594.

Furnham, A., Petrides, K. V., Jackson, C., & Cotter, T. (2002). Do personality factors predict job satisfaction? *Personality and Individual Differences, 33*, 1325–1342.

Furnham, A., Moutafi, J., & Crump, J. (2003). The relationship between the revised NEO-personality inventory and the Myers–Briggs Type Indicator. *Social Behaviour and Personality, 31*, 577–584.

Furnham, A., Petrides, K. V., Isaousis, I., Pappas, K., & Garrod, D. (2005). A cross-cultural investigation into the relationship between personality traits and work values. *Journal of Psychology, 139*, 5–32.

Furnham, A., Rawles, R., & Iqbal, S. (2006). Personality, intelligence and proof-reading. *Personality and Individual Differences, 41*, 1457–1467.

Furnham, A., Eysenck, S., & Saklofske, D. (2007a). The Eysenck Personality measures: Fifty years of scale developments. In G. Boyle, G. Matthews, & D. Saklofske (Eds.), *Handbook of personality theory and testing*. Thousand Oaks, CA: Sage.

Furnham, A., Pendleton, D., Johnson, J., & Hogan, R. (2007b). *Personality traits, personality disorders and job value preferences.* Unpublished paper.

Galton, F. (1869). *Hereditary genius.* Gloucester, MA: Peter Smith.

Gana, K., & Trouillet, R. (2003). Structure invariance of the Temperament and Character Inventory (TCI). *Personality and Individual Differences, 35*, 1483–1495.

Garden, A.-M. (1991). Unresolved issues with the Myers–Briggs Type Indicator. *Journal of Psychological Type, 22*, 3–14.

Gardner, H. (1983). *Creating minds.* New York: Basic Books.

Gardner, J. (1983). *Frames of mind: The theory of multiple intelligences.* New York: Basic Books.

Gardner, J. (1999). *Intelligence reframed: Multiple intelligence for the 21st century.* New York: Basic Books.

Gaudet, F., & Carli, A. (1957). Why executives fail. *Personnel Psychology, 10*, 7–22.

Gay, E., Weiss, D., Hendel, D., Dawis, R., & Lofquist, L. (1975). *The Minnesota Importance Questionnaire – 1975.* Minneapolis, MN: University of Minnesota.

Gelade, G. (1997). Creativity in conflict: The personality of the commercial creative. *Journal of Genetic Psychology, 165*, 67–78.

George, J. M., & Zhou, J. (2001). When openness to experience and conscientiousness are related to creative behavior: An interactional approach. *Journal of Applied Psychology, 86*, 513–524.

Gerstein, M., & Reisman, H. (1983). Strategic selection: Matching executives to business conditions. *Sloan Management Review, 24*, 118–139.

Getzels, J. W., & Jackson, P. W. (1962). *Creativity and intelligence: Explorations with gifted students.* London: Wiley.

Ghiselli, E. (1966). *The validity of occupational aptitude tests.* New York: Wiley.

Ghiselli, E., & Barthol, R. (1953). The validity of personality inventions in the selection of employees. *Journal of Applied Psychology, 37*, 18–20.

Ghiselli, E., & Brown, C. (1955). *Personnel and industrial psychology.* New York: McGraw-Hill.

Giacalone, R., & Greenberg, J. (1997). *Antisocial behaviour in the work-place*. Thousand Oaks, CA: Sage.

Gilhooly, K., Wynn, V., & Osman. M. (2004). Studies of divergent thinking. *Symposium address at the Annual Conference of the British Psychological Society*.

Gillespie, N., Cloninger, C., Heath, A., & Martin, N. (2003). The genetic and environmental relationship between Cloninger's dimensions of temperament and character. *Personality and Individual Differences, 35*, 1931–1946.

Goertzel, M. G., Goertzel, V., & Goertzel, T.G. (1978). *Eminent personalities*. San Francisco: Jossey-Bass.

Goh, D., & Leong, F. (1993). The relationship between Holland's theory of vocational interest and Eysenck's model of personality. *Personality and Individual Differences, 15*, 555–562.

Goleman, D. (1995). *Emotional intelligence: Why it can matter more than IQ*. New York: Bantam Books.

Goleman, D. (1998). *Working with emotional intelligence*. New York: Bantam Books.

Goleman, D. (2006). *Social intelligence: The new science of human relationships*. New York: Bantam Books.

Goodstein, L., & Prien, E. (2006). *Using individual assessment in the workplace*. New York: Pfeiffer.

Goodstein, L., & Schroder, W. (1963). An empirically derived managerial key for the California Psychological Inventory. *Journal of Applied Psychology, 47*, 42–45.

Gottfredson, G., Jones, E., & Holland, J. (1993). Personality and vocational interests. *Journal of Counselling Psychology, 40*, 518–525.

Gottfredson, L. (1997). Why *g* matters: The complexity of everyday life. *Intelligence, 24*, 79–132.

Gottfredson, L. (1998). The general intelligence factor. *Scientific American, 9*, 24–29.

Gottfredson, L. (2002). Where and why *g* matters: Not a mystery. *Human Performance, 15*, 25–46.

Gottfredson, L. (2005). What if the hereditarians' hypothesis is true? *Psychology, Public Policy and Law, 11*(2), 311–319.

Gottfredson, L., & Deary, I. (2004). Intelligence predicts health and longevity, but why? *Current Direction in Psychological Science, 13*, 1–4.

Gottfredson, L. S. (2003a). Dissecting practical intelligence theory: Its claims and evidence. *Intelligence, 31*, 343–397.

Gottfredson, L. S. (2003b). *g* jobs and life. In J. Nyborg (Ed.), *The science of mental ability* (pp. 293–342). Oxford, UK: Pergamon.

Gottfredson, L. S. (2003c). On Sternberg's "Reply to Gottfredson". *Intelligence, 31*, 415–424.

Gotz, K. O., & Gotz, K. (1973). Introversion–extraversion and neuroticism in gifted and ungifted art students. *Perceptual and Motor Skills, 36*, 675–678.

Gotz, K. O., & Gotz, K. (1979a). Personality characteristics of professional artists. *Perceptual and Motor Skills, 49*, 327–334.

Gotz, K. O., & Gotz, K. (1979b). Personality characteristics of successful artists. *Perceptual and Motor Skills, 49*, 919–924.

Gough, H. (1968). College attendance among high aptitude students as predicted from the CPI. *Journal of Counselling Psychology, 69*, 269–278.

Gough, H. (1984). A managerial potential scale for the California Psychological Inventory. *Journal of Applied Psychology, 69*, 233–240.

Gough, H. (1985). A work orientation scale for the California Psychological Inventory. *Journal of Applied Psychology, 70*, 505–513.

Gough, H. (1989). The California Psychological Inventory. In C. Niemark (Ed.), *Major psychological assessment instruments* (pp. 67–98). Boston: Allyn & Bacon.

Gough, H. G. (1961). Techniques for identifying the creative research scientist. In *Conference on the creative person*. Berkeley, CA: University of California, IPAR.

Gough, H. G. (1976). Studying creativity by means of association tests. *Journal of Applied Psychology, 61*, 348–353.

Greenberg, J. (2006). *Insidious work behaviour*. Mahwah, NJ: Lawrence Erlbaum Associates, Inc.

Griffin, R., & O'Leary-Kelly, A. (2004). *The dark side of organisational behaviour*. San Francisco: Jossey-Bass.

Grigorenko, E. L., & Sternberg, R. J. (2001). Analytical, creative, and practical intelligence as predictors of self-reported adaptive functioning: A case study in Russia. *Intelligence*, *29*, 57–73.

Groth-Marnet, G. (1984). *Handbook of psychological assessment*. New York: Van Nostrand.

Guastello, S., Rieke, M., Guastello, D., & Billings, S. (1992). A study of cynicism, personality and work values. *Journal of Psychology*, *126*, 37–48.

Guilford, J., Zimmerman, W., & Guilford, J. (1976). *The Guilford–Zimmerman temperament survey handbook*, San Diego, CA: Editors.

Guilford, J. P. (1950). Creativity. *American Psychologist*, *5*, 444–454.

Guilford, J. P. (1967). *The nature of human intelligence*. New York: McGraw-Hill

Guilford, J. P. (1968). Intelligence has three facets. *Science*, *160*, 615–620.

Guilford, J. P. (1981). Higher-order structure-of-intellect abilities. *Multivariate Behavioral Research*, *16*, 411–435.

Guilford, J. P. (1983). Transformation abilities of functions. *Journal of Creative Behavior*, *17*, 75–83.

Guion, R., & Gottier, R. (1965). Validity of personality measures in personnel selection. *Personnel Psychology*, *18*, 135–164.

Hafer, C., & Begue, L. (2005). Experimental research on just-world theory. *Psychological Bulletin*, *131*, 128–167.

Hakstian, A., & Cattell, R. (1976). *Comprehensive Ability Battery*. Champagne, IL: Institute for Personality and Ability Testing, Inc.

Haley, U., & Stumpf, J. (1989). Cognitive traits in strategic decision making: Linking theories of personality and cognition. *Journal of Management Studies*, *26*, 477–497.

Hall, C. S., & Lindzey, G. (1978). *Theories of personality* (3rd ed.). Chichester, UK: Wiley.

Halpern, D. (1992). *Sex differences: Cognitive abilities*. Hillsdale, NJ: Lawrence Erlbaum Associates, Inc.

Harrell, M., Harrell, T., McIntyre, S., & Weinberg, C. (1977). Predicting compensation among MBA graduate five and ten years after graduation. *Journal of Applied Psychology*, *62*, 636–640.

Harrell, T., & Harrell, M. (1945). Army general classification test scores for civilian occupations. *Educational and Psychological Measurement*, *5*, 229–239.

Harrell, T., & Harrell, M. (1984). *Stanford MBA careers: A 20 year longitudinal study*. Stanford, CA: Graduate School of Business, Research Paper 723.

Hartung, P., Borges, N., & Jones, B. (2005). Using person matching to predict career speciality choice. *Journal of Vocational Behaviour*, *67*, 102–117.

Harvey, M., Novicevic, M., & Kiessling, T. (2002). Development of multiple IQ maps for the use in the selection of impatriate managers: A practical theory. *International Journal of Intercultural Relations*, *26*, 493–524.

Haslam, N. (2007). *Introduction to personality and intelligence*. London: Sage.

Hathaway, S. R., & McKinley, J. C. (1967). *Manual of the Minnesota Multiphasic Personality Inventory*. New York: The Psychological Corporation.

Hattie, J. A. (1977). Conditions for administering creativity tests. *Psychological Bulletin*, *84*, 1249–1260.

Hattie, J. A. (1980). Should creativity tests be administered under test like conditions? An empirical study of three alternative conditions. *Journal of Educational Psychology*, *72*, 87–98.

Hausknecht, J., Day, D., & Thomas, S. (2004). Applicant reactions to selection procedures. *Personnel Psychology*, *57*, 639–683.

Heaven, P. (1996). Personality and self-reported delinquency: Analysis of the "Big Five" personality dimensions. *Personality and Individual Differences*, *20*, 47–54.

Helmes, E. (1989). Evaluating the internal structure of the Eysenck Personality Questionnaire: Objective criteria. *Multivariate Behavioural Research*, *24*, 353–364.

Hemsley, D. (1991). An experimental psychological model of schizophrenia. In A. Hafner, W. Gattaz, & F. Janzarik (Eds.), *Search for causes of schizophrenia* (pp. 179–188). Heidelberg, Germany: Springer-Verlag.

Henderson, J., & Nutt, P. (1980). The influence of decision style on decision-making behaviour. *Managerial Science, 26*, 371–386.

Hennessey, B. A., & Amabile, T. M. (1988). Story-telling: A method for assessing children's creativity. *Journal of Creative Behavior, 22*, 235–246.

Herrnstein, R., & Murray, C. (1994). *The bell curve.* New York: Free Press.

Herzberg, F., Mausner, D., & Snyderman, B. (1959). *The motivation to work.* New York: Wiley.

Heston, L. L. (1966). Psychiatric disorders in foster home reared children of schizophrenic mothers. *British Journal of Psychiatry, 112*, 1103–1110.

Hicks, L. (1984). Conceptual and empirical analysis of some assumptions of an explicitly technological theory. *Journal of Personality and Social Psychology, 46*, 1118–1131.

Higgs, M. J., & Dulewicz, S. V. (1999). *Making sense of emotional intelligence.* Windsor, UK: NFER-Nelson.

Hill, A. (1975). Extraversion and variety-seeking in a monotonous task. *British Journal of Psychology, 66*, 9–13.

Hinrich, R. (1978). An eight year follow-up of a management assessment centre. *Journal of Applied Psychology, 63*, 596–601.

Hirsch, S., & Kummerow, J. (1998). *Introduction to type in organisations.* Palo Alto, CA: Consulting Psychologist Press.

Hirschfeld, R., & Field, H. (2000). Work centrality and work alienation. *Journal of Organisational Behaviour, 21*, 789–800.

Hocevar, D. (1980). Intelligence, divergent thinking and creativity. *Intelligence, 4*, 25–40.

Hochschild, A. (1983). *The managed heart: Commercialisation of human feeling.* Berkeley, CA: University of California Press.

Hodgkinson, G., & Payne, R. (1998). Graduate selection in three European countries. *Journal of Occupational and Organisational Psychology, 71*, 359–365.

Hodgkinson, G., Daley, N., & Payne, R. (1995). Knowledge of, and attitudes towards, the demographic time bomb. *International Journal of Management, 16*, 59–76.

Hofstede, W. (2001). Intelligence and personality: Do they mix? In J. Collis & S. Messick (Eds.), *Intelligence and personality: Bridging the gap in theory and measurement* (pp. 43–60). Hove, UK: Lawrence Erlbaum Associates Ltd.

Hogan, J., & Brinkmeyer, K. (1997). Bridging the gap between overt and personality based integrity tests. *Personnel Psychology, 5*, 587–600.

Hogan, J., & Holland, B. (2003). Using theory to evaluate personality and job-performance relations. *Journal of Applied Psychology, 88*, 100–112.

Hogan, R. (1991). Personality and personality measurement. In M. Dunnette & L. Hough (Eds.), *Handbook of industrial and organizational psychology* (2nd ed., Vol. 2, pp. 327–396). Palo Alto, CA: Consulting Psychologists Press.

Hogan, R. (2005a). Comments. *Human Performance, 18*, 405–407.

Hogan, R. (2005b). In defence of personality measures. *Human Performance, 18*, 331–341.

Hogan, R. (2006). *Personality and the fate of organizations.* Mahwah, NJ: Lawrence Erlbaum Associates, Inc.

Hogan, R., & Blake, R. (1999). John Holland's vocational typology and personality theory. *Journal of Vocational Psychology, 55*, 41–56.

Hogan, R., & Hogan, J. (1989). How to measure employee reliability. *Journal of Applied Psychology, 94*, 273–279.

Hogan, R., & Hogan, J. (1992). *Hogan Personality Inventory manual.* Tulsa, OK: Hogan Assessment Systems.

Hogan, R., & Hogan, J. (1997). *Hogan Development Survey manual.* Tulsa, OK: Hogan Assessment Systems.

Hogan, R., & Hogan, J. (2001). Assessing leadership: A view from the dark side. *International Journal of Selection and Assessment, 9,* 40–51.

Hogan, R., & Roberts, B. (2000). A socioanalytic perspective of person–environment interaction. In W. Walsh, K. Craik, & R. Price (Eds.), *New directions in person–environment psychology* (pp. 1–24). Mahwah, NJ: Lawrence Erlbaum Associates, Inc.

Hogan, R., Hogan, J., & Trickey, G. (1999). Goodbye mumbo-jumbo: The transcendental beauty of a validity coefficient. *Selection and Development Review, 15,* 3–16.

Holland, J. (1966). *A psychology of vocational choice: A theory of personality types and environments.* Waltham, MA: Blarsdell.

Holland, J. (1973). *Making vocational choices. A theory of career.* Englewood Cliffs, NJ: Prentice Hall.

Holland, J. (1985). *Making vocational choices: A theory of vocational personalities and work environments.* Englewood Cliffs, NJ: Prentice Hall.

Hollenbeck, J., & Whitener, E. (1988). Reclaiming personality traits for personnel selection: Self-esteem as an illustrative case. *Journal of Management, 14,* 81–91.

Horn, J. L., & Knapp, J. R. (1973). On the subjective character of the empirical base of Guilford's structure-of-intellect model. *Psychological Bulletin, 80,* 33–43.

Hough, L. (1996a). Can integrity tests be trusted? *Employment Testing, 5,* 97–111.

Hough, L. (2003). Emerging trends and needs in personality research and practice. In M. Barrick & M. Ryan (Eds.), *Personality and work* (pp. 283–325). San Francisco: Jossey-Bass.

Hough, L., & Oswald, F. (2005). They're right, well . . . mostly right: Research evidence and an agenda to rescue personality testing from 1960s insights. *Human Performance, 18,* 373–388.

Hough, L., Oswald, F., & Ployhart, R. (2001). Determinants, detection and amelioration of adverse impact in personal selection procedures. *International Journal of Selection and Assessment, 9,* 152–194.

Hough, L. M. (1992). The "Big Five" personality variable construct confusion: Description versus prediction. *Human Performance, 5,* 139–155.

Hough, L. M. (1996b). Personality at work: Issues and evidence. In M. D. Hakel (Ed.), *Beyond multiple choice: Evaluating alternatives to traditional testing for selection* (pp. 52–65). Hillsdale, NJ: Lawrence Erlbaum Associates, Inc.

Hough, L. M. (2001). I owe its advance to personality. In B. Roberts & R. Hogan (Eds.), *Personality psychology in the workplace* (pp. 19–29). Washington, DC: American Psychological Association.

Hough, L. M., & Furnham, A. (2003). Use of personality variables in work settings. In W. Borman, O. Ilgen, & R. Klimoski (Eds.), *Handbook of psychology* (Vol. 12, pp. 131–169). New York: Wiley.

Hough, L. M., & Schneider, R. J. (1996). Personality trait, taxonomies and application in organisations. In K. R. Murphy (Ed.), *Individual differences and behaviour in organisations* (pp. 31–88). San Francisco: Jossey-Bass.

Hough, L. M., Eaton, N. L., Dunnette, M. D., Kamp, J. D., & McCloy, R. A. (1990). Criterion-related validities of personality constructs and the effects of response distortion on these validities. *Journal of Applied Psychology, 75,* 581–595.

Hovorka-Mead, A., Ross, W., Whipple, T., & Renchin, M. (2002). Watching the detectives. *Personnel Psychology, 55,* 329–362.

Howard, A., & Bray, D. (1988). *Managerial lives in transition.* New York: Guilford Press.

Howard, R., & Howard, J. (2001). *The owner's manual for personality at work.* Austin, TX: Bard Press.

Hudson, L. (1970). The question of creativity. In P. E. Vernon (Ed.), *Creativity: Selected readings.* Harmondsworth, UK: Penguin.

Hulsheger, U., Maier, G., & Stumpp, T. (2007). Validity of general mental ability for the prediction of job performance and training success in Germany. *International Journal of Selection and Assessment, 15,* 3–18.

Hunter, J. (1986). Cognitive ability, cognitive aptitudes, job knowledge and job performance. *Intelligence*, *29*, 340–362.

Hunter, J., & Hunter, R. (1984). Validity and utility of alternative predictors of job performance. *Psychological Bulletin*, *96*, 72–98.

Hunter, J. E., & Schmidt, F. L. (1976). A critical analysis of the statistical and ethical implications of various definitions of test fairness. *Psychological Bulletin*, *83*, 1053–1071.

Hunter, J. E., & Schmidt, F. L. (1990). *Methods of meta-analysis: Correcting for error and bias in research findings.* Newbury Park, CA: Sage.

Hurtz, G., & Donovan, J. (2000). Personality and job performance. *Journal of Applied Psychology*, *85*, 869–879.

Iacono, W., & Patrick, C. (1997). Polygraphy and integrity testing. In R. Rogers (Ed.), *Clinical assessment of malingering and deception* (pp. 252–283). New York: Guilford Press.

Ingleton, C. (1975). Graduate selection. In K. Miller (Ed.), *Psychological testing in personnel assessment* (pp. 61–71). New York: Wiley.

Inwald, R. (1988). Five year follow-up study of departmental terminators as predicted by 16 pre-employment psychological indicators. *Journal of Applied Psychology*, *73*, 1–8.

Jackson, C. J., Furnham, A., Forde, L., & Cotter, T. (2000). The structure of the Eysenck Personality Profiler. *British Journal of Psychology*, *91*, 223–239.

Jackson, D., & Rushton, J. (2006). Males have greater "g". *Intelligence*, *34*, 479–486.

Jacobs, R. (1989). Getting the measure of management competence. *Personnel Management*, *6*, 32–37.

James, W. (1890). *Principles of psychology*. London: Macmillan.

Jamison, K. R. (1989). Mood disorders and patterns of creativity in British writers and artists. *Psychiatry*, *52*, 125–134.

Jamison, K. R. (1993). *Touched with fire: Manic depressive illness and the artistic temperament.* New York: Free Press.

Janowsky, D., Morter, S., & Hong, L. (2002). Relationship of Myers–Briggs Type Indicator personality characteristics to suicidality in affective disorder patients. *Journal of Psychometric Research*, *36*, 33–39.

Jay, R. (2006). *The ultimate book of business creativity*. Oxford, UK: Capstone.

Jeanneret, R., & Silzer, R. (2000). An overview of individual psychological assessment. In R. Jeanneret & R. Silzer (Eds.), *Individual psychological assessment* (pp. 3–26). San Francisco: Jossey-Bass.

Jensen, A. (1969). How much can we boost IQ and scholastic achievement? *Harvard Educational Review*, *39*, 1–123.

Jensen, A. (1998). *The g factor: The science of mental ability*. New York: Praeger.

Jessup, C., & Jessup, H. (1971). Validity of the Eysenck Personality Inventory in pilot selection. *Occupational Psychology*, *45*, 111–123.

Johnson, M. (2001). Changes in job values during the transition to adulthood. *Work and Occupations*, *28*, 315–345.

Johnson, R. (2003). Towards a better understanding of the relationship between personality and individuals' job performance. In M. Barrick & A. Ryan (Eds.), *Personality and work* (pp. 83–120). San Francisco: Jossey-Bass.

Jones, G. (1988). *Investigation of the efficacy of general ability versus specific abilities as predictors of occupational success.* Unpublished thesis, St Mary's University of Texas.

Jones, H. (1997). The Protestant ethic: Weber's model and the empirical literature. *Human Relations*, *50*, 757–778.

Jones, H., Sasek, J., & Wakefield, J. (1976). Maslow's need hierarchy and Cattell's 16PF. *Journal of Clinical Psychology*, *32*, 74–76.

Jones, J. (1991). *Pre-employment honesty testing*. Westport, CT: Quorum Books.

Jones, P., & Poppleton, S. (1998). Trends in personality assessment for the millennium. *Selection and Development Review*, *14*, 16–18.

Jordan, P. J., Ashkanasy, N. M., Hartel, C. E. J., & Hooper, G. S. (2002). Workgroup emotional intelligence scale development and relationship to team process effectiveness and goal focus. *Human Resource Management Review, 12*, 195–214.

Judge, T., Mattocchio, J., & Thorensen, C. (1997). Five-factor model of personality and employee absence. *Journal of Applied Psychology, 82*, 745–755.

Judge, T., Bono, J., Ilies, R., & Gerhert, M. (2002a). Personality and leadership: A qualitative and quantitative review. *Journal of Applied Psychology, 87*, 765–780.

Judge, T., Heller, D., & Mount, M. (2002b). Five-factor model of personality and employee absence. *Journal of Applied Psychology, 87*, 530–541.

Judge, T., Colbert, A., & Ilies, R. (2004). Intelligence and leadership. *Journal of Applied Psychology, 89*, 542–555.

Jung, C. (1953). *The integration of personality*. New York: Farrar & Ruchart.

Karp, S. L. (Ed.). (1999). *Studies of objective/projective personality tests*. Brooklandville, MD: Objective/Projective Tests, Inc.

Karson, S., & O'Dell, J. (1970). *A guide to the clinical use of the 16PF*. Champagne, IL: IPAT.

Kasof, J. (1997). Creativity and breadth of attention. *Creativity Research Journal, 10*, 303–315.

Kaye, A., & Shea, M. (2000). Personality disorders, personality traits, and defense mechanisms measures. In APA Taskforce (Eds.), *Handbook of psychiatric measures* (pp. 713–749). Washington, DC: APA.

Keefe, I. (1988). *Profiling and utilizing learning style*. Reston, VA: NASSP.

Keller, L., Bouchard, T., Arvey, R., Segal, N., & Dawis, R. (1992). Work values: Genetic and environmental influences. *Journal of Applied Psychology, 77*, 79–88.

Kershner, J. R., & Ledger, G. (1985). Effect of sex, intelligence, and style of thinking on creativity: A comparison of gifted and average IQ children. *Journal of Personality and Social Psychology, 48*, 1033–1040.

Kets de Vries, M. (1999). Managing puzzling personalities. *European Management Journal, 17*, 8–19.

Kets de Vries, M. (2004). Organisations on the couch. *European Management Journal, 22*, 183–200.

Kets de Vries, M., & Miller, D. (1985). *The neurotic organisation*. San Francisco, CA: Jossey-Bass.

Kidwell, R., & Martin, C. (Eds.). (2005). *Managing organisational deviance*. Thousand Oaks, CA: Sage.

Kim, J. (1980). Relationships of personality to perceptual and behavioural responses in stimulating and non-stimulating tasks. *Academy of Management Journal, 23*, 307–319.

King, L., Walker, L., & Broyles, S. (1996). Creativity and the five-factor model. *Journal of Research in Personality, 30*, 189–203.

Kirchner, W. (1961). "Real-life" faking on the Strong Vocational Interest Blank by sales applicants. *Journal of Applied Psychology, 45*, 273–276.

Kirchner, W. (1962). "Real-life" faking on the Edwards Personal Preference Schedule by sales applicants. *Journal of Applied Psychology, 46*, 128–130.

Kirton, M., & Mulligan, G. (1973). Correlates of managers' attitudes toward change. *Journal of Applied Psychology, 58*, 101–107.

Klehe, U.-C. (2004). Choosing how to choose: Institutional pressures affecting the adoption of personnel selection procedures. *International Journal of Selection and Assessment, 12*, 327–342.

Klehe, U.-C., & Anderson, N. (2005). The prediction of typical and maximum performance. In A. Evers, O. Smit-Voskugh, & N. Anderson (Eds.), *Handbook of personnel selection*. Oxford, UK: Blackwell.

Klein, P. (1997). Multiplying the problems of intelligence by eight: A critique of Gardner's Theory. *Canadian Journal of Education, 22*, 377–394.

Kline, P. (1978). *OOQ and OPQ Personality Tests*. Windsor, UK: NFER.

Kline, P., & Cooper, C. (1986). Psychoticism and creativity. *Journal of Genetic Psychology, 147*, 183–188.

Knox, L., & Spivak, H. (2004). What health professionals should know: Core competencies for effective practice in youth violence prevention. *American Journal of Preventative Medicine, 29*, 191–199.

Kohn, M., & Schooler, C. (1982). Job conditions and personality: A longitudinal assessment of their reciprocal effects. *American Journal of Sociology, 87*, 1257–1286.

Koke, L. C., & Vernon, P. A. (2003). The Sternberg Triarchic Abilities test (STAT) as a measure of academic achievement and general intelligence. *Personality and Individual Differences, 35*, 1803–1807.

Kornor, H., & Nordvik, A. (2004). Personality traits in leadership behaviour. *Scandinavian Journal of Personality, 45*, 49–54.

Kriedt, P., & Gadel, M. (1953). Prediction of turnover among clerical workers. *Journal of Applied Psychology, 37*, 338–340.

Kuhn, T. S. (1970). *The structure of scientific revolutions.* Chicago: University of Chicago Press.

Kuncel, N., Hezlett, S., & Ones, D. (2001). A comprehensive meta-analysis of the predictive validity of the Graduate Record Examinations. *Psychological Bulletin, 127*, 162–181.

Kuncel, N., Hezlett, S., & Ones, D. (2004). Academic performance, career potential, creativity and job performance. *Journal of Personality and Social Psychology, 86*, 148–161.

Kwiatkowski, R. (2003). Trends in organisations and selection. *Journal of Managerial Psychology, 18*, 382–394.

Landy, F. (2006). The long, frustrating and fruitless search for social intelligence: A cautionary tale. In K. Murphy (Ed.), *A critique of emotional intelligence* (pp. 81–123). Mahwah, NJ: Lawrence Erlbaum Associates, Inc.

Larson, L., Rottinghaus, P., & Borgen, F. (2002). Meta-analyses of Big Six interests and Big Five personality factors. *Journal of Vocational Behaviour, 61*, 217–229.

Lauritzen, E. S. (1963). Semantic divergent thinking factors among elementary school children. *Dissertation Abstracts, 24*, 629.

Lee, K., Ashton, M., & Shin, K.-H. (2005). Personality correlates of work place antisocial behaviour. *Applied Psychology, 54*, 81–98.

Lerner, M. (1980). *The belief in a just world.* New York: Plenum.

Lerner, M., & Miller, D. (1978). Just world research and the attribution process. *Psychological Bulletin, 85*, 1030–1050.

Leuner, B. (1966). Emotionale Intelligenz und Emanzipation [Emotional intelligence and emancipation]. *Praxis der Kinderpsychologie und Kinderpsychiatry, 15*, 196–203.

Lievens, F., van Dam, K., & Anderson, N (2002). Recent trends in challenges in personnel selection. *Personnel Review, 31*, 580–601.

Lievens, F., De Corte, W., & Brysse, K. (2003). Applicant perceptions of selection procedures. *International Journal of Selection and Assessment, 11*, 67–71.

Lilienfeld, S., Alliger, G., & Mitchell, K. (1995). Why integrity testing remains controversial. *American Psychologist, 50*, 457–458.

Lloyd-Evans, R., Batey, M., & Furnham, A. (2006). Bipolar disorder and creativity: Investigating a possible link. *Advances in Psychology Research, 40*, 111–141.

Locke, E. (2005). Why emotional intelligence is an invalid concept. *Journal of Organisational Behaviour, 26*, 425–431.

Long, D. (2004). Competency-based training in neurosurgery: The next revolution in medical education. *Surgical Neurology, 61*, 5–14.

Loo, R. (1979). Role of primary personality factors in the perception of traffic signs and driver violations and accidents. *Accident Analysis and Prevention, 11*, 125–127.

Lopes, P., Salovey, P., & Straus, R. (2003). Emotional intelligence, personality and the perceived quality of social relationships. *Personality and Individual Differences, 35*, 641–658.

Lorr, M. (1991). An empirical evaluation of the MBTI typology. *Personality and Individual Differences, 12*, 1141–1145.

Losey, M. (1999). Mastering the competencies of HR management. *Human Resource Management, 38*, 95–102.

Lounsbury, J., Gibson, L., Steel, R., Sundstrom, E., & Loveland, J. (2004). An investigation of intelligence and personality in relation to career satisfaction. *Personality and Individual Differences, 37*, 181–187.

Lowenfeld, V., & Beittel, K. (1959). Interdisciplinary criteria of creativity in the arts and sciences: A progress report. *Research Yearbook, National Art Education Association*, 35–44.

Lubart, T. I. (1994). Creativity. In R. J. Sternberg (Ed.), *Thinking and problem solving. Handbook of perception and cognition* (2nd ed.). San Diego, CA: Academic Press.

Lubart, T. I. (2003). In search of creative intelligence. In R. J. Sternberg & J. Lautrey (Eds.), *Models of intelligence: International perspectives*. Washington, DC: American Psychological Association.

Lubinski, D. (2004). Introduction to the special section on cognitive abilities. *Journal of Personality and Social Psychology, 86*, 96–111.

Lucas, R., & Diener, E. (2003). The happy worker. In M. Barrick & A. Ryan (Eds.), *Personality and work* (pp. 30–59). San Francisco: Jossey-Bass.

Lynam, D., & Widiger, T. (2004). Using the five-factor model to represent the DSM-IV personality disorders. *Journal of Abnormal Psychology, 110*, 401–412.

Lynn, R. (1999). Sex differences in intelligence and brain size. *Intelligence, 27*, 1–12.

Lynn, R., & Irwing, P. (2004). Sex differences on the progressive matrices: A meta-analysis. *Intelligence, 32*, 481–498.

MacKinnon, D. W. (1961). Fostering creativity in students of engineering. *Journal of Engineering Education, 52*, 129–142.

MacKinnon, D. W. (1965). Personality and the realization of creative potential. *American Psychologist, 20*, 273–281.

MacKinnon, D. W. (1978). *In search of human effectiveness*. New York: Creative Education Foundation.

Mackintosh, N. (1998). *IQ and human intelligence*. Oxford, UK: Oxford University Press.

Magnusson, D., & Backteman, G. (1978). Longitudinal stability of person characteristics: Intelligence and creativity. *Applied Psychological Measurement, 2*, 481–490.

Manhardt, P. (1972). Job orientations of male and female college graduates in business. *Personnel Psychology, 25*, 361–368.

Mansfield, R. (1999). What is "competence" all about? *Competency, 6*, 12–16.

Mantech, P. (1983). *Work Values Questionnaire*. Auckland, New Zealand: ABRA Press.

Marcia, D., Aiuppa, T., & Watson, J. (1989). Personality type, organizational norms and self-esteem. *Psychological Reports, 65*, 915–919.

Marcus, B., Hoft, S., & Riediger, M. (2006). Integrity tests and the five factor model of personality. *International Journal of Selection and Assessment, 14*, 113–130.

Mars, G. (1984). *Cheats at work*. London: Counterpart.

Martin, T., & Kirkaldy, B. (1998). Gender differences on the EPQ-R and attitudes to work. *Personality and Individual Differences, 24*, 1–5.

Martindale, C. (1981). *Cognition and consciousness*. Homewood, IL: Dorsey.

Martindale, C. (1989). Personality, situation, and creativity. In J. A. Glover, R. R. Ronning, & C. R. Reynolds (Eds.), *Handbook of creativity. Perspectives on individual differences* (pp. 3–32). New York: Plenum.

Martindale, C. (1999). Biological bases of creativity. In R. J. Sternberg (Ed.), *Creativity research handbook*. Cambridge, UK: Cambridge University Press.

Martindale, C., & Dailey, A. (1996). Creativity. Primary process cognition and personality. *Personality and Individual Differences, 20*, 409–414.

Martinko, M., Gundlack, M., & Douglas, S. (2002). Toward an integrative theory of counterproductive workplace behaviour. *International Journal of Selection and Assessment, 10*, 36–50.

Matteson, M., Ivancevich, J., & Smith, S. (1984). Relation of Type A behaviour to performance and satisfaction among sales personnel. *Journal of Vocational Behaviour, 25*, 203–214.

Matthewman, J. (1997). Competencies in practice. *Competency, 9*, 11–15.

Matthews, G. (1999). Personality and skill. In P. Ackerman, P. Kyllonen, & R. Roberts (Eds.), *Learning and individual differences* (pp. 437–462). Atlanta, GA: Georgia Institute of Technology.

Matthews, G., & Stanton, N. (1994). Item and scale factor analysis of the Occupation Personality Questionnaire. *Personality and Individual Differences, 16*, 733–743.

Matthews, G., Stanton, N., Graham, N., & Brimelow, C. (1990). A factor analysis of the scales of the Occupational Personality Questionnaire. *Personality and Individual Differences, 11*, 591–596.

Matthews, G., Zeidner, M., & Roberts, R. D. (2002). *Emotional intelligence: Science and myth.* Cambridge, MA: MIT Press.

Matthews, G., Deary, I., & Whiteman, M. (2003). *Personality traits.* Cambridge, UK: Cambridge University Press.

Mayer, J. D., & Salovey, P. (1997). What is emotional intelligence? In P. Salovey & D. J. Sluyter (Eds.), *Emotional development and emotional intelligence: Educational implications* (pp. 3–31). New York: Basic Books.

Mayer, J. D., Salovey, P., & Caruso, D. R. (2000). Models of emotional intelligence. In R. J. Sternberg (Ed.), *The handbook of intelligence* (pp. 396–420). New York: Cambridge University Press.

Mayer, J. D., Salovey, P., & Caruso, D. R. (2002). *The Mayer–Salovey–Caruso Emotional Intelligence Test (MSCEIT): User's manual.* Toronto, Canada: Multi-Health Systems.

McCall, M. (1998). *High flyers.* Cambridge, MA: Harvard University Press.

McClelland, D. (1973). Testing for competency rather than intelligence. *American Psychologist, 28*, 1–14.

McCloy, W., & Meier, N. C. (1931). Re-creative imagination. *Psychological Monographs, 51*, 108–116.

McCrae, R. (1987). Creativity, divergent thinking and openness to experience. *Journal of Personality and Social Psychology, 52*, 1258–1265.

McCrae, R., & Costa, P. (1989). Reinterpreting the Myers–Briggs Type Indicator from the perspective of the five-factor model of personality. *Journal of Personality, 57*, 17–40.

McCrae, R., & Costa, P. (1995). Trait explanations in personality psychology. *European Journal of Personality Psychology, 9*, 211–252.

McDonald, D. A., Anderson, P. E., Tsagarakis, C. I., & Holland, J. H. (1994). Examination of the relationship between the Myers–Briggs Type Indicator and the NEO Personality Inventory. *Psychological Reports, 74*, 339–344.

McHenry, J., Hough, L., Toquam, J., Hanson, M., & Ashworth, S. (1990). Project A validity results. *Personnel Psychology, 43*, 335–354.

McLoughlin, C., Friedson, D., & Murray, J. (1983). Personality profiles of recently terminated executives. *Personnel and Guidance Journal, 61*, 226–229.

Mednick, S. A. (1962). The associative basis of the creative process. *Psychological Review, 3*, 220–232.

Mednick, S. A., & Andrews, F. M. (1967). Creative thinking and level of intelligence. *Journal of Creative Behavior, 1*, 428–431.

Mednick, S. A., & Mednick, M. T. (1967). *Examiner's manual: Remote Associates Test.* Boston: Houghton Mifflin.

Meehl, P. (1992). Factors and taxa traits and types: Differences of degree and differences of kind. *Journal of Personality, 60*, 117–174.

Mendelsohn, E. (1965). Review of the Myers–Briggs Type Indicator. In O. K. Buros (Ed.), *Sixth mental measurement yearbook.* Highland Park, NJ: Gryphon Press.

Merten, T. (1993). Word association responses and psychoticism. *Personality and Individual Differences, 14*, 837–839.

Merten, T. (1995). Factors influencing word-association responses: A reanalysis. *Creativity Research Journal, 8*, 249–263.

Merten, T., & Fischer, I. (1999). Creativity, personality and word association responses: Associative behaviour in forty supposedly creative persons. *Personality and Individual Differences, 27*, 933–942.

Messick, S. (Ed.). (1976). *Individuality and learning*. San Francisco: Jossey-Bass.

Messick, S. (1984). The nature of cognitive styles: Problems and promise in educational practice. *Educational Psychologist, 19*, 59–74.

Messick, S. (1994). The matter of style: Manifestations of personality in cognition, learning and teaching. *Educational Psychologist, 29*, 121–136.

Meyer, J., Irving, G., & Allen, N. (1998). Examination of the combined effects of work values and early work experiences on organisational commitment. *Journal of Organisational Behaviour, 19*, 29–52.

Michielsen, H., Willemsen, T., Croon, M., De Vries, J., & Van Heck, G. (2004). Determinants of general fatigue. *Psychology and Health, 19*, 223–235.

Miklewska, A., Kaczmarek, M., & Strelau, J. (2005). The relationship between temperament and intelligence. *Personality and Individual Differences, 40*, 643–653.

Miller, E., & Chapman, L. (1983). Continued word associations in hypothetically psychosis-prone college students. *Journal of Abnormal Psychology, 92*, 468–478.

Miller, J., Lynam, D., Widiger, T., & Leukefeld, C. (2001). Personality disorders as extreme variants of common personality dimensions. *Journal of Personality, 69*, 253–276.

Miller, J., Woehr, D., & Hudspeth, N. (2002). The meaning and measurement of the work ethic. *Journal of Vocational Behaviour, 60*, 451–489.

Miller, K. (1975). *Psychological testing in personnel assessment*. New York: Wiley.

Millon, T. (1981). *Disorders of personality DSM-III: Axis II*. New York: Wiley.

Mills, C., & Bohannon, W. (1980). Personality characteristics of effective state police officers. *Journal of Applied Psychology, 65*, 680–684.

Miner, J., & Capps, M. (1996). *How honesty testing works*. Westport, CT: Quorum.

Mischel, W. (1968). *Personality and assessment*. New York: Wiley.

Moloney, K. (1997). Why competencies may not be enough. *Competency, 9*, 33–37.

Moore, R., & Stewart, R. (1989). Evaluating employee integrity. *Employee Responsibility and Rights Journal, 2*, 203–218.

Moore, T. (1987, March 30). Personality tests are back. *Fortune*, 74–82.

Morey, L., Waugh, M., & Blashfield, R. (1985). MMPI Scales for DSM-III personality disorders: Their derivation and correlates. *Journal of Personality Assessment, 49*, 245–251.

Morgan, H. (1996). An analysis of Gardner's theory of multiple intelligence. *Roeper Review, 18*, 263–269.

Morgenstern, F., Hodgson, R., & Law, L. (1974). Work efficiency and personality: A comparison of introverted and extroverted subjects exposed to conditions of distraction and distortion of stimulus in a learning task. *Ergometrics, 17*, 211–220.

Mortimer, J., Lorence, J., & Kumka, D. (1986). *Work, family and personality: Transition to adulthood*. Norwood, NJ: Ablex.

Most, R., & Zeidner, M. (1995). Constructing personality and intelligence instruments. In D. Saklofske & M. Zeidner (Eds.), *International handbook of personality and intelligence* (pp. 475–503). New York: Plenum.

Mount, M., & Barrick, M. (1995). The Big Five personality dimensions. *Research in Personnel and Human Resources Management, 13*, 153–200.

Moutafi, J., Furnham, A., & Crump, J. (2005). What facets of openness and conscientiousness predict fluid intelligence scores? *Learning and Individual Differences, 16*, 31–42.

Moutafi, J., Furnham, A., & Tsaousis, I. (2006). Is the relationship between intelligence and trait neuroticism mediated by test anxiety? *Personality and Individual Differences, 40*, 587–597.

Mueller, J. (1992). Anxiety and performance. In A. Smith & D. Jones (Eds.), *Handbook of human performance* (pp. 127–160). London: Academic Press.

Mumford, M., Connelly, M., Helton, W., Strange, J., & Osburn, H. (2001). On the construct validity of integrity tests. *International Journal of Selection and Assessment, 9*, 240–257.

Mumford, M. D. (2003a). Where have we been, where are we going? Taking stock in creativity research. *Creativity Research Journal, 15*, 107–120.

Mumford, M. D. (2003b). Taking stock in taking stock. *Creativity Research Journal, 15*, 147–151.

Mumford, M. D., & Gustafson, S. B. (1988). Creativity syndrome: Integration, application, and innovation. *Psychological Bulletin, 103*, 27–43.

Murphy, K. (1994). *Honesty in the workplace*. Pacific Grove, LA: Brooks.

Murphy, K. (2002). Can conflicting perspectives on the role of *g* in personnel selection be resolved? *Human Performance, 15*, 173–186.

Murphy, K., & Dzieweczynski, J. (2005). Why don't measures of broad dimensions of personality perform better as predictors of job performance? *Human Performance, 18*, 343–357.

Murphy, K., & Lee, S. (1994). Personality variables related to integrity test scores. *Journal of Business and Psychology, 8*, 413–424.

Murray, J. (1990). Review of research on the Myers–Briggs Type Indicator. *Perceptual and Motor Skills, 10*, 1187–1202.

Nardi, D. (2001). *Multiple intelligences and personality type*. New York: Telos Publications.

Neel, R., & Dunn, R. (1960). Predicting success in supervisory training programs by the use of psychological tests. *Journal of Applied Psychology, 44*, 358–360.

Neisser, U. (1967). *Cognitive psychology*. New York: Appleton Century Crofts.

Neisser, U. (1976). General academic and artificial intelligence. In L. Resnick (Ed.), *The nature of intelligence* (pp. 135–144). Hillsdale, NJ: Lawrence Erlbaum Associates, Inc.

Nettle, D. (2006). The evolution of personality variation in humans and other animals. *American Psychologist, 61*, 623–631.

Nettlebeck, T., & Wilson, C. (2005). Intelligence and IQ: What teachers should know? *Educational Psychology, 25*, 609–630.

Newberry, B., Clark, W., Crawford, R., Strelau, J., Angleitner, A., Jones, J., et al. (1997). An American English version of the Pavolovian temperament survey. *Personality and Individual Differences, 22*, 105–114.

Nutt, P. (1986a). Decision style and strategic decisions of top executives. *Technological Forecasting and Social Change, 30*, 39–62.

Nutt, P. (1986b). Decision style and its impact on managers and management. *Technological Forecasting and Social Change, 29*, 341–366.

Nutt, P. (1989). Uncertainty and culture in bank loan decisions. *OMEGA: International Journal of Management Science, 17*, 297–308.

Nutt, P. (1990). Strategic decisions made by top executives and middle managers with data and process dominant styles. *Journal of Management Studies, 27*, 173–194.

Ochse, R. (1990). *Before the gates of excellence*. Cambridge, UK: Cambridge University Press.

Okakue, M., Nakamura, M., & Niura, K. (1977). Personality characteristics of pilots on EPPS, MPI and DOSEFU. *Reports of Aeromedical Laboratory, 18*, 83–93.

Oldham, J., & Morris, R. (1991). *Personality self-portrait*. New York: Bantam Books.

Olson, K., & Weber, D. (2004). Relations between Big Five traits and fundamental motives. *Psychological Reports, 95*, 795–802.

Ones, D., & Anderson, N. (2002). Gender and ethnic group differences on personality scales in selection. *Journal of Occupational and Organisational Psychology, 75*, 255–276.

Ones, D., & Viswesvaran, C. (1998). Integrity testing in organisations. In R. Griffin, A. O'Leary-Kelly, & J. Collins (Eds.), *Dysfunctional behaviour in organisations* (Vol. 23B). Greenwich, CT: JAI Press.

Ones, D., & Viswesvaran, C. (2001). Integrity tests and other Criterion-Focused Occupational Psychology Scales (COPS) used in personnel selection. *International Journal of Selection and Assessment, 9*, 31–39.

Ones, D., Viswesvaran, C., & Schmidt, F. (1995). Integrity tests: Overlooked facts, resolved issues and remaining questions. *American Psychologist, 50,* 456–457.

Ones, D., Viswesvaran, C., & Dilchert, S. (2005). Personality at work: Raising awareness and correcting misconceptions. *Human Performance, 18,* 389–404.

Ones, D., Viswesvaran, C., & Dilchert, S. (2006). Cognitive ability in selection decisions. In D. Wilheml & R. Engle (Eds.), *Understanding and measuring intelligence.* London: Sage.

Ones, D. S., & Viswesvaran, C. (2000). Personality at work: Criterion-Focused Occupational Personality Scales (COPS) used in personnel selection. In B. W. Roberts & R. Hogan (Eds.), *Applied personality psychology: The intersection of personality and I/O psychology* (pp. 63–92). Washington, DC: American Psychological Association.

Ones, D. S., Viswesvaran, C., & Schmidt, F. L. (1993). Comprehensive meta-analysis of integrity test validities. *Journal of Applied Psychology: Monograph, 78,* 679–703.

Organ, D. (1975). Extraversion, locus of control, and individual differences in conditionability in organisations. *Journal of Applied Psychology, 60,* 401–404.

Orpen, C. (1983). Note on prediction of managerial effectiveness from the Californian Psychological Inventory. *Psychological Reports, 53,* 622.

Palmer, W. (1974). Management effectiveness as a function of personality traits of the manager. *Personality Psychology, 27,* 283–295.

Paul, A. (2004). *The cult of personality.* New York: Free Press.

Penny, L., & Spector, P. (2002). Narcissism and counter-productive work behaviour. *International Journal of Selection and Assessment, 10,* 126–134.

Perez, J., Petrides, K. V., & Furnham, A. (2005). Measuring trait emotional intelligence. In R. Schulze & R. Roberts (Eds.), *Emotional intelligence: An international handbook* (pp. 181–201). Göttingen, Germany: Hogrefe.

Perkins, A., & Corr, P. (2005). Can worriers be winners? The association between worrying and job performance. *Personality and Individual Differences, 38,* 25–32.

Pervin, L. (1967). *Personality: Theory and research.* New York: Wiley.

Peterson, J. B., & Carson, S. (2000). Latent inhibition and openness to experience in a high-achieving student population. *Personality and Individual Differences, 28,* 323–332.

Peterson, J. B., Smith, K. W., & Carson, S. H. (2002). Openness and extraversion are associated with reduced latent inhibition: Replication and commentary. *Personality and Individual Differences, 33,* 1137–1147.

Petrides, K. V., & Furnham, A. (2000a). Gender differences in measured and self-estimated trait emotional intelligence. *Sex Roles, 42,* 449–461.

Petrides, K. V., & Furnham, A. (2000b). On the dimensional structure of emotional intelligence. *Personality and Individual Differences, 29,* 313–320.

Petrides, K. V., & Furnham, A. (2001). Trait emotional intelligence: Psychometric investigation with reference to established trait taxonomies. *European Journal of Personality, 15,* 425–448.

Petrides, K. V., & Furnham, A. (2003). Trait emotional intelligence: Behavioural validation in two studies of emotion recognition and reactivity to mood induction. *European Journal of Personality, 17,* 39–57.

Petrides, K. V., & Furnham, A. (2006). The role of trait emotional intelligence in a gender-specific model of organisational variables. *Journal of Applied Social Psychology, 36,* 552–569.

Petrides, K. V., Frederickson, N., & Furnham, A. (2004a). The role of trait emotional intelligence in academic performance and deviant behaviour at school. *Personality and Individual Differences, 36,* 277–293.

Petrides, K. V., Furnham, A., & Frederickson, N. (2004b). Emotional intelligence. *The Psychologist, 17,* 574–577.

Petrie, A. (1967). *Individuality in pain and suffering.* Chicago: University of Chicago Press.

Piers, E. V., Daniels, J. M., & Quakenbush, J. F. (1960). The identification of creativity in adolescents. *Journal of Educational Psychology, 51,* 346–351.

Posthuma, R., & Maertz, C. (2003). Relationships between integrity-related variables, work performance and trustworthiness in English and Spanish. *International Journal of Selection and Assessment, 11*, 102–105.

Potosky, D., & Bobko, P. (2004). Selection testing via the Internet. *Personnel Psychology, 57*, 1003–1034.

Prentky, R. A. (1980). *Creativity and psychopathology: A neurocognitive perspective.* New York: Praeger.

Prentky, R. A. (1989). Creativity and psychopathology: Gamboling at the seat of madness. In J. A. Glover, R. Ronning, & C. Reynolds (Eds.), *Handbook of creativity* (pp. 243–269). New York: Plenum Press.

Prentky, R. A. (2001). Mental illness and roots of genius. *Creativity Research Journal, 13*, 95–104.

Price, L. (2004). Individual differences in learning: Cognitive control, cognitive style and learning style. *Educational Psychology, 24*, 681–698.

Puffer, S., McCarthy, D., & Naumor, A. (1997). Russian managers' beliefs about work. *Journal of World Business, 32*, 258–276.

Quebbeman, A., & Rozell, E. (2002). Emotional intelligence and dispositional affectivity as moderators of workplace aggression. *Human Resource Management Review, 12*, 125–143.

Querk, N. (2000). *Essentials of Myers–Briggs Type Indicator assessment.* New York: Wiley.

Rabbitt, P. (1988). Human intelligence: A critical review of five books by R. J. Sternberg. *The Quarterly Journal of Experimental Psychology, 40*, 167–185.

Rahim, A. (1981). Job satisfaction as a function of personality–job congruence: A study with Jungian psychological types. *Psychological Reports, 49*, 496–498.

Randell, G. (1975). *Selection of salesmen.* Unpublished paper, University of Bradford Management Centre, UK.

Randle, C. (1956). How to identify promotable executives. *Harvard Business Review, 34*, 122–134.

Raven, J. C. (1963). *Standard progressive matrices.* London: Lewis.

Rawlings, D. (1985). Psychoticism, creativity and dichotic shadowing. *Personality and Individual Differences, 6*, 737–742.

Rawls, D., & Rawls, J. (1968). Personality characteristics and personal history data of successful and less successful executives. *Psychological Reports, 23*, 1032–1034.

Ree, M., & Carretta, T. (1998). General cognitive ability and occupational performance. In C. Cooper & I. Robertson (Eds.), *International Review of Industrial and Organisational Psychology* (Vol. 13, pp. 161–189). Chichester, UK: Wiley.

Ree, M., & Earles, J. (1994). The ubiquitous predictiveness of *g*. In M. Rumsey, C. Walker, & J. Harris (Eds.), *Personnel selection and classification* (pp. 127–135). Hillsdale, NJ: Lawrence Erlbaum Associates, Inc.

Ree, M., Earles, J., & Teachout, M. (1994). Predicting job performance. *Journal of Applied Psychology, 79*, 518–524.

Ree, M., Carretta, T., & Teachout, M. (1995). The role of ability and prior job knowledge in complex training performance. *Journal of Applied Psychology, 80*, 721–730.

Reeve, C., & Hakel, M. (2002). Asking the right questions about *g*. *Human Performance, 15*, 47–74.

Reinhardt, R. (1970). The outstanding jet pilot. *American Journal of Psychiatry, 127*, 732–736.

Reiss, S., & Havercamp, S. (1998). Toward a comprehensive assessment of fundamental motivation. *Psychological Assessment, 10*, 97–106.

Reitan, R. M. (1992). *Trail Making Test. Manual for administration and scoring.* South Tuscon, AZ: Reitan Neurological Laboratory.

Rentsch, J., & McEwan, A. (2002). Comparing personality characteristics, values and goals as antecedents of organisational attractiveness. *International Journal of Selection and Assessment, 10*, 225–234.

Rice, G., & Lindecamp, D. (1989). Personality types and business success of small retailers. *Journal of Occupational Psychology, 62*, 177–182.

Richards, R. L. (1976). A comparison of selected Guilford and Wallach–Kogan Creative

Thinking Tests in conjunction with measures of intelligence. *Journal of Creative Behavior, 10*, 178–182.

Riding, R. (2005). Individual differences and educational performance. *Educational Psychology, 25*, 659–672.

Rieke, M., & Guastello, S. (1994). Unresolved issues in honesty and integrity testing. *American Psychologist, 50*, 458–459.

Riggio, R., Murphy, S., & Pirozzolo, F. (2002). *Multiple intelligences and leadership*. Mahwah, NJ: Lawrence Erlbaum Associates Inc.

Rim, Y. (1961). Dimensions of job incentives and personality. *Acta Psychologia, 18*, 332–336.

Rim, Y. (1977). Significance of work and personality. *Journal of Occupational Psychology, 50*, 135–138.

Roberts, G. (1998). Competency management systems – The need for a practical framework. *Competency, 5*, 8–10.

Roberts, R., Zeidner, M. R., & Matthews, G. (2001). Does emotional intelligence meet traditional standards for an intelligence? Some new data and conclusions. *Emotion, 1*, 243–248.

Robertson, I., & Kinder, A. (1993). Personality and job competency. *Journal of Occupational and Organisational Psychology, 66*, 225–244.

Robertson, I., & Makin, P. (1986). Management selection in Britain: A survey and critique. *Journal of Occupational Psychology, 59*, 45–57.

Robertson, I., & Smith, M. (2001). Personnel selection. *Journal of Occupational and Organisational Psychology, 74*, 444–472.

Robinson, S., & Brown, G. (2004). Psychological contract breach and violation in organisations. In R. Griffin & A. O'Leary-Kelly (Eds.), *The dark side of organisational behaviour* (pp. 309–337). New York: Wiley.

Robinson, S., & Greenberg, J. (1998). Employees behaving badly. In C. Cooper & D. Rousseau (Eds.), *Trends in organisational behavior*. (Vol. 5, pp. 1–23). New York: Wiley.

Rodgers, J. (1999). A critique of the Flynn effect. *Intelligence, 26*, 337–356.

Rogers, C. R. (1954). Toward a theory of creativity. *ETC: A review of General Semantics, 11*, 249–260.

Rogers, J. (1997). *Sixteen personality types at work in organisations*. Cambridge, UK: Managers Futures Ltd.

Rokeach, M. (1975). *The nature of human values*. New York: Free Press.

Rolfhus, E., & Ackerman, P. (1999). Assessing individual differences in knowledge. *Journal of Educational Psychology, 91*, 511–526.

Rolland, J.-P., & De Fruyt, F. (2003). The validity of FFM personality dimensions and maladaptive traits to predict negative affect at work. *European Journal of Personality, 17*, 101–121.

Rolland, J.-P., Parker, W. R., & Stumpf, H. (1998). A psychometric examination of the French translation of the NEO-PI-R and NEO-FFI. *Journal of Personality Assessment, 71*, 2689–2690.

Rosse, J., Miller, J., & Ringer, R. (1996). The deterrent value of drug and integrity testing. *Journal of Business and Psychology, 10*, 477–485.

Rotter, J. (1966). Generalised expectancies for internal versus external control of reinforcement. *Psychological Monographs, 69*.

Rousseau, D. (2004). Under-the-table-deals: Preferential, unauthorised or idiosyncratic. In R. Griffin & A. O'Leary-Kelly (Eds.), *The dark side of organizational behavior* (pp. 262–290). San Francisco: Jossey-Bass.

Ruble, T., & Cosier, R. (1990). Effects of cognitive styles and decision setting on performance. *Organisational Behaviour and Human Decision Processes, 46*, 283–295.

Runco, M. A. (2004). Creativity. *Annual Review of Psychology, 55*, 657–687.

Rushton, J. (1995). *Race, evolution and behaviour*. New Brunswick, NJ: Transaction.

Rushton, J., & Jensen, A. (2005). Thirty years of research on race differences in cognitive ability. *Psychology, Public Policy and Law, 11*, 235–294.

Rushton, J. P. (1990). Creativity, intelligence, and psychoticism. *Personality and Individual Differences, 11*, 1291–1298.

Ryan, A., & Kristof-Brown, A. (2003). Focusing on personality in person–organisation fit research. In M. Barrick & A. Ryan (Eds.), *Personality and work* (pp. 262–288). San Francisco: Jossey-Bass.

Ryan, A. M., & Sackett, P. (2000). Individual assessment: The research base. In R. Jeanneret & R. Silzer (Eds.), *Individual psychological assessment* (pp. 54–87). San Francisco: Jossey-Bass.

Rynes, S., Orlitzky, M., & Bretz, R. (1997). Experienced hiring versus college recruiting. *Personnel Psychology, 30*, 309–334.

Sackett, P. (1994). Integrity testing for personnel selection. *Current Directions in Psychological Science, 3*, 73–76.

Sackett, P., Burns, L., & Callahan, C. (1989). Integrity testing for personnel selection. *Personnel Psychology, 42*, 491–530.

Saggino, A., & Kline, P. (1996). The location of the Myers–Briggs Type Indicator in personality factor space. *Personality and Individual Differences, 21*, 591–597.

Saklofske, D., & Zeidner, M. (Eds.). (1995). *International handbook of personality and intelligence.* New York: Plenum.

Salgado, J. (1997). The five factor model of personality and job performance in the European Community. *Journal of Applied Psychology, 82*, 30–43.

Salgado, J. (2002). The Big Five personality dimensions and counter-productive behaviours. *International Journal of Selection and Assessment, 10*, 117–125.

Salgado, J., & Moscoso, S. (2003). Internet-based personality testing. *International Journal of Selection and Assessment, 11*, 194–205.

Salgado, J., Anderson, N., Moscoso, S., Bertua, C., & De Fruyt, F. (2003). International validity generalisation of GMA and cognitive abilities. *Personnel Psychology, 56*, 573–605.

Salovey, P., & Mayer, J. D. (1990). Emotional intelligence. *Imagination, Cognition and Personality, 9*, 185–211.

Salovey, P., Mayer, J. D., Goldman, S., Turvey, C., & Paflai, T. (1995). Emotional attention, clarity and repair: Exploring emotional intelligence using the Trait Meta-Mood Scale. In J. W. Pennebaker (Ed.), *Emotion, disclosure, and health* (pp. 125–154). Washington, DC: American Psychological Association.

Sass, L. A. (2001). Schizophrenia, modernism, and the "creative imagination": On creativity and psychopathology. *Creativity Research Journal, 13*, 55–74.

Saulsman, L., & Page, A. (2004). The five factor model and personality disorder empirical literature: A meta-analytic review. *Clinical Psychology Review, 23*, 1055–1085.

Savage, R., & Stewart, R. (1972). Personality and the success of card-punch operators in training. *British Journal of Psychology, 63*, 445–450

Schinka, J., Dye, D., & Curtiss, E. (1997). Correspondence between five-factor and RAISEC models of personality. *Journal of Personality Assessment, 68*, 355–368.

Schmidt, F. (2002). The role of general cognitive ability and job performance. *Human Performance, 15*, 187–210.

Schmidt, F. L., & Hunter, J. E. (1977). Development of a general solution to the problem of validity generalisation. *Journal of Applied Psychology, 62*(5), 529–540.

Schmidt, F. L., & Hunter, J. E. (1984). A within-setting empirical test of the situational specificity hypothesis in personnel selection. *Personnel Psychology, 37*, 317–326.

Schmidt, F. L., & Hunter, J. E. (1998). The validity and utility of selection methods in personnel psychology: Practical and theoretical implications of 85 years of research findings. *Psychological Bulletin, 124*, 262–274.

Schmidt, F. L., & Hunter, J. E. (2004). General mental ability in the world of work. *Journal of Personality and Social Psychology, 86*, 162–173.

Schmidt, L., & Schwenkmezger, P. (1994). Differential diagnosis of psychiatric disorders using personality tests and questionnaires. *Diagnostica, 40*, 27–41.

Schmitt, N. (1989). Fairness in employment selection. In M. Smith & I. Robertson (Eds.), *Advances in selection and assessment* (pp. 131–153), Chichester, UK: Wiley.

Schmitt, N., Gooding, R., Noe, R., & Kirsch, M. (1984). Meta-analysis of validity studies published between 1964 and 1986 and the investigations of study characteristics. *Personnel Psychology, 27*, 407–422.

Schneidman, E. (1984). Personality and "success" among a selected group of lawyers. *Journal of Personality Assessment, 48*, 609–616.

Schoppe, K. J. (1975). *Verbaler Kreativitäts-Test (V-K-T). Ein Verfahren zur Erfassung verbal produktiver Kreativitätsmerkmale. Handandweisung.* Göttingen, Germany: Hogrefe.

Schotte, C., & De Doncker, D. (1994). *ADP-IV Vragenlijst.* Antwerp, Belgium: Universtat Ziekenhuis Antwerpen.

Schurr, K., Ruble, V., & Henriksen, L. (1985). Relationships of Myers–Briggs Type Indicator personality characteristics and self-reported academic problems and skill ratings with scholastic aptitude test scores. *Educational and Psychological Measurement, 48*, 187–196.

Schutte, N. S., Malouff, J. M., Hall, L. E., Haggerty, D. J., Cooper, J. T., Golden, C. J., et al. (1998). Development and validation of a measure of emotional intelligence. *Personality and Individual Differences, 25*, 167–177.

Schwartz, S. (1992). Universals in the content and structure of value. In M. Zanna (Ed.), *Advances in experimental social psychology* (pp. 1–65). New York: Academic Press.

Schwenkmezger, P., Schmidt, L., & Stephan-Henback, G. (1994). Anxiety, anger and anger expression in psychiatric and psychosomatic individuals. *Zeitschrift für Klinische-Psychologie, 23*, 163–177.

Sen, A. K., & Hagtvet, K. A. (1993). Correlations among creativity, intelligence, personality, and academic achievement. *Perceptual and Motor Skills, 77*, 497–498.

Seymore, D. (2000). Emotional labour. *Hospitality Management, 19*, 159–171.

Shaw, L., & Sichel, H. (1970). *Accident proneness.* Oxford, UK: Pergamon.

Sherwood, D. (2001). *Smart things to know about innovation and creativity.* Oxford, UK: Capstone.

Silva, F., Avice, D., Sanz, J., Martinez-Arias, R., Grana, J., & Sanchez-Bernardos, M.L. (1994). The five-factor model – 1. Contributions to the structure of the NEO-PI. *Personality and Individual Differences, 17*, 741–753.

Simonton, D. K. (1976). Biographical determinants of achieved eminence: A multivariate approach to the Cox data. *Journal of Personality and Social Psychology, 35*, 218–226.

Simonton, D. K. (1999). *Origins of genius.* New York: Oxford University Press.

Skarlicki, D., & Folger, R. (1997). Retaliation in the workplace: The roles of distributive procedural and interactional justice. *Journal of Applied Psychology, 82*, 100–108.

Slocum, J. (1978). Does cognitive style affect diagnosis and intervention strategies of change agents. *Group and Organisational Studies, 3*, 199–210.

Smith, M., & Abrahamson, M. (1992). Patterns of selection in six countries. *The Psychologist, 5*, 205–207.

Smithikrai, C. (2007). Personality traits and job success: An investigation in a Thai sample. *International Journal of Selection and Assessment, 15*, 134–131.

Snyder, M. (1975). Self-monitoring of expressive behaviour. *Journal of Personality and Social Psychology, 30*, 526–537.

Snyderman, M., & Rothman, S. (1987). Survey of expert opinion on intelligence and aptitude testing. *American Psychologist, 42*, 137–144.

Soldz, S., & Vaillant, G. E. (1999). The Big Five personality traits and the life course: A 45-year longitudinal study. *Journal of Research in Personality, 33*, 208–232.

Sparks, C. (1983). Paper and pencil measures of potential. In G. Dreher & P. Sackett (Eds.), *Perspectives on employee staffing and selection* (pp. 349–368). Homewood, IL: Irwin.

Spearman, C. (1904). General intelligence: Objectively determined and measured. *American Journal of Psychology, 15*, 201–293.

Spector, P. (1982). Behaviour in organisations as a function of employees' locus of control. *Psychological Bulletin, 91*, 482–497.

Spitzer, M., & McNamara, W. (1964). A managerial selection study. *Personnel Psychology, 17*, 19–40.

Stanton, N., Matthews, G., Graham, N., & Brimelow, C. (1991). The OPQ and the Big Five. *Journal of Managerial Psychology, 6*, 25–27.

Staw, B., Bell, N., & Clausen, J. (1986). The dispositional approach to job attitudes. *Administrative Science Quarterly, 31*, 56–77.

Sternberg, R. (1985). *Beyond IQ: A triarchic theory of human intelligence.* New York: Cambridge University Press.

Sternberg, R. (1990). *Metaphors of mind.* Cambridge, UK: Cambridge University Press.

Sternberg, R. (1997a). *Successful intelligence.* New York: Plume.

Sternberg, R. (1997b). *Thinking styles.* New York: Cambridge University Press.

Sternberg, R. (2005). There are no public-policy implications. *Psychology, Public Policy and Law, 11*(2), 295–301.

Sternberg, R., & Grigorenko, E. (1997). Are cognitive styles still in style? *American Psychologist, 52*, 700–712.

Sternberg, R. J. (1988). *The triarchic mind: A theory of human intelligence.* New York: Viking.

Sternberg, R. J. (1996). *Successful intelligence.* New York: Simon & Schuster.

Sternberg, R. J. (2003). A broad view of intelligence: The theory of successful intelligence. *Consulting Psychology Journal, 55*, 139–154.

Sternberg, R. J., & Grigorenko, E. L. (2001). Guilford's structure of intellect model and model of creativity: Contributions and limitations. *Creativity Research Journal, 13*, 309–316.

Sternberg, R. J., & Lubart, T. I. (1991). An investment theory of creativity and its development. *Human Development, 34*, 1–32.

Sternberg, R. J., & Lubart, T. I. (1992). Buy low sell high: An investment approach to creativity. *Current Directions in Psychological Research, 1*, 1–5.

Sternberg, R. J., & Lubart, T. I. (1995). *Defying the crowd: Cultivating creativity in a culture of conformity.* New York: Free Press.

Sternberg, R. J., & Lubart, T. I. (1999). The concept of creativity: Prospects and paradigms. In R. J. Sternberg (Ed.), *Handbook of creativity* (pp. 3–15). Cambridge, UK: Cambridge University Press.

Sternberg, R. J., & O'Hara, L. A. (1999). Creativity and intelligence. In R. J. Sternberg (Ed.), *Handbook of creativity* (pp. 251–272). Cambridge, UK: Cambridge University Press.

Sternberg, R. J., Ferrari, M., Clinkenbeard, P., & Grigorenko, E. L. (1996). Identification, instruction and assessment of gifted children: A construct validation of a triarchic model. *Gifted Child Quarterly, 40*, 129–137.

Sternberg, R. J., Grigorenko, E. L., Ferrari, M., & Clinkenbeard, P. (1999). A triarchic analysis of an aptitude–treatment interaction. *European Journal of Psychological Assessment, 15*, 3–13.

Sternberg, R. J., Castejón, J. L., Prieto, M. D., Hautamäki, J., & Grigorenko, E. L. (2001). Confirmatory factor analysis of the Sternberg Triarchic Abilities Test in three international samples: An empirical test of the triarchic theory of intelligence. *European Journal of Psychological Assessment, 17*, 1–16.

Sterns, L., Alexander, R., Barrett, G., & Dambrot, F. (1983). The relationship of extraversion and neuroticism with job preference and job satisfaction for clerical employees. *Journal of Occupational Psychology, 56*, 145–155.

Stewart, G. (2003). Toward an understanding of the multi-level role of personality in teams. In M. Barrick & A. Ryan (Eds.), *Personality and work* (pp. 183–203). San Francisco: Jossey-Bass.

Stone, R. (1988). Personality tests in management selection. *Human Resources Journal, 3*, 51–55.

Strebler, M., Robinson, D., & Heron, P. (1997). *Getting the best out of your competencies.* Brighton, UK: Institute for Employment Studies.

Strelau, J. (1983). *Temperament, personality, activity.* London: Academic Press.

Strelau, J. (1996). The regulative theory of temperament: Current status. *Personality and Individual Differences, 20,* 131–142.

Strelau, J. (1997). The contribution of Pavlov's typology of CNS properties to personality research. *European Psychologist, 2,* 125–134.

Stricker, L., & Ross, J. (1964). Some correlates of a Jungian Personality Inventory. *Psychological Reports, 14,* 623–643.

Super, D. (1970). *Work Values Inventory manual.* Boston: Houghton Mifflin.

Tallett, S., & O'Brodovich, H. (2004). Acquisition of competencies during the pediatric residency: A Canadian perspective. *Journal of Paediatrics, 144,* 289–290.

Taylor, C., Smith, W., Ghiselin, B., & Ellison, R. (1961). *Explorations of the measurement and prediction of contributions of one sample of scientists.* ASO-TR-61–96. Lachland Airbase, USA.

Taylor, E., & Nevis, E. (1957). The use of projective techniques in management selection. *Personnel, 33,* 462–474.

Te Nijenhuis, J., Voskuijl, O., & Schijive, N. (2001). Practice on coaching on IQ tests. *International Journal of Selection and Assessment, 9,* 302–306.

Tenopyr, M. (2002). Theory versus reality: Evaluation of g in the workplace. *Human Performance, 15,* 107–122.

Terman, L. M. (1925). *Genetic studies of genius. Vol. 1: Mental and physical traits of a thousand gifted children.* Palo Alto, CA: Stanford University Press.

Terman, L. M. (1973). *Concept Mastery Test manual.* New York: Psychological Corporation.

Terman, L. M., & Oden, M. H. (1940). The significance of deviates. III. Correlates of adult achievement in the California gifted group. *Yearbook of the National Society for the Study of Education, 39,* 74–89.

Tetewsky, S. J., & Sternberg, R. J. (1986). Conceptual and lexical determinants of non-entrenched thinking. *Journal of Memory and Language, 25,* 202–225.

Tett, R., & Jackson, D. (1990). Organisation and personality correlates of participative behaviours using an in-basket exercise. *Journal of Occupational Behaviour, 63,* 175–188.

Tett, R., Jackson, D., & Rothstein, M. (1991). Personality measures as predictors of job performance: A meta-analytic review. *Personnel Psychology, 44,* 703–725.

Thompson, B., & Borrello, E. (1986). Construct validity of the Myers–Briggs Type Indicator. *Educational and Psychological Measurement, 14,* 745–752.

Thompson, J. (2003). Proactive personality and job performance. *Journal of Applied Psychology, 90,* 1011–1017.

Thorndike, E. L. (1920). Intelligence and its use. *Harper's Magazine, 140,* 227–235.

Thurstone, L. L. (1938). A new rotational method in factor analysis. *Psychometrika, 3,* 199–218.

Tiedemann, J. (1989). Measures of cognitive styles: A critical review. *Educational Psychologist, 24,* 261–275.

Tipper, P. (1985). The negative primary effect: Inhibitory priming by ignored objects. *Quarterly Journal of Experimental Psychology, 37,* 571–590.

Tokar, D., & Swanson, J. (1995). Evaluation of the correspondence between Holland's vocational personality typology and the five factor model of personality. *Journal of Vocational Behaviour, 46,* 89–108.

Toole, D., Gavin, J., Murdy, L., & Sells, S. (1972). The different validity of personality, personal history, and aptitude data for minority and non-minority employees. *Personnel Psychology, 25,* 661–672.

Topp, B., & Kardash, C. (1986). Personality, achievement and attention. *Journal of Police Science and Administration, 14,* 234–241.

Torrance, E. P. (1962). *Guiding creative talent.* Englewood Cliffs, NJ: Prentice Hall.

Torrance, E. P. (1966). *Torrance tests of creative thinking: Directions manual and scoring guide.* Princeton, NJ: Personnel Press.

Torrance, E. P. (1967). The Minnesota studies of creative behavior: National and international extensions. *Journal of Creative Behavior, 1,* 137–154.

Torrance, E. P. (1974). *Torrance tests of creative thinking: Directions guide and scoring manual.* Princeton, NJ: Personnel Press.

Trull, T., Widiger, T., Lynam, D., & Costa, T. (2003). Borderline personality disorder from the perspective of general personality functioning. *Journal of Abnormal Psychology, 112,*193–202.

Truxillo, D., Steiner, D., & Gilliland, S. (2004). The importance of organisational justice in personnel. *International Journal of Selection and Assessment, 12,* 39–53.

Truxillo, D., Bauer, T., Campion, M., & Paronto, M. (2006). A field study of the role of Big Five personality factors in applicant perceptions of selection fairness, self and the hiring organisation. *International Journal of Selection and Assessment, 14,* 269–277.

Tseng, W. S., & Streltzer, J. (2004). *Cultural competence in clinical psychiatry.* New York: American Psychiatric Press.

Turnbull, A. (1976). Selling and the salesman: Prediction of success and personality change. *Psychological Reports, 38,* 1175–1180.

Tversky, A., & Kahneman, D. (1982). Judgment under uncertainty. In D. Kahneman, P. Slovic, & A. Tversky (Eds.), *Judgments under uncertainty: Heuristics and biases* (pp. 3–20). New York: Cambridge University Press.

Tyler, G., & Newcombe, P. (2006). Relationship between work performance and personality traits in Hong Kong organisational settings. *International Journal of Selection and Assessment, 14,* 37–50.

Upmanyu, V. V., Bhardwaj, S., & Singh, S. (1996). Word-association emotional indicators: Associations with anxiety, psychoticism, neuroticism, extraversion, and creativity. *Journal of Social Psychology, 136,* 521–529.

Van de Vijver, F., & Phalet, K. (2004). Assessment in multicultural groups. *Applied Psychology, 53,* 215–236.

Van den Berg, P., & Feij, I. (2003). Complex relationships among personality traits, job characteristics and work behaviours. *International Journal of Selection and Assessment, 11,* 326–335.

Van den Berg, P., Rose, R., Zijlstra, F., & Krediet, I. (1996). Temperamental factors in the execution of interrupted editing tasks. *European Journal of Personality, 10,* 233–248.

Van der Linden, D., Taris, T., Beckers, D., & Kindt, K. (2007). Reinforcement sensitivity theory and occupational health: BAS and BIS on the job. *Personality and Individual Differences, 42,* 1127–1138.

Van Grundy, A. (1988). *Techniques of structured problem solving.* New York: Van Nostrand Reinhold.

Vincent, A. S., Decker, B. P., & Mumford, M. D. (2002). Divergent thinking, intelligence, and expertise: A test of alternative models. *Creativity Research Journal, 14,* 163–178.

Vinchur, A., Schippman, J., Switzer, F., & Roth, P. (1998). A meta-analytic view of predictors of job performance for sales people. *Journal of Applied Psychology, 83,* 586–597.

Vinson, G., Connelly, B., & Ones, D. (2007). Relationship between personality and organisational switching. *International Journal of Selection and Assessment, 15,* 118–133.

Visser, B., Ashton, M., & Vernon, P. (2006). Beyond g: Putting multiple intelligence theory to the test. *Intelligence, 34,* 487–502.

Viswesvaran, C., & Ones, D. (2002). Agreements and disagreements on the role of general mental ability (GMA) in industrial and organisational psychology. *Human Performance, 15,* 211–231.

Viswesvaran, C., Ones, D., & Schmidt, F. (1996). Comparative analysis of the reliability of job performance ratings. *Journal of Applied Psychology, 81,* 557–574.

Wade, S. (1968). Differences between intelligence and creativity: Some speculations on the role of environment. *Journal of Creative Behavior, 2,* 97–101.

Wagner, E. (1960). Predicting success for young executives from objective test scores and personal data. *Personnel Psychology, 13,* 181–186.

Waibel, M., & Wicklund, R. (1994). Inferring competence from incompetence: An ironic process associated with person descriptors. *European Journal of Social Psychology, 24,* 443–452.

Wakefield, J. (1979). *Using personality to individualise instruction.* San Francisco: EdITS.

Wallace, H. R. (1961). Creative thinking: A factor in sales productivity. *Vocational Guidance Quarterly, 9,* 223–226.

Wallace, J., & Newman, J. (1990). Differential effects of reward and punishment cues on response speed in anxious and impulsive individuals. *Personality and Individual Differences, 11,* 999–1009.

Wallach, M. A. (1970). Creativity. In J. Carmichael (Ed.), *Manual of child psychology* (3rd ed., pp. 1211–1272). Toronto, Canada: Wiley.

Wallach, M. A., & Kogan, N. (1965). *Modes of thinking in young children.* New York: Holt, Rinehart & Winston.

Waneck, J. (1999). Integrity and honesty testing: What do we know? How do we use it? *International Journal of Selection and Assessment, 7,* 183–195.

Wankowski, J. (1973). *Temperament, motivation and academic achievement.* Unpublished report, University of Birmingham, UK.

Wareing, B., & Fletcher, C. (2004). Ethnic minority differences in self-assessment. *Selection and Development Review, 20,* 7–10.

Warr, P. (1987). *Work, unemployment and mental health.* Oxford, UK: Clarendon Press.

Watson-Wyatt. (1998). Available at www.personalityresearch.org.pd.html – accessed 19 December 2002.

Weber, M. (1905). Die proestantische Ethik und der "Geist" des kapitalismus. *Archiv für sozialvissenschaft und socialpolitik, 20,* 1–54.

Weisinger, H. (1998). *Emotional intelligence at work: The untapped edge for success.* San Francisco: Jossey-Bass.

Weiss, H., & Adler, S. (1984). Personality and organisational behaviour. *Research in Organisational Behaviour, 4,* 1–50.

Weiss, H., & Kurek, K. (2003). Dispositional influences on affective experiences at work. In M. Barrick & A Ryan (Eds.), *Personality and work* (pp. 121–149). San Francisco, Jossey-Bass.

Welch, L. (1946). Recombination of ideas in creative thinking. *Journal of Applied Psychology, 30,* 638–643.

West, M., & Farr, J. (Eds.). (1990). *Innovation and creativity at work.* Chichester, UK: Wiley.

Whalley, L., & Deary, I. (2001). Longitudinal cohort study of childhood IQ and survival up to age 76. *British Medical Journal, 322,* 1–5.

Wheeler, K. (1981). Sex differences in perceptions of desired rewards, availability of rewards, and abilities in relation to occupational selection. *Journal of Occupational Psychology, 54,* 141–148.

White, J. (2005). Howard Gardner: The myth of multiple intelligences. *Viewpoint, 16,* 1–11.

Widiger, T., & Coker, L. (2001). Assessing personality disorders. In J. N. Butcher (Ed.), *Clinical personality assessment: Practical approaches* (2nd ed., pp. 407–434). New York: Oxford University Press.

Widiger, T. A., Costa, P. T., & McCrae, R. R. (2001). Proposals for Axis II: Diagnosing personality disorders using the five-factor model. In P. T. Costa & T. A. Widiger (Eds.), *Personality disorders and the five-factor model of personality* (2nd ed., pp. 432–456). Washington, DC: APA.

Widiger, T. A., Trull, T. J., Clarkin, J. F., Sanderson, C., & Costa, P. T. (2002). A description of the DSM-IV personality disorders with the five-factor model of personality. In P. T. Costa & T. A. Widiger (Eds.), *Personality disorders and the five-factor model of personality* (2nd ed., pp. 89–99). Washington, DC: APA.

Widom, C. S., & Newman, J. P. (1985). Characteristics of non-institutionalised psychopaths. In J. Gunn & D. Farrington (Eds.), *Current research in forensic psychiatry and psychology* (Vol. 2, pp. 57–80). New York: Wiley.

Wiggins, J., & Pincus, A. (1989). Conceptions of personality disorders and dimensions of personality. *Psychological Assessment, 1,* 305–316.

Wilson, D. (1975). Use of tests in United Biscuits. In K. Miller (Ed.), *Psychological testing in personnel assessment* (pp. 45–60). New York: Wiley.

Wilson, G. (1973). *The psychology of conservatism*. London: Academic Press.

Wilson, G., Tunstall, O., & Eysenck, H. (1972). Measurement of motivation in predicting industrial performance: A study of apprentice gas fitters. *Occupational Psychology, 46*, 15–24.

Wilson, G. D., & Jackson, C. (1994). The personality of physicists. *Personality and Individual Differences, 16*, 187–189.

Wolf, M., & Ackerman, P. (2005). Extraversion and intelligence: A meta-analytic investigation. *Personality and Individual Differences, 38*, 531–542.

Wolfradt, U., & Pretz, J. (2001). Individual differences in creativity: Personality, story writing, and hobbies. *European Journal of Personality, 15*, 297–310.

Wolk, C., & Nikolai, L. (1997). Personality types of accounting students and faculty. *Journal of Accounting Education, 15*, 1–17.

Wollack, S., Goodale, J., Witjing, J., & Smith, P. (1971). Development of the Survey of Work values. *Journal of Applied Psychology, 44*, 331–338.

Woodman, R. W., & Schoenfeldt, L. F. (1989). Individual differences in creativity: An interactionist perspective. In J. A. Glover, R. R. Ronning, & C. R. Reynolds (Eds.), *Handbook of creativity. Perspectives on individual differences* (pp. 3–32). New York: Plenum.

Woodruffe, C. (1993). *Assessment centres: Identifying and developing competencies*. London: Institute of Personnel Development.

Woody, E., & Claridge, G. (1977). Psychoticism and thinking. *British Journal of Social and Clinical Psychology, 16*, 241–248.

Wulf, F. (1922). Transformation of images – Memory and Gestalt. *Psychologische Forschung, 1*, 33–37.

Wuthrich, V., & Bates, T. C. (2001). Schizotypy and latent inhibition: Non-linear linkage between psychometric and cognitive markers. *Personality and Individual Differences, 30*, 783–798.

Yamamoto, K. (1964). Threshold of intelligence in academic achievement of highly creative students. *Journal of Experimental Education, 32*, 401–405.

Young, D., Hamilton, C., & Kirk, A. (2004). Web-based coaching – Lessons from a practical experience. *Selection and Development Review, 20*, 18–23.

Young, S., & Parker, C. (1999). Predicting collective climates: Assessing the role of shared work values, needs, employee interaction, and work group memberships. *Journal of Organisational Behaviour, 20*, 1199–1218.

Zeidner, M. (1995). Personality trait correlates of intelligence. In D. Saklofske & M. Zeidner (Eds.), *International handbook of personality and intelligence* (pp. 299–315). New York: Plenum.

Zeidner, M., Matthews, G., & Roberts, R. (2004). Emotional intelligence in the workplace: A critical review. *Applied Psychology, 33*, 371–399.

Zhang, L. F. (2004a). Does student–teacher thinking style match/mismatch matter in student's achievement. *Educational Psychology, 26*, 395–409.

Zhang, L. F. (2004b). Predicting cognitive development, intellectual styles, and personality traits from self-rated abilities. *Learning and Individual Differences, 15*, 67–88.

Zhao, H., & Seibert, S. (2006). The Big Five personality dimensions and entrepreneurial status: A meta-analysis review. *Journal of Applied Psychology, 91*, 259–271.

Zichar, M. (2001). Using personality inventories to identify thugs and agitators. *Journal of Vocational Behaviour, 23*, 605–633.

Ziller, R. C. (1990). *Photographing the self: Methods for observing personal orientations*. Newbury Park, CA: Sage.

Ziyal, L. (1997). Definition of critical performance demands: A new approach to competency. *Competency, 4*, 25–31.

Zuckerman, M. (1979). *Sensation seeking*. Chichester, UK: Wiley.

Zuckerman, M. (2006). *Psychobiology of personality*. Cambridge, UK: Cambridge University Press.

Zweig, D., & Webster, J. (2003). Where is the line between benign and invasive? *Journal of Organisational Behaviour, 23*, 605–633.

Zweig, D., & Webster, J. (2004). What are we measuring? An examination of the relationships between the Big Five personality traits, goal orientation and performance intention. *Personality and Individual Differences, 36*, 1693–1708.

Author index

Note: *italic* page numbers denote references to Figures/Tables.

Subject index

Note: *italic* page numbers denote references to Figures/Tables.